TRANSFORMING JAPAN

HOW FEMINISM AND DIVERSITY
ARE MAKING A DIFFERENCE

Edited by

Kumiko Fujimura-Fanselow

THE FEMINIST PRESS
AT THE CITY UNIVERSITY OF NEW YORK
FEMINISTPRESS.ORG

Published in 2011 by the Feminist Press at the City University of New York
The Graduate Center, 365 Fifth Avenue, Suite 5406, New York, NY 10016

feministpress.org

This publication is made possible by support from the Japan Foundation.

 JAPANFOUNDATION

First printing February 2011

Cover design and text design by Drew Stevens

Library of Congress Cataloging-in-Publication Data

Transforming Japan : how feminism and diversity are making a difference / edited by Kumiko
Fujimura-Fanselow.
    p. cm.
  ISBN 978-1-55861-699-8
  1. Feminism—Japan. 2. Minority women—Japan. 3. Japan—Social conditions—1989-
I. Fujimura-Fanselow, Kumiko, 1947-
  HQ1762.T89 2011
  305.48'800952—dc22

                                                                    2010047349

To my daughters
Aya Dorothy and Misa Laura

CONTENTS

III MARRIAGE AND FAMILIES

IV CHANGING SEXUALITIES

V ACTIVISM FOR THE RIGHTS OF MINORITIES

Japanese practice places the family name or surname preceding the given or "first" name. However, since the text is in English, many readers will expect the names to appear in Western order. In addition, several authors included as writers, subjects, or references are known in countries outside of Japan where their names have appeared in Western order. Therefore I have followed the Western order of placing the given name first, followed by the family name.

Preface

Almost twenty years ago, I approached Florence Howe, the director of the Feminist Press, with the idea of producing an anthology written by Japanese scholars about Japanese women's lives. The volume took five years to complete. *Japanese Women: New Feminist Perspectives on the Past, Present, and Future* (1995), which I co-edited with Atsuko Kameda, served a worldwide audience interested in the views of Japanese women scholars. The book created a break in the one-way flow of information between Japan and the rest of the world. While Japanese scholars had considerable access to information about women in other countries through translated works by foreign scholars, this book would bring Japanese women's scholarship to readers abroad. *Japanese Women* aimed to close the gap between what feminist researchers, scholars, and activists in Japan write and what the world reads—more often than not distorted, exaggerated, or stereotyped in the mass media.

That first volume, intended for students and scholars studying Japan as well as those interested in gaining a cross-cultural perspective on issues concerning women, was adopted as a text in both undergraduate and graduate courses in women's/gender studies courses as well as Japanese/Asian studies courses in many countries, including Japan and, of course, the US. The essays reflected social, political, and cultural challenges Japanese women have confronted since the end of World War II, as well as the new consciousness that emerged among women beginning in the early 1970s with the birth of the women's liberation movement in Japan and international developments that affected Japanese women.

At the time the book was published, we held some sense of optimism that we could anticipate further progress in women's advancement in the workplace, politics, and education, as described in many of the essays. Such optimism was strongly tempered by other essays that dealt with issues that had yet to be adequately confronted, such as domestic violence and the plight of migrant women, as well as the continuing stagnation of the

Japanese economy that would inevitably affect women's status within both the workplace and the home. Five years after the book's publication, Florence Howe was already encouraging me to update the book to reflect the changes that had taken place in the intervening years. Florence's insistence and encouragement spurred me to take up the task.

Transforming Japan is as comprehensive as *Japanese Women*, and while it retains five historical essays from the previous volume, the perspective here differs substantially. More than half of the essays focus on aspects of women's lives untouched in *Japanese Women*. These essays represent the areas of significant change not only in women's lives, but also in Japanese culture. These topics include: the visibility of single mothers; the visibility of lesbian lives in the past and the present; the changing lives of men especially in relationship to parenthood; the new consciousness about Japan as a multicultural society and what that means for minority women's rights.

This book is directed at readers interested in learning about the diverse faces of women living in Japan, who confront challenges and struggles that in many ways overlap, yet in other ways are unique to specific groups. It does not assume sophisticated prior knowledge of Japan or feminist theories. As a feminist, I am committed to making knowledge and books about women accessible to as many readers as possible, so I specifically instructed the authors to avoid the use of academic and feminist jargon.

While most of the contributors to this volume are academics, some are activists associated with nonprofit organizations supporting single mothers and migrant women, one is a lawyer who advocates for women's rights, and several are politicians. All of the contributors share a strong commitment to identifying and addressing human rights issues, especially as they pertain to women, and to working actively to rectify abuses. In addition, many of the authors and translators are themselves members of marginalized/minority groups, and have worked as researchers and advocates. I sought out these authors in the hope that their possession of an intimate knowledge and understanding of the lives, struggles, and accomplishments of particular groups of women, combined with skills of scholarly analysis, would infuse these essays with personal meaning and immediacy.

In the process of editing this book, I asked students enrolled in my undergraduate and graduate classes dealing with gender issues to read several manuscripts, and I invited the authors and translators to speak to my classes. While I was not wholly surprised, I was nonetheless dismayed to discover that the majority of my students—including graduate students who range in age from the midtwenties to fifty-plus, and who work in a variety of professions—were almost totally ignorant or at most had only a vague awareness or superficial knowledge of many important issues, particularly those pertaining to minority groups. The few who knew of the existence of minority groups in Japan believed that whatever discrimination they may have faced in the past no longer existed, that their problems had been resolved.

A striking moment occurred during Malaya Ileto's visit. A former staff member at the International Movement Against All Forms of Discrimination and Racism (IMADR), she had translated the essay "Buraku Solidarity" by Risa Kumamoto on women of the Buraku community (see chapter 16), who continue to face discrimination in Japan. Ileto came to speak to a group of undergraduates about her initial encounter with the Buraku issue. A number of students thought that she had said "black" and was referring to discrimination faced by black people in the US. While the Japanese pronunciation of "black" is close to "Buraku," the misunderstanding occurred chiefly because these students—like most Japanese—view racial or ethnic discrimination as something that exists in other countries but certainly not in their own society. Despite the presence of people of various nationalities in Japan, to most students they remain "outsiders" with whom they have very little contact and whom they perceive as "different." Few have talked face-to-face with a person of Buraku origin.

I invited Donna Nishimoto, one of the participants in the research project described in Leny P. Tolentino's and Nanako Inaba's essay (see chapter 14, "The Story of Kalakasan and Migrant Filipinas"), who now works as a Filipina activist, to speak to my students.

With Leny P. Tolentino by her side, who at times took her hand to provide support, Donna described her life in the Philippines, and her coming to Japan in search of employment. She described the violence she endured from her Japanese husband, and the bullying suffered by her Filipino-Japanese son in school. She expressed her determination to recover her dignity and to protect her son by appealing to his teachers for help. Upon hearing her story, the students were visibly moved. Previously, most thought scantily clad Filipina women had come to Japan to make money by soliciting customers in front of bars. Meeting Donna and learning about the reasons and circumstances that bring Filipina women to Japan, and the hardships and challenges they encounter living in Japan, helped to dispel the negative images many students held of Filipina women. At the same time, they viewed Donna and others who suffered abuse and exploitation not simply as victims of ethnic discrimination and violence, but as examples of women who possessed strength and pride in their identity with the determination to improve their own lives and that of other Filipina women and their families.

In a course on sexuality, the students met Masae Torai, one of the participants in "Dialogue: Three Activists on Gender and Sexuality" (see chapter 13), who underwent female-to-male gender alignment surgery. He described his life and his efforts to promote understanding about and tolerance toward sexual minorities. About halfway through this course, one student asked for the opportunity to come out to the class about her bisexuality. For many of her classmates, this was their first exposure to a self-identified bisexual. In evaluating the class a number of students later wrote that, in spite of what we had read, studied, and talked about in class, their immediate reaction to the student coming out—however momentary—had been one of shock and disapproval. They admitted that their lack of knowledge, and the experience of knowing people whose sexualities might differ from theirs, had led them to internalize stereotyped images and prejudices against LGBT (lesbian, gay, bisexual, and transgender) people. The student who came out was also affected by the ignorance of her classmates, and decided to increase awareness about LGBT communities and the issues they face by forming an LGBT association on campus. The association serves as a support group and a setting where students, whatever their sexual orientation, could learn more about these issues.

The students became aware of the discrimination faced by Buraku women and migrant women and their children, and LBGT people, and realized their own ignorance and apathy toward people belonging to sexual or ethnic minority groups. Through their readings and direct encounters with authors and translators, they began to recognize the common humanity they shared as women. At times, they saw some of these issues of women's rights violations as overlapping with and being intimately linked with their own lives.

One question, however, continued to nag me throughout: why is it that so many in Japan, including these students, have so little awareness about issues of human rights? The answer, I believe, is that concepts of equality and the violations of human rights are simply not addressed in schools or in the media.[1] Most report they have never been exposed to issues concerning sexuality or minority groups, nor have they engaged in discussions about human rights at any point in their schooling. Many accept practices, such as the entrance exam system, that excessively emphasize competition and inflict strong psychological pressure, or school rules and regulations that attempt to enforce conformity and even infringe on privacy rights (practices that I regard as coming close to constituting violations of children's rights).

If people are unaware of their own human rights, that may account for their lack of concern about how other people suffer violations of their rights. This is to a large extent the result of deliberate efforts on the part of a conservative government and its supporters to prevent the teaching of such topics.[2] The prescribed state-controlled curriculum in elementary and secondary schools, combined with the system of competitive entrance examinations for entry into upper-secondary school and university, limit the scope of "knowledge" students can gain. In addition, large size classes, and a teaching style dominated by a top-down "transmission of knowledge" approach in which students play a passive role, inhibit the development of autonomous, critical thinking. Students are also held back from questioning social norms and practices as well as personal values, perceptions, and assumptions.

The same point can be made with respect to teaching students about women's/gender issues. Incoming students at my university have scant knowledge of the current economic and social conditions of women's lives and the many ongoing changes. Formal education does not provide girls with the opportunity to learn about issues of concern to all women and how changes taking place in society affect women's lives. Students do not learn to question common assumptions regarding gender roles, or to consider different personal and career options for their future. Women's studies, which emerged in the mid-1970s, has gained some foothold within colleges and universities,[3] but it has not made any discernible headway at the elementary and secondary school levels. On the contrary, the gender-bashing which emerged in 2001 has put a brake on efforts to promote gender-sensitivity in schools, with the result that gender-stereotyping and bias persist in textbooks, teaching practices, and guidance/career counseling.

Between 1995 and 2008, the percentage of female high school graduates going on to four-year universities has shown a marked increase, and within that time frame some progress has taken place—at least on the surface—toward promoting gender equality and providing an increased number of employment options for women with the enactment of the Basic Law for a Gender-Equal Society (1999) and other legislation, as well as revisions to the 1985 Equal Employment Opportunity Law.

However, at the same time, recent surveys point to a trend toward conservatism among young women in Japan. In a 2009 survey conducted by the Cabinet Office, *Danjo kyodo sankaku shakai ni kansuru yoron chosa* (Public opinion survey on gender equality), over 35 percent of women in their twenties expressed agreement with the view that "Husbands should work and be the breadwinner, wives should stay in the home." While this figure was about 5 percentage points lower than in 1997, the rate among women of this age group was higher than that among women in their thirties, forties, and fifties. At first glance, this trend appears perplexing; one might anticipate that as more young women enjoy the benefits of higher education, they become less tied to traditional gender role expectations and imbued with an aspiration to play a greater role in various spheres of society. But the majority of incoming female students I teach envision for themselves a life much like that imagined by students fifteen years ago: almost all plan to take a job after graduation, as a way to gain some experience and to make use of their university education; but nearly all of them wish to get married and have a couple of children (Fujimura-Fanselow "College Women Today. . ." 1995). Most of them anticipate quitting their jobs once they have children, and returning to work on a part-time basis once their children enter elementary school. Those aspiring to pursue work on a continuous basis, whether or not they marry or have children, constitute a minority. The dominant expectation among these students is closely in line with what most women in society actually do.

In addition to the fact that schools do little to educate and raise consciousness among female students about issues affecting them, girls and young women have little exposure in their daily lives to diverse role models who can offer alternative visions of women's lives and career patterns as well as alternative models of gender relationships and family arrangements. Their projections and assumptions about the future tend to be based on images they have absorbed from the mass media, which are highly gender stereotyped, or from their immediate familial surroundings. Their expectations also reflect a reluctance to deviate from what they perceive to be the "normal, accepted" life course for women.

The majority of women enrolled at my institution—and in most four-year universities—come from families in which the father earns a relatively comfortable income and the mother is either a full-time housewife or else works part time. The dominant role models for these young women are therefore women who gave up their jobs—willingly or not—to marry and raise families, and who were married to men who held steady jobs that allowed them to earn salaries sufficient to support their families and provide for their children's education.

Of course, not all students in a given class come from similar backgrounds: a few have mothers who have held full-time jobs throughout their adult lives—usually in the civil service or in professional fields such as teaching or nursing or working in the family business. Some have fathers who regularly perform household chores. In a class of thirty or so students, there are usually at least three or four students who were raised by single mothers. When one class read the essay "Single Mothers" by Chieko Akaishi (chapter 8) on single-mother households, a few students shared with the class that they had been raised by single mothers. One student said that her mother divorced her father because of domestic abuse and, subsequently, he had failed to make child support payments.

It is certainly clear that, unless such topics are taken up and unless students are given the opportunity to share their thoughts and experiences in relation to these topics, the diversity of experience that exists within their midst remains hidden. In addition, without such discussion, stereotyped concepts of gender roles and the normative family model remain unchallenged. Masaki Matsuda's visit to my class had a strong impact in this regard. Not only did Matsuda, the author of "My Life as a Househusband" (chapter 10), project a man radically different from the fathers the students were accustomed to, but he also shattered the myth that only mothers can adequately care for small children. Many of the students wrote in their reaction papers that his talk opened their minds to the possibility of combining a career and family by establishing a relationship based on the sharing of childcare and housework responsibilities by both parents. No student had previously encountered this possibility.

Educators engaged in teaching young women, especially those like myself who offer women's studies, need to urge students to examine critically every aspect of accepted thinking and assumptions concerning women and to be receptive to alternative viewpoints; to arouse awareness of conditions and changes taking place in society that are likely to shape their future; to inform them of both the difficulties and obstacles as well as emerging opportunities and options available to them; and, finally, to instill in them the skills, strength, and confidence to confront both. Students at the women's university where I teach are required to take a one-semester introductory course in women's studies; it is probably one of the few institutions in Japan that have such a requirement. The majority take the course in their freshman year, and I have found that many students are stimulated as a result of being exposed to issues affecting women. They also have the rare opportunity to share their views about those issues and their futures in small groups.

In this regard, the authors and translators of the essays who came to talk about their work and their experiences contributed naturally to all of these goals. One common message that seems to have reached and touched many of the students was, "Don't let your ambitions be limited by common notions of what is 'normal' or 'appropriate,' a fear of being labeled as 'different' by others, or a fear of making mistakes or failing. Take risks. If something doesn't work out, you can start over again. Different options will likely appear at various points in your life. Remain open to new possibilities."

To these students, whose educational choices at every level have been determined on the basis of tests consisting of questions with a single correct answer, and who have grown up in a milieu where there is considerable pressure toward group conformity, the fear of being wrong or acting differently from others is very strong. Meeting these authors and listening to them as they related their wide-ranging experiences and professional interests provided encouragement and incentive for many of the students to move beyond their sometimes constricted mode of thinking, and to understand that they have the option to explore a wider range of possibilities and options for their future than they previously thought possible.

Notes

1. The United Nations Committee on the Rights of the Child, in its Concluding Observations on Japan's second periodic report regarding its compliance with the Convention on the Rights of the Child in 2004, recommended that the State party "Include human rights education, and specifically child rights education, in the school curriculum."

2. The Ministry of Education, Culture, Sports, Science and Technology screens all textbooks written by textbook publishers and directs revisions based on evaluation of conformity with curriculum and teaching guidelines. Pressures exerted on the textbook screening committee from reactionary scholars and politicians have led to the deletion of the word "gender" from junior high school textbooks. Likewise the issue of the "comfort women" was included in junior high school history textbooks published by all of the seven publishers and approved by the ministry in 1997, but today, only one of the textbooks includes references to it. In the past the screening committee has directed deletion of references to/depictions of same sex couples in discussions of diversity among families.

3. As of 2008, about a half of all universities and junior colleges in Japan— 614 out of close to 1,200—offered one or more courses related to gender/women's studies. The total number of courses was 4,221 (Kokuritsu josei kyoiku kaikan 2008).

Works Cited

Fujimura-Fanselow, Kumiko. 1995. "College Women Today: Options and Dilemmas." In *Japanese Women: New Feminist Perspectives on the Past, Present, and Future*, ed. Kumiko Fujimura-Fanselow and Atsuko Kameda. New York: The Feminist Press.
Kokuritsu josei kyoiku kaikan (National Women's Education Center). *Joseigaku jendaaron kanren kamoku deeta beesu 2008* (Data base on courses related to women's and gender studies 2008). http://winet.nwec.jp/toukei/save/xls/L113110.xls
Nihon kazoku shakaigakkai zenkoku kazoku chosa iinkai (Family Research Committee of the Japan Society of Family Sociology). 2005. *Dainikai kazoku ni tsuiteno zenkoku chosa* (Second national survey on families).
Ohinata, Masami. 1995. "The Mystique of Motherhood: A Key to Understanding Social Change and Family Problems in Japan." In *Japanese Women: New Feminist Perspectives on the Past, Present, and Future*, ed. Kumiko Fujimura-Fanselow and Atsuko Kameda. New York: The Feminist Press.
UN Committee on the Rights of the Child. 2004. Consideration of Reports Submitted by States Parties Under Article 44 of the Convention—Concluding observations: Japan. February 26. http://www.unhcr.org/refworld/country,,CRC,,JPN,4562d8cf2,41178bd04,0.html

Introduction

The early 1990s were often described as *onna no jidai* or "the era of women." The implication was that women in Japan had not only attained a large measure of equality in a highly affluent society and could exercise freedom in choosing from a variety of options in their pursuit of a fulfilling life, but also that as a result they enjoyed happier, fuller, and more balanced lives than their male counterparts who were tied exclusively to their work.

Support for this notion could be seen in the significant strides made by women in securing greater rights and opportunities in the home, workplace, schools, and the political field, particularly in the decade following the United Nation's International Women's Year in 1975. The passage of the Equal Employment Opportunity Law (EEOL) in 1985 opened up the previously all-male career track within Japanese companies to university-educated women. The Child Care Leave Law of 1991 required companies to grant unpaid leave to either parent until the child reached the age of one. A number of professions and occupations previously open only to men now admitted women, many of whom were coming from four-year universities, and were perhaps affected by the growth of women's studies courses on many college campuses. Local, regional, and national female politicians increased in numbers and visibility. And married women, including those with children, entered the labor force, and also participated in a wide range of activities outside the traditional confines of the home, including adult learning and community-related programs, volunteer work, and environmental, political, and peace movements. While these were tentative steps, the climate seemed charged with optimism. There seemed to be no end to women's increasing ascendance.

Twenty years later, the picture is less rosy, for there is little progress to be seen. Instead one sees regression in aspects of Japanese women's lives. A number of simple facts tell the story. First, the United Nations Development Programme's Gender Empowerment Measure (GEM), which rates the extent to which women participate in economic and political life by assuming positions of leadership and policy-making, reported that, in 2008, Japan's ranking was fifty-eighth out of 108 nations. Further, Japan's ranking on the GEM has shown little improvement over the past twenty years. Other statistics reveal that women occupy only 10 percent of managerial posts, in contrast to women in the US and many European countries, where the figure is 30 to 40 percent. The proportion of seats in the Lower House of the National Diet (legislature) occupied by women in 2010 was just 11 percent (fifty-four out of 480 seats), while in the Upper House the figure was 18 percent (forty-four out of 242 seats). The paucity of women in policy-making positions may be a significant factor impeding national progress. If more women were in positions of national influence, they might provide fresh perspectives on policies relating to the economy, with special attention to employment, social welfare, and social security, as is the case with the two politicians profiled in part VII, "Feminism and Political Power." They might also move the nation forward toward gender equality.

Another negative development during recent years has been the growing poverty of women, treated in chapter 18, "Employment and Poverty" by Mami Nakano. The Japanese economy, which remained in recession for a decade starting in 1990, has taken a dramatic turn for the worse after the global economic downturn that began in 2008. The consequences as seen in salary reductions, bankruptcies among many smaller-sized companies, worker layoffs, and replacement of regular employees by non-regular (temporary, contract, and part-time) workers, together with reductions in government spending on health and social services and the deregulation of certain employment practices, have all wrought increasing hardship on many Japanese. The expressions "*waakingu poa*" (working poor), "*hinkon*" (poverty), and "*kakusa shakai*" (social disparity) have entered the popular lexicon and replaced the formerly popular perception (which may have been inaccurate to begin with) that Japan was a more or less egalitarian society in which the majority of people belonged to the middle class. Income inequality and relative poverty among the working-age population as a whole has risen to the point where it is now above the average found among the thirty member countries of the Organization for Economic Co-operation and Development (OECD 2006, 2008). But the situation for women—who occupy a more vulnerable position to begin with—is more deplorable: earnings for full-time female workers average below 70 percent of earnings for full-time male workers, compared to 70-80 percent among many other OECD countries (Kokuritsu josei kyoiku kaikan 2009, 51, figure 4-1). Finally, 44 percent of working women, compared to fewer than 10 percent of men, earn two million yen ($20,000) or less yearly, with the result that women make up 74 percent of those who live under the poverty line.

Dominating this portrait is the overall deterioration of the status of women in the workplace. What has occurred since the enactment of the EEOL in 1985 is a greater polarization or stratification among women workers. While the status and treatment of some women workers has improved—as seen in the increase in the proportion of women pursuing careers in previously male-dominated professional and technical occupations (from 11 percent to over 16 percent between 1985 and 2006) (Naikakufu 2008a, 71, graph 1-2-3), the situation for the overwhelming majority has worsened, with more women employed as non-regular workers at low wages with few benefits or protections and with limited access to training and little prospect of mobility into regular employment. The percentage of workers in non-regular employment is much higher among women than men: 55 percent of employed women, compared to 20 percent of men are in non-regular employment, accounting for close to 70 percent of workers in this category. The situation faced by women of various minority groups within Japanese society, such as the Ainu, Buraku, Zainichi Koreans, and migrants, taken up in the essays in part V, "Activism for the Rights of Minorities," is still worse. Women within minority communities have less access to good education and employment, and are more likely to suffer economic hardship.

The deterioration of the economy has undeniably been a major factor in bringing about these developments, but it would be more accurate to see it as aggravating an already existing situation—a persistent gender gap in wages and poverty among women. The benefits received by low-income households remain low and are inadequate to help single mothers survive. Other causal factors are the nation's tax and social security systems, and employment practices and policies—all of which are based on the male-breadwinner model, with women viewed as secondary or supplementary workers, assuming that women will be supported and protected by their husbands.

In addition, the expectation that full-time employees will place work at the center of their lives, put in long hours of overtime, meet demanding quotas, and accept transfers to various parts of the country or even abroad, combined with the fact that the overwhelming portion of such unpaid work as child care, elderly care, and housekeeping fall on women—all make it extremely difficult for women to reconcile work with family life. Reinforcing the status quo are prevailing attitudes regarding gender roles, and, more importantly, state policies and practices that serve to reinforce those attitudes through failing to provide adequate facilities for the care of children, the sick, and the elderly. Thus, while most women enter employment after completing their education and tend to continue working after marriage, 70 percent stop working after the birth of their first child. The ability to combine a full-time career with motherhood is limited to highly educated women who work in specific occupations—professions such as teaching or public/civil service work—which provide job security and have comparatively good maternity and child-care leave policies as well as more limited work hours. Among women with college or graduate degrees as a whole, however, the percentage of women who work in regular employment falls from a high of around 80 percent following graduation to 70 percent among those in their thirties, and below 60 percent for those in their forties. The average length of continuous employment for these women is six years, which in part explains why the wage gap between female and male graduates, though initially small, increases in older age groups (Koseirodosho 2009b). On the other hand, minority women described in this volume have no choice but to work throughout their lives.

Many married women re-enter the labor market once their children are older, and in fact since 1997 the proportion of households in which both wife and husband hold jobs has continued to overtake those with working husbands and full-time housewives: 55 percent in 2008. But the jobs available to these women are predominantly part time, with most earning between one and two million yen ($10,000-20,000)[1] annually. Practices such as company allowances for spouses, wage structure based on seniority, and the use of age limits on potential new workers function to discourage, if not to make it nearly impossible, for women, particularly middle-aged and older women, to obtain full-time regular employment after a career break. Because the majority of women have interrupted work careers and low earnings, they receive smaller old age pensions, some reduced to poverty.

Thus, persistent economic inequality, discrimination, and domestic violence (discussed below) prevent women from leading autonomous lives. These factors may also lie at the root of several significant social developments. These include trends toward late marriages and a lowered marriage rate, as well as declining birth rates and increasing divorce rates accompanied by rising numbers of single mothers.

Changing Patterns of Marriage and Declining Birthrates

According to various surveys, ninety percent of young Japanese women and men overall profess a desire or expectation to marry and have children, a figure which has remained unchanged over the past twenty years. In reality, however, there are more late marriages than before, and more people choosing not to marry at all. Even more striking, there has been a rising tendency of married couples to remain childless.

A close look at marriage figures shows that the highest percentage of non-married men may be found among those in non-regular employment, especially "freeters" (a term used to refer primarily to males under age thirty-five, who do not have regular employment), while among single women it is found among those with high levels of education, earning high incomes, and living in large cities. These differences reflect the traditional view of both sexes that men should bear the major responsibility for supporting a wife and children. They also illustrate the point made by Aya Ezawa in chapter 7, "The Changing Patterns of Marriage and Motherhood," that a combination of societal attitudes about motherhood and work and the realistic choices available to educated, advantaged women determines their choices. For example, while women in low-paying, non-career track jobs with little prospect of promotion or higher pay may see marriage as a necessary means of acquiring security and a comfortable standard of living, such a motivation for marriage is less likely to apply to women from more affluent backgrounds with university degrees and careers that enable them to be financially self-supporting. Additionally, they are less likely to feel pressured to marry from family and relatives.

Accompanying the decline in marriage rates has been the continuing decline in the birthrate. Whereas the decline had previously been attributed to the rise in the number of individuals remaining single, it is now linked to the increasing number of married couples who decide not to have children. While numerous factors lie behind this, most important is a strong sense of uncertainty felt by many Japanese about the future in general and in particular about their ability to rear and educate children in a society where the financial costs of day care, higher education, and elder care fall on individual families. The slow and low wage increases and the lack of improvement in the prospective future income of young workers due to the stagnation of the economy are major factors behind this sense of insecurity.

Many other countries—in Europe as well as Asia—also report low fertility rates. Recent studies indicate that countries with high female labor-force participation rates report high fertility levels (e.g., France, Norway, Sweden), while those with the lowest female labor-force participation rates report the lowest fertility levels rates (e.g., Italy, Greece, Spain, South Korea, Taiwan, Japan) (Specialist Committee on the Declining Birthrate. . .2005). The "low-fertility countries" tend to be organized around a male, single-wage-earning model, in which women are expected to leave the labor market when they have children. The "high-fertility countries," in contrast, are characterized by greater gender equality and have shown greater social commitment to day care and other institutional support for working women. They have instituted work policies and practices that are more likely to achieve balanced work and family lives for both women and men.

The fact that the responsibilities associated with housekeeping and child care, as well as elder care, are borne almost entirely by women, is another factor responsible for women's reluctance to have children. Gender attitudes, though, are not the decisive factor determining a husband's participation in housework and child care. Rather, one must note the gender gap in the labor market, specifically that a wife's income might on average constitute only about 10 percent of a total household income (Kokuritsu josei kyoiku kaikan 2009, 83, table 6-3), at the same time that a husband's working hours extend into evenings. Even when young husbands interested in assuming a greater share of housekeeping and child-care responsibilities want to contribute more, long working hours prevent them from spending more time at home (Kiwaki 2006).

The declines in marriage and childbirth rates reflect several intertwined factors, at the core of which are the burdens of family life for women. We must also add the option to marry (or to seek legal recognition and support in the form of civil unions or domestic partnerships) is not available to lesbian and gay partners. Furthermore, children born outside of marriage face not only prejudice but legal handicaps. For example, the civil code grants children born outside of marriage only one-half of the inheritance otherwise allowed.

Rise in Divorce Rates

The divorce rate has risen from 1.28 per thousand population in 1990 to 1.99 per thousand population in 2008. The most noticeable increase has been among couples married for twenty years or more. The majority of divorces take place by mutual consent (*kyogi rikon*), but of the 10 percent or so that take place through the Family Court, 70 percent are initiated by women, and where there are children under the age of twenty, women assume custody in over 80 percent of cases.

Viewed in a positive light, this development reflects changes in women's expectations regarding marriage, as well as women's entrance into the paid labor market, thus enabling women to attain some measure of financial self-sufficiency. On the other hand, the divorce rate may also reflect a downturn in the economy leading to bankruptcies and rising male unemployment rates (5 percent in 2009), accompanied by an increase in the numbers of husbands, burdened by debt, expressing their rage through domestic violence. In the most recent survey by the Cabinet Office on domestic violence, one in three women (33 percent) reported having experienced some form of violence (physical, psychological or sexual); of these women, over 13 percent said they felt their life had been threatened (Naikakufu 2008b). Among the reasons given by the forty-six thousand women who petitioned for divorce in 2007, most frequently cited—by twenty-one thousand women— was "a lack of compatibility." In addition, more than ten thousand women cited each of the following: "use of violence," "psychological abuse," and "refusal to give money for living expenses" (Kokuritsu josei kyoiku kaikan 2009, 27, fig 2-8).

Since the passage of the Law for the Prevention of Spousal Violence and the Protection of Victims (DV Prevention Law) in 2001, greater awareness about domestic violence has undoubtedly spurred many women to seek divorce. At the same time, many women probably remain in violent relationships because they cannot support themselves and their children. This is starkly demonstrated by the plight of single mothers seen in chapter 8, "Single Mothers" by Chieko Akaishi. According to the OECD (2006), more than half of single working parents lived in relative poverty in 2000, compared with an OECD average of around 20 percent. While the overwhelming majority of these women work, lack of access to regular full-time work leaves them suffering considerable financial hardship.

Policies and Laws Related to Child-care Support

The continuing decline in birthrates, with its ramifications in terms of a reduced labor force and a reduced tax base to meet the cost of caring for a growing population of elderly Japanese, has raised alarm, resulting in the introduction of various measures designed to encourage women to bear more children, and at the same time, to promote their participation in the labor market by increasing support for child care, expanding day-care facilities, promoting training and employment opportunities for women wishing to re-enter the labor market after raising children, and promoting a work-life balance. However, these measures have not been particularly successful.

The decline in the fertility rate to an all-time low of 1.57 children in 1989 led to the enactment of the Child Care Leave Law of 1991, which entitled both women and men to take unpaid leave during the first year of a child's life. This law was revised in 1995, becoming the Child Care and Family Care Leave Law. Since that time, the law has undergone a number of revisions. The most recent revision, which went into effect in 2010, prohibits negative treatment of workers applying for or taking child-care or family-care leave, obliges employers to offer exemptions from overtime, and to establish short-ened working hours for those caring for children under the age of three.

The government has instituted several other related measures toward the goal of increasing the birthrate. Among these were the Angel Plan (1994), focused on improving childcare services; the New Angel Plan (1999), on providing support services to enable women to combine work with child rearing; and the Law for Measures to Support the Development of the Next Generation (2005), aimed at bringing about changes in workplace practices so as to make them more "parenting-friendly." New rules included recom-mendations for providing on-site day-care centers, encouraging fathers to take paternity leave, offering financial support for child-care services, developing flexible working conditions, reducing overtime work, and intro-ducing work-sharing schemes. Disappointingly, however, these measures have failed significantly to halt the downward trajectory of fertility rates.

In reality, most women do not make use of childcare leave, since 70 percent leave their jobs after childbirth. Of the 30 percent or so who con-tinue working, about 90 percent take child-care leave. Moreover, this latter figure is higher among women working in large companies than in those employed at smaller firms. Thus, the percentage of employed women who actually make use of child-care leave amounts to between 20 and 30 per-cent of the total number of women in the labor market. As a result, the percentage of women—including both those who take child-care leave and those who do not—who are employed at the same job one year after giving birth as prior to their pregnancy, has remained at 25 percent. As these fig-ures demonstrate, while a system that allows for child-care leave is in place, many women find it difficult to take advantage of it.

The 2005 Revision of the Child Care and Family Care Leave Law made it possible for dispatch and part-time workers who have been at their jobs for at least one year to take advantage of child-care leave. However, even while improvements are made, the ability to take advantage of them has decreased as more women have become non-regular (temporary, contract, and part-time) workers. In addition, despite the fact that employees are legally protected from being penalized for taking child-care leave, there are reports of workers getting fired. Similar incidents have taken place in the case of women who become pregnant or give birth. In many ways, these laws and provisions exist in name only.

In 2009, the percentage of men taking child-care leave was still a mere 1.72 percent (Koseirodosho 2009a). The reasons most often cited for the low rate of men taking child-care leave include the following: particularly in small companies, male employees are needed full-time; further, many men and women continue to believe that men are not suited to the care of small children; finally, the dominant ethos—described by Masaki Mat-suda in chapter 10, "My Life as a Househusband"—insists that a man's primary commitment should be to his work. Ultimately, however, the most significant reason is undoubtedly financial, since employees on child-care leave receive a subsidy equivalent to about 50 percent of their regular wages through their employment insurance. Because men's earnings are generally higher than women's, the reduction in household income resulting from a man taking leave makes this an unviable option for most families. In addition, taking such leave has been shown to result in negative consequences when an employee is being evaluated for bonus payments, periodic pay increases, or promotions. While a lack of social support for child care is one major factor behind the low birthrate, and also the inability of women in their thirties to participate more fully in the workplace, in the case of middle-aged women wishing to return to work, responsibilities associated with the care of elderly and sick parents have been major obstacles to their re-entering the work force.

Basic Law for a Gender-Equal Society

Danjo kyodo sankaku kihonho, the official translation of which is the Basic Law for a Gender-Equal Society was passed by the Japanese Diet in June 1999. Its stated purpose is "to comprehensively and systematically promote formation of a Gender-Equal Society" in which "both women and men shall be given equal opportunities to participate voluntarily in activities in all fields as equal partners in the society, and shall be able to enjoy political, economic, social, and cultural benefits equally as well as to share responsibilities." It lays out five basic principles relating to the formation of such a society: (1) "respect for the human rights of women and men"; (2) "consideration of social systems or practices" so that they have as neutral an impact as possible on individuals' choice of roles and activities to pursue in society; (3) "joint participation by women and men in planning and deciding policies, etc."; (4) "compatibility of activities in family life and other activities" (promoting measures to enable women and men to perform home-related activities together with other activities); and (5) "international cooperation" (formation of a gender-equal society based on international cooperation). The law requires the development of a Basic Plan for Gender Equality to implement the Basic Law, and stipulates the responsibilities of the State and local governments as well as citizens in promoting a gender-equal society.

The national machinery for the promotion of the above measures was put into place with the establishment of the Council for Gender Equality, consisting of twelve cabinet ministers named by the prime minister and twelve specialists (e.g., scholars, lawyers, representatives from labor unions, mass media and women's organizations) appointed by the prime minister and chaired by the chief cabinet secretary. The council's functions include deliberating on basic policies and measures for promoting the goals of the Basic Law; submitting the results of their deliberations to the cabinet ministers or the prime minister for their consideration; and monitoring the implementation of measures taken by the government to meet those goals. In addition, local governments (at the prefectural and municipal levels) are required to establish ordinances and formulate policies to implement the principles laid out in the Basic Law.

One important impetus for enacting this law was Article 2(a) of the Convention on the Elimination of All Forms of Discrimination against Women (CEDAW), which the Japanese government ratified in 1985, according to which signatories agreed to undertake steps "To embody the principle of the equality of men and women in their national constitutions or other appropriate legislation if not yet incorporated therein and to ensure, through law and other appropriate means, the practical realization of this principle." But as noted economist, Mari Osawa, suggests, while some members of the government were genuinely concerned about gender issues, the most significant factor behind the enactment of the law was ". . . the growing perception among LDP [the ruling Liberal Democratic Party] politicians and their colleagues in industry that gender equality is good for business" (Osawa 2000, 4).

In short, reforms were seen as necessary in order to combat and reverse the trend toward a declining birthrate with its economic ramifications, including a reduced labor force, a decline in economic growth and living standards, and a reduced tax base to meet the cost of caring for a growing elderly population. Promoting measures to make it more feasible for women—and men—both to work and to raise families, was seen as necessary for raising the birthrate and also the rate of employment among women, particularly those with small children and those middle aged, both of whom constitute important sources of underutilized labor.

While many women regard the very enactment of the Basic Law as a significant advance, in that it lent political legitimacy to efforts to pursue policies for promoting equality, others expressed considerable skepticism and criticism from the start. It should be noted, first of all, that while the official English translation for the law is "Basic Law for a Gender-Equal Society," and the term "gender-equal society" is used throughout the translated text, the Japanese designation, "Danjo kyodo sankaku kihonho" does not actually include the word byodo, which means "equal" or "equality." The literal translation is closer to, "Basic Law on the Cooperative (or Joint)

Participation of Men and Women in Society." There was much discussion and controversy over the naming of the law, with many women's groups pressing for the term "gender equality"; the designation chosen reflected the antipathy on the part of conservative politicians to terms such as "equality" and "discrimination." Strong resistance to enacting the Basic Law in the first place among conservative elements in Japan became manifested in a strong backlash movement almost immediately following its implementation (see chapter 23, "Backlash Against Gender Equality after 2000" by Midori Wakakuwa and Kumiko Fujimura-Fanselow).

As the noted lawyer, Michiko Nakajima, pointed out, however, ". . . the basic law is far from fulfilling the duties stated in the Conventions [CEDAW and the Workers with Family Responsibilities Convention adopted by the International Labor Organization in 1981 and ratified by Japan in 1995]" (Nakajima 2000, 9). For one thing, the law aims at providing *equality of opportunity* for women to participate in all fields, not "the practical realization" of the principle of equality of men and women, as called for by CEDAW. Nakajima and other prominent feminists have pointed to the contradiction inherent in the idea of expecting women to participate cooperatively with men and to bear equal responsibility in all spheres of society when the government has not taken necessary steps toward equality as demonstrated by the many forms of inequality and sex discrimination that pervade various spheres of society—the family, schools, workplace, legal system, etc. (Nakajima, Makita, et al. 2000).

In 2005, the Minister of State for Gender Equality and Social Affairs was established, and in the same year the cabinet approved the Second Basic Plan for Gender Equality, based upon the Basic Law. The Second Basic Plan set up numerical targets in twelve areas, among them: raising the proportion of women occupying leadership positions in all fields of society (both private and public sector) to 30 percent by 2020; raising the ratio of women on national university faculties to 20 percent by 2010; creating universal (100 percent) awareness within Japan of the term "gender-equal society" by fiscal year 2010; raising the ratio of companies engaging in positive (affirmative) action to 40 percent by fiscal year 2009; raising the ratio of workers taking child-care leave to 10 percent for men and 80 percent for women by around 2014; promoting a strategy of "zero-waiting list" for children seeking admission to child-care facilities, and obtaining universal recognition that the actions of "slapping" and "threatening with a clenched fist" occurring between married couples constitute acts of violence. In fact, however, pressure exerted by proponents of the backlash movement has led to formulation of gender-equal plans by some municipalities that do not reflect the principles set out in the Basic Law. Meanwhile, the numerical targets remain unmet. The Third Basic Plan for Gender Equality is currently in the process of formulation, and it is expected to place greater emphasis on the implementation of priorities set forth in the Second Plan.

The Law for the Prevention of Spousal Violence and the Protection of Victims

One significant by-product of the enactment of the Basic Law was the Law for the Prevention of Spousal Violence and the Protection of Victims (DV Prevention Law), enacted in 2001. In the essay on domestic violence included in *Japanese Women*, the author, Aiko Hada (1995) noted that domestic violence had just begun to gain public awareness in Japan as a social problem. At that time, laws and social measures to respond to domestic violence and help victims were lacking. Pressure by women's groups on the Japanese government to take action regarding domestic violence mounted in the wake of the 1995 United Nations Fourth World Conference on Women held in Beijing, where eradication of violence against women was a major focus. In 1999 the government conducted its first nationwide survey on the subject. The results, which showed that 5 percent of wives had experienced life-threatening violence at the hands of their husbands, spurred the enactment of the DV Prevention Law. The law called for the establishment of Spousal Violence Counseling and Support Centers in prefectures to provide consultation and counseling, temporary protection, and information as well as other forms of assistance. The law enabled district courts to issue six-month restraining orders against abusers and order their eviction from the home for up to two weeks. Abusers who violate court orders could receive sentences up to a year in jail and fines up to one million yen ($10,000).

The law was characterized by several flaws, among them the fact that in order to obtain a restraining order, the victim must carry the burden of proof. The victim must notify authorities and submit either a notarized affidavit or reports from doctors, women's shelters, or the police backing up the claim of abuse. The law was amended in 2004 and again in 2007 to cover not only spouses but also former spouses, to allow for issuance of orders of protection with regard to threats of physical harm, and to extend protection to victims' children and relatives. The revision also made it explicit that the law covered non-Japanese nationals and persons with disabilities. In addition, the law now placed responsibility on national and local governments to prevent violence and to provide protection to victims, as well as support to enable victims to become self-sufficient. The Spousal Violence Counseling and Support Centers were given the additional task of providing support to victims in finding employment and housing as well as information on how to access other types of assistance. Further amendments to the law have been advocated to cover cases of dating violence among unmarried couples and also same-sex partners and to establish shelters for gender minorities and men.

The effectiveness of these laws, whether viewed in terms of contributing to the goal of stopping or reversing the decline in birthrates, advancing women's employment status, increasing women's presence in decision-making positions, or tackling the problem of domestic violence, has been limited for a number of reasons. Foremost among them is the failure to address the fundamental issue of gender inequality and sex discrimination and to provide adequate funding for reforms in such areas as child-care and elderly care, pensions, and support for victims of domestic violence. Also important to note is the emergence, almost immediately following the enactment of the Basic Law, of a strong backlash movement led by conservative politicians, academics, and journalists against policies designed to promote gender equality.

Emergence of Issues Concerning Minority Groups

As is the case in every society, the lives of women in Japan are strongly affected by their social class, educational background, sexual orientation, marital status, place of residence, ethnicity, and nationality. The social, economic, and political realities described earlier, among them employment policies and practices that discriminate against women, discriminatory laws relating to marriage and inheritance, the economic downturn that has continued since the early 1990s and worsened dramatically since 2008, the growing incidence of domestic violence, all have different impacts on different groups of women.

The Japan Federation of Bar Associations (JFBA), in its shadow report to the CEDAW Committee in advance of the examination of the sixth periodic report of the Japanese government to the Committee in July 2009, cites data demonstrating the growing presence in Japan of foreigners and migrants from as many as 190 different countries. The largest number of migrants is Chinese, followed by Koreans, Brazilians, and Filipinos. In addition there are those with Japanese nationality who are indigenous peoples (the Ainu), national minorities, including the Buraku people and the people of Okinawa, as well as descendants of those from former Japanese colonies, including the Zainichi Koreans. The report notes that ". . . Japanese society is already changing into [a] multiracial and multicultural society," and continues, "but Japanese society operates on the assumption that those of other races and cultures will assimilate and integrate into Japanese society in areas such as language, culture, and social systems, and it can be said the notion of coexisting in a multicultural environment hardly exists" (JFBA 2009, 72).

Much the same can be said with regard to issues concerning sexual minorities, which are treated in part IV, "Changing Sexualities." Many Japanese hold negative views toward lesbian, gay, bisexual, and transgender people (LGBT), but these are based primarily on stereotyped and negative images presented through the mass media; very few people are aware of the presence of lesbian, gay, bisexual, and transgender people in their midst. Their low visibility reflects a lack of social support as well as an absence of legal protections and rights. Not until the 1980s did some feminists begin to acknowledge the presence of lesbians in their midst, and this "helped bring a measure of visibility—however limited it may have been at the time" (Sawabe 2008,10). Not until 2007 did issues concerning sexual minorities become a central focus of the annual conference held by the Women's Studies Association of Japan, despite the fact that writings by and about sexual minorities and activism among members of these groups had, in fact, existed for some time, albeit not with visibility among mainstream feminist groups.

Growing attention and scrutiny by the UN in recent years to the rights of minority groups—indigenous peoples, racial minorities, migrants, as well as sexual minorities—have offered some support to minority women in Japan, exposing issues of discrimination and human rights previously hidden from view. The Japanese government has felt pressured to meet their obligations under UN conventions pertaining to human rights, including the CEDAW, the International Covenant on Civil and Political Rights (ICCPR), and the Convention on the Elimination of All Forms of Racial Discrimination (CERD). Japanese NGOs that work on issues of human rights and women's rights—among them GayJapanNews, a Tokyo-based LGBT news source and advocacy group, the Japan Federation of Bar Associations, the Buraku Liberation and Human Rights Research Institute, the Ainu Resource Center, the Women's Active Museum on War and Peace, the Asia-Japan Women's Resource Center, and the Association of Korean Human Rights in Japan—have submitted shadow reports to and spoken before the UN Human Rights Committee (which monitors compliance with the ICCPR) and the CEDAW Committee (which monitors compliance with the CEDAW) in advance of the examinations held periodically by these committees to review the Japanese government's compliance with its treaty obligations as well as previous recommendations made by the committees. These groups have brought international pressure to bear on the

Japanese government to move toward compliance. The UN Human Rights Committee in 2008 urged the Japanese government to amend its legislation to include sexual orientation among the prohibited grounds of discrimination, and to ensure that benefits granted to unmarried cohabiting heterosexual couples are equally granted to unmarried cohabiting same-sex couples.

While issues pertaining to the "comfort women," women from traditionally discriminated groups such as the Ainu, Buraku, and Zainichi Koreans, migrant women, including women trafficked to work in the sex industry, and sexual minorities, have yet to be fully taken up by mainstream media, NGO groups and publications advocating for women's rights have worked to increase the awareness of their identities and the issues they confront. These efforts have produced an awareness among women's rights activists and feminist researchers of the need to incorporate the perspectives of minority women—including sexual minorities—in actions they take or in any research or teaching they conduct, as illustrated in many of the essays contained in this volume.

Note

1. Currency exchange rates between the Japanese yen and the US dollar fluctuate. For simplicity, 100 yen are equated with one US dollar throughout the book.

Works Cited

Hada, Aiko. 1995. "Domestic Violence." In *Japanese Women: New Feminist Perspectives on the Past, Present, and Future*, ed. Kumiko Fujimura-Fanselow and Atsuko Kameda. New York: The Feminist Press.

Japan Federation of Bar Associations (JFBA). 2009. Update Report on Issues and Questions from the Committee on the Elimination of Discrimination against Women with regard to the Sixth Periodic Report of the Japanese Government. http://www2.ohchr.org/english/bodies/cedaw/docs/ngos/Bar_Association_June09_Japan_cedaw44.pdf

Kiwaki, Nachiko. 2006. "Danshi no kosodate" (Upbringing of boys). In *Nijuisseiki ajia kazoku* (Families in 21st century Asia), ed. Emiko Ochiai and Kayoko Ueno. Tokyo: Akashi shoten.

Kokuritsu josei kyoiku kaikan (National Women's Education Center), ed. 2009. *Danjo kyodo sankaku tokei deetabukku—Nihon no josei to dansei—2009* (Gender statistics book—women and men in Japan—2009). Tokyo: Gyosei.

Koseirodosho (Ministry of Health, Labor and Welfare). 2009a. *Heisei nijuichinendo koyo kinto kihon chosa* (Basic survey on employment equality 2009).

———. 2009b. *Josei rodo hakusho 2008* (White paper on female labor 2008).

Naikakufu (Cabinet Office, Government of Japan). 2008a. Danjo kyodo sankaku hakusho (White paper on gender equality). Tokyo: Saiki insatsu.

———. 2008b. *Danjokan no boryoku ni kansuru chosa* (Survey on violence between males and females). http://www.gender.go.jp/e-vaw/chousa/images/pdf/chousagai-you2103.pdf

Nakajima, Michiko. 2000. "The Problems of the Basic Law on the Joint/Cooperative Participation of Men and Women in Society." *Women's Asia 21 Voices from Japan*, no. 6 (Autumn): 9-12.

———. Mayumi Makita, Kimiko Ogasawara, Kaoru Aoyama and Yayori Matsui. 2000. "Women's Movement in Japan: Present and Future—A Roundtable Discussion." *Women's Asia 21 Voices from Japan*, no. 6 (Autumn): 19-23.

Osawa, Mari. 2000. "Government approaches to gender equality in the mid-1990s." *Social Science Japan Journal* (3), no. 1: 3-19.

OECD. 2006. *Economic Survey of Japan 2006.*

———. 2008. *Growing Unequal? Income Distribution and Poverty in OECD Countries.* http://www.oecd.org/document/53/0,3343,en_2649_33933_41460917_1_1_1_1,00.html.

Sawabe, Hitomi. 2008. "The Symbolic Tree of Lesbianism in Japan: An overview of lesbian activist history and literary works." In *Sparkling Rain: And Other Fiction from Japan of Women Who Love Women*, ed. Barbara Summerhawk and Kimberly Hughes. Chicago: New Victoria Publishers.

Specialist Committee on the Declining Birthrate and Gender-Equal Participation, Council for Gender Equality. 2005. "International Comparison of the Social Environment regarding the Declining Birthrates and Gender-Equality." http://www.gender.go.jp/english_contents/siryou/english-1.pdf

I

CULTURAL AND HISTORICAL PERSPECTIVES

The Struggle for Legal Rights and Reforms: A Historical View

Sachiko Kaneko

Japanese women had few individual or political rights before World War II. Under the prevailing *ie*, or family, system, which was the foundation of prewar Japanese society, the proper place for women was considered to be within the home, under the authority of the male family head. Any type of involvement by women in political activities was thought to be contradictory to natural physiological and psychological laws and to the traditions and customs of Japanese society.[1] Yet, in the face of such prevailing attitudes, many women struggled for their rights.

Women's Place

The Political Situation

In the mid-nineteenth century, in the face of pressures from Western countries as well as changes taking place within the country itself, Japan was forced to abandon its policy of seclusion, which dated back nearly three hundred years. With the Meiji Restoration of 1868 Japan began a process of transformation from a feudal to a modern, unified national state. The new government, in order to guarantee the nation's independence and to achieve self-sufficiency, worked to build its power and national wealth through economic and military development, based on knowledge, ideas, and skills from the West, particularly the United States and Europe.

The government, however, shifted away from its Western-oriented policies in 1874, when the Popular Rights Movement was born and people began to call for the establishment of a national assembly. Several women took part in this political cause.[2] It was reported that on the island of Shikoku in 1878 Kita Kusunose, a forty-five-year-old woman, argued that she should have the right to vote because she had been paying taxes as the household head since her husband's death in 1872. She was called the "grandma of people's rights." Toshiko Kishida lectured and wrote about equal rights for women beginning in 1882. Hideko Kageyama (later Fukuda) was influenced by one of Kishida's speeches, joined the Popular Rights Movement, and later became a socialist. At that time women could still attend political meetings and organize political groups.

The government suppressed the Popular Rights Movement, while promising to establish an assembly by 1881. It sought to create a national polity as soon as possible in order to build a modern country that could compete with other nations. In 1889 the Maiji Constitution was proclaimed, establishing a constitutional monarchy with the emperor as sovereign head of state.

During the next year three important events occurred. The first took place when the National Diet, Japan's national assembly, convened with members of the Lower House who had been elected on the basis of limited franchises. Only men who paid a certain amount in taxes had the right to vote. Second was the adoption of the Imperial Rescript on Education, based on Confucian ideas, which emphasized loyalty to the emperor and filial piety to parents. The goal of education was to create subjects willing to serve the nation and the emperor, and pupils were indoctrinated with this family-state ideology. Japan was to be regarded as a family-state and the emperor the head of the Japanese family. Finally, the government issued the Meeting and Political Organization Law in 1890, which restricted all political activities.

Women's political participation became still more difficult under the Police Security Regulations of 1900, which succeeded the Law of 1890. Article 5 prohibited women and minors from joining political organizations, holding or attending meetings in which political speeches or lectures were given, and initiating such meetings.[3] Women were denied all political rights at both local and national levels.

In 1905, a group of women from a small socialist group called the Heiminsha (Commoners' Association) petitioned for a revision of Article 5. They gathered hundreds of signatures and went to the Diet every year until 1909, though without any success.[4]

The *ie,* or Family, System

In 1898 the civil code established a family network of relationships known as the *ie* system. According to this code, the patriarchal head of the family (usually the eldest son) held unquestioned authority over the rest of the family. Together with the privilege of primogeniture, he had an obligation to support the family financially. He could designate the areas where the rest of the family could reside; if they protested, he did not have to support them. Women under twenty-five and men under thirty needed the consent of the head of the family before marrying.

A woman had very few legal rights. When she married she entered her husband's family (and his family register), and control of her property was transferred to her husband. Custody of children was held by the father exclusively. Illegitimate sons (if any) acknowledged by their fathers had prior rights to the family estate over legitimate daughters. For this reason women were expected to produce male heirs.

In the event of divorce there was also severe discrimination. A wife's adultery constituted grounds for divorce, and she could be punished under the new criminal code of 1880. In the case of the husband, only if he committed adultery with a married woman and was sued by her husband and punished would the wife be granted a divorce. Adultery was also defined differently for men and women. Although concubinage was officially abolished in 1880, licensed prostitution still existed, and a polygamous attitude was prevalent across all strata of Japanese society.

Following Japan's victory in the Sino-Japanese War (1894-95) the government promoted girls' education designed to lend support to the family system and the place of women within that system. The Girls' High School Law, issued in 1899, aimed to educate girls to become "good wives and wise mothers." The number of women's secondary schools increased as time passed. However, women were expected to support their husbands, raise children, and not work outside the home.[5]

The Struggle for Political Rights

Shin fujin kyokai (The New Women's Association)
The death of the Meiji emperor marked the beginning of the Taisho period (1912-26). After World War I the universal manhood suffrage movement emerged, and *demokurashii* (democracy) became a key word to characterize the Taisho period. Raicho Hiratsuka formed the New Women's Association—the first organization of female citizens to be established on a nationwide scale—with Fusae Ichikawa in 1920.[6] It had 331 members that first year. During the next year the Sekirankai (Red Wave Society), the first socialist women's organization, was founded in Tokyo by Kikue Yamakawa.

Hiratsuka called for the reconstruction of society. Motherhood, she insisted, should be esteemed, and she criticized the patriarchal *ie* system and demanded rights for women and children. The association called for women's right to political participation through a revision of the Security Police Law, Article 5. It also petitioned the Diet to enact a law to restrict marriage for men with venereal diseases.[7]

The New Women's Association held meetings and lectures across Japan.

The group collected more than two thousand signatures for the revision of Article 5. Hiratsuka and Ichikawa visited legislators, asking for cooperation and support, from early morning to late evening. At the same time, in order to move around and work more efficiently, they took to wearing Western clothes when they went out, instead of the traditional kimono, with its wide sleeves and tight sashes. Hiratsuka and Ichikawa worked diligently, but personal conflicts and differences ended their work together. Hiratsuka withdrew from the movement, and Ichikawa went to the United States in order to observe the women's movement and labor movement there.

Mumeo Oku became the new leader of the movement. In 1922 she visited the infamous Baron Fujimura, who had been a strong opponent of Oku's group. He was impressed by the young mother, who had a baby on her back during the visit. His image of the suffragettes changed, and he thereafter supported the movement. Later in 1922 the petition was approved, and Article 5 was revised. Women were now able to organize and participate in political meetings.

Female schoolteachers and housewives supported this political reform. The most cooperative group was the Nihon kirisutokyo fujin kyofukai (Japan Christian Women's Organization), modelled on the Woman's Christian Temperance Union, originally organized in 1874 in the United States to work for the prohibition of alcohol. Mary Leavitt, of the US organization, gave a series of lectures in Japan, one of which impressed Kajiko Yajima. In 1886 Yajima, president of a girls' school based on Christianity, began organizing for the Kyofukai (literally meaning "reform society") in Japan. She was particularly interested in the issue because she had divorced a drunken husband. The members decided to work for specific reforms because they thought Japanese society was in need of purification. They regarded the polygamous attitude within Japanese society as a social evil and thought concubinage and prostitution should be abolished. They insisted on monogamy and petitioned for a revision of the civil code and the criminal code. They supported the abolition of licensed prostitution, and they built a shelter for prostitutes who had run away from brothels.[8]

In 1916 the Kyofukai began a two-year campaign against building prostitution quarters in Osaka but failed. Ochimi Kubushiro, a successor of Yajima, realized the necessity of securing women's rights and declared that suffrage was indispensable for the success of their cause.

Fusen kakutoku domei (The Women's Suffrage League)
After the Great Kanto Earthquake of 1923, women's groups worked together to help victims and the Tokyo rengo fujinkai (Federation of Women's Association in Tokyo) was formed. Kubushiro saw this as an opportune time

to organize a national women's suffrage organization. Universal male suffrage was drawing near (it was approved in 1925). Fusae Ichikawa worked at the Tokyo International Labor Organization after spending several years in the United States. While working in the United States, she had visited Hull House, founded by Jane Addams, and spoken with various union leaders. She had also met Alice Paul, a leader of the National Woman's Party, who encouraged her to work for women's suffrage in Japan.[9]

In 1924 Kubushiro and Ichikawa established the Fujin sanseiken kakutoku kisej domeikai (League for the Realization of Women's Suffrage). During the next year the organization changed its name to the Fusen kakutoku domei (Women's Suffrage League). After Kubushiro's withdrawal Ichikawa became the general secretary and was regarded as the central figure in this struggle.

The league issued the following manifesto:

> Women, who form one-half of the population of the country, have been left entirely outside the field of political activity, classified along with males of less than 25 years of age and those who are recipients of relief or aid from State or private organizations. We women feel ourselves no longer compelled to explain the reasons why it is at once natural and necessary for us, who are both human beings and citizens, to participate in the administration of our country. . . .We women must concentrate our energies solely on one thing, namely, the acquisition of the right to take part in politics, and cooperate with one another regardless of any political, religious and other differences we may have.[10]

Membership in the league increased each year. There were about 200 members at the beginning, 483 in 1927, and 1,762 in 1932. In the western part of Japan the Zen kansai fujinrengokai (All-Kansai Women's Federation) supported the league. Together they collected fifty-six thousand signatures and sent them to the House of Representatives in 1927. By 1931 the government was on the verge of granting the franchise to women at the local (from village to city) level. It appeared that the acquisition of women's suffrage was imminent.

Family Life—Women's Issues

Taisho Period (1912-26)

While some women became active outside the home, for example, joining the suffrage movement, others were facing family problems inside the home. This is evident in the number of women's magazines and women's columns in newspapers which appeared. Women's issues became popular

early in the Taisho period. *Seito* (Bluestocking) (1911-16) was published
by Raicho Hiratsuka, and in 1914 *Yomiuri shimbun*, a national newspaper,
established a column for women. Two important women's magazines, *Fujin
koron* (Women's review) in 1916 and *Shufu no tomo* (Friends of housewives),
began publishing in 1917. These publications were widely read by women;
the percentage of girls entering school had reached 96 percent by 1907.[11]

Fujin koron was directed at intellectuals and dealt with theoretical issues
of women's liberation such as the famous, ongoing "debate over the protection and support of motherhood."[12] Akiko Yosano, a well-known poet,
advocated the economic independence of married women. Hiratsuka was
more concerned, however, with the protection of motherhood. She had
been influenced by the ideas of Ellen Key, the Swedish thinker and author
of *Love and Marriage* (1903). Hiratsuka emphasized the incompatibility of work outside the home and raising children inside the home. Then
Kikue Yamakawa argued from a socialist point of view that the important
thing was to change economic relations in the existing society. This debate
reflected the fact that increasing numbers of women—including married
women—were working outside the home in silk reeling and cotton spinning mills, contributing to the economic development of their country.

On the other hand, *Shufu no tomo* dealt with various problems women
faced managing the family in their daily lives.[13] Thrift and savings were
emphasized. During the Taisho period the number of people in the middle
class increased as industrialization and urbanization progressed. Nuclear
families emerged, consisting only of the husband, wife, and children, and
young housewives of this class were particularly attracted to *Shufu no tomo*.
It was supported by a wide range of women and obtained the largest circulation among all magazines in 1920, reaching about 600,000 in 1931 and
1,800,000 in 1941.

Shufu no tomo listened to women's voices; letters from readers were welcomed and printed. Eventually, an advice column, or *minoue sodan*, was
instituted to serve the readers. The letters pointed to some of the common
problems women faced. In a typical letter a housewife wrote about how
she suffered from her husband's extramarital affairs and drinking, which
led to the family's poverty. In addition, her husband had infected her with
a venereal disease. Another letter dealt with divorce, from a bride who was
expected to work hard but could not satisfy her parents-in-law and was
driven out of the family. Her in-laws had forced her to divorce her husband and leave their children behind. There were other letters from single
women who suffered from the prospect of forced marriages arranged by
parents or relatives.[14]

The Early Showa Period (1926-45)

The early Showa period saw an increase in social insecurity brought about by the economic depression and the Manchurian Incident of 1931 (which marked a significant step in Japan's expansion into China). Advice columns were also popular at this time. *Yomiuri shimbun* published an advice column from 1931 to 1937 with Natsu Kawasaki as one of the columnists. She was an educator and later became director of the action committee for the first Hahaoya taikai (Mother's Congress) in 1955.[15] Of the 1,248 letters that appeared between 1931 and 1937, Kawasaki answered 954 (76.4 percent), most of them submitted by young women, roughly half of whom were married and the other half single.[16]

Women's problems varied; some were economic, some emotional, and others physical. The largest number of letters from married women were about their husbands' extramarital affairs. The next largest number were about loveless marriages. Single women sought advice about love and marriage: they wanted to marry men whom they loved, but their parents tended to force "arranged" marriages. Many also suffered from rape or sexual harassment. The following is a typical letter from a married woman:

> Age: 22. I was forced to marry at the age of 19. My husband is selfish and drinks a lot. I was mistreated by my mother-in-law so that I lost weight and my breast milk stopped. I came back to my own parents' home, but my parents-in-law refused to allow my child to come to me. (1934.5.3)

Under the *ie* system filial piety and obedience were demanded of women. A bride had to serve her parents-in-law first, then her husband. The parent-child relation was much more important than the relationship between wife and husband. Many women could not even consider divorce, since they were economically dependent on their husbands. After a divorce the custody of children was granted to the father according to the civil code.

Kawasaki's advice, generally, was as follows: she didn't ignore or deny filial piety but limited its meaning. Instead of passive self-sacrifice, women should find their own way, which would eventually comfort their parents. She told young women not to abandon the hope of love in marriage and to try to persuade parents of its benefits. She advised that married women reside separately from in-laws, because the basis of the family should be the husband and wife. She suggested couples trying to live together for the children instead of considering divorce. Economic independence was particularly difficult for divorcees. Finally, Kawasaki believed women's problems could be solved not by women's awareness alone but also by changes in the social system. She supported a revision of the civil code and the protection of motherhood as well as adequate vocational training and sex education.

These letters indicate not only the conflicts that existed under the *ie* system but also that the system itself did not work. Ironically, the *minoue sodan* column in *Yomiuri* was terminated in 1937 when the fighting in China turned into a war.

The Difficulties of War

Japan had taken the first step toward war with the Manchurian Incident of 1931. Militarism swept the country. The government suppressed the growing labor movement and arrested socialists. Those with more liberal ideas found it difficult to speak and write freely in public.

In 1932 the Kokubo fujinkai (Women's National Defense Association) was established and was supported by the army. There was also a group called the Aikoku fujinkai (Women's Patriotic Society), which had been formed in 1901 and played an active role during the Russo-Japanese War (1904-5). These two groups saw soldiers off at train stations and prepared comfort bags for the war effort. Their activities were similar in nature, and they soon became competitive in seeking to increase their memberships. By the end of 1935 the membership of the Defense Association stood at 2.5 million and outnumbered that of the Patriotic Society, 2.2 million.[17]

Japan's militaristic policies affected the activities of Ichikawa's group too. Attainment of suffrage became more difficult, and membership rapidly decreased from 1,762 in 1932 to 690 in 1939. The group had to change its course in order to survive. Instead of suffrage, members emphasized local consumer problems and a reform election campaign for the Tokyo Municipal Assembly. They demanded passage of the Protection of Mother-and-Child Bill in 1934. This bill was approved in 1936 to support poor mothers because the government saw an increase in population as a way to help the war effort. It commended mothers for having a large number of children.

Ichikawa felt depressed when the war with China began, and she wrote: "Under these circumstances, the attainment of suffrage becomes much harder. Yet our purpose of suffrage is to cooperate with the government and men in order to make a contribution to our nation and society."[18] When she came home to Aichi Prefecture to visit her mother, Ichikawa attended a local meeting of the Women's National Defense Association. Many women, young and old, seemed happy to leave their homes to hear lectures by local veterans. She felt that this was a kind of "emancipation." Women in rural villages had never had time of their own in the past, but now they could attend a meeting free from their chores for half a day.

It is ironic that, while Japanese women had no political rights, their social participation was encouraged at the grassroots level. The Women's

Suffrage League had disbanded in 1940. But in 1942, after Japan's attack on Pearl Harbor, Dai Nihon fujinkai (the Greater Japan Women's Organization) was established, and all women's groups were consolidated under the control of government authorities. Awkwardly, the government emphasized that a woman's place was in the home, but at the same time accepted the fact that, because of the war, women began to work outside the home in factories. Thus, the *ie* system, previously insisted upon by the government, collapsed under war conditions.

Postwar Reforms

Japan was defeated and accepted the Potsdam Declaration on August 15, 1945. Fusae Ichikawa established Sengo taisaku fujin iinkai (the Women's Committee on Postwar Countermeasures) on August 25 and once again demanded women's suffrage. It was possible to organize a sizable group in a short time because of women's history of struggle in the prewar period and the existence of the former network.

On October 9, 1945 a new Cabinet came into power, with Kijuro Shidehara as prime minister. On October 10 the group held a conference and decided to enfranchise women.[19] On October 11 the Supreme Commander for the Allied Powers, General Douglas MacArthur, called on the Japanese government to institute five basic reforms in the social order, including the emancipation of women through their enfranchisement and the liberalization of education. His aim was to democratize Japan as well as to pacify and stabilize the country. By the end of 1945 women's suffrage was approved under a revision of the election law, and in the following year thirty-nine women were elected in the first national general election.

The new Japanese Constitution was proclaimed in 1946. It clearly outlined Japan's renunciation of war and respect for fundamental human rights. Article 14 stated that all people are equal under the law and that there would be no discrimination in political, economic, or social relations because of race, creed, sex, social status, or family origin. Article 24 prescribed that marriage would be based only on the consent of both individuals.

With the new constitution it was necessary to revise certain laws. The government set up the Judiciary and Legislative Council, and revision of the civil code was discussed. A heated controversy ensued about whether to abolish the *ie* system. Then, Kawasaki, a member of the council, gave an impressive speech in support of the new system. She explained women's pre-war experiences based on her experience with *minoue sodan*: "I have received as many as 70,000 letters, 90 percent of which were from women. These letters pointed out women's miserable lives. Some suffered because of economic problems, others because of family troubles. All these problems derived from the *ie* system."[20] Kawasaki said that women would raise joyful voices if the *ie* system were to be revised, and she urged council members to listen to those voices. The revised civil code was issued in 1947, and Japanese women became free from the patriarchal *ie* system.

Conclusion

It was not until after World War II that Japanese women finally attained the right of suffrage and legal equality in marriage. Yet, as I have described here, many women actively struggled to seize those rights for themselves from the very beginning of the Meiji period, when Japan embarked on its program of modernization. The welfare and interests of women were constantly subordinated to the interests of the nation-state and the *ie* system. The new Constitution, based on democratic ideals of equality and respect for individual human rights, which was proclaimed following Japan's defeat in World War II, finally granted political rights to women. At the same time, the abolition of the *ie* system allowed women to enjoy equality within marriage and in the home. Women, who had suffered bitter experiences under the traditional system and had fought so long for these reforms, welcomed these changes.

Once women had at last achieved legal equality, the remaining challenge was to bring about actual, substantive equality. It is a challenge that has proven to be much more difficult, requiring, as it does, fundamental changes in individual and social attitudes regarding gender roles.

Notes

1. See Baron Yoshiro Fujimura's speech in 1921 before the House of Peers, in Fusae Ichikawa, *Ichikawa Fusae jiden, senzen hen* (Autobiography of Fusae Ichikawa, the prewar period) (Tokyo: Shinjuku shobo, 1975), 94. In Japanese mythology, however, the Sun Goddess, Amaterasu, ruled the Heaven and commissioned her grandson to govern the Earth—the islands of Japan. According to Chinese historical sources, Queen Himiko ruled a part of Japan around A.D. 250. In the seventh and eighth centuries several empresses engaged in social and political activities. For a brief history of Japanese women in the premodern period, see Dorothy Robin-Mowry, *The Hidden Sun: Women of Modern Japan* (Boulder, CO.: Westview Press, 1983), 5-29.

2. For some individuals in the women's movement during the Meiji period, see Mioko Fujieda's article, chapter 22, "Japan's First Phase of Feminism," in this volume; and Sharon L. Sievers, *Flowers in Salt: The Beginnings of Feminist Consciousness in Modern Japan* (Stanford, CA.: Stanford University Press, 1983).

3. Translation of Article 5 from Robin-Mowry (*Hidden Sun,* 64), with English slightly changed by the author.

4. Katsuko Kodama, *Fujin sanseiken undo shoshi* (A short history of the women's suffrage movement) (Tokyo: Domesu shuppan, 1981), 29-34.

5. For a discussion of women's education in the Meiji period, see chapter 5 in this volume.

6. Hiratsuka became involved in the women's movement after she published *Seito* (Bluestocking), a literary magazine for women, and advocated the appearance of female "geniuses" in 1911.

7. Raicho Hiratsuka, *Genshi josei wa taiyo de atta: Hiratsuka Raicho jiden* (In the beginning woman was the sun: autobiography of Raicho Hiratsuka), (Tokyo: Otsuki shoten, 1973), 2:38-213

8. See Nihon kirisutokyo fujin kyofukai, ed., *Nihon kirisutokyo fujin kyofukai hyakunenshi* (A centennial history of the Japan Christian Women's Organization) (Tokyo: Domesu shuppan, 1989); and Sachiko Kaneko, *Kindai Nihon joseiron no keifu* (The genealogy of ideas and controversies on women in modern Japan), (Tokyo: Fuji shuppan, 1999), 66-87.

9. Ichikawa, *Ichikawa Fusae jiden*, 118.

10. Sen Katayama, "The Political Position of Women," *Japanese Women* 2, no. 6 (November 1939): 2 (with English slightly changed by the author).

11. Masashi Fukaya, *Ryosai kenbo shugi no kyoiku* (Education for good wives and wise mothers) (Tokyo: Reimei shobo, 1966), 212.

12. See Nobuko Kochi, ed., *Shiryo: bosei hogo ronso* (Materials: the debate over the protection and support of motherhood) (Tokyo: Domesu shuppan, 1984).

13. Shufunotomosha, ed., *Shufunotomosha no gojunen* (Fifty years of the Shufunotomo publishing company) (Tokyo: Shufunotomosha, 1967), 41-56.

14. Sachiko Kaneko, *Kindai Nihon joseiron no keifu* (The genealogy of ideas and controversies on women in modern Japan), (Tokyo: Fuji shuppan, 1999), 149-176.

15. See Hikaru Hayashi, *Hahaoya ga kawareba shakai ga kawaru: Kawasaki Natsu den* (If mothers change, society will change: a biography of Natsu Kawasaki) (Tokyo: Sodo bunka, 1974).

16. The following examples of *"minoue sodan"* are from Sachiko Kaneko, *Kindai Nihon joseiron no keifu* (The genealogy of ideas and controversies on women in modern Japan), (Tokyo: Fuji shuppan, 1999), 211-218.

17. Tadatoshi Fujii, *Kokubo fujinkai: hinomaru to kappogi* (The Women's National Defense Association: the rising sun and cooking aprons) (Tokyo: Iwanami shoten, 1985), 95.

18. Ichikawa, *Ichikawa Fusae jiden*, 434.

19. Zenjiro Horikiri, "Fujin sanseiken wa Makkasa kara no okurimono dewa nai" (Women's suffrage was not given by MacArthur), in Fujin sansei jusshunen kinen gyoji jikko iinkai zanmu seiri iinkai, ed., *Fujin sansei jusshunen kinen gyoji jikko iinkai kiroku* (The record of the acting committee for the commemorative event of the tenth anniversary of women's suffrage) (September 1959), in *Seiji* (Politics), vol. 2 of *Nihon fujin mondai shiryo shusei* (Compiled materials on Japanese women's issues), ed. Fusae Ichikawa (Tokyo: Domesu shuppan, 1977), 677-78.

20. Sakae Wagatsuma, ed., *Sengo ni okeru minpo kaisei no keika* (The process of revising the civil code after the war) (Tokyo: Nihon hyoronsha, 1956), 83.

Works Cited

Fujii, Tadatoshi. 1985. *Kokubo fujinkai: hinomaru to kappogi* (The Women's National Defense Association: the rising sun and cooking aprons). Tokyo: Iwanami shoten.

Fujin sansei jusshunen kinen gyoji jikko iinkai zanmu seiri iinkai, ed. 1959. *Fujin sansei jusshunen kinen gyoji jikko iinkai kiroku* (the record of the acting committee for the commemorative event of the tenth anniversary of women's suffrage). In *Seiji* (Politics), vol.2 of *Nihon fujin mondai shiryo shusei* (Compiled materials on Japanese women's issues), ed. Fusae Ichikawa. Tokyo: Domesu shuppan, 1977.

Fukaya, Masashi. 1966. *Ryosai kenbo shugi no kyoiku* (Education for good wives and wise mothers). Tokyo: Reimei shobo.

Hayashi, Hikaru. 1974. *Hahaoya ga kawareba shakai ga kawaru: Kawasaki Natsu den* (If mothers change, society will change: a biography of Natsu Kawasaki) Tokyo: Sodo bunka.

Hiratsuka, Raicho. 1973. *Genshi josei wa taiyo de atta: Hiratsuka Raicho jiden* (In the beginning woman was the sun: autobiography of Raicho Hiratsuka), vol. 2. Tokyo: Otsuki shoten.

Ichikawa, Fusae. 1975. *Ichikawa Fusae jiden, senzen hen* (Autobiography of Fusae Ichikawa, the prewar period). Tokyo: Shinjuku shobo.

Kaneko, Sachiko. 1999. *Kindai Nihon joseiron no keifu* (The genealogy of ideas and controversies on women in modern Japan). Tokyo: Fuji shuppan.

Katayama, Sen. 1939. "The Political Position of Women." *Japanese Women* 2, no. 6.

Kodama, Katsuko. 1981. *Fujin sanseiken undo shoshi* (A short history of the women's suffrage movement). Tokyo: Domesu shuppan.

Kochi, Nobuko, ed. 1984. *Shiryo: Bosei hogo ronso* (Materials: the debate over the protection and support of motherhood). Tokyo: Domesu shuppan.

Nihon kirisutokyo fujin kyofuka, ed. 1989. *Nihon kirisutokyo fujin kyofukai hyanku-nenshi* (A centennial history of the Japan Christian Women's Organization). Tokyo: Domesu shuppan.

Robin-Mowry, Dorothy. 1983. *The Hidden Sun: Women of Modern Japan*. Boulder, CO: Westview Press.

Shufunotomosha, ed. 1967. *Shufunotomosha no gojunen* (Fifty years of Shufunotomo publishing company). Tokyo: Shufunotomosha.

Sievers, Sharon L. 1983. *Flowers in Salt: The Beginnings of Feminist Consciousness in Modern Japan*. Stanford, CA: Stanford University Press.

Wagatsuma, Sakae, ed. 1956. *Sengo ni okeru minpo kaisei no keika* (The process of revising the civil code after the war). Tokyo: Nihon hyoronsha.

Women in Japanese Buddhism

2

Haruko K. Okano
Translated by Kumiko Fujimura-
Fanselow and Yoko Tsuruta

In Japan today, there are still certain designated places that by tradition are barred to women. For example, women are not permitted to climb certain so-called *reizan* (holy mountains) such as Omine Mountain in Nara. Similarly, there is a taboo against women setting foot at the site of a tunnel under construction based on the superstition that, if she does so, the mountain goddess will become angry or jealous and cause an accident.[1] And in 1989, attention was focused on the sumo wrestling association when it refused to allow a female government minister to present an award at the closing ceremony because that would have entailed her stepping up to the sumo ring, which also has traditionally been restricted exclusively to men. On the other hand, some Japanese claim, half-jokingly, that the fact that women's colleges are allowed to exist while previously all-male universities were made coeducational following post-World War II educational reforms is an example of discrimination against males. While at a glance all of these may be seen as manifestations of sexual discrimination, my own view is that, eventually, compromises and solutions will be worked out as we begin to see more women who insist that they want to be sumo wrestlers or men who express a desire to study at a women's university. What is of critical importance is to build and establish a foundation and a social climate that will give emergence to and support individuals who will not feel inhibited or restricted from expressing such liberated aspirations.

Sexual discrimination cannot be measured simply by the extent to which women are excluded from various spheres of life; more often, discrimination is hidden and, therefore, difficult to assess. The assigning of predetermined gender roles as a matter of course in, for example, social organizations such as schools and workplaces, functions to limit women's freedom as well as their abilities. In Japan, as in many other societies, religions—in this case Shinto, Buddhism, and Confucianism—have contributed significantly to the development and maintenance of separate gender roles and of gender inequality. These religions have encouraged people to accept a notion of ethics which proclaims that people are born with differing abilities and into different statuses within society, thereby serving to maintain the prevailing social order. In so doing, religions have served to promote unequal sex roles. This idea, within the context of a patriarchal social system, served to give rise to a distorted image of the relationship between the sexes and the view that women are subordinate to men. For example, every newly ordained head of a temple in the Jodo Shin sect, one of the Japanese Buddhist sects, is given a copy of the manual *Jushokudo* (The way of the religious leader), which states, "The husband is lord and the wife is the servant" (Inoue 1989, 115). In recent years these traditional religions have come under severe criticism by feminists for having accepted and legitimized unequal gender relationships within society.

Similarly, many newer religions, such as Rissho Koseikai and Jissenrin-rikoseikai, which have gained adherents among those who have been unable to find satisfaction in the traditional religions, also maintain the traditional idea of unequal sex roles, their ideal women being wives who obey their husbands. Yet, ironically, these new religions have more women than men both among their leaders or teachers and their followers. In comparison to Western societies, it is often very difficult to discern the presence of gender discrimination in Japanese society. In fact, many of the issues related to sex discrimination in Japan cannot be analyzed through the lens of Western feminism.

Though Shinto, Buddhism, and Confucianism have all played a historically significant role in the formulation, justification, and enforcement of national ideology and state power,[2] this essay focuses on Buddhism as the most influential of the three in shaping the image and role of women and supporting sexism in Japanese society. Following my discussion of Buddhism and its effects on women's position in society, I will examine the history of the salvation of women in religions and clarify the influence these religions have had on the history of women's struggle for liberation in Japan.

Women in Early Buddhism and Mahayana Buddhism

The most important goal in the Buddhist religion is the achievement of satori, or enlightenment. One who reaches the state of enlightenment is called a buddha, and, according to the original teachings of Buddhism, becoming a Buddhist priest means giving up all of one's personal possessions and renouncing the worldly life. Thus, Buddhism in its original form was an ascetic religion. This characteristic seems to suggest that Buddhism has from the first manifested a fear of sexuality and, therefore, certain anti-female characteristics (Okano 1988, 410-26). As we know from historical records, Gautama Buddha himself was ambivalent in his views toward women. While the Pali canon, a collection of sutras from the fourth to third centuries B.C. written in the Pali language, includes various statements ascribed to Buddha which express the common sex discriminatory ideas of the Indian society of his time, he at the same time clearly states that women need to and can be saved. He admitted women into his own religious order as nuns. The various sects of Buddhism which were established after the death of Gautama Buddha follow his sacred teachings in different ways. All of these sects, which fall within the larger category of Theravada Buddhism, however, share the notion that Nirvana—the final, ultimate state of bliss—can be achieved by death and that it is possible only through the renunciation of the worldly life. Originally, then, it was possible for both men and women to become buddhas if they lived accordingly and underwent rigorous religious training. In the first century B.C. a new movement arose among the masses in rebellion against Theravada Buddhism. This movement, which came to be called Mahayana Buddhism, declared that salvation is open to everyone. Mahayana Buddhism spread and became dominant in China, Korea, and Japan.

According to the principles of the Buddhist religion, a Buddha is an entity that is sexless. Yet, since it came to be deified in Mahayana Buddhism, thirty-two characteristics came to be attributed to this entity. One of these characteristics was a hidden penis, which is obviously contradictory to the established sexless nature of a buddha. As a result, the idea that a buddha, including the historical figure Gautama Buddha, must be male became entrenched within the religion. In light of this it is interesting to note that in China and Japan, Avalokiteśvara, the *bosatsu*, or Bodhisattva of compassion, which was originally male, has been represented in female figures (e.g., Hibo Kannon); this was presumably done to balance the masculine-oriented Buddhist pantheon. A Bodhisattva is a personage in an intermediary stage in the evolution of an ordinary person into a buddha. Characteristically, a Bodhisattva tries to answer the appeals of the struggling faithful without asking for anything in return. Such a manifestation of generous love, much akin to that associated with a mother, probably led people to cast these saints in the figure of female statues.

Yet, if buddha were defined as male, then how could women achieve salvation? Yet to deny the possibility of salvation for women was contradictory to the notion of universal salvation preached by Mahayana Buddhism. The possibility of salvation for women was further diminished by the concept of the "five hindrances" stated in the Lotus Sutra, which refer to the five existences that women can never achieve: the four Indian Gods (Brahma, Shakra [Indra], Mara, and Cakravartin) and Buddha. To get around this contradiction, the notion of a "metamorphosed male" was introduced, meaning that women could become a Buddha after becoming a male.

Similarily discriminatory are the "three obediences" for women: "Women must obey their father as a daughter, once married obey their husband, and when widowed, obey their son. Women must not become independent" (Manu Hoten, chap. 5, 148). The idea of three obediences was brought into Japan in the Mahayana sutras, and, hand in hand with a Confucian teaching of a similar nature, crucially influenced women's education in Japan. The Mahayana sutras are not, however, entirely antifeminist. Some of them guarantee equality between the sexes in the process of becoming a Buddha, an idea that goes back to the original teaching by Gautama Buddha. A religion based on an egalitarian concept of human beings would have raised the questions posed in the Chinese sutra: "How could a man achieve Satori if a woman could not?" and "Can there be any difference between the sexes in terms of one's desire to achieve Satori?" (*Hai-lung-wang-ching*, bk. 3 [A.D. 414], qtd. in Iwamoto 1980, 75). The idea, however, that women and men are essentially equal did not become part of the mainstream of Buddhist doctrine.

Acceptance of Buddhism and Rejection of Female Priests by a United Japan

In the middle of the sixth century Mahayana Buddhism was brought to Japan by the scholar Wani, an envoy of the king of the Korean kingdom of Paikche, together with other features of Chinese civilization, including Confucianism and the Chinese writing system. In 584 Buddhist nuns first made their appearance, and soon thereafter the temple Sakuraiji was built in Nara for these nuns. It was not until twenty years later that the monastery Kentsuji was built for monks. This twenty-year gap is interesting in terms of how it signified Japanese attitudes toward Buddhism at the time. When these first Japanese Buddhist nuns were selected, there was an expectation or hope that they would have the kind of shamanic and charismatic powers that had been found in Himiko and other queens of ancient Japan. The nuns were regarded as priestesses or conductors of religious ceremonies.

In 624 all Buddhist monks and nuns were placed under the central control of the Emperor and the government. There is no concrete evidence indicating discrimination between monks and nuns until the middle of the Nara era (646-794). Thus, for example, nuns and monks were allowed to recite sutras in the same place. The Japanese view of women in Buddhism had not been affected by the discriminatory statements found in the Mahayana sutras.

This changed during the eighth century, as more women became nuns and more temples were built for female Buddhists. In Kinai (within the capital district) thirteen nunneries were built, and provincial temples were built for monks as well as for nuns by order of the Shomu emperor and the Komyo empress consort. In this era each monastery had a partner nunnery; Todaiji and Hokkeniji, for example, were treated as a "pair temples," as were Saidaiji and Sairyuniji. There seems also to have been an economic link between the partners: monasteries were in charge of the finances of nunneries. The nunneries had such a dependent status that they were referred to as "the laundry room of monasteries" in the *Nihon sandai jitsuroku*, a record from the ninth century. It seems that nunneries were subordinate to monasteries, and nuns were expected to serve monks and secular men in their everyday life. Thus, the relationship between a monastery and a nunnery, in the eighth century, seems to have been parallel to that between men and women in the secular world.

As Buddhism came increasingly under state control and was used to promote and protect the nation, it became increasingly patriarchal. While priests became functionaries of the state, nuns were regarded as less and less welcome. After the year 730 nuns were gradually banned from chanting in the court and in other official Buddhist ceremonies. In the mid-ninth century, for a period of time women were restricted from entering religious life. These developments parallel the history of women's gradual expulsion from important functions within the Shinto religion in the previous era.

Concept of Female Impurity

In the Heian era (794–1185/1192) the notions of five hindrances and three obediences repeatedly mentioned in the Mahayana sutras, mixed with the indigenous Japanese idea of ritual purity and blood as a source of impurity, led to the establishment of the view that women were sinful and could not obtain salvation. "Blood impurity" refers to the fact that menstruation and childbirth were seen as sources of uncleanliness and, therefore, a cause of ceremonial impurity.

It is debatable when this idea began and whether it originated in Shinto or in Buddhism. In any case there seem to have existed in early Japanese history, special *tsukigoya* ("monthly huts") and "parturition huts," isolated sheds to which women withdrew during menstruation and childbirth. Some say that the reason for this was to avoid defilement by blood, while others, including Shinobu Orikuchi, feel that it was an expression, instead, of the awe of blood and its sacred power (1955, 466f.). Women's bleeding has been viewed ambivalently in many cultures; as a source of life and power, it has been both worshipped and feared. What is clear is that the idea of blood impurity is not found in *Kojiki* or in *Nihon shoki*, which chronicle the beginnings and earliest history of Japan. In the mid-Heian era (ninth to twelfth centuries) "female bleeding" came to be regarded as a source of defilement, and since that time women have been prohibited from taking part in Shinto ceremonies while menstruating.[3]

Following the establishment in the seventh century of a national system of administration, women became excluded from posts in major religious institutions. In Shinto, however, women were not thought to be impure or sinful beings but, rather, impure only during menstruation and puerperium. Today it may appear as if Shinto is free from sex discrimination, since women are able to perform the same religious duties as men within Shinto institutions. Yet the idea of blood impurity is still very much present. Thus, for example, female staff members are required to take hormone pills and control their menstruation schedule in order to avoid polluting religious ceremonies.

Among Buddhists it was thought in ancient India that human birth was defiled because it originated from the parents' sexual pleasure (Nagata 1986, 677). Yet, fairly old Buddhist sutras such as *Choagon Kyo* (Dirghâyama) and *Ashukubukkoku Kyo* (Aksobhyasya tathâgatasya vyûha [A.D. 147]) deal with women's body and childbirth in a positive way, mentioning a possible painless childbirth in the ideal paradise. More ascetic sutras written for monks such as the Lotus Sutra and the Sukavativyuha Sutra (dating back roughly two thousand years), in contrast, inheriting the original Indian idea, state that being born through the vagina involves impurity. Therefore, an ideal birth was a supernatural one. Bodhisattvas, Buddhas, and other religious entities were supposed to have entered their mother's womb through the help of God and to have been born from her right armhole.

Concept of Woman as the "Sinful" and "Unsalvable"

An admixture of the two ideas blood impurity and "impure women" led to the establishment of the belief that women are sinful and cannot attain salvation. Honen (1133-1212), for example, the founder of the Jodo, or Pure Land, sect, regarded women as "being too sinful and facing too many obstacles to acceptance by any of the Buddhist paradises" (Kasahara 1984, 58). This negative view of women is found in writings of women themselves. The mother of General Udaisho Michitsuna (tenth century), writing in her diary, *Kagero nikki*, talks about her conflict with her husband, describes herself as "sinful," and relates how she repeatedly made up her mind to become a nun, confining herself for periods of time in different temples. Even Izumi Shikibu, who is known for her unusually liberated thinking, complains in her diary (ca. 1004) about not being admitted to Mount Hiei because of women's sinfulness. In one of her poems she expresses the wish that she were a flower on the hat of a monk so that she could go on the holy Mount Hiei. Murasaki Shikibu, in her novel *The Tale of Genji* (ca. 1011), analyzes the reasons for women's lack of virtue and unsalvability. She makes the criticism that it is because women only wish to depend on others, and therefore lack the ability to take leadership, that they are said to be lacking in virtue. She seems to have meant to say that a woman should not depend so much on the conditions of her father, husband, and sons that she could not be secure, but rather, she should be independent, just as men were. Her appeal for women's independence seems so insightful that it still is one of the key points in today's feminism.

Concept of Metamorphosis

The image of women as "defiled" and "sinful" grew not only out of the concept of impurity by blood but also from the notions of the three obediences and five hindrances. It was in order to provide a means for women to overcome these obstacles to the attainment of buddhahood and salvation that the notion of "metamorphosis" was proposed. According to this idea, a woman could become a Buddha and be reborn again in the Pure Land after first being changed to a man. This principle, which is prominent in the Lotus Sutra and in the three great Amida Sutras (second to fifth centuries A.D.), has, since the Heian era, represented the only means through which women might obtain salvation.

The idea of metamorphosis became more important in the Muromachi era (fourteenth to fifteenth centuries) with the introduction from China of the folk belief in the Ketsubon Sutra that all women who have given birth to a child will go to the hell of blood. This belief held that blood shed in the process of childbirth polluted the earth, which in turn polluted the rivers, which could eventually pollute monks if they unwittingly took the water for their tea. In the Edo era (seventeenth to nineteenth centuries) the idea of blood pollution was expanded to include menstrual bleeding, so that it came to be believed that all women would go to the hell of blood after death. Despite a general skepticism about the orthodoxy of such a belief, this Chinese idea became widely spread in Japan and thereby functioned to promote negative attitudes toward women.

Exclusion of Women from Buddhist Temples

This belief regarding the impurity and sinfulness of women became manifested in the phenomenon whereby women were excluded from certain of
the state Buddhist temples. In some cases, such as the temple at Mount
Koya and at Mount Hiei, the temple as well as the entire mountain on which
it stood were closed off to women, whereas in other cases, such as Todaiji,
Yakushiji, Horyuji, and Zenkoji temples, only the innermost sanctuary of
the temples were made off limits to women.

Originally, temples excluded women to keep monks free from sexual dis-
tractions. In other words, the rejection of women by Buddhist temples was
introduced for the purpose of maintaining the religious order. A legend that
was passed on to support the orthodoxy of this practice of rejecting women
at Mount Hiei and Kinpusen temples goes thus: when a nun, Toran, tried
to enter the sanctuary, a horrible disaster occurred, and she was destroyed
because of her impurity, and the sanctuary was thereby saved. This legend
and its variants can be read, from a feminist viewpoint, to be paradoxi-
cal; the real force of the religion was revealed only when confronted by the
impurity of women (Abe 1989, 188). Thus, the exclusion of women, which
was originally practiced as a means of maintaining the discipline of monks,
became established as a method of giving added power and authority to the
temples. The temples that followed this practice were precisely those that
were closely connected with the ruling power, which looked to religion as
a means of control.

Criticism of Women's Exclusion

What is clear regarding this practice of female exclusion which served religious and political functions is that, whatever the rationale, it was created
by men. There were some attempts to oppose this absurd practice as early
as the tenth century. Besides the nun Toran, who tried to enter a sanctuary,
additional examples are found in literature such as in the Noh plays *Sotoba
no Komachi*, by Kan'ami, and *Tatatsu no Saemon*, by Zeami (Abe 1989,
189). These cases, however, were exceptional. Even radical thinkers, such
as the founders of the new Buddhist sects of the Kamakura era (twelfth to
thirteenth centuries), Honen (1133-1212), Shinran (1173-1262), Nichiren
(1222-82), and Myoe (1173-1232), did not criticize the exclusion of women
by the temples.

The only exception was the Zen patriarch Dogen (1200-1253). In a
chapter of his *Shobogenzo* entitled "Raihaitokuzui" he clearly criticized the
exclusion of women by ancient Buddhism, claiming that it was an evil prac-

tice and had no grounding in actual religious principles. He even criticized, implicitly, the five hindrances to women's attainment of salvation mentioned in the Lotus Sutra. In this respect Dogen may deserve the title of feminist. However, after he moved to Eihei Temple in Echizen in 1243, he began to claim that leaving the worldly life was sacrosanct and became more supportive of the practice of female exclusion by the temples. Dogen appears to have felt the same ambivalence that Buddha held. And their ambivalence seems to exemplify the dilemma frequently encountered in religious life between asceticism and sexuality. It was not until the seventeenth century that liberal ideas expressed by Dogen in his earlier years reappeared.

The *Ie* Structure of Religious Organizations

In order to understand why it took so long for another liberal philosopher such as Dogen to emerge and why the practice of female exclusion persisted so tenaciously, we need to examine another critical factor, which has to do with the characteristically Japanese-style *ie* (household, or family) social organization of these temples. While the monks lived atop the holy mountains conducting various religious affairs in service of the nation, their wives, mothers, and sisters resided in a separate community called a *satobo* at the foot of the mountains under the protection of the monks, leading a religious life and performing their assigned roles—sewing and washing the monks' clothing and preparing their meals. A *satobo* also functioned as an asylum for women who lacked protection and as a new home for those who had abandoned the worldly life (Nishiguchi 1987, 54). A *satobo* represented the closest connection a woman could have to the religious sanctuary of the mountaintop. Many of these *satobo* originated with the mothers of some famous monks. Legends tell of elderly mothers who lived religious lives under the protection of their sons, who led spiritual lives atop the mountains and eventually died, watched over by their sons, and were believed to be reborn in the Pure Land. Tales of mothers of great monks such as Saicho, Kukai, and Ennogyoja have been loved by the local people, and these women have come to be worshipped as patron saints of safe delivery and nursing.

What we find, then, is that while, on the one hand, the religious sanctuaries atop the mountains were restricted only to men, on the other hand, a separate religious space (*ie*) was created for their female family members. The ultimate wish of these women was to die with their men beside them and be buried at the top of the holy mountain, which represented paradise. Women could reach the top of the holy mountain only after death.

It has been a normal Buddhist practice since the feudal age for a priest to serve at a temple supported at the same time by his own *ie*, or family. In particular, the Jodo Shin sect has had an *ie* within the organization from the very beginning of history. However, the status of the wives, who functioned as the main support within the *ie*, has always been low, and women have never been allowed to become head of a temple, a tradition that is now severely criticized by feminists. Even in the Jodo Shin sect, despite the importance of the *ie* in its philosophy, Shinran, Zongaku, Rennyo, and all the other priests espoused the idea of differentiated gender roles and supported the notion of metamorphosis. This contradictory fact has recently attracted critical attentions of male researchers (Endo 1989).

Women, through their role within the *ie*, have been a source of support behind the development of various Buddhist sects in Japan in greater or lesser degrees.[4] The fact that, in spite of this, women's status has been held down and their freedom of thought restricted is due in large degree to the importance given, at least in principle, to the Buddhist concept of "leaving the worldly life." In reality this idea has been distorted in the process of undergoing assimilation in the Japanese setting, as demonstrated in the discussion of women's presence within the *ie* attached to the monasteries. Japanese Buddhist groups must now undertake a reexamination of how this distortion came about and reconsider the status and position of women.

Sexism in the "New Religions"

Buddhism was imported to Japan, and it became diffused within the population from the top down. On the other hand, the so-called new religions,[5] to which I will now turn, are indigenous to Japanese society. They, too, however, are characterized by sexism.

What is collectively called "new religions" vary considerably in terms of length of existence. Among the older ones membership dates back several generations; others came into being in the period immediately following World War II, amid the social upheaval that prevailed in postwar Japanese society; while the most recent ones were established in the 1970s. These new religions also differ in terms of their belief systems. Yet they also share many characteristics in common. One of them is that their religious authority is derived from the traditional religions, such as Shinto, Buddhism, and Christianity. In this respect, all the new religions can be said to be another sect or offshoots of the traditional ones. A second common characteristic is that these new religions have created a pseudofamily, that is, an organization just like the *ie*, with the founder as the "parent" and the religious community leaders as elder siblings. This characteristic seems to provide a feeling of security to those who might lack the support of a real family and have not found help through traditional religions or from social service organizations. A third common feature shared by these new religions is that most of them have actively sought to play an influential role in national politics.

These religions show a similarity to the traditional religions of Japan such as Shinto and Buddhism in terms of their historical development and structure. The case of Rissho Koseikai, an offshoot of the Nichiren sect of Buddhism, is a good illustration (see Osumi 1989). Rissho Koseikai was originally founded in 1936 by a woman possessing shamanistic charisma, assisted by a man who was in charge of the establishment of laws and doctrines. In the early period following its establishment seven out of eight leaders were women. After the death of the shamanic woman following the war, however, the group began to emphasize systematizing the religious doctrines and building its organization. Today the key figures consist exclusively of men, and there is a fixed division of gender roles within the organization, with men in charge of the bureaucratic functions and women performing the various daily routines at the local chapters.

The concept of unequal sex roles is widely accepted within the new religions. Moreover, their followers are encouraged to emulate this concept in their own family lives, with the husband assuming the role of leader and the wife that of subordinate. For example, Sokagakkai, founded in the 1930s, upholds a domestic role for women, based on the teaching of Nichiren, founder of the Nichiren sect of Buddhism, that "a woman, while subordinating herself to all (including men), is able to control all (including men)" (Inoue 1988, 286). Although a woman must subordinate herself to her husband, an exception is made in the case in which a husband opposes the wife's membership in the religious organization. Another new religion, Jissenrinrikoseikai, which was founded immediately following World War II, compares the roles of the husband and wife to those of the engine car, performing the dominant, active role, and the trailed car, which is subordinate and passive. In these religious organizations women are repeatedly taught to cultivate obedience rather than to be clever, and the religious magazines carry many stories showing how an obedient wife successfully manages to resolve family problems (Numata 1988, 236). The hierarchical distinctions derived from Confucianism, too, are widely accepted among these new religions.

To summarize the ideas common among new religions, the role of women is perceived as that of maintaining the family by taking care of the spirits of ancestors and stillborn children and caring for elderly parents, while the role of men is to contribute toward the maintenance of national prosperity through their work in industry. The picture coincides with the

26   HARUKO K. OKANO

welfare policy of the Liberal Democratic Party, which held power in Japan throughout most of the years following World War II, until 2009. The new religions thus provide ethical support for the maintenance of the present system of Japanese society, which retains a central role for the *ie*.

What reasons account for the fact that the new religions attract so many female followers? According to Inoue (1988) and Numata (1988), the answer can be found in the fact that these religions perform the following types of functions:

1. They offer help and advice on problems housewives commonly confront (mothers-in-law, husbands, children's education).
2. They provide companionship as well as activities for women to fill the void left by husbands who are busily caught up in their work and children who have grown and gone off on their own.
3. Housewives can find a sense of purpose by participating in religious-affiliated activities within their communities.
4. The notion of "obedient wife and responsible mother" espoused by these religions, provides a measure of stability and peace, superficial though it may be, within the family.
5. They provide opportunities for women to engage in self-expression and gain experience in the larger society by allowing them to assume positions of responsibility and leadership within the organization, for example, presiding over or speaking before large groups of followers.

Incidentally, with regard to this last point, giving women opportunities to perform various executive-type functions veils the sexism that is in fact characteristic of these religious organizations.

Conclusion

The women of Japan today constitute a highly diverse population both in terms of the values they hold and the lifestyles they lead. Are either the traditional religions or the new religions capable of responding adequately to the emotional sufferings experienced by these diverse types of women—housewives who suffer from loneliness in spite of living with their families, single women, married but childless women, unmarried mothers, women who are caught in a dilemma between career and family life? What must be done—what changes must be undertaken—in order that women can be truly liberated *as* women, rather than *from* being a woman?

One of the obstacles that has been preventing Buddhism and the new religions from recognizing the various values that women hold is their adherence to family-like structure. The Constitution, which was enacted in 1947 following World War II, contained several provisions aimed at abolishing the traditional family system and securing equality of the sexes within the family. The sexism inherent in Japanese religions will continue to prevail so long as the family system is maintained. The function and meaning of this family system and the role of women within that system, particularly the domestic functions performed by them, must be reexamined and reevaluated in order for women to achieve a solid status within the sphere of organized religion. There is another factor that has prevented feminist issues from being clearly perceived in Japanese society—namely, a lack of individual consciousness and a sense of individuals making decisions for themselves and taking responsibility for themselves. In Western societies one tends to regard things in terms of dichotomies, for example, between sacred and secular, right and wrong, or superior and inferior, and then to proceed to do away with those elements that are seen as negative. In Japan, however, there is a tendency to accept and try to harmonize both the good and the bad rather than to seek to make clear the differences. Within this milieu individual qualities and abilities are often ignored. Social pressures encourage people to be as similar to others as possible and to maintain the status quo rather than seek to change it.

This kind of society, which tends to accept everything without analysis or criticism and to embrace all of its members indiscriminately so long as they stay within the social order, has been labeled a "maternal society" by the psychologist Hayao Kawai (1976). In such a society individuals are not required or encouraged to decide matters for themselves. By extension, in such a society individuals are unlikely to think seriously about feminist issues and to raise such questions as, "Who is wrong?" and "Who are the enemies of feminism?" Men, too, are robbed of their autonomy in the social organizations in which they work and are therefore also victims.

Our society is structured in such a way that all Japanese, of both sexes and at all levels, are forced to surrender their freedom for the sake of maintaining harmony and order within the larger social organization, that is, the nation. The pursuit of feminist issues within the Japanese context inevitably leads to consideration of other fundamental issues. One of these is the responsibility incumbent on those of us who have tended to entrust everything to organizational structures such as the nation, industry, and educational institutions to cultivate our own wills and personalities and to mature into individuals who can exercise independence and initiative in directing our lives.

Notes

1. In March 1992 the technical chief of a local Construction Ministry site became the first female field officer to enter a tunnel being built by the government. In October 1990 a female reporter for a Japanese newspaper had been banned from attending a ribbon-cutting ceremony for a tunnel in Yamagata Prefecture ("Woman defies taboo, enters tunnel," *Japan Times*, March 22, 1992, 3).

2. Christianity was introduced to Japan in 1549 by the Jesuit priest Francis Xavier. While it was initially tolerated and even encouraged under the rule of Nobunaga, following the ascension of Hideyoshi various edicts were issued banning it, and under Ieyasu persecution of Christians became more intense. Christianity vanished from the scene, although it continued to be practiced secretly by converts. It was not until 1873 that complete religious freedom was granted. At present Christians constitute just 1 percent of the total Japanese population. There are several complex reasons that have been set forth to explain why Christianity has not gained a significant foothold in Japan, and it is beyond the scope of this chapter to go into these explanations. One important factor, however, is that the Christian concept of a spiritual, non-blood related brotherhood or family could not compete against the concept of the traditional family system, with its emphasis on the primacy of ties based on blood.

3. See, for example, *Engishiki* (Institutes of the Engi Period), a collection of codes of laws completed in 927, and *Kinpisho*, a book written by Emperor Juntoku and completed around 1221, which records the history and origin of imperial court ceremonies and sets forth the rules and etiquette for carrying out such ceremonies.

4. It should be mentioned that in the seventeenth century temples were established by nuns to which women seeking to sever a marriage (which was extremely difficult for a woman to do) were able to flee.

5. This section is a translation of part of an essay written in German by the author titled "Weiblichkeitssymbolik and Seximus in alten und neuen Religionen Japans" (Feminine symbolism and sexism in old and new religions in Japan), in Japan—*ein Land der Frauen?* (Japan—a women's country?), ed. Elizabeth Gössmann (Munich: Iudicium Verlag, 1991), chap. 5, pp. 124-29.

Works Cited

Abe, Yasuro. 1989. "Nyonin kinsei to suisan" (Prohibition of women and self-imposition). In *Miko to megami* (Maidens and goddesses), ed. Kazuo Osumi et al. Tokyo: Heibonsha.

Endo, Hajime. 1989. "Bomori izen no koto" (The origin of marriage for priests of the Jodo Shin Sect). In *Shinjin to kuyo* (Faith and service for the dead), ed. Kazuo Osumi et al. Tokyo: Heibonsha.

Inoue, Setsuko. 1988. *Shufu o misuru shin shukyo* (The new religions that charm housewives).Tokyo: Tanizawa shobo.

———. 1989. "Bukkyo no josei sabetsu ni tachiatta onnatachi (Women who criticized sexism in Buddhism). *Shukyo joho* (Religious News), no. 32 (June): 115.

Iwamoto, Yutaka. 1980. *Bukkyo to josei* (Buddhism and women). Tokyo: Daisan bunmeisha.

Kasahara, Kazuo. 1984. *Bukkyo ni miru Nihon josei kaiho-shi* (History of women's liberation as seen in Buddhism). Tokyo: Hoso daigaku kyoiku shinkokai.

Kawai, Hayao. 1976. *Bosei shakai Nihon no byori* (The pathology of Japan's maternal society). Tokyo: Chuokoronsha.

Manu Hoten (Laws of Manu). 1991. Trans. Nobuyuki Watase. Tokyo: Chuokoronsha.

Nagata, Mizu. 1986. "Butten ni miru boseikan" (View of motherhood in Buddhist scriptures). In *Bosei o tou* (Questioning motherhood), vol. 1, ed. Haruko Wakita. Tokyo: Jinbun shoin.

Nishiguchi, Junko. 1987. *Onna no chikara* (The power of women). Tokyo: Heibonsha.

Numata, Kenya. 1988. *Gendai Nihon no shin shukyo* (New religions in contemporary Japan). Tokyo: Sogensha.

Okano, Haruko. 1988. "Himmel ohne Frauen" (Heaven without women). In *Das Gold im Wachs* (The gold in wax), ed. E. Gössmann and G. Zobel. Munich: Iudicium Verlag.

———. 1990. "Nihon josei no shukyojo no ichi" (The status of Japanese women in religion). In *Nihon-Doitsu: josei no atarashii uneri* (Japan and Germany: the new surge of women), ed. Tokyo doitsu bunka senta (German Cultural Center). Tokyo: Kawai shuppan.

Orikuchi, Shinobu. 1955. *Oguri Hangan-ron no keikaku* (The plan for a study on Oguri Hangan). *Orikuchi Shinobu zenshu* (Complete works of Shinobu Orikuchi), vol. 3. Tokyo: Chuokoronsha.

Osumi, Kazuo. 1989. "Shin shukyo ni miru josei no katsudo" (The activities of women as seen in the new religions). In *Shinjin to kuyo* (Faith and service for the dead), ed. Kazuo Osumi et al. Tokyo: Heibonsha.

"Woman Defies Taboo, Enters Tunnel." 1992. *Japan Times*. March 22.

Who's Afraid of Kiku Amino?
Gender Conflict
and the Literary Canon

3

Chieko M. Ariga

Kiku Amino (1900-1978) seems to have disappeared from the scene of Japanese literature today. A writer born in turn-of-the century Japan, she was a contemporary of Yuriko Miyamoto (1899-1951), and, like other women writers of her day, wrote semi-auto-biographical fiction ("I-fiction," or *shishosetsu*). During her long and pro-lific writing career, which spanned nearly sixty years, Amino received wide public recognition and many literary prizes and awards. Her works were acclaimed for their detached observations and her style for its unadorned plainness by the critics and writers of her time.

Given this profile, it is curious that Amino is not treated as a major author in literary history books and guides to Japanese literature published today. Most of the books on Japanese authors which have been published in Japan in recent decades do not even mention her name. For example, in *Nihon kindai bungaku no shiso to jokyo* (Ideology and circumstances of modern Japanese literature [Odagiri 1971]), only two women writers, Ineko Sata and Sakae Tsuboi, are represented. In *Nihon no kindai bungaku* (Modern Japanese literature, [Wada 1982]) Amino's name does not appear, while other women writers contemporary to her—such as Kanoko Okamoto (1889-1939), Yuriko Miyamoto, Chiyo Uno (1897-1996), Fumiko Hayashi (1903-51), Taiko Hirabayashi (1905-71), Sakae Tsuboi (1900-1967), Ineko Sata (1904-1998), and Yaeko Nogami (1885-1985)—are all mentioned. Likewise, in *Kindai joryu bungaku* (Modern Japanese literature by women, 1983) the works of Kanoko Okamoto, Fumiko Hayashi, Taiko Hirabayshi, and Ineko Sata are detailed.

There is no question about the artistry of the women writers included, but why is Amino excluded from the canon of Japanese women authors? This essay will maintain that Amino's exclusion from the canon of both male and female Japanese authors stems from the fact the women she depicted in her fiction did not conform to the patriarchal definition of "woman."[1] In the course of this discussion, I will reveal the mechanism of ideological control and exclusion operating in the Japanese literary institution.[2]

Japanese Women's Literature Defined
by the Patriarchal Institution

Before the Meiji period (1868-1912), few women produced literature, except during the Heian period (794-1192), known as "the flourishing age of literature by court ladies." A host of court ladies at the imperial palace—including Murasaki Shikibu, Sei Shonagon, Izumi Shikibu, Michitsuna's mother, and Sugawara no Takasue's daughter—left diaries and fictional tales depicting the lives of the royal family and aristocrats centered around love relationships between men and women. The most well-known works are Murasaki Shikibu's *Genji monogatari* (*The Tale of Genji*) and Sei Shonagon's *Makura no soshi* (*The Pillow Book*), both assumed to have been written in the early eleventh century. In subsequent periods, writing by women disappeared for the most part, a consequence of having a military government whose political foundation was Confucianism.[3] The social order was based upon the Confucian family system in which women's roles were defined solely as those of wife and mother. This left little opportunity for them to participate in the world of letters. It was not until the Meiji period that women started writing again.

In the Meiji period the most recognized women writers were Ichiyo Higuchi (1872-96), who left fictional pieces on the life of an ordinary woman, and the poet Akiko Yosano (1878-1942). The other writers followed, including Yuriko Miyamoto and the writers of her generation, who actively wrote semi-autobiographical fiction in the Taisho (1912-25) and Showa (1925-89) periods. The works of Fumiko Enchi (1905-86) and Aya Koda (1904-90) became popular after World War II. In the 1950s the so-called first wave of women writers emerged. Writers like Ayako Sono (b. 1931), Sawako Ariyoshi (1931-84), Yumiko Kurahashi (1935-2005), and Harumi Setouchi (b. 1922) were followed by a second wave of writers: Taeko Kono (b. 1926), Seiko Tanabe (b. 1928), Setsuko Tsumura (b. 1928), Minako Oba (1930-2007), Takako Takahashi (b. 1932), Taeko Tomioka (b. 1935), Mieko Kanai (b. 1947), and Yuko Tsushima (b. 1947).[4] In the works of these postwar writers, the subject matter expanded to include hatred of motherhood, womanhood, or women's bodies; some wrote on social and political issues, unlike the prewar writers.[5]

In recent years the number of Japanese writers who are women has grown, partly because "women's literature" is now being promoted commercially, sometimes involving lucrative film or television adaptations. The recipients of the prestigious Akutagawa and Naoki literary awards include more and more women. If one includes such contemporary best-selling writers as Mariko Hayashi, Eimi Yamada, and Banana Yoshimoto, it indeed appears that women are flourishing on the Japanese literary scene.

Yet to conclude from this evidence that women occupy a prestigious position in the Japanese literary establishment would not be quite correct. Even though many of them have excellent reputations, their literature is still largely relegated to the confines of women's literature. Compared with men's literature, women's literature occupies only a secondary status in the orthodoxy of the Japanese literary establishment. In fact, as in the West, women's works are almost always classified by Japanese literary scholarship as *joryu bungaku* (female-school literature), which treats subjects peculiar to women, as opposed to *bungaku* (literature), which treats subjects considered universal, serious, and important (Hijiya-Kirschnereit 1986, 11). The arrangement of typical *bungaku zenshu* (complete works of literature series) well proves this point. Women's works are customarily put together in separate volumes, regardless of their differences in style or the time in which they lived.

As pointed out by many female writers and scholars, such categories are clearly a product of male culture.[6] Of course, for generations the very nature of literature that all but excluded women ensured that the pre-Meiji works by women were appropriated by male scholars and philologists. This tradition has continued into present-day literary scholarship. Works after the Meiji period are often divided into *kindai Nihon bungaku* (modern Japanese literature) and *gendai bungaku* (contemporary Japanese literature); the evaluation of these, too, has remained exclusively in the hands of male writers and critics. Among those active in the elite Tokyo coterie (*bundan*) in the Taisho and early Showa periods were naturalist (*shizenshugi*) writers and the White Birch (*shirakabaha*) group. Centering around small-scale literary journals circulated among a small number of literature lovers, these people actively wrote and set the standard of the literature of their day (Fowler 1988, 131-32).

The Tokyo coterie eventually dissipated as political pressure forced them to cooperate with the wartime effort. Also, commercialism gradually took over in the Showa period (1926-89). Publishers became interested in selling more copies of books, rather than small-scale journals and magazines written by specialists (ibid., 141). Next came the age of postwar *bundan*, which includes the established writers and critics, some freelancers, and others belonging to academic institutions. This group includes people such as Hideo Kobayashi, Sei Ito, Ken Hirano, Mitsuo Nakamura, Shuichi Kato, Saiichi Maruya, Jun Eto, and Kojin Karatani, to name a few.

Looking over the past one hundred years of Japanese literary culture, however, one has a hard time finding women who were included in the mainstream literary criticism. In fact, the sheer numbers of Japanese women writers recognized in this century tend to obscure the fact that women have hardly been represented in the evaluative body of the core Japanese literary institutions. In the words of the feminist critic Chizuko Ueno (1993, 5):

> The predominance of men in literature has been fostered and perpetuated by well-entrenched patterns in publishing, reviewing, and marketing literary works. There is only a handful of female critics, leaving men to virtually monopolize the field as well as the screening committees for the major literary prizes given to works considered "superior."[7]

It is normally the case that the critical commentary and introduction attached to a literary work or volume are written by major *bundan* male critics, as is most typically observed in the *bungaku zenshu* published by Chuokoron, *Nihon no bungaku* (Japanese literature, 1964-1970). Even in the eight volumes of *Gendai no joryu bungaku* (Modern women's literature, 1974-1975), published by the Mainichi Newspaper company and edited by women writers, Fumiko Enchi and Ineko Sata, the critical essays about the works are all written by male critics. The most glaring example is *Gendai nihon bungaku zenshu* (Complete works of contemporary Japanese literature, 1956-1959), which includes three volumes containing major critical essays by literary critics from the Meiji period to the 1950s: out of a total of eighty-six critics, there is not a *single* woman.

Books on female-school literature are also often written and edited by male critics and scholars: for example, *Shintei Meiji joryu sakkaron* (A newly revised account of Meiji women writers) (1983) and *Monogatari joryu bundanshi* (An anecdotal history of women writers, vol. 2, 1977)[8]. Almost all book reviews on Japanese literature in major newspapers and magazines are done by *bundan* male critics as well. Even though the recent rise of feminist scholarship is gradually challenging and changing this situation, still, as far as the mainstream literary criticism is concerned, women's participation is extremely limited.[9]

Women's works are evaluated and institutionalized as female-school literature in this heavily male-dominated literary milieu, meaning that, if a writer is not recognized as one of the major writers by bundan male critics, she is more than likely not to be included in the canon of Japanese literature.[10] In what follows I will explore Amino's exclusion from the literary canon by examining the representation of women in her works—women who defy the established category of "woman." For a comparison, I will also look at the representation of women in the works of women writers contemporary with Amino who are considered to be major—namely, Fumiko Hayashi, Taiko Hirabayashi, Yuriko Miyamoto, Sakae Tsuboi, and Chiyo Uno. The investigation will reveal that the major difference between their works and Amino's works is that, in the former case, women are always

constructed in relationship to men. The conclusion suggests that the implication in Amino's work of the "woman alone" and the "female grotesque" in
the context of compulsory heterosexual economy has much to do with Kiku
Amino's exclusion from the Japanese literary canon.

A Profile of Kiku Amino

Kiku Amino was born to the family of a self-employed harness manufacturer in 1900.[11] Her mother was from Tatsuno in Nagano prefecture. Amino's childhood was full of turmoil. Having had an affair with a younger
man, her mother was abandoned by her family and later publicly accused
of adultery in a lawsuit pressed by her father, when Amino was seven. Then
three stepmothers came one after another, all of whom either died or disappeared. Her biography says that, when the second mother died and the
third mother was to come, Amino attempted suicide. Her childhood often
became the subject of her writings. Even though her upbringing was not a
happy one, at least her father's business was going well, especially after the
Russo-Japanese War (1904-5), when war supplies such as harnesses became
in great demand. Amino was allowed to take lessons in classical Japanese
singing and guitar.

After finishing girls' high school, she was to take sewing lessons, but,
because she was a good student, her parents reluctantly gave her permission
to go to a women's college. In 1916 Amino entered Japan Women's University to study English literature. Yuriko Miyamoto was her classmate. After
graduating in 1920, she started publishing her work while serving on the
editorial staff of the university alumnae newsletter. Her first published work
was *Aki* (Autumn, 1920). Between 1922 and 1925 she attended lectures in
the Russian Department at Waseda University. On the recommendation
of Naoya Shiga (1883-1971), Amino's lifetime mentor and friend, her two
works, *Ie* (The Family, 1925) and *Mitsuko* (1926), were published.

In 1930 Amino married and went to Manchuria with her husband.
In 1938 they divorced. This experience is depicted in *Tsumatachi* (Wives,
1943). During World War II she produced such collections of stories as
Wakai hi (Youth, 1942), *Itoko* (Cousins, 1943), and *Yuki no yama* (Snowy
Mountains, 1943). Representative works after the war include *Tsukimono*
(Possessed by Evil Spirits, 1946) and *Kin no kan* (The Golden Casket, 1947),
for which she received the Women Writers' Award. From time to time
she also translated Russian and English works, including children's stories,
such as *Hi no tori* (Firebirds, 1955) and *Semushi no kouma* (A Hunch-
back Pony, 1957). She also wrote a biography of Charlotte Bronte (*Sharotto
Bronte den*, 1942).

Amino's works received more and more public recognition, especially after *Sakura no hana* (Cherry Blossoms, 1961), which brought her yet two more literary awards. The succeeding works, *Yureru ashi* (Blown Reed, 1964) and *Ichigo ichie* (The Crucial Encounter, 1967), which received the Yomi-uri Literary Award, were also successful. The following year she received the Japan Art Academy Award. She continued to write until her death. Her later works include *Enzan no yuki* (Snow in the Distant Mountains, 1971), *Hi no sasu heya* (A Room with Sunlight, 1975), and a collection of essays, *Kokoro no saigetsu* (Years in My Heart, 1972). She died in 1978 at the age of seventy-eight.

Representations of Women in Writings by Amino's Contemporaries

We will now look at the literary representation of women in the works of female-school writers contemporaneous with Amino—namely, Yuriko Miyamoto, Fumiko Hayashi, Taiko Hirabayashi, Sakae Tsuboi, and Chiyo Uno. They provide a good comparison, since they all were born at the turn of the century and, like Amino, wrote semi-autobiographical fiction in one form or another. For this analysis I have selected those works with a reputation for being fairly representative of each author. Let me note at the outset that it is not my intention here to devalue the merits of works by these authors; separate levels of analyses of their works are certainly important. For the purpose of this essay, however, I must risk reducing their texts for representational analysis.

Let us first look at the women in the texts of Yuriko Miyamoto and Taiko Hirabayashi, both of whom were successful proletarian writers. Miyamoto, probably the best known of all, is remembered for her leftist activity in political movements against the dictatorial military government of the prewar period. Despite the active revolutionary "proletarian writer" label put on Miyamoto, the women she constructed in her texts are often faithful and dedicated to the men who are the center of their lives.

For example, *Banshu heiya* (Banshu Plain, 1947),[12] considered to be one of her most successful works, is about the life of a woman, Hiroko, during World War II. It is said to be a political work, envisioning a positive future for communism in Japan. Yet a close reading reveals it to be as much a study of the main character's struggle to be a good, loyal wife and daughter-in-law in a male-centered family system. Hiroko's husband, Jukichi, is jailed for his leftist activities during the war. Hiroko, herself an active member of the proletarian movement, is a good caretaker who supports her husband and his family both financially and morally during his twelve-year absence.

Frequent visits to his prison, more than a thousand letters written to him, and her care for his family matters attest to her devotion as a patient and enduring wife who waits for her husband with heroic martyrdom.

A theme showing the helplessness of women is repeated throughout the text. For example, while helping the husband's family after they are victimized by a flood, the heroine sighs, thinking that, if only her husband or his brothers had been there, the family would not have suffered so. The household of women without men is physically and emotionally vulnerable. In spite of the fact that Hiroko is such a reliable, strong woman, she thinks that it would be difficult to live without her husband. The hope that her husband will be released from prison someday is the only thing that sustains her. She admits, however, that her loyalty and love toward her husband are probably pretty one-sided, because her husband does not need her as much as she needs him: "Hiroko could not think of life without Jukichi. But she knew well that Jukichi would live the kind of life he chose, whether or not she was with him. Hiroko realized this more than once during those hard enduring years" (Miyamoto 1975, 7:346). After the Peace Preservation Law is abolished,[13] the news of the release of political prisoners is announced. Hiroko excitedly set out on her journey east to see her husband who is returning from a penitentiary in Abashiri, Hokkaido.

Fuchiso (The Weathervane Plant, 1947), obviously a continuation of *Banshu heiya*, is about Hiroko and her husband, Jukichi, who has now been released from jail. After a period of recuperation Jukichi returns to his leftist political activity. The book ends with a depiction of a communist meeting, with moving scenes of the release of leftist prisoners, including Jukichi. This text is viewed as another installment in Miyamoto's ardent expression of excitement at building a proletarian society in the new Japan, yet, when one focuses on the interaction between Hiroko and Jukichi, the book seems as much about the relationship and power struggle between a husband and wife.

In fact, most of the episodes that unfold after Jukichi's release clearly show his attitude as the head of a family and Hiroko's puzzlement. One day, for example, the two go out, and, while riding on a train, Jukichi criticizes Hiroko for being "widowlike," for working too hard and losing her femininity. Hiroko's feelings are deeply hurt, and she cries. She has been battling with life alone during his absence; it has been hard to survive and support not only her husband but also his family. She feels she should be appreciated, not criticized. Later, however, she thanks him for pointing out her shortcoming, something she says she did not notice.

In spite of her doubts, outwardly Hiroko never argues, never explains, and certainly never takes issue with him; instead, she simply accepts whatever her husband says to keep peace and any cost. What emerges here is a power play between a husband, who tries to put his wife under his control, and his wife, who struggles to be good and obedient and to submit to him.[14]

Taiko Hirabayashi is another proletarian writer who wrote about her life with a husband engaged in leftist politics. Her noted novel *Seryoshitsu* (At a Clinic, 1927) is about a sick and pregnant protagonist in Dalian, China, shortly before World War II. She, her husband, and his group are arrested and charged with the terrorist activity of bombing trains. She suffers from beriberi, from her pregnancy, and can hardly move. In a basement room at a clinic of a hospital filled with humidity and odor, unattended like a stray dog, she gives birth. The baby soon dies of malnutrition. Though having gone through all these sacrifices, she thinks to herself:

> I will not blame my husband. It was obvious to me that such terrorist activities would certainly result in this kind of messy imprisonment. At the time of planning, my husband and three members laughed at my hesitation, saying that it was the timid conservatism of a pregnant woman. But the outcome is just what I anticipated. Still, if we cannot accomplish anything without terrorism, I guess I must do as they say. That's the obligation of political activists. It is also the duty of a wife to her husband. Hence, I have no regrets. (Hirabayashi and Ohara 1969, 48:8)

A woman protagonist in *Hitori iku* (Walking Alone, 1946) is incarcerated for outlawed activities together with her husband. She has been relocated to a prison in the suburbs of Tokyo from the prison where she was kept with him, because she always looked in the direction of her husband's cell. The new prison is cold, and she suffers from tuberculosis. The only thing that occupies her mind is her sickly husband; she worries about his health and well-being more than her own. A husband to her is a father and child, both at the same time. She says: "I cannot possibly leave my husband and die, a husband who is like my only son and yet like my own father. Thinking this and that about my husband, I really started believing that he is the child I gave birth to" (Ibid., 67).

The women Hirabayashi wrote about are, like Miyamoto's political activists, intellectual women who write and publish. And yet a closer examination shows them to be loyal and faithful women who believe that following their husband is "the way of a wife." To them political interests are often secondary to their concern and preoccupation with their husbands, so much so that they adjust themselves to their husbands' ideas and ways even against their wills. At times doubts do occur to them about their subordinate roles, but they immediately give them up in the name of "feminine virtues." These women are also dedicated, nurturing mothers, lovingly taking care of their husbands, whom they treat as their own children.

In a different view of womanhood Fumiko Hayashi and Chiyo Uno wrote about a woman's intense jealousies toward the "other woman" in love triangles. The story in Hayashi's noted *Ukigumo* (Drifting Clouds, 1951) is about a woman's obsession and suffering in a relationship with a nihilistic and emotionally unavailable man.[15] The heroine, Yukiko, a typist, meets Tomioka, a specialist sent by the Ministry of Agriculture and Forestry in French Indochina during World War II. Their passionate love affair takes place in the utopian village in which they live unaffected by the war. But their promised life is no longer the same after they return to Japan. In the confusion after the war Tomioka has no job and a wife and parents to support. He lacks the courage and passion to divorce his wife and start a new life with Yukiko. They go through several attempts to separate from each other, including affairs with different partners, but Yukiko is obsessed with this self-destructive man and cannot let him go. The only way out is to commit suicide, but they lack courage for this. When his wife dies, and his other mistress whom he met at a hot spring is killed, he decides to live on a small isolated island, Yakushima, south of Kyushu. Yukiko, though not wanted by Tomioka, clings to him and follows him like a beaten dog in the hopes that he will eventually marry her. On the way she becomes ill and dies.

What guides the plot of *Ukigumo* is a woman's masochistic love for a cold and emotionally abusive lover. Tomioka is prone to dangerous affairs: to begin with, he snatches his wife from another man, impregnates a native woman, has an affair with Yukiko, and steals the wife of a tavern owner. He is addicted to a never-ending self-destructive love triangle. Yukiko is constantly jealous of his other women and yet cannot let him go. She is obsessed with this man as much as he is obsessed with the thrill of illicit love affairs that lead nowhere. This fixation ultimately leads to her destruction.

Chiyo Uno's jealous women are often on the other side: wives who suffer from their jealousies for their husband's other women. In *Sasu* (To stab, 1966) the narrator and her husband have a successful publishing business right after World War II.[16] Because the narrator is older than her husband, she is constantly threatened by and jealous of younger women dancers with whom her husband associates, and she takes dance lessons to compete with these girls. Even though she finds that he is having an affair with another woman, afraid to face the truth, she busies herself with a new business venture and with designing their house. When she is on a trip to France, her husband writes that his affair has ended, but he soon begins others. She suffers from burning jealousies and spends sleepless nights in agony. Although they no longer communicate, each living in opposite ends of the house, she does not have the courage to bring up the subject. She cannot confront her husband because of her fear that the marriage would break up if she did. The story ends when her husband finally asks her for a divorce and decides to move out.

In *Ohan* (1957) Uno depicted a very different woman, an all-forgiving, eternal woman who has no feelings of jealousy and thinks only of the happiness of her man.[17] Unlike other works, the story is narrated by Ohan's husband in the manner of flashbacks. At the beginning Ohan and her dissipated husband separate when he has a geisha as a mistress. Some years later they happen to meet on the street, and their relationship is rekindled because of their son. He promises Ohan that they will reunite. When the boy is drowned in a river on a rainy day, however, Ohan disappears, leaving a letter. In it she says that she does not want to disturb the happiness of his life with his mistress and that she has been made extremely happy just by knowing that she was loved by him. She concludes that she only hopes he will continue to care for his mistress. Ohan is a selfless martyr wife, who thinks only of her husband's happiness at the expense of her own life.

This figure leads to the next category, the cultural ideal of the eternal mother, and no writer portrays this ideal womanhood as eloquently as Sakae Tsuboi. In her popular *Nijushi no hitomi* (Twenty-four Eyes, 1952),[18] the protagonist, the teacher Oishi, is a newly appointed elementary school teacher at a small branch school in a village along a cape on Shodoshima Island. At first her students and their parents dislike her and treat her coldly, but after a while they begin to understand her genuine love and concern for their children and change their attitude. One day Oishi injures her leg, and, when commuting becomes difficult, she is transferred to the main branch school in a nearby town. Several years later the village children start commuting to the main branch school, and Oishi's contact with her students resumes.

Soon World War II breaks out, and a hard and enduring wartime life begins. Oishi loses her mother, husband, and a child and is left with her two sons. The whereabouts of her students are unknown. When the war finally ends Oishi returns to work at the old branch school in the village. The story ends when her former students come back and a class reunion is held.

Teacher Oishi's love for her students fits the idea of a nurturing mother. She cries at her students' troubles, and she tries to help them with their family difficulties and financial problems. Oishi represents the all-giving selfless mother-woman who will do anything for her students/children.

Representation of Women in the Writings of Kiku Amino

Unlike the women in the texts of these authors, whose lives largely revolve around men, Amino's women are not in relationships with men, which means they are out of circulation among them.[19] Her early piece, *Umibe* (By the Seaside, 1942), for example, tells a story of two young women on a trip to a nunnery by the quiet seaside. Teiko and Haruko, students in a women's school, visit this nunnery to finish their school theses. There are other female students, their teacher (a woman), and a runaway wife staying there as well. The narration advances by contrasting the quiet life of the nuns and the wishful and yet unsettled lives of young women. Currently, all of these women have little to do with men. Teiko seems to have some interest in men, but nothing is happening in her life; Haruko has several suitors but never takes them seriously. Her housemates, two students and their teacher, are passionately involved in the pursuit of knowledge and the change of women's status in Japan. The runaway wife, a piano teacher, wants to break away from her husband, who does not support her career. And, of course, the nuns carry on a quiet life out of touch with the world of men. The nunnery is a utopian shelter for single women.

Amino's women often express discontent with life centered around a man and marriage. In *Tsukimono* (Possessed by Evil Spirits), for example, the heroine, Hiro, has four different mothers (one real mother and three stepmothers). When her father marries for the fourth time, Hiro talks to herself as follows:

> A year later, Hiro's father married again. Hiro herself, under stress, unwillingly married. This marriage made her realize the constant toil expected of a wife in a Japanese family. About a year after Hiro's marriage, her father and his fourth wife had a baby girl. Looking at the face of the new-born infant, Hiro felt sorry for her, thinking "this baby too will have to go through various hardships in life as a woman." (Nogami and Amino 1965, 337-38)

In *Wakare* (Separation, 1940) Yoshino cannot bear a child and expresses her discontent at the idea of living with her husband's family.[20] This event is in a sharp contrast with Hiroko in Miyamoto's *Banshu heiya* (The Banshu Plain), who tries financially and emotionally to help her husband's family for twelve years during his absence.

Likewise, Amino depicts the internal consciousness of a single woman without children, who is outside of the patriarchal family system. In *Tsumetai kokoro* (Cold Heart, 1946),[21] the heroine's indifference to a sickly kitten is depicted in a detached manner. Ume moves into a small shack, which used to be a henhouse. She does not like cats, but, fearing rats, she decides to keep one. The kitten she has received from an acquaintance demands constant care, but Ume pays little attention to it, and, eventually, the kitten dies. She feels guilty and thinks of a comment by her former mother-in-law: "Childless women are cold." She does not deny it and thinks that it is indeed due to her childlessness that the kitten has died.

In *Hitorigurashi* (Living Alone, 1959), the heroine, Yoshiko, feels a little lonely thinking about her own future when hearing about a writer, Nagai Kafu, who died alone. A cleaning lady found him in the morning. Yoshiko suspects that there might be no one with her when she herself dies, yet she feels encouraged by Kafu, who disliked people and, like her, favored solitude. She takes each day as it comes and lives a quiet, peaceful life.

Above all what uniquely characterizes Amino's women is that they have real bodies—bodies that are not aesthetic or sensual but, rather, bodies that may be injured or diseased, bodies that excrete and menstruate. For example, in *Mitsuko* (1926), which is about the difficult relationship between the heroine, Mitsuko, and her stepmother, the stepmother is hospitalized because of typhoid fever. When Mitsuko visits her in the hospital, a nurse is attending her stepmother. The stepmother does not quite like this nurse, who is not very gentle. When the nurse tries to comb the mother's hair, she cries hysterically, "Stop it, stop it, please!" After a while she says she has to have a bowel movement and asks for a portable toilet. Mitsuko tries not to look at what the nurse is doing, pretending she has no interest. The stepmother, with her eyes closed, appears to have no will to resist and quietly lets the nurse do what she must.

> "I have felt like a movement since this morning, but I couldn't quite. . .," said the mother in a low voice.
>
> Mitsuko, with a show of cheerfulness, said, "Yes, I understand. You are just not used to this."
>
> When the nurse finished cleaning up, the mother said more than once, "Was it okay? Did I do it all right?" Mitsuko asked the nurse.
>
> She said immediately, "Yes, that's fine."
>
> Mitsuko told the mother, "Your nurse said that's fine," but she did not have enough kindness to check it herself. (Amino 1969, 1:64)

Keiko, the protagonist of *Kin no kan* (The Golden Casket, 1947), suffers from a type of fungal infection.

> When she began her translation work, the fungus on her hands and feet spread. Also for some unknown reason her face puffed up like a drowned body. Not only could she not work but she could not do her hair or wear a sash because of the bandage on her hands. She barely survived with the help of a young maid at her father's house. . .By the end of

August her hands healed a little, but the condition of her feet worsened because she had stood for over two hours at the funeral of her friend, a senior woman writer. Keiko applied gauze with ointment to the wound along with oil paper, and then put a thick bandage over it. Still the pus dripped down and it was very unpleasant to her. . .

Keiko and her stepmother did not stay for Takayoshi's wake. Keiko did not go to the seventh day service either. It was partly because of her infected feet which left ugly pus marks on the clean floor of Miyoko's house. (Nogami and Amino 1965, 385 and 394)

In *Akai kaaneishon* (Red Carnations, 1950) the heroine, Yoshiko, is close to her sister, Umeko. This beautiful sister has a disease and goes through an operation for an intestinal obstruction. Umeko's physical condition after the operation is described in great detail:

Feeling wet and uncomfortable, Umeko asked for a bandage change. A nurse told her to just leave it, but Umeko repeated the request. The nurse and Yoshiko undressed the wound.

A bad smell suddenly attacked their nostrils. What they found was that excrement that should be discharged from the anus had come from the old wound [in the stomach].

"Oh, Good! You must feel clean now. I'm sure gas was released too. It's good that all the body waste is gone," said Yoshiko to Umeko. (Ibid., 417)

Umeko was concerned that it was time for the last penicillin shot of the day. The assistant went out of the room to call a duty nurse.

Umeko said to Yoshiko, "Bad timing, my period just started. . ."

"Oh? Even after that big operation? I thought when one is seriously ill, the period normally stops. Well, but, that must mean you are in good physical condition. You cannot eat right now, but the blood transfusion probably is giving you nourishment." So Yoshiko consoled her, while, at the same time, thinking to herself, "What bad timing this is. Even a healthy person becomes weak during a period." (424)

As these examples show, the woman's body in Amino's texts is cast directly and boldly. In the texts of Hirabayashi, too, the woman's body is detailed, but this body is that of a pregnant mother or a wife welcoming her husband. The woman's body of Amino is not for men: it is not the body of a virgin or of a sensual, grown-up woman, nor is this body for reproduction.

According to the theories of body politics as developed in the past decade, the image of the disorderly woman or the bodily grotesque is subversive (Mikhail Bakhtin, 1968; Natalie Z. Davis 1975; Julia Kristeva 1982; Peter Stallybrass and Allon White in 1986; Miriam Silverberg 1991)[22]. It is possible to view the bodies of Amino's women as subverting the body of the woman tamed and appropriated by the dominant ideology of patriarchy. Amino's women assert the otherness of their existence through their bodies, which produce excess, blood, and defecation, having nothing to do with the seducer or the container of penis (Hite 1988, 133-34). Their "grotesque bodies" exist for the benefit not of men but, rather, of themselves. This body demystifies and degrades the idealized femininity prescribed by the patriarchal symbology. As the entity outside the system, it cuts through male codes and rules and therefore has a destabilizing power.

Conclusion

For the past decade the cultural meaning of "single women" in literature and history has been explored by scholars and theorists in conjunction with the critique of patriarchy and compulsory heterosexual economy.[23] In this emerging new discourse the heterosexual system, which has long been considered "natural" and "normal," is increasingly looked at as a cultural construct that marginalizes and excludes from effective participation certain groups of people, including single people beyond an acceptable marriageable age (particularly women), homosexual men, and lesbians. Those groups of people have been often labeled as deviant, abnormal, dangerous, and threatening and have been excluded from society because compulsory heterosexuality must be maintained and enforced at all costs in order to maximize continuing patriarchal control.

Unlike the women commonly portrayed in the works of her contemporaries, Amino's women clearly belong to an excluded group, the category of single women. They are unattached to men; they have no romantic expectations about men; they are disillusioned and disappointed by marriage; they do not want to live with the husband's family; and they have no children. Furthermore, they have life-sized adult bodies that are not sensual or aesthetic nor organized for reproduction. Their bodies are infected, and they menstruate and produce bodily wastes. Amino's women do not fit smoothly into the culturally defined signifiers of acceptable "women"; their very existence and presence subverts and threatens to nullify the patriarchally dictated gender distinctions. These women are self-representations from inside the marginal/woman's territory. Here lies the primary reason for the exclusion of Amino from the female-school literary canon.

The admission of literary works as "major" is a result of "successful critical promotion" (Robinson 1985, 105), and not any single event. It reflects literary sensibilities, values, and ideologies of certain periods and places. The female-school literature canon in Japanese literature is clearly a cumulative product of patriarchal culture; it is a "gentlemanly artifact" (106). It is a site in which the hegemonic power is covertly manifested in the form of academic classification of literary knowledge.

One sometimes hears a comment about Amino as a writer who is "*jimi*" (down to earth, subdued), as opposed to "*hade*" (gay, splashy), because she did not write about matters in terms of gender. This comment seems true, but only on the surface: it does not take into account the underlying subversive nature of her works. Thus, it is no accident that Amino, inconvenient to the patriarchal discourse, has come to be valued less and less as the *bundan* version of the history of modern Japanese literature continues to be told. Amino needs to be brought back into the literary mainstream and to be promoted continuously. Such an endeavor will surely lead to the remapping of the canon of Japanese literature, past and present.

Notes

This chapter is based on the author's Japanese essay "kafuchoseika no josei bungaku: Amino Kiku wa doko e," *U.S.-Japan Women's Journal*, no. 8 (1990): 83-100; and her English essay "Who's Afraid of Amino Kiku? Gender Conflict and the Literary Canon in Japanese Literature," *International Journal of Social Education*, 6, no. 1 (1991): 95-113. Permission to reprint has been granted by the publishers, the U.S.-Japan Women's Center, Palo Alto, California, and the Indiana Council for Social Studies, Muncie, Indiana. Some revisions have been made for the present version.

1. There are many definitions of the word *patriarchy*. I use the term here as Teresa L. Ebert (1988:19) defines it: "The organization and division of all practices and signification in culture in terms of gender and the privileging of one gender over the other, giving males control over female sexuality, fertility, and labor." Though it is said that patriarchy exists transhistorically and globally, it is not one universalizing system; it takes diverse forms and manifestations depending on time and location. The patriarchy in present-day industrial Japan, for example, is intricately intertwined with the development of capitalism. See Ueno 1990.

2. In *L'ordre du discours* (1971) Foucault states that the discursive formation is based upon control and economizing by excluding. It involves external control, internal control, and the control of agents. Within the second category he lists an academic discourse controlled under the name "scholarship" (Uchida 1990:164-66). In all of his writings Foucault targeted the critique of the notion of "human beings" in the modern West, but he rejected any notion of identity politics which replaces "human beings." It is my position that we should learn from the insight of Foucault and other poststructuralist critics who put the subject into critical interrogation, but my essay, which is a feminist analysis of the Japanese literary institution, presupposes a female identity. Of course, noncritical self-identification without a consideration of the marginalized spaces within must be avoided, but I believe that essentializing (identity politics) is a necessary tool for any political movement against oppression. For a feminist critique of Foucault from the perspective of identity politics, see Horowitz 1987 and Hartsock 1990.

3. Female poets such as Abutsuni, who wrote a well-known travelogue *Izayoi nikki* (1277) in the Kamakura period (1192-1333), and *Kaga no Chiyo* (1703-75) in the Edo period (1603-1869) were two of the better-known exceptions. The women who gained any prominence in letters during those periods were generally poets.

4. See Yamada 1985,10-16. For a bibliography on the works of Japanese women writers in English translation, see Mamola 1989.

5. The works of leftist writers such as Yuriko Miyamoto, Taiko Hirabayashi, and Ineko Sata, however, necessarily involve social issues.

6. One female writer, Saegusa Kazuko (1984), however, thinks that *joryu bungaku* is a positive category for women.

7. This scarcity of women in literary criticism in Japan is partly due to the fact that there have been far fewer women in academic institutions. Even today many feminist scholars and researchers are not full-time instructors.

8. *Kindai joryu bungaku* (Modern women's literature, 1983), edited by Nihon bungaku kenkyu shiryo kankokai, is a collection of essays by both male and female researchers, but women account for only 30 percent of the contributors.

9. For the state of art on feminist criticism and research on women's literature in Japan, see Kitada 1991.

10. My project is situated within the emerging feminist discourse in Japan to bring back the female writers buried or forgotten in the patriarchal literary canon. See Kitada 1991.

11. The following sources were used as reference for Amino's life: "Amino Kiku," in Nogami and Amino (1965, 44:515-44); and Nihon kindai bungakukan 1977. Her book, *Yureru ashi* (Blown Reed, 1964), is an autobiography of her life.

12. For an English translation of *Banshu heiya*, see Miyamoto 1963, 1986.

13. The Peace Preservation Law, originally enacted in 1887, was amended from time to time over the years. The new Peace Preservation Law of 1925, designed to suppress communist activities, prohibited groups that harbored dangerous thoughts or might advocate a change in Japanese political forms or the private property system. It remained in effect until it was abolished in October 1945, following Japan's defeat in World War II.

14. Miyamoto wrote about different kinds of women in other works: her most well-known, *Nobuko* (1926), for example, is about the heroine's difficult growth process through marriage and divorce, toward independence.

15. For an English translation of *Ukigumo*, see Hayashi 1957.

16. For an English translation of *Sasu*, see Uno 1991.

17. For an English translation of *Ohan*, see Uno 1961.

18. For an English translation of *Nijushi no hitomi*, see Tsuboi 1983.

19. These authors, however, have some works that do not fit this characterization.

20. For an English translation of *Wakare*, see Amino 1991.

21. This is the date Amino completed *Tsumetai kokoro*. This short story appears in Nogami and Amino 1965, but the date of the first publication is not clear.

22. For a general introduction to the subject and references, see Russo 1986.

23 See, for example, Auerbach 1982, special issue of *Journal of Family History* 1984; Vicinus 1985; Doan 1991; special issue of *Rekishi hyoron* (1992). For a critique of heterosexuality from a lesbian perspective, see Rich 1980.

Works Cited

Amino, Kiku. 1991. "Separation" (Wakare). Trans. Chieko M. Ariga. *Manoa: A Pacific Journal of International Writing* 3, no. 2 (Fall).

———. 1969. *Amino Kiku zenshu* (The complete works of Amino Kiku). 3 vols. Tokyo: Kodansha.

Auerbach, Nina. 1982. *Woman and the Demon: The Life of a Victorian Myth*. Cambridge, Mass. and London: MIT Press.

Bakhtin, Mikhail. 1968. *Rabelais and His World*. Trans. Helene Iswolsky. Cambridge, Mass. and London: MIT Press.

Davis, Natalie Zemon. 1975. *Society and Culture in Early Modern France*. Stanford, Calif.: Stanford University Press.

Doan, Laura L., ed 1991. *Old Maids to Radical Spinsters: Unmarried Women in the Twentieth-Century Novel*. Urbana and Chicago: University of Illinois Press.

Ebert, Teresa L. 1988. "The Romance of Patriarchy: Ideology, Subjectivity, and Postmodern Feminist Cultural Theory." *Cultural Critique* 10:19-57.

Fowler, Edward. 1988. *The Rhetoric of Confession: Shishosetsu in Early Twentieth-Century Japanese Fiction*. Berkeley, Los Angeles, and London: University of California Press.

Hartstock, Nancy. "Foucault on Power: A Theory for Young Women?" In *Feminism/Post-modernism*, ed. Linda J. Nicholson. New York and London: Routledge, 1990.

Hayashi, Fumiko. 1964. *Nihon no bungaku*, vol. 47: *Hayashi Fumiko* (Japanese literature, vol. 47: Fumiko Hayashi). Tokyo: Chuokoronsha.

———. 1957. *Floating Cloud* (Ukigumo). Trans. Yoshiyuki Koitabashi. Tokyo: Information Publications.

Hijiya-Kirschnereit, Irmela. 1986. "Joryu bungaku ga bungaku ni naru hi" (The day when women's literature becomes "literature"). *Asahi shimbun*, 2 September, 11.

Hirabayashi, Taiko and Tomie Ohara, 1969. *Nihon no bungaku*, vol. 48: *Hirabayashi Taiko, Ohara Tomie* (Japanese literature, vol. 48: Taiko Hirabayashi and Tomie Ohara). Tokyo: Chuokoronsha.

Hite, Molly. 1988. "Writing—and Reading—the Body: Female Sexuality and Recent Feminist Fiction." *Feminist Studies* 14 (Spring): 121-42.

Horowitz, Gad. 1987. "The Foucaultian Impasse: No Sex, No Self, No Revolution." *Political Theory* 15:61-81.

Iwaya, Daishi. 1977. *Monogatari joryu bundanshi* (An anecdotal history of women writers), vol. 2. Tokyo: Chuokoronsha.

Joyru bungakushakai. 1975. *Gendai no joryu bungaku* (Contemporary women's literature), vol. 7. Tokyo: Mainichi shimbunsha.

Journal of Family History. 1984. Special issue (Winter).

Kitada, Sachie. 1991. "Feminizumu bungakuhihyo no genzai: Nihonhen" (Japanese feminist literary criticism: state of the art). *New Feminism Review* 2:162-71.

Kristeva, Julia. 1982. *Powers of Horror: An Essay on Abjection*. Trans. Leon S. Roudiez. New York: Columbia University Press.

Mamola, Claire Zebroski. 1989. *Japanese Women Writers in English Translation: An Annotated Bibliography*. New York and London: Garland Publishing.

Miyamoto, Yuriko. 1984a. "Banshu Plain" (*Banshu heiya*, excerpt 1). Trans. Brett de Bary, *Bulletin of Concerned Asian Scholars* 16, no. 2 (April-June): 40-45.

———. 1984b. "The Weathervane Plant" (*Fuchiso*, excerpt). Trans. Brett de Bary. *Bulletin of Concerned Asian Scholars* 16, no. 2 (April-June): 46-47.

———. 1975. *Gendai no joryu bungaku* (Contemporary women's literature), vol. 7. Tokyo: Mainichi shimbunsha.

———. 1969. *Nihon no bungaku* (Japanese literature), vol. 45: *Miyamoto Yuriko*. Tokyo: Chuokoronsha.

———. 1963. "Banshu Plain" (*Banshu heiya*, excerpt 2). Trans. Yukiko Sakaguchi and Jay Gluck. In *Ukiyo*, ed. J. Gluck. New York: Vanguard Press.

Nihon bungaku kenkyu shiryo kankokai, ed. 1983. *Kindai joryu bungaku* (Modern Japanese literature by women). Tokyo: Yuseido.

Nihon kindai bungakukan. 1977. *Nihon kindai bungaku daijiten* (Comprehensive dictionary of modern Japanese literature), s.v. "Amino Kiku."

Nogami, Yaeko, and Kiku Amino. 1965. *Nihon no bungaku*, vol. 44: *Nogami Taeko, Amino Kiku* (Japanese Literature, vol. 44: Taeko Nogami and Kiku Amino). Tokyo: Chuokoronsha.

Odagiri, Hideo. 1971. *Nihon kindai bungaku no shiso to jokyo* (Ideology and circumstances of modern Japanese literature). Tokyo: Hosei daigaku.

Rekishi hyoron. 1992. Special issue on "Rekishi no naka no shinguru" (Singles in history), no. 503 (March).

Rich, Adrienne. 1980. "Compulsory Heterosexuality and the Lesbian Experience." *Signs* 5, no. 4: 631-60.

Robinson, Lillian. 1985. "Treason Our Text: Feminist Challenges to the Literary Canon." In *New Feminist Criticism: Essays on Women, Literature, and Theory*, ed. Elaine Showalter. New York: Pantheon Books.

Russo, Mary. 1986. "Female Grotesques: Carnival and Theory." In *Feminist Studies, Critical Studies*, ed. Teresa de Lauretis. Bloomington: Indiana University Press.

Saegusa, Kazuko. 1984. *Sayonara otoko no jidai* (Good-bye to the age of men). Tokyo: Jinbun shoin.

Sata, Ineko, and Sakae Tsuboi. 1968. *Nihon no bungaku*, vol. 49: *Sata Ineko, Tsuboi Sakae* (Japanese literature, vol. 49: Ineko Sata and Sakae Tsuboi). Tokyo: Chuokoronsha.

Shioda, Ryohei. 1983. *Shintei Meiji joryu sakkaron* (A newly revised account of Meiji women writers). Tokyo: Bunsendo.

Silverberg, Miriam. 1991. "The Modern Girl as Militant." In *Recreating Japanese Women, 1600-1945*, ed. Gail Bernstein. Berkeley, Los Angeles, and Oxford: University of California Press.

Stallybrass, Peter, and Allon White. 1986. *The Politics and Poetics of Transgression*. Ithaca, N.Y.: Cornell University Press.

Tsuboi, Sakae. 1983. *Twenty-Four Eyes* (Nijushi no hitomi). Trans. Akira Miura. Rutland, Vt. and Tokyo: Tuttle.

Uchida, Ryuzo. 1990. *Misheru Fuko* (Michel Foucault). Tokyo: Kodansha.

Ueno, Chizuko. 1993. "The Rise of Feminist Criticism." *Japanese Book News*, no. 2 (Spring): 5, 20.

———. 1990. *Kafuchosei to shihonsei: Marukusushugi feminizumu no chihei* (Patriarchy and capitalism: a horizon for Marxist feminism). Tokyo: Iwanami shoten.

Uno, Chiyo. 1991. "To Stab" (Sasu). Trans. Kyoko Iriye Selden. In *Japanese Women Writers: Twentieth Century Short Fiction*, ed. Noriko Mizuta Lippit and Kyoko Iriye Selden. New York: M. E. Sharpe.

———. 1969. *Nihon no bungaku*, vol. 46: *Uno Chiyo, Okamoto Kanoko* (Japanese literature, vol. 46: Chiyo Uno and Kanoko Okamoto). Tokyo: Chuokoronsha.

———. 1961. "Ohan." In *The Old Woman, the Wife, and the Archer: Three Modern Japanese Short Novels*, ed. and trans. Donald Keene, 51-118. New York: Viking Press.

Vicinus, Martha. 1985. *Independent Women: Work and Community for Single Women, 1850-1920*. Chicago and London: University of Chicago Press.

Wada, Shigejiro. 1982. *Nihon no kindai bungaku* (Modern Japanese literature). Tokyo: Dohosha.

Yamada, Yusaku. 1985. *Joryu bungaku no genzai* (The current status of women's literature). Tokyo: Gakujutsutosho shuppansha.

Yoshida, Seiichi, ed. 1969. *Joryu bungakushi* (History of female-school literature). Tokyo: Dobun shoin.

Unions and Disunions:
Three Early Twentieth-Century
Female Couples

4

Hitomi Sawabe
Translated by Kimberly Hughes

The period between 1910 and the early 1930s was a comparatively peaceful one of economic stability following Japan's victory in World War I. During this time of the Taisho democracy, cities were filled with so-called *mobo* (modern boys), and *moga* (modern girls), young adults who had adopted Western dress and behavior. Fancy operas and musicals were popular, as well as the new Takarazuka Girls' Theater Troupe[1], which was formed as an all-female version of Kabuki theater. Also in fashion during this era were girls' magazines, to which many young women submitted pieces pouring out their hearts. Some of these contributors, including Yoshiya Nobuko, gained an enthusiastic following among girls and young women.

While males and females were strictly forbidden to enjoy each other's company, students at girls' schools, particularly those in boarding schools, were able to forge close relationships with their female classmates and teachers. It was not uncommon for romantic relationships to develop between girls. They were called *esu* ("S"), taken from the first letter of the English word "sister," and used both as a code word and a derogatory term signifying lesbian: or *o-dear*, a Japanese transliteration of the English "dear," using the honorific prefix "o." Although these liaisons usually ended when one or both of the girls married, there were also frequent incidents of *shinju jiken* (same-sex love-pact suicides)[2] among female students and factory workers. While the circumstances differed in each case, such suicides often resulted from the despair that followed when one of the girls was forced into marriage by her parents.

Most boys growing up within this patriarchal system received preferential treatment from childhood, and therefore unconsciously adopted the same attitude as their parents in discriminating against women. In response to such practices, some women set about rejecting these men by creating their own *ai no kaihoku* (space for liberated love) (Horiba 1988, 108) within which they would be free to love other women. From this period in the early twentieth century, I want to describe three famous pairings, one of which remained together until death parted them. In both other instances, the relationship ended when one woman left the other for a male lover.

Raicho Hiratsuka and Kokichi Otake

Raicho Hiratsuka (1886-1971) was a leading figure of the women's movement in Japan, as well as an intellectual and critical commentator. Near the end of the Meiji period, she founded and published *Seito*, a literary magazine by and for women, which called upon all women to wake up to the reality that was facing them. She also worked as a leader of both the women's suffragist and antiwar movements. A collection of her writing fills eight volumes.

Raicho Hiratsuka (born Haru) was born into the family of a high-ranking government official in Tokyo that included her parents, an older sister, and a grandmother. Her father had lived abroad prior to her birth, and her mother wore Western dress and learned English in a manner befitting a woman of the new modern age. While Hiratsuka's early years were spent quite comfortably, the political winds turned as she entered Ochanomizu Girls' High School. As Japanese nationalism began to reject all things Western, her family changed their Western-style house into one more visibly Japanese. They also shed Western-style dress in favor of purple cotton kimono and *hakama*, a formal overskirt.

Hiratsuka displayed a sharp intellect and achieved high grades from the time she was in elementary school. She found herself both bored and disturbed, however, by her school curriculum's almost exclusive focus on homemaking and child-rearing skills, as well as outdated Confucian ideals that instructed women to obey their fathers during childhood, their husbands in wedlock, and their sons in old age. Together with several other classmates, Raicho formed a group of so-called *kaizoku gumi* (pirates). Rejecting the ideals of proscribed femininity, the girls cut class together rather than attend the ethics courses. After graduation, Raicho entered Japan Women's University, which proclaimed an educational philosophy of treating women *hito to shite* (as individual human beings). She was once again completely disillusioned, however, upon discovering that this school offered nothing more than the same fare based upon the dictum of "good wife, wise mother."

Nevertheless, Hiratsuka continued to engage in her own self-study, which included reading and analyzing religious and philosophical texts, as well as personal self-development through Buddhist *zazen* meditation. Such practices enabled her to attain an understanding that the differences between men and women merely dealt with surface-level expression, as opposed to the persona housed within the depths of one's soul—which she recognized as denoting one's true self. As a result of this revelation, Raicho experienced a profound sense of liberation at a relatively young age.

In 1911, Hiratsuka and four other students from her university created a group they termed *Seitosha*—the Japanese approximation of the British women's "bluestocking." Together they began producing *Seito*, Japan's first literary magazine written by and for women. For the inaugural issue, Hiratsuka wrote, "In the beginning, woman was the sun," while such patriarchal customs as the household system then worked to render her "as pale and sickly as the moon." She issued a call for women to realize that "we must restore this sun from its hidden confines to its rightful place."

In response, *Seitosha* was flooded with enthusiastic letters from readers, as well as subscriptions and inquiries from women wishing to join the organization. They also received submissions of all sorts, including essays, poetry, and personal diary entries. Clearly, many women wanted to tell their own stories in their own words, whatever the form.

One such woman was Kokichi Otake (1893-1966), born Kazue. Her nickname "Kokichi" signifies crimson, her favorite color. Born in Toyama City and reared in Osaka, she was the eldest of four daughters born to the family of Japanese-style painter Etsudo Otake (1868-1931). As a youngster, she showed talent in both sports and music, and was also an avid reader. Her mother, who was a descendant of the warrior (samurai) class, disciplined her daughter to follow the traditional values of femininity. At the same time, however, Otake was trained to continue in her father's profession—treatment usually reserved for a son, and she became a talented artist. Following a yearlong association with the *Seito* journal during her late teens, Kokichi Otake published a literary journal called *Safuran* (Saffron).

Otake had been extremely moved after reading Hiratsuka's assertion that "In the beginning, woman was the sun." She was apparently also greatly inspired by Hiratsuka's statement that "we are all—every last one of us—hidden geniuses with the potential to reach genius-level achievements," which she recited each day as if it were a sacred text (Tomimoto 1935, 86). For Otake, Hiratsuka was an absolute role model whom she worshipped and adored. Otake believed that entry into *Seitosha* would "allow me to faithfully express who I truly am," and proceeded to send Hiratsuka a series of passionate fan letters—even once going as far as to recount a personal experience of an erotic nature. Hiratsuka, at first, read these letters with disbelief because it was "not clear whether the sender was a man or a woman," and the prose was full of errors. Having expressed boredom with "the organization's tendency to endlessly attract only a mediocre and uninteresting lineup of women" (Hiratsuka Feb. 1913, 99), however, Hiratsuka's curiosity was admittedly piqued by this "eccentric individual." Finally, she responded and asked if Otake would be interested in designing the cover for an issue of *Seito*.

Hiratsuka and Otake first met on February 19, 1912, six months after *Seito*'s first issue. When Hiratsuka opened the sliding door and entered the room, Otake initially looked her straight in the eyes. Penetrated by Hiratsuka's intelligent and beautiful gaze, she reported later that she was so nervous that her entire body had begun to shake. Although Hiratsuka's colleagues had previously referred to Otake mockingly as "the strange one from Osaka," they found upon meeting her in person that she was in fact a pleasant individual who exuded a quality of childlike innocence. She was uncharacteristically tall for a Japanese woman of her day, and dressed in a male kimono made of *kurumegasuri* cotton with a *hakama*, obi belt, and sandals. Hiratsuka, whose intelligence had already led her to analyze the existing oppression against women, was intrigued by how Otake had cast off the social constraints demanding that women look feminine. "I can't put my finger on it, but this woman seems to have great potential," she commented (Hiratsuka, Dec. 1913, 11).

At the time, Hiratsuka was twenty-six, and Otake was nineteen. After moving to Tokyo on April 9 of that year, Otake began to frequent the *Seito-sha* office and Hiratsuka's home in order to assist with editing and illustrations for the publication. Elated at finding that she could express herself freely and openly within the organization, she walked around laughing and singing in a loud and carefree voice. The others reportedly viewed her as "a natural-born, free spirit," and they began to warm to her. A *Seitosha* meeting was held the following month on May 13 at Otake's home, and she cheerfully prepared a feast of food and drinks for the occasion. This day was to be a historical one for Hiratsuka, who later wrote in her diary: "How could I ever have known the passion with which I embraced her and kissed her as I attempted to bring Otake into my world?" (Hiratsuka, Aug. 1912, 82).

Otake found herself more and more consumed with confusing and yet burning feelings for the older woman, who in turn referred to her by such intimate names as "my boy" and "Raicho's boy" (Hiratsuka, Aug. 1912, 85). Otake wrote the following diary entry in the June issue of *Seito*, titled "One Night and One Morning":

> My heart has been violently thrown about by this older woman who has suddenly dashed out in front of me, and toward whom I feel an intense longing. I feel like a young boy who is a complete prisoner . . . Even if it means becoming a slave or sacrificing myself, I would do it gladly and

willingly, just so long as I know that I would never lose her embraces or her kisses. (Otake 1912, 115-16)

The relationship between the two ended abruptly two weeks later, however, when Hiratsuka announced her intention with the following letter: "I desire to embrace you and kiss you . . . but far more than this, I crave the luxury of solitude and peaceful quiet, such as one might find inside the deep forest. Farewell to you. Farewell!" (Hiratsuka, Aug. 1912, 93)

For Hiratsuka, who cherished solitude and indulged in her own thoughts, the overly enthusiastic Otake—who was clingy and hated being alone—had clearly begun to demand too much of her energy. Similarly, she may also have had doubts about sharing a future with someone who had fallen in love so quickly and easily. Prior to issuing the *Seito* journal, Hiratsuka's past had included a failed double-suicide attempt with her lover, the writer Sohei Morita,[3] as well as an incident in which she had shocked the Zen Buddhist monk Nakahara Shugaku by suddenly kissing him in the midst of meditation. It was likely, therefore, that the "passionate embraces and kisses" that she bestowed upon the young Otake were similarly nothing more than impulsive flings to be added to her already "questionable" past record.

Otake, by contrast, clearly lacked the self-confidence and sense of personal identity that Hiratsuka possessed naturally. She would have given her life for this relationship. In order to strengthen her fragile budding talents, she needed someone who would love her steadily while accepting her for who she was. In a reply to Hiratsuka on June 3, she wrote, "The child inside me has finally died" (Hiratsuka, Aug. 1912, 94). Clearly, Hiratsuka was not the motherly figure that Otake required in order to cultivate her gifts.

In the editor's postscript to the July edition of *Seito*, Otake included references to several of her own recent personal experiences and observations. She described, for example, the dinner that she, Hiratsuka, and fellow *Seito* member Hatsuko Nakano had with an *oiran* (high-class courtesan) called Eizan at the Daimonjiro restaurant in the Yoshiwara red-light district, which they had visited at the invitation of Otake's uncle (the Japanese-style painter Chikuha Otake) in order to see what life was like among lower-class women. In addition, she wrote about the delightfully gorgeous, multicolored liquor she had seen at the *Koh no su* (Goose Nest) restaurant where she had conducted an interview for the magazine.

Otake's openness rendered her completely vulnerable to the malevolent intentions of journalists. She answered questions honestly and without the slightest hesitation, much to the bemusement of the newspaper reporters who interviewed her. Already looking askance at the *Seito* journal, these journalists eagerly leaped at the opportunity to expose what they saw as the scandalous behavior of these "new women" who used vulgar speech, indulged in alcohol, cavorted with prostitutes as if they were men—and even included a mysterious homosexual referred to as "Hiratsuka's boy."

And so began a campaign of criticism and attack against the two women. Hiratsuka received a barrage of threatening letters, and rocks were hurled at the window of her home. Many people began leaving *Seitosha* and canceling their subscriptions to the journal. Otake became the object of severe criticism from members for initiating this chain of events, including an accusation from founding member Yoshi Yasumochi (who went by the pen name of *obasan*, or "auntie") that Otake was "imprudent." Feeling the acute weight of her own responsibility in the matter, Otake soon decided to leave the organization.

At around the same time, on July 12, Otake was diagnosed with tuberculosis. Accompanied by Hiratsuka, she was admitted to the Nankoin sanatorium in the town of Chigasaki in Kanagawa prefecture. Heartbroken and in disarray, Otake slowly began piecing her life back together. She corrected her finicky eating habits, making sure to consume more eggs and milk in order to regain her strength. As long as Hiratsuka was by her side, she felt the will to go on living. Hiratsuka rented a room in a nearby fisherman's house in late August, and the pair worked together to edit September's first anniversary issue of *Seito*.

Fate was already at work, however, in the form of an encounter between Hiratsuka and the young painting student Hiroshi Okumura in the waiting room of the sanatorium. He was five years Hiratsuka's junior, and displayed no overtly "masculine" characteristics. The pair fell in love at first sight—an incident that was not lost upon Otake, who was in the room at the time and witnessed their meeting. When he came to visit a couple of days later, Okumura missed the last train back and ended up sleeping in the sanatorium waiting room. It was a stormy night with rain and lightning, and a concerned Hiratsuka invited him back to her room. Feeling agitation and an uneasy premonition, Otake was unable to sleep the entire night. Confirming first thing in the morning that Okumura was not in the sanatorium, she ran straight to Hiratsuka's house. She went inside and found that the place was empty—but that bedding for two was aligned underneath the mosquito net, with Okumura's sketch box and tripod lying nearby.

Otake walked down to the beach and ended up crossing paths with the two, who were wrapped in a blanket together taking a stroll. "Goodbye, Hiratsuka!" she shouted before running back to the hospital, consumed with jealousy. Hiratsuka's nature was such that once she set her sights on something or someone new, she pursued it with the entirely of her being and never bothered to look back. For Otake, there was absolutely nothing to be done other than to resign herself to reality.

The one-year anniversary issue of *Seito* did not include contributions from Hiratsuka. While Otake wrote a piece called "*Sono kouta*" (That Ditty), it displayed none of her previous mischievous flair. Clearly, her youthful sensibility and energetic tendency to say whatever was on her mind had fled. For the November issue, she wrote an essay titled "*Gunshu ni majitte*" (Mingling with the Crowd), which was essentially a painful self-criticism. Shortly thereafter, she officially left the organization for good.[4]

Becoming Kazue Otake once again, she returned home to continue painting. She was selected for the Thirteenth *Tatsumi Gakai* Painting Exhibition in April of 1913 with her folding screen work titled "Biwa no mi" (Loquat fruit), and she published a literary journal in March of the following year titled *Safuran* (Saffron). By this time, the young persona of Otake had all but disappeared. On October 27, 1914, she wed the ceramic artist Kenkichi Tomimoto,[5] who had just returned from living abroad. From then on, she became known by her married name, Kazue Tomimoto.

Around the time that her daughter was born, she seriously thought of leaving her husband or becoming a Catholic nun—and even found herself considering the possibility of death (Takai and Orii 1985). While she had hoped that her husband would be someone with whom she could share a life in the arts, he viewed her as nothing more than a glorified assistant charged with providing wifely support so that he might become a successful artist.

While she often enjoyed inviting young women into her home for small salon gatherings, the once vibrant Kokichi Otake was never to return. Filled with angst over the chasm between her attraction to women in contrast to her life as mother to three children, and wife to Kenkichi Tomimoto (who was later designated as a Living National Treasure for his ceramic artistry), she lived the rest of her life in quiet isolation (Kurosawa 2001, 16).

As for Hiratsuka, she began writing a three-part essay in 1913 titled "*Ichinenkan*" (For One Year). "I had been wanting to provide these original materials for future research on women," she wrote (Hiratsuka, Feb. 1913, 87), and proceeded to publish a segment of the letters she had received from Otake. She also included partial translations of Ellen Key's *Love and Marriage*, which outlines the ideals of heterosexual monogamy. Hiratsuka had been preparing at this time for her future life with Okumura, and the following year she left her parents' home to live with him. Thus, while she remained critical of institutional marriage, Hiratsuka became a wife and mother and established her identity as a "new woman"—a modern subject characterized by the keywords "woman," "heterosexuality," and "motherhood."

Hiratsuka also wrote dismissively at this time regarding Otake—the person whom she had once referred to as "my boy"—using stigmatizing terminology from the lexicon of modern sexology such as "an almost congenital sexual invert" and "a true sexual invert".[6] In the autobiography that she completed toward the end of her life, titled *Genshi josei wa taiyo de atta* (In the Beginning Woman Was the Sun), she wrote about Otake as follows:

> It is true that the eccentric Kokichi Otake was completely obsessed with me. If one were to look at the situation in the terms of homosexuality, it is likely that what she was feeling toward me was indeed same-sex love. As for myself, though, while I may have been attracted by her unique charm, the feelings that I experienced toward her were most certainly not homosexual ones. Rather, I found her powerful feelings and overwhelming advances toward me to be sweet. I was drawn to her free expression and sense of sharp perception, and my own heart at the time admittedly did feel somewhat mischievous. Although the impact of this encounter between the two of us was certainly not insignificant, it was most definitely not homosexual love—as evidenced by the way Okumura subsequently came along and swept away my heart. (Hiratsuka 1992, 135).

Yoshiko Yuasa and Yuriko Miyamoto [7]

Yoshiko Yuasa (1896-1990) and Yuriko Chujo (later, Miyamoto) (1899-1951), who will be referred to as Yuriko,[8] shared their lives for eight years during their late twenties and early thirties. They first met on April 11, 1924 in the writing studio of a mutual friend, the novelist Yaeko Nogami.[9] At the time, Yuasa was twenty-seven years old. She was auditing courses in Russian literature at Waseda University—where women were not yet allowed to enroll as official students—while also working as an editor of the magazine *Aikoku fujin* (Patriotic Woman). She was steeped in grief at this time, having lost her mother two years previously and also having ended a love affair with the *geisha* Sei Kitamura, whom she had sent off on a traditional singing apprenticeship for four years to obtain a diploma. Today, Yoshiko Yuasa is remembered as a scholar of Russian literature. She translated and introduced to a Japanese audience several Russian novels and plays, including *Sakura no sono* (The Cherry Orchard), *Sannin shimai* (The Three Sisters), and *Kamome* (The Seagull) by Anton Chekhov, as well as *Mori wa ikiteiru* (The Forest Is Alive) by Samuli Marshak. Her Japanese translations were acclaimed, and many were rendered into stage productions following World War II. She also published volumes of essays, including *Ippiki okami* (The Lone Wolf, 1996), and *Okami imada oizu* (The

Ageless Wolf, 1973), as well as a collection of letters called *Yuriko no tegami* (Yuriko's Letters, 1978).

In 1924, Yuriko was twenty-five and an accomplished author, who had published at seventeen *Mazushiki hitobito no mure* (A Flock of the Poor), thus earning a reputation as a young genius. While studying abroad in New York, she had married Shigeru Araki, a scholar of ancient East Asian languages, despite strong parental opposition. In the midst of an unhappy marriage and feeling some frustration about the progress of her writing career, she, too, was depressed when the two women first met.

Their conversation apparently struck the right chord, as was evidenced by Yuriko's remark "What a boring magazine!" after learning of Yuasa's editing work. Such a frank comment was largely unheard of in Japan, where people would choose to say nothing in lieu of a negative comment. Unfazed by the remark, however, Yuasa agreed, "They don't spend enough money to make a worthwhile magazine. The whole thing should just be shut down!" Quickly dispensing with all social formalities in their interactions with one another, the two women became friends. Shortly thereafter, Yuriko wrote an essay titled *"Taisetsu na me"* (Precious Sprout), wherein she spoke of the joy of personal relationships:

> Prospects of good friendship excite me when I find that, while in the presence of such people, I am able to lay aside all pretenses and simply be as I am, without feeling stagnant. Merely talking and spending time with such friends gives me a feeling of contentment and fresh confidence and makes me feel inspired to be able to accomplish things. (Chujo 1924, 72)

The encounter with Yuasa reminded Yuriko that her husband lacked both understanding and empathy. Similarly, Yuasa found her conversations with Yuriko to be intelligent and stimulating. Both women enjoyed their ability to speak openly to each other, in trust and comfort. Their relationship soon deepened.

At the end of May, a month and-a-half after their first meeting, Yuasa paid a five-day visit to Yuriko's writing retreat near Mt. Kaiseizan.[10] There they became lovers. Yuriko wrote of this occasion in her diary, "I could not help but acknowledge that there are elements of *liebe* (love) blended within our friendship. . .The mere thought of her departure the following afternoon was unbearable. . .I became completely lost in my feelings of passion" (Miyamoto 1979, 764).

In a letter to Yuasa, she also wrote, "I plan to hold close and nurture to the fullest extent possible this amazing love that exists between us, as a completely natural part of who we are." (Miyamoto 1983, 34)

Yuasa's reaction to Yuriko's grand words was at first surprisingly cool. She was wary of being used by Yuriko as a means to leave her marriage, and so she asked Yuriko to reconsider what she was thinking and feeling. Her request served only as fuel to the fire Yuriko already felt. She continued to write to Yuasa, describing the transgressions of her younger days, which she had never confessed to her husband. She also wrote to her husband informing him that she wished to begin separate lives. She then immediately promised Yuasa, "Whatever this love may be called, I am going to live my life for your love—for you, the fortress of my heart." (Miyamoto 1983, 40).

Despite the passionate feelings behind this pledge, however, ten days later everything came crashing down. After receiving Yuriko's letter, her husband Shigeru Araki took time off from work and headed straight for Mt. Kaiseizan. He found the studio empty, however, as Yuriko had gone to Tokyo to see Yuasa. Reading the diary that Yuriko had left sitting on the desk, he realized that Yuasa was the reason for Yuriko's leaving him. Araki returned to Tokyo and began to pressure Yuriko to stay with him. Using sex as a tool, he convinced her three days later that they should move into a larger house in the neighborhood. Since Yuriko enjoyed sex with men more than with women, she accepted her husband's proposals. When Yuriko went to see Yuasa that afternoon, she clearly had no idea of the impact this news would have on her new lover. To Yuasa, the move was nothing more than a cover-up whereby Yuriko would continue her relationship with her husband as before—and therefore represented a clear betrayal of Yuriko's promise to her.

The following morning, faced with Yuasa's harsh accusations, Yuriko finally admitted her own cowardice. She told her husband that she had changed her mind about the move, and then, depressed, retreated to Mt. Kaiseizan. Yuasa wrote criticizing Yuriko's drifting indeterminately and then making excuses without acknowledging responsibility. Yuriko reflected deeply on her behavior after reading the letter, and realized that Yuasa's criticism offered her a precious opportunity to become a more decisive person. In a subsequent letter dated June 10, Yuasa wrote, "You make me a better person, as I do you (we complement each other) . . . I love the work that you do, and I love you."[11] Such words of praise for a woman and her talents may rarely be uttered by a male lover—even in this age. For Yuasa and Yuriko, the moment marked the strength of their relationship.

Their correspondence also focused on sexuality, a taboo topic for women of the day. Once, in a response to Yuasa, Yuriko wrote the following with regard to her husband, "The power a man yields over a woman's heart through a sexual relationship is truly vexing." She proceeded to profess her embarrassment, adding: "I can't believe I am writing such a thing!" She then continued:

> Often, just because a man is her sexual partner, a woman hesitates to talk back to him, since that would hurt his feelings. Women often lapse into being completely bound to men in a display of virtuous servility. Most worrisome to me, however, is a woman's willingness to hand over her most precious, precious soul in exchange for the gratification of her physical desire. (Miyamoto 1983, 62)

In response, Yuasa wrote, "It is indeed a sad contradiction that men and women will forever be at odds with one another, yet women cannot live apart from men.[12]

Yuasa's conclusion that "men and women will forever be at odds with one another" was reached not from reading books, but through closely observing the personal experience of people close to her. Her mother Iku had endured the painful reality of her husband taking her own younger sister as a lover, and she also witnessed how her friend, the author Toshiko Tamura,[13] was unable to break off relations with her husband Shogyo despite endless fierce fighting. In Yuasa's view, the "love" that existed between men and women who were sexually involved with each other was nothing more than a bargaining tool that remained steeped in the dynamics of control and subordination. Yuasa was able to reach powerful insights of this sort precisely because she was not bound to the restrictive limitations of "proper femininity." Wearing chic men's clothing, smoking, and using no typically female speech, Yuasa had transcended the boundaries of gender. She recognized that while relationships between members of the same sex were privy to none of the social protections rendered to married couples, such relationships in turn provided freedoms that would be impossible to enjoy within the official system of marriage. She regarded it as a simple matter, then, to leave behind the idea of marriage to a man.

Yuriko found that her correspondence with Yuasa served as a useful important tool of consciousness-raising, which in turn had an enormous impact upon her written works. She destroyed perhaps as many as forty nonpublished pieces and wrote a short novel called *Kikiwakerarenu ashioto* (Inaudible Footsteps), which later became part of a more extensive work titled *Nobuko*, her most feminist work and one that continues to be read today.

At the same time that Yuriko was writing *Nobuko*, she and Yuasa were in the midst of a daily correspondence. They wrote some one hundred and eighty letters, exceeding one thousand crammed pages. A comparison of these letters with Yuriko's diary from the same period clearly reveals that Yuasa's love was a significant source of comfort for her as she wrote her novel. Shortly thereafter, Yuriko ended her marriage to Araki and began officially sharing her life with Yuasa. She found that she was able to stay up late and sleep in late—something she had been unable to do while living with her husband. She also found endless new sources of inspiration from loving conversations with Yuasa, as well as from leisurely activities such as drawing, listening to music, and attending theater performances. Yuasa, ever the realist, often straightforwardly criticized Yuriko for her constant tendency to lapse into idle daydreaming. Yuriko, for her part, was positive and cheerful. Expressing distaste for Yuasa's fondness for singing with *geisha* as "decadent," she sought to focus Yuasa's energies on her translations.

When Yaeko Nogami visited the couple a month or so later, she wrote in her diary that their relationship was an ideal example of cohabitation that seemed "simple, peaceful, and beautiful, with no apparent restrictions or troublesome elements" (Nogami 1986, 209-210). "We brought each other what the other person lacked," Yuasa wrote in her diary. "Living together, we helped, complemented and enhanced each other's lives."[14] But their relationship was not completely rosy. Eighteen months later, Yuriko's diary entries note small quarrels often rooted in her own sexuality. Nogami also mentions some doubts in her diary, "I wonder, however, whether it will be possible for the two to continue living as they are now, with nothing coming between them. I find this quite unlikely, especially since it seems clear that Chujo [i.e., Yuriko] will eventually seek love elsewhere." (Nogami 1986, 209-210) Journalists at the time were writing mockingly about Yuriko and Yuasa as a *doseiai fufu* (homosexual couple). "Let them say whatever they like," shrugged Yuasa, who dismissed the reports as mere gossip that was not worth paying attention to. Indeed, although the pair were lovers toward the beginning of their relationship, Yuriko's sexual interest did eventually begin to cool down. And as their passion evolved into something more resembling affection, Yuriko began to look around for other possible lovers—this time male.

In a diary entry on August 15, 1927, Yuriko writes, "This division between love and passion! I feel I have now achieved maturity. I feel myself flowering as a woman. It's as if the very life inside of me is crying out; as if my inner pistils are begging for the arrival of stamen." Yuriko's references to "flowering," "pistils," and "stamen" suggest heterosexuality. She continues, "Y loves me as much as it is humanly possible to love another, although this has failed to satisfy my passion, which is different from this kind of love. This is not Y's fault; it is simply due to the fact that she is not male."

At least one of Yuriko's stories and one novel include a heterosexual plot built around her actual romantic liaisons during this period, one with Toshihiko Akiba in Japan, another with Teizo Taira when alone in Paris. (Miyamoto 1979, 37; 1980, 296) In preparation for writing the biography of Yoshiko Yuasa, *Yuriko, Do svidanya: Yuasa Yuasa no seishun* (The Vernal Years of Yoshiko Yuasa, 1990), I spent three years interviewing Yuasa toward the end of her life. At this time, she confirmed that the episodes from Yuriko's novels were autobiographical. She said, "Yuriko's weakness for men lies in the fact that she just loses all control when a man gives her pleasure." In numerous diary entries, Yuriko herself admitted that she had a "weakness for men." In my view, having "a weakness for men" means valuing men more than women. As I see it, in sexual relations with men, women tend to assume a passive position, and thereby succumb to the existing social structure that discriminates against women. Sensing Yuriko's betrayal, Yuasa became quite irritated—causing Yuriko in turn to pull further away and withdraw. Caught in a negative spiral, they were ultimately unable to resolve the issue of sexual incompatibility within their partnership. Ironically, their problems were exacerbated by the closeness of their relationship. They went everywhere together, causing Yuriko to comment that their relationship resembled "two train cars coupled together." At times, borders between them became blurred. The relationship also invited a sense of ennui, extremely threatening for any writer.

Yuasa's subsequent decision at the end of 1927 to study in Russia, therefore, represents a deliberate attempt to move forward. For the two women—whose individual characters were both intense—an eventual breakup was inevitable.

For three years, shortly after the Russian Revolution, Yuasa worked hard in Moscow to lay the foundation for her career as a scholar of Russian literature. Yuriko, meanwhile, traveled around the new Communist state and also visited various European countries. After a period of traveling in Europe with Yuasa, Yuriko stayed on in London and then in Paris. A letter she wrote to Yuasa in Moscow in April 1929 seemed to indicate she had decided to reaffirm her partnership with Yuriko. Unfortunately, letters written by Yuasa from this period no longer exist. Yuriko's letters, though, are lively and filled with high energy. She was enjoying seeing the world.

Following her return to Japan at the end of 1930, Yuriko, deeply involved in the proletarian literary movement, met Kenji Miyamoto,[15] a member of the then-illegal Japan Communist Party, who was nine years her junior. Two years later, in the spring of 1932, she moved out of the home she had been sharing with Yuasa to marry him. "You are not a *tovarich* (comrade)" she announced to Yuasa—a renunciation supported by her association with

Communism, and her new husband who embodied the ideals of the party.

Yuriko Miyamoto, as she was known from then on, became an official writer for the Japan Communist Party following the end of World War II. She founded the *Fujin minshu shimbun* (Women's Democratic Newspaper),[16] which served as an important news source for women. Her two autobiographical novels *Futatsu no niwa* (Two Gardens) and *Dohyo* (Signpost),[17] which followed the publication of *Nobuko*, referred to the character Motoko (who represented Yuasa) as a "sexually perverse *petit bourgeois*," thereby invoking the power-laden terminology of both the Communist Party[18] and modern sexology. Clearly, this was a witch-hunt with Yuasa as its target.

When asked by others for her side of the story, Yuasa maintained silence, replying, "It's just a novel," and directing her efforts toward translating works by Chekhov and other Russian writers. She did not reveal her thoughts about the relationship until she was ninety years old, when I approached her to in order to write her biography. Over sixty years had passed since her relationship with Yuriko had ended. Yuriko had died at fifty-one, at least in part because of six imprisonments during the pre-World War II purge of Communists. Yuasa once remarked to me near the end of her life, in her trademark humorous style, "Not being with a man helped me to live longer, you know." When I asked her on her deathbed whether her life had been solitary, her reply was "Solitary, yes, but not lonely. After all, I know other kindred spirits out there."

Nobuko Yoshiya and Chiyo Monma: Partners for Life[19]

Nobuko Yoshiya and Chiyo Monma met first on January 12, 1923, which was Yoshiya's twenty-seventh birthday. A mutual friend Shigeri Kaneko (later, Yamataka), a journalist with the *Kokumin shimbun* (Peoples' newspaper), introduced them. At the time, Yoshiya was depressed about her love affair with an older woman whom she had met four years earlier while living in an all-women's dorm at the YWCA. "Close friendship between women is impossible!" Yoshiya had remarked, to which Kaneko flatly disagreed before proceeding to introduce her to Chiyo Monma. A twenty-year-old math teacher at the Kojimachi Girls' Monma High School, Monma had been a good friend of Kaneko since their school days together at the Tokyo First Girls' High School. Yoshiya and Monma felt an immediate rapport, and they soon began to see each other every day. Monma would go to Yoshiya's house after school, or else the two would meet to stroll through used bookstores in Tokyo's Kanda district. An early letter Yoshiya wrote to Monma expresses her sadness when they could not meet:

Aah. . .if only we did not have to part at dusk!

Will the day come when we will live together under the same roof? How easy things would be if only we were a man and a woman! But alas, you are a woman. . .and so am I. If only our hearts remain resolute, Monma, I am sure we shall soon be able to ensure that our love will live on forever. . .In the meantime, let us put our heads together and figure out a way that will allow us to live together! (Yoshitake 1982, 140)

Nobuko Yoshiya (1896-1973) was born to parents of the former warrior (samurai) class, for whom male domination over women (*danson johi*) reigned supreme. Her father was an ambitious man who began his career first as a police officer, then became a local county government official, with the family following him through several transfers around the country. Yoshiya was the only girl among seven children, and her mother attempted to teach her the virtues of obedience while training her to perform domestic duties.

Displaying talent in writing from the time she was an elementary school student, Yoshiya defied her mother's warnings and spent long hours reading novels from her brothers' bookshelf. When she was twelve years old, she was deeply impressed by a speech she heard given by scholar and writer Inazo Nitobe,[20] who said to women, "Before becoming a good wife and wise mother (*ryosai kenbo*), it is important to develop oneself as an individual." Yoshiya began to publish in various girls' magazines (*shojo zasshi*), and at twenty, in 1916, published a small volume of short stories, *Hana monogatari* (Flower Tales)—depicting female characters who develop supportive relationships with other girls. Young women of prewar Japan, seeking a respite from the bleak realities of the day, were enraptured.

Despite being referred to contemptuously by male critics as a mere "author for young girls" and "popular writer," Yoshiya went on to become a best-selling novelist who produced such works as *Onna no yujo* (Women's Friendship), *Otto no teiso* (A Husband's Chastity), and *Atakake no hitobito* (The Ataka Family). Throughout her life, she explored two major themes: friendship between women, and the idea of "ideal" males. She gained a large female readership, prompting scholar Kimi Komashaku[21] to refer to her as a "closet feminist." (Komashaku 1994)

Yoshiya's partner, Chiyo Monma (1897-1996), also came from a family of the warrior class. Her father was an educator who declared that "higher education for females is nothing but a waste." Siding with Chiyo, however, her mother took on piece-work so that her daughter could continue her studies. Recognizing Chiyo's literary talent, she did not want her daughter to make the same mistake she did—of sacrificing her own life for a husband and children. Accordingly, Monma felt a deep gratitude and empathy for her mother. Monma hated her school sewing courses, and often paid scant attention to how she looked—thereby earning herself a reputation as an intellectual nicknamed "the philosopher." While studying at a teacher training school, she yearned for her friend Kiyo Ueno, but her love remained unrequited. Seeking financial independence, Monma became a mathematics teacher at a girls' high school, and following her mother's death, she looked after and supported her six brothers and sisters who were all underage.

Monma was not as pessimistic as Yoshiya about the idea of love between women. In response to Yoshiya's resentment about the obstacles that same-sex couples faced, Monma responded with optimism, "I don't understand why males and females have no problem getting together, whereas two women are forbidden to do so. Why is love judged on the surface-level rather than by the depth of its quality?" (Yoshitake 1982, 198). Monma attributed her own candor and positive attitude toward women to the wisdom and kindness with which her own mother had protected her.

One year after meeting each other, the two were forced to spend ten months apart when Monma's job sent her away from Tokyo to Shimonoseki on the far west end of Honshu Island. During this time, Yoshiya, who had already made a name for herself with *Hana monogatari* (Flower Tales), was asked to publish a collection of her writings in a magazine known as *Kurobara* (Black Rose). Aware of the difficulty of the undertaking, she nevertheless accepted the job, expecting that Monma might be able to edit for the magazine, and thus return to Tokyo. The employment would help them survive financially.

Things did not go according to Yoshiya's plan, however, for Monma decided not to return to Tokyo. Desperate with loneliness, Yoshiya wrote Monma a letter filled with anger and jealousy. Monma's moderate reply was entirely in character:

> You must try and calm yourself. At the very least, you must realize that whatever happens, things cannot get any worse than they are now. . . . We must strive to build our inner strength as a firm core which will not be destroyed regardless of what happens to each of us or what changes outside of us. Let us use our strength to build this faith and inner power. For what you have described in *Yaneurano nishojo* (Two Virgins in the Attic) is precisely such a model relationship, in which each woman enhances the other's life. (Ibid., 196)

While Monma had previously referred to Yoshiya as *oneesama* (elder sister), in this letter for the first time she called Yoshiya *anata* (my dear). Moved by Monma's calm response to her outburst of emotion, and respecting her dedication to her work, Yoshiya responded in a different tone, "Darling, you are the light of my life; my very conscience. With you, I am truly a better person." She also wrote in a diary entry that "Monma's letters always purify my soul" (Yoshitake 1982, 197). Indeed, throughout her entire life she never lost this sense of respect for Monma.

About one month before Monma returned to Tokyo, Yoshiya mailed the following plan for their life together (Wada 1987):

1. We will build a small house for the two of us.
2. I will become the head of household and will then officially adopt you.[22]
3. We will ask a friend to serve as go-between, and hold a wedding reception.

At the end of the letter, Yoshiya added, "I cannot wait for another month or more for your return. Please come back as soon as possible, and don't ever leave me again! I promise I will stay with you until the day that death parts us. Oh, my dear Monma, how do you feel about this?" (Yoshitake 1982, 199)

Yoshiya kept her promises to Monma, first using her book royalties to build a small home in the neighborhood of Shimo-ochiai. When the pair moved in to begin officially to share their lives together, it was 1926, three years after they had first met. Monma continued to work as a math instructor until 1931, when, seeing how Yoshiya's writing consumed her, she decided to manage the housekeeping and to work as Yoshiya's secretary. They spent half-a-century together, until Yoshiya's death from rectal cancer in 1973. Women writers and other friends often gathered in their home, which was always filled with warm laughter. Near the end of Monma's life, Teruko Yoshitake, author of *Nyonin Yoshiya Nobuko* (Nobuko Yoshiya, the Woman) asked her "how the two women managed this extraordinary achievement," to which Monma replied, "because Yoshiya and I thought alike" (Yoshitake 1982, 134). In other words, both women were staunchly opposed to the existing system of patriarchy, while simultaneously being committed to a way of life based on two women loving and supporting one another as equals.

Given patriarchal Japan, the couple's bond had to be extremely strong. Monma's remark to Kiyoko Horiba, the author of *Seito no jidai: Hiratsuka Raicho to atarashii onnatachi* (The Seito Years: Raicho Hiratsuka and the New Women) is telling, "Honestly, the men of that period were just so arrogant! We would have done anything to live outside of that patriarchal system" (Horiba 1988, 108).

If the relationship may seemed to have mimicked heterosexual marriage, their partnership was defined not according to gender, but based rather on continual consultation and discussion about their particular needs and preferences. In response to journalists who suspected that the two women were lovers and went sniffing around for gossip, Yoshiya and Monma consistently maintained that their relationship was of a writer and her secretary. With friends and between themselves, their relationship was much like that of close friends or a mother and daughter. Their opposition to prevailing communist ideology, and the modern sexual mores stemmed from the importance they accorded their own personal experiences.

Nobuko Yoshiya, whose popularity had reached a level equal to that of a Takarazuka star, used her large royalties to build five homes and, in 1928, to organize a year of travel in Europe with Monma. That these women had the means to enjoy the pleasures of life certainly contributed to the stability of their relationship. With her well-grounded partner by her side, for over half a century, Yoshiya was blessed with success as an author.

Conclusion

What can we conclude about the three very different pairs of women who shared their tumultuous lives during tumultuous times? All six were born in privileged homes, five of them from members of the warrior class, one from a family of merchants. Two of them were sent to university, but dropped out because they found the curriculum meant for wives and mothers boring; a third was denied the education of her brothers. Perhaps one can posit that for these women, the lack of education led them to break loose from proscribed gender roles, and, instead, to live according to their own desires.

The three other women traveled as far down the road of higher education as was possible in their day. Only one of these women, Chiyo Monma, whose father had been especially sexist, thoroughly rejected prevalent ideas of patriarchy. The other two—Raicho Hiratsuka and Yuriko Miyamoto—both had had close relationships with their fathers. Perhaps ironically, therefore, both women ended up wielding the power-laden ideals of modern sexual mores and communism as part of rejecting their female lovers. They behaved no differently from male members of the intelligentsia of the day, assuming homophobic attitudes in order to break up their relationships with their female lovers.

As for the one story with a happy ending, one may note several unusual ingredients that were absent in the other relationships: first, a coherent working relationship between the two; second, ample financial resources; and third, perhaps most ironic, that the couple accepted the compromise many, if not most, lesbian couples today deplore—acknowledging the relationship as if it were between a mother and daughter for the purposes of legal recognition.

Notes

1. Performance group that was formed in 1914 (Taisho 3) in order to provide entertainment at the Takarazuka Shin-onsen hot spring resort. Name was changed in 1940 to the Takarazuka gekidan (Takarazuka Revue Company). Consisting entirely of unmarried females, the troupe performs various drama pieces, revues and musicals, and continues to produce numerous female stars to this day.

2. While this term was originally used to signify double suicides carried out by heterosexual couples, it now commonly refers to two or more people taking their lives at the same time. In this case, I use the term to mean female couples killing themselves together. Well-known cases in this regard include two graduates from a girls' school in Niigata in July 1911, and an incident occurring at Mt. Miharayama in January 1933.

3. Sohei Morita (1881-1849) Writer and translator who made his literary debut with the novel *Baien* (Smoke), based on his attempted double suicide with Raicho.

4. A poignant poem written from Otake to Hiratsuka in 1914 and included in the Seito journal may be found in *Sparkling Rain: And Other Fiction from Japan of Women Who Love Women* (ed. by Barbara Summerhawk and Kimberly Hughes, 2008).

5. Kenkichi Tomimoto (1886-1963) Following graduation from the Tokyo Fine Arts School and a period studying abroad in London, returned to Japan in 1911 and began working as a ceramic artist. Was later designated as a Living National Treasure for his artwork.

6. From the 1913 translation of Krafft-Ebing's *Psychopathia Sexualis*, and Kokyo Nakamura's 1917 work *Hentai shinri* (Psychology of perversion)18.

7. This section includes excerpts from my work *Yuriko, Do svidanya: Yuasa Yoshiko no seishun* (Farewell Yuriko: The Vernal Years of Yoshiko Yuasa). I titled the work as such on behalf of Yuasa, who was unable to gain closure from the pair's breakup prior to Yuriko's death.

8. Editor's note: The reason for referring to Yuriko Miyamoto by her given name is that she was already a published author known as Yuriko Chujo before marrying Kenji Miyamoto at age thirty-four (prior to which she had been married to Shigeru Araki). In addition, calling her simply "Miyamoto" might be confusing since her husband became very famous and lived much longer than she did.

9. Yaeko Nogami (1885-1985) Novelist whose most well read works include *Machiko*, and *Hideyoshi to Rikyu* (Hideyoshi and Rikyu). See also *Nogami Yaeko zenshu* (Complete works of Yaeko Nogami), Vol. 1 (1980-82) and Vol. 2 (1988-91).

10. A mountain located in the Asaka region near Koriyama City in Fukushima Prefecture, where Yuriko's paternal grandfather lived.

11. Portions of the letters written by Yoshiko Yuasa to Yuriko Chujo that are included here were introduced in *Yuriko, Do svidanya*. The completed collection was published by modern literary scholar Ariko Kurosawa (see Kurosawa 2008).

12. Letter written by Yoshiko Yuasa on June 25, 1924 (Taisho 13). Most of the letter is included in *Yuriko, Do svidanya* pp. 44-45 (Bungei shunju version) and pp. 57-59 (pocket edition).

13. Toshiko Tamura (1884-1945) Writer. Her debut novel *Akirame* (Resignation), which she wrote at the urging of her husband Shogyo, won top awards at a newspaper competition. She continued to gain popularity with the works that she subsequently published in the *Seito* and *Chuo koron* journals, and was also friendly for a period of time with Yoshiko Yuasa.

14. Section of Yoshiko Yuasa's diary from February 28, 1932, following Yuriko's abrupt departure. It is included in its entirety in *Yuriko, Do svidanya* pp. 284-85 (Bungei shunju version) and pp. 329-30 (pocket edition).

15. Kenji Miyamoto (1908-2007) Critical commentator and politician. Made his literary debut with *Haiboku no bungaku* (Literature of defeat) while a student at Tokyo University. Entered the Japan Communist Party (JCP) in 1931, and met Yuriko Chujo while working with the alliance of proletarian literature in Japan. Arrested in 1933 in conjunction with the Spy Inquiry incident, and released in 1945. Married his secretary, Sueko Omori, following Yuriko's death. After the war, served as an international leader of the JCP and as a member of the Upper House. *Juninen no tegami* (Twelve Years of Letters) (1983), which documents his correspondence with Yuriko during his imprisonment, provides a clear glimpse of the depth of his patriarchal attitudes.

16. Newspaper put out by the GHQ-supported *Fujin minshu kurabu* (Women's Democratic Club), which was formed following Japan's defeat in the war. Yuriko was one of the founders of the newspaper, which focused on peace and women's issues, and continues today under the name of *Femin fujin minshu shimbun* (Femin Women's Democratic Newspaper).

17. Yuriko rewrote the three-thousand-page manuscript for this full-length novel, *Dohyo* (Signpost) several times until it gained the approval of Kenji Miyamoto.

18. Communism as a doctrine has tended to remain largely intolerant toward homosexuality.

19. This section is based on the work of Teruko Yoshitake (1982) and Kimi Komashaku (1994).

20. Inazo Nitobe (1862-1933). Agriculturalist and educator. Following graduation from Tokyo University, moved to the US for study with the goal of acting as a bridge between the two countries across the Pacific. Became a pious Quaker and married Mary Elkinton. Known for his work *Bushido: The Soul of Japan* (1900), which was published in English. Became the deputy director of the League of Nations in 1920, and attended the World Esperanto Organization Congress the following year.

21. Kimi Komashaku (1925-2007). Modern literary scholar who lived until her death with women's liberation activist Aya Konishi. Wrote several works introducing her unique approach to feminist-style critique, including *Soseki toiu hito: Wagahai wa wagahai dearu* (The Man called Soseki: I am me) (1987), and *Murasaki Shikibu no messeeji* (Murasaki Shikibu's Message) (1991).

22. Editor's note: Partner adoption has been one strategy utilized historically by homosexual couples in Japan in order to secure legal protections.

Works Cited

Chujo, Yuriko. 1924. "Taisetsu na me" (Precious sprout). *Josei kaizo* (June).
Hiratsuka, Raicho. 1912. "Marumado yori" (From the round window.) *Seito* (August).
———. 1913. "Ichinenkan" (For one year). *Seito* (February).

———. 1913. "Ichinenkan" (For one year). *Seito* (December).

———. 1992. *Hiratsuka Raicho jiden: Genshi, josei wa taiyo de atta* (Autobiography of Raicho Hiratsuka: In the Beginning Woman was the Sun) Vol. 2 (originally published in 1971). Tokyo: Otsuki shoten.

Horiba, Kiyoko. 1988. *Seito no jidai: Hiratsuka Raicho to atarashii onnatachi* (The Seito Years: Raicho Hiratsuka and the New Women). Tokyo: Iwanami shoten.

Komashaku, Kimi. 1994. *Yoshiya Nobuko: Kakure feminisuto* (Nobuko Yoshiya: The closet feminist). Tokyo: Riburo poto.

Kurosawa, Ariko. 2001. "Josei geijutsushi: Safuran to Otake Kazue" (History of Women Artists: Safuran and Kazue Otake). *Hosho gekkan* (February). Tokyo: Hirotakasha.

———. 2008. *Ofuku shokan: Miyamoto Yuriko to Yuasa Yoshiko* (Correspondence: Yuriko Miyamoto and Yoshiko Yuasa). Tokyo: Kanrin shobo.

Miyamoto, Yuriko. 1979. *Miyamoto Yuriko zenshu* (Complete works of Yuriko Miyamoto). Vol. 4. Tokyo: Shin Nihon shuppansha.

———. 1980. *Miyamoto Yuriko zenshu* (Complete works of Yuriko Miyamoto). Vol. 8. Tokyo: Shin Nihon shuppansha.

———. 1983. *Miyamoto Yuriko zenshu* (Collected works of Yuriko Miyamoto). Supplemental volume. Tokyo: Shin Nihon shuppansha.

Nogami, Yaeko. 1986. *Nogami Yaeko zenshu* (Complete works of Yaeko Nogami). Tokyo: Iwanami shoten. Part II Vol. I (1980-82).

Otake Kokichi. 1912. "Aru yoru to aru asa" (One night and one morning). *Seito* (June).

Sawabe, Hitomi. 1990. *Yuriko, Do svidanya: Yuasa Yoshiko no seishun* (Farewell Yuriko: The Vernal Years of Yoshiko Yuasa). Tokyo: Bungei shunju.

———. 1996. *Yuriko, Do svidanya: Yuasa Yoshiko no seishun* (Farewell Yuriko: The Vernal Years of Yoshiko Yuasa). Tokyo: Gakuyo shobo.

Summerhawk, Barbara and Kimberly Hughes, eds. 2008. *Sparkling Rain: And Other Fiction from Japan of Women Who Love Women*. Chicago: New Victoria Publishers.

Takai, Yo and Orii Miyako. 1985. *Azami no hana: Tomimoto Kazue shoden* (Thistle Flowers: The life of Kazue Tomimoto). Tokyo: Domesu shuppan.

Tanabe, Seiko. 1999. *Yumeharuka Yoshiya Nobuko* (Distant visions Nobuko Yoshiya). Tokyo: Mainichi shimbunsha.

Tomimoto, Kazue. 1935. "Tsukon no tami: Seishun zange" (People of painful regrets: Confessions of youth). *Fujin koron* (February).

Wada, Naoko. 1987. "Nihon no senpai rezubian tachi: Yoshiya Nobuko to Monma Chiyo" (Japan's lesbian pioneers: Nobuko Yoshiya and Chiyo Monma). In *Onna o aisuru onnatachi no monogatari* (Stories of women who love women), ed. Yumi Hirosawa. *Bessatsu Takarajima* (64). Tokyo: JICC shuppan kyoku.

Yoshitake, Teruko. 1982. *Nyonin Yoshiya Nobuko* (Nobuko Yoshiya, the Woman). Tokyo: Bungei shunju.

EDUCATION

Educational Challenges
Past and Present

Kimi Hara and
Kumiko Fujimura-Fanselow

"Education frees the human spirit."
How often have I, Kimi Hara, been struck by and reminded of the significance of this inscription inside the entrance of Judd Hall at the University
of Chicago. Education, in the true sense of the term, helps develop human
potential, emancipating us from all bindings and restrictions. Education
regenerates one's heart and mind and thereby influences the social and cultural forces and institutions within a society. At the same time, education is
a sociocultural product, reflecting the kind of society and culture in which
women and men struggle to survive.

In this essay, we present a historical review and analysis of the nature
and development of education for girls and women in Japan in the modern
period and the social and cultural forces and factors that have shaped that
education. Female education in Japan prior to the end of World War II can,
by and large, be characterized as gender segregated, gender stereotyped,
inferior, and less valued compared to that of males. In this essay we examine why female education in Japan has been treated in this manner and the
consequences of such a distorted type of education as well as the changes
that have taken place since the end of World War II and the impact of those
changes.

Women's Education prior to the Meiji Period

Prior to the establishment of a nationwide system of education under the
Meiji government in 1872, the type and level of education available to the
Japanese people depended on their social class as well as gender. In the
three hundred years of the Tokugawa (or Edo) period that preceded the
Meiji Restoration of 1868, sons of the samurai, or the ruling military class,
were educated in the *hanko* (domain schools) which were maintained by
each of the roughly 280 feudal *han* (domains) into which the nation was
divided. Very often attendance requirements as well as type of curricula

71

provided differed for different ranks of the samurai. *Gogaku* (local schools) developed rapidly after the middle of the nineteenth century, starting out as a "branch" of the main domain school or soon turning into one. By the end of the Tokugawa era some of these schools included students of both samurai and commoner class (Passin 1965, 19). In addition to these schools, there was also a wide variety of private academies, or *shijuku*, which were institutions of higher education largely for the samurai but, in many cases, also admitted commoners. "By the end of the Tokugawa Period," writes Passin, "it would be fair to say that practically all the children of the samurai class (and of the much smaller court nobility) attended some kind of school for some period of time" (1965, 43). This statement applied, however, only in the case of males. In the case of the daughters of the samurai class, they were usually kept at home and given tutoring either by the family or an outside tutor.

The primary institution for the education of commoners, who constituted the overwhelming majority of the population, were the *terakoya*, which were small, private educational establishments started by public-minded individuals. Teachers—often samurai, priests, or doctors—taught the "3Rs" to groups of thirty to forty pupils in "schools" housed in shrines, temples, vacant buildings, or private homes. By the end of the Tokugawa era the ratio of female to male teachers reached fifty-five to one hundred (Osada 1961, 123). Besides the 3Rs, the basic curriculum included instruction in morals and manners. In accordance with the teachings of Confucianism, from the age of seven boys and girls were treated separately. Osada informs us that the ratio of female to male pupils at *terakoya* was about 1 to 4; attendance was particularly low in the more conservative, rural areas of the country, while in cities like Edo (present-day Tokyo) and other urban areas the proportion of female pupils was much higher, in fact little below that of boys (Ibid., 124). While girls were taught the 3Rs, beyond that the emphasis was on teaching the basic skills required for running and maintaining a household—namely, sewing, weaving, spinning, etc. In some cases instruction was also given in tea ceremony, flower arrangement, and painting. From the middle of the eighteenth century on, slightly higher-level education institutions corresponding to the middle-school level began to be established for the children of the commoner class. Apart from formal education, domestic service was another vehicle of female education of a more informal variety. Many young women of the farming and merchant classes received training in manners and in skills required for running a household by becoming domestic servants in homes of samurai families for a couple of years.

The major school of thought underlying the education of females was the Confucian conception of the role of women, which confined them to childbearing and child rearing and which held that learning was not only unnecessary but, indeed, harmful for women, a thought exemplified in the following statement by Matsudaira Sadanobu, the shogunal chancellor from 1786-93, "It is well that women should be unlettered. To cultivate women's skills would be harmful. They have no need of learning. It is enough if they can read books in *kana* [the Japanese syllabary, as distinct from the more difficult Chinese characters]. Let it be that way" (Karasawa 1956, 105; qtd. in Passin 1965, 46). Notwithstanding the restrictions imposed by such attitudes toward women, in the Tokugawa period quite a few women managed to acquire literacy, and, indeed, as research by feminist historians in recent years has unveiled, many literary works of various genres—diaries, essays, poetry, historical tales—were produced not only by women of the noble class but also by those of the commoner class (Kuwabara 1990, 180-96). In the case of the majority of women, however, the social definition of the women's role which confined them to the realm of the household afforded women little opportunity for applying their education in the larger, social realm.

The Development of Education from the Meiji Period

In the face of social, intellectual, and economic pressures from within as well as threats from the United States and other Western powers, the Meiji Restoration of 1868 marked the emergence of Japan from a feudal society, long isolated from the rest of the world, into a modern nation-state under the monarchical rule of Emperor Meiji. In the words of Beasley, "[It] has something of the significance that the English Revolution has for England or the French Revolution for France; it is the point from which modern history can be said to begin" (1972, 1-2).

The Meiji Restoration also marked the first education reform in modern Japan. Two main streams of educational thought were evident: one was *bunmei kaika*, or "civilization and enlightenment" (Kaigo 1961, 108-12). Education was to be one of the keys to meeting the challenges posed by the Western countries by providing skills required for military and economic development, promoting a common sense of nationhood, and opening the way to the full realization of the intellectual resources of the country. The other stream of thought was a conservative one based on Confucian philosophy, which emphasized loyalty to the emperor. The former was based on the idea of equality of all people and breaking up the existing hierarchy of classes (warriors, farmers, artisans, and merchants). Thus, whereas it had formerly been regarded as unnecessary for girls and women to go to school, under the influence of those espousing "civilization and enlightenment," equality in educational opportunities for both sexes was, in principle, at least partially established.

The nation's leaders were eager to eliminate illiteracy among the people in order to modernize the country and to catch up with the advanced nations of the West. In 1871 the Ministry of Education was established, and in the following year the Fundamental Code of Education was promulgated, making four years of elementary schooling compulsory for all children, irrespective of gender or social status. Plans were announced for the establishment of 53,760 elementary schools, 256 middle schools, and eight universities.

School buildings had to be constructed anew, but neither the government nor the local districts had the necessary financial resources to build them.[1] By 1879 only 52 percent of the planned number of elementary schools had been built. In 1882 the rate of girls' attendance was less than one-half that of boys. Even boys' attendance was only 40 percent of the appropriate age group (Karasawa 1968, 16-17). In the northern prefectures remote from Tokyo there could hardly be seen a single girl in a school. As Karasawa (1968, 41) notes, this reflected the continued dominance of the notion that females need not be literate or learned and that childbearing and child rearing were the only activities worthy for them. Obedience was considered to be a woman's greatest virtue. If girls and women became educated and enlightened, they would be able to think for themselves, thereby causing much trouble and inconvenience to the prevailing social order; such was the generally held view. Therefore, females were discouraged from becoming critical minded and confident. The following statement made in 1887 by Arinori Mori, the first minister of education as well as a great promoter of "civilization and enlightenment," is an expression of these very views regarding women's education:

The fundamental basis for an enriched country lies with education, whose basis is with *women's* education. The success or failure of the country depends upon women's education. This must not be forgotten. In the process of educating girls and women, we must put across the idea of serving and helping their country. The models for women are a mother nurturing her child; a mother teaching her child; her son coming of age and being conscripted to go to war and leaving his mother with a good-bye; a son fighting bravely on the battlefield; and a mother receiving a telegram informing her of her son's death in the war. (Morosawa 1978, 23-24)

Mori recommended that pictures of these models be posted in classrooms because they symbolized the essence of the spirit of women's education.

The Ideology of Japanese Education
prior to World War II

The ultimate purpose of education, as envisioned by the Meiji leadership, was "to enrich the country and strengthen the army." In order to consolidate the foundation of the country against threats posed by the Americans, English, and Russians, who demanded that Japan open its doors to the world, the Japanese government adopted the slogan *fukoku kyohei* (Enrich the country and strengthen the army). This can be restated as making the country (not the people) rich by means of building a strong army. This slogan infiltrated and penetrated into all spheres of Japanese life—political, legal, economic, social, cultural, and educational. Adoption of this slogan as the basis of national policy must be viewed in the sociopolitical context of the extraordinary national crisis that existed at the time.

The political indoctrination of militaristic ideas and thoughts to the younger generation was most effectively carried out by means of the educational system. As Reischauer points out, "In classrooms and army barracks the young Japanese was taught to glory in Japanese military traditions" (1964, 129). Thus, Japanese were taught to sacrifice themselves for the sake of the emperor in order to enrich their country, but not the people themselves.

For girls and women the basic principle was *ryosai kenbo kyoiku* (Education for good wives and wise mothers), which restricted their role primarily to the home and family. In fact, to be a good wife and wise mother was seen as the other side of the coin of "Enrich the country and strengthen the army." It was for men to enhance the wealth of the country and maintain its strength by becoming hard workers and brave soldiers, while women's duty was to serve their men and families and maintain the continuity of the Japanese patriarchal family system.

These ideals were embodied in the Imperial Rescript on Education, which was promulgated in 1890. It was based on a nationalistic ideology that focused on worship of the emperor as the embodiment of the spiritual unity of the nation. The Rescript stressed the importance of such virtues as loyalty to the emperor, filial piety, cooperation and consideration among brothers and sisters, harmony between spouses, trust among friends, and love toward the masses. It is clear that the Rescript was not based upon the principle of universal human rights or the dignity of human beings; rather, it aimed at promoting the interests of the nation-state. A copy of the Rescript, which was considered a sacred document, occupied a prominent place within each school and was read out loud by the principal to the teachers and the student body on ceremonial occasions. This document was the heart of prewar Japanese education, and for nearly fifty years it served as a tool of the state for molding a loyal and nationalistic citizenry.

The Dawn of Women's Education

With respect to the education of girls and women, in 1871, immediately following the Meiji Restoration, when Japan was just opening its doors to the world, a phenomenal event took place. In the early years of the Meiji period thousands of young men were sent abroad or went on their own, to Europe and the United States, in order to study and bring back knowledge and skills that could be put to use in the new society. In 1871 a group of five young girls was included among fifty-nine students sent to the United States and Europe. An account of how this came about is given by Umeko Tsuda, one of the five girls, who later founded a college for women:

> It is said that when Count Kuroda was in America he was struck with the position and influence of women in the country and found that it was because the American women as well as the men receive education. The desire to have Japanese women equally enlightened made him take the step which led to our being sent abroad. It therefore was decided by the Government, through his advice, to send over a number of girl students and the five chosen may have included all those who applied or desired to go. (Tsuda 1980, 77-78)

As noted in Tsuda's account, Kiyotaka Kuroda proposed to Arinori Mori, the high commissioner to the United States, that the government officially send a group of young women to the United States for study. The plan called for a ten-year period of study, with expenses for the journey, tuition, and school costs; living expenses to be guaranteed; and an annual provision of eight hundred dollars for incidental expenses. Initially, there were no parents interested in sending their young daughters to the United States, but a second attempt at recruitment produced five candidates, Ryoko Yoshimasa (aged fifteen), Sadako Ueda (also fifteen), Sutematsu Yamakawa (twelve), Shigeko Nagai (nine), and Umeko Tsuda (seven). Umeko Tsuda's father was a very progressive man who had studied Dutch and English and had accompanied a group led by Yukichi Fukuzawa to Europe and the United States in 1867. He had been much enlightened by the impact of Western culture.

Umeko Tsuda and the others departed for San Francisco on December 23, 1871, accompanied by government officials who were traveling to the United States and Europe in order to negotiate treaties with various governments (the so-called Iwakura Mission). After living in the United States for more than ten years with an American family and later going back again to the United States and graduating from Bryn Mawr College, Tsuda established a small women's college in Tokyo in 1900 called Women's English College (later Tsuda College). Although it was not a mission school, it was based on Christianity and placed high value on the spirit of the Bible. Her vision and ideals were profound and high. She aimed at providing Japanese women with professional, academic training and helping them develop all-round personalities. This was quite different from the prevailing concept of education for "good wives and wise mothers." Emphasis was placed also on providing a thorough and individualized education in small groups, particularly in the teaching of English. Tsuda's ideal has been inherited from generation to generation at Tsuda College. Who would have dreamed of such a woman educator emerging out of the Iwakura Mission? Through Umeko Tsuda a new Western wave was introduced to innovate Japanese higher education for women. (For further discussion of Tsuda, see Oba 1986, 1990; and Furuki 1991).

It is important to note the important role played by Christian missionaries in promoting female education during the Meiji period (see Karasawa 1968, 59-65). Although the Fundamental Code of Education had initially provided for coeducation at all levels, following the Education Act of 1880, which called for the abolishment of coeducation beyond elementary school, women were formally excluded from public middle schools. In fact, as a rule, girls and boys were thereafter segregated after the third year of elementary school.

Christian missionaries pioneered in establishing high schools for girls, such as the Ferris Seminary (1870), Kobe Jogakuin (1875), and others such as Aoyama Gakuin, Joshi Gakuin, Kassui, and Iai in various parts of Japan. The missionary teachers came from the United States, Canada, and Great Britain. It was not until the 1880s that the government took steps to set up secondary schools for girls, and, as late as 1894, only eight public girls' high schools existed throughout Japan (Nihon Joshi Daigaku 1967, 201, table 2). The rapidly expanding industrial economy led to a growing need for female workers not only in factories but also as telephone operators, office workers, teachers, and receptionists, which in turn spurred demand for more education for girls. The Sino-Japanese War (1894-95) also had a significant impact. The plight of women left widowed and forced to find employment pressed home the need to provide greater education and occupational training for women. The Girls' High School Law, promulgated in 1900, called on local governments to establish at least one girls' high school in each prefecture with a four-year course of study, and in 1920 five-year secondary

schools for girls opened which offered more practical and technical subjects. As years went by, these schools spread rapidly, from 156 public and
53 private girls' high schools in 1912, to 487 public and 176 private schools
by 1926, and in the 1920s and 1930s both the number of girls' high schools
and their enrollment caught up with and surpassed the number of boys'
middle schools and their enrollment. The principle underlying secondary
education for girls was, again, primarily that of training them for their role
as homemakers and instilling feminine virtues.

Women were denied admission to universities, yet, as in the case of secondary schools, several girls' colleges were established by the private sector. The first of these was the Women's English College, established in 1900
by Tsuda. The same year saw the opening of a women's medical school in
Tokyo, followed by a school of fine arts and Japan Women's University in
1901. By 1937 forty-two private women's colleges offered three-year courses.
The majority of these institutions were, however, in large cities such as
Tokyo, Kyoto, and Osaka, so that women residing in rural areas had little
access to them. Two national women's higher normal schools were established by the government for the purpose of training teachers for girls' high
schools and women's normal schools, and six public or prefectural colleges
were established prior to World War II. All of these institutions of higher
education for women were regarded as inferior to men's colleges and universities and none of them were accredited as a university. In other words,
women's education was placed not within the mainstream but, rather, on
the periphery.

According to a survey conducted by the Ministry of Education in 1925,
roughly 15 percent of the appropriate age group entered girls' high schools
of various types. Enrollment in institutions of higher education was considerably lower: in 1920 only 1.2 women out of 1,000 were enrolled in such
institutions, though, by 1935 the ratio had increased almost fourfold.

An Ad Hoc Educational Council was convened from 1917 to 1918 in
order to make preparations for meeting changes brought about as a result of
World War I. It proposed, among other things, the need for placing greater
emphasis on moral education in elementary schools, teacher education and
practical education for girls, and the establishment of higher professional
institutions for women (see Osada 1961, 241-44). The council emphasized
that the content of the Imperial Rescript on Education must be taught carefully so that girls would grow up to become "good wives and wise mothers" who were instilled with patriotic feelings. The actual changes that
came about following World War I, however, had profound influences on
the thinking of many young girls, who, transcending the traditional image,
tried to move in a new direction toward self-reliance.

Democratic Influences on Women's Education in the Taisho Period

In the second decade of the twentieth century, which marked the start of the new Taisho era (1912-26), there surfaced in Japan a ferment of democratic liberal thought, which was manifested in many forms: a movement for universal manhood suffrage; the emergence of *demokurashii* (democracy) as a key word; the appearance of numerous women's organizations that espoused various causes, including socialism, political rights for women, and the abolition of prostitution; as well as the development of new schools of educational thought. The so-called New Education Movement that was launched in this period in opposition to the existing nationalistic education reflected the influence of educational ideas and methods that found their way to Japan from Europe and the United States. A number of education leaders—such as Masataro Sawayanagi of Seijo Gakuen, Kuniyoshi Ohara of Tamagawa Gakuen, and Choichi Higuchi, influenced by Ellen Key (1849-1929), Paul Nartorp (1845-1924), and John Dewey (1859-1952)—became interested in child-centered education and freedom-oriented education and introduced the Dalton Plan, the Project Method, and other educational ideas and methods to Japan (Karasawa 1953, 259-62). Not only did numerous existing schools, public as well as private, adopt one or another of these concepts and methodologies into their curriculum, but in addition new schools were founded based on those principles, such as Seijo Gakuen and Jiyu Gakuen (Freedom School), a private high school founded by Motoko Hani, who was one of the first graduates of the First Girls' High School established in Tokyo in 1888 as the first government-sponsored girls' high school. The outbreak of war marked by the Manchurian Incident in 1931, and subsequent growing ultranationalism put an end to these efforts.

My (Kimi Hara's) experiences at the First Girls' High School of Tokyo, which I entered in 1928, exemplify many of the ideas and principles advocated by this New Education Movement. The principal of my high school, Genzo Ichikawa, had traveled throughout the world in order to observe new educational practices, and he served as chairman of the National Association of Principals of Girls' High Schools for many years. The high school consisted of five grades, seventh through eleventh. Each grade consisted of five classes of forty-eight girls. The total number of students was around twelve hundred. Competition for entry into this high school was very keen; generally, there were five to six applicants for each student accepted. Since the school was a public, government-run school, the monthly tuition was quite low- four yen, fifty sen. Nevertheless, in terms of social class background, the students were predominantly from the upper and upper-middle classes.

The symbol of the school was a tower of hope named Almond Tower, soaring high in the sky. The entire building was heated by steam, and the toilets were Western style. The science classrooms (which included physics, chemistry, botany, biology, and zoology), music room, painting and drawing room, history and geography rooms, gymnasium, playground, library, and auditorium were equipped with modern facilities. Each classroom was provided with all the needed dictionaries and books for self-study. A hot lunch program was provided as well. There were also special Etiquette Rooms, one Japanese and the other Western, in which girls learned how to behave in their daily lives. In the Japanese room, students sat straight on the tatami mat floor and practiced repeatedly how to sit, stand, walk, and bow according to the Japanese style. Also, they learned how to behave when invited as guests and how to entertain guests as hostesses as well as how to drink green tea and eat Japanese cakes. The etiquette teacher had been a dancing teacher for the empress and was very strict in training the girls. In the Western room we were taught how to sit in a chair, how to serve and to drink English tea, and how to greet and carry on conversations. We were also taught Western table manners.

Self-government, self-study, and self-reliance were stressed at this school. Each school day, from Monday to Friday, consisted of six forty-five-minute periods, including one period for self-study. On Saturdays there were only four periods. During the self-study period, which was scheduled just before the lunch hour, students were allowed to go to the library if they wished to. Silence was observed as a rule. Students could prepare for afternoon classes as well as review what had been studied in the morning. The classroom teachers were there to help students and answer questions as needed.

The principal and the teachers placed great confidence in the young women's abilities and character. Students were expected to learn and to behave. As people tend to behave as expected, the girls enjoyed school and strove hard to achieve no less than boys. Unlike girls' high schools generally, these students were never treated as not equal to boys. For instance, in English classes two teachers, who were native speakers of English, Mrs. Okamura from Hawaii and Mrs. Tanaka, an American who had graduated from the University of Chicago, taught us English conversation during the extracurricular hour.

The principal was an enthusiastic advocate of women's rights and conducted special classes for the eleventh grade in which discussions were held on current topics of interest to the students. I can remember discussing such topics as suicide, women and smoking, women's suffrage, women's professions, and marriage. In each grade students studied a different religion or belief: *Bushido* (Way of the samurai), Shintoism, Confucianism, Buddhism, and Christianity. The principal's goal was to expose the students to all types of religions so that they could choose their own freely in later years.

Even though the days of militaristic regimentation were approaching and Japan's economic conditions were getting tighter, what went on in these classrooms was challenging and enjoyable. Students were never forced to emulate the virtues of the "good wife and wise mother"; instead, they were inspired and challenged to think about and solve problems. Through such an opportunity for diversified, experiential learning, my classmates and I gained a sense of righteousness and a sense of dignity as women.

The principal and teachers also made special efforts to encourage their female students to enter higher educational institutions. In 1935 only 4.6 females out of one thousand females in the age group pursued education beyond high school, a figure representing a mere one-tenth of the rate among males. At this high school, however, as many as one out of two went on to higher education with the aim of becoming teachers, medical doctors, dentists, pharmacists, writers, artists, or musicians, a figure that surpasses today's.[2]

World War II and Its Impact on Female Education

As the nation endured war for nearly fifteen years, until Japan's defeat in World War II on August 15, 1945, most adversely affected was education for young people. Militarism and ultranationalism were the main thrusts in education (see Kaigo 1961, 148-49). Indoctrination and regimentation were practiced as ways of disciplining the young hearts and minds of students. With the start of World War II in December 1941, educational activities were severely restricted or else suspended. In 1941 students were graduated from institutions of higher education four months earlier than scheduled; in 1942 the length of studies was reduced by six months and in 1943 by twelve months. The same practice was applied to secondary schools as well.

In 1944, when American air raids on Japanese cities became intense, schoolchildren were evacuated with their teachers to the countryside, where they lived in shrines and temples. Discipline was strict, indeed militaristic; youngsters were forced to obey the orders of teachers and upper-grade students without question. Some children died of illness and hunger.

Nearly three million girls and young women were mobilized to replace men in different posts in society at the sacrifice of their education (Fujii 1971, 23). In addition, half a million women worked on farms in place of fathers, husbands, brothers, and sons who had been drafted for the war.

Educational Reforms following World War II

Out of the terrible ruins wrought by World War II and Japan's defeat, the women of Japan were at last able to obtain equality of educational opportunity as a result of a series of educational reforms that were instituted under the influence and direction of the Allied Occupation. In March 1946 the United States Education Mission, consisting of twenty-seven members and headed by chairman George D. Stoddard, arrived in Japan to recommend educational reforms to the Supreme Commander for the Allied Powers, General Douglas MacArthur. Prior to their arrival, at the recommendation of General MacArthur, a committee of twenty-nine Japanese scholars and educators had been organized, headed by Tokyo University President Shigeru Nambara.

The Education Mission from the United States was determined to liberate Japan's education from militaristic and ultranationalistic influences and to bring about decentralization and democratization as well as to remove discrimination against women. The Japanese Education Committee, headed by Shigeru Nambara, also discussed and debated important issues pertaining to the reorganization and democratization of Japanese education. The report, which was submitted to the Education Mission as well as to the Japanese government, was in agreement with the Report of the Education Mission in both spirit and content (Osada 1961, 294-95). Based on the recommendations of the Education Mission, equality of educational opportunity for women was guaranteed in several provisions in the new Japanese Constitution, enacted in 1946, and in the Fundamental Law of Education, established in 1947.

Article 26 of the Constitution defines the basic right of all boys and girls to receive education and the obligation of adults to make sure that they receive such education. The Fundamental Law of Education set forth in more detail the aims and principles of education in accordance with the spirit of the Constitution and provided for nine years of free, compulsory education for both boys and girls; coeducation, which was formerly limited to the elementary school, was now recognized by law and extended to all levels. A common curriculum for both boys and girls was instituted in schools, and women were now allowed to attend the same schools and go on to the same universities as men. Under the new system of higher education which went into effect in 1949, thirty-one of the women's higher educational institutions in existence—two national, three municipal, and twenty-six private—were elevated to the status of college or university. Many of the other existing higher institutions were given the title *tanki daigaku* ("short-term college" or junior college).

In the 1960s Japan pushed headlong toward rapid industrialization, a process that transformed social structures as well as human relations. As technological innovations advanced, economic growth accelerated. It was, in fact, the invisible work of women employed as cheap labor, which sustained the Japanese economy from the bottom to bring about this growth, as it has ever since the Meiji Restoration (Hara 1984, 190-91).

As industrialization and economic growth progressed, there was a concomitant rise in the educational levels attained by the Japanese people. The percentage of girls within the appropriate age group entering upper secondary school (tenth through twelfth grade) doubled within a mere twenty-five-year period, from 47.4 percent in 1955 to 95 percent in 1979. Within the same period the percentage of young women studying at junior colleges increased eightfold and those in four-year universities grew sixfold.

Conclusion

The process of the development of women's education in Japan is none other than a long history of struggle against bondage toward the emancipation of women as individual human beings. In pre-World War II society little attention or respect was accorded to the dignity, personal autonomy, independence, and freedom of choice of women. Instead, the family and the nation were always given priority and exercised dominance over women.

Through the educational reforms that were instituted under the influence of the Allied Occupation following Japan's defeat in World War II, the long-established sex-discriminatory system of education was, at least in principle, destroyed almost overnight. In contrast to the earlier policy of education for "good wives and wise mothers," women were henceforth to be encouraged to develop their potential as individuals and as contributing citizens to society.

In spite of the advances that have been made in women's education, there are still several impediments to the realization of full equality in the sphere of education for Japanese women. Moreover, the prewar concept of gender-differentiated education and the ideology of education for "good wives and wise mothers" has resurged from time to time over the postwar period. Thus, for example, back in the mid-1960s, when rising numbers of women began to enter four-year universities, some educators denounced this trend, charging that it would lead to the demise of the country, since women did not utilize their education for the benefit of society, and urging that the numbers of women admitted to universities be limited. This became a subject of much debate in the mass media (Hara, 1976).

Another example is that in September 1969 the basic principles of an "education suited for the special aptitudes and abilities of females and males" were issued by the Ministry of Education, as a result of which general home economics was made a required subject in upper secondary schools for female students only. At the time, the director of the Bureau of Elementary and Secondary Education of the Ministry of Education was quoted as saying: "This undoubtedly aims at educating women as good wives and wise mothers. No one dares to oppose it" (*Mainichi shimbun*, October 1, 1969). This measure was put into effect in 1973; not until 1989 was the policy reversed, requiring both sexes in upper secondary school to study home economics beginning in 1994.

The backlash against gender equality that surfaced beginning in 2000 led to angry attacks on the policy of teaching home economics to both female and male students, as well as on the inclusion of sex education and the promotion of so-called "gender-free" education (for details see "Backlash Against Gender Equality after 2000" in this volume). In 2006, revision of the Fundamental Law of Education was pushed through under the administration of the conservative Prime Minister Shinzo Abe of the Liberal Democratic Party despite widespread opposition by citizens' groups including teachers, scholars, lawyers, and women. Among the targets of the revision, which emphasized the promotion of patriotism, nationalism, and family education, was the removal of the language on "coeducation" (Article 5): "Men and women shall esteem and cooperate with each other. Coeducation, therefore, shall be recognized in education." Backlash against gender equality was clearly behind this move.

Despite efforts begun more than thirty years ago by women's groups, lawyers, and many teachers to call attention to stereotyping in textbooks (see Kameda 1995), such gender bias continues, as the UN's Committee on the Elimination of Discrimination against Women concluded in its response to Japan's 2009 report (CEDAW 2009). Thus, for example, textbooks continue to be overwhelmingly male-centered. A symposium on history education and gender organized by the Science Council of Japan in 2009 revealed that Japanese history textbooks make very little mention of women and do not write history from the perspective of women—in spite of the outpouring of research since the 1980s in the area of women's history by Japanese scholars (Himeoka 2010; Nagano 2010). This is attributable in part to the fact that textbook authors are overwhelmingly male.

It is not surprising, therefore, that most undergraduate women know nothing about the "First Wave" of feminism and the struggle for social and legal rights undertaken by women in the late nineteenth century, described in this volume by Sachiko Kaneko ("The Struggle for Legal Rights and Reforms: A Historical View"), and Mioko Fujieda ("Japan's First Phase of

Feminism"). Students are equally ignorant about the impact of the women's liberation movement of the early 1970s. Few have even heard the term "feminism," and if they have, it has probably been in a negative context (as in "aggressive, man-hating women clamoring for rights and wanting to be like men") or perhaps confused with the word "feminine," which often appears in women's fashion magazines. Girls and young women have had few opportunities to learn about the struggles of women who preceded them, to identify with them or to feel pride in their accomplishments. Thus they may be unable to understand the problems, issues, and new possibilities confronting women today—all essential for thinking clearly about their futures. Women's studies courses, which made their appearance at Japanese colleges and universities in the mid-1970s, have the potential to fill this gap, but as Tanaka (2009) notes, even after thirty years, few institutions have an organized curriculum or program in women's studies, and it is doubtful that the percentage of students enrolled in these classes has discernibly increased from the two percent found in 1992 (Fujieda and Fujimura-Fanselow 1995, 161).

If many Japanese complacently assume that equality of educational opportunity for girls and women has now been fully achieved, they are looking only at attendance at primary and secondary levels, where there are no differences. But parity falls away as one considers higher education. Although the percentage of female high school graduates advancing to four-year universities has overtaken that of those choosing junior colleges over the last fifteen years—in 2008 reaching 43 percent, that figure continues to be lower than that of males—55 percent (Mombukagakusho 2009). This statistic stands in sharp contrast to most other highly developed countries where female entry into university-level institutions is significantly higher than among males.[3] Female students comprise 40 percent of four-year university enrollment, while they account for close to 90 percent of junior college enrollment. Similarly, the percentage of female university graduates going on to graduate school is about half of that among males—8 percent and 16 percent, and females make up 30 percent of graduate school enrollment. Moreover, female students continue to be concentrated in traditional fields of study: at universities they dominate the student body in the humanities, education, domestic science, and art, but continue to be underrepresented in science—25 percent and engineering—10 percent (Ibid.).

These disparities reflect persisting attitudes about the responsibilities of women and men in the family and in society which many young people and their parents, and often teachers and counseling staff as well, hold, as well as existing inequalities in the labor market (Fujimura-Fanselow, "College Women Today . . . " 1995). Parents continue to assign higher priority to sons when providing university education. This is especially true among those in lower income levels and those whose children have lower levels of academic achievement. The high tuition fees at private universities, which make up more than three-quarters of all universities and enroll a similar proportion of all students, plus the additional high cost for rent and living expenses (since few universities provide student dormitories), mean that young women, whose grades are below average, and who come from lower middle income families, are more likely than their male counterparts to be guided into a local junior college to which they can commute from home or to one of the more than three thousand vocational schools (*senmongakko*) that provide training lasting usually for two years for a variety of occupations (Kobayashi 2008).

A related issue is the underrepresentation of women on university faculties. Among faculty at all four-year universities in 2008, just 19 percent were female (compared to 11 percent in 1995); women made up 12 percent of professors and just 8 percent of university presidents (Kokuritsu josei kyoiku kaikan 2009, 105, table 7-8). The Second Basic Plan for Gender Equality approved by the Japanese Cabinet in 2005 based on the Basic Law for a Gender-Equal Society set a numerical target for national universities to raise the ratio of female faculty to 20 percent by 2010. Yet the figure in 2009 remained at 12 percent. Given that many young women enter college with limited and stereotyped expectations and visions for their futures—combined often with little confidence and a belief ingrained in them by families and schools that they do not measure up to men—we need to have more women teachers who not only can be role models for them, but perhaps more importantly, as Adrienne Rich (1979) put it, "take them seriously." This means setting high goals and expectations for these students and helping them develop the skills and motivations necessary for achieving those goals. In the process they may come to realize they are far more capable than they have allowed themselves to believe.

In many respects Japanese women are still on the periphery rather than the mainstream of education. Educational policy makers, administrators and teachers at all educational levels, guidance counselors, and parents must all first of all acknowledge the biases and inequalities that exist and their responsibilities for perpetuating them. Unless concerted measures are taken by all who are involved to ensure girls and young women full equality of educational opportunity, their ability to develop their full potential and to participate in all aspects of society on an equal footing with men will continue to be restricted.

Notes

1. At the age of sixteen Reijiro Watatsuki, a future prime minister of Japan, taught children, as a substitute teacher, in a makeshift classroom atop a cow shed. He received only 1.5 yen per month in salary. He recalled cows mooing downstairs, while his pupils made a great fuss upstairs (Karasawa 1968, 15).

2. It was most unfortunate that a few years after our graduation the principal was forced to resign from his post due to pressures from the militaristic government because he was considered to be too progressive and liberal. In 1935 some of the alumnae of the First Girls' High School established a private girls' high school named Oyugakuen and invited him to be the principal so that he could bring to a realization his high ideals.

3. On average, among OECD countries, the entry rates to university-level institutions in 2007 were significantly higher among females than males—63 percent versus 50 percent; the opposite was the case for Japan, where the figures were 40 percent and 52 percent (OECD 2009, 59, table A2.4).

Works Cited

Beasley, W. G. 1972. *The Meiji Restoration*. Palo Alto: Stanford University Press.

Fujieda, Mioko, and Kumiko Fujimura-Fanselow. 1995. "Women's Studies: An Overview." In *Japanese Women: New Feminist Perspectives on the Past, Present, and Future*, ed. Kumiko Fujimura-Fanselow and Atsuko Kameda. New York: The Feminist Press.

Fujii, Harue. 1971. *Korekara no josei to joshi kyoiku* (Women and women's education in the future). Tokyo: Sekaishoin.

Fujimura-Fanselow, Kumiko. 1995. "College women today: options and dilemmas." In *Japanese Women: New Feminist Perspectives on the Past, Present, and Future*, ed. Kumiko Fujimura-Fanselow and Atsuko Kameda. New York: The Feminist Press.

Furuki, Yoshiko. 1991. *The White Plum, a Biography of Ume Tsuda*. New York and Tokyo: Weatherhill, 1991.

Hara, Kimi. 1976. "Joshi kyoiku no tenkai to shakai hendo" (Development of women's education in relation to social change). In *Shakai hendo to kyoiku* (Social change and education), ed. Yoshihiro Shimizu. Tokyo: Tokyo daigaku shuppankai.

———. 1984. "Women Workers in Textiles and Electrical Industries in Japan." In *Women on the Move: Women in a World Perspective*. Paris: UNESCO.

Himeoka, Toshiko. 2010. "Rekishi kyoiku ni kazaana o akeru" (Opening an air hole in history education). *Women's Democratic Journal femin*, No. 2922, May 5:5.

Kaigo, Muneomi. 1961. *Kyoiku-shi* (History of education). In *Gendai Nihon shoshi* (A short story of modern Japan), ed. Tadao Yanaihara. Tokyo: Misuzu Books.

Kameda, Atsuko. 1995. "Sexism and Gender Stereotyping in Schools." In *Japanese Women: New Feminist Perspectives on the Past, Present, and Future*, ed. Kumiko Fujimura-Fanselow and Atsuko Kameda. New York: The Feminist Press.

Karasawa, Tomitaro. 1953. *Nihon kyoiku-shi* (History of Japanese education). Tokyo: Seibundo shinkosha.

———. 1956. *Kyoshi no rekishi* (History of teachers). Tokyo: Sobunsha.

———. 1968. *Meiji hyakunen no kyoiku* (One hundred-year history of education since Meiji). Tokyo: Nikkei shinsho.

Kobayashi, Masayuki. 2008. *Shingaku kakusa* (Gap in advancement to higher education). Tokyo: Chikuma shinsho.

Kokuritsu josei kyoiku kaikan (National Women's Education Center). 2009. *Danjo kyodo sankaku deetabukku—Nihon no josei to dansei—2009* (Gender statistics book—women and men in Japan—2009). Tokyo: Gyosei.

Kuwabara, Megumi. 1990. "Kinseiteki kyoyo bunka to josei" (Modern culture and women). In *Nihon josei seikatsushi* (A history of the lives of Japanese women), vol. 3: *Kinsei* (Modern period), ed. Josei-shi sogokenkyukai. Tokyo: Tokyo daigaku shuppankai.

Mombukagakusho (Ministry of Education, Culture, Sports, Science and Technology). 2009. *Gakko kihon chosa* (School basic survey).

Morosawa, Yoko. 1978. *Onna to kyoiku* (Women and education). Tokyo: Heibonsha.

Nagai, Michio. 1961. *Nihon no daigaku* (Japanese universities). Tokyo: Chuko shinsho.

Nagano, Hiroko. 2010. "Kenkyuwa do ikasaretaka" (How has research been made use of?). *Women's Democratic Journal femin*, No. 2918, March 15: 5

Oba, Minako. 1968. "Tsuda Umeko—joshi kyoiku no senkakusha" (Umeko Tsuda, a pioneer in women's education). *Joshi kyoiku mondai* (Issues in women's education). January: 69-76.

———. 1990. *Tsuda Umeko*. Tokyo: Asahi shimbunsha.

OECD. 2009. *Education at a Glance 2009*. http://www.oecd.org/dataoecd/41/25/43636 332.pdf.

Osada, Arata. 1961. *Nihon kyoiku-shi* (A history of Japanese education). Tokyo: Ochanomizu shobo.

Passin, Herbert. 1965. *Society and Education in Japan*. New York: Teachers College Press, Columbia University.

Prime Minister's Office (Tokyo). 1990. *Japanese Women Today*.

Reischauer, Edwin O. 1964. *Japan Past and Present*. Tokyo: Charles E. Tuttle.

Rich, Adrienne. 1979. "Taking Women Students Seriously." In *On Lies, Secrets, and Silence*. New York and London: W.W. Norton.

Tanaka, Kazuko. 2009. "Jissentekina gakumon to shite no joseigaku ga dokuji no gakusaiteki kiban o kochiku surutameni" (Women's studies: its needs to develop its own interdisciplinary foundation). *Joseigaku* (Women's studies) 17: 32-44.

Tsuda, Umeko. 1980. *Tsuda Umeko bunsho* (Writings by Umeko Tsuda). Tokyo: Tsuda College.

UN CEDAW. 2009. "Concluding observations of the Committee on the Elimination of Discrimination against Women - Japan." (Advance unedited version) August 7. http://www2.ohchr.org/english/bodies/cedaw/docs/co/CEDAW.C.JPN.CO.6.pdf

The Advancement of Women in Science and Technology

Atsuko Kameda
Translated by Malaya Ileto

In 2006, female high school students—called "Rocket Girls"—earned headlines in Japanese newspapers reporting that during the summer break the Akita University Innovation Center for Engineering Design and Manufacturing created a project designed to slow the loss of female students from science fields. Thirteen young women from Akita Prefecture and Tokyo participated. One student said, "The joy you get from making something is worth the effort. This is the first time I have experienced such pleasure" ("'Roketto gaaru' sodate. . ."2007).

Other recent newspaper coverage has testified to the efforts of universities and business also trying to encourage young women in secondary schools to major in science. Many experimental classes began to target female students with such slogans as "Backing Young Women in the Advanced Study of Science," and "Young Women, Welcome to Science!" Another, "Come on, Science Girl!" beckons senior high school students to join special school visits, where "Science Angels" introduce the work of women scientists to them. Women's magazines have also begun to focus on technological developments made by women that are used in everyday life, including the i-mode mobile phone, and such household appliances as the refrigerator, and drinks that reduce triglycerides in diets.

If the year 2006 has marked the beginning of activity to encourage the participation of women in the field of science and technology, it has come, in part, as a response to the United Nations Development Program's Gender Empowerment Measure, in which Japan has ranked thirty-eighth, even behind the Philippines, and thus far behind all the developed countries. There is now a Japanese budget specifically to support measures to raise the percentage of women researchers in all science and engineering fields combined from the current 10 percent to the quantitative target of 25 percent. In 2000, the Science Council of Japan compiled a list of demands for improving the work environment for women scientists (Nihon gakujutsu kaigi 2002), and science-related organizations have begun to take specific steps towards new goals. Thus, some sixty years after women were first granted the right to attend university, we are finally beginning to see positive measures to promote the advancement of women's education in science fields, where they have been, until now, very few in number. In this time of declining birthrates, women are finally being recognized as "visible" human resources necessary to maintain the skills base of the nation. In both education and employment, the advancement of women in science in Japan has finally begun.

The Historical Gap between Women and Science

Most people cannot name a Japanese woman scientist. Both historically and today, the link between women and science and technology is extremely weak. Nevertheless, we can glimpse a few women interested in science in the eighteenth and nineteenth centuries. For example, the daughter of Genkei Nakane—whose name is lost to us—was a scientist who researched Dutch astronomy. Similarly, Tozo Chiba, who published the book *Sanpo shojo* (Algorithm girl) in 1775, describing how to make calculations, writes that his daughter helped in the book's creation (Sogo joseishi kenkyukai 1993, 241). In addition, we can name Ineko Kusumoto (1827-1903), daughter of the German physician Philipp Franz von Siebold (1796-1866), who came to Japan in 1823 as the first European to teach Western medicine. Kusumoto studied Dutch medicine and carried out work similar to that of a physician. Certainly some women may have worked in science with their fathers or husbands, but it is safe to say that such women were rare.

Still, among the few exceptions is Umeko Tsuda (1864-1929), a scientist who emphasized the importance of science education for women. In 1871, at the age of seven, Umeko Tsuda and four other young girls were sent by the Japanese government to the United States for study. Ten years later she returned to Japan for a visit, and then went back to the US to enter Bryn Mawr College. Her father, Sen Tsuda, was an agriculturalist with an interest in many things, including English, technology, and agricultural development, and these interests were passed on to his daughter. The expectation was that she would remain at Bryn Mawr College after completing her studies in biology and pursue a career as a scientist, but after graduating she returned to Japan. Her parents' friend, Anna C. Hartshorne, recollected that Umeko Tsuda wanted Japanese women to study science, but that existing conditions did not allow it: "Umeko wanted to return to Japan to encourage the progressive women of Meiji to become interested in the sciences, but the education level of Japanese women at the time was much too low" (Tsuda juku rika no rekishi o kirokusurukai 1987, 142).

In 1900, therefore, Tsuda founded Joshi Eigaku Juku (Women's English College, later named Tsuda College), centered on the teaching of English. Although she was unable to realize her plan of introducing science education at the time, science was introduced at the school in 1943, during World War II, in the form of mathematics and physics. The school principal at the time, Ai Hoshino, was one of the women responsible for the advancement of women in science and engineering. After the end of the war, Tsuda's school became a university offering, in addition to English, science education, still extremely rare at the time. Several other science foremothers deserve mention, including Ginko Ogino, who passed the examination for medical practitioners in 1885, and became Japan's first woman doctor. At the time, women were unable to study medicine or to take the examination, so this achievement marked the overcoming of many barriers. In 1913, the Tohoku University Faculty of Science opened its doors to women as auditors. Three women were admitted: Chika Kuroda and Ume Tange, both in science; and Raku Makita in mathematics. Another woman, Kono Yasui was sent overseas as a scholar by the Ministry of Education in 1913, but in her appointment she was instructed that she must, "In addition to scientific research, add research in home economics," thus making it somewhat difficult for her to concentrate on scientific research. Nevertheless, in 1927, Kono became the first female Doctor of Science for her research in botany, and Kuroda the second for her research in chemistry. Women were unable to enroll in the science and agriculture faculties of public universities until the 1920s and 1930s, and in Tokyo University, not until after the war.

A Statistical Portrait

The percentage of Japanese women researchers in science and engineering fields reached 12.4 percent in 2008, up from 8.9 percent in 1995, 10.6 percent in 2000, and 11.9 percent in 2007. International data clearly show that this figure is extremely low, since the corresponding statistic is 19.2 percent for Germany, 26 percent for the U.K., 27.8 percent for France, 34.3 percent for the US, 37.1 percent for Greece, 46.2 percent for Portugal, and 51.5 percent for Latvia (Naikakufu 2008, 115, fig 1-6-6).

With regard to the percentage of women who are university faculty members in Japan, although about one-fourth of assistant professors are women, only 11.1 percent are full professors (Ibid., 113, fig 1-6-4). When one focuses on women in science fields, the percentages drop precipitously. In Japan, 3.9 percent of professors of science are women; 2.1 percent in engineering, and 1.9 percent in agriculture. In general, only one to five out of one hundred professors are women (Ibid., 116, fig. 1-6-10). The percentage of women who are assistant professors and assistants in the faculties of science and engineering is also very low. As important, the chances of students having a woman science teacher are also very low. According to the 2003 survey, "Trends in International Studies in Mathematics and Science," by the International Association for the Evaluation of Educational Achievement, the average percentage of females among eighth grade science teachers among forty-six countries surveyed was 60 percent. The figure for Japan was extremely low at 20 percent, unlike the US, Korea, and Italy, where the percentages exceed 50 percent. Thus, Japanese high school students rarely meet female role models among their science teachers.

According to the Ministry of Education's 2007 *Gakko kihon chosa* (School basic survey) (Mombukagakusho 2007) 65 percent of elementary school teachers were women, 41 percent in junior high schools, and 26 percent in senior high schools. When one examines subject areas, one finds that in both junior and senior high schools, more women teach Japanese, English, and art, and more men teach mathematics, science and social studies. In general, therefore, one can say that women science teachers are rare.

According to a 2005 survey by the Organisation for Economic Co-operation and Development (OECD 2005), Japan ranked lowest out of 16 countries in terms of the percentage of women studying science and technology, whether as new entrants, graduates, or those obtaining doctoral degrees. The percentage of women studying science is more than 30 percent in most countries, including Australia, Denmark, France, Portugal and Canada, and about 25 percent in Korea. At less than 15 percent, Japan's shortcoming is clear. Doctoral degree holders who are women are more than 25 percent in Europe and over 45 percent in Poland, but in Japan, the figure stands at only 10 percent. Areas of study where Japanese women fall especially short are mercantile marine science (5.6 percent), engineering (10.5 percent), and all areas within the field of science (25.5 percent) (Mombukagakusho 2008). In the 20 years since 1985, the percentage of women studying the social sciences has increased from 9.3 percent to 31.8 percent, with one woman out of three entering this field. Although there has also been an increase in the percentage of women studying science, it has been very small. The percentage of girls studying engineering has exceeded 10 percent only very recently, in 2000.

What Are the Problems?

As Akiko Tsugawa (2006) has pointed out, it seems clear that the dominant reasons for women's reluctance to pursue the sciences are the lack of role models and the absence of a clear understanding of what kinds of jobs such education will lead to. These reasons are in addition to the problems of balancing family and work and managing a workplace environment unfriendly to women. But there are other problems that cause concern.

They begin with the statistical portrait drawn above, especially with the notable paucity of women teachers at the junior high and high school levels. Similarly, the absence of female college teachers of science and researchers in science are also part of the problem, since many studies have pointed to the importance of role models for young people.

In addition, there is also a problem in the awareness levels of and guidance offered by parents. In a Ministry of Education survey (Mombuka-gakusho 2000-2002) targeting junior high school students, 29 percent of male respondents, as opposed to only 15 percent of female respondents, said they thought their mothers would probably be pleased if they were to pursue a career in science or technology. In respect to fathers the statistics were 31 percent and 21 percent. Similarly, when students were asked whether they thought their teachers expected them to achieve good grades in science, 18.5 percent of male students as compared to 6.5 percent of female students responded affirmatively. Seemingly, at least from the point of view of the students themselves, neither parents nor teachers expect that female students will do well in science or pursue work in that field. Seemingly also, despite being surrounded by science and technology in their everyday lives, young women rarely connect science to their interests or careers.

The culture of adolescent youth is yet another aspect of the problem that keeps young women—focused on being "attractive"—far from science education or careers in science. Secondary school adolescents' formative years strengthen the constraints of gender stereotypes in Japan, so that there is basically no encouragement given to girls to increase their science capabilities and so link themselves to future careers in science. Rather, young women are surrounded by an abundance of magazines and other media focused on how to be "attractive" and "feminine." Women's magazines focus on fashion, beauty, and the body, and rarely on science or technology. Comics, animation films, and television dramas only very rarely feature a female central character in a scientific context. Although there are many opportunities to encounter science in everyday life, such information is not expected to be of interest to women, and is ordinarily directly produced for men.

A further problem for Japan is a lack of public interest in science and technology, despite having come to be known for innovations in technology and a high quality of manufacturing. According to "Science and Technology in the Public Eye," a 1996 international report from the Organisation for Economic Co-operation and Development (OECD) about public interest in science and technology in member countries, interest in new scientific discoveries was highest in France at 68 percent. Japan ranked fourteenth at 31 percent, a low score. Sixty percent of Japanese women said they were "not interested," in science, in contrast to 95 percent of American women who selected "interested" (Muramatsu ed. 2004). What we can learn from other international comparative data is that the problem is not that Japanese children are lacking ability in science, for, in fact, they have strong capabilities. Rather, Japanese children follow their parents' leads: they dislike science or they are uninterested in it. Although girls' and boys' test scores indicate their similar abilities, the attitudes of girls toward the sciences are very much more negative than those of the boys. So the pattern begins in youth and mirrors the culture.

In the 1995 and 1999 surveys by the International Association for the Evaluation of Educational Achievement, "Trends in International Mathematics and Science Study" of fourth and eighth grade students, Japan ranked in the top tier despite having fallen from third place (out of forty-one countries) in 1995 to fifth place (out of thirty-eight countries) in 1999 in mathematics, and third to fourth place in science. In the 1999 tests, differences between males and females no longer existed, and Japanese girls ranked second to those in Singapore. In the 2000 OECD Program for International Student Assessment, scientific literacy among Japanese fifteen-year-olds was ranked second after Korea. Although not a significant statistical difference, girls achieved seven points more than boys in scientific literacy. In a survey conducted in 2002 by the National Institute for Educational Policy Research of fifth to ninth grade students, girls achieved higher scores than boys in science and math examinations at nearly every grade level (Kokuritsu kyoiku kenkyusho 2002). The tendency for boys to excel over girls in these areas is no longer the case. Still, the problems noted above with regard to the sharpening of gender distinctions at puberty continue to follow women as they enter science fields as faculty and researchers.

Following a 2002 survey, the Ministry of Education issued a report on research activities in Japan (Mombukagakusho 2002). Women and men researchers were both asked to give reasons to explain the lack of women researchers. Women ranked as the most important reason that it was "Difficult to continue research work because of childbirth, child care, and nursing care" (female respondents 63 percent, male respondents 45 percent). Women also noted that there was "No system in place to accommodate women researchers" (females 57 percent, males 38 percent). Men, on the other hand, claimed that the lack of women in science was due to the "Lack of women studying science" (males 63 percent, females 19 percent). In other words, this group blames women for their absence in science research.

In 2006, the Japan Women Engineers Forum (JWEF) compiled the report, "Working Environment and Career Development for Women Technicians" (Nihon josei gijutsusha fooramu 2006). In the report, a woman who had resigned from her job at a major electrical manufacturer to attend graduate school is quoted as saying in a discussion session, "When I had to dash out of the office at 6:15 to be on time to pick up my child, my colleagues would say 'Why are you in such a hurry? You could be ten minutes late for the nursery! Or do you really miss your child that much?' I figured there was no point saying anything" (Ibid., 9-11). From this anecdote and other data, one can surmise how difficult it is for women to balance work and family, and how little awareness about such problems still exist in the workplace.

Efforts to Effect Change

The 1994 report of the Science Council of Japan (Nihon gakujutsu kaigi), an advisory body to the prime minister, raised the question of diversity in human resources for science and technology and pointed to the need to increase women's participation in various scientific fields. In 1996, Fumiko Yonezawa was appointed head of the Physics Society of Japan, and by the late 1990s several women had been appointed as presidents of scientific organizations: Mizuho Ishida at the Seismological Society of Japan; Tomoko Kusama at the Japan Health Physics Society; Misaho Oi at the Spectroscopical Society of Japan. At the 1999 UNESCO World Conference on Science held in Budapest, the theme of Gender in Science was raised for the first time. The conference declaration emphasized that there was to be no discrimination between men and women, and that the growth of women's participation in science would lead to the changes demanded and expected by society.

In 2000, the Science Council of Japan, which represents scientists throughout the country, began to take specific action, having previously submitted to the government its investigation-based recommendations for measures to improve the situation for women researchers (Nihon gakujutsu kaigi 2002). Even with regard to the gender of Council members, who were mostly male, a goal was set in the Council's statement, "Gender Equal Participation at the Science Council of Japan," to increase female Council members from 3.3 percent to 10 percent in ten years. By 2006, the percentage had reached 20 percent. A system for allowing women to take a leave of absence for childbirth and child care was set up in 2003, and there has been substantial development in providing support for childbirth and child care. The Third Science and Technology Basic Plan, which was put into action in 2006, includes important guidelines on the promotion of women in science, including the establishment of a system in universities and other bodies to help cultivate the next generation, including balancing work and family, creating an environment conducive to this, and raising awareness about the issues involved; the promotion of active recruitment and appointment of women researchers (with a goal of 25 percent in the field of natural sciences); and the provision of activities to stimulate and increase the interest of girls in science and technology and highlight role models in the field.

In 2002, the Ministry of Education established the Super Science High Schools program, whereby certain schools prioritize education in science and mathematics. The program is aimed at fostering future human resources in science and technology. More than one hundred schools have been awarded this status, including such girls' high schools as Gunma Prefecture Takasaki Girls' High School, Saitama Prefecture Urawa First Girls' High School and Miyagi Prefecture First Girls' High School. At Gunma Prefecture Takasaki Girls' High School, individual and group research projects are underway aimed at nurturing women researchers to work internationally. Group research projects, carried out in collaboration with universities and business, include basic genetics experiments and studies of cosmetics for the skin in collaboration with such companies as Shiseido. The program "Women and Science" brings female students and researchers together for lectures and discussion, thus providing an opportunity for students to meet role models and learn about careers in the sciences. The young women at this high school are reported to be showing a strong interest in the study of science, commenting, for example, that "The program is exciting, I can experience many things I normally can't" and "It made me see that science is relevant to my life." Universities have also begun various programs targeting secondary school female students to strengthen the link between high school education and the advanced study of science.

In 2005, the Cabinet Office's Gender Equality Bureau set up the "Challenge Campaign" website to encourage young women to study and work in science and engineering and to offer support for advanced studies and employment (Naikakufu danjo kyodo sankakukyoku 2005). The site features messages posted by people working in different areas of science, as well as information on public seminars. In 2007, the following events specifically targeting junior high school girls were announced on this website:

— Tohoku University held an exchange forum with women researchers
— Nara Prefecture held an event targeting female high school students called "The Summer to Fall in Love with Science at the Nara Science College"
— Yamagata Prefecture initiated "Messages from Women Scientists,"

"The Science and Engineering Challenge" seminar and the newsletter "Let's try Science and Engineering"
— Kobe College held the symposium "Let's Study Science"
— Fukui Prefecture held a seminar targeting female high school students called "An Invitation to Scientists and Technicians"
— The Tokyo University of Agriculture and Technology held the symposium "Empowerment Program for Women in Science"
— Girls' Summer School for Budding Scientists and Technicians

The impetus behind these programs was the Japanese Ministry of Education's Program to Promote Advanced Study of Science among Female Secondary School Students, which began in 2006, providing subsidies of three to five million yen ($30,000 to $50,000) per university, thereby stimulating universities to rouse interest in the sciences.

At the Akita Prefecture Rocket Girl Training Workshop, university students provided guidance to high school girls building a rocket. The faculty member in charge said, "The aim of this is to raise enthusiasm and curiosity in the study of science. We want to capture the attention of girls who would not otherwise be interested in science by showing girls building rockets" ("Kitare rikei gaaru!" 2007).

Tohoku University initiated the "Science Angels Program," aimed at increasing the number of girls who hold positive attitudes about science. Female graduate students visit high schools to share their experiences of studying science and to talk about their career prospects. Unique programs are being carried out in other universities, such as Hokkaido University's "Let's Try Science: Be Ambitious" program for secondary school girls and the Tokyo Institute of Technology's "Experience the Hall of Science." The idea is to make visible the study of science through role models who can help students envision a future working in science. It is fair to add, however, that while there are these specific efforts of universities to ameliorate the problems of sexism in science, there are unresolved problems. When role models are sent in, for example, in engineering, these inevitably are male, and there appears to be little interest in nurturing female technicians. In general, despite the individual projects, there is still very little encouragement and support for women.

Changing the Workplace for Women Scientists

Along with the need to increase the number of female scientists is the need to provide an encouraging workplace that assures the possibility of women's continued employment. In Japan, a general system that would enable

women to continue working long-term is not yet in place. Thus, many
women leave their jobs after marriage because women are still assumed to
be responsible for housework and rearing children. Further, it is difficult
for women to return to full-time employment because of the long working
hours prevalent in most work places. Hence, many women are forced to
take on part-time or temporary work. Few universities in Japan have day-
care facilities, and since most researchers are men, there is no awareness of
the need for facilities that would allow women to continue working while
caring for children.

New efforts, mostly in women's universities, have begun to create a support system for female researchers. Tokyo joshi ikadaigaku (Tokyo Wom-
en's Medical University), for example, has created both child-care facilities
and work-sharing. Ochanomizu University has begun to construct a model
plan for the employment of women researchers; and Hokkaido University
has established the Support Center for Women Researchers, and set a target
for increasing the percentage of women researchers in the university to 20
percent by 2020. Co-educational universities are also implementing measures to support female researchers. For example, Waseda University has
implemented a Plan for Gender Equality in the Cultivation of Researchers.

In addition a special program targeting part-time researchers and post-
doctorates on term appointments has been established to support those
returning to work after leaving for childbirth and child care. The program
offers women an opportunity to engage in research, along with research
subsidies that cover two years of research expenses. Tokyo Women's Medical University, in response to the Ministry of Education's Program to Cultivate Model Women Researchers, has created the Support Center for Female
Medical Scientists. Vice Director Kayoko Saito, describing the importance
of the Center, notes "The support of women doctors who can carry out
medical research while rearing children is our university's mission for the
future" (Tokyo joshi ikadaigaku homepage). The new program has set up
child-care facilities, and in 2006 began work-sharing. Space to accommodate sick children was added to the university's nursery. Opportunities
to carry out research work and present findings have been made possible
through work-sharing and flextime arrangements. The university also runs
a counseling program, with senior doctors and psychologists serving as
"support officers," and provides opportunities for young women medical
researchers to interact with one another.

At Nara Women's University multiple activities support women researchers, including programs to encourage the next generation of women in
science. Activities include the creation of the Network to Support Child
Care, which offers information on child care and consultations; the estab-

lishment of a system to recruit educational support staff to help women researchers who are simultaneously engaged in child care or elderly care; the appointment of a counselor to provide advice on parenting and child care; the creation of a mailing list to disseminate information on research work opportunities and careers for graduate students; and the organization of science lectures for primary and secondary school students. A system to provide women researchers with continued support in their work is beginning to fall in place.

The business community has also begun to encourage secondary school girls to study science, with the main aim of increasing the number of women in their organizations. The International Network of Women Engineers and Scientists (INWES), founded in 1964 in forty countries, including Japan, seeks to encourage women researchers and to support the younger generation of women in science. In 2006, Japan produced a DVD with the support of the Japan Science and Technology Agency entitled "Let's Study Science: You Can Do Anything." The DVD introduces young scientists working in the field, for example, supervising construction work and doing cosmetic product development. Events for secondary school students have been held throughout Japan, using this DVD as a tool to raise interest in science, and bring home an image of the kinds of careers the study of science can lead to.

IBM has been making active efforts to diversify its human resources since the 1990s, but in 1998, women in management positions at IBM Japan stood at 13 percent, the lowest among all IBM offices around the world. The three reasons raised as obstructions to women's career development were: "inability to picture one's future within the organization," "difficulty of balancing work and family" and "the male-centered corporate culture." Discussions of these matters led to company-wide efforts to make better use of female employees through instituting several reforms: discussion seminars about the problems; a mentor system for would-be women executives; and the introduction of child care and flextime. A three-day event for female students called "EXITE Camp" (*Exploring Interests in Technology and Engineering*) has also been developed, during which students may conduct science experiments and hear women engineers discussing their experiences. Women technicians also meet with junior high school girls as volunteer mentors (IBM homepage).

Another business organization seeking to contribute to the advancement of women in science and technology is Agilent Technologies, an electronic measuring instruments manufacturer in Tokyo. Since 2005, it has held a workshop for junior high school girls during the spring break on how to make germanium radios. One student, who took part in the workshop three years in a row, and challenged herself by making an FM radio said, "It's exciting to develop my skills. In the future I would like to major in science" ("Rikei ni joshi irasshai!" 2007).

We can say that Japan has now entered the twenty-first century, having finally begun to prepare for the advancement of women in the fields of science and technology. It has taken a very long time to begin to close the socially and culturally constructed gap between science and technology and women, and overcome the limits imposed by gender. The contributions of women to the fields of science and technology may become a strong force for change in Japanese society.

Works Cited

IBM. http://www.06.ibm.com/jp/accessibility/news/exite2005.html.

"Kitare rikei gaaru!" (Come on, science girls!). 2007. *Nihon keizai shimbun* (Nihon keizai newspaper). July 23(Evening edition).

Kokuritsu kyoiku kenkyusho (National Institute for Educational Policy Research. 2002. *Heisei jusannendo shochugakko kyoiku katei jisshi jokyo chosa* (2001 survey on the implementation of educational curricula in elementary and junior high schools).

Mombukagakusho (Ministry of Education, Culture, Sports, Science and Technology). 2002. *Gakko kyoiku ni okeru jendaa baiasu ni kansuru kenkyu, 2000-2002* (Research on gender bias in school education, 2000-2002).

———. 2002. *Wagakuni no kenkyu katsudo no jittai ni kansuru chosa* (Survey report on research activities in Japan).

———. 2007 & 2008. *Gakko kihon chosa* (School basic survey).

Muramatsu, Yasuko, ed. 1996. *Josei no rikei noryoku o ikasu* (Utilizing women's capabilities in the sciences). Tokyo: Nihon hyoronsha.

——— . 2004. *Rikabanare shiteiru no wa dareka* (Who is it that is moving away from the science courses?). Tokyo: Nihon hyoronsha.

Naikakufu (Cabinet Office, Government of Japan). 2008. *Danjo kyodo sankaku hakusho* (White paper on gender equality). Tokyo: Saiki insatsu.

Naikakufu danjo kyodo sankakukyoku (Gender Equality Bureau, Cabinet Office, Government of Japan). 2005. Website. "Challenge Campaign" http://www.gender.go.jp/c-challenge/.

Nihon gakujutsu kaigi (Science Council of Japan). 2002. *Yoboshо—Josei kagakusha no kankyo kaizen no gutaiteki sochi ni tsuite* (Petition—Regarding concrete measures to improve the working environment of women researchers).

Nihon josei gijutsusha fooramu (Japan Women Engineers Forum). 2006. *Josei gijutsusha shuro kankyo to kyaria keisei* (Working environment and career development for women technicians).

OECD Global Science Forum. 2005. *Declining Enrollment in Science & Technology Studies.*

Ogawa, Mariko. 2001. *Feminism to kagaku/gijitsu* (Feminism and science and technology).Tokyo: Iwanami shoten.

"Rikei ni joshi irrashai!" (Girls, welcome to the sciences!). 2007. *Chugoku shimbun* (Chugoku newspaper). April 23.

"'Rokettogaaru' sodate joshikokoseira sekkeiuchiage" ("Nurturing 'rocket girls': high school girls design and launch rocket"). 2007. *Asahi shimbun* (Asahi newspaper). September 2.

Sogo joseishi kenkyukai (Society for comprehensive research on women's history), ed. 1993. *Nihon josei no rekishi bunka to shiso 3: kindai* (The history, culture and ideas of Japanese women vol. 3: modern times). Tokyo: Kadokawa sensho.

Tokyo joshi ikadaigaku (Tokyo Women's Medical University). http://www.twmu. ac.jp. See Joshi igaku kenkyusha shienshitsu (Support Center for Female Medical Scientists).

Tsuda juku rika no rekishi o kirokusurukai (Society for recording the history of Tsuda College's faculty of science), ed. 1987. *Josei no jiritsu to kagaku kyoiku* (Women's independence and science education). Tokyo: Domesu shuppan.

Tsugawa, Akiko. 1996. *Hiraku: Nihon no josei kagakusha no kiseki* (Opening the way: the road walked by women scientists in Japan). Tokyo: Domesu shuppan.

———. 2006. *Rikei ni iko! joshi chukosei no tame no rikei annai* (Let's study science! A guidebook for secondary school girls about studying science). Tokyo: Kyutensha.

III

MARRIAGE AND FAMILIES

The Changing Patterns of Marriage and Motherhood

7

Aya Ezawa

Recent policy discussions surrounding changes in marriage and family in contemporary Japan evoke a sense of crisis. Japan's fertility rate, with an average of 1.37 children per woman in 2008 (Koseirodosho 2008), is well below the replacement rate, raising fears of a gradual decline in Japan's population. In addition, Japanese women are increasingly delaying marriage and a growing number are remaining unmarried. Marriage is not only declining in appeal, but marriages are also becoming more brittle. Japan's divorce rate has increased significantly in the past decades and in 2008, was similar to divorce rates in Western Europe (Ibid.). In short, there are two interrelated problems: women are having fewer children; and the institution of marriage is changing.

What makes recent debates about family changes in Japan particularly fascinating is that they throw into relief the close connection between family life and the modern nation-state. Marriage and childbearing are not simply personal or private choices, but, as current concerns over the decline in marriage and fertility in Japan show, are public issues with broader social, economic, and political ramifications. The modern nation-state depends on the maintenance of a healthy and productive population (Foucault 1978), and a physical decline in population can cause major disruptions in its economy and social systems. Fewer children means fewer students and workers, which can cause labor shortages, and make it increasingly difficult to maintain a social security and pension system in a rapidly aging population. As women are central to reproducing and educating the population, their "private" attitudes toward marriage and children constitute a major policy concern and public issue. In this essay, I explore this connection between gender and the state by describing the lives and attitudes toward marriage of several divorced mothers.

Comparative Perspectives

A decline in fertility and marriage, and a rise in divorce are noticeable in most advanced industrialized countries, which means that current trends in Japan are by no means unique. Industrialization itself has led to many fundamental shifts in family life (Tilly and Scott 1987), most noticeable of which is the transition from a large, multigenerational family with many children, to a nuclear family composed of a married couple and an average of two children (Goode 1963). In Japan, fertility rates began to decline with the onset of industrialization during the Meiji era (1868-1912), a trend that intensified in the postwar period. Between 1949 and 1957, the total fertility rate in Japan declined from 4.32 to 2.04 children per woman (Koseirodosho 2008). In other words, Japan experienced a shift from families with four or more children to an average of two within less than ten years (Ochiai 2005). While a decline in fertility during a period of industrialization seems universal, in the case of Japan, it occurred at an unprecedented speed.

Even more striking however are the regularity and predictability that came to be associated with women's lives in postwar Japan, also described as the "postwar Japanese family system" (Ochiai 1994). While marriage and childbirth in other countries tended to spread out over a wider range of ages (i.e., from teenage to late thirties), reflecting a diversity of lifestyles, in postwar Japan, they came to follow a predictable and uniform pattern, and concentrated in a narrow range of years (Brinton 1992). In the 1960s and 1970s, women's average age at the time of their first marriage was narrowly clustered around age twenty-four (Koseirodosho 2008), they bore an average of two children, and there was a growing trend for women to become housewives.

Moreover, Japanese marriages until the 1980s were remarkable not only in their timing, but also in their seeming stability. Despite the wide-ranging social transformations of the economy and society during the period of high-speed growth, divorce in early postwar Japan remained remarkably uncommon. That is to say, whereas economic growth and industrialization led to a steady increase in divorce in the industrialized West, in Japan divorce rates were unusually high during the Meiji period, but declined with the onset of industrialization, and dropped to unusually low levels in the 1960s (0.73 per thousand population in 1963), the peak period of Japan's economic expansion (Fuess 2004; Kawashima and Steiner 1960; Koseirodosho 2008). Similarly, while single parenthood and birth outside of marriage are becoming increasingly common in most of Europe and North America, single mothers in Japan remain a small minority, and birth outside of marriage, with 2.11 percent of births in 2008, is a rare event (Koseirodosho

2008). In short, what makes the dynamics of postwar Japanese family life remarkable is the seeming absence of change despite the dramatic social and economic transformations of the postwar era.

It is in the context of these stable and predictable patterns of family life that current concerns over an accelerating decline in fertility, the delay of marriage, and rise of non-marriage and divorce emerge. Viewed in comparison to other advanced industrialized countries, however, recent developments in Japan seem hardly unusual. Fertility rates in many countries have declined to levels that make it difficult to maintain the size of the population (see e.g., Therborn 2004). In the EU, fertility rates have declined from an average of 2.59 in the late 1960s to 1.47 in 2002, and have since remained below the replacement level (European Foundation 2004, OECD 2006). Japan's fertility rate (with 1.37 in 2008) is in this sense not unusual, although it is among the lowest in advanced industrialized countries (Koseirodosho 2008). A delay and decline in marriage, as well as an increase in divorce and the growing presence of single-mother families, similarly, have become significant public issues in Europe and North America (Lewis 1997; OECD 2006). Divorce rates in 2007 were highest in the United States (3.6 per thousand population), followed by the United Kingdom and Germany (2.37), Sweden (2.27), France (2.22), and Italy (0.84) (IPSS 2010; US Census Bureau 2010). Japan's current divorce rate (1.99 in 2008) is thus similar but not higher than that of most European countries (MHLW 2008). Similarly, although the percentage of single mothers in Japan has been increasing (6.4 percent, JIL 2003), this ratio remains significantly lower than in the US (27.6 percent, US Census Bureau 1998), the United Kingdom (17 percent), France (9 percent), and Germany (8 percent) and only somewhat higher than in Italy (4 percent, 2003 figures, Lehman and Wirtz 2004).

Comparison however also suggests important, even if subtle similarities and differences among countries. Japanese family trends are, interestingly, most similar to those in Italy, which stands out as a country with one of the lowest fertility rates, a low divorce rate, and very few single mothers. What are the similarities and differences between these two countries? If Catholicism has a strong influence on family trends in Italy (Bimbi 1997), what is behind trends in Japan? How have different policies and labor market conditions in Japan and Italy influenced marriage and fertility patterns? In contrast to Scandinavian welfare states, which have supported a dual-earner family and have made it easier for married mothers to work, for instance, in Italy and Japan, the state has relied on families and women to provide care for the elderly and children, and has made it difficult for women to combine work and family life (Lewis 1997; Trifiletti 2006). Social policies and institutions, as well as workplace practices create structural conditions and institutional frameworks, which shape women's opportunities and lifestyles, and can influence trends in marriage, family formations, and women's lives.

The Family and the Nation-State

In Japan, perhaps more consciously than elsewhere, policy makers and government officials recognized early the centrality and importance of women and the family for building a modern nation-state. During the period of modernization, the Meiji Code (1898) institutionalized the family as a subunit of the modern state in the form of the *ie* (family/household) and *koseki* (family registration) systems, which gave power to heads of families over other household members, but also made them responsible for their welfare and accountable to the state (Toshitani 1987; 1994). The state also promoted a new ideology of the "good wife and wise mother" (*ryosai kenbo*), of the dedicated woman, devoted to the upbringing of her children and the welfare of her family (Koyama 1991; Uno 1993). Through compulsory education, as well as Daily Life Improvement Campaigns, policy makers promoted a new ideal of motherhood, child rearing practices, and efficient household management, with the goal of strengthening both home and nation (Garon 1997; Koyama 1999). That is, prewar policies positively incorporated women into the modern state, by promoting women as efficient housewives and responsible mothers who would raise healthy soldiers and dutiful citizens (Nolte and Hastings 1991).

Family life and women's status changed significantly as a consequence of the sweeping social, economic, and political changes following Japan's defeat in World War II. With the introduction of the postwar Constitution, women obtained a range of new civil, social, and political rights, ranging from universal suffrage and the freedom to choose their marriage partners, to the right to divorce and receive welfare support from the state. The expansion of the educational system also increased women's access to a high school and college education, and to paid employment. The "good wife, and wise mother" ideology, meanwhile, became associated with prewar and wartime ideology, and the term *ryosai kenbo* fell into disuse (Uno 1993). Instead, a middle-class family, consisting of a full-time "professional" housewife, a hardworking salaried husband and two children, became central to the popular image of the postwar Japanese family (Ochiai 1994; Sakamoto 1997).

Still, in postwar Japan, though the rhetoric has changed, the family has continued to constitute a key unit of society, the economy, and the state.

As Yokoyama Fumino's detailed analysis has shown, from family law, education, taxation, to labor law and child-care services, policies and regulations in postwar Japan have presumed and reinforced a specific model of family with a salaried husband and full-time housewife. In the 1960s, education promoted a gendered division of labor through such compulsory school subjects for girls as home economics. A failure to invest in day care services and the limited availability of maternity leave continued to make child care a private matter and the responsibility of women and families. Pension and tax schemes also provided incentives for women to limit their work activities and income in order to maintain their eligibility for tax deductions and waivers of pension contributions for dependent spouses (Yokoyama 2002, 90).

Such policies have encouraged women to become housewives in a period that was assumed to provide greater opportunities for women to become economically independent from families and husbands. Although women's educational attainment increased, the tendency for women to become full-time housewives and remain dependent on their husbands intensified during the 1960s and 1970s (Ochiai 1994). Most strikingly, women with university or college degrees were, until the 1980s, less likely to be engaged in paid work than high school graduates (Brinton 1993, 38f, see also Tanaka 1995). College graduates were not only over-qualified for typically female jobs, but they were also encouraged to become full-time housewives because of the middle-class status of their husbands (Ogasawara 1998).

Moreover, company practices reinforced women's domesticity by maintaining a gender division of labor in the workplace. The introduction of a family wage, lifetime employment and a seniority-based promotion system assured the male worker of his ability to sustain himself and his family, but also limited women's work opportunities and ability to earn a living wage (Kimoto 2000). In particular, the distinction between permanent employees (*seishain*) with lifetime employment and nonpermanent employees in contractual or part-time positions has led to a gendered segregation of the labor market and has limited women's career opportunities. Until the introduction of the Equal Employment Opportunities Law in 1985, women were routinely offered only monotonous clerical jobs with no opportunity of advancement, and encouraged to quit their jobs upon marriage (Ogasawara 1998). The lack of challenges, promotion, and recognition on the job, as well as low remuneration have not only limited women's economic independence but also made a housewife's life seem more appealing than a job without career prospects.

Today, although an increasing number of women are returning to the workforce after giving birth, they are often not continuing a career. Few women are able to reenter permanent positions, with the consequence that most middle-aged women with children tend to work in part-time jobs (Osawa 1999). University graduates are least likely to return to the work-force, suggesting that some mothers return to the workforce primarily for financial reasons (Nakai and Akachi 2000). Moreover, the few university graduates who continue working without interruption tend to work in specific professions—as school teachers or public servants—jobs which provide security and comparatively good maternity leave policies (Hirao 1999). In short, the ability to combine a career, rather than a part-time job, with motherhood often seems to be limited to highly educated women who work in specific occupations. While the postwar era has provided many new freedoms and opportunities to women, institutional structures have continued to press women into the prescribed life course of early marriage and life as a full-time housewife.

Perspectives on Marriage

Between 1998 and 2000 and again in 2005, I conducted interviews with fifty-nine divorced, unmarried and widowed single mothers in Tokyo. I was especially interested in exploring their ideas about marriage and the chal-lenges they faced during marriage, and when they divorced and became single mothers. The majority of these women were in their thirties and for-ties (i.e., born between the late 1950s and early 1970s) when I met them, and the dominant majority (thirty-one) were taking care of children below school age. In this essay, I will focus only on the thirty-eight who were divorced.[1]

Although most of the women in this study were enthusiastic about mar-riage and becoming a mother while in their twenties, their stories of get-ting married also reflected significant tensions between the wish to find an ideal partner, and pressures to get married in a timely fashion and become mothers. Such tensions are also noticeable in recent surveys on contem-porary attitudes toward marriage among single women in Japan. Whereas arranged marriages were common in early postwar Japan, a preference for "love marriages" or those based on choice and mutual love ranks high among contemporary perspectives. Even when marriages are "arranged" today, they are not unions decided upon by parents or relatives, but rather the result of introductions through friends, relatives, or matchmakers. Sur-veys indicate that women want to marry the partner of their dreams, and that they are willing to wait for the right person rather than marry by a spe-cific age (IPSS 2005a). That is to say, an increasing number of women insist that marriage should be a personal choice, and not an obligation (Bumpass and Choe 2004), and an inability to find an appropriate partner is also the main reason cited for remaining unmarried (IPSS 2005a). In approaching the limit of the ideal marriage age, however, women may feel considerable pressure to get married (Sakai 2003), since remaining unmarried at thirty is a "failure." Under such circumstances, age, rather than finding the perfect partner, may become a more important consideration in getting married.

In addition, although the idea of becoming a mother remains one of the major attractions of getting married, there is also considerable concern about the pressures and high expectations facing women as married mothers. The single most important "benefit" or attraction of getting married cited by single women is the "ability to have children and a family," indicating that motherhood remains central to women's image of marriage. Notably, the "ability to live with a person you love" follows far behind as a third factor, and has been of declining significance over the past years (IPSS 2005a). The major "cost" of marriage cited, meanwhile, is the "loss of freedom in one's personal conduct and lifestyle," imposed by the expectation to become a mother and housewife once married (Ehara 2004; IPSS 2005a; Kamano 2004). As recent studies have shown, an increasing number of women today wish to continue working once married (IPSS 2005a), yet they are also aware that in becoming mothers, they may have little choice but to drop out of the workforce (Nagase 2006). Many mothers thus find themselves in a double bind: on the one hand, many continue to emphasize the importance of being a mother and raising their children at home and motherhood as a source of self-fulfillment (Tsuya, Mason and Bumpass 2004). Yet, while many women are devoted to becoming a mother, they also wish to find sources of self-fulfillment outside of child rearing, which is however made difficult by the demands of full-time motherhood (Ehara 2000). In short, the ability to become a mother is the major attraction of getting married, while the high expectations and pressures facing mothers are also its major detractions.

Personal Stories

The stories of several women provide insights into the motivations and logic behind these puzzling trends. Going beyond statistical indicators, they reveal how women understand the meaning of marriage and envision their lives among the tensions of marriage, motherhood, and work.

Yoshimi Sakai [2]
Yoshimi Sakai is a mother of two in her midthirties, who lives in a public housing unit in Tokyo. Reared in a working-class district in Tokyo, she con-

nects her motivation to get married with the difficult living conditions she faced as a child and teenager. When asked about her personal background, she introduced herself as someone who grew up in a low-income family:

> My mother was a full-time housewife and my father a company employee. I was the second child in our family. But I grew up in a low-income household. We lived in an an old apartment without a bath. . . . When I was a child [in the early 1970s], to live in such a household was still common. Middle-class people usually owned a house with a bath, but about a third of my schoolmates lived in private apartments without baths. We all went to the public bath [*sento*], and I would meet my classmates there and say, "Hey, what's up?" That's how we lived.

Sakai was also aware of her limited educational opportunities. Her mother began to work part-time after she entered middle school, but she knew that her parents could not afford university tuition. Even though she was eager to become a preschool teacher, she was discouraged by her parents even from this path, since they could not afford the piano lessons required to obtain the qualification. Instead of pursuing her interests when she entered high school, she began to work after school in a supermarket to supplement the family income. The work tired her, and she studied just enough to get by. After graduation, she found a job as a clerical worker in a small company. Eager to have her own space, she soon moved out, and rented a small apartment without a bath near her parents' residence. Still, she worried increasingly about her future, aware that her parents were aging, and aware also of the limited income she earned as a clerical worker. She notes:

> Around me, middle-class people were having a nice life but I lived in an apartment without a bath [in the early 1990s]. In order to move into an apartment with a bath, I would have to have a guarantor [required to rent private apartments]. I wondered whom I could ask after my parents passed away. I was really worried. At that time, someone asked me to marry him. He promised I could become a full-time housewife, and we would rent an apartment nearby so that I could take care of my parents. And so I got married.

Despite Sakai's independent mode of life, she was well aware that achieving a higher living standard would only be possible by getting married. Yet her marriage turned out to be quite different from what she had expected, since her husband actually had no stable income, came to live off her, accumulated debts in her name, and eventually became violent. Pregnant, and having just quit her job, she found herself trapped in an exploitative relationship, from which she did not believe she had the resources to escape.

The prospect of becoming a mother, moreover, made her cautious about setting out on her own, aware of the difficulties she would have in supporting herself and her child. In consideration of the welfare of her child, she stayed with her husband for several years, returning to full-time work a few months after giving birth to support the family, and separating only after feeling threatened by another wave of domestic violence.

While Sakai's story is in some respects extreme, her outlook on life and marriage is not unique. Several women from low-income backgrounds similarly had begun working from an early age, and noted the discomfort of living in crammed conditions at home, and expressed the wish to have their own space as married wives and mothers. They had grown up with few toys and luxuries, and recounted hurt feelings about not being able to dress up like other teenage girls in high school, not unlike the working-class childhoods described by Lillian Rubin's study on working-class families in the United States (1976). Under such conditions, marriage was attractive in part because it promised to provide them with their own home and a higher living standard. Fond of children, many aspired to becoming full-time housewives if financially feasible. Yet, although their expectations about their partners in marriage were often quite basic—to provide for the family—they often faced living conditions quite similar, if not more difficult, than those they had experienced as children.

Chikako Nagai

Where Sakai's story underscores socioeconomic incentives for marriage, Chikako Nagai, a mother of a teenager in her midforties, connects her urge to get married and become a mother with the limited sense of accomplishment she found in the world of work. Nagai grew up outside Tokyo in a family that ran a small business. Although her father placed great emphasis on the university attendance of her brother, he saw little meaning in investing in the education or working career of his daughter. Nevertheless, with some persistence, Nagai managed to attend junior college, working part-time to support herself, and then after graduation worked as a clerical accountant in a small company. But she never envisioned a career. She notes:

> I changed jobs quite a bit, always working in accounting. . . . I did not have an image of a woman working for a long time, there were no career-track jobs for women at the time . . . I could not imagine a woman working while raising children . . . It was always the same every day, always the same work, the same employees, and all my friends eventually marrying and quitting . . . There were no female division chiefs, so there was also no role model [for pursuing a career] . . . When the other women quit after a few years, I also decided to quit.

Nagai's experience reflects an employment trajectory typical for women in the 1980s. As visualized by the well-known M-shaped work participation rate of Japanese women (Iwai and Manabe 2000), the majority of women work after graduation from school, but then retire from the workforce with marriage and reenter the workforce as part-time workers in middle-age. Placed in monotonous, noncareer track "office lady" jobs, companies have offered women few opportunities to pursue a career and find recognition through work, making departure from the workplace upon marriage all the more attractive (Ogasawara 1998).

As Nagai remained unmarried even in her midtwenties however, she began to reconsider her options. Bored by the monotony of clerical work, she started looking for a job that would offer her more challenges: "Until then I had been an accounting clerk, but I wanted to do a real job, something that would allow me to become more independent. At the time, there was a job as manager of a shop, rare at the time open to women. . ..So I applied, received training, and became a manager [of a small store]." Yet although she enjoyed the responsibilities of her new job, her excitement soon wore off. Since she had to work long hours and had no independence in decision-making, she quit after two years, and pursued contractual (*haken*) work instead. By then in her late twenties, her priority shifted to marriage, both seemingly urgent as she approached her thirtieth birthday, and potentially attractive, given the limited fulfillment of her work experience. She also emphasized motherhood as a major motivation: "I really wanted children. . . . These days, some people have children later. . . . but in those days, I thought the twenties was the limit, and I wondered, will I just go on without giving birth?"

Nagai's story also highlights how her wish to get married and become a mother was related to the frustrations she experienced in the world of work:

> I didn't find my job interesting or challenging, otherwise things might have been different. But by coincidence, there was someone who proposed marriage to me, and I thought maybe this is the last chance. . . . Well, I made a mistake in getting married. It would have been different if I had a job I enjoyed.

In contrast to Sakai, marriage in Nagai's case enabled her to attain a comfortable living standard, and the much respected status of a middle-class housewife, as her husband was a successful entrepreneur. Yet, the privileges and status of this lifestyle came with its own challenges. Although Nagai had expected to reenter employment after giving birth, she faced strong resistance from her husband. In light of his status as the owner of a company, sending their child to a day care center (which are historically institutions taking care of the children of the working class) was out of question, as it would give the impression that her husband could not adequately provide for her and their offspring. Although marriage provided Nagai with a comfortable lifestyle, the expectations tying her to being a housewife and mother became a source of friction, and brought about an early end to her marriage.

Kyoko Sekiguchi

In contrast to Sakai and Nagai, Kyoko Sekiguchi, a university graduate in her early forties did not share the same sense of urgency about getting married and becoming a mother. Along with a small group of mostly university-educated women in career-track jobs, she was among the few who voiced resistance to an institutionalized ideal of marriage, and articulated an alternative vision of partnership and family life.

Sekiguchi grew up in a family dedicated to their children's education. Both of her parents were professionals who worked full time, and encouraged her to study and pursue her interests from an early age. She was conscious that she was expected to graduate from university, and took it for granted that she would pursue a profession after graduation. She notes: "Because both of my parents worked full time, I did not resist the idea of becoming a working woman. Because I am the eldest daughter, my parents also had high expectations toward me. They were very enthusiastic about my studies. But at university, I did not study much, I joined a [sports] club and did sports most of the time." Unlike Nagai and Sakai, Sekiguchi could take her education for granted, and rather than having to be concerned with earning an income, could pursue her own interests.

As her graduation from university coincided with the introduction of the Equal Employment Opportunity Law and the bubble economy, employment opportunities for women like her seemed abundant. Through an acquaintance, she found a position with a popular magazine publishing company, which launched her career as a writer. This is also where she met her partner: "I was working in a small company. That is when I met him, and I immediately thought I would like to be with him . . . He was working a lot overseas, and I myself had been traveling abroad a lot when I was a student, and I was interested in exploring new places. So I continued my work as a freelancer while traveling with him." While many women envisioned marriage and family life as centered on motherhood and children, Sekiguchi was among the few to talk about the importance of her relationship with her partner.

But neither her relationship with her partner, nor her pregnancy in her late twenties, appeared to make marriage a pressing topic to her. She explains: "We thought one does not have to insist on registering the marriage... so we did not formally get married. When the baby was born, he officially declared his paternity." Sekiguchi's decision not to marry yet live together with her partner in a common-law marriage is part of a recent movement of couples who consciously reject marriage as an institution yet not as a practice (Yoshizumi 1997). Under the family registration system, which governs marriage and family relations in Japan, the key unit of personal identification is not the individual (as is the case with a US drivers' license or Social Security number), but the nuclear family. Women leave their parents' family register with marriage and enter the family register of their husbands as dependents (unless the husband decides to enter his wife's family register). Marriage therefore does not merely consist of a contract between individuals but means that a woman joins her husband's family unit and changes her name to that of the husband.

Couples who live in common-law marriages reject legal marriage because it assumes a hierarchical relationship between husband and wife (in literally making wives dependents of husbands in the family register) and implies a traditional division of labor in the home. Although such couples do not register their marriages, they live together as if legally married and call each other husband and wife. Most are highly educated and tend to have significantly more progressive views of family relationships. Asked about how such couples manage differences in opinion, few women in common-law marriages agree that they must accept their husband's opinions, even though 71.5 percent of women in legal marriages do so. Men in common law marriages also tend to be significantly more involved in housework and child rearing (Yoshizumi 1997 43, 133-134).

While living in a common-law marriage allowed Sekiguchi to assert a different kind of relationship and vision of marriage, she also faced significant disadvantages when she separated from her partner after several years. Since she was not legally divorced (or married), she was ineligible for allowances for single mothers, which were at the time limited to divorced (as opposed to unmarried) single mothers, and so she received no support from the welfare office. Although her partner voluntarily provided child support payments, she would have had difficulties enforcing these without a judicial divorce.

Sekiguchi's story is exemplary for the freedom she enjoyed in pursuing her studies and career, as well as in her relationship with her husband. She did not merely get a job, but could see work as a vocation, and something that enabled her to pursue her interest in travel. Likewise, although she was eager to live with her partner, and to have children, she did not see marriage as necessary in order to confirm her status or relationship.

The stories of the women presented here highlight the contradictory realities faced by women in contemporary Japanese society. They reflect on tensions between ideals and aspirations of personal choice and self-fulfillment, and limited alternatives to the prescribed life course of a timely marriage and life as a housewife and mother. Even though marriage is supposedly a private issue and personal choice, women's often pragmatic decisions about partners, marriage, and motherhood indicate that such personal matters as getting married are also shaped by the opportunities and constraints they face in society and the economy.

As Sakai's case illustrates, for women from low-income family backgrounds, marriage can be a means to find one's own space, and promises a living standard that would be unattainable on a woman's single salary. Marriage, in this case, has a strong appeal because of the potential for upward mobility. For Nagai, this was not just a possibility but a reality. Even though her parents had little education to speak of, her marriage allowed her to attain a typical middle-class lifestyle. Where full-time employment provides little opportunity for women with a high school or junior college education to become financially independent, marriage remains an important means to ensure an adequate living standard.

The decline in fertility and marriage rates, and the rise of the divorce rate are often assumed to be consequences of women's increasing financial independence, pursuit of a career, and changing attitudes toward marriage. While this may be the case for a small minority of highly educated women such as Sekiguchi, the everyday realities of most other women are, as we have seen, often quite different. If there is anything specific about these divorced mothers, it is their rather optimistic pursuit of marriage and motherhood. The crisis surrounding marriage in contemporary Japan can thus be seen as a sign of growing hesitance among Japanese women to follow the prescribed norm, as well as the rather limited opportunities to pursue an alternative lifestyle.[3]

Notes

1. The women interviewed came from a variety of socioeconomic backgrounds. Twenty-nine of the women had earned a junior college or university degree, twenty-six graduated from senior high school, and four did not complete senior high school. Of the fifty-nine women I interviewed, forty-seven were employed and were for the most part working full time. Their occupations included clerical work, elderly care work, accounting, work as a pharmacist and as teachers, as well as self-employment as writer or owner or manager of a small store. Although the women in this study cannot represent a larger population of women or single mothers, their stories allow insight into individual experiences, which inform broader marriage trends.

2. All names as well as minor details have been changed to ensure anonymity.

3. The research for this paper was supported by grants from the Itoh Scholarship Foundation, the Matsushita International Foundation, the University of Illinois at Urbana-Champaign, as well as an Abe Fellowship.

Works Cited

Bimbi, Franca. 1997. "Lone Mothers in Italy: a Hidden and Embarrassing Issue in a Familist Welfare Regime." In *Lone Mothers in European Welfare Regimes*, ed. Jane Lewis, 171-202. London: Jessica Kingsley Publishers.

Brinton, Mary C. 1992. "Christmas Cakes and Wedding Cakes: The Social Organization of Japanese Women's Life Course." In *Japanese Social Organization*, ed. Takie Sugiyama Lebra. Honolulu: University of Hawaii Press.

———. 1993. *Women and the Economic Miracle*. Berkeley: University of California Press.

Bumpass, Larry L., and Minja Kim Choe. 2004. "Attitudes Relating to Marriage and Family Life." In *Marriage, Work, and Family Life in Comparative Perspective*, ed. Noriko O. Tsuya and Larry L. Bumpass. Honolulu: University of Hawaii Press.

Ehara, Yumiko. 2000. "Hahaoyatachi no daburu baindo" (The double bind of mothers). In *Shoshika jidai no jendaa to hahaoya ishiki* (Gender and attitudes of mothers in the age of declining fertility rate), ed. Yoriko Meguro and Sumiko Yazawa. Tokyo: Shinyosha.

———. 2004. "Gender ishiki no henyo to kekkon kaihi" (Changes in gender consciousness and marriage avoidance). In *Shoshika no jendaa bunseki* (Gender analysis of the declining fertility rate), ed. Yoriko Meguro. Tokyo: Keiso shobo.

European Foundation for the Improvement of Living and Working Conditions. 2004. "Fertility and family issues in an enlarged Europe."

Foucault, Michel. 1978. *History of Sexuality. Volume 1: An Introduction*. New York: Vintage Books.

Fuess, Harald. 2004. *Divorce in Japan: Gender, and the State 1600-2000*. Stanford: Stanford University Press.

Garon, Sheldon. 1997. *Molding Japanese Minds—The State in Everyday Life*. Princeton: Princeton University Press.

Goode, William J. 1963. *World Revolutions and Family Patterns*. New York: The Free Press.

Hirao, Keiko. 1999. "Josei no shoki kyaria keisei ni okeru rodoshijo e no teichakusei" (Women's attachment to the labor market at the early stages of their career formation). *Nihon rodo kenkyu zasshi* (Journal of the Japan Institute of Labor), no. 471 (September): 29-41.

IPSS, National Institute of Population and Social Security Research. 2005a. "Dai jusankai shussei doko kihon chosa—kekkon to shussan ni kansuru zenkoku chosa: dokushinsha chosa kekka no gaiyo" (Thirteenth survey of trends in fertility rates—national survey regarding marriage and childbirth: summary of results pertaining to single people). Tokyo: Kokuritsu shakai hosho jinko mondai kenkyujo.

———. 2010. *Jinko tokei shiryo*. Tokyo: Kokuritsu shakai hosho jinko mondai kenkyujo.

Iwai, Hachiro, and Rinko Manabe. 2000. "M-jigata shugyo pataan no teichaku to sono imi" (The hardening of the M-shaped work pattern and its meaning). In *Nihon no kaiso shisutemu 4: jendaa/shijo/kazoku* (Japan's system of stratification, 4: gender, children, family), ed. Kazuo Seiyama. Tokyo: Tokyo daigaku shuppankai.

JIL (Japan Institute of Labor). 2003. *Boshisetai no haha e no shuroshien ni kansuru kenkyu* (Research on work support for mothers in lone mother households). Tokyo: Nihon rodo kenkyu kiko.

Kamano, Saori. 2004. "Dokushin danjo no kaku kekkonzo" (Images of marriage among single men and women). In *Shoshika no jendaa bunseki* (Gender analysis of the declining fertility rate), ed. Yoriko Meguro and Hachiro Nishoka. Tokyo: Keiso shobo.

Kawashima, Takeyoshi, and Kurt Steiner. 1960. "Modernization and Divorce Rate Trends in Japan." *Economic Development and Cultural Change* 9: 213-39.

Kimoto, Kimiko. 2000. "Kigyo shakai no henka to kazoku (Changes in corporate society and the family). *Kazoku shakaigaku kenkyu* (Japanese journal of family sociology) 12: 27-40.

Koseirodosho (Ministry of Health Labor and Welfare). 2008. *Jinko dotai tokei* (Survey of vital statistics).

Koyama, Shizuko. 1991. *Ryosai kenbo no kihan* (The norm of 'good wife and wise mother'). Tokyo: Keiso shobo.

———. 1999. *Katei no seisei to josei no kokuminka* (The creation of families and subjectification of women). Tokyo: Keiso shobo.

Lehman, Petra, and Christine Wirtz. 2004. "Household formation in the EU-lone parents." *Eurostat: Statistics in Focus*.

Nagase, Nobuko. 2006. "Japanese youth's attitudes towards marriage and child rearing." In *The Changing Japanese Family*, ed. Ayumi Takenaka and Marcus Rebick. London: Routledge.

Nakai, Miki, and Mayuko Akachi. 2000. "Shijo sanka/shakai sanka" (Participation in the market/participation in society). In *Nihon no kaiso shisutemu 4: Gender/shijo/kazoku* (Japan's system of stratification, 4: gender, children, family), ed. Kazuo Seiyama. Tokyo: Tokyo daigaku shuppankai.

Nolte, Sharon H. , and Sally Ann Hastings. 1991. "The Meiji State's Policy Toward Women, 1890-1910." In *Recreating Japanese Women, 1600-1945*, ed. Gail Lee Bernstein. Berkeley: University of California Press.

Ochiai, Emiko. 1994. *21 Seiki no kazoku e* (The Japanese family system in transition). Tokyo: Yuhikaku sensho.

———. 2005. "The Postwar Japanese Family System in Global Perspective: Familism, Low Fertility, and Gender Roles." *U.S.-Japan Women's Journal*, no. 29 (December): 3-36.

OECD (Organisation for Economic Co-operation and Development). 2006. *Society at a Glance—OECD Social Indicators 2006*. Paris: OECD.

Ogasawara, Yuko. 1998. *Office Ladies and Salaried Men: Power, Gender, and Work in Japanese Companies*. Berkeley: University of California Press.

Osawa, Machiko. 1999. "Shigoto to katei no chowa no tame no shugyo shien (Work support for harmony between work and family). *Kikan shakai hosho kenkyu* (The Quarterly of Social Security Research) 34: 385-391.

Rubin, Lillian B. 1976. *Worlds of Pain: Life in the Working Class Family*. New York: Basic Books.

Sakai, Junko. 2003. *Makeinu no toboe* (The howling of the loser dogs). Tokyo: Kodansha.

Sakamoto, Kazue. 1997. *Kazoku no imeeji no tanjo* (The birth of family images). Tokyo: Shinyosha.

Tanaka, Kazuko. 1995. "Work, Education, and the Family." In *Japanese Women: New Feminist Perspectives on the Past, Present, and Future*, ed. Kumiko Fujimura-Fanselow and Atsuko Kameda. New York: The Feminist Press at The City University of New York.

Therborn, Göran. 2004. *Between Sex and Power: Family in the World, 1900-2000*. London: Routledge.

Tilly, Louise A., and Joan W. Scott. 1987. *Women, Work, and Family*. London: Routledge.

Toshitani, Nobuyoshi. 1987. *Kazoku to kokka* (Family and the state). Tokyo: Chikuma shobo.

———. 1994. "The Reform of Japanese Family Law and Changes in the Family System." *U.S.-Japan Women's Journal*, no. 6 (March): 66-82.

Trifiletti, Rossana. 2006. "Different paths to welfare: family transformations, the production of welfare, and future prospects for social care in Italy and Japan." In *The Changing Japanese Family*, ed. Marcus Rebick and Ayumi Takenaka. London: Routledge.

Tsuya, Noriko O., Karen Oppenheim Mason, and Larry L. Bumpass. 2004. "Views of Marriage among Never-Married Young Adults." In *Marriage, Work, and family Life in Comparative Perspective*, ed. Noriko O. Tsuya and Larry L. Bumpass. Honolulu: University of Hawaii Press.

US Census Bureau. 2010. *Statistical Abstracts*.

Uno, Kathleen S. 1993. "The Death of the "Good Wife, Wise Mother"?" In *Postwar Japan as History*, ed. Andrew Gordon. Berkeley: University of California Press.

Yokoyama, Fumino. 2002. *Sengo nihon no josei seisaku* (Japan's postwar policies regarding women). Tokyo: Keiso shobo.

Yoshizumi, Kyoko. 1997. *"Kindai kazoku" o koeru* (Beyond the "modern family"). Tokyo: Aoki shoten.

Single Mothers

Chieko Akaishi
Translated by Minata Hara

As an unmarried mother, I have been actively involved in a single mothers' group since the 1980s. Initially called No Cutbacks on Dependent Children's Allowance Networking Group (*Jido fuyo teate no kirisute o yurusanai renrakukai*), we organized to maintain the Dependent Children's Allowance that sustains single mothers. In the 1990s as our goals broadened, we renamed our group the Single Mother's Forum. Our aim throughout has been to create a better life for single mothers and their children by offering useful information and consultations, as well as through policy proposals, surveys, and other research activities.

In Japan, the number of single-mother households is around 1.2 million,[1] 80 percent of which result from divorce. Due to the national recession and the tightening job market, single-mother households have become more and more impoverished over the past decade or so. Given the economy, the Dependent Children's Allowance has been reduced as the government redirects its financial resources toward job support. Although we have resisted strongly, this fiscal policy has been enforced, albeit with slight amendments, so that an increasing number of single-mother households now face financial difficulties. Although social prejudice against single mothers and their children has eased somewhat over the last two decades, it still prevails particularly in the case of unmarried mothers.[2]

Single Mothers Today

A national survey conducted in 2006 by the Ministry of Health, Labor and Welfare found that divorced mothers accounted for a majority—79.7 percent, as opposed to widowed—9.7 percent, and unmarried mothers—6.7 percent (Koseirodosho 2007). The divorce rate declined temporarily around 1990, rose again to reach an estimated 290,000 in 2003, and is again declining slightly (Koseirodosho 2004). Approximately 60 percent of divorced couples have children, and in 80 percent of these cases the mother has assumed custody.

According to statistics of the Ministry of Justice, the major reasons for divorce include personality conflict, violence, and financial problems. Interviews by single-mother organizations, however, reveal that an overwhelming number of divorcees cite financial debts, and violence, including psychological abuse. This may partly be due to the growing awareness of domestic violence after the Domestic Violence Prevention Law was enacted in 2001. Divorces also result from the inability to cope with multiple debts as corporate restructuring affects husbands' jobs or income.

The average single mother is 39.4 years old and has two children; 32.5 percent live with their parents, presumably out of financial necessity (Koseirodosho 2007). Their average annual income is 2.13 million yen or roughly $21,000 (including allowances and widows' pensions), which is extremely low. It amounts to only 37 percent of the average household income of other households, and only about 30 percent of the annual income of households with children (Koseirodosho 2003). Even though 84.5 percent of single mothers work, their income is low.

Housing also presents a major problem. Only 34.7 percent of single mothers own their homes (Koseirodosho 2007). Many live in public housing and a large proportion of their household budget goes toward rent. In cities, public housing is not as readily available to single mothers, as there is greater competition. As their general income is low, many single mothers are barely at subsistence levels. Two case studies illuminate the problems of these women.

Ms. O. is a thirty-year-old single mother living in Tokyo. She has three children who are ten, eight, and six years of age. Her husband's family ran a family business, but as debts piled up under her husband's name, she was forced to divorce. Ms. O. had dropped out of high school and had little work experience. After her divorce, she worked nights at a sushi bar, and through distance learning she tried to acquire the qualifications to work in a medical office. She would pick up her children from day care and put them to bed before going to her night shift. One night, her eldest child, who was then seven years old, woke up in the middle of the night and called her cell phone asking, "Mommy where are you?" She says it was a heart-wrenching moment for her. Partly due to a lack of sleep, she fell ill after three months, and was unable to complete her distance education. After that, she managed to receive public assistance in addition to the income from her job. Three years after her divorce she suffered depression, and quit her full-time job. She is now working part-time from 10 a.m. to 4 p.m. in a retail shipping company for an hourly wage of 800 yen ($8). Because one of her children suffers from severe asthma and needs occasional hospitalization, and also because she herself is sometimes unwell, she is unable to earn much steady income; in fact at times she earns no income.

She somehow makes ends meet with 49,720 yen ($500) per month from Dependent Children's Allowance (*jido fuyo teate*); 13,500 yen per month for each of her three children, which comes to 40,500 yen ($400) per month from the Tokyo Municipal Child Rearing Allowance for Single Parents (*jido ikusei teate*); 20,000 yen ($200) per month from the Children's Allowance (*jido teate*); and 100,000 yen ($1,000) per month in Public Assistance (*seikatsu hogo*). Her former husband has remarried, and does not contribute any child support. Being able to live in municipal housing is helpful since its costs are only 30,000 yen ($300) a month. She incurs considerable medical expenses for her asthmatic child, and for another child who has a developmental handicap and needs to be taken to a hospital some distance away for treatment periodically. She cannot afford the cost of sending her children to *juku* (private after-hours cram school) as many Japanese parents do, but she wants to provide some extra help for them and therefore pays 5,600 yen (roughly $50) per month for each child so they can take correspondence classes.

Ms. O. says she wants to undertake vocational training, but cannot afford to do so. Although her life has somewhat stabilized since her divorce, her children's medical expenses, as well as her own ill health, make it difficult for her family to subsist solely on her earnings.

Ms. Y. is a forty-year-old single mother who works full time managing an elderly care provider service. After her divorce four years ago, she moved nearer to her childhood home. One of her two sons is a third-year student in high school, the other a second-year student in junior high. A university graduate, Ms. Y. worked in an editorial office before marrying and becoming a full-time housewife. Immediately after her divorce she suffered from depression, and was unable to think positively. Later, she took a course for training elderly care providers ("home helpers") and within two years she attained the highest-level of certification possible and secured her current job. Her monthly wage is approximately 200,000 yen ($2,000), and she receives 40,000 yen ($400) in Dependent Children's Allowance and 50,000 yen ($500) in child support from her ex-husband. She has several problems, including difficulties with her eldest son who refuses to go to school. She must also care for her elderly father. Just after the divorce, she used to pay 65,000 yen ($650) a month in rent, but she has now secured subsidized public housing. While Ms. Y's situation is relatively stable, still she says, "I have to work such long hours that I can't do much to help my child who stopped going to school. I also want to qualify for care management but I just don't have the time to study" (Single Mother's Forum 2002).

Problems Faced by Single Mothers—
Income and Employment

Although a high proportion of single mothers work, their income is comparatively low. Securing full time, permanent employment is impossible for those who are unable to work overtime. In order to fulfill their child-rearing duties, single mothers must resort to low paying part-time, dispatch, or contract work. In addition, single mothers tend to have relatively little formal education and they may be without qualifications for skilled jobs (Fujiwara 2005, 2007). Temporary, part-time, and contractual work accounts for 48.7 percent of the labor sector, about 10 percentage points higher than nine years ago. This is not unrelated to the overall increase in non-regular and temporary workers due to the deregulation of Japanese laws that formerly provided protection. Consequently, employment has become unstable, and parents are spending less and less time with their children because they must work overtime in order to keep their jobs. An increasing number of single mothers work at more than one job.

On the other hand, only a handful of fathers are paying child support, and not many fathers exercise visitation rights. This could be due to the lack of social awareness that a father is responsible for his children even after divorce. Although there has been a slight increase in the percentage of those women who negotiate for child support, and reach some kind of an agreement, in about half of the cases the father fails to pay despite the settlement reached. The average amount of child support received by single mothers, if they do receive any child support payments, is 42,000 yen ($400) a month.

Single mothers who have divorced their abusive husbands often suffer from post-traumatic stress disorder and find it difficult to hold a job. While it is now relatively easy to claim welfare assistance via shelters, the shelters are often full. Women are also left to struggle on their own once they have left the shelter, for there is no follow-up support system. Thus, many women hesitate to escape from abuse because they know it will be difficult to earn a decent living on their own. (See Single Mother's Forum 2004, 2005, 2007 for further information.)

Children's education is another major problem. During the period of compulsory education from elementary to junior high school, low-income households are eligible for subsidies for educational expenses. From senior high school onward, however, there is not much financial assistance for education. Equality of educational opportunity is gradually deteriorating in Japan, and children from wealthier homes now tend to have better access to quality education. Moreover, single mothers are usually compelled to work long hours and have little time to spend with their children. They often cannot afford to pay extra for cram schools, and so their children are at a disadvantage when preparing for senior high school entrance exams. Many of them drop out. This limits their employment options later in life, and makes them more prone to poverty. Even those students who are granted scholarships to attend university are shackled with heavy debt after graduation.

Recent Changes in Policies

The Dependent Children's Allowance (*jido fuyo teate*) is a form of state assistance devised for divorced or unmarried single mothers. Since its introduction in 1962 as an allowance to complement the Widowed Mothers' Pension scheme, it has been revised and improved. In 1985, when it was separated from the Widowed Mothers' Pension, the rate of payment was changed into a two-tiered support system based on the level of a recipient's income. Local governments took on one quarter of the financial burden. A proposal to exclude "unwed mothers" from support was eventually rejected. Single mothers across the nation met to debate and then to submit their demands through petitions. This was the period when our activities first intensified.

In 1998, the upper-income limit for eligibility was lowered substantially for single mothers as well as for their parents, siblings, and other cohabiting family members, thus making many cohabiting single mothers ineligible for the allowance. In addition, a government ordinance that required suspending the Dependent Children's Allowance if the father of a child born out of marriage acknowledged paternity was revised to make it possible for such children to continue receiving the allowance. This revision was made in the face of a lawsuit claiming the practice was discriminatory toward children born outside of marriage. Calls for cutting back the Dependent Children's Allowance have become louder as an increasing divorce rate has swelled the national budget. In 2002, sharp cuts to single mothers' support took the form of providing work support and the enforcement of child support payments by fathers. Such a shift supposedly was based on US policies with regard to single parent households.

Thus, a household with one child, and an annual income of up to 1.3 million yen ($13,000) would be eligible for a monthly allowance of 41,720 yen ($417). That amount would be reduced with each additional 10,000 yen ($100) earned, up to an annual income of 3.65 million yen ($36,500). Child support must also be declared, 80 percent of which would be considered as income and would serve to reduce the allowance accordingly. As a result of these policies, nearly 50 percent of single mothers had their allowances reduced. Furthermore, the Dependent Children's Allowance was deemed

a temporary allowance helpful for adjusting to divorce, and would thus be
reduced after five years. Still, the Dependent Children's Allowance remains
crucial as a guaranteed income for single-mother households. As of the end
of 2006, 990,000 households were receiving the allowance and the number
of beneficiaries was increasing, partly due to the economic recession and
restructuring that have caused a drop in the income of single mothers. We
continued to oppose the 2002 revision of the Dependent Children's Allowance. Although we argued strongly that the government should reduce the
allowance only after the work support programs were enforced and proven
effective, we were unable to prevent the revision.

The revision of the Mother and Child Welfare Law enabled a reduction
of the Dependent Children's Allowance up to half the amount in 2008 after
five years. From 2006 through 2007 we lobbied to oppose these cutbacks
by forming a wide-ranging antipoverty network and addressing the issue
of poverty faced by single mothers in a wider social context, thus including
young people and the homeless. As a result, the ruling coalition suffered a
massive defeat in the 2007 elections for the Upper House of the National
Diet (legislature).

By appealing to the media and lobbying the National Diet and the
Ministry of Health, Labor and Welfare, we gained a de facto "freeze" of
the reductions. This is undoubtedly because the election results compelled
not only the opposition parties, but also the ruling parties to revise their
policies regarding the elderly, people with disabilities, and single-mother
households. Still, the new ruling stipulated that from the fifth year onward,
the beneficiaries must submit proof of employment or of job-seeking to
continue receiving their allowance.

Widowed mothers with dependent children, on the other hand, have a
higher annual income compared to divorced mothers, as they are eligible for
the Bereaved Family's Basic Pension (*izoku kiso nenkin*) and the Bereaved
Family's Welfare Pension (*izoku kosei nenkin*), which provide payments that
are substantially larger than those of the Dependent Children's Allowance.

But what of the work-support programs, which were supposedly implemented to compensate for the reduction of the Dependent Children's
Allowance? The shift in focus to work-support programs was accompanied
by assistance for child care. These policies were placed under the jurisdiction of prefectural and municipal governments. Specifically, various vocational education and training programs, aiming to promote self-sufficiency,
were established so that women might gain qualifications, for example, in
nursing or physiotherapy. These programs were accompanied by financial
incentives offered to employers who hire single mothers as regular employees. Support centers for working single mothers were set up in every pre-

fecture, metropolis, and in designated cities with five hundred thousand or more inhabitants, and other urban hubs, offering job placement, consultation, and vocational training courses. Also, a system of compulsory child support was revised along with a new payment calculation chart to help secure payments from fathers.

Even after five years, such policies have not proven effective. Only 58 percent of the budget is actually used for the work-support programs, which shows how difficult it is for single mothers to make good use of them. For example, the subsidy for vocational training programs only provides livelihood assistance in the last year of study; if the subsidy for vocational training were to be provided from the first year of training, more mothers might apply for it. Work support is useless without the provision of livelihood assistance. Every local government has a self-sufficiency support center for working single mothers. However, the majority of so-called single-mother organizations involved are, in reality, conservative groups that consist mostly of war widows and other widowed families. The advisors are ex-labor consultants who have little understanding of single mothers' lives.

As a part of the national and local governments' scheme to employ single mothers, the Ministry of Health, Labor and Welfare is said to hire single mothers as non-regular employees, but a large number of women who have applied have been turned down. The Ministry also claims to be promoting home-based work, but this amounts to an income of 30-40,000 yen ($300-400) a month, and does not appear to improve the overall situation for single mothers. In its bid to focus on work support, the Japanese government has declared that those who are not looking for a job would not be offered any financial assistance. Providing the allowance only to those who are working is said to emulate the American system. However, the meaning of introducing such policies to the Japanese context is currently being questioned since single mothers in Japan are for the most part already working and do not need to be pressed to seek employment; the situation is totally different from that of the United States (see, e.g., Ezawa and Fujiwara 2005). In a survey conducted by the Single Mother's Forum, some described the work-support programs as useless as "a picture on the wall," while over 50 percent of those surveyed had never even heard of the program (Single Mother's Forum 2002).

Ten percent of single mothers receive Public Assistance (*seikatsu hogo*), part of the social security system. Half of these women are also employed. Benefit standards are relatively high, such that a single mother with two children could receive over 200,000 yen ($2,000) a month in living, housing, and educational assistance. A large number of single mother households, however, are not receiving Public Assistance even though they live below this income level. I estimate this ratio to be as high as 70 to 80 percent of single-mother households in Japan. This is probably due to the stigma attached to receiving Public Assistance, the widespread tactics by authorities to discourage application, and the fact that beneficiaries are not permitted to own cars and other assets. These tactics range from telling applicants to come back later with the correct documents, or somehow failing to give an applicant an application. Japan is definitely an exception among advanced industrialized nations in making application for Public Assistance so difficult, as well as in terms of the low ratio of those eligible who actually claim benefits (an estimated 15 percent).

The Public Assistance program was further tightened in recent years. Since 2005, an additional allowance, which single mothers with children aged fifteen or older received in addition to the regular Public Assistance payment, has gradually been phased out. From April 2007, another additional allowance for single mothers (called *boshi kasan*), received by single mothers with children aged fifteen or lower (23,100 yen or $230 for Level 1) was also abolished, and replaced with a work-promotion allowance (which is less than half of the amount of the *boshi kasan*). The reasons for this include the recession, the fluidity of employment, and the rising number of Public Assistance recipients. In addition, the Ministry of Health, Labor and Welfare argued that it was unfair to give recipients of Public Assistance an extra allowance in light of the low income of single mothers who do not receive Public Assistance. If so, however, we in turn argued, they should stop rejecting applications and make the system more accessible to those who need it. With these arguments, the goverment attempted to divide the poor, and incite conflict among different groups. There have already been a number of incidents involving death from starvation caused by rejection of applications, and forced termination of public assistance. Under Prime Minister Yukio Hatoyama, who assumed office in September 2009, the additional allowance was revived in December of that year, as had been promised in the Democratic Party of Japan's election manifesto.

Social Prejudice

Social prejudice toward single mothers has decreased over the years. Single-mother families are less frequently viewed as incomplete or defective. And divorced women are less likely to be referred to as *batsuichi*, a trendy term used in the 1990s to signify the big X (*batsu*) placed over a woman's name on the family register (*koseki*) after a divorce. In public opinion surveys, more than 50 percent of people say that divorce is a viable option if a marriage does not work out. Still, attitudes are harsher in rural areas. Single mothers who move to urban areas after a divorce do so not only to seek employment but also to escape prejudice in their hometowns. How do single mothers see themselves? While awareness fluctuates, a rising number of single mothers have a positive image of their status after a divorce. Even so, many still face prejudice and sexual harassment in the workplace and at school.

There is still a strong prejudice toward bearing a child outside of marriage (Single Mother's Forum 2003). These views are supported by the Japanese legal system, which discriminates against these children in the family register and in the civil code. According to inheritance laws in the civil code, children born to an unmarried couple or an unmarried mother are eligible to inherit only half of what "legitimate" children are entitled to. It used to be the case that the legitimacy of children had to be indicated on their birth registration forms. Perhaps this may be unthinkable in countries without a *koseki* (family register) system, but the family register form had a section to indicate whether the child was, for example, the "eldest daughter" or "second son" (for a child born in marriage), or simply "girl" or "boy" (for a child born outside of marriage)." In 2004 the form was changed to indicate "eldest daughter/ second son" regardless of the parents' marital status.

Unmarried single mothers face even stronger social discrimination than divorced mothers. Their wages are low, and their relatives often shun them. Even the tax system discriminates against them. To receive benefits, unmarried mothers may be required to answer questions, and even write down details regarding their relationship with the father of the child, as well as the background of the pregnancy. A series of lawsuits have fought for a mother's right to privacy, and some discriminatory attitudes toward unmarried mothers appear to have become less pronounced. The national network I work with began in 2007 to address issues of poverty for single mothers, as well as other groups such as the homeless, and people with disabilities. The impact of this network on the government and other political parties has been considerable, and offers hope for positive change in the future.

Notes

1. According to the report by the Ministry of Health, Labor and Welfare of its 2003 survey on single-mother households in Japan, the number of such households was estimated to be 1,225,400, but no figures were given in the Ministry's 2006 report. MHLW appears to have deemed it impossible to reach an estimate through this survey. Instead, the Ministry published the number of independent single-mother households (those who do not live with relatives) as 750,000 according to census statistics. This would increase to 1,200,000 households if dependent single-mother households were included based on the rate of cohabitation (Koseirodosho 2005, 2007).

2. The number of unmarried mothers has increased slightly, although it remains still very small. Only 2.03 percent of children are born outside of marriage (Koseirodosho 2004). While this figure has doubled as compared to twenty years ago, it is still extremely low in comparison to other countries. Although social prejudice has decreased slightly over the years, not many women give birth outside of marriage since deep-rooted legal and social discrimination still prevail.

Works Cited

Ezawa, Aya and Chisa Fujiwara. 2005. "Lone Mothers and Welfare-to-Work Policies in Japan and the United States: Toward an Alternative Perspective." *Journal of Sociology and Social Welfare* 32: 41-63.

Fujiwara, Chisa. 2005. "Hitori oya no shugyo to kaisosei" (Class aspects of work patterns among single parents). *Shakai seisaku gakkaishi* (Journal of Social Policy)13:161-75.

———. 2007. "Boshisetai no kaiso bunka—seido riyosha no tokucho kara mita seisakutaisho no meikakuka" (Class differentiation among single-mother households—distinguishing the targets of policies based on characteristics of the system's clients) *Kakei keizai kenkyu* (Research on household economics) 73:10-21.

Koseirodosho (Ministry of Health, Labor and Welfare). 2004. *Heisei jurokunen jinko dotai tokei* (2004 survey of vital statistics).

———. 2005. *Heisei jugonendo zenkoku boshisetaito chosa kekka hokokusho* (Report of the 2003 nationwide survey on single-mother households).

———. 2007. *Heisei juhachinendo zenkoku boshisetaito chosa kekka hokokusho* (Report of the 2006 nationwide survey on single-mother households).

Single Mother's Forum. 2001. "Boshi katei no nenkin kanyu chosa jittai hokokusho" (Survey on pension membership status among single-mother households).

———. 2002. "Boshi katei no shigoto to kurashi" (Work and life of single-mother households).

———. 2003. "Boshi katei no kodomotachi" (Children of single-mother households).

———. 2004. "Yoikuhi o moraimasho" (Let's get child support payment).

———. 2005. "Wakareta chichi to kodomotachi" (Divorced fathers and the children)

———. 2007. "Boshi katei no shigoto to kurashi 2" (Work and life of single-mother households 2).

The Formation and Growth of the Men's Movement

9

Kimio Ito
Translated by Kimberly Hughes

In 1991, the so-called "men's lib" movement in Japan made its formal debut, when I and four other men living in Osaka and its surrounding area, called Kansai, organized what we called the "Men's Lib Research Group (Tentative Title)." As the last part of our group's name suggests, we were at first completely unsure about how to make our claim. Of course, our work was preceded by earlier examples of men working together on sensitive gender-related issues, such as the "men's lib" allies of the women's liberationists during the 1970s, and the creation of such groups in the 1980s as Ikujiren (Child Care Hours for Men and Women Network), and another organization focused around issues specific to raising boys. These organizations were spearheaded by men who had been influenced by the women's liberation movement and feminist theory, and who wished to begin taking on the responsibilities of child rearing. Also preceding our work were groups of men who raised questions regarding a man's way of life from the perspective of human rights, including an organization working on the issues around the sex trade in Asia (Oyama and Otsuka1999).

These groups naturally gave close consideration to the hardships experienced by men, such as the reality of exceedingly long working hours. But they did not fully expose all of the problems that men faced within a society that could essentially be characterized as male supremacist. This was the task, then, that was assumed by our tentatively titled "Men's Lib Research Group": to build upon the work of previous men's groups by beginning to address and dissect the inconsistencies and contradictions facing men within this male-dominated society. In this respect our group represented a new direction in the men's movement.

Working with the Women's Movement

Insofar as the women's movement itself was the catalyst for the establishment of our group, however, it cannot be said that our movement sprang up solely

131

through the effort of men. Our activities were first launched on the occasion of a conference titled "Can Men Become Feminists?" that was sponsored by the Women's Studies Society of Japan in September 1989. The men attending this conference, most of whom were members of the Kansai branch of Ikujiren, subsequently sponsored a gathering in Osaka the following year in September 1990 that was titled "Symposium By, Of, and For Men: Living and Enjoying Ourselves Free From the Constraints of Masculinity."

Following this conference, I got together with four other male participants—a journalist, a student, a culinary researcher, and a day laborer/activist—in order to consider just how a lifestyle freed from "the constraints of masculinity" could be achieved (Menzu sentaa 2005; Ito 2005). The fact that the catalyst for our movement was our encounter with women's groups in a sense set a certain direction for our movement. In other words, all five of us shared the fundamental ethos of "freeing ourselves from the constraints of gender." Needless to say, however, not all men participating in the men's lib movement share the same philosophy. While many of them sympathize with the ideals of feminism and favor promoting greater participation by women in society, there are others who are strongly against such principles. While we therefore hold debates with regard to our differing opinions, it is important to point out that as a rule, we do not exclude or reject particular viewpoints.

Era of the "Male Problem"

Why did the men's movement come about when it did? What were the social currents at work during this particular period in time? As I have written elsewhere, I began working on what would now be called "men's studies" or "masculinity research" during the late 1970s. Around the end of 1989, I wrote a piece for the evening edition of the *Asahi shimbun* newspaper where I predicted that "we will shortly be entering an era where we will begin fully confronting the 'male problem.'" I felt sure that as men's sense of their gender identity began to waver, they would inevitably confront numerous contradictions in their lives, and that at times this would become manifested in a variety of social pathologies (Ito 1993, 1996).

Indeed, as I had envisioned, the beginning of the 1990s saw the rate of suicides, and suicide-hotline calls begin to climb among middle-aged and older men. In addition, rising numbers of indecent assaults committed by men—clearly the pathological manifestation of their inability to cultivate healthy relationships with women—also dramatically increased at this time, as did divorce rates among older couples.

I believe that one explanation for such changes may be found within the radical shifts in consciousness among women throughout the world after the early seventies, as the women's movement began to grow visible. Demands for gender equality and for equal treatment in the workplace, combined with the strengthening of social services to support working women. Moreover, injustices surrounding a social structure based on male privilege also began to be questioned. At the heart of the issue was a clear indictment of the existence of patriarchy, and all that it represented: not only the traditional familial system of control over households, but also the mechanism of male supremacy that pervaded the workplace, economy, politics, and culture.

A shift of this magnitude with regard to women's awareness and social participation resulted inevitably in the necessity for men to begin changing their ways. At issue were not only men's attitudes toward women: in essence, women were now demanding a structural change of revolutionary proportion with regard to prevailing male lifestyles, which depended on having women perform subordinate, support-level labor. My prediction at the time was that men who were unable to meet these demands for change would run up against various paradoxes: some would resort to an exaggerated assertion of outdated qualities of masculinity, while others would fall prey to severe stress as they experienced an acute loss of confidence in themselves as "men."

Men in a State of Confusion

My forecast of an approaching "era of the 'male problem'" was grounded in a basic presumption that the pending social shift would result in men's experiencing fluctuations or tremors in their heretofore rock-like self-identity. It is often said that, in male-dominated societies, men actually deal with change far less easily than women. Women, growing up in a patriarchy, learn how to survive crashing into the boundaries of gender. They've learned how to make adjustments in their own lives to male-made obstacles, and how to shift direction when necessary. For women, then, the ideas of "change" and "personal revolution" have been familiar ones.

Men in patriarchal societies, however, have never had to face gender-based barriers. For many of them, the issue has been hidden from their consciousness, and some men have continued to remain entirely unaware that patriarchal walls even exist. In a social climate and system that favors men at all stages, men can construct their lives as "men," so long as they follow the conventional pattern. Moreover, any setbacks or problems they might confront could be attributed to individual abilities or pure luck—certainly not to gender. What the shift in awareness and demands for equality among women during and after the 1980s managed to accomplish, therefore, was to introduce a fissure into this existing male life pattern. For the first time in history, men were being asked to make some significant changes.

Economic Growth and Male "Overwork"

This was not the only shift occurring, however. Given the hardship of working sixty or more hours a week required as a norm around the end of the 1970s, men themselves also began to call their own lifestyles into question. In real-life terms, overworking among men in Japan has meant that they have been robbed of their family and community lives. This has resulted in broken familial and community ties, damaged social stability, and men being unable to lead real lives of meaning and value (Ito 2003). It was in the period of the bubble economy in the mid-1980s and the burst of that bubble in 1990 that men started to become dimly aware of the inhuman reality of the lives they were leading. Thus, it was against the backdrop of women's drive to seek greater participation in society and a still vaguely conscious desire on the part of men to recapture a decent, human way of life, that the "men's problem" first surfaced and the "men's lib" movement was born.

The Lib Movement

The movement for men's liberation, born in the Kansai region, spread quickly to other parts of the country. Over fifty groups sprang up at this time, of which many were simply called "Men's Lib," while others might be called "Men's Gossip Group." The pioneering Kansai group would usually hold a meeting once every two months on a specific theme of interest, featuring a guest speaker followed by a discussion. The goal was not to arrive at some resolution or decisive conclusion, but rather to provide a forum in which participants might reexamine their "maleness" and consider how such thinking might affect their daily lives.

These activities have continued. In 2006 Otsuka and Inoue conducted a survey among members of fifty-one different men's lib groups, and in response to a question asking why the men first decided to join the movement, a large number of respondents cited having participated in the "men's seminars" put on by their local government offices. Others credited their attendance at antiviolence programs, or the existence of their own personal desires, including one respondent who cited the wish to "be freed from the burden of masculinity, and pursue a freer way of life."

With regard to the question of what they intended to take away from men's lib activities, noteworthy responses included those such as "rethinking what it means to be a man," "meeting men from other professions and age groups," "stripping myself of the armor of masculinity," and "finding my place as a man." Many respondents described typical men's lib activities as those of "gathering to chat," and cited the benefits gained from their involvement with the movement as including increased communication and understanding with other men, as well as the feeling of liberation experienced from opening up with others regarding their personal issues.

An important element of these meetings is their restriction to men only, since many men tend to fall back on formalities when women are present. This setting also affords an opportunity for men to receive feedback from others, which can help provide important new perspectives from which to reconsider their situations. This serves a function very much like that of the consciousness-raising exercises of the feminist movement during the 1960s.

The meetings have sometimes received criticism for representing nothing other than a bunch of men sitting around and licking each other's wounds, and members have remained very much aware of the potential dangers of restricting themselves to men-only groups. At times we have in fact deliberately arranged discussions that include both women and men. However, in the process of reflecting on the issues men face, I think there is an important value in having men experience sharing their thoughts among themselves, as was the case with the strategy of temporary "separatism" adopted by some women in the women's movement.

Another matter that has struck me powerfully has been the gap in consciousness existing among men of different generations. Most members of the men's lib movement in the Kansai region, including myself, are middle-aged or senior men who were born shortly after the war. This contrasts considerably with groups in Tokyo (where participants also include women) and other cities, whose founding members have included many men who tend to be younger. And while all groups have ostensibly met to discuss the matter of the "male problem," the manner in which this has been approached seems to differ considerably depending upon the age of the members in attendance. Middle-aged and senior members, for example, have tended to focus on marital relations and child rearing, and have usually framed issues within wide social contexts. Younger participants are more likely to discuss issues regarding "the opposite sex," including the "shy male lover," for example, and often discuss other matters relating to the "care of the heart."

Development of the Men's Lib Movement

While the men's lib movement had its initial beginnings in informal discussion groups, it soon expanded to encompass a broad range of activities. First among these was the idea of telephone counseling for men, inspired by similar hotlines that had been set up for women. Once established, and staffed by professionally-trained counselors, the telephone hotlines received calls not only from men but also from women who were having men-related problems. By now, this type of service for men has been established by local governments as part of their gender-equality policy programs. In a society where many men are cloaked in an outer layer of armor called masculinity, such programs convey an important message that may save lives—that it's all right for men to seek help and advice when they feel the need.

In 1995, a men's center was set up in the city of Osaka to serve as a nationwide resource center for men's groups, as well as an international point of contact representing the men's movement in Japan. It was not a large-scale facility such as some women's centers and gender equality establishments set up in Japan, but was rather a shared space in a small apartment that doubled as an office.

The following year, in 1996, a "men's festival" event was held for men and women to come together around common issues of concern. This became an annual event, featuring numerous subgroups that gathered to discuss such issues as domestic violence, couples' relationships, child rearing, fashion, the gay liberation movement, grandparenting, and issues relating to bisexual and transgendered persons. Men and women interested in men-related issues have gathered from around the country, in some years drawing as many as five hundred participants.

An issue that has been of particular interest to participants of these men's festivals, as well as the founders of the men's lib movement, has been "male violence and communication." Members of the men's lib movement have tried to address this issue by setting up communications courses that focus on expressing one's emotions and antiviolence training programs for perpetrators of domestic violence.

Recent popular television programs have touched upon issues such as divorce among older couples, men who want to get married but are unable to, and househusbands. Offerings available at bookstores—while including some conservative titles—have lately begun to include a variety of books that question the dominant lifestyle of men.

Another social phenomenon that has recently been attracting attention is that of climbing divorce rates. The serious struggles faced not only by single-mother households but also single-father households (which now number around two hundred thousand) have both become recognized as significant issues. The greatest difficulty facing single-mother households is that of economic instability, while single fathers face the problem of inexperience in housework and child rearing. At the same time, single fathers are likely to be excluded from jobs that require long hours, with the result that as with single-mother households, the rate of poverty among single-father households is high compared to two-parent households. Because of these issues, single-parent fathers have formed self-help groups. While policies have ordinarily excluded single-father households, as of June 2010 the scope of the Dependent Children's Allowance was revised to cover these families.

Fathers' participation in child care has also spread through activities sponsored by PTAs nationwide. A prime example is the "Fathers' Association," which has received official government endorsement (including a message from then Prime Minister Junichiro Koizumi at its official establishment). These have sprung up across the country.

Thus, the issues that were raised by the men's lib movement in the early 1990s are now starting to be recognized by society-at-large. I do not presume to say that it was the men's movement that prompted this new awareness. Rather, it was the social situation itself—and all of the associated symptoms therewith—that gave birth to the men's lib movement. Still, it would be possible to claim that the men's movement and research carried out in the areas of men's studies/masculinity have made men's lives more visible, through uncovering the thoughts and feelings of many men, as well as women who very strongly wished for men to change. Though the men's lib movement may have been small in scale, its activities have made an important contribution.

Works Cited

Ito, Kimio. 1993. *"Otokorashisa" no yukue* (Locating "masculinity"). Tokyo: Shinyosha.
———. 1996. *Danseigaku nyumon* (Introduction to men's studies). Tokyo: Sakuhinsha.
———. 2003. *"Otokorashisa" to iu shinwa* (The myth of "masculinity"). Tokyo: NHK shuppan.
———. 2005. "An introduction to men's studies." In *Genders, Transgenders and Sexualities in Japan*, ed. M. Maclelland and R. Dasgupta. London: Routledge.
Menzu sentaa (Men's Center Japan) 2005. *Danjo kyodo sankaku de hirogeru otoko no ikikata* (Gender equality and the opportunity for expanding men's lives). Osaka: Menzu sentaa.
Otsuka, Takao and Miku Inoue. 2006. "Dansei undo guruupu no katsudo to kadai—chukan hokoku" (Interim report of activities and issues within the men's movement). *Butsudai shakaigaku* (Bukkyo University Sociology) 30.
Oyama, Haruhiko and Takao Otsuka. 1999. "Nihon dansei undo no ayumi 1: men's ribu no tanjo." (Tracing the men's movement in Japan: No. 1: the birth of men's lib." *Nihon jendaa kenkyu* (Japan gender research) 2.

My Life as a Househusband

Masaki Matsuda
Translated by Kimberly Hughes

I first decided to seek child care hours because I had made an agreement with my pharmacist wife, that, once we married, we would both work outside our home—whether full time or part time—while also dividing responsibilities for housework and child care. When our son was born in July 1992, I was working at a small chemical firm with about forty employees. This was the same year that the Child Care Leave Law came into force, allowing either the father or mother to take child-care leave for one year after the child's birth. My wife took six months of child-care leave, and then, since both of us wanted to continue working, we decided to put him into a daycare center. My wife's commute from home to work was one hour and fifteen minutes, while mine was about five minutes longer. Since my wife had already taken child-care leave, I decided that I should be the one to take our son to and from the daycare center every day. On mornings the baby was cranky, I would often arrive at work late; and when the baby was sick, I would have to take the day off from work. My allotted paid leave time was therefore soon used up entirely, and so I decided to apply for child care hours in order to cover the time spent traveling to the daycare center.

The Labor Standards Law enacted in 1947 specified that, "In addition to allotted rest hours, women with infants less than one year of age are allowed two periods of at least thirty minutes per day to devote to child care." In order to broaden the law to include men, in 1980, Kiyoshi Masuno founded the Ikujiren organization. He also wanted the law lengthened beyond one year. In 1986, Kenji Tajiri, one of the members of Ikujiren (Child Care Hours for Men and Women Network), began a five-year "child-care strike" at the oil company where he worked, resulting in his obtaining child-care leave in order to take his children to and from day care. Since he had begun his "strike" prior to the passage of the Child Care and Family Care Leave Law, his repeated late arrival at work meant that he could possibly have been fired. Tajiri got around this, however, by terming his action a "child-care strike"—a very clever strategy since it is illegal to fire an employee who is striking, and thus he was also able to gain support from his union.

I first heard Tajiri speak about his experience at an Ikujiren symposium held in Tokyo on Father's Day, 1995. He encouraged me to speak up at work about my desire to be involved with child care, and I realized at this time that he was a role model for me. I immediately joined Ikujiren and then wrote a letter shortly thereafter to my boss requesting that I be allowed to take child-care hours. At first, the response was, "There is no precedent, and so your request must be denied." But I persisted, and I was finally given approval in March 1995, by which time our son was two years old. I believe that my request was eventually granted because my desire to participate in the rearing of my child was both genuine and strong. I also emphasized that the child care period would last no longer than ten years. I believe that the child-care leave was finally approved because a small firm could not afford to lose an employee familiar with the company's affairs.

The normal starting time at my office was 8:45 a.m.; I was allowed to arrive at the office by 10:15 a.m. I also refrained from working overtime and from going out drinking with my colleagues, and began leaving the office just after 5 p.m. each day. I also received a compensatory reduction in wages in the amount of 30,000-40,000 yen ($300-$400) per month. I felt that what I had done was perfectly normal. Hence, I was considerably surprised, later, to be featured on television and in newspaper articles. Looking back now, I realize that I was encouraged to work on behalf of Ikujiren in order to support other men who found themselves in a situation like mine.

But not all people were supportive of my behavior. My colleagues' attitudes, for example, turned quite frosty. Some of my superiors and co-workers asked, "Why is it that you are coming in late to work? Why don't you make your wife quit her job and take care of the housework and child care?" or "What has happened to your dignity as a man?" or "Are you really serious about your work?" My department head also was criticized by his counterparts in other departments, who said things like, "What's wrong with your department—do you have a little too much time on your hands or something?"

My relatives also showed no understanding of my life. After they saw me profiled on an NHK (Japan Broadcasting Corporation) television program, they made comments like, "Do you mean to bring shame upon the Matsuda family?" From my perspective, it was precisely because of the birth of our child that I felt I wanted to slow down and spend more time with my wife and child, and that, once my son was grown, I could devote more time to my work. I was thinking in long-range terms about my life over the coming ten-year period. No concept of a "work-life balance" existed at the time, however, and so others simply had no understanding of what I was trying to do.

After I was granted child-care hours, I was able to give my son breakfast and get to the office with plenty of extra time, even if there were occasional mornings when we couldn't get to the daycare center on time. And since I left the office right on schedule, I was able to share the responsibilities of dinner preparation, laundry, and housecleaning with my wife. Of course, I could have left our child for longer hours in daycare in order to focus on my own career advancement, but this would have been hard on a small child, and so I felt my plan was good for my son as well as myself.

Soon, however, I began to realize that taking an hour-and-a-half per day of child-care hours from work amounted to little more than making a small adjustment in the "work-life balance" of my daily life. And so, after having worked for ten years at the same chemical firm, in September 1997 I decided to quit my job and work part-time several days a week at a delivery collection center and a bread baking factory, both located close to our home. In my view, there was nothing wrong with a man giving up a full-time career in order to work closer to home. My wife agreed with this decision, and she also noted, "I might decide someday to return to work in the private sector, or to go for a graduate degree. In that case, I'll be counting on you to support me!"

It was in this way, then, that I took on the challenge of undertaking a work life organized around the need to take care of our child. While my life had previously revolved around my job, and the daily commute between home and work, I now began to get involved with activities at my son's school, including patrol duty when a suspicious individual was seen lurking around the school grounds. My life changed drastically; I had become a male *shufu* or househusband. My son, however, did not view this advent as unusual, since I had been for so many years taking him to the daycare center and picking him up, as well as observing his school classes.

As a househusband, I could have earned a partial tax refund by becoming a dependent of my wife, who continued to work as a public servant. But I decided against this, since I wanted to be able to make my own national pension and health insurance payments as an ordinary member of society. I felt none of the weakened social relations or sense of isolation sometimes attributed to househusbands, which I can explain only by noting that my spouse and I were not dependent upon one another. My independence helped me maintain my sense of personal identity.

While I made choices rare for a Japanese man, I have felt no particular sense of conflict over these decisions. I grew up in a traditional family: my father was an architect during the period of Japan's high economic growth, and he traveled very often all over the country; my mother was a full-time housewife. While I was growing up, I was not interested in housework or raising children, and as a young adult, I had never heard about men's studies. Hence, my unusual choice of lifestyle cannot be attributed either to the influence of my parents or to my sensitivity to gender bias. The major influence on my life, I believe, has been my wife. We met during our university days, when she was very clear that she wanted to work throughout her entire life, even if she married and bore children. Choosing to spend my life with her, then, made my subsequent decisions seem completely natural. I feel very fortunate to have married her, since I have been able to enjoy far greater freedom than most Japanese men.

Working for Change

When I first joined Ikujiren in 1995, I wanted support for seeking release hours from work for child care. Subsequently, my scope of interest has broadened to encompass such issues as male identity, more specifically, what it means to live as a man. One serious problem I have had to think about is the high rate of male suicide—numbering over twenty-three thousand in 2008—and the related problem of *karoshi* (death from overwork). I have come to think that fathers' involvement in caring for their children can provide an invaluable opportunity for men to recognize the value of their own lives, and of the value of life in general. Yet in fact, very few fathers in Japan take part in child care and child rearing.

Enacted in 1992, the Child Care Leave Law allowed for both mothers and fathers to take leave, but even in 2008, only 1.23 percent of male company employees actually took child-care leave. A major obstacle lies in the attitudes of men themselves, who have been brought up to believe that for a man, work must take precedence over one's family and one's personal life. These ideas are taught to male children, consciously and unconsciously. They learn that being absent is a bad thing, and they earn awards for perfect attendance at school. Then as adult males, many will not take even a single day off to attend their wives during childbirth. While some companies have now introduced the concept of flextime, most continue to require that employees come into the office every day. Unpaid overtime work (*saabisu zangyo*) is still prevalent, and some firms still offer their own version of the "perfect attendance award." Moreover, the heads of many Japanese companies, usually men in their fifties and sixties, are generally not receptive to men taking child-care leave. A few venture capital firms, with presidents in their twenties who are fathers themselves, have begun to implement proactive child-care leave policies for their male employees.

Since 2004, I have served in Kanagawa Prefecture as a member of the Association to Promote Policies Assisting the Raising of the Next Generation. We have been working to urge the prefectural government to adopt a "child-rearing promotion measure," which will give first priority to firms with proactive child-care policies when considering which firms to do business with. In addition, we have been trying to persuade companies to become more aware of the need for corporate social responsibility. Finally, we have aimed to encourage business owners to introduce specific action plans that make it easier for both female and male employees to take child-care leave.

Along with another member of Ikujiren, Minoru Omoishi, I have joined the Committee to Promote Child Rearing among Fathers which has been organized by the All Japan Federation of Municipal Health Centers (an organization affiliated with the Ministry of Health, Labor and Welfare). The committee's activities have included creating an educational pamphlet for fathers, and contracting with the Isehara Municipal Health Center to offer a course for fathers five times per year through the parental education program. Since it is too difficult to reach fathers directly through their workplaces, we have attempted to use these health center courses as a vehicle to educate fathers who are working in the corporate world.

The Ikujiren group is also involved in outreach programs aimed at teenage boys and male college students. In order for young men to become involved in the care of children, they need to see alternative models of masculinity, different examples of fathers and husbands. Most men who approach Ikujiren seeking support are in their late twenties, thirties, or even forties. While such men are certainly able to enlighten themselves if they desire to do so, I believe that it is still more important to reach the younger generation. In my own case, I did not change my ideas until I met my wife at age twenty-one—but even this was rather late. I believe that young boys, even still in high school, need to think about what it means to be a decent man, and how they want to live their lives as human beings.

For the past several years, I have been teaching a special class at a local public high school. Male students sometimes come to me for advice concerning sex. Although junior high and high school-aged boys definitely need to be educated about sex, no provision has been made for such education. I also visit high schools in my neighborhood to speak about my own experience, and to impress upon these future parents the importance of the task of raising children. I have also been invited to speak as a guest lecturer at several universities. Through these experiences, I have come to note the glaring omission of sex education for young people. I find it extremely worrisome that students may be getting information about sex from adult videos. Date rape is already a problem among university students and may also be found among high school students, in all cases a reflection of the negative and violent images of masculinity prevalent in film and television.

Finally, despite the efforts of Ikujiren since its inception in 1980 to expand the provision for child-care hours in the Labor Standards Law to include men, it continues to be restricted to women only. Every May Day, Ikujiren continues to hand out flyers calling for child-care leave to be extended to men. Since Ikujiren no longer draws young members, the organization has remained stable. Many men come by only once, and never return. I suspect also that some men do no more than read our website. I think that's completely fine: Ikujiren will welcome all those who come to the organization with a problem. Unfortunately, however, the organization does not exist outside Japan's major cities, where there is a growing need for counseling resources for men. The widespread manifestations of domestic violence and male suicide, for example, call attention to the "male problem" in Japanese society. From my perspective, to deal with these issues, I see an increased need for qualified feminist counselors—both male and female.

Men, such as myself, who choose to become househusbands, are still a rarity in Japan—about 0.4 percent of all married men. In a 2004 survey conducted among high school students, just 12.5 percent of male and 4.7 percent of female students said they confided their problems to their fathers (the figures were 35 and 42 percent in the case of mothers) (Meiji Yasuda seikatsu fukushi kenkyujo 2004). My son, who is now seventeen years old and in high school, seems to feel comfortable coming to me for advice about college and career plans, and I think this is at least in part due to the fact that I have been involved on a day-to-day basis in his care and upbringing. As for his views at this point on the matter of gender roles, it's difficult for me to gauge, but I fondly remember a Father's Day card he gave me when he was in elementary school. Below the drawing he made of my face he wrote, "Thanks, Dad, for taking me to the amusement park the other day. It was really fun!" More striking was the message addressed to his mother on the same card, "Thank you Mom for working hard all the time for Dad and me." To me this showed that my son regarded his mother not in the limited role of "mother" but as the "family breadwinner," and seemed to accept this fact in stride.

I have come to believe it is almost hopeless to try to change the attitudes held by men of my generation of older on issues concerning gender roles. My hope lies in my son's generation, and I view it as my responsibility to endeavor to influence these young people so that they develop more flexible attitudes than their fathers and grandfathers, and feel free to pursue a variety of lifestyles, no longer constrained by traditional views and practices.

Works Cited

Meiji Yasuda seikatsu fukushi kenkyujo (Meiji Yasuda Institute of Life and Wellness). 2004. *Kokosei ishiki ni kansuru ankeeto chosa* (Survey of attitudes among high school students).

IV
CHANGING SEXUALITIES

Defining Lesbian Partnerships

Saori Kamano and Diana Khor

To fully appreciate how lesbians in Japan define and live their lives as couples, it is important to understand the current social and legal environment in which lesbians find themselves. Public opinion surveys show that more people express negative attitudes than neutral or positive ones when explicitly asked about same-sex sexual relationships. As in other countries, more men hold negative attitudes toward such relationships compared to women, and younger people are more open to same-sex relationships and have more knowledge about multiple sexualities. For example, in response to a question in a 2000 national survey on what respondents think about same-sex sexual relationships, slightly over 50 percent of all women and over 60 percent of men expressed negative opinions, but the corresponding figures for women and men in their 20s were only about 20 percent and 30 percent (Iwai and Sato 2002). However, there is some indication that more people express discomfort with same-sex *couples*. For example, two out of three respondents said that they felt a lot or some resistance toward "same-sex couples, such as homosexuals and lesbians" in a 2004 survey (Mainichi shimbunsha jinkomondai chosakai 2005).[1] One cannot tell if such opinions—whether positive or negative—indicate that people are aware of the existence of lesbians and gay men in the abstract or as real people among whom they live. This is because of the low visibility of lesbian, bisexual, and gay people, which is reinforced by the homosocial characteristics of Japanese society. A homosocial and gendered society tolerates or even encourages same-sex socializing and "absorbs" cohabiting lesbian couples into the mainstream world by considering them as friends or roommates, regardless of whether they have the desire to appear as heterosexuals or not.

The low visibility also means a general lack of social support and affirmation, which is aggravated by the lack of legal rights for non-heterosexuals. "Registered marriage" is the only form of couple relationship legally recognized in Japan. Indeed, Article 24 of the Constitution states that "marriage should be based only on the mutual consent of both sexes." There is no partnership law or domestic partnership system for either heterosexual or homosexual relationships. To obtain legal recognition for their relationship, which includes tax benefits, medical benefits, and inheritance rights, same-sex partners may enter into an adoptive relationship *(yoshien-gumi)* or draw up notarized deeds *(koseishosho)* (Maree 2004; Kazama 2003).

Upon a successful adoption, a "couple" would be formally considered a parent and a child, with the rights and obligations expected in any parent-child relationship. In the *koseki* (the family register), the older one would be the adoptive parent and the younger one the adopted child, and the adopted child would take on the surname of the parent. The adoptive law also states that an adoptive relationship is invalid if either party is unwilling to be in a parent-child relationship. If the two parties have a sexual relationship, which is highly likely for same-sex partners, the legal adoptive relationship may be considered invalid. Some lesbians and gay men also dislike the idea of being in a parent-child relationship with their partner because it is against their idea of "partnership." Partners entering into an adoptive relationship, which essentially creates a new family unit, have to be aware that it contributes to the continuation of the family household and the register system and does not necessarily sever the ties, and hence rights and obligations, of the adopted child to his/her existing parents (see Otsuka 1994).

Drawing up notarized deeds involves the registration of various documents at a notary office, including, for example, individual wills and testaments, a joint living agreement that outlines "how partners wish to conduct their personal affairs in times of emergency or death" (Maree 2004, 545). Maree (2004) notes that such agreements are situated outside the family register system and are employed by those who do not wish to enter the institutions of marriage and family. However, it remains to be seen how effective the agreement would be in an actual situation. If one partner is unconscious in a hospital, and the medical practitioners, following usual practice, say that only family members can see the patient, the agreement might provide a solid basis for the other partner to insist that he/she is in a position to see the patient (Nagayasu 2002). Nevertheless, since medical practitioners are not obliged legally to follow the agreement, they may refuse such a request (Tanamura 1997; see also Kamano 2004a).

All things considered, lesbian couples are rendered invisible in Japanese mainstream society and do not have legal rights or social support. In such a context, how do lesbians define and understand their partnerships and live their lives in the larger society? What are the concerns, gratification, and implications? We will explore these questions after explaining the interview process.

Interviews

The following analysis is based on interviews conducted by the first author in 2002 with twenty-one women who were cohabiting with a woman partner. There were nine couples among them and the interviews were conducted with both partners together, whereas the remaining three interviews were conducted with individuals. The interviewees were recruited through personal connections, direct solicitation at various events the first author attended, correspondence with people who had posted messages on Internet bulletin boards, and through these people's introductions.[2]

The loosely structured interviews lasted between one and a half to four hours, covering a range of issues related to the lives of the couples, including the history of their relationship, housework division and practice, management of household finances and relationships with families, friends and colleagues, as well as each person's experiences related to being or becoming a lesbian and experiences in lesbian communities. Questions about their own images or views of lesbian couples were not asked, but the interview participants quite spontaneously shared their opinions about images of lesbian couples and issues involved in forming a relationship. They were asked one question about how their situation and daily lives might be similar to or different from those of gay male couples, but many spontaneously mentioned lesbian partnerships in contrast to gay male partnerships as a topic of its own or in the context of conversing on other issues. Further, although no questions were asked about how lesbian relationships compare to heterosexual relationships, many commented on the latter.

Defining Lesbian Partnership

From the way they consider their relationships either in terms of an ideal or in comparison with gay male and heterosexual relationships, the interviewees appear to be quite deliberately shaping and constructing "lesbian partnership," not only their own, but as a category of relationship. They define lesbian partnership through marking its differences from gay and heterosexual relationships with respect to the basis of partnership, equality and freedom in the relationship, and length of the relationship.[3]

The Bases of Partnership

In discussing commitment to one partner ("monogamy"), the (non-) significance of sex in the relationship, and the effort they put into sustaining a relationship, the women often contrast lesbian with gay male relationships. They comment frequently that sex is a central part of gay male relationships or that gay men in general consider sex as an important component of a relationship. In contrast, for lesbian couples, the sexual part is not as important and most lesbian relationships begin as friends while gay men's relationships begin from "the body."

Nozomi compares lesbian and gay male relationships as follows:

"They [gay men] have totally different ways of constructing a relationship. Women tend to want to be monogamous. Even if there are gay couples in long-term relationships, they tend to practice "polygamy." For women, some couples in long-term relationships say at times that they might want to try "a polygamous relationship," but when they try, they break up."

". . . They [gay men] can have a second lover, sex friends, and so on, a lot more easily than lesbian couples can. On the other hand, I do meet quite a lot of lesbians who actually are asexual."

"Seiko [Nozomi's partner] has an identity as a lesbian, and yet is closer to asexual, but there are others who are asexual without identifying themselves as lesbians. If you think about being asexual in the context of a lesbian continuum, then, partnership between women can be established regardless of their sexual orientation."

"I think this is something that is fundamentally different from gay male couples. For gay male couples, the erotic part of a relationship is extremely important."

Similar observations are made by Yasuko and Mizuho.

Mizuho: "I think how gays begin a relationship is different. They start from physical things."

Yasuko: "Yes, I hear that there are not so many people [gay men] who would develop from being friends to lovers."

Mizuho: "There are many lesbians who start [a relationship] from being friends. I hear that a lot more often."

Mizuho: "Also they [gay men] do not live together, since they instinctively know that it will not continue. If they live together, they cannot have fun. And also it would be difficult to break up. So they do not live together to begin with."

In some way, lesbian relationships are seen as similar to heterosexual relationships, in contrast to gay male relationships. Some explicitly state that *erosu* ("the erotic") is not an important part of their (lesbian) partnership, and they consider the latter a family-like relationship. One interviewee, for example, invokes heterosexual couples, noting that heterosexuals do not break up just because they do not have sex. Instead, intimate feelings dissociated from sex are possible, and important.

Seiko: "For heterosexual couples, too, the nature of a relationship usually changes over time. Even if one does not feel a strong sexual attraction to the partner, they do not necessarily break up. Of course, some do break up, but not necessarily so, and some might have lovers outside, etc. That is because they emphasize a relationship as a family. . . . But for me, I tend to find more meaning in family-like relationships or couple relationships based on other things, like values and interests, the relationship that matures over time, you know. So I feel that there is something wrong with separating just because you do not feel sexually attracted to the partner or the partner has changed appearance over time, and so on. And I don't think I would do that."

At the same time, some point to the negative side of heterosexual relationships, suggesting that they can be maintained without love.

Keiko: "I had thought I could just meet someone through *omiai*[4] and get married, before I met her. *Miai* was no problem for me. There's no need to like the person to marry him."

Nozomi has this to say:

"Our relationship is not protected by anything. What we have is just our "relationship." In that sense, it is very fragile. Without effort, it can easily break."

Nozomi refers directly to the effort lesbians put into building and sustaining a relationship, implying perhaps that precisely because it is fragile, it is also precious. The idea of "fragility" seems logically connected to what some perceive as the instability of lesbian relationships, that they do not last. However, when talking about it, the interviewee participants do not mention the lack of support for their being lesbians. Indeed, some couples regard getting help negatively, and do not seek or obtain support from others. Instead of focusing on the lack of support, our interview participants often refer to *gyokai* ("the lesbian world") in discussing the instability in lesbian relationships. For example, Michiyo makes the following remark:

"In 'this world,' the rate of getting together and breaking up is really high. And most likely, the women who are together today, those who've gotten into a relationship only recently, have known each other from before."[5]

Similarly, Mizuho sees the situation as follows:

"Relationships come and go too quickly in places like [Shinjuku] nichome,[6] and it is probably because the relationship takes the form of romantic love before the women get to know each other. That is not good."

Yasuko: "I guess people do not endure at all these days. Endure and tolerate, you know."
Mizuho: "Yes, if you really love that person, you would."
Yasuko: "But they think that even if they break up, they can find another partner easily."

The explanation strikes us as quite conventional, little different from the way an average person in society talks about problems with (heterosexual) relationships and the increase in the divorce rate today.

Nozomi: "As long as people are just getting together and then breaking up, the societal view of lesbians and gays—that we are just after love affairs and sex—will not change."
Seiko: "There are many of us who do not think so and who are serious about having a relationship."
Nozomi: "I assume that the people you have been interviewing are seriously constructing their relationships. On the one hand, there are people like that, but on the other hand, the tendency [of easily breaking up] stands out."

Despite the fact that the women imply their relationships are short-lived, they seem to think that gay men's relationships are even more so:

Keiko: ". . .My acquaintance, who is seeing a person in his fifties with a wife and children. . .They have been seeing each other for two years, and I heard that it is kind of long for men."

At the same time, no interview participant directly compares gay and lesbian relationships in terms of length and stability.

Equality

So far, the narratives convey that while lesbian relationships might have their problems, they are superior in various ways to heterosexual and gay male relationships. The interviewees are affirmative in particular about the equality in lesbian partnerships. There seems to be an almost immediate association of lesbian partnership with equality by virtue of its consisting of two women. They suggest, indeed assert, that the relationship ought to be equal.

In referring to inequality in the division of housework among most heterosexual couples, Seiko said, "It is such a waste to follow the way heterosexual couples divide housework when you can be so equal between two women." Mizuho does not do a lot of housework herself, but she affirms the possibility and value of equality:

". . .I don't do housework much now, but I can do it if I have time, and I do not approach it with the attitude that takes for granted the housework she does. I feel that if it is impossible to do it, there is no need to force it. And I do things whenever I can, like washing dishes, or cleaning the bathtub. And I never complain if she does not do the work. It is because I can also do the work myself; since we are both women, we both can do the housework, and we both know the burden of the work. There is a big difference between having housework done for you when one is fully aware of how much work it takes, and when one just takes everything for granted. For us, whoever does the work will be thanked and we are always conscious of the fact that whoever is doing it is the person who can do the work at that moment. I think all these are advantages over being with a man."[7]

Here, Mizuho gives a coherent analysis of the "advantages" of a lesbian relationship over a heterosexual relationship, from the perspective of a woman. She emphasizes the "spirit" of equality, rather than an actual 50-50 division, and appreciation and recognition of the amount of work that housework involves.

The understanding of equality is also expressed in relative or indirect terms, and in contrast to gay male relationships. The general understanding is that gay men tend to engage in role-playing behaviors and that there are many gay male couples who do not have an equal relationship, as indicated by some addressing their partners as *okusan* (meaning "a wife," but literally a person "inside" the house), an extremely high level of financial dependency of one on the other, or being in an adoptive relationship.

Seiko describes what she found on gay couples' Internet sites. She notices the following patterns: a big age difference between partners; a partner telling the other that he does not have to work, cook, or do anything but can just stay home; a richer person adopting a younger one; a person paying off a debt of 20-30 million yen (about $167,000 to $250,000, at the December 2002 rate) for his partner, and so on.

Nozomi also says:

"Many long-term [gay] couples have gone through an adoption process. Since men are in a better economic condition than women, they adopt young men whom they fancy, and just devote themselves to them."

Seiko continues on this point:

"These are quite rare among women. It is more common [for women] to want to have equal relationships. Of course, there are some women who do financially take care of the other [partner], but such cases are rare. In that case, the economic basis of a relationship is close to what a man and a woman have [in their relationship], but for women, both need to work in order to survive."

Indeed, in response to a question about the possibility of adoption or drawing up a notarized deed, a few women say that it does not matter to them since they just make ends meet, and have no property or extra money to be concerned about.

Implied in these narratives is that the deliberate effort lesbians put into constructing a relationship has a basis in necessity as well as commitment to equality. They recognize gender inequality in society, and also express a sense of woman-identification. Interview participants also directly comment on the inequality they perceive in heterosexual relationships. Namie, who works for customers in their homes, has this to say:

> "The customers I deal with are mostly newly married couples, or the wife is pregnant, and the couple is buying a new condo. Those people make me mad. Those husbands address the wives 'hey.'"

Namie adds that those in their early thirties are the worst:

> ". . .those working men are so obnoxious: [It is as if they are saying that] I work like a dog and I finally got this condo, so you stay home, and just raise the kids. . .the type of attitude they have."

Individuality and Independence

Resistance against "merging" or "fusion" with one's partner, a phenomenon frequently commented on in extant literature (see, for example, Krestan and Bepko 1980), is also expressed alongside the emphasis on equality. The desire and the struggle for "individuality" in a relationship, and the emphasis on individual identity or one's existence as an individual, are expressed very directly. The idea is that even though they are in a relationship, each person is an individual. They express strong resistance against being treated or thought of as a unit with their partner. In addition, they also react negatively against other couples they perceive as being too attached to each other—as "sticking together" excessively. Such "merging" is seen to result in a woman losing her sense of individuality.

> Aya: "There are people who would say 'my so and so' [about her partner], like people in male-female relationships do. You know, I would listen to her say something thinking that it was her opinion, and then find out that she was just speaking on her partner's behalf."

In response to a question asking whether she has always wished to live with someone, Ikumi says:

"Yes, I did have such wishes. But it was not like becoming a 'set' with someone. Each person is an individual and I question the fact of being a set with another person. At the same time, I also feel it is quite lonely to live alone throughout your life. So I do think that it is my ideal to cooperate with someone I love and live with."

Even when she is referring to the meaning of her relationship, she emphasizes that it is not good to think that she and her partner are complete only as a unit. Similarly, when asked if they have thought about drawing up a contract (notarized deed) for their relationship or considered adult adoption, Akane responds as follows:

"Not at all. Basically, we are separate. We are separate human beings. That is true for our money, too, though we do usually have dinner together."

However, what many lesbians observe in other lesbians is far from the independent ideal. When talking about their general impression of the couples they encounter in places like a community space for sexual minority women (SPACE, hereafter) and in Shinjuku ni-chome, these women note, in a negative tone, that other couples tend to be fused and emphasize that they do not want to be that way themselves. Namie, Mika, Seiko, Nozomi, and Kanako share their observations and experiences, including how others have treated them as "couples." The picture of "couples" that emerges suggests excessive attachment ("too sticky"), excessive public display of affection, lack of individuation to the point that one cannot talk to a person without her partner's permission, and expectations that partners would take primary care of each other under any circumstances.

One can feel palpably Namie and Mika's frustration at not being taken as individuals in some lesbian events they have attended:

Namie: "I thought the couples we saw at SPACE are "sticky" in front of people.... I think, even in comparison to 'regular' couples."

Namie recounts her recent experience at one of the events:

Namie: "Other couples are really stuck together. And when Mika and I were separately talking to different people, I was asked if my partner was not there that day. I pointed out to her that she was over there, and then the woman said, 'Oh, you are sitting separately?'"

Mika: "Right, I've had similar experiences. They would ask if it is okay that I am talking to someone without her presence.... Also, even when I am talking to a friend at SPACE, others think that we are a couple."

Namie: "Yes, there was something like that the other day."

Mika: " . . . we tend to think of ourselves as individuals, so even if something gets communicated to one of us, it does not mean that it will get communicated to the other. Because of their assumptions, people are surprised when some miscommunication occurs and would ask us why [such miscommunication could happen]."

Mika: "So people around us think that the two of us are 'one,' but we think of ourselves as independent individuals and we are attending these events as individuals [rather than as a couple]. So I feel like saying, don't keep putting us together."

Mika and Namie do have friends like them:

Mika: "The couple whom we are close to, Aya and Kanako, aren't like that . . . and we both agreed that we had not seen any other couples like that [i.e. who are not excessively attached to each other] until we met each other."

Aya and Kanako share their view on the same issue:

Aya: "Kanako and I like the other couple [Mika and Namie] because they do not display their affection in front of others and also they do not speak on behalf of each other, unlike heterosexual couples . . . In that sense, they are independent and that is what I like about them."

Kanako: "We like Mika and Namie because they don't treat us as a unit —we could independently relate to either of them."

Kanako also makes the following specific comment:

"I really do not like that. Once we let others know that we are a couple, then they started treating us as a unit. If a person was talking to Aya, she would try to be considerate and talk to me too. I do not want that type of consideration. If she wants to talk to Aya, go head and talk! No need to mind me."

One may observe that an attempt to involve partners in a conversation, particularly when they are sitting close by, does not violate social etiquette. The strong reactions we see here suggest that such a pattern of interaction is only one example of a general atmosphere that does not allow partners in a relationship to socialize or identify themselves as individuals. Nozomi, who organizes some of these events, has many opportunities to observe couples and she corroborates Kanako's and Aya's observations noted above, saying that it is difficult to make friends once one is in a relationship:

"There are in fact couples who don't want anyone to talk to either of them individually. There are people like that, so guarded. On our side, we have no such intention [of splitting them or grabbing her partner], yeah, we are not at all interested in your lover, but if it [i.e. any attempt to interact with the lover as an individual] is interpreted as such, it becomes quite difficult to start a conversation. If I talk to one of them and not to her lover, then, it is not good. So we always have to be careful in interacting with couples."

The observations and ideas about how partners are perceived already touch on how lesbians live their lives as partners in the lesbian community. The next questions to pursue are how lesbians live their lives in the mainstream society, how their partnership is viewed, and how they relate to each other as partners in heteronormative settings.

Living Life as a Couple

The homosocial nature of Japanese society, particularly for women, makes it possible, even easy, for two lesbian partners to "pass" as close friends. The women interviewed observe that physical closeness between persons of the same sex, especially women, is less stigmatized than in the West.

Our interview participants give many examples of this, and many contrast the ease of passing for lesbians with the difficulty of passing for gay men. "Passing" is discussed in both a positive and a negative way, the former consisting in convenience and avoidance of trouble, and the latter lack of recognition, as no matter what they say, they are thought of only as good friends.

The convenience in passing includes the ease of finding a room to share or traveling together when women do not make known the nature of their relationship. Here are some comments by Michiyo and Sachiko:

Michiyo: "Things like social dance, too. When women dance together, people do not look that much, but since it is very rare for men to dance together, people do react."

Sachiko: "Especially in Japan, we can take trips together and no one gives us strange looks at a hotel or *ryokan* (Japanese inn)."

Michiyo: "Regardless of one's sexual orientation, I think women have a higher degree of freedom. Even if we live together, no one says anything."

Michiyo: "For women, we can eat out together, hold hands, and so on."

Sachiko: "Yes, Asian cultures are mostly like that. Men together, women together, etc. Unlike in most Western societies, it is not so common to have male-female couples [socializing together]. So in that way, we have it easy."

Michiyo: "In renting our place, each of us needed to have a guarantor but other than that, no problem. I guess it might be easier for two women to rent a place compared to two men."

The ease of passing is reinforced by conventional assumptions about women's need for company, inability to be on their own, or the idea that it is not safe for women to be alone.

> Michiyo: "Actually, when you see two men together, people do wonder. But when it comes to two women together, people can say that since a woman would be lonely on her own, they are staying together."

Sachiko elaborates on this point:

> "My parents, too, when they find out that Michiyo is not around and that I am alone at home on a particular day, they ask, 'Are you okay? You have to be careful,' and so on. They worry. It seems they think that since I am on my own it is better to have this 'friend' around so that they can feel safer about me. It seems easy for them to accept it. I don't think we have been perceived in any strange manner."

Some also refer to the general image some Japanese people have about lesbian couples or lesbians. Unless one party dresses like a man, people do not recognize the relationship at all.

> Mika: "I am not sure if people knew about us in school. Our school was a girls' high school and maybe it was just in our school—we could kind of be intimate with one another and hold hands, even when we walked around town, we held hands, and that was just understood as being close. Also, parents, too, they are simple-minded, or do not want to believe, so even if we are being intimate, they just keep seeing us as close friends. If one of us had gone around wearing men's clothes, like those shirts or something, then, it might have been different."

While the women do appreciate the ease of passing, they are also ambivalent about it. When they do want to tell that they are a couple or partners, or want to be recognized as such, the ease of passing can backfire and become frustrating. For example, Emiko has told her parents that she likes women, and they seemed, at that time, to have understood it. However, recently, even when she visits her parents with her partner Akane, her parents ask her to seriously think about marriage. Emiko is not the only target—her parents have begun pressuring her partner, Akane, as well.

> Emiko: "These days, they pretend that they have forgotten all about it, and keep asking me when I am getting married."
> Akane: "It is as if they are saying that we should stop our relationship."
> Interviewer: "You mean they think (this relationship) will end eventually."
> Akane: "Yes, exactly. Stop this type of 'playing around with a friend . . .'"

Emiko: "Yes, it is like saying, 'haven't you had enough?' . . . I did tell
them and I thought they understood, but they pretend that they have
forgotten about it."

Similarly, Mayumi has been living with her partner for almost nine years,
and when the partner's mother passed away a few years ago, all the relatives
expected and assumed that she would go back to live with her father. Their
assumption was that since the person she was living with was a woman, and
therefore just a friend or roommate, she would of course return "home" to
help her family.

The Characterizations of Lesbian Relationships:
Interpretation and Implications

We have seen how the interview participants define and live their partnerships. The thoughts and emotions they shared through the interviews indicate that they were very conscious of their relationships: they did not take
their own partnership or lesbian partnerships in general for granted, and
had put much effort in constructing and maintaining their relationships.
They carefully delineated "lesbian relationships" by identifying the differences from gay male relationships, and differences from as well as similarities to heterosexual relationships. Through this process, they painted a vivid
picture of lesbian partnership, the ideal and the frustrating, and the ease and
difficulty of being in a lesbian relationship in "the community" as well as in
mainstream society. We would not say that our interviewees constructed
lesbian relationships through reacting against gay male and heterosexual
relationships; the similarities they saw with heterosexual relationships, and
indeed, their conventional take on endurance and family indicated otherwise. Instead, we detect a strong sense of "woman-identification" embedded in all these ideas and experiences, which is important in helping us
understand more deeply lesbian partnership in Japan.

Our interview participants suggested that being women shapes how
they relate to each other, and what they expect from a relationship with
a woman. That they saw only differences from gay male relationships but
noticed some similarities between heterosexual and lesbian relationships
could mean that they perceive or experience more affiliation with women,
heterosexual or lesbian, than with gay men. This affiliation is constituted
by recognition of gender inequality in society, which has left lesbians less
financially secure than gay men, and with fewer resources to use as a source
of power, and of inequality in relationships, appreciating the work that
women do on a daily basis to maintain a relationship and a home. We may

even detect a certain latent feminism among them, especially in their discussion of equality in lesbian partnerships that they held to be superior to both gay male and heterosexual partnerships, and connected to this, the ideal of independence and individuality, which some adamantly defended as what lesbian partnerships ought to be based on.

If the previous observation is accurate, how can we make sense of lesbian couples who seem to be overly attached to each other, hence violating the ideal our interviewees have about lesbian partnership? We'd propose that both are comprehensible if we understand our interviewees' ideas and lives as a resistance against norms of femininity and the invisibility of lesbians in mainstream society.

The assertion of independence and individuality can be quite easily interpreted as a resistance against the feminine norm of dependence, especially given how some of them criticized the mode of dependence and inequality in gay male and heterosexual relationships. In addition, they also noticed that the ease of passing in mainstream society is predicated partly on the assumption that women cannot be left alone and be safe, and asserting independence and individuality is one way to counter this assumption of the "weak and dependent woman."

At the same time, the ease of passing leaves lesbian partnerships invisible—lesbian couples are conveniently ignored or accepted as friends and roommates, rather than intimate partners. The invisibility in the mainstream world goes in tandem with the fragility of relationship many have noted in the lesbian world. It is possible to think that both forces might have prompted some lesbians to deliberately and conspicuously perform "lesbian partnership" in the safe context of community, as exemplified in couples who are seen as "overly attached" to each other and have become "a set," as described by some of our interview participants. It could be a way of cherishing and making visible lesbian partnerships, in a way that seems impossible in the larger society, where lesbian partners are taken to be sisters, good friends, or roommates.

In other words, we may say that gender is important in influencing the way lesbians construct and live their partnerships, through recognizing connections with each other as women and also in resisting, in different ways that are at times contradictory on an aggregate level, gender norms and expectations regarding women. In some way, they may exemplify the stereotypes of women—valuing and being nurturing, caring, and de-emphasizing the sexual aspect of a relationship, and so on. In other ways, they are resisting the stereotypes, showing a clear recognition of gender inequality, valuing equality and housework in their relationships, and asserting independence and self-sufficiency. They pass in mainstream society as heterosexual women, and at the same time, they recognize the invisibility thus rendered, prompting some to put up an "excessive" performance of lesbian partnership.

Together with the research reported here, we have begun to explore more specifically how lesbians negotiate their partnerships in specific contexts, such as their families of origin, workplace, friendship circles and so on (Kamano and Khor 2006) and how they actually meet and establish a relationship (Kamano and Khor 2008). However, to do justice to the portrayal of lesbian partnerships in Japan, we need more research, not only in terms of a bigger sample covering diverse social and demographic backgrounds, but also in terms of sources of information. We are also intrigued by the "ideal" of lesbian partnership and the critical view some have about how lesbian relationships "are" in the community. To further explore this, and to see if the interpretation we put forward here is valid, it would be fruitful to look at published materials and Internet sites to delineate different modes in which images of lesbian partnership are expressed. Further, interviewing lesbians in different "modes" of partnership would be an obvious next step.

There is still much to learn, and much to be done. It is our hope that this research has taken a step toward understanding and defining what it means to be "lesbian couples" in today's Japan by taking a more "insider's approach," which can add to the works that look at how lesbian couples are seen, represented in, and understood within the larger society.

Notes

1. Further research will unravel the reasons behind the differences in how people perceive individual lesbians and gay men as individuals and lesbian/gay male relationships. However, one may conjecture that comparatively speaking, lesbians and gay men as individuals do not threaten the status quo of heterosexism as much as same-sex couples. The latter, who apparently are committed to living a life resembling heterosexual couples, might accentuate the differences, and hence "unnaturalness," of non-heterosexuals from heterosexuals as an alternative to "deviation" from, and a threat to "normal (heterosexual) family life" (see also Kamano and Khor 1996; Kamano 1995). It has to be noted that there is a six- or seven-year gap between the two surveys cited in the text, and the surveys, with their different samplings and instruments, are not fully comparable. However, there is also no evidence of a dramatic change in opinions even though the "gay boom" in the 1990s did raise people's awareness of lesbian (and gay) existence.

2. The twenty-one interviewees were aged between twenty-nine and fifty-one years at the time of the interviews, with twelve in their thirties, five under thirty, and four in their forties and above. Seven of them had been cohabiting for seven years to eleven years, and the rest from ten months to four years. The majority have educational attainment beyond senior high school, having graduated from vocational schools, junior colleges, or four-year universities. A few among them are in regular full-time employment, but the majority are in irregular employment, including part-time employment and dis-

patch work. All but one reside in Tokyo and its surrounding areas, and the majority of them within the Metropolitan Area. In the text, the interviewees are identified by first names (all pseudonyms).

3. The women used one of the following terms in addressing their "partners": *paatonaa* ("partner"), *isshogai no paatonaa* ("life-time partner"), *kanojo* ("girlfriend"), *aikata* ("my better-half"), *tsureai* ("companion"), *koibito* ("lover"), *yome* ("wife", in the sense of "someone who has married into my family"), and *uchi-no-...* ("my so-and-so or so-and-so of my home"). The most common terms the women used were "partner" and "girlfriend." When they mentioned the relationship itself, they used terms such as *kappuru* ("couple"), *paatonaashippu* ("partnership"), *soiu-kankei* ("that type of relationship"), *kazoku* ("family"), and *katei* ("home").

4. (O)miai refers to meeting a potential husband or wife, generally through introduction by family, relatives, neighbors or a boss, although it is increasingly arranged through matchmaking agencies.

5. This is a frequently made observation about lesbian relationships. See, for example, Weinstock and Rothblum (1996) and Weston (1991).

6. A district in Tokyo where there is a concentration of gay and (some) lesbian bars and shops.

7. Even though the point is not to assess our interviewees' words against research, it should be pointed out here that the literature accumulated so far on lesbians' housework division in diverse countries has borne out this interview participant's words: there is generally an equal division of housework and financial responsibilities in lesbian households, not so much in the sense of a 50-50 split at any one point in time, but a commitment to equality and fluid division of responsibilities over time (see, for example, Dunne 1997; 1998; Kamano 2004b; Khor 2007; Solomon, Rothblum and Balsam 2005).

Works Cited

Dunne, Gillian A. 1997. *Lesbian Lifestyles: Women's Work and the Politics of Sexuality.* Toronto: University of Toronto Press.

———.1998. "Pioneers behind our front doors: new models for the organization of work in partnership." *Work, Employment and Society* 12(6): 273-95.

Iwai, Noriko and Sato Hiroki. 2002. *Nihonjin no sugata: JGSS ni miru ishiki to kodo* (The figures of Japanese people: attitudes and behaviors observed from Japanese General Social Surveys [JGSS]). Tokyo: Yuhikaku.

Kamano, Saori and Diana Khor. 2008. "How Did You Two Meet? The Formation of Lesbian Partnerships in Japan." In *East Asian Sexualities: Modernity, Gender & New Sexual Cultures*, ed. Stevi Jackson, Liu Jieyu and Woo Juhyun. London: Zed Books.

———. 2006. "'Coming Out' for Lesbians in Japan: Meanings and Implications." Paper presented at the International Conference on LGBT Human Rights, Montreal, July 26-29.

———. 1996. "Toward an Understanding of Cross-National Differences in the Naming of Same-Sex Sexual/Intimate Relationships." *NWSA Journal* 8:124-141.

Kamano, Saori. 2005. "Entering the Lesbian World in Japan: Debut Stories." *Journal of Lesbian Studies* 9 (1/2): 11-30.

———. 2004a. "*Rezubian kappuru to gei kappuru: shakaikankyo ni yoru nichijo seikatsu no chigai*" (Lesbian couples and gay couples: how differences in social environment affect daily lives)." In *Suweeden no kazoku to paatonaakankei* (Families and partner relationships: A comparative study of Sweden and Japan), ed. Kyoko Yoshizumi. Tokyo: Aoki shoten.

——. 2004b. *"Nihon no rezubian kappuru ni okeru kajibuntan no kaishaku to kosatsu–intabyu chosa o motoni"* (Interpretation and analysis of housework division among lesbian couples in Japan). Paper presented at the 14th Annual Meeting of the Japanese Family Sociological Association, Tokyo.

——. 1995. "Same-Sex Sexual/Intimate Relationships: A Cross-National Analysis of Interlinkages among Naming, the Gender System, and Gay and Lesbian Resistance Activities." Ph.D. Dissertation, Department of Sociology, Stanford University.

Kazama, Takashi. 2003. "Doseikon no poritikkusu" (Politics of same-sex marriage). *Kazoku shakaigaku kenkyu* (Japanese Journal of Family Sociology) 14(2):32-42.

Khor, Diana. 2007. "Doing Gender: A Critical Review and an Exploration of Lesbigay Domestic Arrangements." *Journal of GLBT Family Studies* 3(1):35-73.

Krestan, JoAnn. and Claudia Bepko. 1980. "The Problem of Fusion in the Lesbian Relationship." *Family Process* 19(3): 277-89.

Mainichi shimbunsha jinkomondai chosakai (The population problems research council, the Mainichi newspapers), ed. 2005. *Choshoshika jidai no kazokuishiki: Daiikkai jinko, kazoku, sedai yoronchosa hokokusho* (Attitudes toward families in the lowest-low fertility era: the first national survey on population, families and generations). Tokyo: Mainichi shimbunsha.

Maree, Claire. 2004. "Same-Sex Partnerships in Japan: Bypasses and Other Alternatives." *Women's Studies: An Interdisciplinary Journal* 33(4):541-49.

Nagayasu, Shibun. 2002. "Dosei paatonaa wa nyuin, shujutsu no kyodaku ga dekiruka" (Can the same-sex partner give permission for his/her partner's hospitalization and surgery?). *Niji* 1(3):2-9.

Otsuka, Takashi. 1994. "Bypass toshite no yoshien-gumi" (Adoption as a bypass). In *Gei no gakuen tengoku!* (Gay's lesson to happiness). Tokyo: Takarajimasha.

Solomon, Sondra E., Esther D. Rothblum, and Kimberly F. Balsam. 2005. "Money, Housework, Sex, and Conflict: Same-Sex Couples in Civil Unions, Those Not in Civil Unions, and Heterosexual Married Siblings." *Sex Roles* 52:561-75.

Tanamura, Masayuki. 1997. "Nihon ni okeru dosei kappuru no hoteki kanosei" (Legal possibilities of same-sex couples in Japan). In *Kuia sutadiizu 97* (Queer studies '97), ed. Kuia sutadiizu henshu iinkai (The editorial board of Queer Studies). Tokyo: Nanatsumori shokan.

Weinstock, Jacqueline S. and Esther D. Rothblum. 1996, "What We Can Be Together: Contemplating Lesbians' Friendships." In *Lesbian Friendships: For Ourselves and Each Other*, ed. Jacqueline S. Weinstock and Esther D. Rothblum. New York: New York University Press.

Weston, Kath. 1991. *Families We Choose: Lesbians, Gays, Kinship*. New York: Columbia University Press.

Increasing Lesbian Visibility

12

Ikuko Sugiura
Translated by Kimberly Hughes

So-called *rezu baa* (lez bars) were pres-
ent in Tokyo as early as the 1960s. When a show by a reputable theater
company portrayed *rezu*-style motifs that featured women dressed in men's
clothing, it was supported by twenty-three lesbian bars in Tokyo (Shiba
1993). If one considers that Tokyo's famous gay district of Shinjuku ni-
chome has only ten *rediisu baa* today (lesbian bars, known also as ladies'
bars), the early figure is impressive. In contrast to present-day establishments, early lesbian bars featured women dressed in men's clothing who
worked as bartenders, also known as *booi* (boys) or *hosuto* (hosts), who
served a clientele consisting of women and men from the larger general
public. Apparently, then, the concept of *rezu* at the time denoted women
who dressed in men's clothing.[1]

At the end of the 1960s, another image of lesbians as vulgar and obscene
began to circulate chiefly through mainstream magazines created by and
for men. In their pages images of women appeared engaged in hardcore
sexual acts, labeled as special "lesbian techniques," said to offer women
levels of pleasure that no man could provide. Not surprisingly, lesbian sex
attracted attention. In these portraits, lesbians did not necessarily dress as
men, nor were they obliged to be the aggressor in sexual activity (Sugiura
2005, 2006a, 2006b). During these early years, therefore, the public portraits of lesbians were limited to the stereotypes of male dressing and car-
nal behavior. Lesbians themselves were isolated, and their most immediate
need was to establish a space where they could meet one another.

In 1971, the lesbian organization known as the Wakakusa no kai (Young
Grass Club) was founded in Tokyo so that lesbians might meet one another.
I believe it is appropriate to say that this group represents the starting
point of lesbian community organizing. It was begun by Michiko Suzuki
(b. 1950), who took out ads in magazines and appeared on television in
order to recruit members. She ran the organization entirely on her own,
publishing a monthly newsletter, responding to letters from people seek-

ing advice, managing inquiries from the mass media, and handling general operating responsibilities. During the group's fifteen-year history, it is estimated that there were a total of at least five hundred members (Hirosawa 1987). Considering the number of years that the group was in existence, it is not surprising that conflicts occurred along the way. As Hirosawa wrote after interviewing Suzuki, the first problems began to surface when, in the midseventies, "a group of lesbians who had become baptized as women's liberationists joined the group and began to criticize its leader" (Hirosawa 1987, 115).

The women's liberation movement in Japan began around the year 1970, and the Ribu Shinjuku sentaa (Lib Shinjuku Center) operated in Tokyo as the movement's central hub from 1972 to 1977. Its membership included lesbians, and in the midseventies, lesbians who had been influenced by the ideals of lesbian feminism began to launch projects, including newsletters, dance parties, and meetings for lesbians in the city of Kyoto.

In contrast to the goal of the Young Grass Club gatherings, which primarily provided a social setting for lesbians to meet one another, the primary aim of these liberationists was educational—to eradicate internalized homophobia among lesbians. This goal clearly appears in the title of their first newsletter, published in 1976, which was called *Subarashii onnatachi* (Wonderful Women) and like others that followed,[2] clearly proclaimed several central ideals of lesbian feminism: that the roots of lesbian oppression could be traced to the existence of patriarchy; that one must value one's own *joseisei* (womanhood), as well as one's relationships with other women; and that the task at hand was to overthrow the patriarchal system itself.

The lesbian feminist critique of the Young Grass Club leader, Michiko Suzuki, was rooted in the ideals described above. Suzuki had apparently made notes regarding individual members on the group's roster using terms such as "feminine," "boyish," "likes to lead her partner," "likes to be led around by her partner," etc., to describe them. This was criticized by the liberationists as replicating the male-created value system (Hirosawa 1987, 115).

The 1980s: Expansion of the Network

All of the newsletters publishing during the 1970s were short-lived, and did not influence lesbian community building. In 1984, however, five lesbians who had been involved with the earlier publications formed a group in Tokyo known as Regumi no gomame. They began issuing a newsletter titled *Regumi tsushin* in 1985, and in March of 1987, they opened an office called the Regumi Studio Tokyo (hereafter referred to as Resta) that remains in existence today. From the beginning, the group named three objectives. First they wished to create solidarity among isolated lesbians throughout the country, and to set up a network aimed at offering them support. Second, they wished to consider what it means to be a lesbian—or a woman who loves women—and to discover the inherent value therein. And third they wished to serve as a source of information for truthful portrayals of what it actually means to be a lesbian, and thereby dispel existing prejudices and discrimination (*Regumi tsushin* 1987, 2-3) Thus, the political goals of Resta, including the construction of a positive lesbian identity, opposing antilesbian prejudice, as well as building a network with which to do so, are clearly stated here. In addition to publishing the monthly *Regumi tsushin* newsletter, members also energetically set about engaging in activities such as organizing events, hosting visitors to the office, and providing a telephone hotline service.

With Resta serving as the contact organization, additional events were also organized such as "lesbian weekends"—retreat-style gatherings that began in 1985—and the second meeting of the Asian Lesbian Network (ALN) in 1992. Lesbian weekends also began to be organized in outlying regions of the country, making this a historical period in which lesbian networks gradually began to expand both nationwide and into the broader Asian region.

In 1987, *Onna o aisuru onnatachi no monogatari* (Stories of Women Who Love Women) appeared, edited by Yumi Hirosawa (b. 1952), one of the founding members of the Regumi no gomame group. The book, which included the compilation of 234 responses by lesbian and bisexual women to a questionnaire, served to portray "the reality of lesbians living in Japan" (Hirosawa 1987, 151). This was the first work by a lesbian made available for purchase in regular bookstores, and it helped dispel existing stereotypes, as well as to foster the network building that had begun.

The end of the 1980s also saw an increase in academic-related pursuits in lesbian studies. This included the establishment of a group within the Women's Studies Association of Japan that began looking at women's sexuality as a question of choice, as well as holding seminars on lesbian feminist writers. Lesbian literary critiques and the study of lesbians in Western countries also began around this time, and six essays from a lesbian feature issue of the journal *Signs* (1985) were translated and published in Japanese in 1990 under the title *Uman rabingu* (Women Loving) (Watanabe et al. 1990). Awareness of lesbianism both abroad and in Japan was furthered through other endeavors during this time.[3]

The 1990s: Lesbian Liberation Comes Out of the Closet

While efforts in the 1980s, which centered around the activities of Resta, sought to inform and educate those outside the lesbian community, the main focus was on lesbians themselves. The only exception was the activism carried out in 1988 against the AIDS Prevention Law, in which Resta joined with gay men's groups to hold meetings and voice opposition to the government and the mass media. Even in this instance, however, the group was very cautious about making its name public (*Regumi tsushin*, 1988, 10).

In order to protect members' privacy, the words "*Regumi*" and "*rezubian*" were not used when holding events at public facilities, and even the most active staff members never openly used their actual names. In other words, almost all lesbians at this time remained closeted. This contrast between active lesbian community life and the inability of members to be outwardly open about their sexuality, revealed the strength of the prejudice toward homosexuals that existed in Japan during the 1980s.

In 1991, Hiroko Kakefuda (b. 1964) began to appear on a television program, talking about her life and about her book, published in 1992, *Rezubian dearu to iukoto* (What It Means to Be Lesbian). In 1994, she also participated in a nine-city performance tour called the LOG Caravan. Kakefuda also helped plan and edit a special feature on lesbians that appeared consecutively in several mainstream magazines, in which lesbians offered stories of their lives.

The relationship between the early Regumi members who came of age during the women's liberation generation, and the lesbians who began participating in community activism along with Kakefuda during the 1990s has been rather weak because of generational differences. However, certain issues that were prominent among early lesbian feminists—such as separatism, criticism of *tachi* (butch) and *neko* (femme)[4] role-playing, and the rejection of "masculinity"—continued to be important to Kakefuda's generation. A controversy that erupted among subscribers to Kakefuda's popular newsletter called *Labrys*—which ran from 1992 to 1995, with a readership of over one thousand six hundred—illuminates the continuity. The article was critical of both bisexual women and *tachi* (butch lesbians). Indeed, until the beginning of the 1990s, the lesbian community was not a comfortable place for bisexuals, since it emphasized a clear lesbian identity and a "wonderful lifestyle that rejects men." One example of this attitude manifested itself with regard to attendance at the lesbian weekends, which—after much discussion—began to be organized as alternately "lesbians only" or "bisexual-friendly." In 1993, a group of mostly bisexual women came together and began organizing separate events that they termed "Women's Week-ends," which were open to women of all sexualities. A group known as the "Women's Bi-Net" also met from 1994 to 1997, and organized various activities that provided affirmation of bisexuality. Hiroko Kakefuda subtitled her *Labrys* newsletter—as well as the LOUD (Lesbians of Undeniable Desire) resource center that she helped establish—with the phrase "for lesbian and bisexual women." Similarly, around the same time, the commercial magazines *Phryné* (1995, Miwa Publishing) and *Anise* (1996-97, Miwa Publishing) utilized the expression "women-loving women" in consideration of the bisexuals within the community, and *Anise* published numerous interviews and essays featuring bisexual writers. In this way, then, the overt criticism toward bisexuals gradually gave way to increased understanding.

The existing fierce condemnation of *tachi* or butch also disappeared around the end of the 1990s, due in large part to the strengthening of the politics of transsexuality, from which emerged the category of *onabe* (women who dress as men), as well as the understanding that some *tachi* were in fact FTMTS (female-to-male transsexual) heterosexuals, rather than a subcategory of lesbians. Conversely, MTFTS (male-to-female transsexual) lesbians, who were at one time categorized as *okama* (men who dress as women), began to join the lesbian community. In addition, FTX[5]—although no longer considered lesbians—have recently become part of the community as well, adding an additional flavor of diversity.

Beginning in the late 1990s, lesbian communities all over Japan—not only in Tokyo—began to feature a wide range of activities that were spearheaded independently by individuals working together. This was a significant change from the previous pattern, whereby one individual alone worked as a community leader. Events that began in the early 1990s, such as the Tokyo International Lesbian and Gay Film Festival (since 1992) and the Tokyo Lesbian and Gay Parade (since 1994), have now moved beyond the capital. Presently, similar events are held throughout the country through the support of numerous volunteer staff members.

Social Opinion and Human Rights

While activities by and for lesbian and bisexual women have been increasing during the past forty years, only some women of a certain educated class, and usually in urban areas, have participated. Far more numerous are others who remain isolated and unable to reach a lesbian community, or whose lives do not permit them the luxury of participating in volunteer activities. Moreover, public opinion remains staunchly negative.

The Japanese General Social Survey (JGSS) of 2000 included a question asking peoples' opinion regarding same-sex sexual relations.[6] Among male respondents, 62.2 percent answered either that it was "wrong without exception" or "wrong in most cases," while 35.2 percent replied that it was "not necessarily wrong" or "not wrong." In the case of females, the replies were 52.9 percent and 41.9 percent, respectively (Iwai and Sato 2002, 226), revealing that women are slightly more tolerant than men. Younger respondents were also more likely to be tolerant. Nevertheless, what stands out is the markedly small percentage of those responding that homosexuality is "not wrong" (6.2 percent of males and 6.9 percent of females).

These figures, then, provide an important backdrop for understanding why homosexuals in Japan have no choice but to remain hidden and to lie about their sexuality at home, in school, among communities, and in the workplace. While public acceptance of homosexuality would resolve this situation, there is now no national law in Japan to prohibit discrimination on the basis of sexual orientation.

In 2002, the first comprehensive legislation proposed in Japan for human rights protection included "sexual orientation." Because the bill sought to regulate reporting activities by the mass media, however, there was criticism that its application could negatively affect citizens' rights to full information disclosure, and the bill was defeated in the Diet (national legislature) in 2005. Also fresh in recent memory is the debacle that occurred with regard to the Tokyo metropolitan government's drafting of a document titled "Guidelines for Promoting Human Rights Measures," which initially included the term "homosexuals." The panel of experts responsible for drafting the document had originally recommended that the guidelines be extended to "people including sexual minorities such as homosexuals, those with gender identity disorder (GID), and intersex individuals." When an outline of the document was published in June 2000, however, the word "homosexuals" had been removed, which the government explained by saying that "consensus does not exist among citizens regarding its inclusion."

When activist groups and individual homosexuals responded with an impassioned protest, the final guidelines released in November included the following single vaguely worded line: "Recently, there have been numerous issues raised with regard to homosexuals." Obviously, the Tokyo metropolitan government's attitude toward protecting the human rights of homosexuals is anything but proactive (Nagayasu 2002, 40-47).

No policies exist in Japan that protect the rights of same-sex couples, such as civil unions or domestic partnerships. Many people have also pointed out that even if such policies were to exist, it would still be difficult, or impossible to use them since this would require coming out at work, to family, and in the community-at-large (Taniguchi 2007).[7]

Work and Employment

So far, there have been no court cases in Japan alleging the loss of one's job as a result of disclosing one's sexual orientation. But there are some indications of harassment in the workplace. The results of a survey published in *Stories of Women Who Love Women*, for example, included such responses as "I was pressured to quit my job after my boss found out I was a lesbian," and "My friend was fired for being a lesbian after being told that it would have a bad effect 'on the general workplace environment.'" Other responses to a questionnaire regarding "work and employment" included comments indicating the stress felt by lesbians asked "about whether or not I am romantically involved with someone," or by "contemptuous remarks about '*homo*' and '*rezu*.'" These were, of course, in addition to the disadvantages faced by women in general in the workplace (Hirosawa 1987; Seiishiki chosa guruupu 1998). High school teacher Kumiko Ikeda, who came out as a lesbian and published a book called *Sensei no rezubian sengen: tsunagaru tame no kamuauto* (A Teacher's Lesbian Declaration: Solidarity Through Coming Out) noted lesbians' inevitable needs to consider their lives and their careers as they approach their late twenties:

> Girls are brought up by their parents to be dependent, and so when they finally figure out that their goal is to live independently and not get married, they are often stunned to find themselves lacking the ability to earn a living. I know numerous lesbians who've gone back to school in order to acquire some type of specialized skills. (Ikeda 1999, 137)

Due to the simple fact that they are women, then, lesbian and bisexual women clearly face difficulties that are different from those of gay men.

School and Human Rights Education

One cause of unstable employment and low pay for women may be found in an education based on traditional gender roles. Scant consideration is given to the fact that the consequences of gender tracking are especially detrimental to the lives of lesbian and bisexual women. Only male-female couplings appear, and heterosexuality seems the only possible lifestyle. Homophobic comments and behavior may appear as part of the classroom's communication patterns between teachers and students and also among students and teachers (Watanabe 2002). An internet survey conducted in 2005 among gay and bisexual men revealed that 54.5 percent of them had been taunted at school with names like *homo* or *okama*,[8] while 45.1 percent had also been harassed nonverbally.[9] In the same survey, 78.5 percent of respondents reported that they had "been taught absolutely nothing at all" about homosexuality in school, 10.7 percent that they had received only "negative information" about it, and 3.9 percent that they had been taught it was "something abnormal." Taken together, then, these figures reveal that 93 percent of the surveyed students had received improper information regarding homosexuality.

But in fact, there is a real need for information regarding sexual minority issues on the part of students themselves—a fact that was made clear by a survey on the topic of sexuality that was conducted among second-year high school students in September 2005 in Akita Prefecture. In response to the question, "What sexuality-related issue would you like to receive advice about?," 6.5 percent of male students responded "gender identity disorder (GID)," which was up from 5 percent in 2003, while 7.4 percent of female students replied "homosexuality" (up from the previous 6.5 percent). Taking these needs into account, moves were made to add information about sexual minorities to the list of topics presented in sex education directed at the entire student body. This proposal was later set aside, however, with the explanation that "there is no one available to teach on this subject."[10]

The Sexual Minority Educators' Network (STN21)[11] was established in January 2001 as a forum for educators, who are themselves sexual minorities, to come together and discuss related issues and problems within the educational field. Since then, members have been working collectively to provide sex and human rights educational curricula focused on the theme "diversity of sexualities" (Sekushuaru mainoritii kyoshokuin nettowaaku 2003; Watanabe 2002).

Familial Relations

Many sexual minorities report that a critical factor distinguishing them from other minorities is their loneliness: no one else in their families knows about their status. Many young people—aware of the social homophobia around them—opt not to disclose their true selves even to their own families for fear of rejection (Tsuzuki 2002). A few who choose to come out to their parents and siblings hope to deepen their family relationships. Some want simply to be understood by those who are important to them, while others want to construct a social safety net to fall back on in times of emergency.

Saori Kamano's 2007 work documents interviews with lesbian couples regarding the construction of personal networks (See also "Defining Lesbian Partnerships," by Kamano and Khor in this volume). Those whom she interviewed said that they did indeed rely upon their parents and siblings,

with whom they either already had, or were striving to build positive relations. Given their recognition of the lack of policies to protect their relationships, "These couples strive to secure support at least from those on
whom they have some influence," Kamano speculates (Kamano 2007). It
is clear that only the most fragile of social policies and awareness exist in
Japan with which to provide support to individuals beyond the ties of the
blood-related family. In reality, the provision of social security in Japanese
society tends to be heavily reliant on family support and unpaid labor.[12] The
hardships suffered by those whose family relations are strained or severed
after coming out, then, are great, especially in the case of lesbian and bisexual women, for whom unstable or discriminatory conditions of employment also place them in financially insecure positions.

Thus, we must conclude that homosexuals have continued to remain
invisible within Japanese society, a condition which most members of society regard with indifference. Perhaps the indifference is responsible for the
fact that the number of hate crimes committed against homosexuals in
Japan is far fewer than those in the United States.[13] Activists who are out
about their sexuality in Japan, moreover, rarely report experiencing fear for
their lives.

Whether at home, school, or the workplace, the automatic social assumption is that homosexuals do not exist. Disparaging comments are made
without hesitation, and almost never does anyone stop to consider whether
a homosexual might actually be present and feel hurt by such remarks. So
commonplace is it to make fun of homosexuals and call them "disgusting,"
in fact, that in reality few people consider this as discrimination. In essence,
homosexuals themselves—as well as the prejudices existing against them—
have both been rendered invisible.

This invisibility is far more prevalent with regard to lesbian and bisexual women, than it is for gay men. At the pride parades, for example, the
sheer number of gay men—as well as the amount of resources that they
have invested into the event itself—is staggering. Additionally, while there
are male entertainers who have come out publicly, there have been few such
examples on the part of women. In terms of the difficulties they confront,
the differences are greater than the similarities between homosexual men
and women—the latter of whom must face certain realities, not as homosexuals but as women, such as employment-related difficulties, the burden
of caring for one's parents, and child rearing.[14]

Lesbian and bisexual women are working steadily in order to find solutions to these sorts of problems. A group of activists in the Kansai region
who came together to research the needs of those seeking legal protections
for same-sex partners and published their results,[15] for example, comprised

a core membership of women (Arita, Fujii and Horie 2006). Osaka prefectural legislator Kanako Otsuji also came out publicly as a lesbian in 2005 (Otsuji 2005), and ran for a seat in the Diet in July 2007 (an election that she unfortunately lost), hoping to secure some sort of legal protection for same-sex partnerships.

Since entering the twenty-first century, centers devoted to this sort of activism continued to increase. In 2003, the Queer and Women's Resource Center (QWRC) was established in Osaka, and the Performance Art/Feminism (PA/F) Space was also launched in Tokyo. While such initiatives continue to struggle with finances, they have succeeded in creating an array of diverse programming. This has included reaching out across the boundaries of gender and generation—a development offering hope that this sort of solidarity will continue on into the future.

Notes

1. While I have heard that *rezu baa* began to disappear one by one from entertainment districts in the late 1970s, my research has not focused on this time period and so I am unable to confirm this or to provide further explanation. Ribonnu, the first bar catering to lesbian and bisexual clientele to hire women who were not dressed as men, opened in June of 1985 in the district of Shinjuku ni-chome (Ribonnu onnashujin 1985). These types of bars are now known as lesbian bars or ladies' bars, as distinguished from those establishments with women dressed as men, which are now referred to as *onabe baa* (*onabe* bars). As indicated earlier, there are only around ten ladies' bars in Shinjuku ni-chome, and no more than two or three each in most other Japanese cities.

2. The three *mini-komi* that were published consecutively during the late 1970s were the following: *Subarashii onnatachi* (Wonderful Women), November 1976; *Za daiku* (The Dyke), January 1978 (issue #1) and June 1978 (issue #2); and *Hikariguruma* (Shining Wheel), April 1978 (issue #1) and September 1978 (issue #2).

3. The contemporary philosophy journal *Imago* also devoted its August 1991 issue to the topic of lesbianism, including a systematic review of the debates around lesbianism that were taking place at the time in the United States, as well as an outstanding overview of lesbian-related works in Japan that analyzed the intimate relations between women that had appeared in works such as *ukiyo-e* (a genre of paintings from the Edo period, 1603-1868, that depicted everyday life), movies, novels, *shojo manga* (manga for girls that often deal with romance), etc. Translator and active Resta member Minako Hara (b. 1956) also rendered several important works into Japanese, such as Pat Califia's *Sapphistry: The Book of Lesbian Sexuality* (1993) and Lillian Faderman's *Odd Girls and Twilight Lovers* (1996).

4. While the origins of the words *tachi* and *neko* are unclear, it is often said that the term *tachi* refers to the role of the leading figure in *Kabuki* theater, although another meaning of the word is to "rise suddenly." *Neko* means "cat", and can also mean "sleeping child" or "geisha".

5. The term FTX refers to women who are female by virtue of biology and *koseki* (family register), but who do not identify as female and yet do not wish to become male either.

6. The survey was conducted among women and men aged twenty to eighty-nine. Responses were utilized from a total of 2,893 individuals.

7. There has been one court case until now alleging homosexual discrimination, filed by gay rights group OCCUR against the Tokyo Metropolitan government. In 1991, while staying overnight at a public facility, OCCUR members were harassed by other guests. While they were able to negotiate with staff regarding the incident, they were subsequently refused permission at other metropolitan government facilities, prompting them to file court action. They won both their case in March 1994, as well as their appeal in September 1997.

8. Slur with a connotation similar to that of "faggot" (translator).

9. Scholarly survey that has been conducted via the internet among gay and bisexual males every other year since 1999, with the support of government funds. The researcher in charge is Yasuharu Hidaka. There were 5,731 respondents to the survey in 2005, for which the results may be viewed at the following site: www.gay-report.jp/

10. In order to provide Akita prefectural officials with information about sex education, this survey was administered to 1,151 male students and 1,098 female students in September 2005. Two years prior, in September 2003, it had been given to 1,121 male students and 1,092 female students. ("Survey among second-year high school students in Akita Prefecture unexpectedly reveals today's students grappling with worries regarding homosexuality, GID." *Asahi shimbun* newspaper [Akita morning edition]. February 15, 2006, 32).

11. The STN21 website address is http://homepage3.nifty.com/stn/

12. For example, those who have family capable of providing financial assistance cannot receive Public Assistance (*seikatsu hogo*). Moreover, the Long-term Care Insurance System that went into force in 2000 put emphasis on home care for the elderly that would be provided by family members free of charge. By constructing a social security system that is based not on the individual but rather the family or household unit, the Japanese government seeks to curb the expanding costs of medical care and social welfare.

13. Until now, the only hate crimes in Japan where the perpetrators were arrested and the incidents received media coverage were those occurring in February 2000, and July 2006, in Tokyo's Yumenoshima Park. The incidents involved attacks on gay men that were motivated by robbery—the first of which resulted in a fatality. In both cases, the crimes were committed by youth who claimed that they "didn't think the incident would be reported to police if it was committed against a gay person."

14. While I was not able to reference the matter of lesbian mothers, they do in fact exist in Japan. Most of these cases involve children born through relationships with men, which reflects the fact that it is extremely difficult in Japan for unmarried individuals to adopt children. Recently, however, there have been cases reported in Japan of lesbians giving birth to children using sperm obtained from sperm banks in the United States.

15. Source: Research Group for Policy Recommendations on Relationships Transcending Blood Ties and Marriage (Volunteer Investigation of Existing Needs). 2004. Volunteer Investigation Project of Needs Regarding Legal Protections for Same-Sex Partnerships. http://www.geocities.jp/seisakuken1003/

Works Cited

Arita, Keiko, Hiromi Fujii and Yuri Horie. 2006. "*Kosho, dakyo, kyozonsuru niizu: dosei-kan paatonaashippu no hoteki hosho ni kansuru tojisha niizu kara*" (The need to negotiate, compromise, and coexist: Learning from the needs of those seeking legal protections for same sex partnerships.) *Joseigaku nenpo* (Women's studies annual report) 27: 4-28.

Califia, Pat. 1988. *Sapphistry: The Book of Lesbian Sexuality.* Translation by Minako Hara. 1993. *Sapphistry: rezubian sekushuaritii no tebiki. Gay and Lesbian Series #4.* Tokyo: Taiyosha.

Faderman, Lillian. 1991. *Odd Girls and Twilight Lovers: A history of lesbian life in twentieth-century America.* Translation by Akemi Fukuoka and Minako Hara. 1996. *Rezubian no rekishi* (Lesbian history). Tokyo: Chikuma shobo.

Hirosawa, Yumi, ed. 1987. *Onna o aisuru onnatachi no monogatari: Nihon de hajimete! 234 nin no shogen de tsuzuru rezubian repooto* (Stories of women who love women: First-ever report in Japan of personal stories from 234 lesbians). *Bessatsu Takarajima* (64). Tokyo: JICC shuppan kyoku.

Ikeda, Kumiko. 1999. *Sensei no rezubian sengen: tsunagaru tame no kamuauto* (A teacher's lesbian declaration: Solidarity through coming out). Tokyo: Kamogawa shuppan.

Iwai, Noriko and Hiroki Sato, ed. 2002. *Nihonjin no sugata: JGSS ni miru ishiki to kodo* (Looking at the Japanese: Consciousness and action as seen through the JGSS [Japanese General Social Survey]). Tokyo: Yuhikaku.

Kakefuda, Hiroko. 1992. *Rezubian dearu to iukoto* (What it means to be lesbian). Tokyo: Kawade shobo shinsha.

Kamano, Saori. 2007. "Rezubian kappuru no paasonaru nettowaaku: sono jittai to hoteki hosho no niizu to no kanren" (Personal networks among lesbian couples: Relationship between existing conditions and need for legal protections") *Shinpojiumu dosei kappuru no seikatsu to seido: kikitori chosa kara kangaeru genzai to mirai—hokoku rejime* (Symposium on lives and policies with regard to homosexual couples: The present and the future as revealed by personal interviews—Summary report delivered on December 15, 2007 at Ochanomizu University.

Nagayasu, Shibun. 2002. "Komyunitii no keiken: Tokyo-to jinken shishin" (Experience in the community: Tokyo metropolitan human rights guidelines." *Niji* 2: 40-47

Naikakufu (Cabinet Office, Government of Japan). 2008. *Danjo kyodo sankaku hakusho* (White Paper on Gender Equality). Tokyo: Saiki insatsu.

Otsuji, Kanako. 2005. *Kamingu auto!: jibun rashisa o mitsukeru tabi* (Coming out! A journey to find my true self). Tokyo: Kodansha.

Regumi tsushin No. 1, March 29, 1987.

Regumi tsushin No.16, July 2, 1988.

Ribonnu onnashujin (Ribonne hostess). 1985. "Ribonnu no yoru: kenso no rezubian baa" (Nights at the bustling lesbian bar Ribonne). *Gekko* (LUNA) (October): 19-21.

Seiishiki chosa guruupu (Research group on sexuality awareness). 1998. *310 nin no seiishiki: iseiaisha dewanai onnatachi no ankeeto chosa* (Sexuality awareness questionnaire conducted among 310 non-heterosexual women. Tokyo: Nanatsumori shokan.

Sekushuaru mainoritii kyoshokuin nettowaaku (Sexual minority educators' network), ed. 2003. *Sekushuaru mainoritii: doseiai, seidoitsusei shogai, intaasekkusu no tojisha ga kataru ningen no tayona sei* (Sexual minorities: Diversity of human sexuality as discussed by homosexuals, those with gender identity disorder, and intersex persons). Tokyo: Akashi shoten.

Shiba, Fumiko. 1993. "Essei showa rokujunendai rezubian buumu: anokoro, rezubian wa osharedatta" (Essay on the lesbian boom in the period 1985-1995 when lesbians were fashionable). In *Tanbi shosetsu, geibungaku bukku gaido* (Aesthetic novels and gay literature guidebook), ed. Eiko Kakinuma and Chiyo Kurihara. Tokyo: Byakuya shobo.

Sugiura, Ikuko. 2005. "Ippan zasshi ni okeru 'rezubian' no hyosho: sengo kara 1971-nen made" (Representations of lesbians in mainstream magazines: Post-World War II through 1971). *Gendai fuzokugaku kenkyu* (Bulletin of Society for Changing Customs in Contemporary Japan) 11: 1-12

———. 2006a. "1970, 80-nendai no ippan zasshi ni okeru 'rezubian' hyosho: rezubian feminisuto gensetsu no tojo made" (Representations of "lesbians" in mainstream magazines during the 1970s and 1980s, until the appearance of lesbian feminist discourse). In *Sengo Nihon joso, doseiai kenkyu* (Research on cross-dressing (female) and homosexuality in postwar Japan), ed. Masami Yajima. Tokyo: Chuo daigaku shuppanbu.

———. 2006b. "Lesbian Discourses in Mainstream Magazines of Post-War Japan: Is *onabe* distinct from *rezubian*?" *Journal of Lesbian Studies* 10 (No.3/4): 127-144.

Taniguchi, Hiroyuki. 2007. "Hoteki hosho no niizu: chosa purojekuto no gaiyo to tomoni" (Overview of research project on the needs for legal protection). *Shinpojiumu dosei kappuru no seikatsu to seido: kikitori chosa kara kangaeru genzai to mirai—hokoku rejime* (Symposium on lives and policies with regard to homosexual couples: The present and the future as revealed by personal interviews—Summary report delivered on December 15, 2007 at Ochanomizu University.

Tsuzuki, Masami. 2002. "Kazoku to nayami o kyoyusuru konnan: seiteki mainoritii kara no meeru sodan" (Difficulty of sharing personal problems with family: Emails received from sexual minorities seeking advice). *Kikan sekushuaritii* (Sexuality quarterly) 6: 56-59

Watanabe, Daisuke. 2002. "Gakko bunka to iseiaishugi" (School culture and heterosexism). In *Doseiai, tayona sekushuaritii: jinken to kyosei o manabu jugyo* (Homosexuality and diverse sexualities: Courses for learning about human rights and coexistence), ed. "Ningen to sei" kyoiku kenkyujo (Research center on education about "human beings and sex"). Tokyo: Kodomono miraisha.

Watanabe, Mieko, et al. 1990. *Uman rabingu: rezubianron sosei ni mukete* (Woman loving: Toward the creation of lesbian theory). Tokyo: Gendai shokan.

Dialogue: Three Activists on Gender and Sexuality

13

*Edited by Ikuko Sugiura
and translated by Minata Hara*

**Chizuka Oe, Masae Torai,
and Aya Kamikawa, with Kumiko
Fujimura-Fanselow, Moderator**

Moderator: We would like to begin this panel discussion by asking each of you to introduce yourself, and tell us about your community involvement, starting with Chizuka Oe.

Oe: I am the main representative of Lesbians of Undeniable Desire (LOUD), a center for lesbian and bisexual women since 1999. As an activist, I have lectured at a number of universities throughout Japan, and I have also co-authored several books on sexuality.

I first made contact with the lesbian community in 1988, when I visited the Regumi Studio Tokyo (hereafter, Resta), one year after it had opened. The reason why it took me a whole year to go was because I didn't know any other lesbians, and I was hesitant to go alone. In those days, Resta held monthly meetings, study groups, and recreational events. I thought it would be easier to start with something recreational rather than academic, so I signed up for an ice skating outing. I was so nervous. I was worried that I might not recognize the group at the meeting place, but when I got there, I immediately knew that it had to be the group of women with short hair, no makeup, and dressed in trousers. Everyone was very friendly, and I really enjoyed myself that day. That was how I first became involved in Resta and subscribed to the newsletter they published called *Regumi tsushin*.

In 1986 and 1987, the people at the center of the lesbian community were activists influenced by women's liberation and American feminism. They often talked about what it was to be a "good (or politically correct) lesbian." Also, I think there were separatist ideas, that a clear line should be drawn between gay men and lesbians. Still, on the other hand, a feminine appearance was not acceptable. At the time, I had long hair, and I was told, "You won't fit in here if you have long hair or wear makeup," and, "When you start coming to places like this, your hair gets shorter and shorter, you know." Even though I thought they looked nice and neat, I was interested in fashion, so this negative attitude toward dressing up was a little difficult for me to accept.

In those days, I had never been in a relationship with a woman, but the general atmosphere did not encourage one to say, "I am looking for a partner." Partly I felt pressured for not having been deeply involved with someone. However, for some reason, most of the activists there were in relationships already, and there was no support for lesbians who were single like me. I told myself "to do what I can," but I also felt uneasy because I wasn't sure whether I could be a lesbian like them.

Eventually, a clash of opinions appeared among Resta's staff members, and even the subscribers were caught up in the major breakup that ensued. It was a great shock for me, and after that I gradually distanced myself from Resta.

Moderator: You mentioned that, when you participated in the Resta event, everyone had short hair. Did you get the impression that they were "butch"?

Oe: I wouldn't go so far as to say that because the "butch/femme" schism had been rejected as mimicking male/female relationships. I guess long hair, makeup, and skirts were generally seen as a coquettish appeal to men. However, many people resisted this attitude behind the scenes. In 1992 Akiko Mizoguchi organized "Salon Positive," which was a very dressy event that reflected various streams of pop culture encouraging women to enjoy themselves "with style and pizazz."

Moderator: Do you think that was due to feminist influences? There was a similar trend during the early stages of the feminist movement, wasn't there?

Oe: Although Resta was a lesbian group, at that time, I think it was largely under the influence of certain feminists, and its focus was on political issues and women's liberation. It felt like you would be scorned if you talked about "romantic love." Many other initiatives began to emerge from those people who felt rather uncomfortable with Resta. For example, there were club nights held in Shinjuku ni-chome (Tokyo's gay neighborhood). Also, there were special weekends organized through the initiative of Western lesbians residing in Japan. The problem was, even if I distanced myself from Resta, there was nowhere else for me to go. I couldn't really get into the commercialized atmosphere or the extraordinary fervor of the club nights and lesbian bars in Shinjuku ni-chome. I stopped participating in any of the community activities for a while. Then, in 1994, a friend of mine asked me to help her organize a social group for those mainly in their thirties, and I eagerly accepted the invitation. That was how I began working in the administration of the "Group daruma." We organized a recreational get-together once a month.

For indoor events like socializing over a cup of tea, we used Malaika, a small space managed by lesbians started in 1988 located in Tokyo, until LOUD was set up in 1995. Then we began to hold events there at LOUD, and that's how I got to know the three founding members, Hiroko Kakefuda, Akiko Mizoguchi, and Toshiko Sekiguchi. They eventually left LOUD for different reasons, and the management of LOUD was handed over to me in 1996.

Many of the staff members were resistant to the kinds of hierarchical structures associated with male-dominated organizations, and our policy was to discuss all issues until we could come up with a compromise that reflected everyone's opinions. To have all ten staff members reach a consensus, however, was a truly difficult and time-consuming endeavor. Furthermore, everyone wanted to have a say but nobody wanted to take on major responsibilities. When the founding members said they wanted to withdraw their names from the tenant contract, nobody else wanted to take over because it would mean shouldering rent and all the other burdens. We also needed a co-signer, but couldn't find anyone willing to take on that responsibility. We talked of closing it down, but couldn't reach any decision regarding where to relocate such a large archive. In the end, I signed the renewed contract and Yoko Ogawa, the current vice-representative, became the co-signer so that we could continue running LOUD.

Not that signing the tenant contract gave me more say in the group. It was somewhat liberating for both Ogawa and me, though, and we became firm in our resolve to disclose our identities, open this place to the public, and deal with the media if necessary. At that point, all the members agreed to establish the post of representative and vice-representative, thereby making clear where responsibilities resided. This was in 1999. Since then, I have been open about my sexuality, going out in public using my real name. I think this is one of the major characteristics of LOUD. There are many groups that support its members within the community. That is valuable work in itself, but I also know from experience that it is important for us to be visible and socially active. Unfortunately, there still are not enough people who are active under their real names. We get called upon by many sectors, but managing this place takes up all our time and energy. There are so many things I envision, but it is frustratingly difficult to actualize any of them.

Moderator: What kinds of activities take place at LOUD?

Oe: LOUD is a place that sexual minorities as well as their supporters can use for a variety of purposes. For example, from the very beginning we have offered a monthly workshop for translating lesbian novels. Eiko Kakinuma, a translator, has been training translators virtually on a voluntary basis. Some of her students now do draft translations for Harlequin Romances. We also have a social group for women who are over forty, a fortune-telling group for sexual minorities, and an English conversation class that discusses topics on feminism and the environment. These groups could use other public facilities, some of which may be available free of charge, but they use our facilities because they want to contribute to our running costs.

LOUD also provides an administrative base for various organizations. The Tokyo International Lesbian and Gay Film Festival based their office here for many years. In addition, we have a mailbox service for the groups who base their activities here. Those who are reluctant to have mail delivered openly to their home address can use LOUD as their contact address. We also hold open days twice a month—these are lively events with about twenty-thirty people on Sunday afternoons and about forty people on Saturday evenings.

Moderator: Am I correct in my assessment that lesbians are still quite invisible in Japanese society?

Oe: Yes, I think lesbians are completely invisible in Japan. I was interviewed for the "Gay in Japan" feature in the January 2007 issue of the Japanese edition of *Newsweek* magazine. The reporter told me at the time that the same feature had appeared in the US twenty years ago. With the exception of Kanako Otsuji, who is now giving national politics a try, virtually no other politician, artist or celebrity has come out as a lesbian.

Moderator: You have become publicly active in various ways since the late 1990s haven't you?

Oe: Right. LOUD was taken up in a weekly journal called *Shukan kinyobi* (Friday Weekly) (December 17, 1999 issue). Then my partner Ogawa and I did a photo interview in three parts, as a part of a special feature on sexual minorities made up of thirty articles, in *Sankei shimbun* (Sankei newspaper) (March 30, 31, and April 5, 2000), a newspaper with nationwide circulation.

Moderator: For a conservative paper like *Sankei*? That is a surprise.

Oe: A highly motivated female reporter was instrumental in publishing this special feature. It was a hot issue within the newspaper company and won the "Desk Award." Since our exposure in the media, more and more people have been contacting us.

Daito Bunka University was the first university that invited me as a guest speaker. Barbara Summerhawk, a professor in English and American literature there who has come out as a bisexual, invited me to speak. I was an object of great interest at that time, since they had previously had a gay guest, but it was their first encounter with a lesbian. The large lecture hall overflowed with students, and we had to organize a second lecture so that nobody missed out.

The students I've spoken to generally seem to hold negative perceptions of lesbians as women who want to be men, women who can't get married, or women who aren't attractive to men. In particular, I think that there are still many who think that lesbians want to be men. Meeting people like me seems to take the wind out of their sails because they realize, "Oh, she's just an ordinary middle-aged woman."

Of course, prejudices and preconceptions are deep-rooted, and when I speak of the domestic partnership system, some students respond with comments like "Such a system would destroy Japan," "Why don't you just go to a country where it's legal?" or "Oh, no, not in Japan!" When I speak of same-sex partners raising children, there are students who say, "That's not fair for the child." However, after ten years of lecturing at universities, I think that I am receiving more and more positive feedback from students who say that they feel the existing discrimination is irrational.

Moderator: It seems that heterosexual feminists have not really supported lesbian activism. Would you agree?

Oe: Yes, I would. Heterosexual feminists seem to get along very well with gay men. Some of them also seem to have contact with people with gender identity disorder (GID). However, they rarely seem to support lesbian activities.

Moderator: Why do you think that is the case? I heard it was considered to be quite a breakthrough when sexual-minority issues were addressed at the conference held by the Women's Studies Association of Japan in June 2007. I was really surprised to hear that. In the US and Europe, lesbians have been involved in mainstream feminism since at least the 1980s. So I don't understand why lesbians are hardly present at academic conferences in Japan.

Oe: Heterosexual feminists, especially, academics/researchers, seem to distance themselves from us. My personal opinion is that heterosexual feminists are particularly concerned about their relationship with men. I think they find it difficult because being feminists, they feel that they should be on an equal footing with their male partners, but this does not work well in reality. One woman told me that, to be truly equal, the partner would have to be another woman, not a man. However, that isn't possible for heterosexuals, so she felt a sense of guilt toward lesbians. It is my impression that it is perhaps such feelings of guilt that cause feminists to distance themselves from lesbians.

Moderator: We will move on now to Masae Torai and Aya Kamikawa, members of the transgender community in Japan. Mr. Torai, would you begin?

Torai: After graduating from university I went to the US to undergo female-to-male sex reassignment surgery. I write and speak on gender identity disorder (GID). I am editor of *FTM Nihon* (FTM Japan), a small-circulation magazine for people with GIDs launched in 1994, and now widely read by researchers and educators within and outside Japan.

I did not set out to become an activist; I just wanted to become a writer. I thought that if I wrote of my own experience, I would have more chance of being published, so I sbmitted my story, "Henseishosha no shuki" (Memoirs of a Transsexual), to a magazine called the *Asahi jaanaru* (Asahi Journal). It was published in two parts in 1987.

After the story appeared, I received about eight large boxes of letters from people of both sexes around the nation saying they were just like me. At first I talked to people who visited me, and had them stay in my house. But then my parents complained, and I ended up not having time for anything but work. That's why I decided to start the small-circulation magazine. In the beginning, I received some help from gays and lesbians. As a matter of fact, the first ten volumes or so of *FTM Japan* were printed at LOUD. There still was no Internet, so we started with a circulation of about sixty-three copies. This has now increased to four hundred. After that, Noriaki Fushimi,[1] a gay writer, introduced me to a publishing company called Seikyusha. I took an erotic FTM novel with me, but the editor said, "If you write a book about yourself, it will sell." I said, "I want to start out as a fiction writer," but the editor said, "Sell your name first before writing fiction." That's how I first started with the publication of *Onna kara otoko ni natta watashi* (My Transformation from Woman to Man) in 1996.

It was around 1995 when I received a letter, through *FTM Japan*, from Takao Harashina, a medical doctor at Saitama Medical University, saying, "I have an FTM patient who wants penis reconstruction surgery. I would like to hear how you had it done in the US." So I visited Dr. Harashina's home with four other MTFs and FTMs who had received genital reconstruction surgery overseas to talk about how it was done. After that, on July 2, 1996, Saitama Medical University publicly announced its intention to perform sex reassignment surgery. That's when the word that described us changed from "*henseisho*," until then used as a Japanese equivalent of "transsexuality" to "*seidoitsusei shogai*," (a medical term equivalent to GID).

Since then, the media's treatment of us has changed, too. The media used to treat me as a freak of nature who was neither man nor woman. But after Saitama Medical University made the announcement, the media started to treat us as "disabled people who need compassion." Even television features on "*new-half*" and "*onabe*"[2] now focus on people "coming out in tears to their families." The perception has really changed completely.

When a journalist named Honoho Morino, who was then active as a lesbian along with Kakefuda, went to interview the doctors at Saitama Medical University, a number of them apparently told her they had never met a transsexual patient before. So a self-help group called *TS to TG o sasaeru hitobito no kai* (Trans Net Japan: TNJ) was started in 1996 as a platform for discussion between physicians and patients. A number of other transgender groups sprouted at about the same time as TNJ, but many of them have folded since, and there are only a few committed groups today. *FTM Japan* has survived precisely because it is a "one-man band." There really aren't many groups left that are run by a collective. But all these groups, including LOUD, G-FRONT Kansai[3] and Sukotan kikaku[4] started around the same period. Nineteen ninety-five was certainly the year when "the god of the LGBT movement" descended upon us. But public interest was focused mostly on GID, particularly on the medical issues, and the human rights issues were completely ignored. After the medicalization of GID I challenged the judicial system in order to enable me to officially change my gender designation on the family register. At first I filed a claim on my own, but it was rejected.

It was around this time, 2000, that Chieko Nono, a LDP (Liberal Democratic Party) member of the House of Councillors, formed a study group about creating new legislation. Learning about GID at a sexology conference prompted Nono to think about whether she had not been mistaken, in her previous work as a midwife, in judging the gender of a newborn simply by looking at the infant's genitals. She asked us whether she could be of any help to people with GID. We immediately formed a project team and started a study group but we couldn't attract enough national assembly members. Many LDP assemblywomen came, but not a single middle-aged male member would come. Then the group was brought to a halt because Nono was appointed Vice-Minister of Health, Labor and Welfare.

It was a big disappointment, but thanks to the encouragement of Toshiyuki Oshima, who had been researching laws related to GID for over twenty years, I got together with my colleagues to file a collective claim to change one's gender designation on the family register in 2001. We gathered GID patients who had undergone surgery at Saitama Medical School, because we thought they might have more chance of being accepted, but to no avail. I was just beginning to think that this was just not going to work, when, in October 2001, the long-running popular television drama series, *San'nen B gumi Kimpachi sensei* ("Mr. Kimpachi, Teacher of Third Year Class B"), which depicts the lives of a class of third-year junior high school students, started airing episodes centering on FTM. It was a story the scriptwriter Mieko Osanai had wanted to write for some time because she had a friend who was an MTF transsexual. After she and I had a number of discussions, Osanai decided to feature an FTM rather than an MTF character, since MTFs had already received quite a bit of media coverage, and to use some episodes from my book. That was how the character Nao Tsurumoto, an FTM junior high school student was created.

When these episodes began to be aired, the number of emails and phone calls I received increased dramatically. I held consultations eight hours a day, 364 days of the year, with my only break being New Year's Day. Whereas the majority of people who consulted me before were those with GID who were college students or older, people of all ages, from seven to seventy, started contacting me once the drama series began, including primary and secondary school students and their mothers. But no fathers, not one. I assume no father was watching "Mr. Kimpachi," or even if they were, they relegated the problem solving to their wives.

But just in the last week of the "Mr. Kimpachi" series, a speedboat race driver named Chinatsu Ando (now known as Hiromasa Ando), who had been registered as female until then, declared the wish to register as a male athlete. News of Ando's coming out as a transgendered person was published in the tabloids. Anyone reading the column "What is GID?" at the time would have understood that GID was different from homosexuality. Fathers may well have read these articles.

I think "Mr. Kimpachi" helped mothers and children to understand a little more about GID, just as the Ando story helped men, both young and old, and I believe the two led up to the introduction of the new law, which I will ask Aya Kamikawa to describe as she continues the discussion from here.

Kamikawa: After I publicly disclosed my GID in 2003, I was elected to Tokyo's Setagawa Ward Assembly, the first self-disclosed sexual minority person to hold public office in Japan. In April 2005, my request that my gender on the family register be changed from male to female was approved under the Law Concerning Special Cases in handling Gender Status of People with Gender Identity Disorder. But I must go back to the beginning when I knew nothing about the possibility of a division between mind and body.

Since my romantic interests had always drawn me to men, I assumed I was homosexual. But even before my first experience of love at the age of thirteen, I felt some sense of discomfort. I could not call myself "*boku*" or "*ore*" (masculine first person pronouns in Japanese). And it somehow didn't feel right to be treated like a boy. I found it difficult to accept the rapid changes in my body as I experienced love and puberty in junior high school. I was also confused by the fact that I was constantly attracted to boys, but I was too scared to face up to these issues at the time. In my case, this fear lasted a long time. I ended up going to university after attending an all-boys high school and then becoming a white-collar worker for five years and three months. I felt I had to conduct myself within the confines of normative behavior, and so up to the age of twenty-seven, I posed as a heterosexual male who liked women.

Until I resigned from my first job at that age, I suffered from a number of problems, including a loss of hair, some impairment to my taste, hives, and duodenal ulcers. I finally realized I had to face up to my pain. There was no happiness in my life, and I began to question whether I could continue to live a life full of lies. So what I decided to do was to go to Tokyo's gay neighborhood, Shinjuku ni-chome, and approach male passersby saying, "Please be my friend." But I managed only to frighten the office workers I approached. Then in 1994, I went to a gay men's hiking circle, hoping I would at last meet someone with whom I could talk about myself, but the men there were all at ease with their bodies and with being treated as men. As hard as I tried to explain my situation, their reaction was, "Why do you need to become a woman?" They said they didn't "understand," and asked, "What's wrong with men liking men?" I realized this was not the place for me.

I was in my late twenties and I had no words with which to express myself, though I was sure that the root of my problem was "sexuality," so I continued to prowl the streets of Shinjuku ni-chome. Then, one day I came across a notice in a gay magazine that said, "Do you know about transsexuality?" So I participated in the first transsexual (TS) study group session on February 12, 1995. This study group was organized by Honoho Morino before TNJ started up in 1996.

I mustered up my courage to go there, and that was where I met

Masae Torai. At first, I assumed this person also wanted to be a woman, and wondered, "Why try so hard to be masculine?" Then when he told me it was the "opposite," my eyes popped. I had heard of the "new-half" phenomenon, of men who wanted to become women, and thought perhaps I was like them. I never thought of the possibility, however, of the opposite phenomenon. But after meeting him, I realized there were also people in a situation opposite to myself, and it offered me a hint to start analyzing my own case.

Torai: Yes, yes that's right. Aya Kamikawa looked the same, except her hair was short. Really beautiful: I knew straight away this person wanted to become a woman.

Kamikawa: The discomfort I felt with my body was so severe that I decided to start estrogen hormone injection therapy, recommended to me by people I'd met at the TS study group. Subsequently, I decided to go to Singapore to undergo surgery. When I came back to Japan the following year, Saitama Medical University's Ethics Board had already delivered their policy report saying it was legitimate to provide medical treatment for those with GID, and declared its intention to formulate guidelines for performing sex reassignment surgery. Opening the door to the first sex reassignment surgery, performed in 1998, the Japanese Society of Psychiatry and Neurology published the first edition of its guidelines. Public perception of these issues had changed dramatically during this time. This gave me hope that I might be able to live a full life in my own country.

From 1997, Honoho Morino, who had begun TNJ, began holding public symposiums involving the media, and bringing in all kinds of people—legal experts, sociologists, clergy, *manga* artists, and makeup artists. This helped us look at our issues from different perspectives, and to gradually understand our position in this society. From 2000 through 2003, I served as an official member running the TNJ, and in 2001 Mr. Torai and five others filed a claim in four separate family courts, seeking a change in their gender designation on the official family registers. These requests were rejected.

After I started living as a woman, I worked for four years as a full-time office worker, but as with others like me, getting a job as a regular, permanent employee was out of the question because most official documents, including those for employment insurance, workers' accident compensation insurance, corporate health insurance and the pension system, indicate the bearer's gender as recorded on the official family register, and of course the inconsistency between what was recorded, and my appearance caused many problems. So I went to the Social Insurance

Bureau and asked them to change my gender record because it hindered my chance for regular employment. I also asked the city council to change my gender on my residential records as it prevented me from renting a house. I also asked the Ministry of Health, Labor and Welfare and the unemployment office "Hello Work" to change the gender recorded on my health insurance card and employment insurance, respectively. Each time I spoke with the people in charge, they were taken aback and said they'd never heard of such a request. They all listened to my story, and some of them even advised me how to get around the rules. I eventually realized, however, that nothing would change without laws, government notices, or precedents. I thought it was ridiculous that I had to keep on refusing offers for regular employment and settle for part-time work. So when the courts rejected Mr. Torai's claim, it came to me as a great shock that even the judicial system was unwilling to consider our needs. That's when I realized we needed to make a new law on our own, and at the end of 2002 we began to lobby the National Diet (legislature) members, though we got to see only about twenty of them.

Torai: We visited the offices of about one hundred Diet members, you know.

Kamikawa: But we couldn't get past their secretaries, and even they didn't give us much of their time. On January 22, 2003, though, we were able to meet with Councillor Satoru Ienishi, who was elected to the Diet after suing the national government as the representative of a group of plaintiffs in Osaka who had been infected with HIV due to their defective transfusions. He spoke to us for many hours, based on his own personal experience, telling us, "Assembly members won't support you unless there is more social awareness. And you can't improve social awareness unless you lobby more publicly. . .Many of us endured public scrutiny in order to appeal to the public about HIV issues."

His advice really hit home. Even though we were running a support group at the time, none of us had made our names and faces public. Even when we received media coverage, we asked them to hide our faces, omit our real names, and change our voices. I realized that was not the way to go. Then, a local assembly member who had helped us with our lobbying suggested that I run for public office myself.

I then began to think that we shouldn't be expecting others to do the job when we were the ones who knew how we were treated in society, and in what ways we needed to change society. When I asked my parents' advice regarding my candidacy, they told me, "Don't worry about us. Just do your best to make you and your friends happy." That was how I became resolved to run for public office.

My partner is an FTM, like Mr. Torai. He donated the money he was saving for his surgery to my electoral campaign, and quit his job in order to work in the campaign. We began making speeches at train stations and street corners. The very first reaction we got was an outburst of insult from a stranger yelling, "What kind of upbringing did your parents give you!" Every visit to the shops in the commercial district was an ordeal. One after another people would say to us, "The problem is not with society. It's with your way of life." But finally two hundred people volunteered to help us and I was able to win the election in April 2003.

Talk of a "member's bill," also known as lawmaker-initiated legislation, emerged two weeks after I was elected. Now that I was elected, it seemed the perfect time to aim for approval of the "member's bill" by the end of the Diet session. I was able to meet with one hundred members of the Diet who had until then refused to hear our case. The Law Concerning Special Cases in handling Gender Status of People with GID was enacted in July 2003, effective July 2004. As of the end of 2006, more than five hundred people have changed their gender designation. More than three years have passed since the law came into effect, and it is about time we discussed changes, especially to the amendment attached to the law having to do with a person's "status regarding children." Changes of gender in the family register had to meet the following conditions: the applicant had to be twenty years or older, unmarried, sterile, having completed sexual reassignment surgery, and childless.[5]

Torai: On learning of the inclusion of the so-called "status regarding children" as one of the conditions for getting approval for a change in gender status, some GID people with children threatened to kill themselves, while others even warned us, "Watch your back." We felt at the time that we might not have a second chance if the bill didn't get passed at that time. We consulted with many people, including women involved in the enactment of legislation on domestic violence. Their advice was to "poke a small hole and spread it wide." But in the back of our minds we did have a concern that even if the law passed, it would be difficult to amend it.

Kamikawa: The bill had to gain unanimous approval from an LDP intra-party review by three bodies—the Judicial Affairs Division, the Deliberation Commission, and the General Council. If even one person in this process disapproved of the idea that people with children would be allowed to change their gender, the entire bill would have failed.

Oe: The enactment of this law created large ripples in the gay and lesbian community as well. There was great objection and protest from those who considered the Special Law as stipulating an explicit ban on same-sex marriage. This is because the condition that the subject "must not be married at the time" can be interpreted as an intention to avoid recognizing same-sex marriage. Still, others applauded this law as the first of its kind recognizing sexual minorities in Japan. In any case, the actual enactment of this law has certainly raised the public visibility of GID.

Kamikawa: It has become a critical human rights issue today.

Oe: But the issue of homosexuality has unfortunately fallen out of this picture. Since the Special Law was enacted, lesbian and gay issues have become increasingly invisible. The number of requests for lectures by lesbians and gays at various events has declined.

Kamikawa: I once spoke in front of eight hundred government officials at a research conference. I wanted to use the title "Sexual Minorities and Human Rights" but someone from the Ministry of Justice expressed disapproval. "GID" is permissible but not "sexual minorities." I was told it was all right to talk about sexual minorities in the lecture but that it would not be appropriate to put it in the title. The Ministry of Justice is strongly reluctant to take up any issues pertaining to lesbians and gays, and even more so when it comes to putting anything in writing. I was very much struck by a comment made by the Director of the Human Rights Bureau that, "Other human rights groups ask us not to put their issues in the same boat as homosexuality, though this is another form of discrimination."

It is easier to address GID for the local council because it has been recognized by the National Diet, and also publicly recognized as a disorder that requires assistance. I took up lesbian and gay issues repeatedly in the local assembly and finally managed to have lesbian and gay issues addressed as a footnote to the "Sexual Minorities" part of the ten-year plan. But the presence of one assembly member is not going to effect much change. The problem is that those affected by discrimination remain invisible. In the present system, the government will consider you to be nonexistent unless you speak out. What we need is to be seen, and to gradually but surely convey our demands and make those in charge become aware of the problems. No one can forget the efforts and passion of people who appear right in front of you. We must keep appealing to the empathy of more and more people. I've realized the importance of this since becoming an assembly member.

Moderator: As Mr. Torai mentioned previously, GID is considered a disorder that requires medical assistance. Homosexuality, however, tends to be seen as a matter of personal preference. Medicalization is one strategy for gaining social recognition, but since homosexuality is no longer considered to be a pathology, the position of lesbians and gays is weak in that sense.

Torai: I heard that there even was a move to use the term "Sexual Orientation Disorder."

Everyone: What! A disorder?

Kamikawa: I think "SOD" is neither viable nor correct as a strategy. I still
think the number one strategy is to promote visibility. According to a
study on gay and bisexual men conducted by Yasuharu Hidaka of Kyoto
University (AIDS Research Project funded by the Ministry of Health,
Labor and Welfare), one half of the subjects have never come out, and 90
percent of the subjects have not come out to their parents. In the 1999
survey, 64 percent of subjects had considered suicide and 15 percent had
attempted suicide. The sad reality of our society today is that their families don't realize their deep sufferings even when they are on the verge of
killing themselves.

Oe: I agree that visibility is very important, as you say, and more lesbians
and gays need to come out. But it isn't encouraged in reality because
some feel that visibility makes you vulnerable to attack, and coming out
may sever your relationship with family and friends. Furthermore, having a strong lesbian identity isn't encouraged either, as exemplified by an
argument awhile back saying strong lesbian identification would only
fortify the idea of gender dualism. So it is difficult.

On the other hand, "coming out" is being re-examined by some
people. The recently published *Kaminguauto retaazu* (Coming Out Letters) (RYOJI and Sunakawa, eds. 2007), includes letters about coming
out exchanged with close friends and family, as well as discussions by
parents of lesbians and gay men. It's a book that helps people understand
how to respond to someone who comes out to them. But, still, many
people hesitate to come out.

Torai: I guess it can't be helped. Even among FTMs, a clear line is drawn
between those who refuse to come out and those who do not hesitate to
come out from the beginning. It all depends on whether you want to live
as a "man" or as an "FTM." But isn't it the gay men who are not so enthusiastic about coming out and the domestic partnership law?

Oe: Right. Women are more enthusiastic about it.

Moderator: Why is it that many gay men don't want to come out?

Oe: Men generally hold higher status in society, so they have more to lose.
One significant reason why more women support domestic partnership
laws is that more than 50 percent of women work in part-time nonreg-
ular employment, and so many need to share their income with their
partners in order to maintain a decent standard of living. Of course,
some women find the couple-oriented lifestyle unacceptable, while oth-

ers stress the importance of woman's independence and self-sufficiency as an individual.

Moderator: Don't students learn about sexual minorities in school at all? When I talk to university students, I get the impression they are totally unfamiliar with the issue.

Oe: From time to time senior high school teachers bring small groups of students to LOUD as an extracurricular activity. They come to hear about discrimination against lesbians. When I talk to them, their first impression seems to be, "Oh, she's not that different from us. She's a normal person." First-year high school students are very flexible—they may be really tense at first, but after listening to my talk their view changes completely, and they become quite open and friendly. University students are more conservative. That's why I think it would be best to start talking about sexual minorities in junior high school.

Moderator: In the book *Tayonasei ga wakaru hon* (Understanding Diverse Sexualities) (Ito and Torai, eds. 2002) a young man recounts that as a high school student he was so troubled about his homosexuality that he contemplated suicide. We really need a comprehensive, supportive education to help similarly troubled young people.

Oe: My partner told me she spent her youth in that kind of darkness. She felt she was not needed in this society, and so she just couldn't wait to get old. She couldn't bear to be an object of sexual interest to men.

Moderator: Are there people in the community who are actively involved in educational efforts?

Kamikawa: I am often invited to speak to educators, from the junior high school to university level. GID seems an easier topic to address in public because of the law enacted in 2003. I always take advantage of these opportunities to deal as well with issues of diverse sexualities because I want to promote understanding of those issues among students and teachers alike. But if I try to use a title like "Sexual Minorities and Human Rights," the school administration will ask me not to use it.

Torai: I'm familiar with efforts to promote sex education in many parts of the country, but not much is being done in Tokyo. They can do it as long as the school principal approves, but I have a feeling they don't report it to the board of education. Given the current governor of Tokyo, who espouses the view that "men have to be manly," it's a difficult situation. In certain areas of Japan such as Saitama, Osaka, Kyoto, and Fukuoka, where efforts to deal with Buraku discrimination are more prominent[6] and there is more awareness of human rights, sexuality is taught as a part of human rights education. But in Tokyo, teachers shy away from anything that touches on sexuality, whether it is homosexuality or GID.

Kamikawa: Teachers seem very apprehensive about taking up the issue.

Oe: I think parents are a big issue for teenagers who are junior or senior high school students. The younger they are, the more important it is for parents to understand, and support them. There is an organization called AGP (Association of Gay Professionals in Counseling and Medical Allied Fields) made up of professionals in health care and education. They provide support and information to parents of sexual minorities.

Kamikawa: Yes, that is crucial. When I propose that the issue of sexual minorities be addressed in school sex education classes, the usual response is "We don't know how the parents will react." Sexuality is one area where big discrepancies exist in values and perceptions among adults. That's why schools can't just go ahead and act on their own. They first need to seek the approval and understanding of the parents.

Moderator: Kids don't talk to their parents about sexuality, and parents just tell their kids things like "Make sure you don't get pregnant," but there is a taboo against talking about sexuality. On the one hand, the sex industry is booming, but on the other hand, talking seriously about sex and sexuality is considered taboo.

Oe: When I speak before an audience of college students who are women, I always start by saying, "My discussion will include some sexual content. Some of you might be repelled, but if that's the case, I'd like you to think whether your feelings are directed toward sex and sexuality in general, or specifically homosexuality." While some young college women may dislike talking about sex in general, others have already been sexually active since junior or senior high school.

Kamikawa: There is heightened interest in sexual matters, and they are talked about a lot among youth. Although they are exposed to a flood of information about sex, they lack the literacy skills to judge and to interpret the information. Recently, there was an incident in which a senior high school student gave birth in the toilet, and left the baby in the toilet bowl. There were two similar cases in my election district. The young women didn't know they were pregnant until they gave birth. They said they had a stomachache, and when they got to the school toilet . . .The school boards don't seem to understand the severity of the situation, but the school nurses certainly see it as a serious problem.

Moderator: The percentage of senior high school students who've had sexual experience is quite high now, isn't it?

Kamikawa: A friend of mine who works as a school counselor at a public high school told me, "Having sex is a daily occurrence for many girls. It's a big problem." And the adults don't even teach these young women how to protect their own bodies. A number of assembly members, mainly women, consider the lack of accurate sex education a problem. But I never use words like "gender" or "sex education" when I address the issue in the assembly. As soon as I mention those words, the voices of the conservative faction drown my words, and I can see the shutters rattling to a close before my eyes. So instead I say things like, "Over 30 percent of women who receive examinations at health centers in Tokyo have been diagnosed with chlamydia. This puts them at twice the risk of contracting HIV." I also tell them, "The number of women diagnosed with cervical cancer in their twenties is increasing, and this is because human papillomavirus is contracted through sexual intercourse. Given that the virus is dormant for several years, women in their twenties may suffer from cancer contracted by sex in their teens." When I put it that way, even the middle-aged male assembly members begin to take it seriously. But if begin by talking about sex education, it just doesn't register on them.

Moderator: Do you think there is a growing interest regarding the same-sex partnership system? I assume there are differences according to generation.

Oe: Many, even those who have been in a long-term relationship, say they weren't really interested in a domestic partnership system before. But it seems as they get older, they start to face problems of ageing and feel the need for a system that will provide protection and benefits for them.

Moderator: In the transsexual community, is there a growing interest in the same-sex partnership system?

Torai: Among some MTF lesbians there is considerable interest, but most people have their hands full trying to save up money for surgery.

Kamikawa: Are there any FTM gays?

Torai: Well, very few that I know of. Even if there were, they would probably be working hard to save money for their own surgery. I also think most of the FTMs who say they are "lesbian" still have FTM and lesbian mixed-up.

Kamikawa: Coming to terms with one's own gender identity is such a big hurdle that I don't know how many people think of an LGBT coalition after that. The term "LGBT" that unites us has spread considerably in the past two or three years. But I don't know how many people recognize the importance of forming a coalition and are sufficiently motivated to become actively involved.

Oe: The situation is similar with lesbians. They can hook up easily through the Internet, so some couples have never met any other lesbians at all.

Kamikawa: There was a time when trans-people were a stronger force, with support groups holding special events several times a month. Now

they have lost their power considerably. People can have surgery overseas without being diagnosed by a psychiatrist, buy hormones through
the Internet, and access information from books without having to join
a support group. There is none of that unifying centripetal force that
brings people together due to social pressure.

Torai: For example, some MTFs are still married to their wives and are
therefore unable to change their gender to female on the family register.
How do you think people like that could join forces with lesbians?

Oe: In such cases, the wife of the MTF would not consider their union to
be that of a "lesbian couple." These wives do not feel they are married to
a woman, or that they themselves are lesbians. I think some wives would
be against easing the conditions of the GID Special Law. The condition
may be even necessary in order to protect the spouse and children.

Kamikawa: GID is so focused on the issue of right to self-determination
that the wives feel they and the children are left behind, and don't know
what to do. That is the problem.

Moderator: Could we have a word from each of you on future prospects?

Oe: Though we are undergoing financial difficulties, we can't close down our
operations immediately. In order to be able to keep operating, we need to
extend and expand the range of lesbian establishments and enterprises,
so that money can circulate effectively within the LGBT community.
It's great that the know-how of LOUD is being made use of in various
areas. If a similar place is created, I think we should each focus on different characteristics instead of competing against each other. LOUD, for
example, could continue to be a place for first-timers.

Another thing I would like to do is to create a database of resources
that can be accessed by many different people. I think it's difficult for any
group, not only LOUD, to effectively manage and make use of resources
and books. I'd like to put all that together in one database system, and
make it available to anyone who is interested.

Kamikawa: Now I am an assembly member, but who knows what I will do
next? Since I have been re-elected for a second term, I intend to fulfill
my responsibilities for the next four years. Now that the GID Special Law
has passed, I do have some say in the assembly, and I am often asked to
speak before various government bodies, so I want to make use of those
opportunities to speak out, not only about GID, but also about diverse
sexualities, and the desire to live a life true to oneself.

We can't change anything by being silent. There is always a risk
involved when we stick our head out and speak up, but even if you don't
go so far as to stand for election, there are many things one can do, such
as writing a public comment, or emailing local or national government

assembly members. Once silent myself, I ran for public office to become an assembly member. But I think there are many ways in which we can convey our needs and demands to society. I want to continue communicating this to everyone.

Torai: I can no longer lay back and say, "I will continue with the small circulation journal until I'm seventy, and do my writing, and give lectures." I opened an office in January 2007. I pay the rent and all expenses out of my own pocket, so I've been sending about ten emails a day to various places asking for work, and my workload is gradually increasing. With the money I'm saving, my goal eventually is to establish a college with a single department—in human rights. I don't know if it's possible but I now have five preliminary steps in mind. First, I'd like to create a free space for GID children and their mothers. There are children suffering from social withdrawal due to GID. They are often talented, for example in music or art. Some of them quit school because they don't want to wear the school uniform. So I want to give such children a place to spend their time. A place where ten-twenty such children could learn, or just do what they want. A place to stop them from going the wrong way. I want to create a place that could help them obtain high school or college qualifications.

Moderator: I would like to thank all of you for your time today.

Notes

1. Noriaki Fushimi, a writer, came out nationwide by publishing a book called *Puraibeeto gei raifu* (Private Gay Life) in 1991, which carried a photo of the author. At this time, the simple fact that straight media published a picture of a gay man was epoch-making.

2. "*New-half*" is a professional category describing MTF cross-dressers or (ex-male) transsexuals who work as bar hostesses, dancers in show business, sex workers, etc. "*Onabe*" is an often derogatory term for women who have strongly masculine elements and is used to refer to FTM cross-dressers, FTM transsexuals, butch lesbians, etc. Recently the term is used mostly to indicate FTM cross-dressers who work as bartenders and bar "hosts" (as opposed to hostesses).

3. G-FRONT Kansai was set up in 1994 as an association for sexual minorities in Osaka. http://www.5e.biglobe.ne.jp/~gfront/

4. Sukotan kikaku was set up in 1994 (Representative: Satoru Ito). Now renamed "Sukotan Social Service," it continues to be active. http://www.sukotan.com/index.html

5. In June 2008, this last item was revised to apply only to children under age twenty.

6. For discussions of Buraku discrimination see Risa Kumamoto's essay, "Buraku Solidarity" and Yuriko Hara's essay, "Ainu, Buraku, and Zainichi Korean Activists Rise Up" in this volume.

Works Cited

Fushimi, Noriaki. 1991. *Puraibeeto gei raifu* (Private Gay Life). Tokyo: Gakuyo shobo.

Ito, Satoru and Masae Torai, eds. 2002.*Tayonasei ga wakaru hon* (Understanding Diverse Sexualities). Tokyo: Kobunsha.

RYOJI, and Hideki Sunakawa, eds. 2007. *Kaminguauto retaazu* (Coming Out Letters). Tokyo: Tarojirosha editasu.

Torai, Masae. 1996. *Onna kara otoko ni natta watashi* (My Transformation from Woman to Man). Tokyo: Seiyusha.

V

ACTIVISM FOR THE RIGHTS OF MINORITIES

The Story of Kalakasan and Migrant Filipinas[1]

Leny P. Tolentino and
Nanako Inaba

In 2007, roughly 2.15 million foreigners —or about 1.7 percent of the country's total population, coming from 190 different countries—lived in Japan. Not surprisingly, over nearly four decades, marriages per annum between Japanese and foreign nationals have steadily increased from around 5,500 in 1970 to more than 40,000 in 2007. In 2007, such bicultural marriages accounted for 5.6 percent of all marriages in Japan. In addition, over a long period, there was still another significant shift. Up until 1975, in the majority of such marriages, Japanese women were marrying foreign men. Beginning in 1975, however, the pattern changed: in 80 percent of these couples, numbering about 32,000, Japanese men married foreign women. A large proportion of these women came from other Asian countries, the largest number Chinese, roughly 12,000, or about 38 percent, followed by 9,200 Filipina women, or 29 percent (Kokuritsu josei kyoiku kaikan 2009, 24; 25, table 2-10).

Filipina women began coming to Japan in the mid-1980s seeking work. Some came on special six-month visas to work as "entertainers," mostly in bars and so-called "snacks," while the majority entered the country on short-term tourist visas, and stayed on, working illegally. Still others have come to Japan as brides through marriages brokered by marriage agencies. Some of the women who initially came to Japan to work temporarily have subsequently married Japanese men, and settled down in Japan. In total, about 130,000 Filipina women married Japanese men between 1992 and 2008 (Koseirodosho for various years).

A significant problem associated with these marriages begins with the foreign wives' dependence on their husbands, since they have to sign off on their wives' annual visas, without which they cannot legally remain in Japan. Automatically, therefore, foreign wives become extraordinarily dependent on their husbands. Furthermore, should a wife decide to divorce, she would find it very difficult to retain her legal residence in Japan unless she were raising children fathered by a Japanese man.[2] Finally, should a wife lack proficiency in Japanese, her opportunity for employment would be limited. While there are no statistics concerning the number of foreign women who fall victim to domestic violence in Japan, a survey by the Ministry of Health, Labor and Welfare reveals a growing increase in the number of non-Japanese women victimized by domestic violence receiving temporary protection at Women's Consultation Centers (Fujin sodanjo): in 2007 that figure was 407 or nine percent of the total number (4,549) of these women (Koseirodosho 2008, 42-43).

What follows is an account of the process through which a group of Filipina women, suffering discrimination, abuse, and violence at the hands of their Japanese male partners, reclaimed their strength and self-respect, reconstructed their lives, achieved personal empowerment, and, moreover, recognized the need for collective action to overcome discrimination. The account focuses in particular on their participation in the Feminist Participatory Action Research (FPAR) conducted by the Kalakasan Migrant Women Empowerment Center, a nonprofit organization located near Tokyo. Through this experience, they gained an opportunity to share their stories and to study, analyze, and reflect on their lives. They managed to achieve an understanding of the forces that had directly caused or indirectly contributed to their victimization and oppression, as well as to summon strength within themselves to feel empowered, and to appreciate the resources which had supported them through this process.

The Kalakasan Migrant Women Empowerment Center

When the Yokohama Catholic Diocese Solidarity Center for Migrants (SOL)[3] was closed in March 2002, its staff, together with abused, migrant Filipina women, who were then volunteers in SOL, continued to feel the need to help migrant women and their children gain a dignified, humane, secure, and vibrant life in Japan. Migrant Filipina women faced harsh realities in Japan. Cultural differences, insufficient fluency in Japanese, unfamiliarity with customs and governance, social and economic pressures, and gender bias—all contributed to the marginal and impoverished lives of migrant women and their children. In most cases, being Filipinas meant that they would face discrimination. The need seemed great, and there were resources, especially among the staff that had worked at SOL. Therefore, on December 7, 2002, the Kalakasan Migrant Women Empowerment Center was launched, with many programs aimed to help Filipina women, including crisis intervention, follow-up care, education and training, home visits, and programs especially for children, as well as advocacy and lobbying.

Feminist Participatory Action Research (FPAR) conducted at Kalakasan

The word "Kalakasan" is Tagalog for "strength," thus providing the organization with its overarching goal: to help women recognize their inner strength, which, when reclaimed, will lead them to personal empowerment and collective action. Among the volunteers and staff of Kalakasan are former victims of domestic abuse who initially came to Kalakasan to seek help and eventually stayed on to participate in its activities. One of these projects is called Feminist Participatory Action Research (FPAR). This program responded to the critiques of migrant women who were displeased when they were treated by researchers as objects of interviews, not as human beings with feelings and interests of their own. Inspired by the realization that women could study and analyze their experience from their own viewpoints, and hoping that they would then take action together to change the lives of abused migrant Filipina women in Japan, FPAR organized its first study group.

Each of the five Filipina women who participated in this first group had been abused by their Japanese partners. One of the participants was a migrant with five children, all of them undocumented. She still lived with her Japanese partner; they were not married. The four other women had already divorced their Japanese partners and had the rearing and custody rights of their Japanese children, which allowed them to remain in Japan. Three women needed to renew their long-term residence visas regularly, and one had a permanent visa that she had acquired before her divorce. For many years before the study, I, Leny P. Tolentino, the facilitator, had accompanied and supported migrant Filipina women in their struggles. In this report, four of the women have used pseudonyms; Donna Nishimoto chose to use her real name.

Donna, who had been an activist on behalf of migrants since long before 2003, and who had worked as a staff member since 2003, was now serving as co-director of Kalakasan. The newest member of the group first came to Kalakasan in 2004. Donna and three other women first received support from the former office of SOL. They had stabilized their legal status for residence in Japan, along with their children's, and had improved the poor images they had once had of themselves. Commonalities connected the group: all were Filipina migrants in Japan, speaking the same native language, and coming mostly from an economically deprived social class. Although I, the facilitator, had not entered into an intimate relationship with a Japanese man nor had I been abused, I had worked on behalf of abused migrant Filipina women for sixteen years. The women had come from different locations in the Philippines, with different family and educational backgrounds, and with different levels of consciousness. We met as a group nine times between July 2004 and January 2005 for four- to five-hour sessions. Once we met overnight, talking for eight hours. All but one member of the group had been friends for many years, and thus, could speak openly.

We called the first four meetings "The River of Life," for we were each telling our individual stories to each other. On a long piece of paper we wrote our life stories, beginning in childhood. We looked at different stages of our lives, both in the Philippines and Japan. We asked ourselves, "What have we learned as women and migrants?" In the Philippines, women were expected to do housework and farm-work or earn money to support the family if they were to be respected. Two women had been sexually harassed and abused, while three had witnessed their mothers being abused by their fathers. The women had been taught to believe that men were more powerful and intelligent than women, and that God had made it so. They also described their experiences with their Japanese partners, remembering that the relationships were enjoyable and egalitarian before marriage, but restricted severely after marriage.

We agreed to listen and to ask questions, but not to contradict or judge. We also set an informal tone and setting; we could lie down, sit, or stand. Emerging from our religious tradition as Catholic Christians, we sometimes started and ended sessions with a prayer.

As facilitator, I (Leny P. Tolentino) was the last to share my story. I could have escaped that, and probably no one would have pressured me to speak. I shared my story, however, because I wanted to make the women feel that we were equals, and to build our relationship. My experience also made clear that whatever their particular circumstances, all women may share the same oppression. Two of the participants commented, "This is a different kind of study because the one studying us is also sharing her story."

During the last sessions, we tried to understand ways to reclaim power and recreate lives. We used the final meeting to confirm what we had learned as well as to make our recommendations to Kalakasan. We had illuminated both the oppression and subordination we had experienced in the Philippines, and then again, in a heightened form, in Japan. We were able to claim that participants could reverse their status as victims through the use of their inner strength and the support of other individuals and groups.

Recollections of Life in the Philippines

The women who participated in this study came from the three major islands of the Philippines: Anna and Belen from Luzon, Donna and Celia from the Visayas, and Ester from Mindanao. Growing up, only one of the women lived in a family with a stable source of income: Anna's mother was a high school teacher and her father worked for a drug company. The other four women's families depended on mining, farming, operating small stores, and assisting custom officers at ports.

Celia's family had enough income when she was in preschool, but when she was about to start elementary school, her parents' store went bankrupt. Celia believes it was because her father was spending money on other women. Life became very difficult, especially when her father started to abuse her mother. Her mother left when Celia was in fourth grade, then reconciled with her father twice, but he continued to abuse her. Finally, her mother ended the relationship. Now her parents live separately, each with a new family. Celia, the third of seven siblings, was the main breadwinner of her family after her mother first left them. At the age of ten, she started working as a fruit and fish sidewalk vendor, and when there was no supply of fruits and fish, she worked on a poultry farm. Her economic contribution to the family had been recognized and respected, especially by her father, who used to favor her over her siblings.

Donna is the fifth child in her family. Her father was an assistant to a port customs officer. It was not the amount of money he earned that made their life difficult, but his behavior. He liked alcohol, so it was hard for them when he was drunk, because he became violent. Her father did not hand his salary over to her mother. When her mother talked to him about this, he abused her. To avoid being hurt, her mother took a laundry job so she could use her own income for family expenses. Donna remembered her mother sending her and her younger brother to harvest vegetables from the swamp to sell to the neighbors. At the age of fourteen, Donna left her family and took different jobs to survive—as a housemaid, babysitter, cook, and food vendor. She left because she was rebellious toward her father, and she promised that she would help improve her family's standard of living.

Regarding education, the highest formal attainment among the participants was Anna's two years at a university, but she was unable to finish her studies when she married. Belen finished high school with her parents' support, and Celia sold fish and fruit during the day and enrolled in night school to finish high school. Donna received a scholarship during high school, but because of her family situation and her rebellious feelings toward her father, she left home.

Ester finished a midwifery course with the support of an uncle. "I realized that I am not brainless, which I used to believe about myself," Ester said. "Before, when I was in high school," she continued, "I planned to marry a foreigner, perhaps an American because I saw our neighbors' daughters, who had married foreigners, returning to our village wearing good clothing and jewelry. Passing the board exam made me change my mind. I wanted to work abroad, using my capabilities, rather than be a wife."

In spite of economic hardship and the restrictions and abuses experienced growing up, all participants tried to find solutions to change their oppressed and subordinated situation. Their coming to Japan as entertainers, and as wives, was mainly an economic alternative, not only for them, but also for their loved ones in the Philippines.

Recollections of Life in Japan

All the participants were in their twenties when they first came to Japan. Anna, Celia, and Ester met and married Japanese men in the Philippines, then entered Japan on spousal visas. The husbands of Belen and Donna had been customers at the "snack" bar where they had worked as entertainers. Belen had entered Japan on an entertainer's visa, while Donna came as a tourist.

Except for Anna, the women were in their twenties when they entered into relationships with their future Japanese spouses. Anna said that love was the main reason for her marriage. Celia, who had three Filipina children from a previous relationship in the Philippines, met her Japanese husband through a friend. Her desire to be married in the church and to have a typical family life were her main motivations for marrying, but as they lived together, she began to feel love for him. Ester met her husband through a marriage agency in the Philippines, where there were five Japanese men looking for wives. She felt proud to have been selected.

Belen and Donna, who had met their husbands in their Japanese workplace, entered into their relationships for similar reasons. Belen accepted a marriage proposal because she was tired of performing at auditions as well as moving through annual immigration procedures, which allowed her to work as an entertainer, always fearful that she would be refused entrance. After marriage, Belen's husband did not facilitate her migration to Japan, so she had to apply to enter Japan once more as an entertainer. When she phoned her husband on her arrival, he hung up on her, and then changed his number, so that Belen was unable to find him. She found work increasingly unbearable, especially the pressure to reach the required quota of customers in order to produce the money she had to pay management. To escape, she eloped with her partner, then a customer, and now father to her five children, but not her husband.

Donna was tired of having to travel to and from Japan as a tourist, and like Belen, feared that at some point, she would not be allowed to enter

Japan. Were that to happen, she would not be able to support her two children and other family members in the Philippines. Donna, who had lived for eight years with a Filipino man (the father of her two Filipina daughters) before her two failed marriages in Japan, stated that after three (attempted) relationships, she was convinced that marriage was not for her.

At the time of the sessions, only Belen was living with her partner. The others had divorced their partners and were living with their children. Anna, Celia, and Donna had long-term resident visas, and Ester a permanent visa, which she had received before her divorce. Belen was overstaying her visa. Belen, Celia, and Donna had children in the Philippines with Filipino partners. Celia had to support her three children because they were still young. Donna did not worry much because her daughters had their own family. Belen wanted to send support for her son's education, but could not because she was raising five children in Japan without the ability to find a good job. Belen's situation was most precarious, since she had overstayed her visa, and since her five dependent children did not have a legal right to stay in Japan because they did not have legal recognition from their Japanese father.

All of these women knew that women with some of these problems were denied ordinary public protection or support. But it was a revelation that their problems were not unique, that other Filipina women suffered similar domestic violence, and other kinds of abuse. It did not matter whether one was in love, or had met one's partner through the workplace, an agency, or friends. It did not matter whether or not they had children from previous relationships. The participants became especially aware of the difficulties faced by Filipina women with children and without documentation.

Unequal Intimate Relationships

Our discussions confirmed that the Japanese men who met their wives in the workplace were aware of the indignity of harassment that women suffered in the workplace. They were also sensitive to women who worried about their uncertain legal status for remaining in Japan. Such Japanese men, the women said, intended to help women escape their miseries. Donna told one story:

> Even when I found out that I was the fifth wife of my first Japanese husband, I still married him because I had experienced his kindness when we lived together before marriage. He understood my situation. He offered marriage so that I could have a visa. In return, he asked me to take care of him. He understood the need to send money to the Philippines for my children and parents. But after our marriage, when we

came back to Japan, he started to control me. I was like a prisoner who had to obey him. He chose the color of my dresses and jewelry, and I could not go anywhere without him.

Such men thought that helping a Filipina woman meant turning her into a Japanese woman. After marriage, husbands became very controlling and critical of their wives' behavior. Women whose marriages were arranged by a friend, or a marriage agency, seemed to feel especially strong pressure to behave as a Japanese woman. The men paid for these women they chose, and expected them to be obedient wives and to act according to the Japanese way. Ester described her experience:

> My husband used to say, "I am ashamed of you," for not using the right things, such as the appropriate umbrella. He wanted Japanese manners to be observed, such as when we were eating—he would say I was messy. He also became very angry, and did not talk to me for days when I fried dried fish from the Philippines, causing so much smoke that it set the fire alarm ringing. I was of course hurt by what he said and by his attitude toward me.

We thought that deep in the consciousness of the Japanese partners laid the belief that all things male, or Japanese, were superior to any others. The system of domination and subordination, based on one's race, class, and gender, pervades the Japanese way of life. For Hisako Kinukawa, this is a reflection of patriarchy[4] penetrating into family life as a small-scale model of the emperor system. In every household, the father is viewed as the authority and the rest of the family, including his wife, are subject to him as head of the household (Kinukawa 1994, 19).

Migrant women have been abused for their inadequate Japanese language skills, their unfamiliarity with Japanese culture, and for being non-Japanese and poor. We found Kinukawa's statement helpful in clarifying this point, "Patriarchy in Japan has become notorious for its racial exclusivity promoted for the purpose of maintaining ethnic purity" (Ibid.). What does this mean to us? It signifies a mindset that believes that "ours is the best," meaning Japanese. It generates a conscious or unconscious tendency to pressure others who are different to act and think as the majority does. Even with the onset of a Japanese internationalization policy and an influx of non-Japanese migrants in Japan, this mindset has not changed much. Before a migrant can be afforded acceptance and respect in Japanese society, he or she has to become Japanese in ways and attitudes. We confirmed this through years of accompanying migrant women and listening to their stories, and through relationships with Japanese colleagues and staff of public and private institutions concerned with the issues of migrants, children, and women.

Anger and the Decision to Break Away
from Abusive Relationships

In the course of group discussions, participants grew aware of the anger that had developed as an expression of their resistance to the stereotyped characterization of women in the Philippines as "obedient and docile wives." The anger expressed their reaction to their treatment as non-entities, neither informed nor consulted, automatically judged, never appreciated as they were because "there was a better way to do it." They expressed their anger not only for their own sakes, but also for the lives and dignity of their children.

The group realized the importance of identifying, owning, and expressing their anger as key to their empowerment. By referring to the article, "The Healing Power of Anger," we tried to understand anger more deeply, and how to use it positively (Saussy and Clarke 1996, 116-120). Since skills in handling anger constructively need time and practice, the participants were challenged to incorporate the need to understand anger in their daily lives. Is anger a reaction, a projection, or something stemming from one's belief system? Do individuals hate or respect themselves and their anger? And can they express their anger directly and responsibly to the target of their anger? The participants acknowledged the importance of avoiding the projection of their anger onto innocent others, their children, for example, which would continue the cycle of violence and disrespect.

"I had had enough," various women said, "when I saw my partner slapping my eight-year-old daughter; when he attempted to inject me with heroin; when he threatened me with a knife; when he sat on my belly during my second pregnancy; when my daughter became pregnant because my partner sexually assaulted her; when he pushed me onto the floor in front of my visitors; when I regained consciousness to find that his worst assault had impaired my hearing and sight; when he had relationships and was spending money on other women." The accumulation of many abusive incidents aroused intense anger, and thus marked a turning point for some of these women who then left their partners to seek a safe place for themselves and their children. In some cases, a woman tried to end the abuse many times. Anna tried to bear it for five years. Her parents had been opposed to her marriage, and she had promised them to make that marriage a success. She tried her best, but when the violence became close to lethal, she escaped with the help of a Japanese friend, and finally decided to divorce her husband.

Celia, Donna, and Ester had made many attempts to end their respective relationships. They pointed to three factors that had made it difficult.

First, the absence of emotional readiness, recognized as the effect of threats and demeaning categorizations heard by the women every day during their lives with their abusive partners. Deeply ingrained in their minds was the thought that they could not live without their partners. This was strengthened by an inability to communicate and to read and write in Japanese. The fact that they could not legally stay in Japan without the sponsorship of their Japanese partner contributed markedly to their dependence. Ester said that, when she received her permanent visa, she became more secure.

The second factor was the seeming inability of the Philippine Consulate to help Filipina women, though this may no longer be the case. One woman recalled that, when she approached the Philippine Consulate in the city of Kobe in the late 1980s, she was told that it was beyond their authority to do anything about her marriage problems, and that she should inquire at the ward office. When she did, she was told that hiring a lawyer was expensive and she would not be able to afford it, that to stay in Japan, she would have to return to her partner.

The third factor was the absence of clear information regarding support available to wives who divorce their partners, including their rights with regard to their children. Information about economic support was critical to their ability to make the decision to end abusive relationships.

The Support of Kalakasan Changed Consciousness

Anna, Celia, Donna, and Ester had been helped to take the step of divorcing their husbands, and overcoming various obstacles through the sustained support of Kalakasan and other groups and individuals. These women discovered that they could decide their futures. They could plan to work for their own welfare and that of their children. They knew also that they were able to learn Japanese, and to grow more familiar with the culture, for they would initiate that action, rather than feel pushed by their husbands. Once they had left their partners, they pursued many different life-giving strategies, including finding appropriate support groups, because they understood that they could not manage alone. They came to realize that empowerment was not an individual endeavor but that it emerges through relationships. They needed other individuals or groups who cared enough to give them space to be themselves, to help them sort out, and identify their anger and the figures that had insisted that they repress that anger. Belen testified to the importance of her experience at a critical moment:

> Here at Kalakasan I came to know that I still have a chance to stay in Japan. I was afraid of my marriage—that I was married to one man yet

living with another. At one point I surrendered; I agreed to go back to the Philippines because I thought nothing could be done. Before I knew about Kalakasan, I could not sleep at night. But now I can sleep well. Is this what is called "peace of mind"? I said to my sister on the phone. Now that I know the sisters at Kalakasan, it is as if ten stones had been removed from my head, making my weight much lighter. My sister cried to hear me.

Donna testified also, "Encouragement—if there is somebody encouraging us, it helps us to reclaim our powers and recreate our lives. If there is encouragement, you go out, you speak, and you know how to face people. If you do not do it, your voice cannot come out. The things that I don't see in myself, I see in others." Donna told us that, in the beginning, she had attended meetings and informal gatherings at Kalakasan without really understanding the issues being discussed. She cooperated because she was determined to continue being involved in actions for justice and peace. Donna said that she appreciated the support of others through meetings, conferences, and training sessions. At the same time, she gave credit to herself for changing her life, "The support was important, but most important was my strong determination to change my life, and act to change the system that discriminates against migrant women."

Donna was the first to disclose her experiences as a migrant woman in Japan. Fearlessly she shared these experiences before student groups at universities, to gatherings of migrants, and in training sessions or workshops. She also described how, when lawmakers were discussing revisions to the Law for the Prevention of Spousal Violence and Protection of Victims, she and others from Kalakasan lobbied members of the National Diet, or legislature, to express the concern of migrant women that the law be amended to apply to them.[5]

Collective Action to Reconstruct Lives

In the process of taking part in this FPAR study, the five women developed a sense of sisterhood. Especially energizing was the experience of telling one's own story. Ester felt that the circle of women became her family, and that the regularity of the sessions made it possible for her to recollect and describe her past life, including even those events which she had sought to forget. Donna said, "Things that were deeply buried inside were unearthed, shared, and processed, resulting in a deeper understanding of ourselves in relation to others." She added that, "Even those who had had no voice were able to tell their stories once trust had developed among us." For her, Donna said, "The experience was beautiful, seeing survivors empowered by the process." In the beginning, some women were not expressive, but "as we met regularly, they became passionate as they told their stories and discovered their strengths."

These women have been able to encourage other abused women to resist violence and injustice, and to work for the transformation of their lives, their children, and even their communities. Ester passionately shared with the group that, within her circle of Filipino friends and her neighbors, women suffering from domestic abuse consult her about their problems. She described how she shared her own experiences with them, and then advises them about where they can go for support. She reported that she was frustrated at first when women hesitated or changed their minds about leaving their abusive partners, but she also knew how difficult such decisions can be. Ester remembered a woman who came to see her, "with black eyes and bad bruises. I told her to report immediately to the ward office. I even offered to accompany her. She told me we would go the next day. But again, she changed her mind. Her partner promised to change, and gave her money. How could I make her understand? But I know now how difficult it is to end a relationship with the abuser."

Donna told the group that she visits survivors who are starting to establish their lives in Japan, assuring such women that they are not alone. She encourages both mothers and their children to visit Kalakasan or to join Kalakasan's church-sponsored activities. To accompany someone in difficulty is very much a part of Filipino culture, which is why Donna's visits are important to help put back together the broken pieces of abused migrant Filipina women's lives. During our sharing sessions, the participants described how outside support helped them at different points of the process of reconstructing their lives. The four women who left their partners regretted that there had not been someone earlier, perhaps even speaking their own language, to listen to them in a non-judgmental way when they had decided to leave their husbands. Donna said, "Listening to other victims gives a woman the chance to clarify her own position in a relationship. Also having the necessary information about where to go, and whom to approach, would allow abused women to plan the next steps in their lives."

The decision to leave a relationship may occur suddenly, and at that point a woman is likely to seek the support of Filipino friends at least for a short time, especially if she decided to escape at night, when most public and NGO offices are closed. She might choose to go to the police, who are supposed to protect victims of domestic abuse. They are supposed to punish the batterers, but on occasion, the police have instead, arrested an undocumented woman, and charged her with violating immigration laws. Two weeks of free accommodation at shelters is available both to documented and undocumented migrant women. Those with legal permission to live in Japan can also apply for Public Assistance (*seikatsu hogo*).

A woman's time in a shelter may be either life affirming or repetitive of the abuse already experienced. Anna, for example, described one occasion when "The shelter staff were kind and helpful, always there to support me and my daughter, especially when I was under medical care for emotional and physical treatment." Ester, on the other hand, expressed dissatisfaction, for she did not have enough time to think about her future. The system, she said, forced her to decide to divorce so that she could avail herself of livelihood assistance. Celia said that she was told in an angry manner that she "could not send money to her children in the Philippines from the livelihood assistance, because that money comes from the taxes of the people." This made her feel as though she was stealing other people's money, and she decided to go back to her husband.

After a woman has escaped an abusive relationship, one may think that the worst is over, but this stage is dangerous, for she has now to begin to manage her life alone with her children, after being totally dependent on her partner for many years. Fears, insecurities, and the cultural expectation of correct family behavior may weaken a woman's determination to change her life. At this moment she urgently needs support.

Kalakasan's staff and volunteers offer basic support related to housing, visa status, child care, education, and medical matters, together with follow-up care in the form of telephone calls, home visits, self-help groups, and workshops and gatherings that allow for mutual sharing. Through formal and informal processes, we aim to help women reclaim their own inner beauty and goodness, so that they can identify forces, personal and structural, that have harmed the expression of their strength. All these processes, including talking about conflict and anger, are important steps in removing internalized negative energies and transforming them into positive forces. Networking with other groups concerned with women in general, and migrant women in particular, can also be empowering.

Notes

1. This is a condensed and edited version of "Breaking Free from Victimization: The Making of Empowered Actors," by Nanako Inaba, and "Transformed Lives: Abused Migrant Women in Japan Blaze a Trail towards Empowerment," by Leny P. Tolentino (2006). In *Transforming Lives: Abused Migrant Women in Japan Blaze a Trail towards Empowerment*, ed. Kalakasan Migrant Women Empowerment Center and The International Movement Against All Forms of Discrimination and Racism Japan Committee (IMADR-JC).

2. The number of divorces among international couples has increased considerably

over the past ten years. Looking specifically at Filipina-Japanese couples, in 2008, marriages between Filipina women and Japanese men numbered 7,290, while divorces among such couples numbered 4,782. The number of children born to couples in these marriages that year was 4,623 (Koseirodosho).

3. A diocesan center of the Catholic Yokohama Diocese established in 1992 to respond to the needs of migrants and to network with various groups concerned with social issues.

4. Patriarchy in Japan, is highlighted by emperor worship, and was forced upon the people as the principle of national unity, of legitimizing all sorts of unscrupulous invasions and of supporting paternal lineage. It penetrated deeply not only into the political and social life but also into each family's life (Kinukawa 1994).

5. The Law for the Prevention of Spousal Violence and Protection of Victims was amended in 2004 to make explicit that all persons regardless of nationality or presence/absence of handicaps.

Works Cited

Asian Migration Center. 2000. "Reviewing Gains, Understanding Empowerment, Deepening Strategies." In *Asian Migrant Yearbook 2000: Migration Facts, Analysis and Issues* in 1999. Hong Kong: AMC.

Kinukawa, Hisako. 1994. *Women and Jesus in Mark: A Japanese feminist perspective.* Maryknoll, NY: Orbis Books.

Kokuritsu josei kyoiku kaikan (National Women's Education Center), ed. 2009. *Danjo kyodo sankaku deetabukku—Nihon no josei to dansei—2009* (Gender statistics book—women and men in Japan—2009). Tokyo: Gyosei.

Koseirodosho (Ministry of Health, Labor and Welfare). *Jinko dotai chosa* (Vital statistics). For various years.

———. 2008. "Ichijihogo ni okeru zaishoshasu no uchi gaikokujinsu-hiritsu" (Number and proportion of foreigners among women receiving temporary protection at women's consultation centers). *Heisei nijunendo zenkoku fujinsodanin shinrihanteiin kenkyukyōgikai gyoseisetsumei* (2008 Report to the government of research on counselors and psychological evaluators at women's consultation centers). Nov. 20.

Saussy, Carroll and Barbara J. Clarke. 1996. "The Healing Power of Anger." In *Through the Eyes of Women, Insights for Pastoral Care*, ed. Jeanne Stevenson Moessner. Minneapolis: Fortress Press.

Revisiting the "Comfort Women": Moving beyond Nationalism

15

Yeong-ae Yamashita
Translated by Malaya Ileto

Between 1931 and 1945, women from Japan, Korea, and China, as well as from other areas under Japanese occupation, were forced into sexual servitude at "comfort stations," set up for the sexual release of Japanese soldiers. Ironically, the women were called "comfort women." The cruelty with which the women were treated was not mentioned at postwar trials, and the issue was hushed up, and did not surface until half a century after the Second World War.

I became active in the movement initiated by Korean women activists to bring to light, and seek a resolution to the "comfort women" issue in September 1988, when, after completing my master's degree at a Japanese university, I went to Korea to do further study in my specialty, Korean women's history, at Ewha Woman's University. While immersing myself in feminism and gender studies, I began to research the state-regulated prostitution system in Korea under Japanese rule, and became interested in the "comfort women" issue. Though I was a foreign student, I worked in the movement with enthusiasm from its start through its first ten years.

After a brief history of the "comfort women" system, I will discuss the problem I saw developing in the approach taken by Korean activists. I was distressed that, as the movement took on an increasingly nationalist tone, the gendered aspect of the issue—namely, the state-sanctioned sexual exploitation and violence perpetrated against women—became diminished, even obscured. Finally I will reflect on a personal aspect of the process, on how working in this movement allowed me also to master my own identity crisis. As a person born of a Korean father and a Japanese mother, I had to learn to live in a world insistent on single national identities.

A History of the "Comfort Women"

When the Japanese military intensified its invasion of the Chinese continent in the early 1930s, they began to establish "comfort stations." By 1938 "comfort stations" had been established not only in China, but also in Manchuria, Hong Kong, the Philippines, Malaysia, Singapore, French Indochina, the Dutch East Indies, British Borneo, Burma, Thailand, Eastern New Guinea, Koror, Saipan, Truk, Halmahera, Guam, Taiwan, Korea, and Japan. As the locations expanded, so too did the nationalities vary of the women forced to have sex with Japanese soldiers. Just how many women were recruited is still unknown even today, but the foremost expert on the history of the "comfort women," Yoshiaki Yoshimi, estimates the number between fifty thousand to two hundred thousand (Yoshimi 1995, 79).

One reason offered for the establishment of so many "comfort stations"— to prevent civilians from being raped in areas occupied by the Japanese Imperial Army—cited such incidents, as the Rape of Nanking.[1] The raping of civilians, officials believed, would damage the "dignity of the imperial army" and lead to retaliation from the local population (Hayao 1939, in Yoshimi 1992). A second reason offered had to do with saving soldiers from sexual diseases, were they to frequent local brothels. In either case, providing for the sexual pleasure of soldiers was the essential reason for establishing "comfort stations," referred to as "hygienic public convenience facilities" (Aso 1939).

Although "comfort stations" were run directly by the military as well as privately, Japan's state-regulated prostitution system, established in the late nineteenth century, lay at their foundation. If the prostitutes seemed to be engaged in commercial transactions of their own volition, in reality, they were slaves bound by debts incurred by their impoverished families. As Japan continued its invasion of Asia after the Sino-Japanese War (1894-1895) and the Russo-Japanese War (1904-1905), this state-regulated prostitution system also spread. Norio Hayakawa has indicated that a similar system to the "comfort stations" had already been designed prior to the Russo-Japanese War, and that this practice could be traced back to the 1910s (Hayakawa 2002).

The system of prostitution adopted for wartime use "ranked" the women, using Japanese women for commissioned officers, and Korean, Taiwanese, Chinese, and Southeast Asian/Pacific women for noncommissioned officers and ordinary soldiers. Allegedly, many of the Japanese women had been prostitutes, and certainly many who were brought to the war zone came believing that they would be able to pay their huge debts. On the other hand, the same brokers also recruited poor rural Korean women, as well as young girls, many of them tricked by talk of good work opportunities, unaware of the "comfort stations."

Korea had been aggressively colonized by Japan in August 1910, and had remained a colony until the defeat of Japan in the Second World War in

August 1945. While brokers in the state-regulated prostitution system knew how to evade the laws related to prostitution in Japan, they could even more easily mobilize Korean women for distant "comfort stations," since applications of the rule of law were far less likely to be scrutinized in colonized areas (Totsuka 2004). One distinctive feature of the Japanese military's "comfort stations" was that a large number of "comfort women," particularly from colonized Korea, were mobilized to places to which the Japanese army was advancing. To manage the program all had to be involved—the military, government, police, colonial authorities, and the chain of those working in the sex industry. Further, the Japanese military's sexual violence did not end with the "comfort station" system, for it was merely part of an organic structure of violence that included systematic rape and rape stations.

Breaking their Silence

Among the Confucian norms firmly embedded in Korean society at that time was the duty of women to remain chaste. Unmarried women, therefore, who had left home, and been forced to work as "comfort women," faced being labeled "defiled." Even if they were somehow able to return home after the war, they could not reveal the truth about their experience. Were the truth known, women would despair.

In May 1990, Korean women broke the forty-five-year silence when a Korean women's organization demanded that the issue be brought to light by the Japanese and Korean governments. The Japanese government first denied that it had any responsibility, arguing that civilian contractors had run the "comfort stations." The campaign in South Korea continued to grow, and in the following year more former "comfort women" emerged to join in. The issue received media coverage throughout Japan and Korea, and became an unresolved political issue between the two governments. The movement then spread rapidly through other Asian countries in which women had suffered similar abuse. Then women began to petition such international bodies as the United Nations and the International Labor Organization.

As the movement spread, documents surfaced revealing the Japanese army's participation, and the Japanese government admitted a certain degree of involvement in the "comfort stations." But it refused to make an official apology or to set up a legal mechanism for reparations, as demanded by the women. Previous conservative prime ministers from the Liberal Democratic Party of Japan had asserted that the "comfort women" had not been forced to have sex but, rather, had volunteered to prostitute themselves—and there are members of the Japanese Diet (national legislature) who continue to make this assertion today. For this view, the Japanese government has been criticized internationally. At a meeting of the United Nations Committee against Torture held in Geneva in May 2007, for example, a participant pointed out that the Japanese government should provide redress for the "comfort women." Bills criticizing the Japanese government have been introduced in the US House of Representatives (which passed a resolution in July 2007), as well as in the Canadian and Australian parliaments. Thus, the "comfort women" issue, first raised by Korean women's groups, has become an international issue of human rights.

My Involvement in the "Comfort Women" Movement

Before going to South Korea in 1988 to start my studies at Ewha Woman's University, I had visited former Japanese "comfort women" with Yuko Suzuki, a Japanese woman researching the issue. Through her, I met Professor Yun Jeong-Ok at Ewha in the fall of 1989, and my interest in the issue deepened further. Professor Yun had been single-handedly researching the Korean "comfort women" issue for the past ten years. I met with Professor Yun frequently. With several other graduate students, in 1990 we established a small research group in the Department of Women's Studies. Previous to that, many of the same students had been instrumental in getting a Korean women's organization to issue a statement demanding that President Roh Tae-woo take up the issue of the "comfort women" publicly, as an unresolved issue of the Second World War on his visit to Japan in May of that year.

In November of the same year, our research group succeeded in organizing Chong-dae-hyeop, the Korean Council for the Women Drafted for Military Sexual Slavery by Japan (hereafter "the Korean Council"), marking the beginning of a new phase for the movement. I became very involved in the research group and the Korean Council. The work was key to all my interests, and I felt very good working hard to facilitate communications between Japanese civil society groups and the Korean Council.

In the course of my involvement in the Korean movement, a number of conflicts and differences of opinion and approach arose. First was the conflict over the question of whether or not Japanese "comfort women," who were mostly licensed prostitutes, should be included in the same category as the "comfort women" who were sex slaves. The second conflict centered on the Korean strategy of opposing the Asian Women's Fund. Both were, in my view, intertwined with Korean nationalism—that is, the tendency on the part of Koreans to approach the issue of the "comfort women" as a national issue, and one of an affront to national pride and honor. My position, on the other hand, was that at its core was the issue of gender.

The concerns of students at Ewha Woman's University, when we first began to call attention to the "comfort women" issue, can be summarized into the following two points: first, anger that Korea and Japan, both male-dominated societies, had neglected it because it was considered a "women's issue," and, second, the failure of both countries to adequately settle the past. It was not until the democratization of Korean society in the late 1980s, and the strengthening of the women's movement that followed, that an end was brought to the long held silence about the "comfort women" and the "comfort women" movement was founded. Exposure of the 1986 incident of sexual torture at the Buchon police station (in Korea)[2] in particular, gave the women's movement an opportunity to discuss gender issues directly, and an awareness of sexual violence increased in the early 1990s, together with an analysis of its social causes, part of the theoretical development of women's studies in Korea. The efforts of former "comfort women" to uncover materials about what had happened to them, and of Christian women's organizations who were interested through their earlier work opposing *kiisen* tourism (sex tours to Korea),[3] were also important in increasing public awareness of the issues.

In addition to demanding that Japan apologize and provide reparations, the movement's members also attempted, in the process, to confront Korean society's patriarchal character—the reason why the issue had not surfaced for half a century following the end of World War II. As the movement evolved, however, both those in the movement and the general public gradually came to emphasize issues regarding nation and state, and the issue of women's rights receded to the background.

"Comfort Women" versus "Prostitutes"—A False Dichotomy

In January 1992, at around the time of Japanese Prime Minister Miyazawa's visit to Korea, an entry for "*yoja chongshindae*" (female workers in military factories) was found in an elementary school record from the colonial period in Seoul. Under the headline "Even young elementary school pupils were drafted as *chongshindae*," nearly all newspapers in Korea reported that twelve-year-old girls had been forced to become "comfort women."[4] This type of reporting led to a new wave of anti-Japanese sentiment in Korea, and the "comfort women" issue was used to emphasize Japanese brutality. To increase nationwide outrage over the "comfort women" issue, and thus increase pressure on the Japanese government, the Korean women's movement emphasized that this was by no means an issue limited to Korean women, but rather one that reflected a "national suffering." Professor Yun Jeong-Ok, representative of the Korean Council, said the following in a newspaper interview:

The issue of women drafted for military sexual slavery by Japan is by no means past history nor an issue that concerns only women. It remains a problem today because the remnants of colonial history have not been fully dealt with. In the past, Japan trampled upon our people with their military uniforms and swords. Today, they are replaying history with their suits and money, under the pretext of *kiisen* tourism. The issue of women drafted for military sexual slavery affects not only women but also Koreans as a whole, and this state-sponsored violence continues today.[5]

In response, Japanese neo-nationalists subscribing to the so-called "liberal view of history" (jiyushugi shikan), argued (and still continue to argue) that there is no evidence or testimony proving that the women were taken by force and deny any responsibility on the part of the Japanese government. This issue became the focal point for both Korea and Japan. In August 1993, in the Japanese government's second report on its study of the issue, Chief Cabinet Secretary Yohei Kono commented that "recruitment, transfer, and control [of the Korean comfort women] were conducted generally against their will, through coaxing and coercion" and "They lived in misery at comfort stations under a coercive atmosphere." The Korean government took these comments as the Japanese government's general admission of the coercive nature of the system.

The point I wish to emphasize is that the focus of the issue, whether by the Japanese or Korean governments or its peoples, became whether or not the women *were forced to work* in the "comfort stations." This point of view logically led to the suggestion that the women could become "comfort women" of their own volition, so that there could be no responsibility on the part of the Japanese government. The argument was that the "comfort women" system was a variety of Japan's state-regulated prostitution system at the time, so that "comfort women" and licensed prostitutes were the same. Rejection of this argument by the Korean side is clearly stated in a statement issued by the Korean Council in response to the Japanese government's second report:

> Unlike Japanese prostitutes licensed under the state-regulated prostitution system, the "comfort women" were sex slaves forced by the national authorities to provide sex to soldiers. The Japanese government's report states: "As for the origin of comfort women who were mobilized to war areas, aside from the Japanese women, those from the Korean Peninsula accounted for a large part." It is clear that the nature of forced mobilization of Korean women as sex slaves is different from what happened with Japanese women. Japanese women became "comfort women" under the state-regulated prostitution system in Japan. They received money, made

contracts, and could quit when their contracts were up. Including the Japanese "comfort women" in the report like this is an attempt to obscure the coercive nature of the military's comfort women system.[6]

Because this statement emphasizes the coercive nature of the Korean "comfort women" experience, it asserts by comparison that this was very different from the case of Japanese "comfort women" who were originally prostitutes.[7] Not only was this assertion based on a misconception, but it also led dangerously to the logic that because Japanese "comfort women" were originally prostitutes, they could not be considered sex slaves under the "comfort women" system. This began to sound similar to male-centered assertions by the Japanese right wing in their bifurcation of women into categories of "virgin or prostitute," and "forced or voluntary," in their attempt to downplay the criminality of the "comfort women" system.

This perception of the "comfort women" held by most Korean activists and scholars differed critically from my own. As I discovered in the process of debates, it was based on a misconception of Japan's state-regulated prostitution system that existed at the time in Japan and in its colonies, such as Korea and Taiwan, specifically, that the Japanese women were engaged in commercial transactions of their own volition.

Prostitution in licensed quarters had been allowed in Japan since the sixteenth century. Most of the women were trafficked. The Maria Luz incident[8] in 1872 became a trigger for the Meiji government to declare the so-called Emancipation Decree for Prostitutes, which banned human trafficking, restricted apprenticeships, and rendered advanced loan contracts invalid. The government and society at the time, however, did not consider prostitution itself inhumane. The year after the decree, Tokyo Prefecture issued Official Decree No. 145 on regulations for brothels, prostitutes and female performers, and the modern state-regulated prostitution system took shape. The core logic behind the ordinance was that prostitution was allowed if it took place "with the desire" and "from the intentions" of the person in question.

Can it be claimed, however, that such women's desires and intentions were the result of an exercise of their "free will"? Under the prevailing patriarchal legal order, women were not recognized as being entitled to the same social and legal rights as men, and the patriarchy extended also into regulation of the home. Even applying for a license to engage in prostitution required the consent of a close male family member, and in the case of a minor, the consent of the parents or grandparents. Adult women were not acknowledged as individuals with the ability to make their own decisions. Clearly, a woman's will could easily be dominated by the family patriarch.

No doubt, her freedom was extremely limited. Furthermore, selling one's daughter into prostitution was one way to relieve family poverty, and some may have considered a daughter virtuous to sacrifice herself for her family. Perhaps women internalized such values. Perhaps women had no choice but to become prostitutes to save their families.

A contract for sexual services was not made on free, equal, and fair terms between the prostitute and customer, for the brothel owner held the real power in the exchange of money. The prostitute was not in charge of the commercial transaction, but merely the "goods" being exchanged. This treatment of the women was nothing short of slavery. Prostitutes lived in designated quarters and needed permission from the police to leave the area. In 1900, the Interior Ministry issued a decree whereby prostitutes could freely leave the trade, the first law to expressly state this, but doing so was difficult in practice. Except for the rare circumstance in which a woman could borrow money to pay back her debt (in most cases incurred by her family) all at once, she was a caged bird until discarded as disabled or diseased. Were she to attempt escape, she would risk her life.

The Japanese state-regulated prostitution system was, in short, a contrivance to evade the law prohibiting slavery, using the pretext of the women's "free will" to justify human trafficking, the exploitation of licensed prostitutes, and the slave-like conditions of their service. My effort to explain this, and to point out the pitfall of attempting to make a sharp differentiation between "comfort women" and women in "voluntary prostitution," was not very successful at the time, though over the years I have gained more understanding. As complex, was a second problem inside the movement: the incapacity of either government to respond to the women as victims of sexual violence.

The Asian Women's Fund: Response to Women's Suffering

From the beginning of the movement, the Japanese government adamantly refused to offer an official apology or to provide reparations. Instead in 1995, the Japanese coalition government created by the Liberal Democratic Party, Socialist Party, and Sakigake Party set up the Asian Women's Fund, through which it tried to demonstrate "moral responsibility."[9] However, it met full opposition from the Korean government and from Korean activists in particular, who saw it as merely "hush money" and an attempt by the Japanese government to evade responsibility. Given the reality of conservative Japanese politics at the time, the establishment of this fund can be regarded to some degree as a demonstration of sincerity directed at the victims who survived the war.

Problems arose when some Korean women decided to accept the Japanese payments. As part of its efforts to obstruct the Asian Women's Fund, in October 1996, the Korean movement established the Coalition of Citizens for Resolving the Issue of Sexual Slavery under the Japanese Military, composed of figures from different spheres of society. They began collecting their own relief funds domestically in Korea to try to discourage women from accepting money from the Asian Women's Fund.

The call for funds was promoted as a way for "healing the sacrifices and wounds through the support of our people" and "caring (for the survivors) with our own hands." Opposing the Asian Women's Fund was a point of struggle not only for the survivors but also for Koreans as a whole, for the message claimed that defending the "comfort women" victims was the same as defending national pride. The character of the movement was made manifest in a public address on March 1, 1997, as part of Movement Commemoration Day[10], calling for funds from fellow countrymen to help the former "comfort women":

> The Japanese Government continues to deny the facts constituting their crime and evade legal responsibility, including the payment of reparations. Taking advantage of the poor economic circumstances of the victimized *halmoni* (Korean word for "old woman"), it is offering consolation payment to the poor, elderly women through civilian funds, sacrificing them yet again for its own political ends instead of taking legal responsibility for its crimes. This ridicules the dignity and human rights of the victims, as well as our national pride. . .Calling to mind the past sufferings of our people under Japanese colonial rule, we must now care for the *halmoni* with our own hands, and together heal the wounds from the unfortunate past. We intend to protect our *halmoni* so that they are not hurt again by imperialistic Japan's dirty money, so that our national pride is not insulted. This will be the beginning of our efforts to make Japan deal with the dregs of the colonial past and complete the establishment of our independent nation.

This meant, then, that rejecting the Asian Women's Fund was a movement "together to heal the wounds from the unfortunate past," and those who chose to accept the money were seen as abandoning the national movement, and thus were disqualified from receiving domestic funds. While there were some survivors who were able to benefit from the movement both materially and spiritually, and regain their national identity, the survivors who were disqualified expressed dissatisfaction at being alienated by the organizations that purported to support the victims.

I had no objection to the collection of domestic funds as a way to oppose the Asian Women's Fund started in Japan, but I was opposed to the exclusion of women who had accepted payment. I believed that, were there true concern for our compatriots, it should be directed at the victims, and that the movement should not prioritize national pride but, rather, the interests of the victims. The fact that they were Korean nationals was not the central issue, I believed. Their suffering was physical and mental, through sexual violence, which had no simple ending, but continued to cause survivors great agony. To help these women required an understanding of their suffering and the provision of professional treatment. One might suggest that activists wanting the trust of survivors needed a keen understanding of their years of suffering.

My own understanding of the situation of "comfort women," though by no means complete, includes sharp regret for the fact that nationalist interests have overwhelmed the actual lives of the women themselves, not to mention the discrimination they have suffered. I found the work of Judith L. Herman (1996) on the trauma suffered by raped or battered women and survivors of war zones or forced detention camps very useful in this regard. The "comfort women" became sex slaves because of ethnic discrimination under colonial rule and a society that looked down on women. It is very difficult to treat the trauma sustained from sexual slavery when national issues—unresolved issues regarding colonial rule—are placed at the forefront. At the same time, activists have incurred suffering not only from confronting the Japanese government's adamant denial of its culpability but also from their strained relationship with the survivors. The pain experienced both by Korea's "comfort women" survivors and by activists is a legacy of the dual suppression endured both as colonized subjects and also as women. Both the colonial experience and the "comfort women" experience have left behind deep and complicated wounds that endure despite the passage of time.

Moving beyond Nationalism to Resolve My Identity Crisis

When I initially went to study at Ewha Woman's University, I had one other purpose in mind: to explore my identity. This crisis of identity began with the revelation, just prior to my graduation from elementary school which was run by Chongryon, a pro-North Korean organization in Japan,[11] that my mother—who I had always assumed to be a Zainichi Korean (Koreans or those of Korean roots residing in Japan), as was my father, who had been born in Korea during Japan's occupation of that country and lived in Japan since the end of the Second World War,[12] was in fact Japanese. And because my parents had not legally married I was registered in my mother's family register,[13] and my brother and I had Japanese nationality. The revelation forced me to change my view of life radically, and led to the collapse of my sense of values, upon which essential elements of my identity were based. After having taught me that Japan was an enemy, my parents placed me in a Japanese middle school, at which point I began to use the Japanese name "Eiai Yamashita," the name that was recorded in the family register but one with which I felt no familiarity at all, rather than my Korean name "Choi Yeong-ae."

From then on, I found it difficult to find a comfortable space either in the community of Zainichi Koreans or the Japanese community. My identity was always divided between the North Korean, Zainichi Korean, and Japanese communities. Later, in college, when I joined Zainichi Korean groups, I always used my Korean name, which raised further confusion in my mind. Around that time I attended a series of monthly public seminars held by the *Ajia no onnatachi no kai* (Asian Women's Association, which later became the Asia-Japan Women's Resource Center), and when I spoke about my name and identity problem at one of the seminars, a woman suggested I use "Yeong-ae Yamashita," a combination of my Korean given name and my Japanese mother's family name. I had never thought of this before, and I felt as though a new door had opened for me. Using my new "double" name, however, did not solve my problem of identity, since neither Japan nor Korea accepts dual nationality, and both profess to be homogeneous states. Moreover, I continued to feel strong pressure from both the Japanese community and the Korean residents in Japan to choose either my Korean or Japanese first and family names.[14]

Although I had traveled to Korea several times, I had never lived in South Korea, had never fully experienced its culture and atmosphere. I hoped to resolve my crisis in my father's native land where I could acquire his Korean language and culture, and become fully "Korean."

The conflicts of opinion with my Korean colleagues in the course of my participation in the "comfort women" movement rekindled my identity crisis. On numerous occasions when I voiced differing views, I was told, "You are not Korean, so you can never understand our way of thinking." This is when I realized that I was reliving what my Japanese mother had experienced in the past with Zainichi Korean women's groups. When I was young, my mother was an active member of a branch of the organization of Zainichi Korean women and even served as an officer. In the summer of 1966, however, the organization decided that all Japanese women, including my mother, could no longer serve as officers. My mother told me that the reason given to her was that the Japanese and Korean wives were "of different blood" so they could not both be at the heart of the movement. She was very hurt by this, and left the organization. My father could not understand her pain, and this led to the beginning of their separation.

A feminist perspective gave me important hints to finding solutions to the dilemmas I confronted and also helped end my identity crisis: I realized that the four groups I had tried to identify with—the Zainichi Koreans, Japanese, North Koreans and South Koreans—were all male-dominated societies. The insistently exclusive nature of both Korean and Japanese social ideologies compels persons of mixed heritage, like myself, to choose between their dual identities. Having clearly understood this led me to think that it was not worth being troubled by it anymore. Similarly, I began to see my differences with colleagues in the Korean movement in a new light. I realized that rather than identifying totally with them, I had to acknowledge our differing views. I had to understand their ways of thinking and their backgrounds from which such differences may have arisen. Most of all, I need to engage in dialogue to build relationships of trust.

The Movement Continues

Twenty years have passed since I participated in the Korean movement in 1990 that raised the issue of "comfort women" in Korea, Japan, and internationally. In that time, the movement has changed. The Korean sector of the movement is struggling to provide care for aging survivors. Weekly Wednesday demonstrations before the Japanese embassy in Seoul allow young people to learn about the movement's history. And another aspect of the movement focuses on establishing a museum to prevent such crimes from happening again. Today some Korean women cartoonists see "comfort women" not simply as a national issue, but rather an issue of sexual violence in war. Despite all the changes, what remains the same is Japan's denial of legal responsibility. In addition, Korea and Japan remain male-dominated societies.

Because of the "Korean Wave" or craze for Korean culture that was sparked by a Korean television romance drama series called "Winter Sonata" that aired in Japan in 2003, and the fact that I share my name with the internationally famed Korean actress Yeong-ae Lee, my name "Yeong-ae," which was so unfamiliar in the past, no longer seems so strange.

Further, with the influence of Hines Ward[15] in 2006 and the increase in migrant workers,[16] we can see a recent move toward dispersing the myth of homogeneity in Korea.

The struggle to resolve the "comfort women" issue will no doubt continue in Korea and Japan, and in other countries where women were victimized. It goes without saying that the goal of the movement is not only to obtain an official apology and reparations from the Japanese government. Such actions would ameliorate the suffering of the survivors, and would begin to uncover the truth. With the lessening of tensions and the rise of active exchanges between North and South Korea, we can also hope for useful change. As nationalism, globalization, and conservative patriarchal ideologies continue to manifest themselves in different ways around the world, those involved in the "comfort women" issue must join together under the banner of feminist thinking. The future calls not just for a solidarity that goes beyond borders, but for awareness-based mutual understanding and feminist solidarity.

Notes

1. Many women were raped during the Japanese invasion and occupation of Nanking (modern-day Nanjing) in 1937. According to the testimonies of foreigners living there at the time, more than twenty thousand women were raped (Matsuoka 130). Individual soldiers as well as groups carried out rapes, and other crimes such as robbery, massacres, and arson were also committed. It is said that the Japanese military formally established the "comfort stations" because of fear that these incidents would lead to a Chinese backlash. (Hayao 1939).

2. Kwon Insuk, a university student at the time, was arrested in June 1986 by the Buchon police for forging an identification card to work at a factory, and while under investigation, sexually tortured. Kwon publicized what had happened and took the case to court. The incident became a trigger for the strengthening of the democratization movement, leading to the struggle for democracy the year after.

3. A *kiisen* was a type of prostitute from the Choson Dynasty (1392 to 1910). Originally these women not only performed sexual services but also had skills in medicine, needlework, singing and dancing, etc. After Korea became a Japanese colony, they assumed the role of entertainers performing singing, dancing, and sexual services. The Korean government actively promoted *kiisen* tourism from the 1970s to 1980s as a way to acquire foreign currency. Most of the clients were Japanese men. Women from Christian women's groups and female university students organized protests against *kiisen* tourism in the 1970s.

4. *The Dong-a Ilbo*. January 14, 1992. The term *"yoja chongshindae"* refers to women who, toward the end of the war, were forced under Japanese government decree to work in military factories. Most of the young women drafted from Korea were in their early teens. Misunderstanding of the term resulted in falsely equating *"yoja chongshindae"* to "comfort women," though in fact they were clearly different.

5. *The Dong-a Ilbo*. "Of course there must be reparations at the national level for the women drafted for military sexual slavery." January 16, 1992; *The Korea Times*, January 16, 1992.

6. Korean Council for the Women Drafted for Military Sexual Slavery by Japan. "Our response to the Japanese government's second report on its study of the issue of women drafted for military sexual slavery" (in Korean). August 4, 1993.

7. The notion that the Japanese "comfort women" were all prostitutes is an inaccurate stereotype. For details see Yamashita (2009).

8. A dispute between Peru and Korea in 1872 that occurred when a Chinese "coolie" laborer jumped ship from the Peruvian ship Maria Luz when it docked in the port of Yokohama. Japan let the man go, reasoning that the slave trade was unjust, to which Peru

pointed out that Japan's sex trade system was problematic. This incident led the government to pass the so-called Emancipation Decree for Prostitutes the following year.

9. The coalition government created in 1994 by the Liberal Democratic Party, Socialist Party and Sakigake Party accepted moral responsibility for the "comfort women" and set this fund up in 1995. The main undertakings of the fund were to give the former "comfort women" funds collected from the Japanese people and conduct health and welfare schemes for the women. In executing these programs, the Japanese government expressed its "apologies" and compiled materials on the "comfort women" as historical evidence, to be used as a lesson of history. Many survivors who sought legal compensation and an apology, however, rejected the fund. The fund ceased its activities in March 2007.

10. In March 1, 1919, leaders gathered to read the Korean Declaration of Independence and demonstrations against the Japanese took place throughout the country, calling for the independence of Korea. This is commemorated as a public holiday, and various events, both public and private, are held every year to celebrate it.

11. In 1945, the Korean Peninsula, having been liberated from Japanese colonialism, was divided along the thirty-eighth parallel by the United States and the Soviet Union. On August 15, 1948, the Republic of Korea (South Korea) was unilaterally created in the American military-administered southern half of the peninsula. In response, on September 9, the Democratic People's Republic of Korea (North Korea) was established. Chongryon was created in 1955 as an activist group of Koreans in Japan who supported the policies of Kim Il Sung, the leader of the Democratic People's Republic of Korea.

12. For more about the life of my father and his family prior to liberation, see Choi Suk-ui 1990.

13. The family register is a record kept for each family unit that details date and place of birth and names of parents and children. This forms the basis for the family in Japanese society. Under the old civil code, women who wed would be recorded under their husband's register, but after the war, the law was changed to formally allow a choice of whose register to be recorded under. In most cases, however, the woman is recorded in the man's register and the woman and children take the man's name. Children who are born out of wedlock are registered in their mother's register and take their mother's name.

14. Since the beginning of Japanese colonial rule of Korea in the 1910s, the Japanese had discriminated against Koreans, and after the war, consistently attempted to assimilate Korean residents in Japan. To become naturalized, Koreans were required to change their names and abandon Korean culture and become "more Japanese." Many people had no choice but to adopt Japanese names to avoid social discrimination. Thus, the recovery of their original names became the struggle for second and third generation Zainichi Koreans, and this became a measure of how much one was able to restore their "Korean-ness." The surname was particularly important, though there was a tendency to be forgiving if one's first name was Japanese. For this reason, Korean activists in Japan never welcomed my strategy of using a combination of names, with my surname being Japanese.

15. Hines Ward is an American football player who was born to a Korean mother and US military father. He was selected MVP player at the 2006 Super Bowl, making him popular in Korea as well. On a visit to Korea, he announced the establishment of a fund for mixed-race children in Korea and criticized the discrimination in Korean society against them.

16. As of 2006 there are about one million foreigners living in Korea (including illegal residents), making it 2.5 times higher than ten years ago, when it stood at three hundred

and eighty thousand. Of this, three hundred thousand are industrial trainees. There is a rapid rise in international marriages between Korean men and Asian (Chinese, Vietnamese, Filipina, Thai) women, and in the children they produce. One out of ten marriages is an international marriage, and there are approximately ten thousand women who migrate through marriage.

Works Cited

Aso, Tetsuo. 1939. "Karyubyo no sekkyokuteki yoboho" (Law for the Prevention of Sexually Transmitted Diseases). Reprinted in 1990 in *Gun ikan no senjo hokoku ikensho* (A collection of reports and commentary by medical officers from the battlefield), ed. Ryuji Takasaki. Tokyo: Fuji shuppan.

Choi, Suk-ui. 1990. "Watashi no gentaiken: Osaka kobayashicho chosen buraku no omoide" (What has shaped me: Memories of living in the Korean community of Kobayashi town, Osaka). In *Zainichi chosenjinshi kenkyu* (Research on Zainichi Korean history) (20), ed. Zainichi chosenjin undoshi kenkyukai.

Hayakawa, Norio, ed. 2002. *Rikugun ni okeru karyubyo* (Sexually transmitted diseases in the army). Tokyo: Fuji shuppan.

Hayao, Torao. 1939. "*Senjo ni okeru tokushu gensho to kitaisaku*" (Unique phenomena in the battlefield and measures for dealing with them) (June). In *Jugun ianfu shiryoshu* (Materials on the military comfort women), ed. Yoshiaki Yoshimi. 1992. Tokyo: Otsuki shoten.

Herman, Judith Lewis. 1997. *Trauma and Recovery*. New York: Basic Books.

Suzuki, Yuko, Masaru Tonomura, and Yeong-ae Yamashita, eds. 2006. *Nihongun ianfu mondai shiryo shusei* (Materials on the Japanese military comfort women.) Tokyo: Akashi shoten.

Totsuka, Etsuro. 2004. "Senjijosei ni taisuru boryoku e no Nihon shiho no taio, sono seika to genkai—hakkutsusareta Nihongun ianfu rachi shobatsu hanketsu" (Results and limitations of Japan's legal response to violence against women during war: Uncovered punishments for kidnapping of the "comfort women" by the Japanese military) (1936). *Senso sekinin kenkyu* (Research on War Responsibilities) (43).

Yamashita, Yeong-ae. 2009. "*Nihonjin 'ianfu' o meguru kioku to gensetsu—chinmoku ga imisurumono*" (Memories and discourse concerning Japanese "comfort women": what silence signifies). In *Jendaashi sosho daigokan—boryoku to senso* (Gender history series vol 5—violence and war), ed. Chikako Kato and Makoto Hosoya. Tokyo: Akashi shoten.

Yoshimi, Yoshiaki, ed. 1992. *Jugun ianfu shiryoshu* (Materials on the military "comfort women"). Tokyo: Otsuki shoten.

———. 1995. *Jugun ianfu* (The military "comfort women"). Tokyo: Iwanami shoten.

Buraku Solidarity

Risa Kumamoto
Translated by Malaya Ileto

The word "Buraku," which literally means "hamlet," refers to the people from particular communities in Japan, as well as the communities themselves. Their history goes back to seventeenth-century Japan, when several legally determined social castes were designated *senmin*, or "humble people," and charged to do specific jobs considered "impure," such as processing dead cattle and leatherwork. They were restricted in where they could live, and those areas today are designated as "discriminated Buraku communities" or "Buraku." An 1871 Emancipation Edict abolished Japan's feudal class system, but the Meiji government failed to introduce policies to eliminate discrimination. Hence, Japanese society continued to discriminate against the Buraku, whether or not they remained in their traditional living areas. The exclusion of Buraku people continued, bringing with it poverty as well as alienation. Even after the Second World War, democratization did not reach into the Buraku areas, and Buraku people were excluded from Japan's economic recovery. Prevented from gaining secure employment, they struggled to survive.

Since the enactment in 1969 of the Law on Special Measures for Dowa Projects (which expired in 2002),[1] many improvements have taken place, and visible results can be seen, but problems still exist in such areas as education, marriage, and employment. Deep-rooted prejudice against the Buraku people continues today. Pre-modern discriminatory beliefs, including ideas of purity versus impurity, nobility versus a common lineage, and the patriarchal household have been difficult to erase. To these beliefs one can add such contemporary phenomena as resentment over perceived reverse discrimination and special treatment. Several other ideas—eugenics, meritocracy, and an overemphasis on academic achievement—also help to keep discrimination against the Buraku alive today.

My Own Story

My mother was born in 1949 into a Buraku community consisting of forty households located at the foot of a mountain. She is still there today, living by herself in Dowa-sponsored public housing, a stone's throw away from where my grandmother and my brother's family live. My grandparents were born in this Buraku, and lived their whole lives there. I lived there for twelve years, from the age of six, when my parents divorced, until I left for university at eighteen.

My parents were high school sweethearts, but because my mother was of Buraku origin, their marriage met fierce opposition from my father's family. My parents eloped, and began their new life together. Later, however, my father's company went bankrupt. The large amount of debt that my parents had to bear caused their relationship to change. My father's family looked coldly upon my mother's plea for help, blaming everything on my father's having married a Buraku woman. No matter how much they criticized my mother's precious home, her family, and her life, however, my mother continued to believe in my father. But then my father disappeared, leaving only the debt behind for my mother to bear.

As a woman alone and with children, my mother had to work long hours at several jobs to pay back the debts. She could secure only low-paid or nightshift jobs, part-time, with no insurance or holidays. Sometimes she was refused work because of her Buraku origins. She also had to endure repeated background checks, and discriminatory slurs when at work. Because my mother found it hard to rear children and work at the same time, she sent my brother and me to live with my grandparents in the Buraku where my mother had grown up. We moved there in 1978, when I was six years old. I became so accustomed to Buraku negative images that I came to internalize and reproduce the stigma against Buraku people. I wanted to leave the Buraku behind and refused to get involved with Buraku people.

I went to a well-known private girls' junior high school far away from home. There, I measured everything by the standards of wealth and status, and experienced feelings of inferiority and superiority, measuring this environment against the Buraku community. I went on to attend a senior secondary school that had a high rate of students going on to college. For the next three years there, I continued to experience these same feelings.

It was difficult to maintain my living expenses, but my family, who had already been through their share of struggles, gave me their full support. They had already had their dreams shattered, their own rights to education, and the freedom to work and to marry taken away because they were Buraku, and because they were women. Non-Buraku people often told me,

"Women don't need to study," or "If you go to university, you won't be able to marry," or "You're a Buraku person/a woman, so even if you go to school, you won't be able to get a job or enter a good marriage," or "Buraku people are lazy—they don't study or work" or "Buraku people are of common lineage and low status. They are vulgar and useless."

My family, and the people from my community, however, cheered me on, telling me that I was the "treasure of the community." They told me, "Study hard and learn life skills, because you are from a Buraku," and "Work hard and learn to become independent, because you are a woman," and "See many different societies and meet many different people."

When I began to learn about the feelings of other people who had been discriminated against, I became proud of and grateful for the support that my family and community had given me. At the time, though, I continued to deceive my friends and hide the fact that I was from a Buraku, and I never invited them home to visit. I judged myself and others in the light of academic background, money, status, and occupation, and struggled with my feelings of inferiority and superiority. That is how I was as a child. In the Buraku, I was sometimes the discriminated against, and sometimes the discriminator. I internalized the image of the "discriminated Buraku" that society had created, and eventually lost sight of the relationship between myself, and others, and between society and myself.

The same was true with regard to being a woman. I could not accept my grandmother's way of life, which was according to the Buddhist teaching of *sanju*, whereby a woman should obey her father at home, her husband after marriage, and her child (in practice the eldest son) after the husband's death. My grandfather, who went to school and became a civil service employee, used to make fun of my grandmother who could neither read nor write. She cannot forget the occasion when my grandfather said to her, "You can't read this, can you?" as he held in his hands the book that she found solace in, a book of Buddhist teachings. She told me how miserable she had felt, as she recalled the incident with frustration and resentment. After my mother's divorce, she faced financial hardships that led to her becoming dependent on the men with whom she had relationships. Sometimes, they were violent toward us. I rejected the lives of my mother and grandmother: I didn't want to live as they had.

Before I knew it, I was making men my role models in life. Having learned about life through them, I was eager for their recognition and approval and sought their attention. I learned the male way of how to survive in this man's world. By using male standards, being privileged, and holding myself up above others, I put women down. I could not establish a relationship based on equality with anybody.

Encountering the Buraku Liberation Movement

In my university years, wanting to escape and seeing endless possibilities overseas, I went to Canada. There I met a group of indigenous peoples whose land had been taken away from them, whose pride in their culture and traditions had been denied. They asked me to explain the Buraku liberation movement to them, so that they could make use of it in their work, but all I could explain to them was the wretched history of the Buraku people and the situation today.

"It is society," they told me, "that creates the negative images that see you as scary, dangerous, poor, bad, smelly, dirty, and lazy. This makes everything more convenient for people who discriminate, because they can turn everything around and make discrimination the fault of the people they are discriminating against. Why internalize their perspective?"

They had wanted me to tell them about the history of the Buraku people's movement, and how, despite discrimination, oppression, and domination, Buraku people are able to live with dignity and connect with others to change society. They wanted to know about the strength of the movement today, and the experiences and hopes held by the people. This was a pivotal encounter for me.

The International Movement against All Forms
of Discrimination and Racism (IMADR)

I began working at IMADR in 1996 after returning to Japan and graduating from university. IMADR is an international nongovernmental organization founded in 1988 to help eliminate all forms of discrimination through forging links among discriminated peoples around the world. The Buraku Liberation League (BLL), which had been founded in 1955, was central to the establishment of IMADR, viewing its responsibility as fulfilling the mission of promoting equality enshrined in the Declaration of the National Levelers' Association of Japan (Zenkoku Suiheisha). Buraku people had founded the National Levelers' Association as early as 1922, with the goal of eradicating discrimination.

Through my work at IMADR, I encountered the history of these movements for Buraku liberation and women's liberation. I learned that there was a structure in this discriminatory society that made me mistakenly think that my mother's and grandmother's experiences were personal issues, problems they encountered because they were women or of Buraku origin. So long as I believed that such problems were "personal," I could never reach self-realization or self-liberation. Once I understood the social dynamic at the root of discrimination, it became important for me to do what I could to decrease discrimination's power, and thus to help transform society. When I realized that social structures are responsible for both Buraku and gender discrimination, I also came to understand that without the elimination of all forms of discrimination in our society, we can never be free—not as Buraku people or as women, but as a human beings.

While sharing these thoughts and experiences with others like me, I became conscious of the issues that I had to deal with. I learned that when I began pondering what was needed for society to change, I was using standards that I had learned, which were that of the strong, the majority, and those in power. I began to take back my history and identity as a woman and a Buraku person. Through interactions with different people and their own layers of history and identity, I learned that I needed also to look at social structures and consciousness, which together create, preserve, and encourage different forms of discrimination.

Multiple Forms of Discrimination in a Global Society

From 1999, therefore, I became involved with the IMADR Japan Committee to help create a network on the theme of such multiple forms of discrimination against women as class, race, ethnicity, religion, language, age, and sexuality, all of which mutually affect each other. One might point to American feminist theory, in the writing, for example, of Audre Lorde (1984), bell hooks (1984, 1989, 1990, 1992, 1999), Angela Davis (1981,1989), Barbara Smith (1983), Gloria Hull (1982), and others. Or one may look back to the nineteenth century's Sojourner Truth. Closer to home, one may cite Hiroko Hagiwara's compilation of Black Feminism's critique of liberation ideas and movements, including how views on labor, family, and relations with men differ according to race and class (Hagiwara 2002, 421-422).

In my interactions with other groups of minority women fighting discrimination both in Japan and abroad, I have heard questions raised regarding the political nature of solidarity. Some of these often left me wondering whether solidarity was really possible. I was told by a female Zainichi Korean (Koreans or those of Korean descent residing in Japan), for example, that if I, a person with suffrage and Japanese citizenship, did not become conscious of my historical and societal position and fight discrimination against Zainichi Koreans, and if I did not question my status as an aggressor in the context of colonial rule, they could not work easily in solidarity with me, just because I happened to be a woman. I was told point blank that, because the women's movement in Japan did not have a long history, colonialism continues today. When I used the term "we," I was challenged to name whom I was referring to exactly.

Even today, I have a clear memory of the Okinawan women I was meeting with, who emphasized that "*Yamatonchu*, or people from the mainland, might talk about solidarity but they don't practice it." As they saw it, only Okinawans were sacrificed in the Battle of Okinawa, which took place toward the end of World War II in April 1945. And yet only the *Yamatonchu* enjoy peace. Seventy-five percent of US military bases in Japan can be found in 0.6 percent of its land, in Okinawa. And only the *Yamatonchu* are economically and politically prosperous. They pointed to my arrogance. How could I think it would be simple to work in solidarity if I said, "I'm a minority woman, too," when I had Japanese citizenship, and lived a privileged life in a place free of military bases? I had to hear this critique of an ethnocentric women's movement, for talking about their experiences regarding sex and gender as if those experiences were universal.

In 2001, at the World Conference against Racism in South Africa, representatives of a group of nongovernmental organizations discussed different forms of multiple discrimination, including race and gender. Women from developing countries and indigenous peoples' groups protested that they were being treated like specimens on display, lined up on stage as supplemental material to show that such-and-such is going on in their communities. At negotiations with their governments or when raising their issues at the United Nations, they were always represented by people with English skills, connections, organizing ability, and money. As a result, some women left the conference room, saying that they could not work together in this way. They said that the concept of "gender" did not reflect their realities. If "multiple forms of discrimination" and "gender equality" were the focus, and equality, human rights, anti-discrimination, and justice were the goals, where, they asked, can their voices be heard? Whom were they fighting against?

I also heard accusations from indigenous women in developing countries that I was part of the privileged, prosperous "North," no matter that I was describing discrimination against Buraku people and women in Japan, and calling for solidarity. Solidarity, they said, with discriminated peoples around the world is not possible at all when the people who hold the power in historical events and present-day social structures don't realize where they stand. In doing this, they end up trampling on the feet of others. This was what they accused me of. Encountering the concept of multiple forms of discrimination and meeting different minority women through such networks have allowed me to rethink my historical and social existence.

Reencountering My Mother and Grandmother

Coming to terms with myself inevitably led me to revisit my family history and present status. My grandmother, who suffered from poverty and discrimination because she was born in a Buraku, was not guaranteed an education because she was a woman. She had to work from a young age, and is still unable to read and write today. She lived in a Buraku, worked with Buraku people, married a Buraku man, and never left that place. A few years ago, when I began to record my grandmother's life history, I was overcome by the power of words in which my grandmother—who had been labeled "illiterate"—had chosen to tell her story. I was astonished by her power of communication, her sensuous and detailed descriptions, her memory, her capacity to listen, and her power to express herself. When she spoke of Buraku discrimination, it was mainly about her frustration, bitterness, and sadness that she had not been able to go to school, as well as that her teachers and other students had treated her badly during the few days that she was able to attend. I am not, of course, saying that being unable to write is fine. But I learned from listening to my grandmother that we must not judge a person's worth only through the lens of those who are privileged to be literate. When I told my grandmother about the people I encountered in Japan and other countries and the activities I was taking part in, she said:

> I don't understand all your talk about "human rights" and "fighting against discrimination." Government officials, researchers, and school teachers come to us saying, "Please tell us about your experiences of being victimized by discrimination." We oblige, though not without mixed feelings. After hearing our stories, they say, "We have learned a great deal from listening to you. We understand how difficult life must be for you, but we hope you will continue in your struggle." Yet when it comes to making laws and ordinances or setting up action plans, we are never consulted. Later they hand us the finished documents—which we can't read or understand. The attitude of these people seems to be, "Laws and action plans are to be made by those who understand these matters. Those who can't understand don't need to. All they have to do is tell us about their experiences of discrimination." Did these people acquire education so that they can look down on and exclude others like us? Is that the reason why you got all that education?

My grandmother's accusations made me think about the real meaning and purpose of learning and education. What she had been deprived of was more than the opportunity to learn to read and write: it was her dignity as a human being. The education she undertook throughout her life was that of recovering and restoring that dignity by becoming aware of her own strength and ability to survive, striving to find solutions to the problems within her community, and freeing herself from the negative attitudes and self-images she had unconsciously internalized from the dominant society. This was her schooling, her education, and it was the Buraku liberation movement, the rich culture, warmth, and mutual support existing within the Buraku community, that made this education possible.

My mother suffered discrimination in employment, as well as in marriage. But because of the Buraku liberation movement, my mother's generation enjoyed more opportunities than my grandmother's. My mother could interact with non-Buraku people in school, and even marry outside the community. After her divorce, my mother worked very hard to house, feed, and raise us while working in an environment that did not protect women. When I began to record my mother's life history, as I had my grandmother's, she did not talk about her experiences and feelings within the framework of Buraku and gender discrimination. As we discussed our relationship as mother and daughter, we shared each other's pain. Later, she wrote in a letter to me:

> I was born amid discrimination, and don't have bad feelings about it. I am very glad I was born and raised this way. I feel fortunate to have been able to know the perspective of both those who are discriminated against, and those who discriminate against others. I have pride in being born in a Buraku and as a woman. It has taught me that I am capable of performing any type of work in order to survive, and that I am a truly wonderful human being, with so many encounters with people and with nature, and with the capacity to feel pain. It has taught me how wonderful it is to work and to learn. I can evaluate myself and not only be evaluated by others. All of this has given me confidence and strength to live. I have gained additional strength in talking about what I have experienced and felt, and in having people listen to what I have to say.

As this essay has made clear, the multiple and overlapping problems faced by women in Buraku communities cannot be dealt with simply by applying external frameworks such as gender mainstreaming or gender equality and putting them into categories such as "women's issues" or "gender discrimination." We need, rather, to examine carefully, through the outlook and experiences of Buraku people—including their relationships with work, family, and men—existing theories and ideas, including those of feminism and the concept of the Buraku liberation movement. In that way, the mutual relationships and synergies between different forms of discriminatory structures will become clear. Moreover, an understanding of how Buraku women have sought to deal with their problems, will lead to a reappraisal of feminist theories and practices.

I have come to believe that we can reconstruct the models of "family," "community" and "culture," which have been created within the existing social and political structure so that they are more respectful of diversity, and of the history and lives of the Buraku people. By deciding within the community what to get rid of and what to keep, new social values and human values can be consciously cultivated to restore human dignity. The rich and vibrant culture Buraku people have created amid poverty and discrimination can be drawn upon to create new values and ideas. For this to take place, education is needed, as well as adequate work opportunities so that people may have the resources with which to work on social reform.

I have come to understand the importance of resisting stereotypes and the definitions others use to portray us. I have come to refuse to be defined by others' perceptions. We must find ourselves again, confirm who we are, positively accept and express ourselves. Some Buraku women have achieved their dignity as human beings because they gained confidence and self-esteem through cooperation with others within their local community. For them, living together with others in the community itself has created shared spaces in which they can work together for community development. I hope that we can regain and develop connections and solidarity to create a liberation movement that is personal to all persons in it, and that does not get buried in the logic of the movement or organization. I also hope that we can turn a vertical, individual-focused style of anti-discrimination activism into a horizontal one that focuses on groups.

Notes

1. As described by the Buraku Liberation and Human Rights Research Institute (BLHRRI), the term *Dowa*, consisting of two Chinese characters "same" and "harmony," "was coined by the Japanese government during the Second World War in the early 1940s in an attempt to foster harmonious relations among soldiers. Buraku soldiers were discriminated against by non-Buraku soldiers, and such conflicts were regarded as impediments to efficient mobilization of the military forces," and the term has since been employed to refer to administrative policies and services related to Buraku issues (BLHRRI homepage).

Works Cited

Buraku Liberation and Human Rights Research Institute. http://blhrri.org/blhrri_e/dowaeducation/de_0003.htm

Davis, Angela Y. 1981. *Women, Race and Class*. New York: Random House.

———.1989. *Women, Culture and Politics*. New York: Random House.

Hagiwara, Hiroko. 2002. "Black Feminism. " In *Iwanami joseigaku jiten* (Iwanami dictionary of women's studies), ed. Teruko Inoue, Chizuko Ueno, Yumiko Ehara, Mari Ohsawa, and Mikiyo Kano. Tokyo: Iwanami shoten.

hooks, bell. 1984. *Feminist Theory: From Margin to Center*. Boston: South End Press.

——. 1989. *Talking Back: Thinking Feminist, Thinking Black*. Boston: South End Press.

——. 1990. *Yearning: Race, Gender, and Cultural Politics*. Boston: South End Press.

——. 1992. *Black Looks: Race and Representation*. Boston: South End Press.

——. 1999. *Ain't I a Woman: Black Women and Feminism*. Boston: South End Press.

Hull, Gloria T., Patricia Bell Scott and Barbara Smith, eds. 1982. *All the Women Are White, All the Blacks Are Men, But Some of Us Are Brave: Black Women's Studies*. New York: The Feminist Press.

Lorde, Audre. 1984. *Sister Outsider*. Berkeley: Crossing Press.

Smith, Barbara, ed. 1983. *Home Girls: A Black Feminist Anthology*. New York: Kitchen Table: Women of Color Press.

Ainu, Buraku, and Zainichi Korean Activists Rise Up

Yuriko Hara
Translated by Malaya Ileto

"We exist." This is what one Zainichi Korean[1] woman asserted in a nongovernmental organization report to the Committee on the Elimination of Discrimination against Women, which oversees the United Nations Convention on the Elimination of All Forms of Discrimination against Women (CEDAW).[2] She was also directing her words toward the Japanese government, and Japanese society in general. But why did she have to say those words? A non-Japanese reader may understand that minorities exist in all countries, and may also be interested in how they came to be there, and what their relationship with the host country is like today. But few Japanese know or care about these issues. Japanese schools do not spend much time on the history of Japan's past feudal, caste-like social system, or its assimilation policies for indigenous peoples, or its colonizing. Perhaps therefore, many are unaware of Japanese minorities today. Hence, Doudou Diene, special rapporteur on racism of the UN Commission on Human Rights, reported in January 2006, following his visit to Japan on a formal mission, " . . . racial discrimination and xenophobia do exist in Japan, and these affect three circles of discriminated groups: the national minorities—the Buraku people, the Ainu, and the people of Okinawa; people from and descendants of people from former Japanese colonies—Korea and China; and foreigners and migrants from other Asian countries and from the rest of the world" (Diene 2006).

Especially absent in Japan is awareness regarding the lives of women in minority communities. At the 1995 United Nations Fourth World Conference on Women held in Beijing, and in the five-year review of the implementation of the Beijing Declaration and Platform for Action (Beijing+5) held in the UN General Assembly in 2000, indigenous women[3] strongly criticized the platform for action, pointing out that regarding women's equal access and full participation in decision-making, equal status, equal pay, etc., "These objectives are hollow and meaningless if the inequality between nations, races, classes, and genders, are not challenged at the same time."[4]

239

The United Nations took up the issue of multiple discrimination only recently, for example, in General Recommendation twenty-five of the UN Committee on the Elimination of Racial Discrimination (CERD) on "Gender-related dimensions of racial discrimination," adopted in March 2000 (UN CERD 2000). CERD pointed out that "There are circumstances in which racial discrimination only or primarily affects women, or affects women in a different way, or to a different degree than men" and that "Certain forms of racial discrimination may be directed towards women specifically because of their gender." This included "sexual violence committed against women members of particular racial or ethnic groups in detention or during armed conflict; the coerced sterilization of indigenous women; abuse of women workers in the informal sector or domestic workers employed abroad by their employers."[5] CERD made clear that it is important for each state to collect information on these issues, and analyze and make appropriate policies in response. Since then, signatories of the International Convention on the Elimination of All Forms of Racial Discrimination have begun to include the perspective of gender, and information regarding gender, in their reports.[6] Resolutions and agreements regarding multiple forms of discrimination were passed at the same time in various bodies of the UN.[7]

In 1985, Japan ratified CEDAW. Yet, the government seemed unaware of its duty to comply with the convention and to seek to eradicate discrimination against all women in Japan, regardless of nationality, ethnicity, civil rights, or legal status.[8] Despite minority women's efforts to communicate their situation and demands to the government, for a long time, the government showed no willingness to listen.[9]

In late 1999, minority women from different communities began taking part in a yearlong series of workshops on multiple discrimination against minority women sponsored by the International Movement Against All Forms of Discrimination and Racism—Japan Committee ((IMADR-JC).[10] At each monthly session, one of the participants would raise a topic for discussion, giving Ainu, Buraku, Zainichi Korean, Okinawan, migrant, and disabled women the opportunity to learn from each other about multiple forms of discrimination, and recognize their shared concerns. Unfortunately, however, they lacked specific data to support descriptions of their realities and to allow them to work toward seeking solutions to problems.

The examination by the CEDAW Committee in July 2003 of Japan's fifth periodic report on the implementation of the convention provided the impetus for these women to take action. The government had not undertaken official surveys or collected data on Buraku, Ainu, Zainichi Korean and foreign women, including migrant workers; nor had they established policies affecting these women. Indeed, in its report to the CEDAW Committee, the government did not mention these women at all. Fortunately, during the previous year, the Japan Network for CEDAW (JNNC) had been formed to collaborate on producing an alternative NGO report to the CEDAW Committee on the situations of Buraku women, Zainichi Korean women, Ainu women, women with disabilities, and women's shelters. In addition Buraku and Ainu women attended the examination in New York to appeal directly to CEDAW Committee members. As a result, multiple forms of discrimination against minority women in Japan became an important agenda item for the CEDAW Committee.

Among the issues taken up in the alternative report was that because of structural discrimination and their deprivation of rights in the past, Buraku, Zainichi Korean, Ainu, and Okinawa/Ryukyu women face restrictions in their opportunities to participate in political and public life, education, and training and employment. They raised the need to improve policies in these spheres, and the obligation of the Japanese government to take all appropriate measures, including legislation, to ensure the full development and advancement of women in all fields, in particular in the political, social, economic, and cultural fields.[11]

The CEDAW Committee criticized the lack of information in the Japanese government's report regarding the situation of minority women. The committee's concluding observations, issued to the government in August 2003, expressed concern over the multiple forms of discrimination and marginalization these groups of women may experience with respect to education, employment, health, social welfare, and exposure to violence, both within their own communities and in the wider society. In addition, the committee called for the inclusion, in the government's next report, of comprehensive information, including disaggregated data on the status of minority women in Japan, including Ainu, Buraku, Zainichi Korean, and migrant women, with respect to the abovementioned areas.

Rising Up and Joining Forces: The Survey by Ainu, Buraku and Zainichi Korean Women

Unfortunately, though, regardless of how much the importance of this issue of minority women was raised at the international level, because it had been a marginalized issue for so long, it continued to be ignored at the domestic level. Even the consultations between the Japanese government and minority women that had been promised at the CEDAW examination in 2003 did not take place, with the government saying it was just not possible to meet minority women separately from other women. Moreover, it showed no will to execute the survey that was discussed at the examination.

With their demands for justice backed by the CEDAW Committee, the women decided that if the government would not execute a survey, they would do it themselves. From 2004 to 2005, three organizations—the Sapporo Branch of the Ainu Association of Hokkaido, the Buraku Liberation League Central Women's Division, and the APEURO Women's Survey Project, carried out their own surveys under the coordination of IMADR-JC. The survey was carried out through a questionnaire that was developed in discussions among the women of these three communities, and focused on the spheres of education, employment, social welfare, health, and violence.

This survey was the first ever undertaken *by* minority women *for* minority women, with Ainu, Buraku, and Zainichi Korean women coming together to discuss and delineate items of common concern. It was the crystallization of joint efforts by the women to record for the first time what the women were experiencing and turn them into words and numbers.[12,13]

The Buraku People

The Buraku people are not a racial minority but rather ethnic Japanese who are descendants of an outcast minority within the caste-like system that was established in the seventeenth century and which persisted into the mid-nineteenth century. These people were forced to undertake specific jobs such as processing dead cattle and leatherwork, and were restricted in where they could live. Those areas are what are today designated as "discriminated Buraku communities" or "Buraku." According to the last government survey of Buraku areas in 1993, there are 4,442 Buraku communities in Japan and around nine hundred thousand Buraku people (Somusho 1993). Buraku organizations and research bodies put their estimates at six thousand areas and three million people. While the feudal caste system was abolished in 1871, discrimination against the Buraku people as well as poverty within Buraku communities persists to this day. (See chapter 16 for a more detailed discussion and analysis of Buraku issues.)

Indigenous Peoples: The Ainu

The Ainu originally lived in Ainu Moshiri ("Land of Humans"), a wide area comprising the north and northeastern part of Japan's mainland, Honshu, to Hokkaido, the Kuril Islands, and Southern Sakhalin. They possessed their own distinct religion and culture. The Meiji period saw the assimilation of the Ainu, with their lands unilaterally taken in 1869 and named "Hokkaido," and their annexation in 1877 as a "no man's land." Reduced to a minority status with the government-promoted immigration from the mainland that followed, the Ainu were robbed of their land, and suffered the destruction of their traditional lifestyle and livelihoods. The 1899 Law for the Protection of Native Hokkaido Aborigines (Hokkaido kyudojin hogoho) treated the indigenous Ainu as second-class citizens, and it was not until 1997 that the law was abolished, when Japan recognized the Ainu as an ethnic minority for the first time, under the Law for the Promotion of the Ainu Culture. The Japanese government had refused to recognize the Ainu as an indigenous people on the ground that there was no international consensus on the definition of an indigenous people, but the adoption by the UN General Assembly in 2007 of the Declaration on Rights of Indigenous Peoples lent strong support to the demands for the recognition that the Ainu people had been pursuing for many years. The Japanese government at last formally recognized the Ainu as an indigenous people following the passage of a resolution to that effect by the National Diet. The number of Ainu, according to a 2006 survey (Hokkaido kankyo seikatsubu somuka . . . 2007), was 23,782, but this is limited to those who identify themselves as Ainu, and live on the island of Hokkaido. The actual number is probably several times higher.

Zainichi Koreans

In 1910, Japan colonized Korea and denied Koreans their lands and ways of life. To survive poverty, many came to Japan alone or with their families. At the height of the Sino-Japanese War in 1937, many Koreans were forcibly moved from their homes to work in Japan's coalmines, munitions factories, construction industry, and harbors. Some had no choice but to remain in Japan after colonization ended in 1945, because of the partition of Korea and the Korean War. Under Japan's colonial policies, Korean people were forced to fully assimilate by speaking Japanese, and using Japanese names. Although forced to become Japanese, Koreans were treated differently under the law and suffered discrimination.[14]

Koreans unilaterally lost their Japanese nationality in 1952 with the San Francisco Peace Treaty, in which Japan formally abandoned its territorial claim to the Korean peninsula. As non-nationals, they had limited rights to education and welfare, and for a long time suffered discrimination in housing, marriage, and employment. Employment was particularly harsh, with no-hire policies against Koreans, exclusion from public office positions, and work being limited to specific areas.

Today, 90 percent of Zainichi Koreans use Japanese names, regardless of nationality, pointing to the discrimination and disadvantages that still result from using one's real (i.e., Korean) name. Zainichi Koreans are now in their fourth and fifth generation, and without becoming naturalized, and obtaining Japanese nationality, they do not have the right to vote, not only at the national level but also at the local level (except in a number of municipalities). Further, because ethnic education is not systematically guaranteed, there are few opportunities to learn about their roots or Korean history and culture. There were about six hundred thousand Zainichi Koreans in Japan at the end of 2006,[15] of which roughly four hundred and forty thousand were special permanent residents. The total number of people naturalized up until 2006 was 288,259.[16]

The Surveys

While the surveys of three minority communities represented a historic first step, one must be clear about their limitations as well as their accomplishments. Since they were not based on a random sample, and since the ages of the respondents were not well distributed, the numbers are not representative of each group as a whole. Moreover, each survey was taken at a different time, and under different conditions, so that it is inappropriate to compare them to each other. In short, each must be viewed as preliminary to a formal, large-scale future study. More important perhaps than their actual findings were the experiences of the women who planned, executed, and responded to the survey. The Zainichi Korean women reported, for example, that the process of distributing and collecting the questionnaires led to building new face-to-face relationships among Zainichi Korean women. For all who participated, the experience may have allowed for the expansion of a movement. Ryoko Tahara, Under Secretary-General, Sapporo Branch of the Ainu Association of Hokkaido, said, for example, "Many of the women who took part in the survey were empowered by it. They came to have pride in their identity as Ainu." The participants reported how they came to realize that their personal experiences of suffering were neither trivial nor the norm.

Perhaps most important was the awareness gained by those planning the surveys and reviewing the results of significant commonalities as well as differences in the histories and present condition of the three groups, thus deepening mutual trust, and strengthening their partnership and basis for working together. We did this fully aware of the danger of lumping all groups, including Ainu, Buraku, and Zainichi Korean women, together into the category of "minority women," and how difficult it is to work in solidarity. We present some of the findings as reported by representatives of each of the three minority groups.[17]

For Ainu women, Ryoko Tahara, Under-Secretary-General, Sapporo

Branch of the Ainu Association of Hokkaido, reports that previous surveys conducted by academics have usually focused on whether the Ainu can recite *yukara* (epic poems) or speak the Ainu language. The Japanese government spends millions of yen to conduct a survey about cranes every year, but says that it does not have the budget to execute one about the Ainu. All that existed before this study is a survey conducted by the Hokkaido government every seven years with a budget of about three million yen ($30,000). It is a random sample and deals only with households, so it says nothing about the lives of women specifically.

In the present survey, the respondents were predominantly members of the Ainu Association of Hokkaido, with 241 women from fourteen branches and one district among the Association's fifty-four branches. Twelve women took on the task of traveling throughout the expansive island of Hokkaido to conduct the survey between October 2004 and February 2005. Seventy-seven percent of the participants were over the age of forty, partly because we did not say in advance that we wanted to reach women of various ages. In addition, since ample time was required to take part in the survey, respondents tended to be older women who were not working or who had the day off. Another factor controlling the age of respondents was that the main targets of the survey were members of the association. Young Ainu women tend not to participate actively in the association, partly since doing so would require them to "come out" to society about their roots. Many women wait until their children have grown up before joining Ainu-organized activities, so that their children will not become targets of discrimination.

Sixty percent of the respondents had completed elementary or junior high school, while 36 percent had finished high school, with four percent having completed college or university. We have heard that the number of those unable to attend school is actually higher than what we were able to glean. Many reported they were unable to attend school because of discrimination from students and teachers. Poverty was another reason. The spiral of discrimination continues, with education affecting employment, and employment affecting marriage and income.

The same can be said for literacy rates. Seventy-two percent said that they were "able to read normally" and 67 percent "able to write normally." It is hard to swallow one's pride and respond, "cannot read or write." However, one-third gave responses indicating they have difficulty in reading to some extent. We do not know whether these figures are higher or lower than the rest of society because there is no national survey on literacy rates.

Over half of the respondents (56 percent) were currently employed, but only 6 percent were full-time company employees, while 26 percent worked part-time, 4 percent as contract or temporary employees, and 10 percent were self-employed (including farming). The fact that almost a third of these women were employed as part-time or temporary workers reflects the instability of their employment. Many worked in the service industry, and not many had employment insurance because they were employed by small businesses.

With regard to social security, as many as 16 percent of the women were not enrolled in any type of pension plan, and will thus be unable to receive a pension in the future. This means that the rate of people receiving Public Assistance (*seikatsu hogo*) will also rise. According to the 2006 Hokkaido survey on the conditions of Ainu, about 4 percent of respondents, both male and female, were receiving Public Assistance (Hokkaido kankyo sei-katsubu somuka. . .2006). In our survey, 12 percent were receiving benefits, which points to a more severe situation; another 9 percent had received such benefits in the past.

Asked about discrimination against the Ainu in Japanese society, a fourth of the 241 respondents cited "An environment making it difficult to share that one is an Ainu," and another 20 percent cited other examples, such as "obstacles in marriage." Yet many indicated they had never experienced discrimination. We should be wary of accepting this response at face value.

Thirty-seven percent of the Ainu women surveyed said that they had suffered physical violence from their spouse or partner. But more than half did not mention whom they were consulting regarding this, although fourteen percent said that they were consulting doctors.

For Buraku women, Reiko Yamazaki, a member of the Buraku Liberation League Central Women's Division, reported on the difficulties of surveying six thousand Buraku communities totaling three million Buraku people, spread very widely throughout the country, both in cities and farming villages. Ultimately, the survey was conducted among 1,405 Buraku women who gathered for the Buraku Liberation League's Fiftieth National Women's Rally held in Tottori Prefecture on January 1, 2005. As a result, 30 percent of the respondents were from Tottori and 60 percent from the nearby regions of Chugoku and Kinki. In addition, 90 percent of the women were over the age of forty.

Discrimination related to marriage was named as a serious problem: 29 percent of the respondents said they had experienced such discrimination, with engagements cancelled by the non-Buraku partner or future in-laws upon learning of the Buraku origins of the woman. Nearly 26 percent answered that they had experienced discrimination after marriage, by neighbors and relatives, as well as their partners.

The percentage of single-mother households was a little over 11 percent, which is much higher than the national rate of 6 percent as found in the Ministry of Health, Labor and Welfare's 2004 Kokumin seikatsu kiso chosa (Basic survey on living conditions). Single-parent households are a major issue in Buraku communities.

At roughly 45 percent, the highest level of education attained by most respondents was high school, followed by junior high school at 34 percent. The number of women who went on to high school rose sharply among respondents in their 50s, probably attributable to a 1969 law allowing high school scholarships, which the Buraku Liberation League had fought hard for. School attendance rates are linked to literacy, and there were women who said that they were unable to read or write at all. The Buraku Liberation League has been involved in literacy education across Japan to deal with this problem.

While the employment rate of women in Japan usually declines upon marriage and childbirth, after which it recovers again, our survey pointed to a big difference in the case of Buraku women: the percentage of women working was 100 percent (23 women) among those in their twenties; over 90 percent among those in their thirties and forties; 82 percent for those in their fifties; and 28 percent among women over the age of seventy—all indicating that Buraku women work their entire lives. Buraku women were found to have experienced various forms of domestic violence. Yet only 19 percent said they had approached someone for help after falling victim to violence, while 38 percent said they had not sought help, and 43 percent did not indicate whether or not they had ever consulted anyone.

Aisun Yang, of the APEURO Women's Survey Project, ("Apeuro" means "forward, to the future" in the Korean language), reports that for Zainichi Korean women, this survey began with a group of five concerned women from the Osaka-Kyoto region and then expanded to forty-two women, ultimately obtaining responses from 818 women between July 2004 and May 2005. The Zainichi Korean community has faced several demographic changes in recent years, including Japanese naturalization and marriage to Japanese nationals and generational change, resulting in a shrinking of the population. Such recent changes in the Zainichi Korean community made it all the more important to conduct a survey to assess its current situation and also to gauge current sentiment about Korean identity.

Those of South Korean nationality were about 71 percent, Chosen (North Korean)[18] 20 percent, and Japanese nationality 7 percent. Respondents were 60 percent third generation, 34 percent second generation, and 3 percent fourth generation. Seventy-eight percent were between the ages of twenty and forty-nine years. Most of the survey participants were therefore relatively young, and had a strong sense of ethnic identity, as well as a strong interest in political issues. Many were actively involved in various community and local school related activities.

Over 20 percent reported experiencing discrimination on the basis of nationality or lineage in the process of job seeking or in the workplace.[19] While more than half the respondents reported using their Korean names in some capacity, only one-third use these names in the workplace, though 9 percent said they wanted to use their Korean names in the workplace in the future.

Twenty-three percent said that they were suffering financial difficulty. In this regard it should be pointed out that Zainichi Koreans in their eighties and older are ineligible for pension payments. Women taking maternity or child-care leave from work are limited to those earning a relatively high income, and the overwhelming majority do not work in environments where they can easily take such leave.

There is little information about how Zainichi Korean women are affected by domestic violence, but of the 818 women we surveyed, 20 percent said they had been subject to physical or verbal forms of violence.

To eliminate discrimination against women within the Zainichi Korean community itself, 34 percent said that it was necessary to eliminate discrimination in Japanese society as a whole and create a society that would make life better for both Zainichi Korean men and women; 25 percent said that it was necessary to eradicate male-dominated values in society, while 11 percent said that we needed to stop teaching children to be feminine or masculine.

Although the Korean traditional rite and memorial service called *Chaesa* tends to require more labor from women than men, 66 percent of women reported that they want to honor and continue *Chaesa* rites, even in simplified form.[20] Together with the survey responses regarding other cultural characteristics (ethnic name, language, consciousness as a Zainichi Korean), this is one more indication of the importance women place on ethnic identity and on being themselves.

Even third-generation Zainichi Koreans, who today comprise the majority of Zainichi, still suffer human rights violations. They would like to live in a receptive social environment, which will accept the use of Korean names at school or in the workplace. They would like to see women able to walk down the street wearing a *chima chogori* (traditional Korean attire) without being attacked.

All three surveys captured aspects of a discriminatory social system, which has established assimilation policies for minority and indigenous peoples, thus firmly rooting colonialism in Japan's legal system along with people's consciousness. New policies need to address underlying causes and interrelationships. The following recommendations come as key to issues common to the three groups. There needs to be a strong antidiscrimination law as well as the development and implementation of policies that reflect the perspectives of minority women; preferential appointments for minority women at decision-making agencies; regular surveys, including the subject of domestic violence and the establishment of structures to address and deal with the violence; and an effective human rights training of counselors and a continuing discussion between minority women and relevant government representatives.

Specifically, Ainu women requested the protection of their rights as indigenous peoples, including the right to ethnic education, and the ratification of the Convention concerning Indigenous and Tribal Peoples in Independent Countries (ILO 169). Buraku women urged that steps be taken for urgent ratification of ILO Convention 111 and Convention 175, which provide for the elimination of discrimination in recruitment and employment, and urged support for literacy education programs. Zainichi Korean women pushed for the urgent implementation of voting rights in local elections, the abolition of the nationality clause for posts such as district welfare officer, securing funding for ethnic education programs, and the application of scholarship money to students enrolled in Korean schools.

Most important, as a result of formulating these recommendations based on the survey results, for the first time the minority women succeeded in getting a representative of the Gender Equality Bureau of the Cabinet Office to listen to them explain their situation. Ainu women from Hokkaido, together with Buraku and Zainichi Korean women from different parts of Japan, participated in the March 2007 negotiations; they were confident as they made their specific demands to the government. The government representative showed an understanding of the situation, and responded in a way far different from what we had experienced previously. However, the representative continued to argue that racial discrimination was not within the jurisdiction of the Gender Equality Bureau. Lack of understanding about multiple forms of discrimination, coupled with inadequacies inherent in the vertical administrative system, have led to issues of discrimination and human rights being dealt with separately from those concerning women. As a result, minority women's issues have fallen between the cracks, with neither side willing to view them as within their jurisdiction. It is not that multiple forms of discrimination are invisible, but that no one will look at them.

When the survey results and recommendations were published, we witnessed some changes. Armed with data, we participated in another government negotiation in September 2007, and for the first time, fifty government representatives from seven ministries attended to listen to what we had to say. We asked the government representatives a number of questions based on the twenty-three themes raised in our survey recommendations. Through these lobbying sessions with government representatives, minority women, backed by statistics and case studies, emphasized their view that the improvement of government policies toward minority women is critical to improving the overall human rights situation in Japan. The responses by government representatives were limited to the framework of existing domestic law and generally passive.

At the press conference that followed, one minority woman participant said, "Although we are less than satisfied with the results of today's negotiations, considering that there have been no measures in place until now to address our specific needs, today's discussions represent the first step toward the creation [of such policies] and must be continued." Another woman added, "If we don't speak out, society will not change. This burden [to speak] is shared by all minority women; it helps us grow [and] gain courage. By speaking out, we have found others willing to speak out with us. We must shed this burden and persevere in this fight."

Strengthening and Expanding the Minority Women's Movement

To see each of our recommendations become a reality, we need a stronger voice and persistent advocacy. We must use the survey and recommendations—the fruits of a struggle to give words and numbers to our experiences—to push for action from the Japanese government and local authorities, women's organizations, people in the women's movement, researchers and minority groups.

In the 1980s, when the issues of domestic violence and sexual harassment were little understood in Japan, women who suffered them began their own movement to survey their experiences, and this became the force behind groups, organizations and local governments conducting their own surveys all around the country. Social awareness of these issues grew, leading to legal measures being enacted in 2001. We can thus say that our movement has just begun. The Buraku Liberation League has already begun new surveys in several areas based on what was learned from the first survey. Reiko Yamazaki, a key person in our survey, was heavily involved in executing a survey of Buraku women in Aichi Prefecture and its findings were published in March 2007. She was appointed member of the Nagoya City Gender Equality Council, which was the first in Japan to put out a report calling for a survey of minority women. We can anticipate that this will become a model case for local authorities to carry out surveys based on the experiences and advice of the women themselves. The Ainu women have discussed plans to expand the reach of the survey to a wider age range and to Ainu women who are not members of the Ainu Association of Hokkaido, and later to Ainu women living in the Kanto and Kansai areas. Our hope is that the minority women's movement will grow stronger and expand in the future, not only through surveys, but also through other kinds of awareness raising and activities, as well as consistent and persistent governmental advocacy.

When the survey results were publicized at an event in March 2007, about two hundred people—most of whom are not part of a minority—participated and many expressed feelings of being inspired, and said the presentation fostered a change in their consciousness. Even though many attended the session believing they already understood the issues, many felt that meeting and connecting with the women showed them that it was an issue that they had to do something about. Those in the women's movement in particular had a new awareness that led them to promise to include activities about minority women in their work, and raise the issue with the Gender Equality Bureau. If these efforts are successful in the future, Japan's women's movement will make big strides forward on an issue that has never been in their framework of action before.

Notes

1. "Zainichi Korean" refers to people whom, regardless of nationality, have Korean roots and/or who regard themselves as descendents of people from the Korean peninsula. Most are people who have come to live in Japan as a result of Japan's colonization of Korea, or their descendents.

2. The Convention on the Elimintion of All Forms of Discrimination against Women (CEDAW) was adopted in 1979 by the UN General Assembly. Consisting of a preamble and thirty articles, it defines discrimination against women, and sets up an agenda for national action to end such discrimination.

3. Both declaration texts are available at the website of the International Indigenous Women's Forum (best known as FIMI, its Spanish initials): http://www.indigenouswomensforum.org.

4. The Beijing Declaration of Indigenous Women states, "Equal pay and equal status in the so-called First World is made possible because of the perpetuation of a development model which is not only non-sustainable but causes the increasing violation of the human rights of women, Indigenous peoples, and nations elsewhere."

5. The "comfort women," who were colonized women forced into sexual slavery during the war by Japan are one example of this. See chapter 15 for more on the "comfort women."

6. Note that because a gender perspective and information regarding gender was found to be lacking in the Japanese government's report when in the deliberation of

the International Convention on the Elimination of All Forms of Racial Discrimination held in March 2001, CERD issued an admonition regarding this problem in its Concluding Observations (UN CERD 2001).

7. In November 2000, an Expert Group Meeting on "Gender and Racial Discrimination" was held in Zagreb (Croatia), and the resulting documentation is the most comprehensive study of the issue of multiple discrimination at the UN level. It points out that it is inappropriate to deal with gender and racial discrimination as two separate issues, and that in some cases, this could even result in worsening the situation. See http://www.un.org/womenwatch/daw/csw/genrac/report.htm

8. From a government response to a question asked at the 2003 exchange session with the government.

9. The word "minorities" encompasses sexual minorities, the physically challenged, migrant workers, refugees, and others, but in this essay, I use the term to refer to Buraku, Ainu, Okinawan and Zainichi Korean people, who have experienced a long history of racism and colonial rule by Japan. The lack of protection of their rights is linked to the lack of protection of the rights of the so-called "new-comers" to Japan, such as migrant workers and refugees, as well as foreigners and sexual minorities.

10. IMADR is an NGO founded in 1988 through a call for action by the Buraku Liberation League for minority groups to work together to eliminate all forms of discrimination and racism around the world. IMADR places importance in the empowerment of minorities and promotes their linkages so that they can work together to combat discrimination and racism. IMADR-JC is the Japan Committee that carries out IMADR's work in Japan.

11. The women also pointed to the lack of protection of reproductive health/rights, and absence of sufficient measures to combat violence against girls and women, particularly at a time when violence and harassment of girl students was rampant, including violence and hate crimes against those attending ethnic North Korean schools in Japan.

12. At the same time that we were undertaking the survey, migrant women from the Philippines were becoming empowered through participating in a study undertaken by the Kalakasan Migrant Women Empowerment Center whereby they shared their difficult life experiences with each other. Kalakasan entrusted IMADR-JC with the task of translating the report of their study to make it available to a wider audience, and this became the joint bilingual publication *Transforming Lives: Abused Migrant Women in Japan Blaze a Trail towards Empowerment* (Kalakasan and IMADR-JC 2006) (See chapter 14 for more on Kalakasan and migrant Filipinas). What they valued in their study, and the impetus behind it, as well as their goals and the insights and experiences they gained, were the same as in the case of our survey.

13. Okinawans were also interested in participating in the survey, but decided not to because Okinawa Prefecture already has surveys about Okinawan women, including public opinion surveys conducted by local authorities on the effects of the US bases on the situation of women in Okinawa and practices that unfairly burden women. Briefly, the people of Ryukyu/Okinawa maintained the Kingdom of Ryukyu from the fourteenth century, but its end came in 1879 when the Japanese government exercised military pressure to annex the territory, making it the Japanese prefecture of Okinawa. Japan's policies to colonize and assimilate the people of Ryukyu began. They banned the use of *Uchina-guchi*, the Ryukyuan language, as well as traditional customs, beliefs, and practices. Okinawa sustained immense damage in 1945, at the end of the Second World War, experiencing the biggest ground war in the country with not only military, but

also countless civilian casualties. With the defeat of Japan in the Second World War and the US occupation of Okinawa, Ryukyu fell under US rule, but was "returned" to Japan in 1972 after much protest. Seventy-five percent of US military bases in Japan are located in Okinawa, which occupies 0.6 percent of Japanese territory. Since the bases were set up, the environment has suffered, and the culture and traditions rooted in the land are not respected; moreover, the human rights of Okinawans are also being violated by the US military, with crimes such as violence, rape, and murder. Because Okinawa is a prefecture in Japan, many people in Okinawa think within this framework and not many advocate for their rights as indigenous peoples. Despite this, many Okinawans are demanding the Japanese government reduce or remove US bases from Okinawa and revise the Japan-US Status-of-Forces Agreement on the basis of past and continuing injustices in the discrimination and human rights violations against Okinawans.

14. For example, many Koreans were slaughtered in the aftermath of the 1923 Great Kanto Earthquake and government authorities persecuted those involved in the Korean liberation movement, though they had done nothing wrong. Directly after the end of World War II, in August 1945, Koreans set up schools across Japan to teach their children about their history, language, and culture, but the government and the General Headquarters (GHQ) of the American Occupation forces ordered their closure as part of efforts to step up control over the Korean population. Several of the schools were later re-established.

15. Those registered as foreign residents under the category of "Korean" (Homusho 2007).

16. Calculated by adding up each year's total according to the yearly publication of *Hoso jiho* (Legal times).

17. A joint report of the survey findings was published in 2007, and an English version was published in 2009. See IMADR-JC et al. 2009.

18. "Chosen" does not refer to a citizenship but a status determined by the 1947 Foreign Registration Decree (1947). At the time, the Japanese government registered all Koreans as such. Since the 1965 Korean-Japan agreements and the normalization of relations between Japan and the Republic of South Korea, those who do not obtain South Korean nationality continue to be registered as "Chosen," and remain stateless today.

19. A university student in Kyoto wrote in the survey that she was hired for a job when she used her Japanese name, yet rejected when she used her Korean name.

20. *Chaesa* is a traditional Korean rite of ancestor worship in the Confucian way. It is practiced by families in Zainichi Korean society to honor lost loved ones.

Works Cited

Beijing Declaration of Indigenous Women. NGO Forum, UN Fourth World Conference on Women. 1995. Huairou, Beijing. 1995.

Diene, Doudou. 2006. Report of the UN Special Rapporteur on contemporary forms of racism, racial discrimination, xenophobia and related intolerance, Addendum, "Mission to Japan," E/CN.4/2006/16/Add.2

Hokkaido kankyo seikatsubu somuka ainu shisaku suishin guruupu (Hokkaido Department of Environmental, Lifestyle and General Affairs, Ainu Policy Promotion Group). 2007. *Heisei juhachinen Hokkaido Ainu seikatsu jittai chosa hokokusho* (Survey report of the living conditions of Ainu in Hokkaido in 2006).

Homusho (Ministry of Justice). 2007. *Heisei jukyunendoban zairyu gaikokujin tokei* (Statistics on foreign residents in Japan, 2007).

Hoso jiho (Legal times). For various years. Tokyo: Hosokai.

IMADR-JC et al. 2009. *Minority Women Rise Up: A Collaborative Survey on Ainu, Buraku and Korean Women in Japan.* Peoples for Human Rights: 12. Tokyo: IMADR.

Kalakasan and IMADR-JC. 2006. *Transforming Lives: Abused Migrant Women in Japan Blaze a Trail towards Empowerment.* Tokyo: Buraku Liberation Publishing House.

Somusho (Ministry of Internal Affairs and Communications). 1993. *Dowa chiku jittai haaku to chosa—chiku gaikyo chosa hokokusho* (Survey of dowa districts—report of general conditions in the districts).

UN CERD. 2000. "General Recommendation No. 25: Gender related dimensions of racial discrimination," Contained in document A/55/18, annex V.

UN CERD. 2001. "Concluding observations of the Committee on the Elimination of Racial Discrimination: Japan," CERD/C/304/Add.114.

VI

DOORS TO EMPLOYMENT OPEN AND CLOSE

Employment and Poverty

Mami Nakano
Translated by Minata Hara

In 1985, the Japanese government ratified the Convention on the Elimination of All Forms of Discrimination against Women (CEDAW) and introduced legislation to abolish discrimination against women in all fields. The Equal Employment Opportunity Law (EEOL), passed in the area of labor the same year, marked a significant turning point for the Japanese employment system. Since its enactment the EEOL has undergone two major revisions, in 1997 and in 2006, to strengthen the provisions prohibiting discrimination against women.

Yet the gender disparity in employment status and wages has not narrowed. Increasing dualism in the labor market or the replacement of regular full-time workers by non-regular workers that has been promoted through deregulation of labor laws has proceeded at a quick pace centered on women's labor, causing a rapid increase in low-wage, unstable employment. Even within regular full-time employment, the spread of the dual-track employment management system that was set up after the passage of the EEOL has widened and consolidated the disparities.

While the overall relative poverty rate in Japan has risen to 15.7 percent (Koseirodosho 2009)—the fourth highest among the thirty Organisation for Economic Co-operation and Development countries (OECD 2008), it is particularly high for women—especially elderly and single-mother households. Rise in low-paid labor, coupled with lack of adequate social spending on low-income households, has been directly linked to women's growing impoverishment.

Establishment of Equal Opportunity Laws and the Deregulation of Labor Laws

Originally, the EEOL required that employers "endeavor" to give equal treatment to women and men. In 1997, a revision sharpened the language so that employers were "forbidden to discriminate against women" both in hiring and in type of contracts offered to male and female employees in the same recruitment or employment categories. Details of the regulations were not specified in the law itself, but rather stipulated in the guidelines. Hence, so long as a company could explain that existing gender differences were a function of a "difference in the form of contract," it was able to evade being charged with discriminatory practices. Furthermore, once the EEOL had become law, many companies set up different tracks for employees based chiefly on three criteria: "job category" or assigning employees either to core decision-making jobs or auxiliary routine work; "transfer eligibility" or assigning an employee to another domestic or international site; and "promotion eligibility" or seeing an employee as a potential manager.

In reality, only a small number of women have been let into what continues to be the predominantly male *sogoshoku* (career track), while the overwhelming majority of women have been relegated to the *ippanshoku* ("auxiliary work" track) and denied opportunities for promotion, upgrades, or training. These practices have served to further entrench and widen the disparities between women and men. A survey conducted in 2007 of 123 companies that have the dual-track management system revealed that women comprised just 6 percent of those in the career track (Koseirodosho 2008a). The percentage of companies promoting women to managerial positions and the percentage of women among all management-level workers has shown a small increase since the EEOL was enacted. However, the number of corporations that have women in positions of assistant manager or equivalent has actually decreased, and the percentage of companies that have female managers/department heads or their equivalent was only 7.1 percent in 1995, and 8.8 percent in 2006. The proportion of women among managers/department heads remains low at just 2 percent, while even among assistant managers they make up fewer than 7 percent (Koseirodosho 2007).

At the same time, with the enactment of the EEOL, work hour restrictions for women were eased or abolished in Japan. Since the working hours for males were far longer than prescribed in international labor standards, bringing them to the women's level would have resulted in gender equality. Deregulation advocates, however, purposely set the criterion at "maximum work hours" and eased or abolished work hour restrictions for females, which had barely complied with international levels, by deeming the restriction on women "sexist." This decision compelled women employed full time to work the same long hours as men if they were to achieve parity. On the other hand, married women who desired "work-life balance" had to give up full-time jobs and retire temporarily from the labor force upon marriage, pregnancy, or childbirth, encouraged to return to the labor force only as "part-time" workers.

The employers' needs to retain the gender disparity and exploit women's work for lower wages apparently "matched" the needs of women who found it difficult to continue working after the work hour restrictions were eased and/or abolished for female workers. The EEOL framework thus promoted the diversification of women's labor and evaded the claims of discrimination against women to make way for the further exploitation of women, forcing them to work for low wages.

Rise in Non-regular Employment among Women

The numbers of employed women have increased significantly, from roughly sixteen million in 1987 to twenty million in 1997 and twenty-three million in 2007. Since the numbers of women employed on farms or in other family business has decreased through those years, it is clear that women are working mostly outside the home. This increase, furthermore, arises from the number of women in non-regular employment—part-time, temporary/contract, and dispatched workers. The proportion of non-regular employees among all female workers rose from 37 percent in 1987 to 44 percent in 1997, and 55 percent in 2007. The comparable figures among male workers were 9, 11, and 20 percent (Kokuritsu josei kyoiku kaikan 2009, 43, table 3-8).

While 90 percent of males aged thirty-five to fifty-four were working as regular employees in 2007, the comparable figure for women was only 42 percent. Particularly striking has been the rise in non-regular employment among females under age thirty-five since the latter part of the 1990s—from 29 percent in 1997 to 47 percent in 2007 (compared to 13 and 23 percent among males of the same age group) (Ibid., 43, figure 3-6). Increasing numbers of women are therefore now working at low wages with few benefits or protection and with limited access to training and little prospect of mobility into regular employment.

While women accounted for close to 70 percent of all non-regular employees in 2007, over three-quarters of these women were part-time workers, with average hourly earning amounting to less than half—48 percent—of that earned by regular male employees (Ibid., 50, table 4-1; 51, table 4-2). The National Pension Law, amended in 1986, the year the EEOL was first enforced, also accelerated an increase in women's part-time employment. The law introduced the category of "No. 3 insured persons," aimed at dependent spouses of insured salaried workers. With this scheme, the full-time housewife (married to a salaried worker) who stays home to raise a family does not have to pay premiums for pension coverage. The pension cost is borne not by the dependent spouses but by everyone participating in the pension scheme, including women who work full time. Guaranteeing a pension to "No. 3 insured persons" resulted in a further acceptance of and actual rise in low-paid part-time workers who, no matter how long they worked, could not earn enough to lead a self-sufficient life. The scheme encouraged housewives to work part time, while they were also responsible for their families, carefully limiting their work hours and earnings to below the threshold where taxes and pension payments would be required.

The Worker Dispatching Law, which was also enacted in 1985, further hastened the replacement of full-time regular employees with non-regular employees by legitimizing a supply of labor previously regarded as illegal, following the "principle of direct hiring" espoused by the earlier Employment Security Act. This new law defined dispatched work as a style in which workers employed by the dispatching agency would be sent out to work in client companies. Roughly 8 percent of female employees in the category of non-regular employment are dispatched workers, and they account for 62 percent of all dispatched workers (Ibid., 43, table 3-8). A large number of dispatched female workers are registered at dispatching agencies and then employed for a period at their client companies, and they are concentrated in clerical and sales work, whereas a majority of men are hired by dispatching agencies on a permanent basis and are found in skilled jobs, or in such relatively high-income sectors as data processing and marketing. This accounts for a wage gap between male and female dispatched workers that is wider than the gap for regular employees.

The commercial trade of dispatched labor involves three parties, namely the dispatching agency, the client company, and the dispatched worker, an arrangement that allows the client company to lower wage levels considerably. This kind of unstable work style with no guarantee of a steady income spread quickly among women in diverse kinds of jobs. The Worker Dispatching Law underwent further, large-scale deregulation. Initially allowing the dispatching of only some professionally established jobs, those, for example, requiring special management and controlled by the Ministry of Health, Labor and Welfare ordinance, the Law eventually approved the dispatching of workers to jobs of any kind. Thus, dispatched workers placed on production lines changed the atmosphere of the workplace dramatically, even sending women workers onto late night shifts.

Wage Disparities

Wage disparities have not changed: in 2008, not including part-time workers, wages of female general workers were 69 percent of men's wages (Koseiro-dosho 2008b). Such disparity in wages appears to be directly proportionate to the size of the corporation. The number of companies practicing the dual-track management system increased after the enactment of the EEOL. From 1998 through 2003, the number of such companies decreased, but subsequently the number increased again among corporations of all sizes, reaching a record high 11 percent in 2006 (compared to 3 percent in 1989). The larger the company, the more likely it is to have adopted the dual-track system, and studies of the male-female wage disparities have concluded that it has been more difficult to minimize the wage gap for companies with dual-track systems compared to those that do not practice this system.

According to a survey of top leaders of management associations and trade unions, and of hearings held with corporate representatives, the main factors that create wage disparities between men and women are: 1) the low number of women in management positions, 2) women's relatively short length of continuous employment on a job, 3) differences in level of work performed by women and men, 4) differences in job type, 5) low fringe benefits and allowances, 6) differences in terms of their track, 7) inability to accept job transfers. The problem was found not with the wage system itself, but rather in how it is implemented, including personnel evaluations, how work is assigned to employees, and the positions in which they are placed in the course of their careers. These problems would arise outside the wage system, as issues of managerial administration.

The cases mentioned above deal with gender disparities manifested solely within scheduled earnings of regular, full-time employees. The gender gap would widen, especially after the EEOL, if we were to include regular workers employed on a part-time basis. The gap would widen even further if we were to include non-regular workers under fixed-term contract. This is because regular workers may benefit from periodic pay raises and benefits, whereas temporary workers under fixed-term contract usually do not benefit from wage increases based on length of service, and in fact, may even be subject to pay decreases when their contracts expire.

In corporations today, part-time labor now accounts for about 40 percent of female and 9 percent of male employees, but wage levels have not increased. The government amended the Part-time Workers Law in 2007 to prohibit discrimination against part-time workers whose job description is equivalent to that of a regular full-time worker. Although it stipulates that business operators should endeavor to achieve equal treatment of all part-time workers, it still allows each firm to retain wage differentials in accordance with the extent to which overtime and work transfer requiring relocation are compulsory, as well as policies such as those relating to long-term career development of their employees.

The disparity between regular full-time employment and part-time employment originally stems from the premise that full-time lifelong employment should guarantee a full, ascending wage scale for the male breadwinner who is the head of the household. In contrast, part-time employment was deemed an "employment status pursued to balance work with family life, with weak ties to the company's interests," and its treatment was based on the premise that "part-timers work to supplement the household income, and not as primary bread-winners." Certainly, these distinctions constituted discrimination against women from their onset and precluded the establishment of a nonsexist employment system.

Any ban on discrimination regarding "part-time employment" would backfire and further widen the gender gap as long as it operates based on the "male breadwinner model." Thus, the bipolar structure of full-time vs. part-time workers remains solid—the former suffer from an increasingly heavy workload and find it difficult to achieve work-life balance, whereas the latter are confined to low-paid jobs precisely because they seek to achieve this work-life balance.

Part-time wage rates are nowhere near self-sufficient levels. Those wage rates do not even reach the minimum wage levels stipulated by the Living Protection Law, established to support self-sufficient living based on Article 25 of the Constitution. A part-time worker earning nine hundred yen ($9.00) per hour would have to work over 3,300 hours a year to earn three million yen ($30,000) per annum, which would be about the standard living protection rate payable to a single-female-parent household of three.

These low wages are quite "unconstitutional" in view of the government's goals to reduce total annual working hours to 1,800 hours and the amount of unpaid "service" overtime. We must radically question a society in which people who devote the majority of their time to paid labor are compelled to be financially dependent upon others. This serious contradiction affects single working mothers most severely. The hardships these women go through in managing paid work, child rearing, and other household chores are beyond imagination. Single working mothers who are forced to work part-time are the prototype of the modern day "working poor" who cannot support themselves no matter how many hours they work.

Fixed-term and indirect hiring practices have further intensified gender-based discrimination. Labor laws and labor union regulations often do not apply to the increasing number of female non-regular workers who are affected by the effects of globalization and advancements in information technologies. Wages of women in part-time, dispatched, fixed-term and home-based employment have been falling rapidly in the past few years. Fixed-term employment is highly convenient for employers since contract renewal allows for the cutting down of wages and other terms of employment.

In addition, from the latter part of the 1990s, many companies have adopted a system of personnel evaluation and wages based on outcome/ output or performance. This outcome-based evaluation system reflects the preexisting gender gap and simply presents it as "the outcome based on ability," so it is overwhelmingly disadvantageous to women who have been relegated to "auxiliary work" that does not get directly reflected in figures (i.e., profit). Only a small number of women who are fortunate enough to develop their potentials and have been exempted from discrimination or violence (for example in the form of sexual harassment) have benefited from this system. This outcome-based evaluation leaves those women going through pregnancy, childbirth, child rearing, and care of the elderly at a particular disadvantage.

Fixed Gender Roles and Long Work Hours

The firmly entrenched traditional division of gender role is a major obstacle to improving women's situation in the workplace. Thus, for example, the percentage of workers who actually take child-care leave out of all eligible workers has increased from 56 percent in 1999, to 72 percent in 2005, and almost 91 percent in 2008 in the case of women; the comparable figures in the case of men show little change—0.42 percent, 0.50 percent, and 1.23 percent, respectively (Naikakufu danjo kyodo sankaku kyoku 2009, 25). Moreover, according to data compiled by the Gender Equality Bureau of the Cabinet Office, men who have children under six spend an average of just thirty-three minutes per day on child care, out of a total of sixty minutes spent on various domestic activities, including housework. These figures are significantly low when compared to the US (sixty-five minutes and over three hours) and many European countries (about one hour and three hours in Germany, Sweden, and Norway) (Ibid., 25).[1] The low ratio of men taking child-care leave and the little time men spend on daily housework and child care indicates that gender-based division of labor is far from being remedied.

The excessively long working hours expected of workers is another major factor impeding women's attainment of parity in the workplace and sustaining the wage gap. As companies continue to embrace the "male breadwinner" model, minimum labor standards have also developed along the prevailing "masculine style of work." The Japanese labor contract comes in an all-in-one package that invariably requires long working hours and high geographical mobility, making it difficult for the employee to achieve any kind of work-life balance. While, as noted earlier, the Japanese government has set the goal of limiting working hours to 1,800 per year, the total hours actually worked per year by the average full-time worker in Japan has again gone up in recent years, from 1,990 hours in 2001 to 2,024 hours in 2006. These data, however, are based solely on the Monthly Labor Survey of the Ministry of Health, Labor and Welfare that reflects paid work hours only, leaving out a vast amount of overtime, including so-called "service" overtime work. In the Labor Force Survey conducted by the Ministry of Internal Affairs and Communications in 2008, over 20 percent of male full-time employees in their thirties and forties were found to be working sixty hours or more per week (about 6 percent among female workers)—in spite of the fact that the Labor Standards Law has set the standard of a forty-hour work week at eight hours a day (Ibid., 24).This means the burden of the work is falling heavily on those who are also raising small children and accounts in large part for the low rate of labor force participation among Japanese women in their thirties.[2] Most women in Japan are compelled to withdraw from the labor force during childbearing and child-rearing years, at least temporarily, in order to bear, almost single-handedly, the responsibility of child care, and in fact, 70 percent stop working after the birth of their first child.

Until now, unlimited "service" overtime and unpaid labor have been male issues. The new wage and treatment system based on outcome evaluation further increases long and intense working hours, and is a backdrop for further unfair treatment of workers with pregnancy and childbirth needs. On the other hand, long working hours are no longer a male phenomenon, as low wages and unstable employment force part-timers to take on multiple jobs. In 2007, close to 40 percent of female part-time workers were working more than thirty-five hours a week—equivalent to full-time hours, and over a quarter of temporary, dispatched and contract workers were working more than forty-two hours a week (Kokuritsu josei kyoiku kaikan 2009, 54, table 4-5). Because these job contracts involve intermittent hours and short work periods under multiple employers, they do not meet the coverage requirement of the employment/pension/health insurance systems. Because Japan's social security system has developed based on the company and the household unit rather than on individuals, those working long hours in multiple jobs are not eligible for social security payments, even if they are on the verge of death from overwork.

Gender Mainstreaming Policies

Alleviating gender-based polarity in jobs and income is impossible without gender mainstreaming reforms. The reforms required in the Japanese-style employment system would involve changing the discriminatory employment structure that has firmly fixed low wages for women and long working hours for men. Policies would have to allow men and women to participate equally in the workplace, the home, and community, with equal rights and responsibilities. Wages of part-time workers would have to be raised to self-sufficient levels, along with equal treatment based on job assessment that is fair and rewarding. To achieve these objectives, all forms of discrimination (based on gender, disability, age, ethnicity, nationality, social standing, belief, family status or responsibilities, job status, etc.) must be eliminated and equal treatment guaranteed for all. In addition, work-hour regulations need to be reviewed according to the basic human right of "freedom from work" in order to enable all to fulfill familial responsibilities regardless of gender. We need to conduct a structural reform of the Japanese employment system to relieve both discrimination against women with regard to income, and discrimination against men with regard to long hours. Measures need to be formulated to alleviate the gender-based polarities and promote new systems of income- and work-sharing.

Toward Achievement of Systematic Reform

Reductions in total working hours for both male and female workers, as well as the enactment of the Child Care and Family Care Leave Law, brought into our labor laws the idea of "familial responsibilities" as a condition of "gender equal" employment. The Basic Law for a Gender-Equal Society was enacted to strategically set up a gender-neutral system that would replace the current gender-based systems in all walks of society. But these reforms, in tune with international gender-mainstreaming policies, have left unchanged the existent structural framework of "equal pay for equal work" of the EEOL, which compares only those men and women who belong to identical categories in recruitment and hiring. The huge number of women in low-paid, part-time work has continued to increase, and no system that would eradicate—or even diminish—discrimination has been established. Progress toward reducing working hours has also been very slow. Indeed, deregulation has led to the introduction of irregular or discretionary working-hour systems. Flexible working hours have conveniently allowed employers to compel their employees to work over eight hours a day, forty hours a week, without paying overtime. Moreover, workers' rights under the Child Care and Family Care Leave Law may not apply at all to those who work in fixed-term piecemeal employment.

In 2006, when the EEOL was revised again, one change made the law applicable both to female and male workers with regard to prohibiting certain forms of indirect discrimination that were officially recognized in the

Ministry of Health, Labor and Welfare's ordinances. Under this provision, "transfer eligibility," which had long been a major condition differentiating those on career tracks from those on non-career tracks, was recognized as a form of "indirect discrimination." Thus, should an employee lodge such a complaint, the employer must provide a rationale for the transfer, or the condition must be abolished. The law, however, is limited in its scope.

The Part-time Workers' Law Amendment Bill was approved by the 2007 Diet. It prohibits discrimination against those who are hired as short-term part-time workers, provided that their positions are the same as full-time employees (part-time workers with long-term employment prospects, who are subject to transfers in the same way as the full-time worker). Yet, this has had only a limited effect, since all other part-time workers are granted only "equal treatment." Since the application of this regulatory framework is based on the male model of full-time employment, it could, in effect, widen the gender gap. Similarly, a ban on age limits stipulated by the Employment Promotion Law allows for a fixed age limit for regular employees in a long-term career pattern. Such new policies not only widen the gap between regular and non-regular workers, but also negatively affect women in particular.

New forms of poverty arising from deregulation, along with the gap between regular and non-regular employment patterns, affect most severely women and the elderly, especially in certain regions of the country and among certain industries. We recommend a new focus not only on alleviating discrimination and securing equal treatment for all workers, but also on the entire process of vocational training and access to the labor market in order to ensure that people can work effectively and with a sense of security. We suggest the following in order to implement such policies: first, expose and add on the numerous existing forms of indirect discrimination that are not included in the current Ministry of Health, Labor and Welfare ordinances; second, apply the "equal pay for equivalent work" principle to eliminate gender-based discrimination clad as differential treatment for different types of work or employment patterns; third, eliminate gender discriminatory evaluation criteria from the new wage system; and fourth, institutionalize positive action through specialized education and training. We believe that only changes in the political climate will make these policy changes a reality.

Notes

1. The data are based on Somusho (Ministry of Internal Affairs and Communications), *Shakai seikatsu kihon chosa* (Basic survey of social lifestyles (2006); European

Commission and Eurostat, *How Europeans spend their time—Everyday life of women and men* (2004); and US Bureau of Statistics, *American Time Use Survery Summary* (2006).

2. Data compiled by the National Women's Education Center, Japan, based on ILO LABORSTA Internet data (2007), tells us that the labor participation for women ages 30 to 34 is 62.7 percent in the 2005 Labor Force Survey conducted by the Ministry of Internal Affairs and Communications, which is quite low compared to between 70 and 80 percent in Germany, France, Finland, and the US (Kokuritsu josei kyoiku kaikan 2009: 38, fig. 3-2, 39, fig 3-3).

Works Cited

Kokuritsu josei kyoiku kaikan (National Women's Education Center), ed. 2009. *Danjo kyodo sankaku tokei deetabukku—Nihon no josei to dansei* (Gender statistics book—women and men in Japan—2009). Tokyo: Gyosei.

Koseirodosho (Ministry of Health, Labor and Welfare). 2007. *Heisei juhachinendo josei koyo kanri kihon chosa* (Basic survey of female employment and management 2006).

——. 2008a. *Koosubetsu koyo kanri seido no jisshi shido to jokyo* (Conditions pertaining to dual-track employment and management and guidance by local government labor bureaus). Dec. 24. http://www.mhlw.go.jp/houdou/2008/12/h1224-1.html

——. 2008b. *Chingin kozo kihon tokei chosa* (Basic survey on wage structure).

——.2009. *Sotai hinkonritsu no kohyo ni tsuite* (Publication of relative poverty rate). October.

Naikakufu danjo kyodo sankaku kyoku (Gender Equality Bureau, Cabinet Office, Government of Japan). 2009. *Danjo kyodo sankaku shakai no jitsugen o mezashite* (Toward realization of a gender-equal society).

OECD. 2008. *Growing Unequal? Income Distribution and Poverty in OECD Countries.* http://www.oecd.org/document/53/0,3343,en_2649_33933_41460917_1_1_1_1,00.html

Japanese Women Professional Wrestlers and Body Image

Keiko Aiba

Since the 1990s, scholars interested in gender have been attending to issues of the body. Martha McCaughey, for example, argues that gender is not only a matter of the mind but of "embodied social values" (1997, 7). Similarly, Moira Gatens (1996) holds that people construct and confirm their masculinity and femininity not only in their minds, but also through their physical activities and through experiences to which are attached social and cultural meanings. Such studies have also focused on the development of the ideal female body. Sandra Bartky (1990), for example, contends that many women discipline themselves to shape their bodies in specific ways considered to be especially desirable. Since attaining a particular body may be a significant part of a woman's sense of herself "as a sexually desiring and desirable subject," (Bartky 1990, 77), it is difficult for women to resist shaping their bodies into a form recognized as desirable.

The ideal female body is not only constructed but also transformed by physical practice. Studies on gender and sport have shown that many women empower themselves through sports and fitness (Dworkin 2003; Heywood 1998; Markula 1995). Such studies illuminate the importance of the body for theories about the construction and reproduction of femininity and masculinity. Here, I will examine some studies of female bodybuilders in English-speaking countries because there are no academic studies in Japan that focus on the relationship between women changing their bodies and their perceptions of the ideal female body. I will focus on bodies of Japanese women professional wrestlers because they also transform their bodies as female bodybuilders do. I will describe the transformation of their bodies and consider whether the perceptions of the women professional wrestlers themselves regarding the ideal female body become transformed as a result of their bodies undergoing transformation.

Transformed Bodies and Gender

Female bodybuilders have gained attention among scholars in English-speaking countries because these women challenge generally accepted sexual differences (St. Martin and Gavey 1996; Schulze 1997). Female bodies with bulging muscles make an impact on spectators and lead them to believe that they are not, in fact, looking at women's bodies (Schulze 1997). Some research on female bodybuilders suggests that female bodybuilding actually contains both resistance to and compliance with normative femininity (Bolin 1992a; Hall 1996; Johnston 1996; Mansfield and McGinn 1993; St Martin and Gavey 1996). On the one hand, muscular women disturb dominant notions of femininity, which hold that men are muscular and women are not; on the other, their challenge to social norms is set back by other aspects of dominant femininity, such as the notion that women should be beautiful, which is inconsistent with being muscular (Bolin 1992a).

Some ethnographic research on female bodybuilders has explored the question of whether female bodybuilders feel empowered and/or how female bodybuilders construct their identities. Female bodybuilders interviewed by Leslee Fisher were very conscious that "they challenged existing notions about appropriate physical appearance for females" (1997, 150). But they were not completely confident in describing themselves as far from normative femininity. They felt ambivalent about themselves (cf. Lowe 1998). According to Jennifer Wesely (2001) and Grogan et al. (2004), identity negotiations of female bodybuilders are complex and contradictory. As a result, "their self-definitions included both traditional and nontraditional components of femininity" (Fisher 1997, 151). In contrast, Bolin shows that since competitive female bodybuilders claim that "I am a woman, therefore I am feminine" (1992b, 382), they redefine and personalize concepts of femininity based on self-identity. Thus, it is possible for female bodybuilders to transgress their normative gender identities.

Have female bodybuilders succeeded in subverting gender? Bolin (2003) points to public and private splits on this issue. Based on her own experiences as a bodybuilder, Bolin (1992b) examines the dieting process and interactions among male and female bodybuilders. During pre-contest dieting, for example, both men and women followed the same diet "in order to appear more dense and muscular" (1992b, 395). Female bodybuilders aimed to construct "a male morphological ideal" (Bolin 1992b, 394); the muscles they developed were, on average, less powerful than those developed by males (i.e., a quantitative distinction). According to Bolin (1992a), however, muscles represent the masculine domain, supposedly "owned" by males. Bolin claims, therefore, that women bodybuilders have "seriously subverted the dominant conception of muscle as a qualitative gender distinction to one of a quantitative distinction" (1992b, 395).

This transformative nature of bodybuilding, however, is confined to the gym. Maria Lowe (1998) shows that bodybuilding institutions, which are dominated by male officials and judges, determine how female bodybuilders should look. Since female bodybuilders' muscular appearance at the 1991 Ms. Olympia contest was not well received by viewers (this was the first time the contest had been televised on ESPN), officials altered the judging guidelines to discourage female bodybuilders from developing muscles, encouraging them instead to express their stereotypical femininity. As a result, according to Lowe, while "female bodybuilders appear to embody an empowering image of women—one that exudes physical strength and emphasizes impressive musculature" (1998, 159), their power is considerably undermined by the bodybuilding organization.

In addition to changing the judging guidelines, bodybuilding organizations have started to hold competitions in the "Fitness" class, which is different from the "Physique" class described in this essay (Choi 2003). By encouraging women to compete in the "Fitness" class, which requires women to be less muscular than "Physique" competitors and emphasizes being beautiful and sexy, especially to a male audience, bodybuilding organizations have repositioned female competitors as desirable heterosexual objects (Choi 2003).

Japanese Women Professional Wrestlers

Japanese women's professional wrestling (joshi puroresu) has developed a distinctive style. The first performance of women's professional wrestling was in a show presented at a US military camp in 1948 by a pair of comedians, the Igari brothers, and their sister, Sadako Igari (Kamei 2000), six years before the first men's professional wrestling exhibition in Japan. The popularity of one of the male wrestlers, Rikidozan, generated enormous interest in men's wrestling, with organizations and promoters showing great interest. Some promoters held quasi-strip shows and called them "women's wrestling." Even when some organizations tried to present women's professional wrestling as a genuine sports event, they were barred from using public gymnasiums for their matches (Kamei 2000) because of the negative image that had been created by promoters offering sexually oriented shows under the name of women's professional wrestling.

Not until 1968, when the predecessor of Zen Nihon Joshi Puroresu Kogyo Kabushikigaisha (All Japan Women's Professional Wrestling Corporation) —called Zenjo for short, was established, did the public image of women's professional wrestling change. Zenjo generated three periods of intense interest in women's pro wrestling: the first was the era of the "Beauty Pair" (Maki Ueda and Jackie Sato) from 1977 to 1979; the second was that of the "Crush Gals" (Chigusa Nagayo and Lioness Asuka) from 1983 to 1989; the last was the "Inter-Organizational Battles" of 1993 and 1994. During these periods, Zenjo drastically changed the image of women's professional wrestling from a sexually oriented show to an aggressive fight. In the first two periods in particular, women's professional wrestling became extremely popular among female junior high and high school students.

Fuji Television in Japan was instrumental to the success of the Beauty Pair. The network had been airing women's professional wrestling matches since 1975, on the condition that wrestlers would sing songs in the ring (Redisu shukan gongu, 2003, May 14). Fuji aimed to create an image of women's professional wrestling as a colorful, bright, and healthy sport in order to attract female viewers (Kamei 2000). In 1974, a producer in Fuji's entertainment section, inspired by the success of the Takarazuka Theater Group's Roses of Versailles,[1] paired Jacky Sato as an otokoyaku (male role) wrestler with Maki Ueda as a musumeyaku (female role) wrestler (Rediisu shukan gongu, 2003, May 14). The Beauty Pair first became popular because of a song they released. Female junior high and high school students initially idolized the Beauty Pair as singers, and then later became interested in their wrestling. The Crush Gals also followed this strategy of not just doing professional wrestling, but also singing popular songs, and behaving like entertainers in order to solidify their popularity among female junior high and high school students.

Today, the popularity of women's professional wrestling is in decline. Zenjo went bankrupt in 2005, ending its thirty-seven-year history. As of 2004, when I conducted interviews with most of the women wrestlers in this study, there were seven women's professional wrestling organizations in Japan (Rediisu shukan gongu 2005, Jan. 4). In the Tokyo area, several women's professional wrestling organizations still hold matches almost every weekend. As of January 1, 2004, 103 women wrestlers were active in Japan.[2] While most women wrestlers either belong to women's wrestling organizations or work independently, nine of them belong to men's wrestling organizations, participating in all-female or mixed matches.[3]

Bodies and the Process of Transformation

The figures of women wrestlers are more varied than those of female body-builders. Some wrestlers are small but muscular; others are larger. Aja Kong, for example, weighs about 220 pounds, and Eagle Sawai (retired) weighed about 264 pounds. While not all wrestlers work to increase their body size, 12 out of 17 of the wrestlers between the ages of twenty and twenty-nine whom I interviewed for this study have a Body Mass Index (BMI) greater than twenty-five, which means that they are considered obese by Japanese standards.[4] On the other hand, the nationwide proportion of obese women in the same age group was 5.6 percent in 2005 (Ministry of Health, Labor and Welfare 2007). Clearly, the bodies of women wrestlers are very different from the bodies of ordinary women in Japan.

Becoming a Japanese woman wrestler is a painful and challenging process. It requires trainees to survive a long, hard, daily regimen of practice. After the trainees' debuts, they become rookies and start to interact with senior wrestlers through assuming the role of a "second." This role involves, among other tasks, constructing an anteroom, guiding wrestlers from the anteroom to the ring, washing senior wrestlers' costumes, and cheering them on during a match. Some rookies disappear because of the stress caused by the hierarchical relationships with senior wrestlers.

Although there are minor differences among organizations with regard to the training process, the basic procedure of transforming an ordinary girl into a professional wrestler is the same. The first step is to conduct basic physical training, including sit-ups, squats, and other exercises to strengthen the back and neck muscles. The bodies of new trainees are usually not strong enough to learn any wrestling techniques (Kamei 2000). In particular, many techniques used in Japanese wrestling subject the wrestler's neck to massive impact; strengthening the neck muscles is therefore crucial for wrestlers. Basic physical training lasts all day. Most wrestlers I interviewed recalled being exhausted by the repetitiveness of the training. They reported suffering from muscle pain throughout their entire bodies during the training process.

The second step for trainees is learning "*ukemi*," since the first and most important characteristic of professional wrestling calls for receiving one's opponent's moves. Through using ukemi techniques, a wrestler can reduce the impact of moves and attacks by the opponent and thereby protect the head and neck especially. One example of "*ukemi*" consists of the "backward roll," in which the wrestler keeps her head and neck straight while looking down at her stomach, and stretches her arms horizontally so that she can hit the ground with them to break a fall. By doing this, she can avoid hitting her head directly when she falls. At this stage, trainees practice ukemi most of the time every day, another painful process. One wrestler I interviewed said that her legs, when smashed into the ring tens of times a day, became blackish purple as capillaries broke on impact.

The third step calls for "rope work" and learning how to execute basic rope techniques. In the professional wrestling ring three ropes, one on top of the other, stretch around the ring like a fence. "Rope work" is the technique through which wrestlers cast their bodies or their opponent's body against these ropes. For example, if wrestler A throws wrestler B to the ropes, wrestler B bounces back to wrestler A. Usually, when wrestler B bounces back to wrestler A, one or both wrestlers will try to execute a technique. Learning rope work is also painful at the beginning. New trainees run toward the ropes, turn their backs, hit the ropes with their backs, and bounce back to the opposite ropes. These "ropes" are actually wires wrapped in rubber, against which, a new trainee must hit her back. Though the practice is painful, she has to continue doing the same thing day after day. Several wrestlers I interviewed said that they eventually had three lines of bruises on their backs made by the three ropes. One day they would have scabs on their bruises; the next day during practice they would hit their scabs on the ropes, and the scabs would break and bleed upon impact. As the skin on their backs gradually became thicker and stronger, they could finally bounce back and forth between the ropes without pain. One wrestler "really believes" that human bodies are amazing.

Several wrestlers trained by Zenjo mentioned that new trainees were usually taught a limited number of basic techniques such as the dropkick[5] and the body slam.[6] While learning those techniques, new trainees "spar" in practice matches with other trainees or senior wrestlers. After a new trainee passes a "pro test" conducted by her organization, she makes her debut.

An example of such training on women's bodies can be seen in the film GAEA Girls, a documentary about the Japanese women's professional wrestling organization called GAEA Japan (Longinotto and Williams 2000). The film contrasts the body of a senior wrestler with that of a trainee named Sato, who has just joined the organization. As the two appear doing squat exercises together, Sato's thighs, which have neither fat nor muscle, look thin and fragile next to the large, muscular ones of the senior wrestler. A body like Sato's will be completely transformed by the intensive training required of her.

Since women wrestlers must gain the stamina to fight aggressively usually for twenty or thirty minutes, and since they must be able to execute professional wrestling techniques requiring physical strength, they need some fat on their bodies, since muscle alone cannot absorb impact (Nakano

1998). Fat, which is the foe of bodybuilders, is an important friend of wrestlers, since their bodies need to be large and thick both in muscles and fat. Thus, thinness is clearly not a priority.

The Ideal Female Body in Japan

What is the ideal female body in Japan, especially among young women who are not professional wrestlers? Ogino (2002) argues that the norm of female beauty has focused on thinness since the 1960s. The equation "thinness equals youth equals beauty," has not changed, even though in the 1970s, normative female beauty evolved to include other forms, such as healthy bodies and strong bodies. Fujita (2005)[7] and Tanaka (1997), in their studies of body image among young women similar in age to new trainees joining wrestling organizations (i.e., from late teens to early twenties), show that, for these women, the ideal body is a thin body. Thus, many wrestlers' physiques deviate from the feminine ideal perceived by most young women.

How Do Women Wrestlers Perceive Their Own Bodies?

Do professional wrestlers, who transform their bodies as bodybuilders do, transgress "the ideal female body"? How do they see their bodies as deviating from the feminine ideal? The results of lengthy, two- to three-hour-long interviews with twenty-two active professional wrestlers between the spring of 2004 and the fall of 2005, provide ample evidence regarding these women's self-images.[8] The sub-groups will emerge below as I describe the responses of women wrestlers, seventeen in their twenties, and five in their thirties. I asked specific questions about changes in their bodies from childhood to the present, and about their experiences in professional wrestling. Although this study analyzes the wrestlers' narratives in response to various questions, two questions in particular were most relevant to this study: Do you think your body is attractive as a wrestler? Do you think your body is attractive as a woman? The first two groups described below answered "no" to both questions; the second three groups answered "yes" to at least one of them. All the wrestlers' names are pseudonyms. I have changed some identifying information regarding these wrestlers, but these changes have not affected my analysis.[9]

Acceptance of One's Body

Sanac Izumi believes that her body is not attractive as a wrestler, because her physique is not immediately recognizable as that of a wrestler. For her, an attractive wrestler's body is a large and muscular body like that of Kazuko Kawabata (pseudonym), a professional wrestler. Izumi decided to become a wrestler when, in the sixth grade, she saw Kawabata at a professional wrestling match. She tried to develop a body like Kawabata's, but she was unable to gain muscle mass even by increasing her caloric intake; Izumi's body is still not like Kawabata's.

Having accepted the fact that her physique cannot be like Kawabata's, Izumi wears "flimsy outfits with lace and ruffles" to stand out and to attract male fans. Izumi believes that if a wrestler is not built like Kawabata, she "should also have a feminine body." A feminine body for her is a buxom body. Izumi admits, however, that her breasts are not big. Another wrestler lent Izumi some pads for her breasts, telling her, "Since you're not big-breasted, use these." Izumi was wearing the pads during a match, and they popped out. A spectator who had been sitting close to the ring noticed this, and after the match, asked her, "Did something pop out of your costume?" Because she does not have large breasts, Izumi regards her body as unfeminine.

While Izumi regards her body as unattractive both from a wrestler's perspective and from a woman's perspective, she is neither insecure about her body nor dissatisfied with it. She retired once and returned to professional wrestling a few years ago. It was not easy for her to come back to a professional wrestling ring. Her current satisfaction with coming back as a wrestler may be one factor that has kept her from feeling discontented with her body.

Conflicts About One's Body

Like Sanae Izumi, women in this group also regard their bodies as unattractive, both as wrestlers and as women, but unlike her, they experience complex emotional conflicts. Akiko Ichikawa, for example, describes her physique as being like a "Whippet tank" rather than like a wrestler, because she is short and stocky. Her most noticeable features as a wrestler are her thick arms and her dyed-brown hair. She says that her body is not attractive as a wrestler. This is because she believes that she "needs to further tone up [her] body, of course."

> I figure that as long as I'm called a pro wrestler, there's a certain way that people look at you as some sort of idol, with expectations they have of you, I guess. So according to that sort of standard, I'm far from being the ideal. I'm a bit of a loser in that respect (laughs).

She says that her views as a woman named Akiko Ichikawa and as a wrestler named "Dash Ichikawa," "sometimes converge, sometimes diverge."

Akiko Ichikawa wants to tone her body further and wear cute clothes. "Dash Ichikawa," on the other hand, is a wrestler whose major appeal is her laid-back warmth, so she should "be a bit on the pudgy side." Also as a wrestler, there is a part of her who thinks that it's fine to be a bit pudgy, but there's also a part of her who thinks that she should shape up a bit more so she can be a figure people look up to. Among the five perspectives presented here, her view is the most deeply conflicted.

A Wrestler's Body

Women in this group see the wrestler's body in opposition to the female body. They regard their wrestlers' bodies with high esteem, and though they recognize that their bodies are not particularly feminine, they do not place much importance on that fact. Sachi Mihara is among the wrestlers who see their bodies in this way. She is confident that her body, as a wrestler, is attractive, because "Well, I've got pretty good height—nothing to brag about, but I've got a fairly good build." On the other hand, she does not think her body is attractive as a woman, since her body is "not cute." She believes that "cuteness" is a requisite for a typically attractive female body. The body that Mihara can be proud of as a wrestler is subject to critique as a female body if she is stripped of her title as a professional wrestler. She concludes, "Well, for most people, you know, a body like mine is a bit too much, I think (laughs). I'm lucky to have the title of 'pro wrestler,' I think." She continues:

> When I'm walking down the street or something, people think there's something different about my physique, and I'm like, well, I'm a pro wrestler, and people are like, oh, of course . . . It feels good to be told that you look strong, doesn't it? Yep. So in that sense, I'm pretty happy with my body the way it is now.

Sachi Mihara, then, is proud that the body she is aiming to develop is different from the one that ordinary women aim to develop. At first, she had trouble gaining weight. But she says, "Once you do gain weight, though, it's like you could gain forever . . . and I think I've got a tendency to gain weight." Now she aims at increasing her weight, saying, "A woman, you know, especially doesn't want to gain weight. But for myself, in my occupation gaining weight is something that you can be proud of, so I think I might try to gain a little more weight."

Among most women, who are unable to free themselves from the ideal of the "thin" body that pervades contemporary Japanese society, Mihara seeks to take pride in her body by further increasing her weight. When she thinks about it, she realizes with glee, that even though she is different from women whose goal is to have a "thin" body, her body is still admired by the professional wrestling community.

Just an Ordinary Girl Who Can Do Professional Wrestling

Wrestlers with this perspective regard their bodies as attractive from the standpoint of being a woman. Besides having attractive bodies as women, they can also practice professional wrestling. Although their bodies look like those of other women of the same age, they have wrestlers' muscles. Mika Matsubara, for example, says that she "does not dislike" her body from a wrestler's standpoint. She acknowledges that there are parts of her body that she does not like as a woman, but she still views it positively. Because she is neither as big nor as tall as other wrestlers, she sees that "my physique ordinarily, well, how do you say, fades into the crowd." People are often surprised to learn that Mika Matsubara is a wrestler. She takes pride in this, and it makes her happy. When she reaches out to grab a plastic bottle, and people comment that her muscles are remarkable, she is very glad to hear that. Even during a wrestling match, she finds it very satisfying to prove to the audience that she is indeed a wrestler by casually showing off her muscles. She does not intend to build her muscles further or focus on muscle definition. She feels that she does not fit the typical image of a wrestler. For her, it is good enough to be regarded as a wrestler when people notice her offhanded display of strength, even though she looks like an ordinary girl.

The New Ideal Female Body

For those who subscribe to this view, the concepts of an attractive wrestler's body and an attractive female body may seem opposed to each other. But to reconcile the differences, women in this group redefine the ideal female body. Rie Hayama follows this line of thinking, seeing her body as "rugged," muscular and solid. She is proud of the "ruggedness" of her body and considers it "cool." When she realized that she could put her body to good use, she began to gain confidence in it. Through judo and professional wrestling, she came to take pride in her large build, although she may still not consider her body attractive as a wrestler, since her muscles don't bulge and are therefore not especially visible. She wants to find "a way to build muscle so that it is more visible."

On the other hand, from "a commonly held perspective," she believes she does not have an attractive body as a woman. She thinks of female attractiveness as being "soft, thin, and you know, cute." Thus, according to

those standards, her body is not attractive, for it has become "masculine."
Nevertheless, she is not dissatisfied with her unfeminine body:

> I wonder why. I guess it's different when it comes to being a strong
> woman. When you talk about being a strong woman, a cool woman, it
> comes down to having a body that you can believe in, and I guess that's
> what I'm aiming for.

In other words, Rie Hayama thinks that if she "builds up" her body with
muscle that is more visible, she will have a body that she can "believe in" as a
wrestler. At the same time, she is proud of the fact that her body is developing into the strong and "cool" female body she speaks of.

As an example of her confidence in her body, Rie Hayama describes an
experience on the street, "When a guy tries to pick you up and you try to get
away, you know, sometimes he even grabs your arm. At times like that I've
been told 'what's with your thick arms!?'" she says, laughing. You can see
she gets a big kick out of the surprise the guy gets when he grabs hold of her
and tries to pick her up. She says she gives this guy a big nod, as if to challenge him, "You still want me to come with you? I'm tougher than you are
. . . I wouldn't be weaker than most of the guys around here." When she sees
his surprise—not just because her arms are thick, but because of her confidence that she's as strong as "most of the guys around here" are—she thinks
she looks good. While she thinks that "thin and beautiful" women have a different "coolness," she regards a "rugged" body as "cool" as well. While "soft,
thin, and you know, cute" bodies are typically considered feminine, she says,
strong, cool bodies are also attractively feminine. She is proud of the fact that
she is getting closer to having a body that is both strong and "cool."

Conclusion

Clearly, even wrestlers whose vocation does not allow them to be thin are
not entirely free from equating thinness with the ideal female body. With
the exception of those who accept their bodies as they are, all others consider
the appropriate female body to be necessarily thin. Akiko Ichikawa, with
"conflicts about her body," believes that even a wrestler should shape up a bit
more. Sachi Mihara, with a "wrestler's body," and Rie Hayama, with the "new
ideal female body," both point not only to being thin but also to being "cute"
as requisites of the ideal female body. Both Sachi Mihara and Rie Hayama
see the wrestler's body as being in opposition to the female body.

Chie Asano argues, "female bodies are not sources of women's power
but alienated bodies as objects to be rated, to be attacked and to be desired"

(1996, 210). Is it impossible for female bodies to become a source of power for women as Asano (1996) argues? Some wrestlers view their bodies as a source of power and are able to evaluate their bodies in a positive way. Even as they perceive that their bodies are different from "thin" female bodies, Sachi Mihara and Rie Hayama, despite their differences, both feel confidence in their own bodies.

Like the bodybuilders studied by Fisher (1997), Sachi Mihara perceives that her physical characteristics are different from the normative female body. By gaining more weight, she intends to expand her confidence in her wrestler's body, and to downplay the fact that her body is not stereotypically feminine. Her intention is to minimize the importance of the normative female body, rather than to transcend her gender category as a woman. "When I try to act feminine, it's not attractive at all," she says, and she adds that now that she is a wrestler, "I've given up on trying" to be outwardly feminine. She has begun to think that, having become a wrestler, she should not wear feminine clothes. I interpret her narrative as follows: although she admits that her current appearance is seen as being unfeminine by others, she nevertheless maintains her position that she still wants to be regarded as a "woman."

Among the five perspectives, Rie Hayama's view in particular claims the existence of a body which is different from the dominant female body. She acknowledges that, outside of the professional wrestling community, a thin body is the ideal female body, and she respects such a body. However, she also believes that a thin body is not the only attractive female body, and that strong and "cool" bodies are also attractive as female bodies. This perspective transforms the ideal female body. Hayama believes it is possible to be confident in a body which is different from a thin body. On the other hand, wrestlers who share her view are in the minority among the wrestlers I interviewed. As bodybuilders in Bolin's study (1992b) transgress their gender only inside the gym, Hayama's view remains valid only in the limited world of the professional wrestling community. Does this mean that women wrestlers' bodies are unable to weaken the gender division? The answers are not yet fully clear.

While this study examined only the perceptions of wrestlers about their bodies, my future research will undertake a comprehensive examination of wrestlers' bodies and professional wrestling as performance, with special consideration on the wrestlers development of fighting skills. In professional wrestling, women must use and display their fighting skills, even though fighting is ordinarily perceived as a male domain. Furthermore, wrestling is different from combat sports such as judo and boxing, in that a wrestler has to be able to receive the full brunt of her opponent's attack

(Kamei 2000), whereas in combat sports a fighter tries to overpower an opponent while sidestepping an opponent's attack. Wrestlers express their physical and psychological power by being able to eventually overpower their opponents despite their receiving the full strength of opponents' attacks. Thus, wrestlers must take ukemi. When a wrestler takes ukemi, her body must be strong enough to receive it, and her form and timing must be perfect, or she can be badly injured.[10] Clearly, the techniques that wrestlers execute and receive have massive destructive power. Hence, I would like to examine whether women professional wrestlers with fighting skills transgress normative femininity as being passive. Perhaps only then will we be able to understand whether women wrestlers do weaken the gender division through their bodies.

Notes

1. The Roses of Versailles was based on a best-selling comic book of the same name published by Riyoko Ikeda. Set just before the French Revolution, the story centers on the adventures of Oscar, a woman who was raised as a man in order to assure the patrilineal continuity of a family of generals (Robertson 1998).

2. I have used four sources to identify the number of women wrestlers: *Joshi puroresuraa zen senshu meikan 2006* (Directory of all female pro wrestlers, 2006), *Rediisu shukan gongu* (Ladies' gong weekly, 2006, November 14), *Ooru karaa 2005 Nihonjin resuraa meikan* (Full color directory of Japanese wrestlers, 2005), and *Nisenninen joshi puroresu ooru sutaa suupa a katarogu* (Super catalog of all-star women pro wrestlers, 2002). This was not an easy task, for several reasons. A few women wrestlers who are associated with independent men's organizations may not be covered in those sources. Furthermore, it is difficult to be sure that some wrestlers are indeed active, because they go back and forth between retirement, temporary leave, and returning to competition. I also excluded women who only perform in "cat fights," sex shows where women wearing skimpy underwear or bikinis try to expose each other's genitals.

3. In mixed matches, a man and a woman, or several men and women, team up on a "tag team" and fight with another tag team that also includes men and women. Most of the time, women fight against women in tag team matches, but women occasionally fight against men from the opposing team.

4. The BMIs (Body Mass Index is calculated by weight [kg] divided by the square of height [m]) of sixteen of these wrestlers were calculated by weight and height as shown in *Ooru karaa 2005 Nihonjin resuraa meikan* (Full color directory of Japanese wrestlers, 2005). The BMI of one wrestler who was not shown in the directory was calculated by referring to *Nisenninen joshi puroresu ooru sutaa supaa katarogu* (Super catalog of all-star women pro wrestlers, 2002).

5. This is a basic professional wrestling technique in which the wrestler jumps up and kicks her opponent with the sole of her foot.

6. This is another basic technique in which the wrestler slams into her opponent's body onto the mat from behind.

7. Although Fujita (2005) interviewed both male and female high school students, I refer only to the ideal female bodies described by female students.

8. I actually interviewed twenty-five wrestlers including three who were retired. I only used the twenty-two active wrestlers for this study because the questions focused on their present bodies. Aiba (2007) provides the details of this research method and partial findings of this study.

9. The following characteristics of the five wrestlers discussed in this study are given: name (given name and family name); length of wrestling career; organizational affiliation; and age as of January 1, 2004. To avoid identification of these wrestlers based on their exact age and length of career, I have given only approximate numbers. Due to space limitations, I have omitted details regarding the other wrestlers interviewed.

i. Sanae Izumi, two years, independent, early twenties;

ii. Akiko Ichikawa, seven years, member of an organization, early thirties;

iii. Sachi Mihara, ten years, member of an organization, early thirties;

iv. Mika Matsubara, six years, member of an organization, early twenties;

v. Rie Hayama, four years, member of an organization, late twenties.

10. In the Japanese pro wrestling community, more than a few women wrestlers have injured their neck vertebrae. Notable cases include that of Akira Hokuto (retired), who broke her neck vertebrae in 1987; and Toshiyo Yamada (retired), who suffered a herniated disc in her neck in 1990.

This study is a part of the research project, "Henyo suru shintai to jendaa: Nihon no joshi puro resuraa no kosatsu" (Transformed bodies and gender: consideration of Japanese women pro wrestlers) with Grant-in-Aid for Scientific Research by Japan Society for the Promotion of Science from FY 2003 to FY 2004.

Works Cited

Aiba, Keiko. 2007. "Henyoshita shintai e no jiko ishiki: joshi puroresuraa no shintai to jendaa" (Self-perceptions toward transformed bodies: Bodies of professional women wrestlers and gender). *Supootsu to jendaa kenkyu* (Journal of Sport and Gender Studies) 5: 4-17.

Asano, Chie. 1996. *Onna wa naze yaseyo to surunoka—sesshoku shogai to jendaa* (Why do women want to be thin?: eating disorder and gender). Tokyo: Keiso shobo.

Bartky, L. Sandra. 1990. *Femininity and Domination: Studies in the Phenomenology of Oppression*. New York: Routledge.

Bolin, Anne. 1992a, "Vanalized Vanity: Feminine Physiques Betrayed and Portrayed." In *Tatoo, Torture, Adornment, and Disfigurement: The Denaturalization of the Body in Culture and Text*, ed. Francis Mascia-Lees. Albany: State University of New York Press.

———. 1992b, "Flex Appeal, Food, and Fat: Competitive Bodybuilding, Gender, and Diet." *Play & Culture* 5: 378-400.

———. 2003, "Beauty or the Beast: The Subversive Soma." In *Athletic Intruders: Ethnographic Research on Women, Culture, and Exercise*, ed. Anne Bolin and Jane Granskog. Albany: State University of New York Press.

Choi, Precilla Y. L. 2003. "Muscle matters: maintaining visible differences between women and men." *Sexualities, Evolution & Gender* 5, no. 2 (August): 71-81.

Dworkin, Shari L. 2003. "A Woman's Place is in the...Cardiovascular Room?? Gender Relations, the Body and the Gym." In *Athletic Intruders: Ethnographic Research on Women, Culture, and Exercise*, ed. Anne Bolin and Jane Granskog. Albany: State University of New York Press.

Fisher, Leslee A. 1997. "'Building One's Self Up': Bodybuilding and the Construction of Identity among Professional Female Bodybuilders." In *Building Bodies*, ed. Pamela L. Moore. New Brunswick: Rutgers University Press.

Fujita, Tomoko. 2005. "Seinenki ni okeru shintaizo to jendaa—kokoseino katariyori" (Body images in adolescence and gender: from narratives of high school students). In *Jendaa to kosasuru kenko/shintai kenko to jendaa III* (Health/body intersecting gender: Health and gender III), ed. Naomi Nemura. Tokyo: Akashi shoten.

Gatens, Moira. 1996. *Imaginary Bodies: Ethics, Power and Corporeality*. London: Routledge.

Grogan, S., Ruth E., Sam W. and Geoff H. 2004. "Femininity and Muscularity: Accounts of Seven Women Body Builders." *Journal of Gender Studies* 13: 49-61.

Hall, M. Ann. 1996. *Feminism and Sporting Bodies: Essays on Theory and Practice*. Champaign, IL: Human Kinetics.

Heywood, Leslie. 1998. *BodyMakers: A Cultural Anatomy of Women's Body Building*. New Brunswick: Rutgers University Press.

Johnston, Linda. 1996. "Flexing femininity: Female body-builders refiguring 'the body'." *Place & Culture: A Journal of Feminist Geography* 3: 327-340.

Joshi puroresuraa zen senshu meikan 2006 (Directory of all female pro wrestlers, 2006). Tokyo: Nihon supootsu shuppansha.

Kamei, Yoshie. 2000. *Joshi puroresu minzoku shi: monogatari no hajimari* (Ethnography of women pro wrestling: the beginning of the story). Tokyo: Yuzankaku.

Longinotto, L. and Williams, J. 2000. *Gaea Girls: A Film of Courage, Transformation and Dreams of Glamour*. Vixen Films for BBC, 106 mins 35mm.

Lowe, Maria. 1998. *Women of Steel: Female Bodybuilders and the Struggle for Self-Definition*. New York: New York University Press.

Mansfield, Alan and McGinne, Barbara. 1993. "Pumping Irony: The Muscular and the Feminine." In *Body Matters: Essays on the Sociology of the Body*, ed. Sue Scott and David Morgan. London: The Falmer Press.

Markula, Pirkko. 1995. "Firm but Shapely, Fit but Sexy, Strong but Thin: The Postmodern Aerobicizing Female Bodies." *Sociology of Sport Journal* 12: 424-453.

McCaughey, Martha. 1997. *Real Knockouts: The Physical Feminism of Women's Self-Defense*. New York: New York University Press.

Ministry of Health, Labor and Welfare. 2007. *Heisei junananen kokumin kenko eiyo chosa kekka no gaiyo* (Summary of national health and nutrition survey in 2005).

Nakano, Keiko. 1998. *Buru nakano no daietto nikki—jukyugo saizu no watashiga kyu go saizuni* (Dieting diary by Bull Nakano: changing from size 19 to size 9). Tokyo: Bukkumansha.

Nisenninen joshi puroresu ooru sutaa suupaa katarogu (Super catalog of all-star women pro wrestlers, 2002). Tokyo: Nihon supootsu shuppansha.

Ogino, Miho. 2002. *Jendaaka suru shintai* (Gendered Bodies). Tokyo: Keiso shobo.

Ooru karaa 2005 Nihonjin resuraa meikan (Full color directory of Japanese wrestlers, 2005). Tokyo: Nihon supootsu shuppansha.

Rediisu shukan gongu (Lady's gong weekly). 2003. (May 14). Tokyo: Nihon supootsu shuppansha.

———. 2005. (January 4).

———. 2006. (November 14).

Robertson, Jennifer. 1998. *Takarazuka: Sexual Politics and Popular Culture in Modern Japan*. Berkeley and Los Angeles: University of California Press.

Schulze, Laurie. 1997. "On the Muscle." In *Building Bodies*, ed. Pamela L. Moore.New Brunswick: Rutgers University Press.

St. Martin, Leena and Gavey, Nicola. 1996. "Women's Bodybuilding: Feminist Resistance and/or Femininity's Recuperation?" *Body and Society* 2: 45-57.

Tanaka, Reiko. 1997. "Wakai josei no soshin zukuri ni kansuru shakaigakuteki kosatsu—joshigakusei kyunin no jirei o toshite" (Sociological consideration of how young women shape a thin body: nine case studies of female students). *Taikugaku kenkyu* (Japan Journal of Physical Education, Health and Sport Sciences) 41: 328-339.

Wesely, Jennifer K. 2001. "Negotiating Gender: Bodybuilding and the Natural/Unnatural Continuum." *Sociology of Sport Journal* 18: 162-180.

Migrants and the Sex Industry

Kaoru Aoyama

From the mid-1980s to the mid-1990s trans-border trade in the sex industry emerged as a social issue, and at the same time globalization, the feminization of labor, and migration also expanded. Yayori Matsui described the problem succinctly in 1995:

> Many of the women who come to Japan as migrant workers are not in the position of being able to raise their own travel expenses to Japan or find jobs there on their own. What usually happens is that they are signed up by brokers in their own countries, given an advance in the form of a round-trip plane ticket, and sent to Japan with a promise or contract stating that they will work as receptionists, waitresses, models, or ordinary bar hostesses (not engaging in prostitution). In reality, however, brokers often sell them to promoters in Japan, many of whom are connected to organized crime syndicates, better known as *yakuza* (1995, 310, parenthesis and italics in original).

In the first half of the 1980s, the trans-border migration of women in East and Southeast Asia began to be studied by academic women. The actual movement of migrant women increased as their labor for caring of the young, the ill, and the elderly, as well as housework came to be recognized as "new gold" extracted from the Third World to the First World, to borrow Arlie Hochschild's lexicon (2002/03, 26). At the macroeconomic level, the so-called Plaza Accord at the end of 1985 changed the global climate, when the finance ministers of the G5 nations decided to devalue the US dollar against other currencies, and the relative values of the German mark and the Japanese yen then increased, enticing not only economic but also cultural and human transactions, particularly between Japan and other Asian countries. As a result informal labor migration in this area increased (Aoyama 2009, esp. introduction and chapter 1).

However, one must note that these shifts were unequal, based on other economic disparities such as sex, class, and race, as well as the differences between people from the North or the South. Further, as the persons involved were women in the informal sector of the economy, they did not carry with them the status of "migrant worker." If they were sex workers, moreover, they were treated both in state legislation and public discourse either as "victims" of trafficking, or "criminals" violating immigration law and the Prostitution Prevention Law of Japan.[2] This is still true today. Until the latter half of the 1990s, the number of such undocumented migrants was estimated to be on the increase, and as the police also recognized, these women were exceedingly vulnerable, deprived of social welfare and the basic citizens' right to equal treatment before the law (Keisatsucho ed. 1994, 99-104). Notably, numbers of Thai women were reported by the mass media to have been involved in criminal cases, such as killing their managers in order to escape from their enslavement (see e.g. Shimodate jiken 1995). Feminists like Yayori Matsui and their supporters documented accounts of these women as victims of sexual and economic subordination, and organized rescue and advocacy activities against this trade.[3]

Now, more than a decade later, and early in the new century, while the politics surrounding trafficking as organized crime has gained more attention at the international level, the lives of migrant women in the global sex trade and the sex industry in Japan have not improved. I can testify to this as a feminist researcher of sex work and migration, who, with deep respect, worked briefly with Ms. Matsui. I dare say that feminists who have been analyzing the issue, rescuing the victims, and leading actions and legal amendments, need now to question our methods and the outcomes of our analyses and practices. Most of all, I believe that we need to search for more complex contexts behind the global sex trade, since targeting the structural subordination of poor women to the rich, male prerogatives have not, in the end, offered better and different job opportunities with improved social positions for these women. What has been lacking seems to be enough attention to the particular actions and non-actions of migrant women in the sex industry, especially in terms of their motives, intentions, and perceptions, all of which together might form the basis of their abilities to act against, or comply with a given situation (based on Giddens 1984/2001, 9).

It is also true that treating women's active will—or "agency"—as an empowering compenent for migrant women has tended to ignore the intractable structural force derived from institutionally based unequal relationships, as other research, such as those of JNATIP (Japan Network against Trafficking in Persons) and F-GENS (Frontiers of Gender Studies) have pointed out.[4] However, we still need to remember that the participants consist not only of the state, or private entities that hold the power to control socioeconomic conditions of the disadvantaged, but also the participation of the disadvantaged themselves. We must factor in *both* structure and individuals as social agents if we are to grasp long standing social phenomena, paying close attention to the process of production and reproduction of the structure. Then in order to construct effective pragmatic strategies, we need to seek a way to involve those in disadvantaged positions— in this case migrant women in the sex industry—in a central role as active discussants on the issues, not merely as victims. Below are my suggestions on how to do this *with* migrant women in Japan's contemporary sex industry.

Trafficking and Anti-Trafficking Discourse

The word "trafficking" and the discourse of anti-trafficking recently became hegemonic when talking about the global sex trade. From my fieldwork in Thailand and in the vicinity of Tokyo, together with the reading of previous research and documentaries,[5] I would define "trafficking" in brief as the movement of people across national borders outside state regulations, mediated by collectively organized others motivated by their own gain. There are migrant women in the sex industry who state that they came to Japan without the help of mediators, but it would be safe to say that the majority came via trafficking as mentioned above, especially after the 1990s.

"Trafficking," however, does not necessarily mean that the women or young girls involved are deceived or kidnapped, and sold to the sex industry market without their consent. Empirical research shows that after the 1990s, women often dealt directly with traffickers, agreeing to sell their sexual services as "prostitution" for financial compensation (c.f. Nyota and Aoyama 2007, 72-77; JNATIP and F-GENS 2005, 2-5, 24, 87-88). At one end of this deal in a potential migrant woman's community is often a relative, brother, sister, friend, neighbor, etc. who may offer an impression of kindness or genuine intention to help introduce a good job opportunity to the woman and/or her family. This person then expects a share of money in advance, and perhaps the potential migrant is willing, for multiple reasons, to comply, and the exchange occurs as a socially sound survival arrangement for all parties, and possibly for the community as a whole.

In trafficking there is no guarantee whatsoever that the migrant will not fall into a slavelike situation in which s/he is deprived of wages and other material compensation, as well as the security and freedom to lead her/his life. But we also have to recognize that the issue is complex: some of these "trafficked" women are quite happy working and earning a sizable amount of money as a result (e.g. a case study in Aoyama 2007). Others are married to Japanese men and working in the sex industry without worrying about deportation, even if prosecuted under the Prostitution Prevention Law (e.g.

SWASH 2007). But some are caught in dire situations of extreme violence and exploitation, which they desperately seek to escape from (e.g. Aoyama 2009, chapters 3 and 4). By now, the diversity within trafficking has gradually become evident, as research, support, and networking has developed between Japan, as a receiving country, and other Asian countries such as Thailand and the Philippines, as sending ones (e.g. Kokuritsu josei kyoiku kaikan 2007; JNATIP and F-GENS 2005).

In 2000, the General Assembly adopted The United Nations Convention against Transnational Organized Crime and defined "trafficking in persons" in its Protocol to Prevent, Suppress and Punish Trafficking in Persons, Especially Women and Children as follows (Article 3): "'Trafficking in persons' shall mean the recruitment, transportation, transfer, harboring or receipt of persons, by means of the threat or use of force or other forms of coercion, of abduction, of fraud, of deception, of the abuse of power or of a position of vulnerability or of the giving or receiving of payments or benefits to achieve the consent of a person having control over another person, for the purpose of exploitation." The protocol explicitly denies the relevance of "consent": "The consent of a victim of trafficking in persons to the intended exploitation set forth in subparagraph (a) of this article shall be irrelevant where any of the means set forth in subparagraph (a) have been used."

Japanese support groups and researchers, as well as lawmakers and others have gradually adopted the UN's definition. At the same time, international views assumed that migrant women who come to Japan were mainly to be found in the sex industry (Otsuki et al. 2007, 217), though this industry also included a wide range of different businesses. In addition, under pressure from the recommendations of the UN Convention on the Elimination of All Forms of Discrimination Against Women (Arts 27-28), the Japanese government revised laws with major impact on migrants in the sex trade in order to ratify the above protocol, including the Entertainment and Amusement Trades Law, and the Immigration Control and Refugee Recognition Law, together with the Passport Law; and established Trafficking in Persons Prohibition Articles within the Penal Code (see Kamino 2007, 87-93 for details) among other minor amendments in relevant laws. [6]

The revised Entertainment and Amusement Trades Law made it obligatory for the employer to confirm the validity of employee visas and work permits. With the Trafficking in Persons Prohibition Articles, the selling, buying, and trading of persons for trafficking within and to Japan was criminalized for the first time in Japan's legal history, although trafficking *from* Japan *to* other countries had already been designated illegal. In keeping with the establishment of the Trafficking in Persons Prevention Articles, the Immigration Control and Refugee Recognition Law was also revised, so that the overstayer (presumed female), if found to be a victim of trafficking, could potentially be granted permission to arrive in Japan retrospectively, to remain in Japan, and to receive assistance for return migration and support for rehabilitation in her country of origin.

There was still another reason for these revisions: to meet the standard of the *US Trafficking in Persons Report* published annually since July 2001, in which the US Department of State ranks other nation states in terms of efforts being made to eliminate human trafficking. Japan's ranking at the Tier 2 Watch List in 2004—with special requirements for the government to undertake research into trafficking, to protect its victims, and to fight organized crime, including the *yakuza* syndicate (2004, 28)—alarmed the Japanese government so as to create a basic plan of action to demonstrate its efforts to control trafficking by amending the relevant laws (The Cabinet Secretariat, Japan 2004, Dec. 17). [7] This development contributed to changes in the language and discussion of trafficking, and policies for policing it, which now favored protecting the victims, and focused punishment on organized traffickers. All of these changes aligned with the demands of advocates hoping to help trafficked women in Japan, who had long called for "protection, not criminalization" of the victims, and who had focused on trafficking as a structural violence against and exploitation of women as the women lose their autonomy once caught up in it.

Some support groups have been rescuing trafficked women in dire situations. Women's shelters, with more than twenty years of history, provide support not only to migrant women, but to women in general who have fled from violence against them. Their help includes such material support as housing, as well as psychological and emotional counseling for migrants in their native languages (see Babior 1996). Another type of assistance consists of support groups, networks established in the eighties and nineties for undocumented migrant women in the sex industry, mainly from the Philippines and Thailand, who came to Japan via trafficking. These support groups have constructed arguments in opposition to trafficking, as well as the sex trade itself, as they have faced the specific but horrendous reality of those who are trafficked and enslaved in forced prostitution. They have also opposed the state's treatment of these victims as criminals, as "illegal" migrants, thereby depriving them of most civil rights (e.g. JNATIP and F-GENS 2005, 10, 107).

I would add that criminalization further deprives trafficked persons of access to such social and financial resources as networking with others outside the sex industry. Without the means to seek other job opportunities or public support, women cannot change their lives. Combined with physical constraints and psychological threats, criminalization has, in extreme cases, driven some victims to despair. Some have found no other way to survive but to kill their managers for imprisoning them. Supporters who have tried to prevent the victimization of such trafficked women, as well as their criminalization, have reported feeling such extreme rage against the injustices these women suffer, as to suffer in empathy themselves (Aoyama 2009, chapter 4).

Ambiguous Categorizations, Incoherent Realities

Needless to say, conventional accounts of anti-trafficking leave little space in which to explore women's agency, even the agency of supporters. While there is a need to protect victims, and to achieve social justice, such needs may blind us from looking at the complicated nature of women's participation in migration and the sex industry, and thus lead to reproducing the structure that perpetuates the global sex trade. As Laura Agustin claims, based on her hands-on research experience with migrants and sex workers in Europe and Latin America, "There is no single truth for all migrant women, whether they work in the sex industry or not, as there is none for all migrants in general." This is the case in Japan, too. To tackle the unequal structural causes, and improve the actual situation of disadvantaged persons affected, we need to recognize that there are a "wide variety of ambiguous situations where clear-cut good and evil do not exist" (Agustin 2003, 84).

The diversity of these women's experiences, I would also emphasize, stems from different methodological biases involved in different research conditions, as much as the diversity of the migrants' realities itself. Particularly influential are the goals of the research and the relationship between the researcher(s) and the subjects in each study. To make a comparison, I introduce here specific examples of the situations and accounts of "victims," as recorded by JNATIP and F-GENS vis-à-vis research experiences of the sex worker group SWASH (Sex Work and Sexual Health), which carries out research on migrant sex workers, and with whom I work.

Searching for Victims to Rescue: JNATIP and F-GENS

JNATIP is a network striving toward the elimination of trafficking in persons, and F-GENS is a university-research project working toward gender equality. Involving academics, lawyers, NGOs, and individual supporters, the two organizations formed a team to conduct research together, and in 2005 and 2007 published their analyses on trafficking victims and support needed in the Japanese context. In both the 2005 report *Research on the Damage by Trafficking in Japan,* and the 2007 report *Research and Activ-*

ism on *"Creating a Support Alliance for Trafficking Victims beyond Regions and Borders"* (author's translation), the migrant women's accounts came to the supporters' knowledge because the women had originally been in search of rescue. They were also gathered for the purpose of establishing empirical evidence of the damages and results of trafficking, as the titles of the two reports suggest, to identify victims for effective support and good policy practices (see JNATIP and F-GENS 2005, 13-16; JNATIP 2007, 4-5 for methodology).

As both reports highlight, the nationality of the largest number of migrants found by the police as victims has changed in recent years: from Thai in 2001 and 2002, Colombian in 2003, Thai again in 2004, Indonesian in 2005, and Filipina in 2006, with those who were indicted as "brokers," or traffickers significantly increasing since 2005, supposedly as a result of the implementation of the newly established Trafficking in Persons Prohibition Articles (see Table 1). The changes in the nationalities of victims allegedly have depended upon changes among the organized traffickers, although Thai nationals have occupied a steady majority throughout these years, and especially since the beginning of the 1990s (Aoyama 2009, introduction).

TABLE 1: CASES RELATED TO TRAFFICKING IN PERSONS (2006)

Year	2001	2002	2003	2004	2005	2006	Total
Number of Arrest Cases	64	44	51	79	81	72	391
Number of Arrested Persons	40	28	41	58	83	78	328
Brokers within the Arrested	9	7	41	58	83	78	276
Number of Victims	65	55	83	77	117	58	455
Filipina	12	2	0	13	40	30	97
Indonesian	4	0	3	0	44	14	65
Taiwanese	7	3	12	5	4	10	41
Thai	39	40	21	48	21	3	172
Korean	0	0	0	3	1	1	5
Romanian	0	0	0	0	4	0	4
Australian	0	0	0	0	1	0	1
Estonian	0	0	0	0	1	0	1
Colombian	3	6	43	5	1	0	58
Russian	0	0	0	2	0	0	2
Lao	0	0	0	1	0	0	1
Chinese	0	4	2	0	0	0	6
Cambodian	0	0	2	0	0	0	2

Source: Consumer and Environment Protection Division of National Police Agency: http://www.npa.go.jp/safetylife/seikan34/20070216.pdf (original in Japanese: author's translation)

All support groups who participated in JNATIP and F-GENS' 2005 research claim the 1990s as the peak period for their rescue activities (JNATIP and F-GENS 2005, 86). Trafficked women's voices were recorded as cries for help from outright enslavement. A rescued woman was reportedly threatened by a manager who said she would be killed should she try to escape. Another woman reported seeing a colleague being captured and lynched, and yet another said that she saw a colleague being ordered to cut her own face with a knife (Ibid. 87, author's translation). In the second half of the 1990s, one heard that "There are growing numbers of women who know what kind of job they will be doing in Japan." Such women "also knew they would be debt-bound by five to six million yen ($40,000 to $50,000)" and that "Repeaters [of migration] are increasing," although some people recalled that knowing such things beforehand does not necessarily mean that these women could anticipate the full extent of the exploitation they would experience, or the debt they would be unable to repay, or that they would be unable to reject any of their customer's demands (Ibid.). After the 1990s, the number of women coming into Japan as brides for Japanese men increased, chiefly through the mediation of organized brokers, who were suspected of being traffickers transforming their trade to escape the tightening net of anti-trafficking policy practices. The shelters have also reported the existence of such women, fleeing from domestic violence (Ibid. and JNATIP 2007, 11, 15).

But the reports often note some ambiguity beneath the identification of respondents simply labeled "victim." For instance, the 2007 JNATIP report points to the difficulty of recognizing the trafficked persons as "victims," when following the arbitrary judgment rendered by various external parties, including women's shelters, *fujin sodanjo* (prefectural women's consultation centers), embassies, as well as the police. The report states that, under the UN protocol, personnel know that they are supposed to interpret the all-embracing categories of trafficking and its victims on a case-by-case basis. Staff members of shelters have said, "[I thought that] they were not victims if they had large sums of money," or "They are not victims if they knew beforehand what their job would be," or "Some of the victims are not aware of their own victimhood [. . .] They were just raided but do not want to go back to their own country" (Ibid: 19, author's translation). Also an important point is that the label of "victim" does not account for time during which migrants may experience changes in their social position and even their identity (c.f. Aoyama 2009, chapters 2-4). A shelter staff member reportedly asked how to treat someone who was a victim (in her own eyes) but who would not submit to immigration control, since she was employed (in the sex industry) and thus was no longer a victim. At the same time, she had no legal visa status and did not want to be deported (Ibid. See also a detailed case study of such Thai women in Aoyama 2007).

Searching for Peers to Work with: SWASH

Different voices have emerged from the research work of SWASH. They have been conducting outreach work, surveys, and in-depth interviews with migrant sex workers in the Tokyo and Osaka areas. The purpose of their research is different from that of JNATIP and F-GENS: rather than finding and presenting evidence of victimization, they seek to learn how migrant workers can protect their human rights, health, and safety *as workers*. The relationship between the researcher and the subjects here is also significantly different, as this is probably the first peer research on migrant women in the sex industry in Japan. These women have seldom been approached as sex workers and not as trafficking "victims."

SWASH's research has not been completed at the time of this writing, but it is significant to mention that SWASH argues thus far that the strengthened policing of trafficking, and, as a consequence, of the sex industry, has driven migrants in the sex industry into an even more vulnerable position. In a workshop organized on migrant sex workers in Hong Kong in May 2007,[8] they determined that stricter visa inspection after 2005 had led to increased deportation,[9] even though the migrants did not want to return to their countries of origin, and the airfare home often poses an additional debt for them. More critically, corresponding to the revised Immigration Control and Refuge Recognition Law, those who are not considered victims of trafficking by the relevant law enforcement body, as arbitrarily as its judgment is, face job losses and become more vulnerable to exploitation and control by underground organizations even if they are not deported.[10] They find themselves in worse conditions generally, as more and more workplaces that have, until then, been willing and sympathetic employers of migrant workers have been shut as regulations of the revised Entertainment and Amusement Trades Law have become more strict (partly in SWASH 2007, 2-4).

Particularly alarming, SWASH members say, is the fact that businesses such as so-called "fashion health," or massage parlors, that have not necessarily been offering direct sexual intercourse, and are thus not illegal, now tend to move frequently to avoid harsh police raids. The nexus for consultation and support for its workers are lost each time. This also means more pressure on workers to earn as much and as quickly as possible, which then makes some "choose" to conduct more dangerous services for extra tips, including unprotected vaginal intercourse and oral sex. When these kind of premises shut, the workers typically resort to "delivery health" business, which can still operate legally under the revised Entertainment and Amusement Trades Law (Art. 4) if registered, but also well underground; "delivery health" dispatches workers directly to customers by phone orders, hence, has no need to have anything publicly visible, perhaps other than a car and a mobile phone. This type of business is known for its danger, as it isolates the worker with an unknown customer in a closed space under unknown conditions, from which it is difficult to escape once dispatched. In practice, the law has thus far backfired on the worker, whether s/he is a victim or worker, a migrant, or Japanese national.

"Prostitution," meaning "to have sexual intercourse with indiscriminate others for compensation or the promise of compensation," is illegal under the Prostitution Prevention Law in Japan (1956, Art. 2). This criminalization makes all sex workers live in fear of police raids, even if she or he is not offering direct intercourse as a service (see other accounts and analyses based on empirical studies in various cultures: e.g. Campbell and O'Neill eds. 2006; Kempadoo, Snghera, and Pattanaik eds. 2005). But if a migrant worker without a long-term permit to remain in Japan is found guilty of violating this law, which can depend on another off-the-cuff judgment by a police or an immigration control officer on the spot, she or he will be deported for violating the Immigration Control and Refugee Regulation Law, as well (Art. 24-4). Those found guilty (judged not as victims of trafficking), suffer job loss, and thus become more prone to exploitation and control by underground management. They must have some sort of residential status in Japan in order not to be deported. According to some workers and managers who came in contact with SWASH's outreach program, there are cases where managers state that they no longer employ those without residential status such as those with spouse, student, and business visas after the stricter inspection imposed by the 2005 amendments to the law, and migrant women in the sex industry state that they have spouse visas so they are relatively relaxed about police raids (SWASH 2007). Such claims confirm the suspicion of JNATIP and F-GENS that "marriage" with Japanese men, though perfectly legal, can be another way of trafficking women from abroad, and one more enticing to potential victims.

Then again, there are accounts that vigorously question this notion of "victimhood" in marriage. Some SWASH respondents state that they wanted to get "married" legally via a broker's arrangement because this process was approved by their circle of friends as a safer way to come to Japan, with fewer "handling fees" and without police harassment. They added that they *also* wanted to get a job in the sex industry, which not only makes much more money but also gives them more financial autonomy than "just get-

ting married to a man." Some are in "real" marital relationships, meaning
that they do their household chores and have sexual intimacy with the husbands. One stated that she is in a long-distance marriage relationship, living
in Tokyo, and going to her husband's house once in a while, and enjoying
her freedom in the city. Others are planning to divorce in the future since
their marriages were for convenience from the start *for both of them:* their
husbands wanted to have sexual partners, or farm workers, or domestic
workers, and elder-caretakers.

These accounts reminded me of three respondents in my previous study
on Thai migrant women in and out of the sex industry in Japan (Aoyama
2009). One of the women talked about her legal marriage with a Japanese
man after having worked in the sex industry; she lived happily with him for
some time but divorced because he had a sexual relationship with another
woman. Another spoke about living with an "*ojiichan*" (old man, literally
"grandpa") after quitting sex work; the only reason she did this was to stay
somewhere discreet to avoid deportation, but she later found herself quite
enjoying life with him and felt lonely and insecure without him. Yet another
got married after being engaged in sex work and settled in Japan; now with
permanent residency, she has lived as a wife, daughter-in-law, mother of
two, and part-time factory worker in a Japanese community for more than
fifteen years at that time.

Even involving a contemporary factor of trans-border migration, marriage here might *not* be drastically different from a typical marriage in
Japan, with its sociological thrusts of upward mobility, and social and economic security, while filling the needs for emotional and sexual intimacy, as
well as household labor. In addition, if we consider a statistic showing that
an average Japanese woman earns 17,802 USD per annum while her male
counterpart earns 40,000 USD (UNDP 2007, 326), marriage for economic
purpose in Japan is not a motive unique to migrant women.[11] Of course, if
violence or deception prevails in their marriages, social aid and possibly
an intervention by law enforcement bodies might be required. My research
allows me to agree with JNATIP and F-GENS that migrants are more disadvantaged in cases where their "marriage" involves debt bondage and/or
where racism marks the attitudes of husbands and in-laws (JNATIP and
F-GENS 2005, 11): a lack of money would prevent the migrants from leaving their marriages, and the racism would expose them to severe violations
of human rights and dignity. Should they divorce, as a rule they would lose
their spousal visa, although they could still apply for the right to remain
in Japan. In practice, though again this is arbitrary, such rights have been
given when the judges can view the marriage as having been satisfactorily
genuine before the breakup—all in accordance with the Immigration Con-

trol Law. Or the migrant woman in question may gain residence if she continues to live with a child or children from the marriage (Arts. 2-4, 21, 22). Clearly, neither migration nor trafficking *per se* drives migrant women who come to Japan via arranged marriage, whether working in the sex industry or not, into insecure social positions. The driving force seems to be immigration rules and practices.

An uneasy hypothesis by SWASH members concludes that, in their outreach work, they have not come across many migrant women who do not hold a legal status to be in Japan, not because most of them have returned to their countries, but because they have gone underground. The members say that during their outreach work, since 2005 they have more often found a commercial sex business shut down and perhaps moved to an unannounced location.

Revisiting the Importance of the "Agency" of Migrant Women

It is difficult, if not impossible, to separate "authentic victims" of trafficking from "illegal migrants," "criminal prostitutes" or those in "genuine marriages," because, in reality, there are few or no permanent black-and-white cases. Still, law enforcement bodies and the sex industry as a whole continue to play cat-and-mouse games in order to punish the bad, and rescue the good, in what is actually a field of graded shades of grey. To make the matter messier, the mice in the game come in at least three sizes, each ranked according to the degree of power in which they can act: the big business owners and employers; the medium-sized Japanese sex workers; and the small migrant sex workers (or trafficking victims).[12] When the large mouse gets away with changing his business style or going underground, the medium-sized and smaller ones are dragged around by the large one and pulled out of sight from supporters, researchers, law makers, and law enforcers. Worse still, if they are small undocumented migrant workers, who are much more vulnerable to human rights violations in the first place, they may disappear underground, and even become invisible to peer workers like SWASH members. That is unless their disappearance means that the law enforcement bodies have succeeded in completely eliminating them from Japanese soil in only three or so years after the implementation of the government's plan to tackle trafficking in 2005. In the game, the small mouse never wins, and is seldom rescued.

Compare Table 1, with the numbers of those in police custody as victims of trafficking (presumed female), and Table 2, below, with the estimated numbers of "illegal" female overstayers. We can surmise that those who have been dealt with under positive revisions to the Immigration Control and Refuge Recognition Law, which includes exemption from deportation and assistance for return migration, and rehabilitation if found to be victims of trafficking (see above), are a tiny minority among the potential population who might or might not have been in dire situations underground. To take only the example of 2006, there are 30 Filipina victims *vis-à-vis* 20,165 overstaying Filipinas, 14 Indonesian victims and 1,965 overstaying Indonesian women, 10 Taiwanese victims and 3,338 overstaying Taiwanese women, 3 Thai victims and 6,164 overstaying Thai women and 1 Korean victim and 25,637 overstaying Korean women. These are estimates based on conservative figures of the Ministry of Justice, and overstayers are working in a variety of industries. So, the realities for migrants in the sex industry and other industries would lie dispersed in between three hypotheses: those who fled and were rescued from enslavement had rare luck and are a tiny minority among undocumented migrants on the whole; there are many more women suffering but invisible to supporters, researchers, lawyers, peer workers, and the law enforcement bodies; and there are many women leading more or less unruffled lives, even without legal status in Japan, if not caught as criminals violating the Immigration Control and/or the Prostitution Prevention Laws.

If there is a possibility that it is the tightened regulations in the sex industry and migration control that have driven these migrant women more underground, as SWASH argues and I support, we might as well abandon the current policy and practice aiming for the elimination of trafficking together with the global sex trade on the whole, in the way implemented over the last few years.

TABLE 2: NUMBERS OF ILLEGAL OVERSTAYERS
BY YEAR AND NATIONALITY (AS OF JANUARY 1 EACH YEAR)

Year	2002	2003	2004	2005	2006
Total	224,067	220,522	219,418	207,299	193,745
Men	118,122	115,114	113,066	106,279	100,562
Women	105,945	105,438	106,352	101,020	93,183
Filipina Women	19,193	19,859	20,957	20,374	20,165
Indonesian Women	1,757	1,806	1,989	1,998	1,965
Taiwanese Women	4,644	4,758	3,832	3,832	3,338
Thai Women	8,905	8,386	8,186	7,513	6,164
Korean Women	34,417	31,392	29,613	27,781	25,637
Chinese Women	11,833	13,227	15,447	14,838	13,787

Adapted from Immigration Bureau (2006) "Illegal Overstayers in Japan", Ministry of Justice: http://www.moj. go.jp/PRESS/060324-2/060324-2.pdf (original in Japanese: author's translation). The estimate is created from accumulated numbers of the difference between those who entered Japan and left Japan within their valid periods of visas. Available nationalities only.

Another problem arises when anti-trafficking language insists on defining migrants either as "victims" or "criminals," for that labels them as "good"
or "bad." This is a classic method to control the dominated—divide and
rule—and does not appeal to me as a feminist in support of migrants, as
well as Japanese women, in the sex industry. As an alternative, I would put
forward the importance of the women's "agency," or "ability to act" against
or in compliance with the situation. I value a suggestion in the 2005 report
of the JNATIP and F-GENS emphasizing the danger in the thesis which
"blames the victim" (JNATIP and F-GENS 2005, 2-3), a view that is in line
with the UN Protocol which makes clear that a woman's consent should be
irrelevant to whether she is identified as a victim or not. However, I have
also argued that this idea is double-edged: to ignore agency altogether or
reject any claims to it leads to a narrow definition of the "ideal victim." Such
a definition is already being used to divide trafficked women into "bad" and
"good" for the convenience of law enforcers. And, we should be aware that
this is a subtle way of labeling such women as social outcasts.

In passing, I would note that the Japanese word for "victim" that feminist
supporters now use is *higaisha*, and their sensitivity in using this word is lost
in translation by them as well as the relevant Japanese authorities. *Higaisha*
is a less value laden legal word than "victim." It should be translated literally
as the "aggrieved party" or a "sufferer from (a particular) harm." The word
for "victim" in the English sense is closer to another Japanese word *giseisha*,
which might be used to relate to innocent and powerless "victims" of natural disasters or accidents. A confusion between the two senses of "victim"—
in translation from the English protocol to the Japanese context—may well
have exacerbated the difficulty feminists have had trying to claim and retain
the trafficked women's authority, "agency" or "ability to act."

I want also to note that when the JNATIP and F-GENS report of 2005
occasionally uses the term "subjective agency" (e.g. 2) to describe migrant
women's "ability to act," they cause further confusion. "Agency," I would
insist, does not always have to be subjective. "Subjectivity" connotes determination by the one and only subject, awareness of her/his situation,
acknowledgement of conditions of her/his actions and fixity of all these.
On the contrary, "agency" connotes flexibility and versatility of what the
agent perceives and does in interaction with her/his changing social environment, depending on time and place (c.f. Stones 2005: 100-109). Thus,
employing the concept of "agency, " always in relation to a given situation
under particular social conditions, separate from "subjectivity," would help
us to avoid thinking in the dichotomous framework of defining them as
either victims or not—actually more applicable to varied accounts reported
by JNATIP and F-GENS' fieldworkers as much as SWASH's as above. This

would also enable us to avoid understanding the women in focus as having false consciousness, as in "they think they are working," implying that they do not realize that they are victimized, or having sole responsibility for their situations, as in "they came here by their own will, then, they are responsible for the consequence, too" (JNATIP and F-GENS 2005, 2).

They are not necessarily misunderstanding their situations but shifting their perceptions accordingly to meet with the shifting contexts, regardless of whatever legal or moral identification is imposed upon them. Thus, while a woman might find herself labeled as a victim or criminal, she may not see herself that way. She may simply see herself as a person doing what she has to do then and there. She may also see herself trapped and forced to do what she does as she moves from one life-stage to another (c.f. Aoyama 2009, chapters 3 and 4). Recognizing she is an agent of migration in this way, with the ability to *act against or comply with* a given situation, makes us want to avoid forcibly identifying her as fitting into one category, as the law enforcers do, and consider, rather, the state of her circumstances, as they grow better or worse from time to time. This approach would, I believe, help to move toward pragmatic strategies to improve the situation of migrant women in the sex industry by pulling them out of the outcast groups—labeled either victims or criminals. In this way, we may begin to see such women becoming able to exercise their agency against violence, exploitation, and/or degradation.

In practice, we need to get closer to the population of migrant women in and out of the sex industry, through outreach work and action research, for instance. This is not to ignore that the sex industry and women's migration are organized within patterns of powerful structural disparities that exist between women and men, between the haves and have-nots, and possibly between racial groupings. But, precisely because such structures of power control or determine a woman's decision to be involved in the global sex trade, and because power relations are resistant to change, I suggest as above that we refuse to categorize these women either as criminals or as victims of mainstream society in order to encourage them to act on their own initiative, while still within the sex-trade structure.

Notes

1. I dedicate this chapter to Yayori Matsui, with anticipation that she will be furious in the other world, at least initially, with my conversion into now thinking of migrant sex work as work. Her death came only a year after organizing the Women's International War Crimes Tribunal on Japan's Military Sexual Slavery, a people's tribunal (voluntary tribunal conducted by a network of people aiming to recover human rights abandoned by the states' justice system). Her name, among others, occupies a significant place in

history for putting the issue of the "comfort women" during World War II on the international agenda of state violence against women as a crime against humanity.

2. However, the Prostitution Prevention Law prohibits only "sexual intercourse with indiscriminate others for compensation or the promise thereof" (Art. 2). Other commercial sexual acts such as striptease or sexual massage without direct intercourse are offered legally in many such premises controlled by the Entertainment and Amusement Trades Law (Arts. 1 to 4).

3. See for example, YWCA APT (2001), Fukami (1999), Kamarado (1998), HELP (1996), Shimodate jiken (1995, 1992)

4. See Stones (2005, 66-67) for intractable dualism of structure and agency, and Nussbaum (2001, 84-86) for capability as innate ability.

5. See Aoyama (2009), JNATIP (2007), Kokuritsu josei kyoiku kaikan (2007), JNATIP and F-GENS (2005), Kyoto YWCA (2001), Caouette and Saito (1999), Karamado (1998), and Shimodate jiken (1995). Also, I refer here to a piece of unconcluded research on migrant sex workers in Japan I am involved in. This project is currently conducted by SWASH, an advocacy group of sex workers, former sex workers and their supporters.

6. The English translations of the various laws and articles are not official translations.

7. However persuasive such criticisms of the Japanese government's failure to protect the human rights of trafficking victims are, there are at least two major difficulties in freely accepting this Report: its US-centrism and its incorporation of anti-trafficking into the military strategy of the then Bush administration. On the former, the standard set for the "right" efforts is based on a single US domestic law (the Trafficking Victims Protection Act 2000). Further, the Department of State declared that while the US Government would consider sanctions on nation states ranked at Tier 3, it did not evaluate the US itself on the subject until 2009. On the latter, the then State Secretary Condoleezza Rice has written that ending trafficking in persons is more of a matter of global security governed by US strategy than a human rights issue (Aoyama 2007: 109-10).

8. Organized by Ziteng, a Hong Kong based advocacy group of sex work, and funded by TEMERP (European Network for HIV/STD Prevention and Health Promotion among Migrant Sex Workers) formed by 24 EU nations.

9. As touched upon in the text above, the revision of the Entertainment and Amusement Trades Law made it obligatory for the management of entertainment premises in the case of migrants to confirm and record their employee's date of birth, nationality, and status, and period of residence (author's translation).

10. In a positive light, an exception of "those who are under control of others by such acts as trafficking" has been added to the regulation of forcible deportation by the state, which includes "those who clearly engage with income generation activities, business management or activities for compensation as a main means of living in conflict with their residential statuses" and "those who engage in prostitution, soliciting it, enticement of it, offering its premises and/or engage in occupations directly related to prostitution" (author's translation).

11. We should, however, recognize that marriage is not only a result *but also a cause* of this economic gap: thus, e.g., women who marry in some cases lose full-time jobs or forgo opportunities for promotion.

12. It is on my future research agenda to consider the finer hierarchical divisions seemingly existing in the Japanese sex industry alongside colonial construction of race and ethnicity: White Western Europeans and North Americans probably enjoy far better working conditions than "the rest," including most Japanese nationals, and White

Eastern Europeans would come after Japanese and before other Asians, and so on.

Works Cited

Agustin, Laura. 2003. "The Disappearing of a Migration Category: Migrants Who Sell Sex." *Journal of Ethnic and Migration Studies* 32(1): 29-47

Aoyama, Kaoru. 2007. "Beyond the Fixed Identification of 'Victim' or 'Criminal': A New Look at Debates and the Policies Surrounding Trafficked Women in Japan." In *Gender and Law in Japan*, ed. Miyoko Tsujimura and Emi Yano. Sendai: Tohoku University Press.

———. 2009. *Thai Migrant Sex Workers: From Modernisation to Globalisation.* Basingstoke: Palgrave Macmillan.

Babior, Sharnan L. 1996. *Josei e no boryoku: Amerika no bunkajinruigakusha ga mita Nihon no kateinai boryoku to jinshin baibai*(trans.Shizuko Oshima,Carolyn Francis, et al. 1993). (*Women of a Tokyo Shelter: Domestic Violence and Sexual Exploitation in Japan).* Tokyo: Akashi shoten.

Campbell, Rosie and Maggie O'Neill, eds. 2006. *Sex Work Now.* Devon: Willan Publishing.

Caouette, Therese and Yuriko Saito. 1999. *To Japan and Back: Thai Women Recount Their Experiences.* Geneva: International Organisation for Migration (IOM).

Fukami, Fumi. 1999. *Tsuyaku no hitsuyo wa arimasen: Dogo Tai-jin josei satsujin jiken saiban no kiroku* (There is no need for translation: A record of the Dogo homicide case of a Thai woman). Matsuyama: Sofusha shuppan.

Giddens, Anthony. 1984/2001. *The Constitution of Society: Outline of the Theory of Structuration.* Cambridge: Polity Press.

HELP Josei no ie (Women's House HELP), ed. 1996. *Ajia no josei ni yotte Nihon no mondai ga miete kita: Josei no ie HELP 10 nen no ayumi* (Revealing problems existing in Japan through Asian women: A ten-year history of Women's House HELP). Tokyo: Nihon kirisutokyo fujin kyofukai (Japan Christian Women's Organization).

Hochschild, Arlie Russell. 2002/03. "Love and Gold." In *Global Woman: Nannies, Maids and Sex Workers in the New Economy*, ed. Barbara Ehrenreich and Arlie Russel Hochschild. London: Granta Books.

JNATIP. 2007. *Jinshin baibai higaisha shien no rentai no kochiku – chiiki, kokkyo o koeta shien ni mukete: Chosa oyobi katsudo hokokusho* (Report of research and activities: Constructing alliances for supporting trafficking victims – Towards providing support beyond regional and national borders). Tokyo: JNATIP.

JNATIP and F-GENS. 2005. *Nihon ni okeru jinshin baibai no higai ni kansuru chosa kenkyu hokokusho* (Research report on trafficking victims in Japan). Tokyo: JNATIP and F-GENS.

Kamarado, Josei no Jinken (Women's Rights Companion), ed. 1998. *Tai kara no tayori: Sunakku "mama"satsugai jiken no sonogo* (Letters from Thailand: Aftermath of the homicide case of a snack "mama"). Tokyo: Pandora.

Kamino, Tomoya. 2007. "Japanese Law and Policy against Human Trafficking." In *Gender and Law in Japan*, ed. Miyoko Tsujimura and Emi Yano. Sendai: Tohoku daigaku shuppankai.

Keisatsucho (The National Police Agency, Japan), ed. 1994. *Keisatsu hakusho: Heisei rokunenban* (Police White Paper: 1994 edition). Tokyo: Okurasho insatsukyoku.

Kempadoo, Kamala, Jyoti Sanghera, and Bandana Pattanaik, eds. 2005. *Trafficking and*

Prostitution Reconsidered: New Perspectives on Migration, Sex Work, and Human Rights. Boulder and London: Paradigm Publishers.

Kokuritsu josei kyoiku kaikan (National Women's Education Center), ed. 2007. *Ajia-taiheiyo chiiki no jinshin torihiki mondai to Nihon no kokusai koken: Josei no enpawaamento no shiten kara* (Issues of trafficking in the Asia Pacific Region and international contribution of Japan: From the perspective of women's empowerment). Saitama: Kokuritsu josei kyoiku kaikan.

Matsui, Yayori. 1995. "The Plight of Asian Migrant Women Working in Japan's Sex Industry." In *Japanese Women: New Feminist Perspectives on the Past, Present, and Future*, ed. Kumiko Fujimura-Fanselow and Atsuko Kameda. New York: The Feminist Press at The City University of New York.

Nussbaum, Martha C. 2001. *Women and Human Development: The Capabilities Approach*. New edition. Cambridge: Cambridge University Press.

Nyota, Mari and Kaoru Aoyama. 2007. "*Tai okoku Chenrai ken ni okeru kikoku josei ichiji chosa*" (Preliminary research on returnee women in Chiangrai Prefecture, Thailand). In *Ajia-taiheiyo chiiki no jinshin torihiki mondai to Nihon no kokusai koken: Josei no enpawaamento no shiten kara* (Issues of trafficking in the Asia Pacific Region and international contribution of Japan: From the perspective of women's empowerment), ed. Kokuritsu josei kyoiku kaikan. Saitama: Kokuritsu josei kyoiku kaikan.

Otsuki, Nami, Keiko Hatano, and Kimio Ito. 2007. "*Jinshin torihiki mondai ni taisuru Nihonjin no ishiki*" (Japanese people's consciousness on the issue of trafficking). In *Ajia-taiheiyo chiiki no jinshin torihiki mondai to Nihon no kokusai koken: Josei no enpawaamento no shiten kara* (Issues of trafficking in the Asia Pacific Region and international contribution of Japan: From the perspective of women's empowerment), ed. Kokuritsu josei kyoiku kaikan. Saitama: Kokuritsu josei kyoiku kaikan.

Shimodate jiken Tai san josei o sasaeru kai (Support group for three women in the Shimodate case). 1995. *Kaishun shakai Nihon e: Tai josei kara no tegami* (Dear Japan, buying-sex-society: Letters from Thai women). Tokyo: Akashi shoten.

Stones, Rob. 2005. *Structuration Theory*. Basingstoke: Palgrave Macmillan.

SWASH (Sex Work and Sexual Health). 2007. *The Globalization of the Policy to Prevent Transnational Organized Crime and Growing Insecurity of Sex Workers* (Pamphlet). Tokyo: SWASH

UNDP (United Nations Development Plan). 2007. *Human Development Report 2007/08*. New York: UNDP.

US Department of State. 2004. *US Trafficking in Persons Report: 2004*. Washington DC: US Department of State.

YWCA APT (Asian People Together) ed. 2001. *Jinshin baibai to ukeire taikoku Nippon: Sono jittai to hoteki kadai* (Human trafficking and Japan as a major receiving country: Its reality and legal issues). Tokyo: Akashi shoten.

The Nonprofit Sector

21

Nami Otsuki
Translated by Malaya Ileto

The nonprofit sector in Japan has expanded in recent years, as has the importance of people working in nonprofit organizations. A major force behind this expansion was the 1995 Great Hanshin-Awaji (Kobe) earthquake in which over six thousand people lost their lives. Following the earthquake, more than a million people from across the country converged on the city of Kobe to work in relief projects, perhaps thereby awakening the idea that citizens might voluntarily make contributions to society. Very soon after the earthquake the National Diet began to explore new legislation to support volunteerism. In 1998 the Law to Promote Specified Nonprofit Activities ("Nonprofit Law") was passed to encourage the development of citizens' nonprofit activities that would enhance the public interest. The law named institutions carrying out nonprofit activities as "designated nonprofit organizations." Thus, ordinary people conducting socially useful activities could gain the legal and social recognition as nonprofit corporations.

The Nonprofit Law lists seventeen activities of organizations that fall under its scope. Most numerous—accounting for half the total nonprofits—are organizations registered under the designation calling for the "promotion of health, medical treatment, or welfare." Many of these carry out nursing care insurance programs for the elderly. Other purposes of nonprofits include the "promotion of social education," the "promotion of community development" and the "welfare of young people." In 2003, the number of nonprofit organizations certified under the law surpassed ten thousand. This number rose to over twenty thousand in 2005, and by November 2008, 37,605.[1]

Understandably, these organizations work to assuage increasingly diverse and complicated social problems, including a falling birthrate and an aging population, the depopulation of rural communities, and increasing anxiety regarding child rearing, youth unemployment, and global warming. Government-initiated action may be, in the end, required for solving most of these problems, but the support offered within local communities by individuals working in nonprofits may also make a difference.

Nonprofit organizations in Japan are still relatively small in scale. A 2004 survey by the Cabinet Office found that 20 percent of them reported no income, while 50 percent earned under one million yen ($10,000). Close to half—47 percent—had between ten to twenty members and another 14 percent had twenty to thirty members with voting rights. Moreover, almost half had no full-time staff, and of those, one-quarter did not pay their full-time staff (Naikakufu 2005). As Iwata (2004) points out, most of the work carried out by these nonprofit organizations is normally of little interest to the corporate sector. Such mission-based activities include helping to weed the gardens of elderly people in the community while also providing companionship, or providing assistance in disaster and poverty-stricken areas where there are international cooperation projects in place.

While there has been a rise in the number of "business-model" nonprofits in Japan, which earn income through their programs and have organizational structures and membership that are more like commercial enterprises, the majority operate on the basis of donations and membership dues. Donations given by individuals to nonprofit organizations amount to a mere fraction of those found in the US. One reason is that the current tax system offers much less incentive in terms of tax deductions for such contributions. Recognizing this, the government has recently proposed changes in the system that would promote such contributions. A more fundamental factor, though, is the lack of a culture of individual gift giving for such purposes. Another relevant factor is the lack of social recognition for financial compensation paid to people working in nonprofit organizations. Some people mistakenly believe that work at nonprofit organizations is strictly voluntary.

Given these circumstances, it is difficult for those engaged in nonprofit work to receive compensation, and even if funds are available, the amounts are modest. A survey conducted in 2005 by the Japan Institute for Labor Policy and Training found that income earned by those in certified nonprofit organizations varies little by either age or gender: the average annual salary of paid directors of nonprofit organizations was two million three hundred and fifty thousand yen ($23,500) and that of regular staff members two million two hundred and forty thousand yen ($22,400) (Rodo seisaku kenkyu kenshu kiko 2006). In comparison, the average annual income of males employed in private enterprises in 2008 was five million three hundred and thirty thousand yen ($53,300), and that of females two million seven hundred and ten thousand yen ($27,100). The marked gender disparity in earnings is due primarily to the fact that women tend to be recruited into the non-career or clerical track, rather than the career track that leads to managerial positions. In the case of male workers, salaries customarily increase with age as they become promoted, so that among those between fifty and fifty-four, who are at the earning peak, the average annual salary was six million seven hundred thousand yen ($67,000), which is almost three-times the average income of both male and female workers in the nonprofit sector. In the case of female workers in private enterprises, salaries do not show much increase with age, so the highest average earning—of roughly three million yen ($30,000) is found among females between thirty and thirty-four (Kokuzeicho 2009). Yet, even this figure is higher than the salaries earned by those working in nonprofits.

It is not surprising, therefore, to find that 60 percent of those working in nonprofit organizations are women (Somusho 2005). According to the Cabinet Office survey cited above, in more than half of nonprofits, most or all staff members were women, the majority (including both male and female staff) over age fifty. Okamoto (2005) suggests that many women choose nonprofit work because gender roles still control their lives so that they are freed—or excluded—from earning money. Hence, nonprofit work is more suitable for them than for men. Okamoto also sees nonprofit organizations as new providers of services that are not offered by male-led private enterprises and government agencies. The extent to which men wield power in the conduct of nonprofit activities is therefore minimal and peripheral, thus making it easier for women to participate. Finally, Okamoto also notes that welfare and education, currently mainstream themes for nonprofit work, are commonly understood as appropriate for the work of women rather than men.

Yamauchi (2001), studying the significance of the wage gap between employment sectors and the wage differential between men and women, concludes that women's participation in the nonprofit sector is actually fostered by the low status of women workers in the for-profit sector. In other words, if women know that they are not likely to receive very much remuneration in the for-profit sector, then the remuneration they can possibly receive in the nonprofit sector does not, relatively speaking, seem so bad, even if it is low. Furthermore, of course, there is also the fact that many women can afford to work for low or no pay because their husbands are the breadwinners in their households.

Ono (2005) similarly points to the huge gap between the wages that men can earn in nonprofit organizations and in private companies. He further notes that the wage gap between men and women in nonprofit organizations is small when they perform the same duties, so that the institutions may offer an environment in which labor conditions are gender-equal. Such desirable workplace conditions—which are difficult for women to find in the corporate sector—lead women, Ono asserts, to choose work at non-profit organizations.

Middle-aged women in Japan suffer especially severe disadvantages when attempting to enter the labor market. They find few opportunities for full-time employment, and perhaps only part-time vacancies at low wages. Japanese companies prefer to hire fresh graduates so that they may nurture them within the company. Such policies reduce the need for midcareer recruitment. In particular, companies tend to avoid hiring those trying to return to work after they have been out of the labor market for a period of time. While setting an age limit in hiring is prohibited, companies tend to prefer younger recruits. Further, companies seem to be attempting to reduce the hiring of regular full-time workers and to rely instead on temporary, contract, and part-time staff. This trend has been particularly pronounced in the case of women: among all women employees, those who were "regular staff/employees" declined from 67.9 percent in 1985, to 58.3 percent in 1997, and 46.7 percent in 2009 (for men, the figures were 92.6 percent, 89.5 percent, and 81.6 percent, respectively) (Somusho 2010). Women's dominance in the nonprofit sector thus reflects prevailing attitudes and practices regarding gender roles, including views about what type of work suits women, including older ones trying to return to the workplace. Thus, for middle-aged married women in particular, nonprofit work may be viewed as a pathway to meaningful work that allows them to use their life experience and to make a difference in the community. They may thus construct a "career"—defined broadly as "a lifelong sequence of role-related experiences" (Hall 2002).

Closeup: Three Nonprofits

Between 2003 and 2005, the National Women's Education Center conducted a survey called *Shogaigakushu o ikashita josei no kyariakeisei ni kansuru chosa kenkyu* (Survey of Women's Career Building through Lifelong Learning).[2] The twenty-one respondents selected were from organizations representative of twelve of the seventeen areas of nonprofit activity classified under the Nonprofit Law: child-rearing support (two), nonprofit organization support (three), promoting gender equality (two), community building (two), promoting the participation of women in politics, support for single mothers, support for victims of domestic violence, support for children with learning disabilities, support for learning, support for non-Japanese residents, nursing-care services, food services, support for women's economic independence, drama, third-party evaluation of welfare facilities, and community building.

The histories of the twenty-one women selected varied somewhat. Eight had run independent businesses which they or their families had set up. Several of the other women were employed in specialized, technical, and administrative professions—that is, in jobs of relatively high social status. Further, fourteen of the women had been engaged in community service work, which had led directly to their work in this particular nonprofit. Of the twenty-one women surveyed, eight were receiving income directly from the organization. The number could rise to thirteen were we to include those receiving income through nonprofit work-related activities. Six women received no income from their nonprofit work or related activities. One must note that, even for those receiving payment, the amounts were small.

According to the regulations governing nonprofit organization, one-third of its officers may be remunerated for their work; there is no rule about payment of those performing actual work. In other words, officers carrying out activities of the organization can receive financial compensation. Among this group of twenty-one, there were sixteen officers (president, director, auditor), but only four of them were being paid. One might conclude that, although women might establish nonprofit organizations and work as officers for them, they would not necessarily be compensated. Each of the four women who received wages was secretary general of the organization and remunerated as "paid full-time staff." Of the twenty-one organizations, ten had "paid full-time staff," suggesting that their operations were sizable, since smaller nonprofits usually hire "paid part-time staff."

Organization Delivering Meals to the Elderly and Disabled

In 1999, six housewives who had been involved in a consumer cooperative became central to the launch of an organization providing meal delivery service to households with elderly and disabled members. It became certified as a nonprofit organization in 2000. The organization prepares lunch and dinner daily except Sundays but including public holidays. They pack one hundred and ninety meals into lunchboxes for delivery to their clients. Each meal costs between five hundred and fifty and seven hundred yen ($5.50 to $7.00). The meals are prepared from food grown using minimal insecticides and no additives. The organization recycles waste products. All twenty-two members of the organization (twenty-one women and one man) receive remuneration as paid staff, eight as "paid full-time staff" and fourteen as "paid part-time staff." The staff hourly rate, which had been two hundred yen ($2.00) at first, has now risen to six hundred and thirty yen ($6.30). This amount is not much different from the hourly rate for other kinds of part-time work in the community. Moreover, the hours are more flexible than the usual part-time job and the women have the satisfaction of knowing they are engaged in valuable activities, which draws them to the organization.

Ms. Saito, in her early fifties at the time of the survey, and one of the organization's founding members, has been key to the expansion of its activities as well as to the raising of the staff's hourly wage. Her background differed significantly from others in the organization, most of whom had no previous employment history. She had worked full time for six and a half years following graduation from high school, but was forced to leave her job when her husband, whom she had married at age twenty-two, was transferred to another part of the country. Once Ms. Saito's children had gotten a bit older, however, she always managed to find jobs, working part time taking information for the national census, or as sales assistant at a supermarket, for example. At the age of twenty-five she also acquired qualifications as a day-care provider.

In her midthirties, she joined a consumer cooperative, and served as a director there for almost ten years. Her involvement with the cooperative led, in turn, to her running as a candidate for city council in order to advocate for such issues as abandoning the use of synthetic detergents in places where school lunches were prepared. She served on the city council for one term, but failed to win re-election for a second term. As she considered what other ways to serve her community, she recalled a time, when she was serving on the city council, people had appealed to the city to set up a meal delivery service. Recalling also her experience of preparing mass amounts of food during her election campaign, she, together with five other women—also members of the consumer cooperative who had helped out in her campaign—decided to start the meal delivery service.

Ms. Saito's work history can be regarded as a driving force behind the organization's growth and its increase in earnings. From her years of working with the consumer cooperative, she realized the importance of increasing the organization's earnings, and giving people financial compensation for their work, and she used her ingenuity to find ways to raise profits. She listened carefully to requests made by customers and worked on publicity, inserting advertisements in circulars put out by neighborhood associations. The neighborhood association circulars proved effective, leading to a significant rise in food deliveries. Similarly, while serving on the city council, Ms. Saito had learned about dealing with the government administration and had established various networks. These previous experiences helped her gain a contract from the city that would allow her organization to provide services. At the time of her interview, more facilities for food preparation were being built in anticipation of getting this contract, which would lead to an increase in the organization's earnings by ten to twelve million yen ($100,000 to $120,000), making the entire business more stable. The organization was, in fact, awarded the contract.

Ms. Saito recalled that, when she was working part time, she had often made suggestions for improvements in her workplace, but there was little she could really do about the situation since she was not in management. In her current work, all staff members discuss matters and make decisions together. She believes that she is now making full use of her skills, experience, and abilities, and that moreover she now enjoys a sense of solidarity with others in her nonprofit work.

Organization Supporting Women's Economic Independence

This organization was founded by Ms. Yoshida, who, in addition to serving as its director, owns and manages an esthetic salon as well as a Japanese restaurant. The organization began as a voluntary association in 2003, and received nonprofit status in 2005. Its purpose is to provide support and training mainly for women who are either thinking about launching their own business, or have actually decided to do so, as well as for women who have already launched businesses and want to develop them further. Specifically, the organization can help women in four different ways. First, it rents out property in the building it owns, at half the market rate, to women aspiring to open their own shop. Thus, women may first try to sell their goods in this convenient and supportive space. Second, through a contract with the municipality, it organizes training seminars on business etiquette, conducting telephone transactions, and basic computer skills. Third, it organizes training seminars sponsored by nonprofit organizations that target women who are thinking of launching their own business. Fourth, it undertakes consulting work.

The organization's annual income amounts to eleven million yen ($110,000). Uniquely, it consists of professionals from a variety of occupations. All are women, and the directors include a person who runs a company, a tax accountant, a judicial scrivener, and a lawyer. They serve as speakers for their seminars and as professional consultants. The organization has only one paid staff member; nine others, including the president and directors, serve as officers who receive no remuneration. Even when they serve as speakers at one of their events, most of the income generated supports the organization's operational costs.

Ms. Yoshida, who was in her early sixties at the time of her interview, had, at the age of twenty-five, married into a family that owned and managed a Japanese restaurant (different from the one she now owns), which she ran together with her husband and in-laws. In her forties, however, she divorced, taking her two children with her. Although she sought to become self-supporting, there were few full-time job openings for women of her age with no special qualifications. She took courses at a vocational training school but found it very difficult to find employment. While working part time at an event planning company, she undertook training as an esthetician (which at the time could be acquired in a short span of time) and she eventually set up her own esthetics salon business, which is currently running successfully.

Her success led to frequent invitations to speak at seminars on entrepreneurship. As she gave these seminars, however, she came to feel that they were not enough, and that she wanted to use her own resources to nurture a new generation of business entrepreneurs. She recalled that, when she was setting up her own business, she had not found these seminars useful. She remembered that the amount of start-up capital assumed essential was much higher than what she had in mind, and the seminars were too sophisticated for some one just starting out. Similarly, what she had learned at the training school for estheticians had not adequately prepared her for daily work. She realized from her own experiences that seminars by themselves were insufficient, and that providing field experience was essential. When she met other people, including municipal government officers, who shared her views, she decided to offer the "Workshop for Women Seeking to Launch their own Business" in 2003. Its success became the impetus for Ms. Yoshida to establish a voluntary association, now a certified nonprofit organization.

Questions of salaries for nonprofit workers continue to be discussed. Ms. Yoshida and her colleagues work without financial compensation because they firmly believe in their organization's mission. They believe that their organization must provide support for women's economic independence. They also believe that the sense of satisfaction they derive from their work compensates for the lack of remuneration. While Ms. Yoshida believes that the considerable work of members ought to be compensated, she knows that many people support the organization by donating funds or renting at low fees precisely because Ms. Yoshida and others are "working free." Were they to be paid, they might be seen as lining their own pockets, and the organization would lose support. This is why none of the members take payment for their work. She believes that unless people stop thinking of nonprofit workers as volunteers, they will never be paid appropriately for their work.

Organization Promoting Gender Equality

This nonprofit began as a voluntary association mainly of housewives some twenty years ago. In 1998, the group functioned within one of three executive committees established in different locations to organize a national convention for the Women's Association for a Better Aging Society, an organization that had been founded in 1983. Ms. Maeda, in her early forties at the time of this interview, was a member of the voluntary association who planned this event. Subsequently, she transformed the association into a certified nonprofit organization, its major function to create a more gender-equal society, which would use all person's abilities. The nonprofit's activities consist mainly of organizing and hosting seminars and symposia on themes related to gender equality. Such programs called "Re-entering the Workforce" or "Cooking with Dad," for example, are typical. The organization also initiates research on issues related to women's rights.

After graduating from university, Ms. Maeda had worked at a stock market listed company, and then left her job to look after her children. The company she had worked for was progressive, in that it allowed women to return to work after taking child-care leave. While Ms. Maeda had intended to go back to work, her husband's job transfer—which brought her to the community where she now lives—made this impossible. As a full-time housewife raising small children in a new community, she found herself isolated. This is when she joined "Time for a Chat," an event run by a local voluntary association, where she began to appreciate the importance of forging links within one's community. She also began to think about women's lives and their social responsibilities.

Ms. Maeda had been an active member of this voluntary association for two years when she was given the opportunity to serve on one of the executive committees planning the 1998 national convention. The three executive committees met monthly through a two-year period. To host the thirty million yen ($300,000) event, they asked local governments and companies for cooperation and donations. Through this work, Ms. Maeda learned about conference management, planning, and staff assignments, and felt she was able, in her words, "to gain experience that an ordinary female office employee in a company would never have had—experience that cannot be exchanged for money." Two years after the convention, she founded this nonprofit organization based on the activities of its predecessor and became its director.

The connections she had made with a local government agency as a member of one of the executive committees proved invaluable to her being able to get a contract from the municipal government that would allow her organization to plan and conduct seminars and workshops offered at the municipal women's center. This work is currently the pillar of the organization's activities. As director, Ms. Maeda is paid two hundred thousand yen ($2,000) per month, the "paid part-time staff," made up of twenty women, are paid an hourly rate of eight hundred yen ($8.00).

The organization's revenues have grown and its finances have been stabilized by the work for the municipality, although few of its staff have managed to become financially self-supporting. Ms. Maeda believes it is important for women to receive remuneration for their work, but that is not to say they should become financially independent or that there is anything wrong with part-time work. She thinks it is important to evaluate the ways in which women work. She believes that we must accept the reality of existing social structures, which place domestic responsibilities on the shoulders of housewives, many of whom cannot take on other work. Given this fact, the organization can serve both as a place to help women who are in the process of finding work, and a support for those who already have jobs. In addition, as a workplace where money can be earned in a flexible manner, the organization may also influence how women live and work.

The income Ms. Maeda earns for her work with the organization is not commensurate with the amount of time and labor she expends, and in fact, she covers many expenses out-of-pocket. But she has built a network with people from organizations around the country and with government officials, who have given her a new way of thinking and a new energy. She has been able to taste the "real attraction of nonprofit work." For her, it is not work or duty. As she put it, "I am learning things here." In her view, while income from an occupation represents "compensation for labor," income derived from nonprofit work consists of "compensation for labor plus the sense of satisfaction and purpose one derives from such work." She feels that the conventional work style is less attractive, for it would not allow her to use her abilities fully. Ms. Maeda's attitudes reflect both her pleasure in working as a volunteer, as well as the fact that she does not have to support herself financially.

Conclusion

If we view nonprofit work from the perspective of career building, we can see that such work—whether it is akin to a professional career that provides financial compensation or to community volunteering—can provide opportunities for women to apply a variety of experiences and skills to problems of the larger society. For Ms. Saito, nonprofit work providing the delivery of meals has become a way to continue a career that was interrupted when she married and moved to another community. She receives compensation for her work, making nonprofit work a profession for her. Moreover, her efforts have borne fruit as the organization has grown, and its earnings have increased, and with that, wages paid to staff members have gone up. In Ms. Maeda's case, the compensation she receives is small in comparison to what a full-time worker in a for-profit organization would be paid, but, even so, her nonprofit work has served to enhance her professional life experiences. In contrast, Ms. Yoshida earns money both from her esthetic salon business and her restaurant, but she is not paid for her work with the nonprofit organization. Subsequent to her interview, the Office of the Prime Minister gave Ms. Yoshida a commendation for her contribution to promoting women's participation in society.

Certainly, it is difficult to derive adequate income from nonprofit work in Japan. Under these circumstances, married women who do not need to earn an income are the ones primarily undertaking the work. For them, even if the pay is low or nonexistent, the work offers greater satisfaction than most of the other types of work available to middle-aged women.

Notes

1. These numbers refer to organizations certified as "nonprofit organizations" based on the Law to Promote Specified Nonprofit Activities. See http://www.npo-homepage. go.jp/data/pref.html. Organizations referred to as "nonprofit organizations" in this essay are those that have been certified as such under this law.

2. In this survey, semi-structured interviews lasting about one and a half hours long each were conducted between October 2004 and January 2005. Respondents were women in their thirties (2), forties (4), fifties (12), sixties (2) and seventies (1).

Works Cited

Hall, Douglas T. 2002. *Careers In and Out of Organizations*. Thousand Oaks, CA: Sage Publications.

Iwata, Katsuhiko. 2004. *Koyo to jiei, borantia—sono chukan ryoiki de no tayo na shugyo jittai to mondaiten* (Employment and independent businesses, volunteer work—diverse working styles and problems in this intermediary sphere). JILPT Discussion Paper 2004. Rodo seisaku kenkyu kenshu kiko (Japan Institute for Labor Policy and Training).

Kokuzeicho (National Tax Agency). 2009. *Minkan kyuyo jittai tokei chosa* (Survey of salaries in the private sector). http://www.nta.go.jp/kohyo/tokei/kokuzeicho/minkan2008/minkan.htm

Koseirodosho (Ministry of Health, Labor and Welfare). 2008. *Heisei jukyunenban hataraku josei no jitsujo* (The status of working women 2007).

Naikakufu (Cabinet Office, Government of Japan). 2005. *Heisei jurokunen shimin ka-*

tsudo dantai kihon chosa hokokusho (Report of basic survey on civic organizations 2004).

Nakata, Yoshifumi and Miyamoto, Dai. 2004. "Nihon ni okeru NPO to koyo—genjo to kadai" (Nonprofit organizations and employment in Japan—present conditions and issues). *Kikan kakei keizai kenkyu* (Household Economic Studies Quarterly) No. 61.

Okamoto, Hideo. 2005. "Josei no kyaria to NPO katsudo" (Women's careers and non-profit work). *Josei no kyaria birudingu to NPO katsudo ni kansuru chosa kenkyu hokokusho* (Report of research on women's career building and NPO work). Saitama: Kokuritsu josei kyoiku kaikan.

Ono, Akiko. 2005. "Naze NPO wa josei o hikitsukeru no ka—chingin kara no kosatsu to sono kadai" (Why women are drawn to nonprofit organizations—examination based on wages and related issues). *We learn* No. 634.

Rodo seisaku kenkyu kenshu kiko (Japan Institute for Labor Policy and Training). 2006. "NPO no yukyu shokuin to borantia—sono hatarakikata to ishiki" (Paid workers and volunteers in NPOs: their style of work and attitudes). *Rodo seisaku kenkyu hokokusho* (Report on Labor Policy Research) No. 60.

Somusho (Ministry of Internal Affairs and Communications). 2005. *Heisei jurokunen jigyosho/kigyo tokei chosa hokoku daiikkan jigyosho ni kansuru shukei zenkoku kekka* (2004 Report on survey of businesses/corporations volume 1, nationwide results on businesses).

———. 2010. *Rodoryoku chosa* (Labor force survey). http://www/stat/go.jp/data/rou-dou/longtime/zuhyou/lt51.xls

Tsuji, Yutaka. 2004. "NPO de hataraku imi to sutaffu no rikiryo keisei" (The meaning of working at nonprofit organizations and the building of staff members' abilities). In *NPO no kyoikuryoku—shogai gakushu to shiminteki kokyosei* (The power of non-profit organizations to educate—lifelong learning and community benefit), ed. Katsuko Sato. Tokyo: Tokyo daigaku shuppankai.

Yamauchi, Naoto. 2001. "Jendaa kara mita hieiri rodo shijo—shufu wa naze NPO shijo o mezasu no ka" (Nonprofit labor market from the perspective of gender—why housewives aim for the nonprofit labor market). *Nihon rodo kenkyu zasshi* (Japanese Journal of Labor Studies) No. 493.

VII
FEMINISM AND POLITICAL POWER

Japan's First Phase of Feminism

Mioko Fujieda

In 1868 the new Meiji government was established in Japan, replacing the Tokugawa shogunate, whose rule had lasted for two hundred and sixty years. A new Japan, with the emperor as head of state, abolished feudalism,[1] introduced a capitalist system, and pursued a path toward modernization, following the models of Western countries. Japan's start as a capitalist country lagged behind the Western countries by more than a century. To catch up with the West, the political leaders of the time embarked on militaristic expansionism with the slogan "Enrich the nation, strengthen the army." Under this policy Taiwan and Korea were colonized successively.

Internally, the Emperor system and the feudalistic patriarchal family system, which formed the fundamental basis for achieving this political end, were placed on a firm ground by the end of the nineteenth century with the promulgation of the Meiji Constitution in 1889, and the civil code in 1898. Thus, total subjugation of women to the head of the household, and to men in general, was given legal justification. Women were placed, so to speak, outside the hierarchical order of society, regardless of the social class to which they belonged.

Women had to wait until the end of World War II in 1945 to see restrictions on their rights as human beings removed in all spheres. In the meantime, however, many women continued to struggle for their emancipation from all the miseries and injustices inflicted upon them by society and the state, through speeches, writings, and actions. Their struggle began in the earlier years of the Meiji period, often inspired and encouraged by the struggles and achievements of their sisters in the West.

It seems that outside Japan very little is known about Japanese women today, let alone about Japanese consciousness of issues concerning women. This lack of knowledge about Japan's "First Phase," or "First Wave," as it is called in the West, holds true among most Japanese also, as the history of early feminism is totally absent from school curricula, except for a few

women who are occasionally mentioned here and there, such as Akiko
Yosano, poet and essayist (1878-1942), and Raicho Hiratsuka (1886-1971),
who started *Seito* magazine (Bluestocking) in 1911.

Although such international developments in recent years as the International Women's Year and the United Nations Decade for Women have
had an impact on the Japanese government, school textbooks, subject to
rigorous inspection by the Ministry of Education prior to publication, are
still filled with gender bias and sexual stereotyping, and ignore the contributions made by women. Gender issues, including those having to do with
the "hidden curriculum," are simply absent as a category from this inspection procedure, and thus textbooks function as an important vehicle for
the perpetuation of gender bias with the Ministry's authorization. This is
further compounded by the fact that for the most part textbook publishers
are unaware of gender issues.

In this essay it is impossible to undertake a comprehensive discussion
of the hundreds of notable women who were active in different ways during
the First Phase. Therefore, what I will do here is to portray briefly the lives
of the following six women: Toshiko Kishida (later known as Shoen Nakajima) (1864-1901), [2] Hideko Kageyama (later Fukuda) (1865-1927), Toyoko
Shimizu (later Kozai, also known by her pen name, Shikin) (1868-1933),
Suga Kanno (1881-1911), Kajiko Yajima (1833-1925), and Fusae Ichikawa
(1893-1981). This list is not intended to be all-inclusive, but rather a selec-
tive illustration of different areas of commitment, persuasion, and inclina-
tion. One characteristic common among these women, however, though in
different ways, is that they were all rebels.

A Real First: Toshiko Kishida

Toshiko Kishida (1864-1901) was a real first: she was the first woman to
give public addresses in support of the Popular Rights Movement which
focussed around issues of political freedom, individual rights, and representative government. Born to a wealthy merchant family in Kyoto, in 1879,
at the age of fifteen she was called to Tokyo to give lectures on Chinese clas-
sics to the empress.[3] Having grown up in a merchant family, however, she
found the court life too conventional, superstitious, and unbearably hierarchical. After two years Kishida resigned, citing poor health as an excuse.

After resigning from her post, Kishida traveled extensively with her
mother all over Japan, meeting people. It was a time when the Popular
Rights Movement, which lasted from the 1870s to the 1880s, was at its
height. Among the people she met during her travels were leaders in this
movement, and she immediately became involved in it.

In 1882 Kishida made her appearance before the public as the first female speaker for the cause of women's rights, giving a speech entitled "Fujo no michi" (The way for women). She seems to have been a very good speaker, with an electrifying effect on the audience. In addition to being brilliant, articulate, and beautiful, the fact that she had served at the imperial court probably gave her a special aura. Her appearance on the political scene definitely had an impact on many women across the country, who were drawn to the popular rights ideas, many of them joining the movement.

This was the period immediately after the start of Japan's modernization, and feudal conventions prevailed. Life was based on Confucianist moral principles, a convention in which women were held to be biologically inferior to men. They were there to serve men, and to maintain the family line. Kishida criticized this situation and called for changing it.

Alarmed by the heightening influence of the Popular Rights Movement, which attracted not only men but also quite a few women, the government embarked on a campaign of harsh repression. A speech Kishida made in 1883 titled "Maidens in Boxes, or the Imperfection of Marriage," which criticized marriage based on a hierarchical relationship, led to her arrest, and indictment on the grounds of violating the Ordinance on Meeting.

It may seem extraordinary that a daughter from a merchant class could do such things, escaping the pressures from the family, but it was a period of transition and social change. Things were moving very fast in many directions. Prior to the Meiji Restoration of 1868 the samurai, or warrior class, had been the ruling class, followed by peasants and artisans, with the merchant class at the very bottom, in spite of their wealth. Toward the end of the feudal era, however, it was the merchants who controlled the whole economy. The samurai class was impoverished, and in debt to the merchants. Among the merchant class one could say that there was a considerable liberalism as well as criticism of the feudal system. In addition to these factors, in the case of Kishida, her mother's supportive role was extremely important in terms of her intellectual development. It was her mother who encouraged her to study and pursue her ideas.

Kishida's most representative article is one entitled "I Tell You, My Fellow Sisters," which appeared in a Liberal Party newspaper in 1884.[4] In it she refutes the commonplace argument that "men are strong and women are weak, therefore they can't be equal," saying that, if this contention refers to difference in physical strength, it reflects nothing but barbarism on the part of the speakers, whereas if it means differences in mental capabilities, it is only a distinction between the educated and uneducated. While urging women to be more self-confident, she turns to men, saying, "You men, alas, when you open your mouth you talk about reform or change, but then why are you so obstinately attached to old conventions when it comes to the issue of equal rights [between the sexes]?" Kishida continues to argue that the primary happiness for any human being will be realized only in a relationship built on love and compassion between equal men and women, and that an imperious attitude on the part of men is sure to destroy this happiness.

To Kishida, however, *kokken* (meaning "nationalism/patriotism," the rights of the state) *minken* (people's rights), and *joken* (women's rights) were all identical, and they coexisted without any contradictions in her mind. This attitude was not unique to her but was shared commonly by most of the Popular Rights activists and theorists, for whom the rights of the state and those of the people were indistinguishable from each other. In Kishida's article, for instance, she explains why she wants to call to her fellow sisters, saying, "There are good reasons for this. . . . I do this from a deeply felt concern for the state and the country." Also, toward the end of the article, speaking about equal rights between the sexes, she says, "It should be a duty for any patriot concerned with our country's fate to make our country more civilized by adopting what is good from the West and making up for our shortcomings."

In 1884 Kishida married a politician, a Liberal Party leader, and withdrew not only from speaking engagements, but also from direct involvement in politics.[5] Around this time Kishida and her husband were baptized and became Christians. Though in later years her writing lost the sharp edge it had in her earlier works, her rational and critical thinking did not wither until the end of her life. Their marital relationship seems to have been quite close to what she held as ideal—a relationship based on mutual love and respect. Kishida died of tuberculosis when she was thirty-seven (or forty, if she was born in 1861), two years after her husband, who also died of tuberculosis.

From a Popular Rights Advocate to a Socialist: Hideko Kageyama (later Fukuda)

One young woman who was very much inspired by Toshiko Kishida was Hideko Kageyama (1865-1927). She heard Kishida give a fiery speech in Okayama on the emancipation of women when she was about seventeen, and the speech made her determine that she would follow Kishida as a Popular Rights advocate.

Feeling the need for women's economic independence and an education that would enable them to achieve it, Kageyama founded a private school (of a family business nature) for girls and women from ages six through the sixties, but it was closed down by the authorities within a short time. Her involvement in a subversive plot, a planned putsch in Korea in 1885, which has come to be known as the Osaka Incident, resulted in her arrest, trial, and imprisonment. As she was the only woman among all those involved, this incident made her famous as "Japan's Joan of Arc." This incident only reveals how narrow and superficial her Popular Rights ideas were, however, as this putsch conspiracy was a manifestation of chauvinistic, interventionist nationalism. It took quite some time for Kageyama to abandon her narrow patriotism.

Her own financial predicaments drove her to become more acutely aware of women's need for economic independence, and this brought her to the Christian faith at one time. Later, her association with the then emerging socialist groups led her to socialism. In 1907, with the help of some of her male friends, she issued *Sekai fujin* (Women of the world) under the banner of women's emancipation. In a front page editorial of the first issue, she described the purposes for publishing this newspaper, "When we look at the conditions currently prevailing in society, we see that virtually everything is coercive and oppressive to the true nature of women. This necessitates that we women rise up and form a social movement of our own." [6] And in the third anniversary issue (no. 32, January 5, 1909) she claimed that the paper was meant for a readership of neither "good wives and wise mothers" nor "the successful" but, rather, for "the losers, the weak and the so-called hoodlums" for whom the paper wished to be a friend. [7] The paper was not, however, an undertaking exclusively of women, as was to be the case of *Seito* magazine published about four years later.

In 1890 the government had prohibited women from attending political meetings. This was in response to the growing campaign by women against licensed prostitution as well as to their increasingly active participation in political discussions. And in 1900 the Police Security Regulations were introduced. The notorious Article 5 of the Regulations placed a total ban on every sort of political activity by women. This made it impossible for women to hold meetings, make speeches, and attend meetings and conferences, let alone form political organizations. All women working for the improvement of women's status became involved in a campaign against Article 5. Kageyama's journal *Sekai fujin*, also took up this issue. While Kageyama's argument was based on the "different but equal" theory, in one of her articles she referred to a "dual struggle." According to this argument, women are subject to the rule of the "male class" and the "aristocrat and rich class," and this dominance is founded on "the society's class structure itself" (no. 4, February 15, 1907). In the meantime, she discussed elsewhere, the male-centered legal system "holds us women in contempt and abuses us," and men, who greatly benefit from this system, are dead set against women's rights. In order to change this she urged that women courageously stand up (no. 30, November 4, 1908). [8] Yet she did not elaborate on this argument. Her dedication and commitment to her paper allowed for it to continue to be published for two years in spite of severe repression by the government authorities.

Kageyama was a woman of action rather than a deep thinker. Her life was always a financially difficult one, as she was the main supporter of her family most of her life—her parents, her children, and her sick husband who died of syphilis in 1900, after eight years of marriage. She "always fought, never wavering because of any setback," as she triumphantly writes in her autobiography.[9] She died in extreme poverty at the age of sixty-three.

Independence versus Marriage:
Toyoko Shimizu (later Kozai)/ Shikin

From the same generation as Kishida and Kageyama there is Toyoko Shimizu, also known by the pen name Shikin (1868-1933), who was influenced by the Popular Rights ideas, though she came upon the scene a little later than Kageyama. Known as a woman's rights advocate, journalist, and novelist, Shikin was a feminist pioneer in the earlier half of her life. "*Koware yubiwa*" (A Broken Ring), her earliest story, published in 1891, and believed to be based on her own life experience, is strikingly feminist in that she portrays a woman who leaves her marriage out of her own will when she finds out that her husband had been married to another woman with whom he had continued to maintain a relationship.[10] The story was literally a feminist declaration of independence, very much advanced for the period.[11]

As in the story, in her real life, in 1899, she walked out of her first marriage, which had been arranged by her father, because of her husband's involvement with other women. This unhappy experience helped awaken her to the cause of women's rights, and she joined the Popular Rights Movement. The way in which she developed her own thinking distinguishes her from her predecessors such as Toshiko Kishida and Hideko Kageyama.

In 1890 Shikin moved from Kyoto to Tokyo and worked as a journalist for the *Jogaku zasshi* (Journal of women's education), and that was where she wielded her critical pen against the repressive government and against society's "common sense," which backed the government's contemptuous attitude toward women. All her editorials, such as "Why are not women allowed to attend political meetings?" and "In tears I call you, my sisters," were written along this line.[12]

Her best novel, *Imin gakuen* (School for Migrants), published in 1899, dealt with the issue of the Burakumin (Buraku people), or the "untouchables," for the first time in the history of Japanese literature. (See chapter 16 for a discussion of Buraku issues.) Although the story was idealistic, the ways in which she described society, and the relationship between men and women reveal how accurate and farsighted her observations were.[13]

Earlier, around 1891, while she was engaged in the Popular Rights Movement, Shikin was proposed to by one of its leaders. It turned out that this same man had also seduced Hideko Kageyama with a promise of marriage, keeping silent about his wife. Both women, without knowing this and trusting what he had told each of them, became pregnant, and gave birth to a child out of wedlock. The two women, who had been close friends at one time, were dismayed. A striking difference between them, however, was that Kageyama reviled and slandered Shikin in her autobiography, whereas Shikin remained completely silent.[14]

Around 1892 Shikin again received a proposal of marriage from an extraordinary man, a natural scientist, who was later to become president of Tokyo University. He proposed to her with passion, and wrote beautiful love letters in which he talked about his own feelings, something that was quite rare for that period. Obviously, she was moved, but she did not want to fall into the trap again. So she told him everything—not of her feelings but of the facts in the past. This man accepted her history, saying, "I'm not interested in your past. I love you as you are now." This rational approach and respect for their own feelings rather than for conventions and other people's feelings were remarkable for the period.[15]

The marriage did not work out, however, because she suffered within it. Shikin had to retreat from her writing. She stopped writing in her early thirties. She retreated into oblivion completely, only to be reread in the 1970s. She suffered all through the rest of her life because of the lack of a social life of her own. Her writing career was a brief ten years, and, ironically, she ended up being a model of a good wife and mother.

One of their sons, a well-known Marxist philosopher, and editor of his mother's works, recalled his mother in the 1970s, saying that his parents got along perfectly well, except on one point. His father never understood how frustrated his mother felt about giving up her writing career. He writes how his father would tease her, while his mother kept silent, her eyes full of tears, saying, "You are now a fool. You who used to be a genius are now a fool."[16]

Japanese Women and the Influence of Christianity

Christianity, particularly in the form of Protestantism, greatly contributed to Japan's modernization, particularly in the early years of Meiji. This was especially notable in the area of education for girls and women and advo-

cacy of improved status for women. Most of the girls' secondary schools
established in the early Meiji years were started by either foreign missionaries, quite often American women, or by Japanese Christians. The kind
of education they sought for girls was to create "modern women," replacing Confucian values, which had been the guiding principle of education
for women. What was meant by *modern women* was the type of women
who would have independence of mind, which would allow them to think
and act as freely and actively as men. In particular, Protestantism provided
moral support for the monogamous marriage, a union between two equal
and free persons.

Protestantism emerged as a progressive ideology in support of the
development of a modern society at a time when the creation of a new
social order and culture following the dissolution of the feudal system was
set as a prioritized task for the new nation, in the early Meiji period. As
the Emperor state system became firmly entrenched, however, toward the
end of the nineteenth century, with the promulgation of the Meiji Constitution and the civil code, there was a reaction against Westernization,
and Protestantism gradually lost its impact as a reformist and progressive force. Nevertheless, directly or indirectly, it had a great impact on the
thinking of the Meiji intellectuals, becoming an impelling force for various
social movements, developing into humanitarianism, or human emancipa-
tory ideas, and socialism. Among leading female believers were Toshiko
Kishida and Kajiko Yajima (who will be referred to later), and among those
who were directly influenced by Christianity one can cite Hideko Fukuda,
Toyoko Shimizu/Shikin, Suga Kanno, the "first political martyr," and many
others.[17]

The First Female Political Martyr: Suga Kanno

Suga Kanno (1881-1911), an anarchist and political martyr,[18] was the only
woman among the twelve people who were executed in 1911. Kanno,
together with eleven men, were hanged on the charge of attempted assas-
sination of the Emperor Meiji, known as the Great Treason Incident, which
was trumped up by the state power determined to crush the socialist/anar-
chist movement. Until the very last moment of her life she is said to have
remained calm as well as firm. At the time of her death she was twenty-nine
years old.

It is quite often the case that a woman's reputation is affected by men's
words, a reflection of the power relationship between women and men, and
this is exactly what happened to Kanno. For she is described even to this
day as a seductress, even to the point of being called a prostitute, an image

far removed from what she really was. Even serious studies on her, including those by women writers, mostly follow this pattern, not to mention the novels about her: all bring disgrace upon her.

Where does this distortion come from? One finds that Kanno's allegedly degrading reputation originates in the autobiographies of a highly respected socialist, Kanson Arahata (1887-1981), who was married to her for a very short period. He was a dedicated socialist whose autobiographies are considered to provide valuable testimony about socialist ideas and the socialist movement in Japan from the Meiji through the Taisho and Showa periods. These works are also regarded as masterpieces of autobiographical literature. This is why his reminiscences about Kanno have been taken as truthful and dependable. Her case presents an excellent example of how male bias can affect a woman's reputation and honor.

As a result of the fact that Arahata kept republishing his autobiography, there are several versions of it. The first was *Kanson jiden* (The autobiography of Kanson), published in 1947, and subsequent ones were published in 1954, 1961, 1965, and 1975.[19] Every version contains a section on Kanno, but a careful examination of these versions reveals significant changes between the first and second versions in the ways she is described. In the second version, titled *Hitosuji no michi* (Earnestly on the way), one finds that there are additions to, and deletions from, the first version, and the subsequent versions more or less follow the line of the second version. What is to be noted here is that Arahata's revisions emphasize that he was just "a novice to the world of eroticism (or love)" and was seduced and driven mad by Kanno, who, according to him, was "a veteran in these matters." All these alterations were made in order to make this assertion sound more truthful.

In the first version Arahata writes that to get money Kanno turned to Bunkai Udagawa in return for sexual favors and that, after separating from Udagawa and becoming a journalist, she had affairs with one man after another. In short, "such a licentious life" became "second nature" to her, and she continued to repeat the same error. But in the later versions changes in wording, additions, or deletions are made in such a way that the examples he lists to demonstrate her "immoral" conduct are used to reinforce the impression on the readers' part that she became a Christian seeking salvation from her sinful life.

Much more significant was an addition Arahata made to the second version explaining Kanno's approach to socialism. He relates the story that, when Kanno was in her early teens, her stepmother arranged to have Kanno raped by a miner who worked for her father, and that this traumatic experience was chiseled in her mind as an indelible memory, leading to a loss of her own self-respect. Much later, according to Arahata, she read a response by the socialist leader Toshihiko Sakai to a letter from an agonized rape victim which was printed in the newspaper *Yorozu choho* (All-out morning paper), in which Sakai said, "It is nothing but an accident, just like a person attacked by a rabid dog on the street; though the victim is definitely unfortunate, it's not something for which the victim should be held responsible." Arahata conjectures that Kanno was deeply moved by the sympathy exhibited by Sakai for women, and that it was a main motive for her interest in socialism. In this way her involvement with socialism is explained in the context of emphasizing a sexual experience in Kanno's life, and the "loose morals" she displayed in her later years are traced back to the assault she suffered earlier.

Except for Arahata's accounts, however, there is no evidence to indicate that her "wicked" stepmother schemed to have her raped. Also, no article, such as Arahata claims Sakai wrote, has been found. And nowhere in Kanno's own writings, in which she quite frequently refers to her family life and her own life, as well as in the police records drawn up at the time of her trial, is there evidence to prove that she harbored any resentment toward her stepmother.

Later, when he learned that Kanno had begun to live with Shusui Kotoku, a senior socialist/anarchist, who was later executed together with Kanno in the same frame-up incident, the infuriated Arahata tried to kill both Kanno and Kotoku with a pistol but failed. Obviously, what consumed him was jealousy, possessiveness, and intensely ambivalent feelings of love and hatred toward Kanno.

In any case, all these accounts of Kanno by Arahata seem to be based on hearsay and rumors, the sources of which are unidentifiable or based merely on his own conjectures. Nevertheless, most of the biographical accounts of Kanno have relied, and still rely, on his words, quite often embroidering his stories further.

What, then, is the truth concerning Kanno? Born in Osaka, she grew up in a wealthy family as a brilliant, tomboyish daughter. After her father, originally from the samurai, or warrior, class, failed in his mining business, the family suffered hardship and misery, and Kanno was forced to give up plans for continuing education beyond primary school, despite her desire to do so. The pride and spirit she held as a samurai's daughter seem to have sustained her through all the difficulties she endured in her life. Her mother died when she was eleven years old, and she had to take care of various members of her family who fell sick—her grandmother and her brother, followed by her father and sister.

In 1899 she married Fukutaro Komiya, a Tokyo merchant. But this marriage did not give her a sense of fulfillment, and her father's illness gave her an excuse to walk out. She returned to Osaka in 1902, and in the same year, was hired as a reporter for the *Osaka choho* (Osaka morning paper) on the recommendation of Bunkai Udagawa (1848-1930), an important figure in the world of journalism and literature in Osaka in the early and middle period of Meiji, under whom Kanno's younger brother was studying as a houseboy. Kanno respected Bunkai highly, and he in turn recognized talent in her, and encouraged her to pursue a writing career. But, as already mentioned, Arahata conjectured that she had become Bunkai's mistress.

Writing for *Osaka choho*, Kanno mounted a strong campaign against licensed prostitution, and the political circles that publicly sanctioned and were closely connected with it as well as social conventions that accepted it as a necessary evil, instead of denouncing it. To appeal to a much wider audience, she worked with eminent Christian and socialist figures, one of whom was the Christian socialist Naoe Kinoshita, and organizations, including the Osaka Women's Reform Society, a local branch of the Japan Christian Women's Organization, which was founded in Tokyo by Kajiko Yajima and others in 1886.

Kanno's success in persuading the Osaka Women's Reform Society, which up until then had been active primarily in the cause of temperance, to take a stand on the issue of prostitution led to her becoming an important figure within the organization. In November 1903 she was baptized a Christian, and in December she was elected to serve as one of the officers of the Osaka Women's Reform Society, responsible for documents and materials.

Kanno's involvement with and commitment to the activities of the Reform Society led her to contacts with socialists, because at the time socialists and Christians were seeking ways to forge unity in their work—though this proved to be impossible by the end of 1907. Her meeting with the socialist leader Toshihiko Sakai had an especially great impact on the subsequent course of her life.

In 1906, on Sakai's recommendation, Kanno moved to Tanabe, in Wakayama Prefecture, in order to work for *Muro shimpo* (Muro news), a socialist and antiwar newspaper. This is where she met Kanson Arahata, who had already been working there as a reporter. After her assignment was over she returned to Kyoto with her sister, who was ill, in May 1906, and in the summer Arahata came to see her. To fulfill her promise to marry him, she moved to Tokyo later that year, again with her sister, and was hired by another newspaper, the *Mainichi dempo* (Mainichi telegraph). The following year, her sister died. After her funeral Kanno collapsed, and her own tuberculosis was diagnosed. The relationship between Kanno and Arahata disintegrated several months after they began living together.

Her worsening tuberculosis, the loss of her job with the newspaper as
a result of the Red Flag Incident (though she was found innocent and later
acquitted),[20] the increasingly reactionary stance of the government, which
was determined to annihilate socialists, and her anger at all of this drove her
to commit herself even more strongly to the socialist/anarchist cause.

Shusui Kotoku, an advocate of anarchism who was also suffering with
tuberculosis, tried, with Kanno, to rebuild the socialist movement, which
had been crushed by the Red Flag Incident. Kanno and Kotoku needed each
other's support, and they became lovers. Their alliance was not welcomed
by the socialist community because of the misunderstanding about Kotoku
having stolen Kanno from Arahata during the latter's confinement in jail.
Kanno and Kotoku were left isolated, both ideologically and personally. (It
can easily be surmised that Arahata's accounts of Kanno had very much to
do with his jealousy.) The situation worsened for them, almost to a point
of suffocation. Kanno (and also Kotoku, at least in the initial stage) was
pushed to be part of a scheme devised by Takichi Miyashita to manufacture
explosives with the aim of assassinating the Emperor Meiji. But their plot
was no match for the efficient police authorities, and it was uncovered. The
incident was blown up as a major conspiracy to bring about a wholesale
revolution. Charges were trumped up against Kanno and others, eventually
leading her, Kotoku, and ten other men to the gallows.

Suga Kanno, sustained by lifelong pride in her own integrity and spirit
as a woman from the former samurai class and led by new ideas, first Christianity and later socialism/anarchism, challenged head-on the state power
as well as the society that did not care about the human rights of women
and men.

An Outstanding Organizer of Women's
Social Work: Kaijko Yajima

One of the most notable among the Christian women of the time was Kajiko
Yajima (1833-1925). Yajima was the first president of the Tokyo fujin kyofukai (Tokyo Women's Reform Society), founded in 1886, which evolved
to become the Nihon kirisutokyo fujin kyofukai (Japan Christian Women's
Organization) in 1893. The Reform Society, was, in fact, the starting point
of the women's movement seeking emancipation and respect for women's
rights as human beings in modern Japan. It was she who pioneered in organizing the women's movement and developing women's social work.

After ten years of marriage, during which she gave birth to three children, Yajima divorced her drunken husband, and moved from Kumamoto
Prefecture in Kyushu to Tokyo, where she studied hard to obtain a teach-

JAPAN'S FIRST PHASE OF FEMINISM

ing license. When she was promoted to principal of a Christian girls' high school she was forty-six years old, and it was from this point that her second life began. She was a woman possessed of an exceptionally independent mind and vitality, standing resolute when necessary; at the same time, she was patient and far-sighted.

One of her nephews, also a Christian and a well-known literary figure, did not hide his dislike of his aunt, calling her a haughty woman who did not have the heart to sympathize with her poor old husband. But his brother, also a very famous writer, had to admit that she was a woman "who does not fail to do what has to be done, and who does not do what needs not be done."[21]

Since its inception the Japan Christian Women's Organization, under her leadership, actively campaigned against drinking and for the abolition of licensed prostitution. It was also actively engaged in petition campaigns for the revision of the criminal and civil codes. While undertaking a campaign, together with other groups and individual women, to repeal the notorious Police Security Regulations, which prohibited women from participating in any form of political activities, the society organized petition campaigns for the abolition of licensed prostitution, organizing speech meetings, and establishing refuge centers to which prostitutes could go for help. Other issues it took up included abuses inflicted upon factory women, a campaign against large-scale pollution of the Ashio Copper Mines area, the first of this kind brought about by industrial development, as well as aid projects extended to women in the polluted area.

The matrix of the Fujin sanseiken kakutoku kisei domeikai (League for the Realization of Women's Suffrage), in which Fusae Ichikawa played a leading role, was in fact the Japan Women's Suffrage Association, which was founded by the Japan Christian Women's Organization in 1921, and headed by Ochimi Kubushiro in pursuance of its platform of action adopted in 1893. [22] In 1921, at the age of eighty-nine, Yajima traveled to Washington, D.C., where the Naval Arms Reduction Conference was being held, and she submitted signatures collected from more than ten thousand Japanese women petitioning for peace. She never ceased to work for the cause of women up until the very end of her days, at the age of ninety-three.

From Suffrage to the Second Phase of Feminism: Fusae Ichikawa

Since 1918, when she founded the New Women's Association, together with Raicho Hiratsuka and others, until the end of her long life, Fusae Ichikawa (1893-1981) continued to remain a leading figure in the women's movement and in the movement for suffrage. Ichikawa went to the United States in 1921, and during her three-year stay she met a number of people, including female leaders. Her meeting with Alice Paul of the National Woman's Party had a particularly great impact on her.[23]

Upon her return to Japan in 1924 Ichikawa opened a branch office of the International Labor Organization in Tokyo and also founded the League for the Realization of Women's Suffrage. She led the campaign for women's suffrage over the following sixteen years, until the League was forced to dissolve under militarist pressures just prior to the outbreak of World War II. What made her distinctly different from other suffragist leaders in the prewar days was her pragmatic strategy. Her primary goal was to improve the status of women by obtaining suffrage, and she sought to realize this goal by working on and through all the political parties, irrespective of their political directions.

Universal suffrage—ironically so called, even though women were excluded from it—was finally promulgated in Japan in 1925. And the first election under this law was carried out in 1928. Ichikawa headed the election campaign committee of the League for the Realization of Women's Suffrage for this election. The committee decided, first of all, to request all political parties and their candidates to explicitly include suffrage for women on their platforms, and, second, to send speakers from the League in support of the particular candidates who placed women's suffrage on their platforms, and to issue letters of recommendations from the League to such candidates, if so required. Requests for female speakers came from all corners, from conservative parties to proletarian ones. The number of speeches women gave in support of various candidates amounted to 276. Especially when Ichikawa was the speaker, the halls were filled with audiences anxious to hear her speak.

This League policy created quite a stir. Many suffragists, particularly those who argued that women should stand at least on the side of proletarian parties, bitterly criticized Ichikawa's position. Mumeo Oku, another suffragist leader, for instance, criticized her severely, saying, "In the morning they speak for the conservative party, and in the evening they speak for the socialist party. They behave themselves just like a prostitute." [24] But Ichikawa remained unperturbed because, for her, it was purely a matter of strategy.

In an essay titled "The Suffragist Spirit" (1934) Ichikawa wrote:

> What I mean by the suffragist spirit is our attitude, our faith. We detest time-serving attitudes. We will not support the policies or the claims of the government or the municipal authorities. We will put them to careful

scrutiny as we understand them, and then direct our effort toward what we believe to be right. I believe this is exactly the attitude that suffragists, those of us who demand women's political participation, must assume... Our job is to struggle through all the difficulties, and to open up a thorny path. Only then, time-servers, so-called ladies of high ranks and the masses, will follow after us along the path we have opened. Our job is to sow the seeds and to fertilize the land, and harvesting is done by those who come later. We are the ones who make efforts and spend our own money, and even so we are ill-spoken of, and the result thus achieved is carried off by others. In this sense, we have not much to gain, but who cares... Speak ill of us if they want to. As long as we have this suffragist spirit, our campaign will keep moving on.

Her pragmatism with regard to women's suffrage turned out to be all too naïve in the face of the state's mounting interventionist/expansionist policy. This policy, which had been pursued since the Meiji period, entered a new phase in 1931, with the outbreak of the so-called Manchurian Incident. In July 1937 Japanese troops invaded China. In September, Ichikawa wrote in her autobiography:

I felt deeply depressed when I saw the [Japan-China] incident develop into a total war...Now we are forced to choose one of three alternatives. The choices are: to go to prison by publicly opposing the war, to withdraw completely from the [women's] movement, or to cooperate with the state to a certain extent by acknowledging things as they are.

And then she quotes an article in which she wrote the conclusion she had reached at the time:

Under the present circumstances, there's no denying that obtaining women's suffrage—a legal reform campaign—will become even more difficult than ever before. However, the objective of our demand for suffrage is to enable women to cooperate with the government as fully as men, so that women can be of service to the state and society at large from the women's point of view. Therefore, when women demonstrate their merits with their own abilities in the face of the most serious national emergency the country has ever experienced, it would be a way to achieve the ultimate goal of suffrage, and it can be a step forward toward obtaining suffrage in legal terms. Let's take up the post women are expected to assume, overcoming sorrow and pain. [25]

It was a decision Ichikawa made in deep anguish. Not only Ichikawa, but also other eminent leaders of the women's movement—such as Ochimi Kubushiro, Tomiko Kora, Shigeru Kaneko (Yamataka), Hideko Maruoka,

Tsuneko Gantoretto (probably Gauntlet), Waka Yamada, and Motoko Hani—were all co-opted by the government and the military through clever maneuvering. They were all swallowed up in some way or another into a war footing called "Kokumin seishin sodoin taisei" (System for an all-out mobilization of the national spirit), though not necessarily actively or willingly. These women were all products of the era of Taisho democracy—Taisho being a brief period from 1912 to 1926, when liberal sentiments prevailed in Japanese society. How, then, could they have collaborated with the war effort? one might ask.[26]

They were made to collaborate with the war effort partly by political maneuvering by the military and the government, which were well aware that, without involving women in their scheme, it would be impossible to carry out the war. These female leaders at the same time harbored an illusionary hope. As Ichikawa's article, quoted in her autobiography, illustrates, they were made to think that their cooperation with the government and men might help improve women's social position, which had been kept deplorably low, with little improvement made since the Meiji period. While the extent of their self-deception was remarkable, the way they felt was, in a way, understandable, though not justifiable.

As soon as World War II ended, with Japan's surrender to the Allied Powers, Ichikawa went to the prime minister and other cabinet members, persuading them that women should get the vote immediately. That was before the American Occupation forces ordered the granting of general suffrage as part of their strategy to demilitarize and democratize Japan. Ichikawa immediately established the Women's League for New Japan (now called the League of Women Voters of Japan) but was expelled from public office by the Occupation forces on grounds that she had cooperated with the country's war efforts.[27] As soon as the purge was lifted in 1950, she made a comeback to the League's presidency.

In 1953 Ichikawa ran for the House of Councillors (the Upper House of the Diet) with the slogan of "An Ideal Election," meaning an election campaign that would be carried out in strict observance of the Election Law, and she was successfully elected. Since then she was successively elected to the Upper House (one term of office lasting six years), developing a grassroots campaign for cleaning up elections and politics. And since the International Women's Year in 1975, she represented the Liaison Committee for the International Women's Year, a nongovernmental organization consisting of forty-eight women's groups. In this way her commitment to the cause of women continued up until the last days of her life.[28]

Conclusion

In the days prior to World War II, the women's movement was characterized essentially by rebellion, or resistance against conventions, to the way society was structured and run. During the early 1940s, as Japanese forces advanced into Asia, an all-out war effort was undertaken. The women's movement was either prohibited or co-opted, with the exception of a patriotic campaign by women to collaborate with the nation's war efforts. A large number of women were successfully mobilized, as exemplified by the case of Fusae Ichikawa.

Yet, when the war ended with Japan's surrender, the women's movement was suddenly out in the open, recognized as an indispensable part of the effort to democratize the society. With equality between the sexes declared in the Constitution, the change was so dramatic that many women felt there was not much to be learned from the past. This may partially account for the fact that the history of women in the prewar period was not given much attention until recently. And, of course, in a male-dominated society, it is the history of men that is taught and remembered.

As in many other countries, Japan saw a women's liberation movement emerge in 1970, which questioned the issue of gender division, a question the First Phase was not able to ask. Although, contrary to what happened in many other countries, the women's liberation movement per se lost its visibility as early as the first half of the 1970s, the emergence of the women's liberation movement marked the beginning of the so-called Second Phase.

And it is in the Second Phase that the history of Japanese women is being reexamined with new interpretations, and efforts have been made to reevaluate and restore to their rightful place the past contributions and achievements of women. As seen in the case of Suga Kanno, however, much has yet to be done to straighten out the historical records.

Notes

1. Although feudalism as a political institution was officially abolished, the feudalistic patriarchal values in society remained intact, keeping women bound to traditional conventions.

2. Kishida's year of birth is generally believed to be 1864, but there are some differing views. Yuko Nishikawa recently came up with new evidence showing that Kishida was born in 1861, instead of 1864. Yuko Nishikawa, *Hana no imoto—Kishida Toshiko-den* (Flower's sister—a biography of Toshiko Kishida) (Tokyo: Shinchosha, 1986).

3. If Kishida was born in 1861, as Yuko Nishikawa argues, then it was at the age of eighteen that she was summoned to the Tokyo Imperial Court. This sounds more plausible.

4. "I Tell You, My Fellow Sisters" was published serially (in ten installments) in "Jiyu no tomoshibi" ("The light of freedom," a Liberal Party paper) from May to June 1884. Incidentally, this article is translated as "To My Brothers and Sisters" in Sharon L. Sievers's *Flowers in Salt—The Beginnings of Feminist Consciousness in Modern Japan* (Stanford, CA: Stanford University Press, 1985), 37. Judging from the text, however, it is evident that Kishida was specifically addressing women.

5. The period during which Kishida was politically active was very brief. The period in which she spoke publicly on women's issues was even more brief, limited only to three years, 1882 through 1884. But her public speeches were the first ever delivered by a woman with such logical and persuasive power that they had a great impact on many women who followed her path.

6. *Sekai fujin* (Women of the world), the first issue, January 1, 1907. Reprinted in *Josei—hangyaku to kakumei to teiko to* (Women—rebellion, revolution, and resistance: an anthology of works by women pioneers), ed. Hiroko Suzuki. (Tokyo: Shakai hyoronsha, 1990).

7. See Ko Yamada, *Joseikaiho no shisokatachi* (Thinkers of women's emancipation) (Tokyo: Aoki shoten, 1987).

8. Ibid.

9. Hideko Fukuda, *Warawa no hanseigai* (Half my life) (Tokyo: Iwanami shoten, 1983).

10. Shikin Shimizu, *Koware yubiwa* (A broken ring), in *Shimizu Shikin zenshu, zen ikkan* (Complete works of Shikin Shimizu in one volume), ed. Yoshishige Kozai (Tokyo: Sodo bunka, 1983).

11. Ibid. Also refer to Kiyoko Takeda, *Fujin kaiho no dohyo* (Some signposts for women's emancipation) (Tokyo: Domesu shuppan, 1985). In the story the heroine relates that, inspired and encouraged by Western thoughts on women's rights, she came to ponder the deplorable conditions of Japanese women, whom she thought should be able to enjoy human rights as well as their happiness. Incidentally, the first translation of John Stuart Mill's *The Subjection of Women* appeared in Japan in 1878 as *On the Equal Rights between Men and Women*.

12. Kozai, *Shimizu Shikin zenshu*.

13. It is alleged that Toson Shimazaki's *Hakai* (Broken commandment) (1906), highly acclaimed as the first novel dealing with the issue of discrimination against the Buraku people, was actually an adaptation of Shikin's *Imin gakuen*, though Shimazaki did not give any acknowledgment to it. See Takeda, *Fujin kaiho*.

14. Ibid. See also Nobuhiko Murakami, *Meiji joseishi chukan zenpen—joken to ie* (History of Meiji women, the first part of the middle volume—women's rights and *ie*) (Tokyo: Rironsha, 1970).

15. Takeda, *Fujin kaiho*; and Murakami, *Meiji joseishi 1—bunmei kaika* (History of Meiji women, vol. 1—Westernization) (Tokyo: Rironsha 1969).

16. Takeda, *Fujin kaiho*; and Kozai, afterword, *Shimizu Shikin zenshu*.

17. Takeda, *Fujin kaiho*; and Murakami, *Meiji joseishi 1*. Also see Sumiko Tanaka, ed., *Josei kaiho no shiso to kodo, senzen hen* (Ideology and action of women's emancipation—the prewar period) (Tokyo: Jijitsushinsha, 1975).

18. See Toshio Itoya, *Kanno Suga* (Tokyo: Iwanami shinsho, 1970); and many others. Among those works that help straighten out the record on Kanno are: Unosuke Shimizu, ed., *Kanno Sugako zenshu* (Collected works of Suga Kanno), vols. 1-3 (Tokyo: Koryusha, 1984); Hiroko Suzuki, ed., *Shiryo heiminsha no onnatachi* (Documents: women of the Commoners' Association) (Tokyo: Fuji shuppan, 1986); Hiroko Suzuki, ed., *Josei—*

hangyaku to kakumei to teiko to (see n. 6). I am particularly indebted to Wataru Oya, *Kanno Suga to Isonokami Tsuyuko* (Suga Kanno and Tsuyuko Isonokami) (Osaka: Toho shuppan, 1989). Oya's detailed examination of Kanson Arahata's autobiographies provide a valuable contribution in terms of shedding a new light on the life of Suga Kanno.

19. Kanson Arahata, *Kanson jiden* (The autobiography of Kanson) (Tokyo: Itagaki shoten, 1947); *Hitosuji no michi* (Earnestly on the way) (Tokyo: Keiyusha, 1954); *Kanson jiden* (The autobiography of Kanson) (Tokyo: Ronsosha, 1961); *Shimpan Kanson jiden* (The autobiography of Kanson—a new version) (Tokyo: Chikuma shobo, 1965); *Kanson jiden* (The autobiography of Kanson) (Tokyo: Iwanami Pocket Library, 1975).

20. At a gathering of socialists from all over the Tokyo area, some members of a group called the Friday Society brought banners reading "Anarchism" and "Anarcho-Communism," which they sought to carry into the streets at the close of the meeting. The police took this as an opportunity to arrest several socialists for allegedly violating the Police Security Regulations. Kanno was one of four women picked up and jailed in this incident, which came to be called the "Red Flag Incident." See Sharon L. Sievers, *Flowers in Salt—The Beginnings of Feminist Consciousness in Modern Japan* (Stanford, Calif.: Stanford University Press, 1985), 135-36.

21. Tanaka, *Josei kaiho.*

22. Takeda, *Fujin kaiho.* Incidentally, the Anti-Prostitution Law was won in 1956 at long last. Takeda emphasizes that here, also, long years of struggle carried out by the Japan Christian Women's Organization since its inception cannot be overlooked.

23. In her autobiography Ichikawa writes that Alice Paul persuaded her to "devote herself to the cause of women's suffrage." Paul repeatedly said to her: "Leave the labor movement business to men. Women's issues are something that only women can take up. You cannot do [two] different things at one time." Ichikawa recalls this, saying, "This advice of Alice seems to have had a great impact upon my later campaign" (Fusae Ichikawa, *Ichikawa Fusae jiden—senzen hen* [The autobiography of Fusae Ichikawa—the prewar period] [Tokyo: Shinjuku shobo, 1974], 118).

24. Ibid., 171.

25. Ibid., 339, 433, 434.

26. Ichikawa describes herself in her autobiography as "one of the liberals baptized by Taisho democracy" (*Ichikawa Fusae jiden*).

27. The reasons for Ichikawa's expulsion from public office are, in fact, uncertain. According to a surmise of Kiyoko Takeda (*Fujin kaiho*), it might have been because of Ichikawa's involvement with Dai Nihon genron hokokukai (The Greater Japan Association for Patriotism through Speech). Emma Kaufman (of Canadian origin) of the Tokyo YWCA was one of those who wrote letters in defense of Ichikawa to the General Headquarters (GHQ) of the Occupation forces. According to Takeda, Ichikawa was very grateful to Emma Kaufman and often talked about her even in her later life. This episode is one more indication of the fact that Ichikawa worked closely with Christian women and that her work was highly respected by them.

28. Fusae Ichikawa remained single throughout her life.

Works Cited

Arahata, Kanson. 1975. *Kanson jiden* (The autobiography of Kanson). Tokyo: Iwanami bunko.

———. 1965. *Shimpan Kanson jiden* (The autobiography of Kanson—a new version). Tokyo: Chikuma shobo.

————. 1961. *Kanson jiden* (The autobiography of Kanson). Tokyo: Ronsosha.

————. 1954. *Hitosuji no michi* (Earnestly on the way). Tokyo: Keiyusha.

————. 1947. *Kanson jiden* (The autobiography of Kanson). Tokyo: Itagaki shoten.

Fukuda, Hideko. 1983. *Warawa no hanseigai* (Half my life). Tokyo: Iwanami shoten.

Ichikawa, Fusae. 1974. *Ichikawa Fusae jiden—senzen hen* (The autobiography of Fusae Ichikawa—the prewar period). Tokyo: Shinjuku shobo.

Itoya, Toshio. 1970. *Kanno Suga*. Tokyo: Iwanami shinsho.

Kozai, Yoshishige, ed. 1983. *Shimizu Shikin zenshu, zen ikkan* (Complete works of Shikin Shimizu in one volume). Tokyo: Sodo bunka.

Murakami, Nobuhiko. 1970. *Meiji joseishi chukan zenpen—joken to ie* (History of Meiji women, the first part of the middle volume—women's rights and *ie*). Tokyo: Rironsha.

————. 1969. *Meiji joseishi 1—bunmei kaika* (History of Meiji women, vol. 1—Westernization). Tokyo: Shinchosha.

Oya, Wataru. 1989. *Kanno Suga to Isonokami Tsuyuko* (Suga Kanno and Tsuyuko Isonokami). Osaka: Toho shuppan.

Shimizu, Unosuke, ed. 1984. *Kanno Sugako zenshu* (Complete works of Suga Kanno), vol. 1-3. Tokyo: Koryusha.

Sievers, Sharon L. 1985. *Flowers in Salt—The Beginnings of Feminist Consciousness in Modern Japan*. Stanford, Calif.: Stanford University Press.

Suzuki, Hiroko, ed. 1990. *Josei—hangyaku to kakumei to teiko to* (Women—rebellion, revolution, and resistance: an anthology of works by women pioneers). Tokyo: Shakai hyoronsha.

————, ed. 1986. *Shiryo heiminsha no onnatachi* (Documents: Women of the Commoner's Association). Tokyo: Fuji shuppan.

Takeda, Kiyoko. 1985. *Fujin kaiho no dohyo* (Some signposts for women's emancipation). Tokyo: Domesu shuppan.

Tanaka, Sumiko, ed. 1975. *Josei kaiho no shiso to kodo, senzen hen* (Ideology and action of women's emancipation—the prewar period). Tokyo: Jijitsushinsha.

Yamada, Ko. 1987. *Joseikaiho no shisokatachi* (Thinkers of women's emancipation). Tokyo: Aoki shoten.

Backlash Against
Gender Equality after 2000

23

Midori Wakakuwa and
Kumiko Fujimura-Fanselow
Translated by Minata Hara

In *Backlash: The Undeclared War Against
American Women*, Susan Faludi warned feminists that the antifeminist
movement headed by leaders of the New Right began as early as the late
1980s. Paul Weyrich, co-founder of the conservative US group The Heritage
Foundation, for example, described the feminist threat in the journal *Conservative Digest*: "[T] here are people who want a different political order,
who are not necessarily Marxists. Symbolized by the women's liberation
movement, they believe that the future for their political power lies in the
restructuring of the traditional family, and particularly in the downgrading
of the male or father role in the traditional family" (Faludi 2006, 244). The
backlashers declared that "Satan has taken the reins of the 'women's liberation' movement and will stop at nothing" and that "'America's rapid decline
as a world power is a direct result' of the feminist campaign for equal rights
and reproductive freedom." They labeled feminists as "'moral perverts,'
'enemies of every decent society,'" and "destroyers of the family" (Ibid).

Two interesting points should be noted here. First, following the conservative victory in the US Congress, the backlashers proposed the Family Protection Act, which would have "eliminate[d] federal laws supporting
equal education; for[bade] 'intermingling of the sexes in any sport or other
school-related activities'; require[d] marriage and motherhood to be taught
as the proper career for girls; den[ied] federal funding to any school using
textbooks portraying women in nontraditional roles; repeal[ed] all federal
laws protecting battered wives from their husbands; and ban[ned] federally
funded legal aid for any woman seeking abortion counseling or a divorce"
(Ibid 247-8). Other legislative proposals included a complete ban on abortion, censoring birth control information until marriage, and the "chastity"
bill. As Faludi points out, their keywords were "pro-motherhood" and "pro-
family," and their real objective was to exercise a man's "God-given responsibility to lead his family" (Ibid 217). It is also noteworthy that the main
dictum of the American backlashers was their criticism of feminism for

eliminating "the gender gap" and thus attempting to neutralize differences between the sexes.

A Japanese backlash similar to the American one emerged in 2001, as we saw a rising antifeminist movement that sought to oppose women's right to sexual self-determination, otherwise known as the right to choose; advocate "chastity" education; and honor the preservation of "hearth and home" (Ogino 2001). This is by no means a coincidence. The mainstay of political forces in Japan today, both for the ruling Democratic Party of Japan (DPJ) and the Liberal Democratic Party (LDP), which held power almost uninterruptedly for more than fifty years until its defeat by the DPJ in the election for the House of Representatives (Lower House of the National Diet or legislature) in August 2009, belong to political factions upholding the ideologies of post-Thatcher neoliberalism and post-Reagan neoconservatism. Thus, what has been occurring in Japan is essentially part of the same global current as the American backlash.

Yet, if some differences do exist, they are due probably to the fact that Japanese politics have not, until very recently, had the dialectic dynamism of a bi-party system, and also because public knowledge and awareness of gender equality issues are still limited. One of the central premises of the current backlashers in Japan, whose views are voiced publicly even by prominent government officials, is that "gender" is a term imported from the US, which does not suit the "beautiful tradition of our nation." Indeed, the Japanese backlash movement is distinguished by its strong links to nationalists, such as those who advocate prime ministerial visits to the Yasukuni Shrine,[1] and it has progressed in tandem with other movements since the 1990s, for example, to revise the Constitution,[2] and the Fundamental Law of Education,[3] to promote legislation on the national flag and national anthem,[4] and revive the traditional Confucian-based family model. Suppression of gender equality has been carried forth by specific groups with nationwide networks and conscious, fixed ideologies. Thus, they are not simply arbitrary, personal, or emotional reactions of a transient nature, but rather deliberate actions on a national scale by factions with definitive political influence and power to determine the future direction of the Japanese nation and society.

A Decade of Backlash History

In contrast to their counterparts in the US, Japanese conservative factions in the 1980s did not initially seem to believe that feminism could jeopardize traditional male authority. Despite a few early rumblings, the backlash against feminism only took hold at the end of the twentieth century after the implementation of the Danjo kyodo sankaku shakai kihonho (Basic Law for a Gender-Equal Society) in 1999. In the US, the 1970s movement that opposed the ratification of the Equal Rights Amendment, according to which "Equality of rights shall not be denied or abridged by the US or by any state on account of sex," later formed the core of the backlash. Similarly, the backlash in Japan was spurred by the nationwide implementation of the Basic Law for a Gender-Equal Society (hereafter referred to as the Basic Law).

In 2001 the backlash focused its attack on the teaching of home economics to both female and male students in schools, and then on sex education during the following year. In 2003, sex-education bashing was carried out in local assemblies and school boards throughout Japan. In 2004, "gender-free" education came under siege, involving educational administrators. The backlash peaked in 2005 with the "anti gender-free" policy of the then ruling LDP and the conservative faction. According to Michiyoshi Hayashi, who is a major spokesperson for the backlash, the Japanese people had studied and absorbed feminism in the pre-1990s era, after which the movement for gender equality took power (referring to the fact that feminist economist Mari Osawa and other feminists were involved in drawing up and implementing the Basic Law). It was not until the twenty-first century that a number of men, who had not taken feminism seriously before, became aware of the threat it posed and began their counterattack, leading to an "all-out war" between the opposing sides from 2005 to 2006. In the autumn of 2006, the backlash became national policy when the figurehead of Japanese neoconservatism, LDP member Shinzo Abe, came into office as Prime Minister.

What follows is a summary of the major currents of the backlash following the implementation of the Basic Law and drafting of the Basic Plan for Gender Equality in June 1999. (See introduction for full description.)

In April 2001, the Ministry of Education, Culture, Sports, Science and Technology (MEXT) authorized junior high school history and civics textbooks compiled by the nationalist organization Atarashii rekikshi kyokasho o tsukurukai (Japanese Society for History Textbook Reform), commonly referred to as "Tsukurukai," and published by Fusosha. These texts glorified Japan's past war of aggression and omitted any mention of wartime "comfort women."[5] The civics textbooks emphasized "the significance of the home and family" and contained "a celebration of housework" by women.

In September 2001, the highly influential Nippon kaigi (Japan Conference), the largest nationalist group in Japan with a huge network made up of Shinto and other religious groups, as well as conservative politicians and academics, initiated a petition protesting a bill that would legalize the use of separate surnames by married couples. Proposed by opposition parties, the bill was eventually scrapped. The protesters called for reviving "family bonds," the so-called Japanese virtues, and national pride.

In November 2001, the neoconservative Tokyo governor Shintaro Ishihara issued his infamous "*babaa hatsugen*" (statement about old women). In the popular women's weekly magazine *Shukan josei* (Women's Weekly), Ishihara expressed support for a statement made by a planetary physicist in an article to the effect that "old women who no longer have the ability to reproduce are useless and their lives represent a crime against civilization." Such a comment would undoubtedly be considered political suicide in the US. Yet, despite the fact that Ishihara was sued for defamation (the plaintiffs subsequently lost the case), many women re-elected him to office in 2007. This came as a great shock to feminists because they could see that the idea of women's rights had not permeated public awareness in Japan, even among women.

In 2002, Eriko Yamatani (later named Prime Ministerial Aide of Shinzo Abe) launched a systematic attack on sex education in the House of Representatives' MEXT Committee. Since the 1990s, education specialists, doctors, and groups promoting gender equality had worked earnestly alongside junior and senior high school teachers to set up sex education programs in Japanese schools. As part of the basic gender equality education program, they aimed to prevent STDs, unwanted pregnancies, and abortions by promoting physical autonomy and "a woman's right to sexual self determination." However, in 2002, Yamatani and other Diet members attacked the "Love & Body Book," a sex-education pamphlet for junior high school students compiled by the Boshi eisei kenkyukai (Mothers, Children, and Families' Health Education Group) as "extremist pill education" because it contained information on birth control pills and abortion. It was eventually withdrawn from circulation.

In 2003, a number of local assembly members began to criticize sex education and a heated debate followed. In April of the same year, the opinion journal *Seiron* (Sound Argument) featured an article entitled "Background of the Ideal—Free Sex, Homosexuality and Extreme Sex Education" by Shiro Takahashi (then Chairman of the Japanese Society for History Textbook Reform). Although the Basic Plan for Gender Equality covers many general principles of gender equality, its critics focused on sex education. In July 2003, forty posters slandering sex education were put up in the city of Fukuoka, accusing the Basic Plan of "encouraging sex crimes." This claim was by no means trivial, since it appeared in the conservative journal *Nihon jiji hyoron* (Japan Publicist).

In the summer of 2003, members of the Tokyo Metropolitan Assembly who were critical of sex education visited the Nanao Tokyo Metropolitan

School for Handicapped Children, and claimed that its sex education program was "extremist." The intellectually disabled often become easy targets for sex offenders because of their innocence; hence the school was using dolls to teach students about body parts. The assembly members labeled these dolls "pornographic" and took photos, which they then released to the newspapers. Two months later, the Tokyo Metropolitan Government Board of Education reprimanded and/or demoted 102 principals and teachers at twenty-two schools, including the principal of the Nanao School for Handicapped Children.[6] Since then, teachers have become very reluctant to approach sex education.

Also in 2003, the mayor of Arakawa ward in Tokyo criticized gender equality education, claiming that "formalistic and perfunctory application of the theory of gender equality will destroy the family and the home, weaken the moral fiber, deny traditional culture, and render education ineffective. It therefore contains dangerous ideas that may lead to the destruction of Japanese society." In December, the mayor appointed several members of the Japanese Society for History Textbook Reform to the newly established Council for a Gender Equal Society in Arakawa ward. The group included Shiro Takahashi of Meisei University, Michiyoshi Hayashi of Tokyo Woman's Christian University, and Hidetsugu Yagi of Takasaki Economics University. These three men subsequently infiltrated local governments as critics of gender equality (Hayashi 2002; Takahashi 2002b, 2004a, 2004b).

Takahashi was elected to similar committees in Tokyo and Sendai Prefecture, and became a central spokesman at government-led meetings for educational reform following the establishment of the Abe cabinet in September 2006. One of the most influential backlash spokespersons, Takahashi graduated from Waseda University Graduate School, and was a visiting scholar at the Stanford University Hoover Institution. With his slogan "Breaking free from postwar education," he argued that moral degeneration in Japan stems from the rush to embrace individualism and the loss of traditional culture after Japan's defeat in World War II and the subsequent American Occupation. Takahashi aimed to effect a third educational reform by re-examining knowledge-biased Western education and postwar individualism in order to bring back the education of the inner soul and sensibility, and revive such institutions as the Family and the State. He stressed the need not only to educate children, but also to re-educate teachers and parents. Takahashi attempted to intervene in every aspect of education: schools, children, teachers, and textbooks. He has established re-training facilities for teachers as well as "parenting" centers to teach the correct way of parenthood. In Saitama Prefecture, he advocated that schools become a place for parenting programs.

According to Takahashi, parents are causing the degeneration of children and schools (e.g., truancy, juvenile delinquency). Family bonds, he says, have disappeared due to the absence of the father, and a nagging, interfering mother, since desirable role models for fatherhood and motherhood have been destroyed by misguided postwar education. Fathers should teach children a sense of order and rules, while mothers should nurture children. Fatherhood and motherhood, discipline and tenderness, must be divided between men and women. This division of gender roles must be kept intact (Oyagakkai, ed. 2004). It follows that these parents and their children form the foundation of the Nation. Therefore, Takahashi thoroughly attacks the teaching of home economics to both female and male students, as well as the content of home economics textbooks, and he decries the idea of "democracy within the family" and the "diversity of families." He proclaims, "Gender-free ideology will clearly bring about the destruction of culture, namely the home, the family, and the sense of community. We urgently need to start a national movement opposing the home economics textbooks" (Takahashi 2002a). Such arguments directly contradict the Basic Law and the policies for child rearing, child support, and child care by state and local governments.

Furthermore, Takahashi opposes the aim of sex education for sexual autonomy, a fundamental human right: "Behind the radical sex education with its emphasis on sexual autonomy lurks a dangerous ideology that aims to dismantle the community of Family and the State" (Takahashi 1994). Takahashi advocates "chastity education" (chastity until marriage, fidelity after marriage), and, based on this, criticizes the gender-free education program for sexual autonomy, and denies the right to the awareness of one's sexuality, information on STDs and contraception, as well as rights to reproductive health. He regards feminism and gender theory as the roots of all evil, claiming, "We should not overlook the fact that feminism is ideologically linked to radical sex education, which advocates sexual autonomy and human rights education."

In 2004, gender-free education came under growing siege. In February, the then Chief Cabinet Secretary Yasuo Fukuda declared to local governments that the term "gender-free" would not be used in government policies, citing a number of reasons. He said the term "lacked clarity of meaning, expressed biased opinion, and is not used in any official document domestically or internationally." According to the *Asahi shimbun* newspaper of May 2004, both the national and local governments "did a turn around and began suppressing" the movement to promote gender equality and gender-free education, which had been pursued after the Basic Law came into effect. For example, criticism against the concept of "gender-free" emerged at the

Four Metropolitan Governors' Council meeting (the governors of Tokyo, Chiba, Kanagawa, and Saitama prefectures) and the Chikugo City Council in Fukuoka Prefecture added special wording to regulations "to avoid mistaking the distinction between genders for gender discrimination."

In Japan, the term "gender-free" has been used since the 1990s to indicate freedom from a "gendered division of labor" as well as a description of "socio-culturally constructed male and female roles." However, this term came to be interpreted as "denying all physical differences between male and female" and to be attacked especially for "denying masculinity and femininity altogether." Earnest efforts of feminists to explain that such attacks are based upon misinterpretations have not been successful.

In 2004 the word "gender" was removed during the screening of junior high school home economics textbooks as "an expression that is highly prone to misinterpretation." On August 26 of the same year, the Tokyo Metropolitan Board of Education stated that "the term 'gender-free' should no longer be used in gender equality education," and that "students' name lists should not be gender-mixed based on the erroneous gender-free thinking which denies all forms of 'masculinity' and 'femininity.'" This statement shocked all educators who had been conducting gender equality education under the banner of "gender-free education," as well as feminists who had been working to promote the Basic Plan. The government's sudden move to ban the use of a term, and concept that had been in circulation for the past ten years, was an abnormality in a democratic society. There was not much opposition, however, from the general public, since the ban was carried out at the local government level by the Board of Education, which had jurisdiction over compulsory education. Furthermore, on the same day that this Board of Education banned the use of the term "gender-free," it also certified the use of a textbook compiled by the previously mentioned Japanese Society for Textbook Reform in metropolitan junior/senior-integrated high schools. In September of the same year, the Kanagawa Prefectural Board of Education also approved a proposal to avoid using the term "gender-free," saying "it is inappropriate as it categorically removes all differences between male and female."

In 2005, the various backlash groups that had been dispersed until then came together under the government's leadership and began an organized campaign with the launch of the "Extreme Sex Education and Gender-Free Education Survey Project" by the ruling Liberal Democratic Party. On May 26, a symposium and exhibition were held to reexamine issues regarding "extreme sex education" and gender-free education. Here, Eriko Yamatani declared that education is getting out of control in schools: "Unbelievable destruction of our children's' character is under way in disregard of their ages and level of maturity." Chief Cabinet Secretary Abe, who chaired the symposium, declared, "Those who promote the term gender-free categorically deny the value of marriage and the family. The Liberal Democratic Party is opposed to radical gender-free ideas. Not only the term 'gender-free,' but also the term 'gender' is prone to misinterpretation. . .Perhaps some abusive DNA is built into the Basic Law and therefore we also intend to review the Basic Law itself." Subsequently, the project team conducted a nationwide study collecting "extreme" and "inappropriate" examples of sex education. This campaign successfully fostered fear as well as a sense aversion to gender-free education.[7]

The effect of the study has been significant. In my (Wakakuwa's) nationwide lectures to promote new perspectives of gender, I have frequently seen ordinary citizens speak out furiously against schools conducting thoughtless education by "telling kids to bring condoms to school" and "teaching young children things they don't need to know yet." In response to this, sex education professionals Haruo Asai, Atsuko Tsuruta, Jun Koyasu, Aya Yamada, and Kazuko Yoshida, have countered with publications such as *Jendaa/sekushuaritii no kyoiku o tsukuru* (Creating Gender and Sexuality Education) (Asai, et al. 2006).

The "inappropriate cases" gathered by the project team largely dwelled upon how children were being taught "prematurely" about contraception and other aspects of sexuality. Other topics that were seized on as scandalous included "boys and girls changing into and out of gym clothes in the same classroom" and "boys and girls being made to pair up in certain competitive sport events." The latter charge proved false. The former was found to have been caused by the absence of locker rooms in Japanese public schools, rather than as a result of gender-free education. At the "Symposium on Gender" held on March 25, 2006, two women of the wartime generation,[8] Sayoko Yoneda and Mikiyo Kano, revealed that "girls were made to exercise shirtless during the war," and that "in both primary and secondary schools we never had separate changing rooms for girls and boys. Mixed changing rooms are a part of the true Japanese tradition"—all of which drew a roar of laughter from the audience. At the time, I (Wakakuwa) proposed that "Now is the time to push the government for funding to build changing rooms in public schools."

Into this growing vortex came the so-called "Kokubunji incident involving Professor Ueno." In the summer of 2005, the Kokubunji City Council in Tokyo decided to engage Chizuko Ueno of Tokyo University to give a keynote lecture titled, "Survey Research for the Promotion of Human Rights Education," as part of a project commissioned by the Ministry of Education. The Head of the Sports-for-All Division of the Tokyo Metropolitan Government Board of Education Secretariat voiced his apprehension, however, that Ueno, as an authority on "Women's Studies" would most likely use the banned term "gender-free" in her lectures and was therefore not an appropriate choice. As a result, Kokubunji retracted their original invitation to Ueno. Gender studies scholars protested to the Tokyo Metropolitan Government offices on January 27, 2006, with a petition signed by nearly 2,000 scholars and citizens, declaring that the removal of Ueno was an infringement upon freedom of speech and thought. This incident demonstrated that the ideological control exerted by the Board of Education was not limited to school teachers, and roused a sense of urgency among academic researchers and gender studies educators regarding the threat of censorship. As a result, there was a nationwide chorus of protest not only from university scholars, but also from educators, politicians, citizens, journalists, and various other groups actively engaged in promoting the Basic Plan. This triggered the formation of a wide-ranging network "Against the Gender Backlash," the first meeting of which took place at the above-mentioned "Symposium on Gender" held on March 25, 2006. A report that collected the opinions of citizens and educators was also published as *Jendaa no kiki o koeru* (Overcoming the Crisis of Gender) (Wakakuwa, et al. 2006). This symposium marked a significant turning point, pulling feminist scholars out of their university research centers and from behind their desks to work together with other women and educators in a joint countermovement to fight the progressively erosive backlash.

Still, the backlash continued its movement. In May 2006, the Fukui Lifelong Learning & Women's Center removed one hundred and fifty publications related to feminism and sex education from the Center's 2,600-volume library because a prefectural assembly member for Gender Equality Promotion objected that "the content of some books is too radical." The authors of those publications joined with Fukui prefecture citizen representatives in protest and appealed to the Cabinet Minister for Gender Equality.

Another significant initiative was taken in June 2006, when the cabinet headed by Prime Minister Junichiro Koizumi drew up the policies of the "'National Movement to Restore Family and Community Links in Support of Child Rearing." Specific measures included the establishment of a "Day of the Family" (November 8) and a "Family Week" (November 11-24). Certain events were to be held by state and local governments to build ties within the family and with the local community. The creation of a national movement was to bring about changes in attitudes of worker and management regarding lifestyles, such as to emphasize the value of children and human life generally. While some of these goals may have been admirable, feminists and other educators have held strong reservations about these initiatives, since they were reminiscent of policies carried out by the totalitarian state that existed in pre-World War II Japan.

With the ascension of Shinzo Abe to the office of prime minister in September 2006, the backlash movement gained further momentum. Since Abe was a key figure among neoconservatives, the policy of the government became antigender *per se* as members of the backlash were granted positions within the government or on various policy-making committees. Its policies were driven by their ideology, the keywords of which were the "family" and the "state," with "education" linking the two. Under Abe's leadership, a number of councils and groups promoting the backlash emerged. Abe sought to implement all of these policies with the aim of constructing a totally conservative state by nurturing the next generation of citizens and strengthening the family, teaching children to be patriotic, making the home a place for their instruction, as well as making women mothers and men fathers.

Abe set up a key strategy council called Kodomo to kazoku o oensuru Nihon (Japan Supporting Children and Families) to address the issue of the declining birthrate, and included among its members the Chief Cabinet Secretary, Minister of State for Measures to address the Declining Birthrate, Minister of Education, Culture, Sports, Science and Technology, Minister of State for Economic and Fiscal Policy, the Minister of Health, Labor and Welfare, and the Minister of Economy, Trade and Industry. At a meeting of the council held on April 27, 2007, one of the members, Michiko Hasegawa—a professor at Saitama University and one of the most outspoken female critics of the Basic Plan for Gender Equality—presented a report describing how to link policies addressing the declining birthrate to achieve an effective work-life balance. Her report declared that an ideal work-life balance could be secured only by regarding the nuclear family as the basic unit. This would be easily achieved were men to work as full-time salaried employees and women to dedicate themselves to child rearing as full-time housewives. Were women to work outside the home, her report maintained, the result would be work-life imbalance, since "women will always bear the burden of giving birth." In addition, she wrote, "Single-parent families are definitely at a disadvantage in terms of giving birth and raising children." In conclusion, she claimed that the Basic Plan contradicted the measures designed to counter the declining birthrate.

Even though Hasegawa's report did not solve the problem, the government continued to consider the question of work-life balance urgent, this time deciding to establish a special task force. "Public & Private Sector Joint Council for Promotion of Work-Life Balance" called upon representatives from management and labor organizations as well as local governments.

Still another governmental initiative launched in February 2007 was the Utsukushii Nippon o tsukurukai (Committee for Building a Beautiful Japan), whose conservative members created the slogan, "Working towards the Abolition of the Basic Law for a Gender-Equal Society." They opposed the Basic Law because its aim of promoting gender equality would "eliminate the distinctions between the sexes." Unconcerned that their view misinterprets gender theory, this committee aimed to revive a patriarchal state based on polarized male-female attributes and a gender-based division of labor.

The launch of the Committee for Building a Beautiful Japan was followed, in April 2007, by the founding of the Japan Family Value Society (FAVS), now a registered nonprofit organization. The chair was Tokyo Metropolitan Assembly member, Toshiaki Koga, and other governmental officials were prominent in its organization. FAVS's main objective was to promote a family-focused campaign after a spate of parent/child killings and the news of a rising divorce rate had brought family-related issues to the foreground. In his opening remark, Chairman Koga stated, "After the war, the Allied Forces implemented a thorough policy to weaken our nation. As a result, we witness today the disturbing trend to disregard the family and the state." With regard to the yearly suicide rate of approximately thirty thousand, he claimed, "If families are strong and more secure, people will think twice before committing suicide." He called for a practical campaign that focused on protecting the family bond, and added, "We should appeal for the prevention of divorce, which causes child abuse and wounds our children's hearts."

Suicide in Japan is caused largely by difficulties in making ends meet in the case of adults and, in the case of children, the negative effects of a knowledge-biased and uniform education system with categorical emphasis on academic performance. That is, "the logic of the fittest" in the adult world also ravages the world of children. A simplistic reduction of all these problems to "family responsibility" drew opposition from the general public. Moreover, no verifiable data could be found to support the claim that child abuse is caused by divorce. A number of factors are indeed involved in child abuse, including financial difficulties and psychological problems. Their resolution lies in initiatives by the child welfare office to separate the abuser from the children and to provide adequate counseling for the abusers. Attempting to resolve such serious family problems by "preventing divorce" is totally retrogressive.

One must note that it has been impossible to sensibly debate with FAVS, since it aims to prevent women from exercising freedom of choice with respect to their lives and careers. According to this group, a criticism of "gender-free" is insufficient; one must eliminate the Basic Plan itself, and for many reasons. It would destroy our country's bi-gendered culture; it would destroy the traditional family structure by imposing state power over the private sphere of the family; it would encourage women to work and thus accelerate the problem of the declining population; and it would increase the risk of domestic violence and child abuse by denying the separate spheres of masculinity and femininity. Ultimately, however the government might claim that the Basic Plan neither "neutralizes the male and the female," "denies masculinity and femininity," nor "puts down the identity of housewives," the committee rejects these statements and the Basic Plan as deceptions that belie the government's actions. FAVS claims, "It is a false notion of gender equality that aims only to expand women's rights. Japan has no future unless we abolish or rewrite the Basic Law for a Gender-Equal Society with a correct gender-equal perspective." Following such views, the organization has declared opposition, for example, to ratifying the Optional Protocol to the Convention on the Elimination of All Forms of Discrimination against Women (CEDAW), which gives individuals and groups of women the right to directly lodge complaints of rights violations to the CEDAW Committee. Needless to say, FAVS also opposes the revision of the civil code, which, among other provisions, would give married coupes the choice of retaining separate surnames.

The most important keywords of the Abe Cabinet were "educational reform," and its spotlight was on "education in the home." To this end, in October 2006, immediately upon taking office, Abe established the Kyoiku saisei kaigi (Educational Rebuilding Council), composed of the Prime Minister, Chief Cabinet Secretary, the Minister of Education, Culture, Science and Technology, and seventeen experts from business, academia, and government. The First Report of the Council (chaired by Ryoji Noyori, 2001 Nobel Prize laureate in chemistry), submitted in January 2007, included a proposal for "parenting education." Shiro Takahashi was the instrumental figure behind this proposal, supported and advocated by Prime Ministerial Aide Eriko Yamatani. The report focused on "child rearing instructions" with such recommendations as "sing lullabies, breastfeed, peer into the eyes of infants," "no television at mealtimes," and "early to bed, early to rise, eat breakfast." Opposition from many fronts, including cabinet members, such as the then Minister of Education, Culture, Sports and Technology, Bunmei Ibuki, who criticized such "condescending instructions" that "impose specific values" and "intrude into family life," as well as ordinary working women, educators, and experts in child rearing, resulted in the eventual exclusion of this proposal from the Council's First Report. The Second Report of the Council, submitted in June 2007, presented a more toned-down version with a view to the upcoming election for the House of Councillors (or Upper House of the National Diet) in July 2007. The recommendation stated in the Report was to "Aim at a society that supports parental learning and child rearing—promote relevant moral education through the cooperation of schools, families, and communities, enhance support for education at home and parenting counseling. . . ." (Education Rebuilding Council 2007).

The Second Report, however, also contained a proposal to incorporate "*tokuiku*" (moral education) into the compulsory education curriculum: "Give all children a strong sense of discipline—Designate moral education as a school subject and seek its enhancement compared with current 'moral education classes'" (Ibid.) According to Prime Ministerial Aide Yamatani, "Its major pillar is to incorporate moral education into the compulsory education curriculum as a subject. Children will learn such essential life skills as honesty, kindness, diligence and parental respect, both at home and in the community."

Prime Minister Abe abruptly resigned from office in September 2007 soon after his party suffered a major defeat in the July Upper House elections, and his support rating plunged amidst a row over pensions and a series of financial scandals involving some of his cabinet ministers. His replacement, fellow LDP member Yasuo Fukuda, though basically a conservative, had held the post of Minister of State for Gender Equality from 2001 to 2004 while serving as Chief Cabinet Secretary under Prime Minister Koizumi, and he was to some extent sympathetic to the cause of gender equality. After the Education Rebuilding Council submitted its Third Report in December of 2007, and its final report in January 2008, to Fukuda, the council was dissolved, to be replaced in February by a committee called the Kyoiku saisei kondankai (Meeting on Education Rebuilding). Fukuda also resigned after one year in office in September 2008, and another member of the LDP, Taro Aso, replaced him. The global financial crisis that ensued soon after Aso took office became the overriding issue during his year in office, which ended with the historic defeat of his party by the DPJ in the House of Representatives election of August 2009. In November 2009, the new government dissolved this committee.

Though the backlash movement's visibility diminished somewhat following the departure of Prime Minister Abe, its undercurrent has remained strong, as the following examples demonstrate.

Opposition to the Domestic Violence Prevention Law

The revised Law for the Prevention of Spousal Violence and the Protection of Victims (known as the DV Prevention Law), which went into effect in

January 2008, placed greater responsibility on national and local governments to prevent violence and to provide protection and support to victims, including the establishment of counseling and support centers. Various conservative groups, among them the DV boshiho gisei kazoku shien no kai (Association Supporting Families Victimized by the Domestic Prevention Law) and Shuken kaifuku o mezasukai (Society to Seek Restoration of Sovereignty), have attacked the law, characterizing it as a "display of radical feminism" that would "lead to the breakdown of families."

An incident that drew national attention was the last minute cancellation by the municipal government of Tsukubamirai in Ibaraki Prefecture of a lecture on domestic violence scheduled to be given by Kazuko Hirakawa, head of the Tokyo Feminist Therapy Center and a member of the Expert Examination Committee of the Cabinet Office's Gender Equality Council in January 2008. Through emails and faxes, opposition groups called on the city government officials to cancel the lecture, accusing Hirakawa of being "ideologically biased." Four days before the scheduled event these opponents held demonstrations in front of the city hall chanting slogans, and on the same day the mayor made the decision to cancel the lecture. Tsukubamirai City's giving in to intimidation by opponents threatens to weaken the foundation of the DV Prevention Law under which local governments are entrusted with prime responsibility for providing support for victims and ensuring protection for victims, their families, and supporters. Concerned groups and individuals, including the Asia-Japan Women's Resource Center (AJWRC), conducted a signature-petition campaign through the Internet and other media, submitting over 2,600 signatures to protest the city's cancellation of the lecture and to seek to re-open proceedings ("Lecture on DV canceled. . ." 2008, 38).

As many feared, this incident led to a number of similar incidents. In the same month, a public high school in neighboring Tsukuba cancelled a class dealing with date violence that was to be conducted by a nonprofit organization, apparently fearing similar protests (Ibid.). Opponents of the DV Prevention Law also sought to prevent a lecture by Hirakawa sponsored by Nagaoka in Niigata Prefecture, sending one hundred or so protest emails and faxes to the city office. In this case city officials stood firm, and the gathering was held as scheduled, but several members of the above-mentioned Association Supporting Families Victimized by the Domestic Prevention Law showed up and made unruly comments. The fear many held was that the prospect of similar protests might well inhibit local governments and other bodies from hosting events dealing with domestic violence (Ueno 2008).

"Comfort Women" As a Feminist Issue

The Japanese government has been repeatedly criticized by United Nations bodies, most recently by the Convention on the Elimination of Discrimination against Women (CEDAW) Committee for its failure to "find a lasting solution" for the situation of the so-called "comfort women" who were victimized under the Japanese military's system of sexual slavery during the Second World War. Specifically the CEDAW Committee has criticized the government's refusal to accept legal responsibility for the systematic abuse of "comfort women," and for failing to prosecute perpetrators, provide compensation to victims, and educate school children and the general public about this history. The CEDAW Committee has also noted that some politicians and members of the mass media continue to defame victims or to deny that the events ever occurred (UN CEDAW 2009; also UN Human Rights Committee 2008). Cabinet members and important politicians, including former prime ministers Abe and Aso, have repeatedly made statements denying such historical facts as the coercion involved in the "comfort women" system.

In the face of the government's continued refusal to act in accordance with the recommendations made by UN bodies, a number of city councils throughout Japan have taken the initiative of passing resolutions calling on the government to take required measures. Takarazuka in Hyogo Prefecture was the first to pass such a resolution in March 2008, and by December 2009, twelve more cities had passed similar resolutions ("City Councils Call. . ."2009; "Sennanshi, Kokubunjishi. . ." 2009). An alarming incident took place in the summer of 2009 when Mitaka (in Tokyo), which had recently passed such a resolution, announced a scheduled exhibit at the city center planned by a local citizens' group designed to teach teenagers about the "comfort women." Claiming that the "comfort women" were "paid prostitutes," and that Mitaka should not be providing space to "teach children about prostitution and pornography," the racist, nationalist groups Zaitokukai (Association Not to Allow Foreigners to Enjoy Privileges in Japan) and the aforementioned Society to Seek Restoration of Sovereignty sought to prevent the city from holding the event. During the exhibit held in August (which was reduced from a week to three days), over one hundred members of Zaitokukai blocked the entrance to the city center, intimidating visitors with racist and sexist remarks and in some cases threatening visitors with physical force. Although about four hundred people managed to get in and view the exhibit, AJWRC's Hisako Motoyama points out that ". . . the Mitaka City authority and the police failed to act adamantly against this most violent attack on citizens and the mass media maintained silence, which is [a] worrisome sign for civil liberty in Japanese society." Part of the problem, Motoyama points out, is that "There is no law in Japan prohibiting speech or deeds that may promote discrimination" (Motoyama 2009, 33-4).

A similar incident occurred the same month in Toyama, where the mayor withdrew sponsorship at the last minute of an event on the theme "Reflecting on war and women's human rights," declaring, "My position is that the 'comfort women' did not exist . . . " Although the event was held as scheduled, subsequently the steering committee submitted a letter of protest to the mayor demanding an explanation for taking an action that amounted to yielding to protest from certain groups and violating the freedom of thought, expression, and gathering ("Toyama-shi dewa koen torike-shi" 2009; Horie 2009).

Related to these attempts by rightist nationalist groups to block efforts to bring the issue of the "comfort women" to public attention is the rise in the number of schools throughout Japan adopting textbooks compiled by the conservative, nationalist organization Tsukurukai (Japanese Society for History Textbook Reform) mentioned earlier, which, among other things, omits any reference to the "comfort women." The Education Ministry authorized junior high school history and civics textbooks compiled by Tsukurukai and published by Fusosha in 2001, and again in 2005, and the textbooks were adopted for use in a number of schools throughout the country.[9]

This created a ripple effect on other textbook publishers. Up until 1993, when the then Chief Cabinet Secretary Yohei Kono issued an official statement (the "Kono Statement"), which acknowledged the involvement of the government and military of Japan, and the use of force in the "comfort women" system none of the textbooks included references to this fact, but by 1997 references had appeared in all seven textbooks authorized by the Ministry of Education, Culture, Sports, Science and Technology and Science for use in junior high schools. Since then, however, references to the "comfort women" issue have gradually disappeared, to the point where in the textbooks used in 2006, the phrase "comfort women" was completely erased, and weakened descriptions remained in only two textbooks.

A liaison group campaigning to have references to the "comfort women" restored to junior high school history textbooks has collected several thousand signatures from groups and individuals, and approached a number of textbook publishers with their request (Yamashita 2009).

Conclusion

In its concluding observations concerning the Japanese government's report to the CEDAW Committee in 2009 referred to earlier, the UN's Committee formally expressed its concern about "the reported 'backlash' against the recognition and promotion of women's human rights in the State party, despite the persistence of inequality between women and men" and "the persistence of patriarchal attitudes and deep-rooted stereotypes regarding the roles and responsibilities of women and men in the family and in society in Japan, which threaten to undermine women's exercise and enjoyment of their human rights." It called upon the government to take proactive and sustained measures, including "enhanc[ing] education and in-service training of the teaching and counseling staff of all educational establishments, and at all levels with regard to gender equality issues," and "speedily complet[ing] a revision of all educational textbooks and materials to eliminate gender stereotypes." The committee also expressed alarm over "the high incidence of gender discriminatory statements and sexist remarks made by public officers and the lack of steps taken to prevent and punish verbal violence against women," and urged the Japanese government to "take measures, including the criminalization of verbal violence, to ensure that Government officials do not make disparaging remarks that demean women and contribute to the patriarchal system which discriminates against women" (UN CEDAW 2009).

Japan has no specific legislation on antidiscrimination or violations of human rights, and no independent national institution outside the government to ensure the protection and promotion of human rights. The UN Human Rights Commission as well as the CEDAW Committee have repeatedly called on the Japanese government to establish such an institution (in accordance with the Paris Principles, General Assembly resolution 48/134, annex) that has a mandate to consider and act on complaints of human rights violations by public authorities, and to allocate adequate financial and human resources to the institution. In addition, the Japanese government has yet to ratify the Optional Protocol to CEDAW, referred to previously.

In its 2009 election manifesto, the Democratic Party of Japan (DPJ) pledged to establish a "Human Rights Violations Relief Agency" as an extra-ministerial agency of the cabinet office, and also to ratify the optional protocols to the relevant human rights treaties. The DPJ manifesto did not mention the "comfort women" issue, but it did set forth the objective of making "the greatest possible effort to develop relations of mutual trust with China, South Korea, and other Asian countries" (Democratic Party of Japan 2009).

Soon after assuming leadership of the newly formed coalition government, Prime Minister Yukio Hatoyama spoke of establishing an "East Asia community" through strengthening cooperation in various fields. As he himself implied, this cannot be achieved without achieving reconciliation with the Asian neighbors on whom Japan inflicted suffering during World War II. Diet members from the DPJ, the Social Democratic Party, and the Communist Party held a gathering in October 2009, and pledged to cooperate in proposing a bill to promote a resolution to the "comfort women" issue, which would include provision to make public compensation to the surviving women (Shoji 2009). Such a bill had failed to be passed by the Diet while the conservative Liberal Democratic Party dominated it.

On another issue, the newly appointed Justice Minister in the Hatoyama cabinet, Keiko Chiba announced her intention to introduce to the Diet a bill to amend the civil code, which, as mentioned earlier, would give married coupes the option of retaining separate surnames. Mizuho Fukushima, leader of one of the DPJ's coalition partners, the Social Democratic Party, who was appointed Minister of State for Consumer Affairs and Food Safety, Social Affairs, and Gender Equality in the Hatoyama cabinet, had long advocated these measures (see profile of Fukushima in chapter 25 of this volume). Fukushima's tenure in the Hatoyama Cabinet was cut short when Hatoyama dismissed her from the cabinet in May 2010 for her refusal to support a resolution on relocating a US airbase within the Japanese island of Okinawa. In June of the same year Kan Naoto of the DPJ replaced Hatoyama as prime minister. The extent to which the Kan government can or will take decisive action in regard to these and other gender-related issues, however, is questionable given not only strong opposition from backlash groups and conservative elements in the opposition LDP, but also the fact that the DPJ itself includes several conservative members who share similar ideologies.

In order to resist attempts to reverse the progress that has been made toward promoting a more gender-equal society, and in order to press for strengthening reforms to resolve remaining issues, it will be essential that all women's groups forge strong, broad networks that include advocacy and support groups for ethnic and sexual minority women, single mothers, migrant women, trafficked women, and women with handicaps. Working together, they must establish channels for cooperation and communication so that they can mobilize to make demands and exert pressure when crises or controversies develop that affect any of them. These efforts may pave the way for a revitalization of the feminist movement that began in Japan in the early 1970s.

   Internationally, the scale of this struggle is larger than ever before, and is inevitably meeting headstrong resistance. Unlike many previous revolutions, this one involves no violence or bloodshed. It is a political struggle that ultimately requires political reform of the customs and system established by the sex that has long held privileges and power. Important issues that remain to be addressed include promoting equality in the field of policy determination (raising Japan's standing in terms of the Gender Empowerment Measure), equality in the workplace, in the home, in sexuality (to eliminate compulsory heterosexuality), and in creative cultural spheres. All these are already specified in the international and domestic laws for gender equality. We must join hands and work together throughout all spheres, both domestic and international, in order to protect the Basic Law for a Gender-Equal Society, and to realize all the reforms and policies that support it.

Notes

1. Yasukuni Shrine is a Shinto shrine in Tokyo dedicated to worship the soldiers and others who died fighting on behalf of the Emperor of Japan. The shrine's history museum contains accounts justifying Japan's actions in World War II. Visits to the shrine by prime ministers and cabinet members have been a source of national controversy and protests abroad, especially after Class A war criminals condemned by the Tokyo International War Tribunal were enshrined there in 1985.

2. Article 9 of the Japanese Constitution, which came into effect on May 3, 1947, prohibits an act of war by the state, and also forbids Japan from maintaining an army, navy, or air force. Under Prime Minister Koizumi the drive began to change this pacifist clause, and in May 2007, under Prime Minister Abe, the Diet passed legislation to hold a national referendum to revise the constitution and amend Article 9.

3. Under Prime Minister Abe, the Fundamental Law of Education (referred to also as the Basic Act on Education), which was established in 1947, setting forth the basic principles and doctrines of education in postwar Japan, was amended despite strong opposition in 2006. Of particular significance was the addition, among "educational aims," of the importance of instilling "respect for tradition and culture" and "love for our nation and homeland," and the deletion of Article 5 (Coeducation) which stated, "Men and women shall esteem and cooperate with each other. Coeducation, therefore, shall be recognized in education." The CEDAW Committee, in its concluding observations on Japan's report to the committee in 2009, expressed concern over the removal of Article 5, and recommended its reintegration in the law.

4. In 1999, the controversial Law Concerning the National Flag and Anthem was promulgated, designating the flag and anthem—both considered by many as a symbol of Japan's imperialist, militaristic past—as Japan's national flag and anthem, and the display of the flag and singing of the anthem was made obligatory at school ceremonies.

5. Criticism of these textbooks and factual errors contained in them are taken up in Oguma and Ueno 2003; Rekishigaku kenkyukai 2005; Kyokasho ni jiyu o renrakukai 2005; Kodomo to kyokasho zenkoku netto 2005. With regard to gender issues see Kano

and Yasumaru 2001; Wakakuwa 2001, 2005). An early work that primarily critiques Japanese denials of the "comfort women" issue and the Rape of Nanjing is VAWW-NET Japan 2001.

6. The Tokyo District Court ruled on March12, 2009, that interference by the three members of the Tokyo Metropolitan Assembly violated Article 10 of the Fundamental Law of Education (1947) which states "Education shall not be subject to improper control," and ordered the three members and the Assembly to pay two million one hundred thousand yen (roughly $21,000) in damages to the thirty-one former teachers who had brought suit against them.

7. The survey conducted by the Liberal Democratic Party was called "Prefectural breakdown of extreme sex education cases" ("*Kagekina seikyoiku kenbetsu jirei*"). See also Hayashi and Yamamoto 2005; Asai, et al. 2003. Major feminist discussions on the backlash include Kimura (2005); Ueno, ed. (2006); Nihon josei gakkai jendaa kenkyu-kai, ed. (2006); Wakakuwa, et al., eds. (2006).

8. Refers mainly to those born in the 1920s and 30s, who spent their adolescent years during the Sino-Japanese War.

9. In April 2009, the Ministry of Education approved textbooks put out by another publisher (Jiyusha), also compiled by Tsukurukai, the contents of which are basically the same as those put out by Fusosha. While the percentage of schools that have adopted textbooks compiled by Tsukurukai make up a small percentage of the total, the fact that their numbers have grown is alarming ("Yokohama-shi, Suginami-ku, Tokyo-to nadode ..." 2009, 41-42).

Works Cited

Asai, Haruo, et al. 2003. *Jendaa furii sei kyoiku basshingu* (Bashing of gender-free sex education). Tokyo: Otsuki shoten.

———.2006. *Jendaa/sekushuaritii no kyoiku o tsukuru—basshingu o koeru chi no keiken* (Creating gender/sexuality education—experiencing knowledge that transcends gender-bashing). Tokyo: Akashi shoten.

"City Councils Call for the Government's Sincere Apology to 'Comfort Women' Victims." 2009. *Women's Asia 21—Voices from Japan*, no. 23 (September): 33.

Democratic Party of Japan. 2009. "2009 Change of Government The Democratic Party of Japan's Platform for Government—Putting People's Lives First." www.dpj.or.jp

Education Rebuilding Council. 2007. *Second Report: Education Rebuilding by Society as a Whole—A Further Step toward the Rebuilding of the Public Education System and the Reconstruction of the Basis for a New Era of Education.* June 1. http://www.kantei. go.jp/jp/singi/kyouiku/houkoku/eibun0601.pdf

Faludi, Susan. 1991, rev. ed. 2006. *Backlash: The Undeclared War Against American Women.* New York: Three Rivers Press. Translated into Japanese by Yukiko Ito and Makiko Kato. 1994. Tokyo: Shinchosha.

Hayashi, Michiyoshi. 2002. "Danjo byodo ni kakusareta kakumei senryaku: kazoku/ dotoku hakai shiso no haigo ni ugomekumono" (The hidden revolution strategy behind gender equality: What lurks behind ideologies that destroy the family and morality). *Seiron* (Sound Argument) (August).

——— and Akira Yamamoto. 2005. *Kokoga okashii danjo kyodo sankaku—bososuru "jendaa" to "kageki na seikyoiku"* (What's wrong with the Plan for Gender Equality—uncontrollable gender policies and extreme sex education). Tokyo: Sekai nipposha.

Horie, Setsuko. 2009. "'Puchi Ishihara' no Toyama shicho o yurusanai!" (We cannot excuse the actions of the 'petit Ishihara' Toyama mayor). *Wam dayori* (News from Women's Active Museum on War and Peace) 13 (November): 13.

Kano, Mikiyo and Yoshio Yasumaru. 2001. "Kindai no josei, kazoku, jendaa o do egaite irunoka" (How are modern women, family and gender depicted?). In *Rekishi kyokasho nani ga mondaika* (What is problematic about history textbooks?), ed. Yoichi Komori, et al. Tokyo: Iwanami shoten.

Kimura, Ryoko. 2005. *Jendaa furii toraburu* (Gender-free trouble). Tokyo: Hakutakusha.

Kodomo to kyokasho zenkoku netto (Children and textbooks nationwide network), ed. 2005. *Kokoga mondai "tsukurukai kyokasho" Tsukurukai shinpan rekishi/komin kyokasho hihan* (The problems of Tsukurukai's textbooks—criticism of Tsukurukai history and civic textbooks, new edition). Tokyo: Otsuki shoten.

Komori, Yoichi, Yoshikazu Sakamoto, and Yoshio Yasumaru, eds. 2001. *Rekishi kyokasho nani ga mondaika* (What is problematic about history textbooks?). Tokyo: Iwanami shoten.

Kyokasho ni shinjitsu to jiyu o renrakukai (Liason group for truth and freedom in textbooks), ed. 2005. *Tettei hihan—kokumin no rekishi—* (Thorough criticism—history of the people—). Tokyo: Otsuki shoten.

"Lecture on DV cancelled in face of protests." 2008. *Women's Asia 21—Voices from Japan*, no. 20 (Winter): 38

Meeting on Education Rebuilding. 2009. *Third Report Summary of Discussion*. February 9. http://www.kantei.go.jp/jp.singi/kyouiku_kondan/houkoku/singi-matome3-eiyaku.pdf

Motoyama, Hisako. 2009. "Rightist group violently attacked 'comfort women' exhibition." *Women's Asia 21—Voices from Japan*, no. 23 (September): 33-34.

"Naze kuni ga 'katei kyoiku'—kyoiku saisei kaigi, dainiji hokokuan" (Why is the State proposing 'family education'? — second report of the Education Rebuilding Council). 2007. *Asahi shimbun* (Asahi newspaper). May 19.

Nihon josei gakkai jendaa kenkyukai (The Women's Studies Association of Japan, Gender Studies Group). 2006. *Q&A Danjo kyodo sankaku/jendaa-furii basshingu—bakkurasshu e no tettei hanron* (Q&A on gender equality/gender-free bashing—refuting the backlash). Tokyo: Akashi shoten.

Ogino, Miho. 2001. *Chuzetsu ronso to amerika shakai—karada o meguru senso* (The abortion debate and American society—the war concerning the body). Tokyo: Iwanami shoten.

Oguma, Eiji and Yoko Ueno. 2003. *"Iyashi" no nashonarizumu—kusanone hoshu undo no jisshoteki kenkyu* (Nationalism for "healing"—an empirical study of grassroot conservative movements). Tokyo: Keio gijuku daigaku shuppankai.

Oyagakkai, ed. 2004. *Oyagaku no susume—taiji, nyuyojiki no kokoro no kyoiku* (An encouragement of parenting—spiritual education during the fetal, infant and childhood period). Supervised by Shiro Takahashi. Kashiwashi: Institute of Moralogy.

Rekishigaku kenkyukai (Research group on history), ed. 2005. *Rekishi kenkyu no genzai to kyokasho mondai—"tsukurukai" kyokasho o tou* (Current study of history and the school textbook debate—questioning the textbooks of Tsukurukai). Tokyo: Aoki shoten.

"Sennanshi, Kokubunjishi, Nagaokakyoshi, Funabashishi de 'ianfu' ketsugi o saitaku" (Resolutions on the "comfort women" adopted in Sennan, Kokubunji, Nagaokakyo, and Funabashi cities). *Onnatachi no nijuisseiki* (Women's Asia 21) no. 60 (December): 55.

Shoji, Rutsuko. 2009. "Shinseiken ni kitaisuru" (Our expectations for the new govern-
    ment). *Wam dayori* (News from Women's Active Museum on War and Peace) 13
    (November): 1.
Takahashi, Shiro. 1994. *Machigaidarake no kyushinteki seikyoiku* (The gross mistakes of
    radical sex education). Tokyo: Reimei shobo.
——. 2002a. "Faros o tamete kuni tatazu" (Bending the phallus won't erect the nation).
    Shokun! (June).
——. 2002b. "Hijojitaini ochiitta Nippon—jichitai to kyoikugenba de shinkosuru
    bunkadaikakumei" (Japan in a state of emergency—cultural revolution permeates
    local governments and the classroom). *Seiron* (Sound argument) (August).
——. 2004a. "Fusei/bosei ga oyagaku no genten" (Fatherhood/motherhood are the
    point of departure for parenting studies). In *Oyagaku no susume—taiji, nyuyojiki no
    kokoro no kyoiku* (An encouragement of parenting—spiritual education during the
    fetal, infant and childhood period), ed. Oyagakkai. Supervised by Shiro Takahashi.
    Kashiwashi: Institute of Moralogy
——. 2004b. "Oyagaku no gendaiteki igi" (The contemporary significance of parenting
    studies). In *Oyagaku no susume—taiji, nyuyojiki no kokoro no kyoiku* (An encour-
    agement of parenting—spiritual education during the fetal, infant and childhood
    period), ed. Oyagakkai. Supervised by Shiro Takahashi. Kashiwashi: Institute of
    Moralogy.
"Toyama-shi dewa koen torikeshi" (Lecture cancelled in Toyama City). *Onnatachi no
    nijuisseiki* (Women's Asia 21), no. 59 (September): 40.
Ueno, Chizuko. ed. 2006. *Bakkurasshu! naze jendaa furii wa tatakaretanoka* (Backlash!
    why has "gender-free" been attacked?). Tokyo: Sofusha.
——. 2008. "DV higai ni tsuite no koen ga totsujo chushi ni?! Tsukubamiraishi koen
    chushi to jendaa kogeki" (Sudden cancellation of lecture on damage caused by
    DV?! Cancellation of lecture in Tsukubamirai City and attack on gender). *Mu-shi
    no oto tsushin*, no. 66 (July 25): 8-11. http://www.ktroad.ne.jp/~tera-t/net/midori/
    news/66-2.html
UN CEDAW. 2009. "Concluding observations of the Committee on the Elimination
    of Discrimination against Women—Japan." (Advance unedited version) August 7.
    http://www2.ohchr.org/english/bodies/cedaw/docs/co/CEDAW.C.JPN.CO.6.pdf
UN Human Rights Committee. 2008. *Consideration of Reports Submitted by States Parties
    Under Article 40 of the International covenant on civil and political rights. Concluding
    observations of the Human Rights Committee - Japan.* December 18. http://daccess-
    dds-ny.un.org/doc/UNDOC/GEN/G09/401/08/PDF/G0940108.pdf?OpenElement
Violence against Women in War-Network Japan (VAWW-NET Japan), ed. 2001. *Koko-
    made hidoi! "Tsukurukai" rekishi/komin kyokasho—josei besshi/rekishi waikyoku,
    kokka shugi hihan* (Going way too far! Tsukurukai's history and civics textbooks—
    criticizing the contempt for women, distortion of history and nationalism). Tokyo:
    Akashi shoten.
Wakakuwa, Midori. 2001. "Jukyoteki kazoku kokkakan e no gyakko" (Retrogression into
    Confucian view of family and state). In *Rekishi kyokasho nani ga mondaika* (What
    is problematic about history textbooks?), ed. Komori, et al. Tokyo: Iwanami shoten.
——. 2005. "Tsukurukai kyokasho o jendaa no shitenkara hihansuru" (A critique of
    Tsukurukai's textbooks from a gender perspective). In *Rekishi kenkyu no genzai to
    kyokasho mondai—"tsukurukai" kyokasho o tou* (Current study of history and the
    school textbook debate—questioning the textbooks of Tsukurukai), ed. Rekishigaku
    kenkyukai. Tokyo: Aoki shoten.

———, Shuichi Kato, Masumi Minagawa, and Chieko Akaishi, eds. 2006. *Jendaa no kiki o koeru!—tettei toron! bakkurasshu* (Overcoming the crisis over gender—a thorough discussion of the backlash). Tokyo: Seikyusha.

Yamashita, Fumiko. 2009. "Chugaku rekishi kyokasho ni 'ianfu' kijutsu no fukkatsu o—koremade no koto to korekara ni mukete" (Restoring references to the 'comfort women' in junior high school history textbooks—movement up to now and future directions). *Wam dayori* (News from Women's Active Museum on War and Peace) 13 (November): 8.

"Yokohama-shi, Suginami-ku, Tokyo-to nadode 'tsukurukai' henshu kyokasho o saitaku" (Textbooks compiled by "Tsukurukai" adopted in Yokohama city, Suginami ward, and metropolitan Tokyo). *Onnatachi no nijuisseiki* (Women's Asia 21), no. 59 (Sept): 41-42.

The Politicization of Housewives

Yoko Kunihiro
Translated by Kimberly Hughes

Women did not gain the right to vote in Japan until just after the country's 1945 defeat in World War II. As a result, women's suffrage in Japan is often remarked to be a "gift from MacArthur," a reference to the American General Douglas MacArthur, who oversaw the Occupation of Japan by the Allied Powers following the end of World War II, and under whose supervision the liberation of women was pursued as one of the most important policies of Japan's democratization. According to Kazuko Sugawara, cabinet members at the time conjectured that the political participation of women, who could be expected to show moderation in their views and actions, would serve to suppress or offset the revolutionary movements that were visible in this chaotic postwar period. Women's forays into politics, in other words, occurred amid the disorder of Japan's wartime defeat, as well as the intricate bargaining that was taking place between those striving to put in place Occupation policies and domestic forces who wished to see the imperial system continue (Sugawara 2002). At the same time, however, the foundation of the movement for women's suffrage—which had begun in the Meiji period, forged among women's groups—must not be minimized. Women activists, including Fusae Ichikawa and others, continued to bring the concerns of women to the political forefront (Shindo 2004).

For the elections of 1946, seventy-six women announced their candidacy to seats in the Lower House (House of Representatives) of the National Diet and thirty-nine were elected.[1] Although the 67.8 percent of women who voted was around ten percent less than the figure for men (78.5 percent), it was nevertheless considerably higher than what had been anticipated. From then on to the 1980s, however, the number of female legislators in the National Diet remained quite low,[2] with only some ten women elected to the Lower House, representing a mere one to three percent of the total membership. Thus, the number of women elected to the Lower House in that first election, given subsequent history, was exceptional. It may be said, in fact, that the numbers of female members in the National Diet from then on up to the 1980s was abnormally low. Signs of improvement appeared from the 1990's, and the figure rose to 4.6 percent in the 1996 election, 7.3 percent in the 2000 election, 9 percent in the 2005 election, and 11.3 percent in the 2009 election—surpassing 10 percent for the first time. While women's representation in the Upper House (House of Councillors) of the Diet has been slightly higher compared to that in the Lower House, prior to 1986 women comprised less than 9 percent of its membership. The political world remained firmly male-dominated, in which the absence of women from the political decision-making process was taken for granted, even by researchers.[3]

Between 1955 and 1993, the Liberal Democratic Party (LDP) ruled continuously as the dominant political party. Political scientist Misako Iwamoto provides one explanation for the absence of women in both the LDP as well as the opposition parties, "The opposition Japan Socialist Party (JSP) and Democratic Party of Japan (DPJ) were essentially vacating seats for retiring labor union leaders in what is known as the system of 'amakudari' [literally "descent from heaven": an institutionalized practice whereby senior bureaucrats retire to take on high-level positions in the private and public sectors]" (Iwamoto 2003, 26). Since very few women reached these positions within the labor unions, seats in the legislature also continued to elude them.

Despite the fact that many single women (in addition to married ones) were employed at this time, the view that "women belong in the home" pervaded not only the workplace but also the political sphere. The minimal level of participation by women in politics, then, was a direct reflection of the prevailing dominant gender ideology. And while a number of female legislators from the LDP were elected to the Lower House during the 1960s and 1970s, women were completely invisible in national-level politics beginning in 1980 until the election of Seiko Noda in 1993.[4]

Changes between the 1980s and the First Decade of 2000

At the end of the 1980s, a change occurred in the National Diet whereby the opposition Socialist Party of Japan (SPJ)—as it was known until January 1996, at which time its name was changed to the Social Democratic Party (SDP)—attempted to regain its political strength. Rather than focus on labor unions, it sought to cultivate strong ties with ordinary citizens, and to do this work positioned female legislator Takako Doi as party head—a move that was termed the "Madonna strategy." For the Upper House election in 1989, Doi's candidates were elected all across the country. In all, twenty-two women were successful in this election (eleven of whom were from the SPJ). Given the fact that this election of women coincided with the reversal of the majority and minority parties in the Upper House, many people asserted that women indeed possessed the potential power to change politics. The Lower House election that followed in 1990 resulted in an increase in the number of female legislators from seven to twelve. Called the "Madonna Boom," this political revolution was thought able to end political corruption.

In 1993 the LDP's single party dominance collapsed, and it was forced to form a coalition government with non-LDP political parties. Three women were appointed to Prime Minister Morihiro Hosokawa's Cabinet—the largest number in history—as Ministers of Education, the Environment, and the Economic Planning Agency. From this time forward, female cabinet ministers were not unusual. In 1996, however, the LDP was restored to power and formed a single-party cabinet, quite willing to use women, despite their formal opposition to affirmative action policies, if so doing ensured the continuation of its rule. Second- and third-generation politicians, television newscasters, and female actors: such were the women with solid organized voting bases who were ushered into office on the LDP ticket. Party officials explained the reasoning behind this strategy in this way, "This is a merit system; we do not practice gender discrimination. If there are qualified women, we will put them forth as candidates. Unfortunately, however, there aren't many qualified women at this point."[5] The operative definition of "merit" in this case referred to voting blocs, visibility or name value, and funds.

The election system reform[6] that took place in 1996 did in fact end up contributing to a rise in the number of female legislators[7]. A total of twenty-three women were elected in the 1996 Lower House contest—seven in the single-member districts, and sixteen through proportional representation. While only two women from the LDP were elected through proportional representation that time, effective utilization of this system resulted in twenty-six women getting elected in the Lower House election of 2005, when Prime Minister Junichiro Koizumi recruited a variety of female candidates.

Teiko Kihira, a representative of the Japan's League of Women Voters, voiced criticism of these women—bureaucrats, professionals, and others, for being "quick to heed the orders of a man, i.e., Prime Minister Koizumi" (Ichikawa Fusae kinen kaikan 2005, 8). However, this action did, in fact, serve to weaken the LDP's stance of excluding women. Moreover, in a political climate that seemed to portend the beginnings of a two-party system consisting of the LDP and the DPJ (Democratic Party of Japan), the field of politics had become more open to women wishing to pursue politics as a career. While the political system had heretofore tended to use women expediently toward its own ends, this period saw increasing numbers of women do the same thing in reverse: utilize the realm of politics to further their own personal goals.

Participation of Women in Prefectural, Municipal, and Town/Village Assemblies

For many years, the number of women gaining a spot in their local assemblies was even lower than that of the National Diet. Considering the average figure for local councils taken as a whole, moreover, it seems clear that the number of women who have broken into politics remains low even today. The percentage of women in local assemblies only recently surpassed 10 percent (the figure was 10.6 percent as of December 2008).[8]

A data analysis of the 1999 nationwide local elections revealed that 100 percent of cities and wards with populations of one hundred thousand or more had at least one female assembly member. For smaller locales with populations between fifty thousand and one hundred thousand, the figure dropped to 94.7 percent; and for those between thirty thousand and fifty thousand, the figure dropped further to 63.9 percent. Among cities with smaller populations, many had no women in their local legislatures at all—a phenomenon found also at the town/village-level (Ichikawa Fusae kinen kaikan 1999a: 6). Oyama reports, moreover, that there is an inverse relationship between the percentage of women legislators at the prefectural level and the percentage of women in the child-rearing age group participating in the workforce (Oyama and Kunihiro 2007, 33).

Discriminatory gender-based norms are more firmly entrenched in communities where the traditional village model persists. Speaking from a cultural standpoint, then, in regions where politics and culture are strongly dominated by traditional standards of gender, women will have a harder time making inroads into political life than in regions where this is less true. This helps explain why the percentages of women in the Tokyo metropolitan ward assemblies were the highest from early on. While the urbanization of communities would appear to bear a causal relationship to the increase of women's political participation, in reality, however, no direct connection exists between the process of urbanization and that of the economic empowerment of women. With regard to married women, in fact, urbanization actually works to take away economic independence—a process that is in turn referred to as "housewife-ization."[9]

Politicized Housewives

It is widely acknowledged that urbanization brought along with it other phenomena such as the rise of *sarariiman* ("salarymen," or office workers) and the trend toward nuclear families, and of women becoming full-time housewives (Yazawa 1993). At the same time more women began to attain higher education and seek paid employment. Nevertheless, social and economic policies promoted urbanized lifestyles, in which men were the primary wage earners and married women the primary child rearers.[10] Unlikely though it may seem, this urban setting, excluding women from the labor market, turning even formerly employed women into housewives was, in my analysis, key to propelling women into the legislature.

Women's forays into legislative politics began with housewives in urban areas during the 1980s.[11] These housewives were not women whose activities were limited to the domestic sphere.[12] Many married women were involved in part-time work outside the home. The political consciousness of such women developed through their involvement in PTA-related activities, in courses on women's issues offered at community centers, and in work with *seikyo* (consumer cooperative groups). Subsequently such women created movements that revolved around issues of immediate concern to them such as education, gender discrimination, food additives, and rampant development leading to environmental destruction. They also created both domestic and international networks to combat environmental pollution and its rapid escalation into a global problem.

At this time, moreover, groups of women organizing across the country realized that their legislators were not hearing their concerns. Losing hope in local assembly members who were concerned exclusively with regional profits as subcontractors to the national government, these women's groups began electing members from within their own ranks instead (Kunihiro 2001, Kanda, Kimura and Noguchi 1992, Yazawa 1992, Sasakura, Nakajima and Sugawara 1990). Thus, the election of women to local assemblies in the larger cities and their environs was fueled largely by a cadre of housewives who were knowledgeable about social issues, and who had time for organizing. While somewhat ironic, then, the "housewife-ization" of women in these urban centers actually served to motivate them to enter politics.

The percentage of women in local assemblies within Kanagawa Prefecture was 20.1 percent, second only to the metropolitan Tokyo statistic of 22.8 percent. Kanagawa Prefecture also has a higher percentage of non-employment among women with young children than the national average, thereby serving as typical of a local government with a simultaneously low rate of employed women, and a high number of female assembly members.

Indeed, a portrait of Kanagawa Prefecture will be instructive for under-standing the post-1980s phenomenon whereby women's political participa-tion was essentially synonymous with the politicization of housewives.

The Case of the Kanagawa Network

Nuclear families comprised of *sarariiman* and full-time housewives living in and around large urban cities such as Tokyo, Kawasaki, and Yokohama (the latter two in Kanagawa Prefecture) often owned their own homes in areas known as "new towns"—prototypes for regions based upon a fixed, gender-based division of labor. These "new towns" had insufficient child-care facili-ties, and it was assumed that non-employed mothers would become involved with PTA activities. There were limited opportunities for women to re-enter the work force. Leading isolated lives in these communities, housewives, aware of social issues, sought out other like-minded women. Immersed in their communities twenty-four hours a day, while performing the unpaid labor of housework and child rearing, these women came into direct contact with such social concerns as environmental dangers and food safety.

The movement of these housewives into the political arena during the 1980s, however, did not occur spontaneously. This was the same period that marked a turning point in Japan's social movements, which had evolved with the labor unions at their base. When the men leading these unions realized that the capacity for their organizations to effect true social reform was limited, they went in search of community leaders organizing various social movements to join their cause. They "discovered" that these were in fact the non-employed married women living in these same communities, and recruited them as resources for their movement.[13]

The result was the establishment not of labor unions, but rather, con-sumer unions. The key word in this regard was not that of *shufu* (housewife), but rather *seikatsusha* (which may be loosely translated as "consumer" or "citizen"). As opposed to the strictly female category of *shufu*, *seikatsusha* was a gender-neutral term identifying the ideal citizen, female or male. For women, the idea of the *seikatsusha* was highly appealing, offering a new identity, not unfamiliar to women conscious of the ideals of gender equal-ity. Many of them had previous workplace experience, and had also rejected the behavior expected of traditional daughters-in-law, as well as the con-cept of *ryosai kenbo* (good wife and wise mother). These women preferred the term *seikatsusha* to that of *shufu*.

Joining newly organized consumers' cooperatives, such women were able to broaden their focus from that of a single family to the wider issues of their communities, and beyond, to such global issues as the environment.

At the time, however, existing local assemblies were run almost exclusively by men unconcerned with daily lives. When they failed to consider these issues, politically minded women began to elect women into office.

Following the 1983 municipal assembly election in the city of Kawasaki (in Kanagawa Prefecture), these women formed a local political party in 1984 known as the Kanagawa Network Movement (NET). Local branches were established in various jurisdictions around the prefecture, and certain regulations were laid down, namely, a limitation of two terms (eight years) for its assembly members, and a central administration of annual salaries.

Regional consumers' cooperatives served as NET's voting bloc, and volunteer supporters performed campaign activities. Having learned through experience that politics were part of daily life, it was not difficult for women to overthrow the idea that politics was a male domain. The husbands of these women were often not at home from morning until night, and some husbands lived away from the family because of assignments to a different location (*tanshin funin*). While it was therefore impossible in such circumstances for businessmen to be elected to office, paradoxically their wives could pave their own paths into the political playing field. NET continued to gain recognition for producing a steady succession of female candidates elected to office from among various local community associations.[14]

Organizations similar to NET also appeared in Tokyo, followed by other regions including Chiba, Saitama, Fukuoka, and Hokkaido. It bears noting, however, that NET remained almost exclusively separate from the women's movement, with suspicion existing on both sides. Feminists strongly criticized NET for being led by men, and accepting existing gender bias. It was true that NET did not criticize the system of gender-based division of labor, since that was the premise on which the movement itself was built. NET did not begin actively incorporating a gender-based policy analysis into its politics until the latter part of the 1990s, following the Fourth World Conference on Women (Kunihiro 2006). More recently, NET has cooperated with other local women's networks within the prefecture during elections.

Post-Beijing 1995: Increasing Moves to Send Women to the Legislature

Many Japanese women participated in the 1995 Fourth World Conference on Women held in Beijing, where they realized anew how few women there were in policy-making positions in Japan, compared to many other countries. Upon their return, these women began to encourage more women to run for political office. They also established a "school for politics," aimed at providing support for female candidates and their supporters, and organized a campaign around the principle of "no more prefectural legislatures with zero female representation!"

By 1999, with the help of local women's movements, there was a considerable rise in the number of women who ran and were elected at the prefectural level. While the percentage among the 3,299 local assemblies across the country reporting at least one female member reached 54.2 percent (an increase of 11.1 percentage points over the previous election), this still meant that nearly half of all local assemblies did not have a single female member (Ichikawa Fusae kinen kaikan 1999b, 13).

The elections of 2003 and 2007 resulted in increased numbers of female legislators. In fact, there had been some concern that the large number of municipal mergers taking place between 2000 and 2005 would have a negative impact on the proportion of elected female assembly members, since voting districts were enlarged while the numbers of local councils and their members were both reduced. Hiroko Kubo writes that this was not the case, however (Kubo 2006), since the widened districts and fewer number of legislators meant that it became more difficult to elect candidates by default. For women who were motivated to go into politics, this was a significant development.

While the number of female mayors and governors also increased, change in conservative regions was slow. Even within Kanagawa Prefecture, several areas (mostly in agricultural regions) had less than 10 percent female representation on their local councils. While Japan ranks relatively high on the United Nations' Human Development Index (HDI) and its Gender-related Development Index (GDI), its ranking in terms of the Gender Empowerment Measure (GEM) remains consistently low. In response, the government, in its Second Basic Plan for Gender Equality (2005) set the following target, "In all fields of society we can expect to see the proportion of women occupying positions of leadership increase to at least around 30 percent by 2020." Legislatures seem far from being able to fulfill this ideal, however, as political parties have continued to craft their policy objectives while leaving untouched specific plans to increase the number of women lawmakers. The question I must ask is whether women who are conscious of the need for female legislative representation will initiate a movement to bring this about or will women wait for men to move in this direction?

Still another question remains: will women's political participation continue in the pattern opened by the politicization of housewives in urban areas? While members of NET participated in the Beijing World Conference on Women, where they were able to educate themselves further regarding gender-related issues, what of their successors? The rate of employment for married women living in urban areas continues to rise, signifying a reduction in the numbers of women whose lifestyles can be focused on community activism. Similarly, the continuing urbanization of the so-called "new towns" has seen a growth in commercial facilities that provide work opportunities for married women.

While many of these women quit their jobs following childbirth, many wish to return to the workforce after their children are older. Moreover, unlike the women of the immediate postwar (baby boomer) generation, many of whom were involved with the women's liberation movement and/or political activism such as the anti-ANPO[15] and Vietnam war movements, this younger generation shows little interest in becoming involved with social action, nor do they seek to link the frustrations and dissatisfactions they confront in raising children to political activism (Yazawa, Kunihiro and Tendo 2003). Even NET, whose members participated in politics while accepting a gender-based division of labor, now includes few full-time housewives. Most members are employed outside the home in some form, and some have come together to form workers' collectives.[16] Hence, NET has fewer members working on behalf of local community movements to elect female assembly members, thus weakening NET's unique characteristic as a political movement focused on specific political proposals of concern to local communities. In other words, the decline in the number of members who are nonemployed (their "de-housewife-ization") has stalled the momentum of the movement.

By the time of the unified local election of 2003, many local NET assembly members had reached the limit of their two-term, eight-year maximum period in office. Many of them then ran—and lost—in prefectural assembly elections. In what was clearly a criticism of these term limits, one such person whom I will call "A" commented as follows: "NET has not been proactive in terms of career design[17]. If they do not start making a move in this direction, young people are likely not to want to become involved anymore."

Because the female legislators elected from NET were "wives supported by their husbands," NET refrained from focusing on achieving economic independence for these women, or building their careers as politicians, but instead concentrated on solidifying the finances of the organization and casting a wide net to acquire new talent. In so doing, NET grew as an organization for a period of time. On the other hand, NET could not empower individual women. As a political party originally designed to work as a horizontal network, it gradually found itself becoming more and more centralized as it enlarged, which led to defections among those who objected to policy decisions passed down from the top. The organizational design, built on the premise that *seikatsusha* or citizens were equivalent to *shufu* or

THE POLITICIZATION OF HOUSEWIVES

housewives, had undergone a case of institutional fatigue since its inception in 1980. Six members of the Yokohama City Assembly were instrumental in establishing a new organization that was independent of NET, called "Network Yokohama."

These organizational changes were partly responsible for the fact that while seven of the eighteen women members of the Yokohama City Assembly were members of NET prior to the 2006 election, only one woman from NET and three from Network Yokohama succeeded in getting elected in the next election. Inevitably, it had become difficult for "politicized" housewives to earn votes in a political climate in which many different types of women (including conservative ones) were running for office.

After leaving NET, however, some women did find it possible to become elected as independent candidates and build successful careers as lawmakers. Many women also went on to use their careers as local legislators to become National Diet members, governors, and mayors.[18]

"Housewife-ization" and the Local Legislatures: New Issues

Among the town and village assemblies in Kanagawa prefecture, as of May 2007, there was one village assembly in the whole of the prefecture—Kiyokawa—with no female representation whatsoever. The percentage of females among the town assemblies in the prefecture varies considerably, ranging from over 50 percent to one single woman or even none. While large numbers of women members were sent to their local assemblies via NET, this has not been universal. One woman legislator, for example, explained that it was unrealistic in this society for male salaried workers to serve on local councils. With salaries for small-town assembly members being comparatively lower than those in urban areas, supporting a family on a legislator's wage is unsustainable over the long term. And since it is impossible for male company workers to serve on local councils at the same time, the situation remains one whereby the only people who are available to serve as candidates are those who are either self-employed, engaged in agriculture, or women.

In the town of Oiso, where the majority of assembly members are women, even without the organized action of such groups as NET, it has become quite common for women active in the PTA, children's associations, or nature-viewing excursions, to run for local office. On the whole, moreover, those town councils with the highest number of female members have tended to be in the so-called "bedroom towns" with increasing numbers of citizens who are free from the constraints of local ties. In these towns, women, who have interrupted their careers to raise children or who have moved into a new community because of their husband's work, may want to supplement their volunteer activities with paid work. Thus, working as a local legislator may be a viable career option. While middle-aged businessmen might find the salary, around 5.5 million yen ($55,000) per year in Oiso, to be too low, middle-aged and older women might see it differently and enjoy rejoining the work force.

Women who hope to enter national politics may see the local-level assembly as a stepping-stone for a future career and the bedroom town as an ideal locale in which to cut their political teeth without being held back by existing social constraints. Among the female legislators from Kanagawa prefecture I interviewed with Oyama (2007), those who began their political careers at an early age included not only those with progressive views, but also more conservative women who wished to pursue a long-term career in the political world. We may speculate that women's advancement into local legislatures will accelerate from the small bedroom communities to other places in the country.

In agricultural regions where the population has declined, on the other hand, we often heard that "men are reluctant to become political candidates, since being a politician requires establishing and maintaining connections in the community (e.g. attending weddings and funerals). These social obligations are too much of a financial drain." With the additional trend toward the decentralization of authority, there has also been a reduction in the numbers of legislators, as well as their salaries. Was it the loss of enticing perks that drove men away from political office? If women are to reverse the special interest politics practiced in the past, the task before female legislators is to take on the caretaker role of restoring the environment and the very life of their communities. This phenomenon ought perhaps be viewed as the "housewife-ization," rather than the "feminization" of legislatures.

Conclusion

In the general elections of 1946, just after women received the right to vote, thirty-nine women were elected to office. In every subsequent election, however, the total number of women elected failed to match this inaugural figure. The record was finally broken fifty-nine years later with the Lower House election of 2005, when forty-three women won seats—a figure that therefore marks a milestone in terms of women's political participation in Japan.

Those concerned with the realization of equality between men and women, however, viewed this increase in the number of women legislators with mixed feelings. Sixty percent of the women elected were from the LDP, which is the most conservative among Japan's political parties. All twenty-six women candidates from the LDP were successful in winning their seats. At the time, Prime Minister Koizumi worked to reverse his party's previously weak support for female members. He backed women candidates—dubbed "Koizumi's children"—with the clear and strategic goal of promoting his postal privatization agenda—and he succeeded.

On the other hand, the Democratic Party of Japan—which had boasted the highest percentage of female electees (40 percent) in the previous election of 2003—lost half of its female members. Moreover, Takako Doi—the former head of the Social Democratic Party and longtime symbolic representative of female politicians, who also personified the image of "woman as pacifist"—failed to be reelected.

Among the female Liberal Democratic Party politicians are those who actively maintain an antifeminist stance. When these women gained key posts, many feared they would overturn policies implemented to promote gender equality following passage of the Basic Law for a Gender-Equal Society in 1999. To their dismay, Prime Minister Koizumi's successor Shinzo Abe proceeded to appoint conservative women to key posts—including Sanae Takaichi as Minister for Gender Equality, and Eriko Yamatani as education advisor.

In the 2007 Upper House election, however, the LDP suffered a historical defeat. In contrast to the Lower House election of 2006, the DPJ surged. A record number of twenty-six women were elected to office, sixteen from the DPJ and seven from the LDP.[19] In the Lower House elections held in 2009, the DPJ won a majority of the seats and assumed leadership of the government. In that election, many of the women among "Koizumi's children" who had been elected to office for the first time in 2005 lost their seats. On the other hand, women helped to bring about the DPJ's landslide victory: out of the total of fifty-four women elected, forty (74 percent) were from the DPJ, in contrast to just eight (15 percent) from the LDP. Moreover, twenty-six out of the forty women from the DPJ were first-time candidates (Ichikawa Fusae kinen kaikan 2009, 4-5).

I believe that, even in the case of the conservative political parties, the exclusion of women from elections is no longer viable. In the past, Japanese women have seen an increase in the number of female politicians lead to a reversal of gender-fair policies. They have learned that it is naïve to assume, as we did in the past, that women's participation in politics would advance peace or equality for women. Among the DPJ women newly elected to the legislature in the 2009 election, some were chosen, despite their lack of adequate experience and preparation, because of the general assumption that the DPJ would through them make a strong showing. Many of these women—some quite young—defeated rival veteran male incumbents from the LDP.

The media mocked these women, calling them "*Ozawa gaaruzu* (girls)" in reference to Ichiro Ozawa, the key DPJ election strategist. The challenge facing women, whose presence has grown in national politics, is to demonstrate by their actions and achievements that they are not some male politician's "children" or "girls." We have finally arrived at the stage where voters' attention is focused not on the numbers of female legislators but rather on their quality.

Notes

1. Among the thiry-nine successful candidates, twenty-five served one-term only. The backgrounds and activities of the thirty-nine women are discussed in Ogai (2005).

2. Under the electoral system in place at the time of the 1946 election, voting districts were exceptionally larger than those in subsequent elections, featuring a large-constituency system and a multiple-entry ballot system that allowed several (up to two or three) candidates' names to be entered. The following year, in 1947, the voting system was changed to one of multiple-seat constituencies and single ballots—thereby reducing the number of successful female candidates. According to the opinion of some, this revision was deliberately carried out as a direct response to the unexpectedly high numbers of women entering the political field (Iwamoto 2003). In any case, the single-ballot system has proven to be extremely problematic for candidates representing minority political parties.

3. See Mikanagi (1999, 20-32) for a discussion regarding the delay of women's participation in politics in Japan.

4. Also in 1993, two women, Makiko Tanaka (daughter of former LDP Prime Minister Kakuei Tanaka) and Sanae Takaichi ran and won their elections as nonparty affiliates.

5. Spoken in a 1999 interview conduced by the author (Yoko Kunihiro) and Nao Oyama with an official of the LDP's Fukushima prefectural association. At the time there were no women from the LDP in the Fukushima prefectural assembly.

6. At this time, the voting district system was changed from one of multiple-seat constituencies (whereby multiple assemblypersons could be elected from a single district) to that of single-seat constituencies (whereby only one candidate can be elected). This became known as the "single-seat proportional representation parallel system."

7. While it was feared that the system of single-seat constituencies would result in a decreasing number of females being elected, the number of females could actually increase if political parties were to put the names of female proportional representation candidates toward the top of their list of candidates. Even if candidates were to be eliminated through the single-member district system, they could still be elected through that of proportional representation.

8. There are still some local assemblies that have no women representatives: as of June 2007, 6.7 percent among city and ward assemblies, 2.1 percent of prefectural assemblies, and 38.7 percent of town and village assemblies (Ichikawa Fusae kinen kaikan 2008).

9. The term *shufu* ("housewife") indicates those subject to the gender-based division of labor characterized by unpaid or low-paid care work such as household chores, child

rearing, etc. "Housewife-ization" refers to the institutionalization of a system that casts individuals into performing this *shufu* role. Put differently, "housewife-ization" connotes an effective plundering of existing care work resources.

10. These refer to taxation, pension, and other policies advanced during the 1980s, when few women could be found as legislators in the National Diet (as I have explained already).

11. For more detailed treatment of women's social action and participation in the political process during the 1980s, see Sato (1995).

12. The "housewife-ization" of women that occurred during the period of high economic growth does not mean that they withdrew completely from social action. Because the mass media promoted stereotypes of women as belonging exclusively within the home, women themselves found it difficult to identify themselves as *shufu* (Kunihiro 2001). Moreover, the idea of women being involved in social action was nothing new. Nihon shufu rengokai (Japan Housewives' Association) was formed when commodities were scarce following Japan's defeat in World War II, using the symbols of a cooking apron and a *shamoji* (spoon-shaped utensil used to scoop rice) to spearhead a movement concerned with consumer issues. The wives of coal mine workers also have a history of social protest, forming an organization to work together on behalf of labor rights (Suzuki 1994).

13. Women entering politics were more often single women in the case of the National Diet, and married *shufu* in that of local assemblies. The "*Midori* (Green) Consumers' Cooperative," which was the precursor to the Seikatsu Club Kanagawa Consumers' Cooperative, was established in 1971.

14. In Kanagawa Prefecture, where unified local elections take place every four years, the number of women elected from NET was nine in 1987, eighteen in 1991, twenty-nine in 1995, twenty-eight in 1999, and thirty-two in 2003 (Kanagawa nettowaaku, 2004).

15. Anti-ANPO was a citizen movement against the signing of the Japan-US Security Treaty in 1960, and then against its automatic renewal in 1970.

16. A workers' collective is a form of productive cooperative in which all the members put up capital and management is based on equality among members who, through joint participation in decision-making, self-manage the organization. Many of these workers' collectives have been set up by women who discontinued working to rear children, and primary importance is placed not on profit-making but rather on making a contribution to the local community (Yokohama-shi joseikyokai 1997, 148-9).

17. This comment refers to the crafting of a satisfying career spanning the entirety of an individual's life. Such comments reveal a lack of any sort of systematic organization whereby legislators may use the experience gained during their eight-year two terms of office, as well as the lack of any existing social support for them on a personal level after leaving their post.

18. To cite several examples: a former NET assembly member ran in the mayor's race in both the cities of Yokohama and Atsugi; the two-term mayor of Kunitachi, Hiroko Uehara, was a former member of a Tokyo Seikatsusha NET; and three-term Tokyo Seikatsusha NET Tokyo Metropolitan Assembly member Masako Ohkawara (see her Profile in this volume) ran for election to the Upper House in 2007 from a Tokyo area voting district with the endorsement of the Democratic Party of Japan (DPJ) and won, receiving the highest number of votes among all the candidates.

19. Fourteen proportional representation candidates were elected to the LDP, of which six were women.

Works Cited

Ichikawa Fusae kinen kaikan (Ichikawa Fusae Memorial Association). 1999a. *Josei san-sei shiryoshu 1999 nenban zenchiho gikai josei giin no genjo* (1999 Report on women legislators in local assemblies nationwide).

———. 1999b. *Josei tenbo* (Women's perspective) (Nov/Dec).

———. 2005. *Josei tenbo* (Nov/Dec).

———. 2008. *Josei sansei shiryoshu 2007 nenban zenchiho gikai josei giin no genjo* (2007 Report on women legislators in local assemblies nationwide).

———. 2009. *Josei tenbo* (October).

Iwamoto, Misako. 2003. "Josei o meguru seijiteki gensetsu" (Political discourse regarding women). *Nenpo seijigaku* (Annual political science) 54:15–44.

Kanagawa nettowaaku undo joho henshushitsu (Kanagawa Network Movement information and editorial office). 2004. *Rookaru paatii no nijunen* (Twenty years of a local party). Kanagawa: Kanagawa Network.

Kanda, Michiko, Keiko Kimura and Masayo Noguchi. 1992. *Shin gendai josei no ishiki to seikatsu* (Women's consciousness and lives in a new era). Tokyo: Nihon hoso shuppan kyokai.

Kubo, Kimiko. 2006. "Shichoson gappei to joseigiin no shinshutsu jokyo" (Women's Venture Into Politics Amidst the Mergers of Cities, Towns and Villages). *Josei tenbo* (Women's perspective) (June):14-17.

Kunihiro, Yoko. 2001. *Shufu to jendaa—gendaiteki shufuzo no kaimei to tenbo* (Housewives and gender: explanation and outlook of the modern housewife). Tokyo: Shogakusha.

———. 2006. "Chiiki keisei shutai toshiteno josei—shufu no paradokkusu" (Women as builders of the community: the housewife paradox). In *Gurobarizeeshon/posuto modan to chiiki shakai* (Globalization, postmodernism and community), ed. Toshiaki Furushiro. Tokyo: Toshindo.

Naikakufu danjo kyodo sankaku kyoku (Gender Equity Bureau, Cabinet Office, Government of Japan). 2007. *Danjo kyodo sankaku hakusho heisei jukyunenban* (White paper on gender equality 2007 edition). Tokyo: Nikkei insatsu.

Ogai, Tokuko. 2005. *Jendaa to seiji sanka* (Gender and political participation). Yokohama: Seorishobo.

Oyama, Nao. 2004. *Seito, toha no josei kohosha ni oyobosu eikyo* (Impact of political parties and factions on female candidates). Proceedings of the Tokai University Literature Department, no. 80.

——— and Yoko Kunihiro. 2007. *Seiji ariina ni okeru jendaa kozo no kenkyu* (Research into the construction of gender within the political arena). Funded by Kagaku kenkyuhi joseikin kiban kenkyu C (Grant-in-Aid for Scientific Research Agency for the Advancement of Science Grant-in-Aid for Scientific Research C), 2004-2006.

Pado Women's Office. 2002. *Ganbare! Josei giin* (Go for It, women legislators!). Tokyo.

Sasakura, Naoko, Satomi Nakajima and Kazuko Sugawara. 1990. *Onna ga seiji o kaeru* (Women changing politics). Tokyo: Shinsensha.

Sato, Yoko. 1995. "From the Home to the Political Arena." In *Japanese Women: New Feminist Perspectives on the Past, Present and Future*, ed. Kumiko Fujimura-Fanselow and Atsuko Kameda. New York: The Feminist Press.

Shindo, Kumiko. 2004. *Jendaa de yomu Nihon seiji* (Reading Japanese politics through the lens of gender). Tokyo: Yuhikaku.

Sugawara, Kazuko. 2002. *Ichikawa Fusae to fujin sanseiken kakutoku undo* (Fusae Ichikawa and the movement for women's suffrage). Yokohama: Seorishobo.

Suzuki, Yuko. 1994. *Onnatachi no sengo rodo undoshi* (History of the postwar women's labor movement). Tokyo: Miraisha.

Yazawa, Sumiko. 1992. *Toshi to josei no shakaigaku* (Sociology of cities and women). Tokyo: Saiensusha.

——, Yoko Kunihiro, and Mutsuko Tendo. 2003. *Toshi kankyo to kosodate* (Urban environment and child raising). Tokyo: Keisoshobo.

Yokohama-shi josei kyokai (Yokohama Women's Association), ed. 1997. *Josei mondai kiiwaado 111* (111 key words pertaining to women's issues). Tokyo: Domesu shuppan.

Profiles of Two Politicians

25

Yoko Kunihiro
Translated by Kimberly Hughes

Masako Ohkawara: Upper House Lawmaker[1]

In 2007, the elections in the Upper House of Japan's National Diet, or legislature (House of Councillors), resulted in serious losses for the ruling
Liberal Democratic Party (LDP), accompanied by impressive gains for the
Democratic Party of Japan (DPJ). Thus, the election shifted the balance
of power significantly, since actions taken by the LDP-dominated Lower
House (House of Representatives) could be voted down in the Upper
House, where the LDP lacked a majority, a phenomenon that became
known as "the twisted Diet," in which different political parties controlled
each House. The conduct of the Diet was thus significantly changed, with
increased importance accorded to the Upper House.

In every election, what happens in Tokyo, the capital, draws national
attention. The DPJ, seeking a political turnaround, decided to increase the
number of its candidates running for the Upper House from the Tokyo electoral district—where the number of seats apportioned had been increased
from four to five. Thus, in addition to the party's male incumbents, it put
forward a new candidate—Masako Ohkawara, a fifty-four-year-old mother
of three.

Ohkawara, sporting an official campaign color of naturally-dyed olive-
green, and speaking powerfully on behalf of consumers' rights, earned a
stunning victory of 1,087,743 votes in this election—more than the other
four candidates. She exceeded her own personal expectations as well as those
of her supporters. Considering that she had no particular existing claim to
fame, and that she ran as a self-titled *obasan* (a middle-aged woman), this
represented an amazing achievement.

In Ohkawara's own words, prior to first entering politics in 1993, she had
"been just an ordinary mother." While her words convey an image worlds
away from politics, in fact, the experience of motherhood served first to

draw her into politics. And while she came to the Diet completely new to national politics, her experience of serving three terms in the Tokyo Metropolitan Assembly, helped earn her a seat on the Committee on Health, Welfare and Labor which she had coveted.

Rearing Children and Working for a Co-op

Ohkawara's social activism flowed from her life as a student and then as a mother. She grew up in Yokohama, first studying at Ferris Seminary, an all-girls' school founded in 1870 by Christian missionaries, and then going on to attend International Christian University. As a first-year student, she became interested in environmental issues after reading such works as the classic *Silent Spring*, as well as Sawako Ariyoshi's bestselling *Fukugo osen* (Multiple pollution) on Japan's environmental problems. She was the kind of student whose sense of justice prompted her to action. She joined demonstrations, for example, against a proposed increase in university fees, explaining that "This was the first instance in Japan of an attempt to establish a system whereby tuition and fees would be automatically adjusted to changes in the cost-of-living. I joined the movement against it out of my youthful sense of justice that in the long run the system would work to the students' disadvantage."

The fervor of the sixties' student movement was beginning to fade during Ohkawara's university days in the early 1970s. Finishing all coursework except for her final thesis, she chose to put off graduation in order to spend a semester studying in the United States. At an English-language school on the West Coast, she met students of various ethnicities. Some were Mexican, Taiwanese, Irish, and she was aware of meeting people with value systems different from her own. She began to value being open to new ideas.

After graduating in 1977, Ohkawara worked in film and stage production, first serving as an assistant to a film producer. She married a fellow student who had also studied abroad and had had experiences like hers. Her husband worked for a research institute after finishing graduate school, and the family moved into housing run by his company. Following the birth of their first child, Ohkawara quit her job.

Most of the families living in the company's housing were members of the consumer cooperative organization (co-op) known as the Seikatsu Club, and Ohkawara decided to join as well after her neighbors recommended the quality of its food. As a result of this experience, she became closely interested in food safety and environmental health. As she explains, "It's hard to get out and go shopping when you have small children. The other members of the housing unit advised me about which foods were safe, and also talked with me about aspects of child rearing. This was my first experience living in a close-knit community."

Sometimes, wives living in company housing describe negative experiences, in part because hierarchical working relationships among their husbands filter into relationships they may try to establish with the other wives. But perhaps because Ohkawara's husband worked for a research firm in which relationships among employees were easygoing, she found the communal experience a wholly positive one within which to live and rear children. As Ohkawara put it, "It was as if my previously existing values actually became more solidified. For example, I had just begun to be concerned about food issues—particularly in relation to our bodies, when I learned about the co-op from the other women." The books she had read as a student—*Silent Spring* and *Fukogo osen*—now had an impact on her life: "For example, the food production process as a whole clearly prioritizes the desires of the producers and sales agents rather than those of the consumer. This is a huge limitation, and it made me realize just how important the consumer co-ops really were."

The Seikatsu Club Consumers' Cooperative Union operates on a system in which food producers and consumers have an open line of communication regarding the collective purchase of safe, quality food. Ohkawara, impressed by this alternative economic initiative and its products as compared to the mainstream market economy, felt that similar gains might be able to be achieved within the political system as well. Indeed, the political movement that she then joined, which is known as the Seikatsusha Network, differed from existing party politics in that it aimed to render *seikatsusha*—or ordinary citizens—as central to the political field. Ohkawara's involvement with politics came as a natural extension of her work with the co-op, and she pursued both in ways that were intricately linked.

Ohkawara continued her work with the movement after moving from Chiba Prefecture to Tokyo's Setagaya ward in 1987. She apparently experienced no conflicts regarding her life as a "regular mother" and as a politician. Her identity as a *seikatsusha* and her belief in the inextricable relationship between politics and everyday life have consistently reinforced one another. When she ran for national political office, in fact, the slogan printed on her campaign materials read: "I am now the exclusive candidate who is able to bring the concerns of *seikatsusha* to the national political fore!" (*Minshu* 166, Democratic Party of Japan Press, DPJ Editorial Committee).

Tokyo Metropolitan Assembly: Candidacy and Action

In 1989, as a board member of the Seikatsu Club, Ohkawara worked tirelessly to collect signatures on behalf of a campaign urging the Tokyo metropolitan government to pass an ordinance ensuring food safety. This was the first experience that led her to view herself as a political person. Until that time, the Tokyo Seikatsusha Network in Setagaya ward (which I will refer to from now on as the "Network") had sent (women) candidates only to the local-level legislature. In 1989, however, it named Mieko Shiota as its first woman candidate to the Tokyo Metropolitan Assembly. Although this was a time in which female candidates from the (then) Socialist Party were benefiting from the so-called "Madonna Boom," Shiota lost the election by a slim margin. While Ohkawara was not actively involved in politics at this time, within two years her experience would change. She describes how it happened that she became involved in local ward elections. For one thing, her children had grown a bit older, and hence she was able to get more involved: "One of the Seikatsu Club board members was running for office in the local ward assembly, and so I started doing things like putting up posters and making announcements from campaign car loudspeakers. I had become aware of the glaring lack of women represented in the assembly, and I also realized just how exciting it was to get involved with the campaign to put one of our own members into office." The candidate that Ohkawara had supported was elected to office, allowing her to experience the thrill of victory. Although she returned to concentrating on co-op related activities rather than political work in conjunction with the Network, her name was subsequently put forth as a possible candidate for the Tokyo Metropolitan Assembly election that occurred two years after the ward election.

The Network's rules allowed a candidate who was put forth at the local election district level to be nominated at the Metropolitan Assembly level after being recommended by the Network as a whole. Ohkawara, whose previous work with the co-op, and with election organizing had been noted, was approached by an executive of the selection committee and asked what her plans were for the following four years. Although her goal had been to return to paid employment as a casting director or scenario writer in the film industry after her children were older, they were still in the first, third, and fifth grades at the time that this question was posed to her in 1993. Realizing that she would not be able to return to work within the next four years, she replied that she was free. She was promptly urged to run for the Metropolitan Assembly as the Network candidate, and decided to accept the challenge.

She describes her thinking at that time:

Long before the DPJ started saying, "Politics is life," I had been point-ing out that the work of the Network embodied the close relationship between politics and issues of an everyday nature. As a result, I under-stood the very real need to put someone into office who shared the per-spectives of ordinary citizens. I myself had been going around urging others to vote for such persons in the ward elections, and I also knew that this was a temporary, four-year position, after which time I could reassess the situation. For these reasons, I honestly felt that there was no justifiable reason why I could refuse this opportunity.

Ohkawara's husband also supported her decision, "saying that I would be busy with the campaign even if I weren't the actual candidate, and if this was what I wanted, it was fine with him." On the other hand, her father "was strongly opposed, since he viewed the political world as dirty, and didn't think I should be involved with it while I was still raising children." Her mother wondered only how she could meet the expenses of running for political office on her husband's salary. But Network candidates did not have to bear financial costs on their own, since individual legislators con-tribute their salaries to the Network, and the Network in turn distributes to each legislator two hundred thousand yen per month ($2,000) plus travel and other expenses related to official duties.

Ohkawara ran as a Network candidate for the Metropolitan Assembly four times, losing once; she served a total of ten years in three terms. Dur-ing this period, she worked on such critical issues as children, education, medical care, social welfare, and the environment. She also spearheaded certain projects, including the creation of Tokyo metropolitan governmen-tal guidelines regarding the impact of chemical substances on children, and a citizen's petition for an audit of a dam project considered unnecessary. Throughout her tenure, she consistently maintained a style of working col-laboratively with members of the community.

While Ohkawara's life may seem to have moved along without difficul-ties, she sustained a major disappointment when she lost her bid for re-election for a second term of office in the Metropolitan Assembly. She notes that "losing the election was indeed a bit of a shock. While many people in a similar position might have gone into withdrawal mode, this just wasn't possible with three children. During the same week that I lost the election, for example, I had to make the rounds giving post-election speeches—and I also had to attend functions for the PTA. In retrospect, it's probably best that I didn't have time to go and get depressed." Ohkawara was urged by her supporters to try again, and so she ran for office during a special election held two years later in 1999. She won this time, as well as in the next regular election held in 2001. Her support base was comprised largely of the membership of the Seikatsu Club, mostly women but also a considerable number of men. With at least twenty thousand votes from within Setagaya ward required in order to win the election, Ohkawara's victory was attributed to an increase in the number of citizens who reported being impressed by her consistent presence in the community—as well as her tireless work on behalf of such local party causes as food safety and assistance with home nursing care.

While still in elementary school, Ohkawara's children, who grew up in a household with two working parents, as she herself had done, learned to cook their own rice and miso soup. These days, in her position in the National Diet, she has no problem attending hearings for the Committee on Health, Welfare, and Labor, for example, beginning at 8 a.m., since her children are now much older.

The World of National Politics

In accordance with its philosophy of encouraging as many of its members as possible to experience serving in the legislature, the Network places term limits on its party members. After completing the maximum of three terms in the Metropolitan Assembly, therefore, Ohkawara began serving as director of a nonprofit organization. When she was asked to run as a candidate of the DPJ in the Tokyo metropolitan district in the Upper House elections of 2007, she was surprised. She said, "I really never thought that I would work in the political sphere again. But I was eventually persuaded to run for office in the Diet when it was pointed out to me that if I wanted to make use of my experiences, there was really not much difference between working for a nonprofit and working as a legislator."

In many previous national elections the policies advocated by the DPJ and the Seikatsusha Network had been quite similar, and the Network had endorsed a number of DPJ candidates. The DPJ catch phrase of "Politics is Life" also represented exactly what Ohkawara and others had identified with. Since the DPJ was not a popular party among most women, moreover, Ohkawara figured that she had been chosen as a candidate because the Network was the only place for the party to turn in order to locate candidates who could embody this slogan. She was also afraid that, if she refused, this sort of opportunity would not be offered to the Network a second time.

The number of votes required to win a seat in Tokyo was estimated to be seven hundred thousand votes. The Network's base of somewhere between one hundred and thirty thousand and one hundred and eighty thousand voters amounted to about one-third of that figure. In addition to the fact that Ohkawara could be expected to count on this constituency, her experience in local politics as well as her numerous personal connections were viewed as valuable assets. She had the advantage of career experience and wide-ranging personal connections. As the Network had never before sent one of its members into national politics, Ohkawara viewed this as an opportunity to forge ties between citizens and the legislature.

The decision to put Ohkawara forth as a candidate was not without internal dissent, however, especially from those who strongly objected on the grounds that participation in the National Diet would betray the Network's philosophy of focusing on local communities and staying away from direct involvement in national politics. "While I certainly understood the desire to concentrate on local issues, it was precisely this sort of work that led us to believe that changes had to be made at the national level," Ohkawara commented. "This is why we pushed for various policy changes, such as including our demands in the political manifestos of national governmental elections. Some people may have thought that we were going to be turning ourselves into some sort of subcontractor to the national government, but in fact, they were completely wrong."

After Ohkawara was approved as a DPJ candidate, she officially separated from the Seikatsusha Network while simultaneously retaining their backing for the election. Most of her pre-election expenses were provided by the DPJ following her approval as an official candidate, while the rest were covered by money borrowed from family members. After winning the election, she has continued to be extremely careful about the use of her annual salary. "I am trying to bring a clear citizen's perspective to finances by being completely open about the way funds are being used," she explains. "Basically, I have the same approach to fiscal issues as I've always had. I now move in far broader circles than I ever did in the past, however, and the reality is that I cannot show up to the Diet wearing jeans. Therefore, I will probably retain for my personal use about twice the amount I used to get from the Network."

Life as a National Diet Member

It remains to be seen what Ohkawara will be able to accomplish before the end of her six-year term in office, at which time she will be sixty years old. She reports feeling that she entered the world of national politics at an extremely intriguing historical juncture, while bearing the clear objective of helping to reconstruct the framework of the Diet in order to make it more transparent to the public. She also notes the need to reform the election system so that anyone may have the chance to run for a seat in the legislature, in contrast to the present system, which remains closed to most women, as well as to most men who are not already second- or third-generation politicians, and to those who lack ample financial resources. While an open recruitment system is a step in this direction, she is openly critical about the clear bias toward putting forth younger candidates.

This very tendency, however, may have had the reverse effect of working to her advantage:

> Whenever I introduced myself while on the campaign trail, I always told people that I was 54 years old. Everyone always wondered why I said my age, which is unusual for a woman. I felt it important to mention, however, that what mattered was not only youth: what was needed was someone with real life experience, good judgment, and a background including the hard knocks of life. For this reason, I deliberately pointed out that I was 54 years old and had three children. I wanted to put forward the image of a solid, trustworthy middle-aged woman.

Having been educated in an all-girls secondary school, Ohkawara grew up without giving particular thought to the fact that she was a female. However she strongly feels there is need to have more female politicians in Japan, and that when the DPJ assumes power, half of the cabinet ministers appointed should be women. In terms of her work as a female politician, Ohkawara views as most important the responsibility to develop policies promoting an enhanced work-life balance. She emphasizes that:

> Providing support to make it possible for both women and men to balance work and life responsibilities is the most important issue. As a female politician, I have the responsibility to address the situation whereby men are forced to work excessively while many women cannot get jobs even if they want to work and their pay remains low. And while recommendations have been made to rectify the problem of indirect discrimination, the reality is that such discrimination persists in many workplaces.

Ohkawara cites the importance of increasing the number of female Diet members, as well as their influence within the DPJ—two goals toward which she plans to direct her future energies, "Given my position, I have a real chance to work toward increasing the number of women legislators." She is thinking of women who are not from such privileged positions as second- or third-generation politicians, special interest groups, or *tarento giin* (popular entertainer/star politicians). She continues:

In my opinion, the foremost function of politics should be that of helping both men and women live out the 80 or so years of life that they have
been given in ways that are most fulfilling to them. From this point of
view, I think it is eminently clear that we cannot entrust the conduct of
politics only to certain people, as has been the case in the past.

Japan's National Diet still has only a few female members with experience in local politics. Only when many people with substantial life
experience like mine begin to fill the local and the national legislatures,
will the phrase "Politics is life" become something meaningful instead
of a mere slogan.

In the 2009 election for the Lower House, the DPJ won an overwhelming victory. Its slogan, "From concrete to people," refers to an emphasis on
improving people's daily lives rather than spending money on construction
projects, which is precisely what Ohkawara has always championed. For
Ohkawara, who ran for the Upper House based on her belief in the importance of the DPJ assuming reins of power, the DPJ's victory has opened up
great possibilities. She has sought to bring about political reforms based
on her frame of mind that "It's not a matter of being used by the party for
its advantage, but rather using the party for the pursuit of my goals." What
kind of post she assumes within the DPJ remains to be seen. Voters who
sent her to the national legislature hold strong expectations for this experienced woman of action.

Mizuho Fukushima: Leader of Japan's Social Democratic Party[2]

Mizuho Fukushima has been the leader of Japan's Social Democratic Party
(SDP) since 2003. Following the landmark victory in 2009 by the Democratic Party of Japan (DPJ) over the Liberal Democratic Party (LDP), which
had held power for half a century, the SDP became part of the coalition
government headed by DPJ leader Yukio Hatoyama. In September 2009
Fukushima was appointed Minister of State in charge of consumer affairs
and food safety, the declining birthrate, and gender equality, while maintaining her position as SDP chair. She served in the Hatoyama Cabinet until
May 2010.

Background

Mizuho Fukushima was born in 1955 and grew up during Japan's period of
high economic growth. Growing up in Miyazaki prefecture, in the southern
part of Japan, Fukushima already knew at the age of fifteen that she wished
to become a lawyer. Her father had told her repeatedly since childhood that,

although foreigners and women faced handicaps in Japanese society, by equipping herself with top qualifications, she could pursue a career without encountering discrimination.

Fukushima's grandfather had immigrated to the United States, and her father and his younger brother were both born in Hawaii. In addition, her grandfather's younger brother was sent to a wartime internment camp in the US for being of Japanese ancestry. From as early as she could remember, she heard stories about the reality of the discrimination faced by her father and grandparents—as well as the efforts and the solidarity that were necessary in order to overcome it.

Another reason for Fukushima's desire to enter the legal profession was her own passion for social activism. From an early age, she had a strong interest in the environmental contamination that was brought about by the economic growth taking place around her, as well as the serious problem of pollution. Watching reports that detailed the work of US environmental advocate Ralph Nader, she found herself drawn to this kind of work at a very early age.

When Fukushima was a first-year high school student, she had the opportunity to travel around the world as a junior representative of a publishing company. Influenced by her older sister while in high school, she also began reading such authors as Raicho Hiratsuka[3] and Simone de Beauvoir, and cultivated an interest in the movement for women's liberation. At Tokyo University there were few women in social science fields, and she was one of fourteen among six hundred and thirty law students.

Strongly influenced by such other women's liberation activists of the day as Mitsu Tanaka,[4] Fukushima's own interest in women's issues continued to deepen as well. Her role model was the late Michiko Nakajima, a highly respected lawyer who arduously fought discrimination against women in the workplace.[5] Fukushima found the lawyers' qualifying examination to be quite challenging. When she passed the bar at age twenty-eight, after many attempts, Michiko Nakajima and other feminist lawyers celebrated her achievement.

At age thirty, Fukushima gave birth to a daughter. Though she had been living with a partner who was also a lawyer, they had not entered into a legal marriage, since that would have required, according to Japan's civil code (Art. 750), that they assume a single surname. Their daughter was therefore considered to be a "child out of wedlock." In Japan, discrimination against such "illegitimate" children persists in several ways including the fact that they are entitled legally only to half the portion of an inheritance granted to legitimate descendants. The women's movement in Japan has for many years endeavored to eradicate this discriminatory law, and Fukushima has been one of the central figures in this regard. She once wrote, "If people have enough time on their hands to talk about how sorry they feel for children born to unmarried parents, why don't they instead direct their energy toward getting rid of the discrimination these children are subjected to?" (Fukushima 1998, 143).

As a lawyer, Fukushima's central focus was on revising the civil code in order to allow married couples to keep separate surnames. In addition, she worked on eliminating the prejudices that were directed toward children born to unmarried couples (see Fukushima 1992, 1997). Due to the pervasiveness of traditional stereotypes existing toward women and children in Japanese society, however, these efforts have borne not success but backlash. According to Fukushima:

> . . . legislation pertaining to women that is proposed in the Diet falls into three types. The first relates to such issues as domestic violence, child abuse, and stalkers—that is, those involving victims. Such legislation has few problems being approved. The second deals with issues that are very abstract and difficult to understand—and for that reason they tend to get passed. This was the case with the Basic Law for a Gender-Equal Society,[6] which was approved in 1999. The third type, however, which includes those concerning such issues as allowing separate surnames for couples, or ending discrimination against children born out of wedlock—these never get passed.

Fukushima regards the revision of the civil code as her life's work.

The Road to the Legislature

Fukushima was forty-two when she became a member of the House of Councillors (or Upper House) of the Diet. Since she had always viewed her life's calling as that of a lawyer, it was not a rapid move for her to enter politics. Several months of persuasion by former Social Democratic Party head Takako Doi convinced her to make the move, although now she faced new obstacles. "It was a totally alien world," she said. "I told Ms. Doi that my own personal policy was to make sure that I enjoyed every day of my life to the fullest, but that I seriously doubted this would be the case if I became a politician. She responded by telling me that although every day might not necessarily be pleasant, the work itself was extremely fulfilling."

Fukushima also noted the obvious in a conversation with Ms. Doi: "The political sphere seemed to be an exclusively male world. I knew I would be an easy target, and I found the thought of entering it to be extremely intimidating. I'm a coward! I'll never be able to handle the bashing that politicians get!" Moreover she was also concerned because her daughter was in elementary school at the time, and she thought she might not be able to spend much time with her. She concluded, "For me, gender equality did not translate into working as hard as men did. It was equally important for me to enjoy my personal life, and I knew that if I had less time to share with my daughter, she and I would both suffer for it."

Takako Doi, who became the first female leader of a political party with her appointment in 1986 as leader of the Japan Socialist Party—renamed the Social Democratic Party (SDP) in 1996—had been hard at work trying to protect Article 9 of the Japanese Constitution[7] and to preserve the nation's policy of renouncing war. With the worrisome move on the part of the ruling Liberal Democratic Party to enact the emergency defense legislation and to also bring about revision of Article 9, Doi had high hopes for Fukushima to take over as her successor. And with the SDP in a weakened position, Fukushima's growing popularity on the mass media outlets of television and radio—along with her effervescent personality—made her a valuable asset to the party.

Despite the challenges facing her, Fukushima finally made the decision to announce her candidacy. Doi placed her in the top rank of the proportional representation candidate list for the Upper House election, which basically ensured her a winning seat—thereby clearly indicating Doi's positive expectations for Fukushima as a politician. When Fukushima was elected to the Upper House in 1998, she reflected,

> "While I had thought my life's calling was to enjoy myself while being involved with civic activism, I realized that the Constitutional revisions being proposed threatened the very foundation of my work and my ability to continue engaging in these activities, and this made me decide to run in the election. Looking back now, taking on that challenge was definitely the right decision."

Working in the Legislature

While Fukushima felt that working as a lawyer was for the most part a solitary pursuit, she realized upon joining the Diet that the world of politics was most definitely a case of team playing. Moreover, she also discovered that in direct contrast to court trials, another reality of politics was that the idea of what constituted success was often an unclear one. Although her accomplishments, including the creation of the Law for the Prevention of Spousal Violence and the Protection of Victims (which went into force in 2001) and its subsequent revisions, have given her great satisfaction, she also has the sense that there is no end to the work that needs to be done—an experience she likened to that of simply passing a collection hat round and round with no foreseeable end in sight.

Fukushima quickly ascended to the SDP party leadership, becoming its chief secretary in 2002, and its top leader in 2003. Others noted, moreover, that she exuded none of the rigidity that was common among political figures. She began appearing regularly in mass media channels as the public face of the SDP, which was comparatively more open than other political parties to being led by a woman since Takako Doi had already paved this road. Still, however, the political world as a whole remained decisively a male domain.

Fukushima was reelected for a third term as SDP party head in November 2007. She is aware that she "proceeded to the position relatively quickly, rather than slowly climbing the ladder," and she has had to rely on "on-the-job training." She notes that "Most men in politics are thoroughly steeped in the ways of operating organizations. But because my roots are set in social activism, I bring a very different, fresh perspective. Yet I have to avoid being viewed as a mere 'decoration' or 'retained madam.' I feel I am now at a critical stage in which I need to rule our party effectively while at the same time to work effectively with other political parties to bring about changes in the political system."

Working as a Politician

Fukushima cites her legal career as the experience that has served as the most helpful resource for her work as a politician, since tasks such as preparing legislation and questions for the Diet floor are closely related to her previous work as a lawyer. She says she enjoys "the process of formulating legislation. Asking questions in the Diet is a bit different from doing so in the courtroom, but both consist of cross-examination. Although the field of law differs from that of national legislature, the difference is not radical. The legal profession is rather conservative, and the courts are most definitely a bureaucracy, which meant that I did not experience much of a culture shock coming to the Diet. I enjoy being a member of the Diet and I love the process of lawmaking." Fukushima also professes a love for asking questions in committee meetings and during full Diet sessions, both indispensable facets of the legislature, which she again attributes to her previous experience as a lawyer. In addition, her close ties with civic activist groups have been an important source of strength in her work.

If legal experience is her first resource, her second, she says, consists of her "networks with NGOs and other citizens." The Law for the Prevention of Spousal Violence and the Protection of Victims, for example, she says, "was more a case of citizen legislation than it was lawmaker legislation, since it was the survivors of domestic violence (DV) themselves who understood the problems and the contradictions that were associated with the issue. This kind of on-the-ground support is a valuable resource."

Fukushima contrasts such support as she enjoys from community groups with "the most powerful lobbyists in the political arena, the government bureaucrats who initiate most legislation." As she sees it, the bureaucrats'

> "explanation of the necessity of a piece of legislation or the appropriateness of its content may sound quite convincing and valid. But if we turn our attention to the actual experiences of DV victims and their supporters, we realize that very real problems and issues may not be dealt with by these bureaucrats, and we come to understand better what needs to be incorporated into legislation. In this regard, again, the networks I have with various citizens' groups as well as the Bar Association are invaluable."

The fact that Fukushima has named her campaign support organization "Let's go to the Diet With Mizuho!" reflects her desire and commitment to always work together with ordinary citizens.

Welcoming More Women to the Legislature

Fukushima began working as a lawyer during the 1980s, when, against the backdrop of pressures from the international community in the wake of the United Nations Decade for Women, Japanese women's advancement into society became more visible and numerous women's activist groups began to flourish. This period was dubbed the "Era of women," and Fukushima became a National Diet legislator during the height of this social shift. As she recalls,

> "This was the time period when people suddenly began to realize that it was okay for young girls to express themselves in an outward and confident manner. As a high school student myself, I remember reading an article in the newspaper about boys beginning to study home economics along with girls. When I entered university, there were many women older than I who had begun to work as lawyers, and they became my mentors. People like Keiko Higuchi[8] and Teruko Yoshitake[9] took extremely good care of me, and encouraged me a lot. It was a real sisterhood."

Since 2000, however, a backlash against gender equality has grown strong enough so that even some female Diet legislators have openly opposed policies designed to promote gender equality and revise the civil code. Fukushima regards the increased number of women legislators as "a good thing," and she continues:

> "Of course, there is diversity among these women, but the advantage of having more women in the Diet is that it can bring about a change in policy priorities. Already, greater numbers of women legislators have led

to the implementation of the DV Prevention Law, and in addition, issues such as those concerning lack of adequate medical care, particularly the shortage of physicians in obstetrics and gynecology, problems faced by single mothers and the growing ranks of part-time employees, and the revision of Article 772 of the Constitution[10] have been brought to the fore. While there are certainly male lawmakers who take an interest in such matters, on the whole women demonstrate far greater concern."

She continues, evoking some straight political talk,

"Generally speaking, people are most concerned with what affects them directly. Different people have different priorities. For example, some politicians think their job is to fund the building of new roads as a public works project. If we can get more women into the Diet, we will start to see a shift in priorities—and this will have a huge impact. Within the limited amount of time available for asking questions, for example, the matter of which are asked is an extremely important one.

"I've been working together with people like (LDP member) Seiko Noda to establish regulations for issues like child prostitution and child pornography. Laws are created in many instances on a nonpartisan basis, and so the political party simply doesn't matter. In fact, I've learned that it's important to broaden your perspective as much as possible while still remaining true to your own ideals. And while we often don't agree with other opposition parties on certain issues, we do try to work with them as best as possible.

"Really, I feel that being a woman is an advantage. Since we are able to speak male lingo in addition to our own natural language, it's as if we are bilingual and therefore a broader range of possibilities are available to us. If the male viewpoint were the only one operating in this society, there would be little sensitivity to issues like child care or the environment. As women, therefore, I think it would be a real pity for us not to possess gender sensitivity."

As the head of an opposition party holding few seats in the legislature—just twelve in the Lower and Upper Houses combined, and as a women's rights activist, Fukushima has a realistic perspective for which issues to tackle. She feels, moreover, that the party must try to expand its power with both determination and flexibility. The political system which she thinks most beneficial to women is that of Northern Europe in which proportional representation allows minority voices to be heard.

Bringing Minority Concerns to the National Diet

When asked whom she viewed herself as representing in her role as politician, Fukushima responded at first by dismissing the word "representing" as "presumptuous, even arrogant." But then she noted

"I am aware of many people with no access to the political system, and no one at all to speak for them. By contrast, something like 40 percent of the members of the LDP are second- and third-generation—so-called 'hereditary' legislators, while the figure for representatives from the DPJ is around 25 percent. They have a solid constituency, and the system is set up whereby they win with 51 percent of the single-seat constituency vote. In my view, these people do not experience the hardships of running for office. Politics for them is like running a family business. Honestly, it's as if everyone who is vying for the position of Prime Minister has either a father or a grandfather who occupied that position in the past."

The political system is a heartless one. Honestly speaking, people who don't have voting rights or political clout—or who are otherwise regarded by those in the Diet as unimportant—end up being entirely ignored. I'm talking about people like foreigners, refugees, non-regular employees, children, and young people who don't regularly go to the polls to vote, for example. I want to speak on behalf of all these people, precisely because they represent no large voting bloc, do not possess large sums of money, and have no lobbying power at all. In particular, though, I would like to work on behalf of the women."

Fukushima says she listens especially to people who have high hopes for the political process to make positive social changes. She has also offered assistance with court cases for people seeking refugee status. Her expressed wish is to continue offering support to those who do not—or in some cases cannot—have Japanese citizenship.

In terms of Japan's political structure, Fukushima is especially concerned about the possible strengthening of a trend toward a two-party system. As the leader of the SDP, Fukushima views this potential political model of the "LDP vs. DPJ" as a troubling one. She explains:

"I am someone who supports the existence of plural values, which I also believe is one of the answers to preventing wars. If the DPJ makes a major gain in the upcoming Lower House election, the model of the two-party system will be strengthened even further—and there will probably be talk once again of forming a grand coalition of the LDP and the DPJ—which share the same stance with regard to the issues of national defense and Article 9. This is a frightening prospect, and that's why I want to appeal to voters to elect more members from the SDP."

Although it is likely somewhat difficult for voters to tell the difference between the SDP and the DPJ, the two parties do differ distinctly with regard to the issues of social democratic values and the protection of Article 9 of Japan's Constitution. Recognizing that the predominant image of her party is that of standing for the latter single issue, Fukushima has traveled around the country speaking about the concrete policies that the SDP plans to implement with regard to issues of concern to everyday life, such as medical care and employment, and trying to widen support.

The Challenge of Widening Support among Women in this Crisis Period

In what can only be called a twisted phenomenon, numerous female voters are today offering their support to Tokyo metropolitan governor Shintaro Ishihara, despite statements that he has made that reflect contempt for women. When asked whether this reveals a simple lack of consciousness on the part of such voters, Fukushima replies that she views the situation as more complex than this. She explains,

> "When the same people who were negatively impacted by former Prime Minister Koizumi's structural reform scheme were the same ones who applauded this move, I realized that something was seriously wrong. Obviously, with the increase in poverty and the gap between rich and poor, people do not have time to be interested in or involved with politics. In Japan right now, one in four workers earns a yearly salary below two million yen ($20,000). One important factor, therefore, is that many women are working extremely hard and facing great difficulties. They certainly are not idle. If we want to earn people's support, we need to appeal to them by formulating policies that address their anxiety around issues such as (the obvious one of) gender equality, as well as the shortage of obstetricians/gynecologists, dwindling Dependent Children's Allowance payments to single mothers, cutbacks in support for social welfare, and so on.
>
>   "Politics is not about doing what you want to do; politicians are entrusted with the task of responding to peoples' needs. People are experiencing great hardship and pain, and we need to respond in ways that will allow us to earn their trust."

Political Life and Family Life

Fukushima's initial hesitation to enter political life was due to her fear that she would not have enough time to spend with her daughter. Since Upper House legislators have a fixed term of six years, however, and since she had already been busy with her work and social organizing activities, the time spent with her daughter did not dramatically decrease after she became a member of the Diet. Her daughter is now twenty-three years old, and hopes to have a career as a lawyer. As she looks back, Fukushima admits that "Yes, I was definitely busy, but in retrospect I was able to eat dinner at home much of the time. And because I was also able to speak with my daughter about many different topics, she is now interested in many different issues including human rights. She has also been influenced by her father, who works on issues concerning prisons and human rights, and has gone with him on overseas visits to prisons. She views gender equality as 'mom's issue,' and so she'll probably decide to focus on something else in her own career."

Fukushima describes her job in the political world as highly rewarding, because despite an endless amount of work, there is also the potential to bring about enormous change.

Life as Cabinet Minister

Since assuming her post as Cabinet minister in September 2009, Fukushima's life has become even more hectic. She was appointed to the Cabinet headed by Prime Minister Hatoyama of the DPJ—even though her party holds only seven seats in the Lower House and five in the Upper House—because the DPJ was seven seats short of having a majority in the Upper House and therefore required the support of the SDP and another minor opposition party, the People's New Party. Thus, a coalition government was formed under Hatoyama's leadership. Some members of the SDP were opposed to entering into a partnership with the other two parties since their policies—notably with respect to such issues as national defense and revision of Article 9 of the Constitution—are at odds with those of the SDP.

Fukushima's appointment as Minister of State responsible for gender equality and other issues was greeted with enthusiasm by feminists who saw some hope that progress would be made toward realizing a number of long-awaited goals, such as the amendment of the civil code (setting the minimum age for marriage at 18 for both women and men, rather than eighteen for men and sixteen for women as it now stands; abolishing the six-month waiting period required for women but not men before remarriage; allowing married couples the option to have separate surnames; and abolishing the discrimination against children born out of marriage in provisions of inheritance.) They were hopeful also about the ratification of the Optional Protocol to CEDAW, which had been held up during the many years of rule by the conservative LDP, especially since the one other woman appointed to the Hatoyama Cabinet, Justice Minister Chiba Keiko, had also demonstrated strong support for ratifying the Optional Protocol.

In December of 2009, just a few months after assuming office, Fukushima made a strong stand against the implementation of a 2006 agreement with the US on relocating a US Marine airbase on the southern Japanese island of Okinawa to another site within Okinawa. Her threat to withdraw her party from the coalition forced Hatoyama to postpone making a final decision regarding the proposed relocation. Six months later, however, on May 28, 2010, Fukushima was dismissed from her Cabinet post by Hatoyama when she refused to sign the Cabinet resolution approving the relocation of the airbase. Subsequently her party withdrew from the coalition government. While she encountered strong criticism for her action from many sides, including members of her own party, from her standpoint, it was a principled decision.

Notes

1. For Masako Ohkawara's profile, Yoko Kunihiro and Kumiko Fujimura-Fanselow interviewed her at Toyo Eiwa University Graduate School in Tokyo on December 22, 2007. Developments subsequent to the interview have been incorporated.

2. For Mizuho Fukushima's profile, Yoko Kunihiro and Kumiko Fujimura-Fanselow interviewed her at her office in the Hall of the House of Councillors on December 26, 2007. Developments subsequent to the interview have been incorporated.

3. Raicho Hiratsuka (1886-1971) was a leading figure of the women's movement in Japan, as well as an intellectual and critical commentator. She published Seito, a literary magazine by and for women, near the end of the Meiji period. She subsequently worked as a leader of both the women's suffrage and antiwar movements. Her works include the eight-volume *Hiratsuka Raicho no chosakushu* (Collective writings of Raicho Hiratsuka). See also chapter 4 in this volume.

4. Mitsu Tanaka was a charismatic member of the women's movement in the 1970s. In 1971 she co-founded the Ribu shinjuku senta, which served as a refuge for women and provided consultation regarding birth control and abortion. In 1975 she went to Mexico to live for a period of time and following her return to Japan became an acupuncturist and opened a clinic.

5. Michiko Nakajima, who passed away in 2007, was also involved in the making of the Equal Employment Opportunity Law (passed in 1985), establishing shelters for female victims of violence, and fighting gender discrimination in schools and the courts.

6. Although the official English translation for *Danjo kyodo sankaku kihonho* is "Basic Law for a Gender-Equal Society," the Japanese designation for this law does not include the word "equal" or "equality," which women's groups had pressed for. The literal translation is something like "Basic Law on the Cooperative Participation of Men and Women in Society"—a designation "more abstract and difficult to understand," as Fukushima says, and also, or perhaps therefore more palatable to conservative politicians. (Editor's note)

7. Article 9 of the Japanese Constitution, which came into effect on May 3, 1947, prohibits an act of war by the state and also forbids Japan from maintaining an army, navy or air force. Japan does, however, maintain Self-Defense Forces (SDF). The emergency defense legislation proposed allowing the Self-Defense Forces to use or destroy private property in the event of a foreign attack on Japan.

8. Keiko Higuchi (b. 1932) is a noted social critical. She is a former professor of Tokyo Kasei University and ran unsuccessfully for the office of Tokyo metropolitan governor in 2003. She is currently the director of an NPO called Koreishakai o yokusuru josei no kai (Women's association for improvement of the ageing society).

9. Teruko Yoshitake (b. 1931) is a writer and social critic who became the first female

advertising producer in Japan.

10. Article 772 of the Constitution stipulates that a child born to a woman within two hundred days following a marriage, or three hundred days following a divorce, is the child of the woman's legal husband. In cases of lengthy divorce proceedings, therefore, it is possible that a child born to a woman and her new partner will nevertheless be regarded as the child of her ex-husband. Because of this article, there are couples that have opted not to officially register the birth of their child.

Works Cited

Fukushima, Mizuho. 1992. *Kekkon to kazoku—atarashii kankei ni mukete* (Marriage and family—towards new kinds of relationships). Tokyo: Iwanami shinsho.

———. 1997. *Fukushima Mizuho no fufubessei seminaaru* (Mizuho Fukushima's seminar on separate surnames for married couples). Tokyo: Jiyukokuminsha.

———. 1998. *Fukushima Mizuhoteki bengoshi seikatsu nooto* (Notes on Mizuho Fukushima's life as a lawyer). Tokyo: Jiyukokuminsha.

Notes on Contributors

Keiko Aiba, who received a PhD in sociology from Washington State University, is currently associate professor in the Faculty of International Studies at Meiji Gakuin University. She has researched various aspects of gender relations in Japan and her writings include "Refreshing Beers and Caring Skin: The Construction of Gender in Japanese Television Commercials" (with Raymond A. Jussaume), in *Journal of National Women's Education Center* (1998), and "Job-Level Sex Composition and the Sex Pay Gap in a Large Japanese Firm" (with Amy Wharton) in *Sociological Perspectives* (2001). She is currently looking at how gender and body are intertwined through an ethnographic study of Japanese women professional wrestlers. Besides her essay in this volume, she has published several other articles on Japanese women professional wrestlers such as "*Tatakaku gino to jiko boei: joshi puroresuraa no shintai to jendaa*" (Combat skills and self-defense: gender and the bodies of wrestlers), in *Jendaa & sekushuariti* (Gender & Sexuality) (2008), and *Joshi puroresuraa no kega to itami* (Injuries and pains of Japanese women professional wrestlers), in *Supootsu to jendaa kenkyu* (Journal of sport and gender studies) (2010).

Chieko Akaishi, who received a BA from the Department of Sociology at Tokyo University, is an activist and writer. Herself a single mother, she is involved in single mothers' self-support efforts, the movement to bring about change in inheritance laws in the civil code pertaining to children of unmarried couples or mothers, and also movements to fight poverty. She is a director of the nonprofit organization *Shinguru mazaazu fooramu* (Single Mothers' Forum), an editor for *Femin fujin minshu shimbun* (Femin Women's Democratic Newspaper), and a representative of *Han-hinkon netto* (Antipoverty network) and *Josei to hinkon netto* (Women and poverty network). Her writings include *Shinguru mazaa ni kanpai* (Cheers to single mothers) (2001), *Shinguru mazaa no anata ni kurashi o norikiru 53 no hoho* (53 ways for single mothers to overcome hardships of living) (2008), and *Jendaa no kiki o koeru* (Overcoming the crisis of gender) (2006).

Kaoru Aoyama obtained her PhD in sociology from the University of Essex, UK, in 2005. She has specialized in issues of gender/sexuality, social inclusion/exclusion, transborder migration, and sex work/trafficking. Striving to create theoretically and methodologically sound social research that will be useful for those being researched, she has been involved in team research projects including one on women returnee migrants in northern Thailand and another on migrant sex workers in Japan, both led by migrants and/or sex workers themselves. In addition, her activism with a Tokyo-based independent organization called People's Plan Study Group, revolves around networking of socially committed academics and activists toward participatory democracy beyond national and other hierarchical borders. She is currently an assistant professor at the Graduate School of Inter-cultural Studies, Kobe University. Her monograph in English, *Thai Migrant Sex Workers: From Modernisation to Globalisation*, was published by Palgrave/Macmillan in 2009.

Chieko M. Ariga is a research faculty at the Department of Languages & Literature, University of Utah. She received her PhD from the University of Chicago. Her special research areas are Edo literature, women's literature, feminist criticism, and cultural studies. Her essays and translations have appeared in such journals as the *International Journal of Social Education, IRIS, Journal of Asian Studies, Manoa, Monumenta Nipponica*, and *U.S.-Japan Women's Journal* (for which she served as the journal's associate editor, 1990-2002). She is the author of *Jendaa kaitai no kiseki: bungaku, seido, bunka* (Strategy of degendering: literature, institutions, and culture) (1996).

Aya Ezawa received her PhD in sociology from the University of Illinois at Urbana-Champaign and is currently university lecturer in the Sociology of Modern Japan in the Japanese Studies Program at Leiden University in the Netherlands. Her research focuses on the gender and class dimensions of social policy, as well as their implications for the living conditions of single mothers in contemporary Japan. Her most recent research has been funded by an Abe Fellowship from the Japan Foundation Center for Global Partnership, and has been published, among others, in *Japanstudien, Kikan shakai hosho kenkyu* (Japanese Quarterly for Social Security Research), and *Social Class in Contemporary Japan: Structures, Sorting and Strategies*, edited by David Slater and Hiroshi Ishida.

Mioko Fujieda, professor emerita of women's studies and dean of the faculty of humanities at Kyoto Seika University, has written widely on Japanese feminism. She is the supervising translator in Japanese of the books *Sexual Politics*, by Kate Millet, and *The New Our Bodies, Ourselves*, by the Boston Women's Health Book Collective.

Kumiko Fujimura-Fanselow (editor), who received a PhD in comparative and international education from Columbia University, is a professor of education and women's studies at Toyo Eiwa University and its graduate school in Tokyo, where she has taught for over twenty years. Her primary interest has been to explore and develop ways of teaching/learning that promote critical thinking and consciousness regarding not only women's issues but human rights issues in general. In addition to *Japanese Women: New Feminist Perspectives on the Past, Present, and Future* (1995), co-edited with Atsuko Kameda, she has also written widely on the topic of feminist pedagogy, women's lifelong learning, women's colleges, and Japanese higher education, and contributed articles/chapters to *Women of Japan and Korea, Japanese Schooling: Patterns of socialization, equality and political control; Asian Higher Education: An International Handbook and Reference Guide; International Comparative Research on Women's Learning Needs and Practices* (National Women's Education Center, Japan, ed.); *Gender and Education; Women's Studies Review* (Korea Women's Institute, Ewha Woman's University); *Comparative Education Review*, and co-authored *Danjo kyodo sankaku shakai ni muketa gakushu gaido—shakaikyoiku shidosha ni jendaa no shiten o* (Guide for promoting gender sensitivity among adult/lifelong education leaders to bring about a gender-equal society), and *Gakushushien handobukku: kyodo no jidai no manabi to jissen* (Handbook for promoting learning based on the principles of cooperation and collaboration).

Kimi Hara, who received a PhD in sociology of education from Michigan State University, was president of Okinawa Christian Junior College from 1991 to 1999. Currently professor emeritus of OCJC and International Christian University, she is now retired and lives with her family in Tokyo. Born in 1916, she graduated from Tsuda College and began teaching English to junior high school students. She worked as an interpreter for the GHQ of the occupational forces and was appointed as a tutor to the youngest daughter of the imperial family. One of the first women scholars in post-war Japan to be sent to study in the United States, she received her MA at the University of Chicago. She taught at Tsuda College, International Christian University, Shikoku Gakuin University, and Tokyo Union Theological Seminary, and served as director of the Japanese Studies Program at Ateneo de Manila University (Philippines), and visiting professor in the Japanese Studies Programs of Padjadjaram University (Indonesia) and the Philippine Women's University. Her major works include *Joshi no kotokyoiku to shokugyo oyobi katei no mondai* (Higher education for women and the occupational and domestic issues they face) (1961), as well as several articles that have appeared in the journals *Contemporary Japan* and *Kyoiku shakaigaku kenkyu* (Journal of sociology and education).

Minata (Minako) Hara (translator) is a bi-gendered translator and interpreter of Japanese, English, and Spanish. Dropping out of school at the age of fourteen due to gender discomfort, Minata is a self-taught and self-employed language specialist whose published works include the Japanese co-translations of *Odd Girls and Twilight Lovers: A History of Lesbian Life in Twentieth-Century America* by Lillian Faderman (1996) and *The Courage to Heal: A Guide for Women Survivors of Child Sexual Abuse* by Ellen Bass and Laura Davis (1997, 2007). Also known as a community organizer/activist on gender, sexuality, and anti-violence issues since the 1980s, Minata now leads the advocacy group "Kyosei-Net for LGBIT" set up in 2008. Minata thanks her niece Sara Kitaoji for her valuable collaboration in translating the articles included in this book.

Yuriko Hara holds an MA in the theory and practice of human rights from the University of Essex. After serving as media coordinator for the Women's International War Crimes Tribunal held in Tokyo in 2000, she joined the International Movement Against All Forms of Discrimination and Racism—Japan Committee (IMADR), where she now serves as secretary general. She is also a steering member of the Japan NGO Network for CEDAW (JNNC), and the Japan Network Against Trafficking in Persons (JNATIP) and also teaches part time at Soka Women's Junior College and Meiji University. She has authored/edited such works as *Koza jinshin baibai* (Seminar on human trafficking) (2007); *Tachiagari tsunagaru mainoriti josei: ainu josei, buraku josei, zainichichosenjin josei ni yoru ankeeto chosa hokokusho to teigen* (2007) (*Minority Women Rise Up: A Collaborative Survey on Ainu, Buraku and Korean Women in Japan* [2009]); *Mainoriti josei no shiten o seisakuni, shakaini—joshi sabetsu teppai joyaku iinkai Nihon hokokusho shinsa o toshite* (Toward inclusion of minority women's perspectives in policies and in society—the process and results of CEDAW's examination of Japan's report to the Committee) (2003); and *Iju josei ga kirihiraku enpawamento no michi* (*Transforming Lives: Abused Migrant Women in Japan Blaze a Trail towards Empowerment,* 2006).

Kimberly Hughes (translator) received a BA in Japanese studies from Arizona State University and an MA in cultural anthropology from the University of California at San Diego. She is a freelance writer, translator, and educator/learner who aspires to be an organic gardener someday. Her previous translations have included *The Diary of Azuma Shiro* (2006) and the anthology *Sparkling Rain: And Other Fiction from Japan of Women Who Love Women* (2008). She has also written several articles regarding peace and LGBT issues in Japan that have appeared in such publications as *Kyoto Journal, Fridae: Empowering Gay Asia, Anise* and *LOTL.* She is originally from the United States and has lived in Tokyo since 2001.

Malaya Ileto (translator) holds an MA in international relations from Columbia University and a BA in law and Japanese from James Cook University. She is also a graduate of the Inter-University Center for Japanese Language Studies, run by Stanford University. A freelance translator and editor, she specializes in serving the nonprofit and academic community in the areas of human rights and humanitarian affairs, international development, political science, social science, education, public health, and women's studies. She has worked at a number of Japanese nongovernmental organizations, including the International Movement Against All Forms of Discrimination and Racism (IMADR), Global Village, Japan-US Community Education and Exchange, and Peace Boat, and has published widely on human rights and gender in Japan, including translating *Minority Women Rise Up: A Collaborative Survey on Ainu, Buraku and Korean Women in Japan* (2009), and editing *Human Trafficking and Racism: Exploring the Links between Marginalization and Exploitative Migration* (2006), both by IMADR. She is originally from the Philippines.

Nanako Inaba is an associate professor in the faculty of humanities at Ibaraki University. As a member of the Division of International Human Rights of the Solidarity Network with Migrants Japan she is actively engaged in networking with various overseas nongovernmental organizations. She is also a board member of Kalakasan Migrant Women Empowerment Center, where she directs research based on FPAR (feminist participatory action research). Her focus of activities is protection of the rights of female migrants and residents without legal status. Her publications include *Kokkyo o koeru—tainichi musurimu imin no shakaigaku* (Crossing borders—sociological analysis of Muslim migrants in Japan) (2007), and *Shakai undo to iu kokyo kukan—riron to hoho no furontia* (Public spaces of social movements: frontier of theory and method) (2004).

Kimio Ito is professor of sociology at Kyoto University's Graduate School of Letters and also heads the public relations committee of the Center for Women Researchers at Kyoto University. He is also president of the Japan Society for Sport Sociology and vice president of the Japan Society of Gender Studies. He is known as a founder of men's and masculinities studies in Japan, offering the first-ever university course in men's studies at Kyoto University in 1992. He has also worked as a member of the Japanese government's Specialist Committee for Gender Equality (on Basic Issues and on Violence against Women). His writings include *"Otokorashisa" no yukue* (Locating "masculinity," 1993), *Danseigaku nyumon* (Introduction to men's studies) (1996), *"Otokorashisa" to iu shinwa* (The myth of "masculinity," 2003), "The Invention of *wa* and the Transformation of the Image of Shotoku in Modern Japan," in *Mirror of Modernity: Invented Traditions of Modern Japan* (1998), and "An introduction to men's studies," in *Genders, Transgenders and Sexualities in Japan* (2005).

Saori Kamano, who received her PhD in sociology at Stanford University, is a senior researcher at the National Institute of Population and Social Security Research in Tokyo and teaches a course on families and sexualities at Hosei University. Her research interests are families, sexualities, and gender. In her current project, she explores various issues on lesbians/lesbian couples, entering lesbian communities (in the *Journal of Lesbian Studies*, 2005), housework division (in *Women's Studies International Forum*, 2009), starting a relationship (in *East Asian Sexualities*, 2008) and personal networks (presented at the Women's Worlds 2008). Her most recent work "Raising Questions about 'the Conventional Family': An Exploration of Lesbigay Families" was published in the *Japanese Journal of Family Sociology*, 2008. Together with Diana Khor, she has also edited *"Lesbians" in East Asia: Diversity, Identities and Resistance* (2006). She has served on the executive committee of the Women's Studies Association of Japan, and is a founding member of The Japan Association for Queer Studies that was inaugurated in 2007.

Atsuko Kameda, who holds an MA in sociology of education from Ochanomizu Women's University, is professor of women's studies at Jyumonji Women's University. She is also director of the Research Center on Women and Information and member of the planning committee in the archives division at the National Women's Education Center. She is coeditor (with Kumiko Fujimura-Fanselow) of *Japanese Women: New Perspectives on the Past, Present, and Future* (1995), and *Gakko o jendaa furiini* (Making schools free of gender bias) (2000), and

co-author of *Josei kocho no kyaria keisei* (Career formation of women school principals) (2009).

Aya Kamikawa, a graduate of Hosei University, publicly disclosed her gender-identity disorder in 2003, and was elected to Tokyo's Setagawa Ward Assembly, becoming the first self-disclosed sexual minority person to be elected to public office in Japan. In April 2005, her request to change her gender on the family register from male to female was approved under the Law Concerning Special Rules Regarding Sex Status of a Person with Gender Identity Disorder. In April 2007, she was re-elected for a second term in the Setagaya Ward Assembly, coming in second (highest rank for incumbent) among seventy-one candidates. She is author of *Kaeteyuku yuki—"Seidoitsusei shogai" no watashi kara* (The courage to change—from me, who has GID) (2007) and co-author of *Seido-itsusei shogai to koseki* (GID and the family register) (2007), and *Tayona "sei" ga wakaru hon* (Understanding diverse sexualities) (2002).

Sachiko Kaneko, who holds a PhD in history from International Christian University in Tokyo, was a professor of gender studies at Nagoya College for many years, and now teaches part time at Japan Women's University. She is the author of *Kindai Nihon joseiron no keifu* (The genealogy of ideas on women in modern Japan, 1999). She is also coauthor of the three-volume *Nihon josei no rekishi* (A history of Japanese women, 1992-93) and *Higashi ajia no kokumin kokka keisei to jendaa* (The formation of the nation-state and gender in East Asia, 2007), and coeditor of *Nihon joseishi daijiten* (The great dictionary of Japanese women's history, 2008).

Diana Khor received her PhD in sociology from Stanford University. She is currently professor at the Faculty of Global and Interdisciplinary Studies at Hosei University. She adopts an intersectional approach in her teaching, and teaches mostly classes related to race, class, gender, and other axes of inequality. Her dissertation on a crossnational analysis of women's movements and the incorporation of women into the public sphere led her to analyzing feminist organizing in Japan, and more recently, the development of women's studies in Japan. She has a general interest in the social construction of gender and has analyzed public opinion questions in the United States and Japan from this perspective. In the area of sexuality, she has worked primarily with Saori Kamano, and explored various aspects of the lives of lesbians in Sweden and Japan, including the household division of labor, personal networks, and the processes through which lesbians authenticate their identities. She is co-editor with Saori Kamano of *"Lesbians" in East Asia: Diversity, Identities, and Resistance* (2006), and her work has appeared in *Feminist Studies, National Women's Studies Association Journal, LGBT Family Studies,* and *U.S.-Japan Women's Journal.*

Risa Kumamoto holds an MA in sociology from Bukkyo University and is currently working on a doctorate in International Social Development at Nihon Fukushi University. She worked for a number of years with the International Movement Against All Forms of Discrimination and Racism-Japan Committee (IMADR-JC) and since 2002 has been on the staff of Kinki University Center for Human Rights. Her publications include *"Fukugo sabetsu, kansetsu sabetsu"*

(Multiple discrimination and indirect discrimination), in *Jinken seisakugaku no susume* (Toward the pursuit of human rights policy studies) (2003), "*Jinken shiso kara mita soosharu inkuruujon*" (Social inclusion from the viewpoint of respect of human rights), in *Soosharu inkuruujon—kakusa shakai no shohosen* (Social inclusion—prescriptions for a society with growing disparity) (2007), "*Jinken to jendaa no fukugo sabetsu o megutte—Daaban kaigi de towareta mono*" (Regarding multiple discrimination based on race and gender—issues raised at the Durban Conference), in *Sengo, boryoku, jendaa (2) Datsu boryoku e no matorikkusu* (Postwar, violence, and gender Vol. 2 Matrix for rejecting violence) (2007). She resides in a small Buraku commuity in Osaka where she is involved in activities related to promotion of human rights, social welfare, and community building. As a researcher and educator, she is also working to involve those outside the Buraku community—the "majority"—so that they become aware of their ignorance of minority groups, which has fueled and sustained prejudice and discrimination.

Yoko Kunihiro, who holds a PhD in sociology from Keio University, is a professor at Tokyo Woman's Christian University, where she teaches courses in women's studies and gender and communication. She previously worked at NHK (Japan Broadcasting Corporation) and was also on the faculty of Musashi University. Her primarily research has been on the topic of political and social activism among housewives, and the images of housewives depicted in the mass media. She is author of *Shufu to jendaa* (Housewives and gender) (2001), co-author of "Super-aging Regional Community and the Feminization of Politics and Social Welfare" (in *Journal of Asian Women's Studies*, 1999), and co-author/editor of *Toshi to josei no shakaigaku* (Sociology of cities and women) (1993), *Toshi kankyo to kosodate* (Urban environment and childraising) (2003), *Terebi to gaikoku imeeji* (Television and images of foreign countries) (2004).

Masaki Matsuda is a graduate of the University of Shizuoka Faculty of Pharmaceutical Sciences. He fought a long battle to be granted ninety minutes of childcare leave daily from the company at which he worked—an event that received considerable media coverage. He later left full-time work and became a househusband. He currently works part time while taking an active role as a staff member of the organization *Ikujiren* (Childcare Hours for Men and Women Network). He was profiled in a video produced by the Tokyo Women's Foundation called "*Otokotachi ga kawarihajimeru*" (As men begin to change) and is a co-author of *Mirai o sodateru kihon no ki* (Foundation for nurturing the future generation) (2002).

Mami Nakano, a graduate of the law faculty at Hokkaido University, is an attorney and director general of the NPO Dispatched Labor Network and board member of the Japan Labor Lawyers' Association. Her publications include *Rodo danpingu—koyo tayoka no hateni* (Labor dumping—beyond diversification of employment) (2006), *Rodosha haken no horitsu sodan* (Legal consultation regarding dispatched workers) (2001), and *Nijuisseiki no danjo byodoho* (Sex equality laws for the twenty-first century) (1997). She has been an advocate for women rights in the area of labor law.

Chizuka Oe has been the main representative of LOUD (Lesbians of Undeniable Desire), a center for lesbian and bisexual women since 1999. A lesbian activist, she has lectured at a number of universities throughout Japan and also co-authored several books dealing with sexuality, including *Doseiaitte nani?* (What is homosexuality?) (2003), *Judai kara no seifaasekkusu nyumon* (Introduction to safer sex for teens) (2005), and *Paatonaashippu seikatsu to seido: kekkon, jijitsukon, doseikon* (Partnership life and systems: marriage, common-law marriage, same-sex marriage) (2007).

Haruko K. Okano holds a PhD in comparative religion from the University of Bonn and is president of the Catholic women's university, Seisen University in Tokyo. She is the author (in German) of *Die Stellung der Frau im Shinto Eine religionsphänomenologische und soziologische Untersuchung* (1976) and *Christliche Theologie im japanischen Kontext* (2002), and coauthor (in German) of *Wörterbuch der Feministischen Theologie* (1991/2002) and *Japan—Ein Land der Frauen? (1991)*, and (in English) of *Women and Religion in Japan* (1998), *Ecclesia of Women in Asia—Gathering the Voices of the Silenced* (2005), and (in Japanese) of *Shukyo no naka no joseishi* (Women's history in religion) (1993) and *Kirisutokyo to jinken shiso* (Christianity and human rights thought) (2008).

Nami Otsuki, who holds a PhD in sociology from Sophia University, was formerly a researcher at the National Women's Education Center, and is currently an associate professor at the University of the Sacred Heart. Her specialization is sociology of work and gender and work. Her writings include *Shokumu kakusa no mekanizumu* (Mechanism of differences among job tasks) (2009), "*Koyo fuanteika no naka de dansei no kasegite yakuwari ishiki wa kawarunoka*" (Will men's attitudes regarding their role as breadwinners change with the instability in employment?) in *Koyo fuantei to dansei no jendaa ishiki* (Instability in the employment market and men's attitudes regarding gender) (2009), and "*Jinshin torihiki mondai ni taisuru Nihonjin no ishiki—seiteki saabisu no 'juyo' to higai-sha taisaku ni kansuru bunseki*" (Japanese attitudes regarding human trafficking—research on "demand" for sexual services and policies toward victims) in *Social Science Japan Journal* (2009).

Hitomi Sawabe received her BA from Waseda University's Department of Japanese literature and completed her course requirements for a doctorate in the field of Japanese language and culture. After teaching Japanese for eight years at a junior high school, she became a nonfiction writer. She is the author of *Yuriko, Do svidanya: Yuasa Yoshiko no seishun* (Farewell Yuriko: The vernal years of Yoshiko Yuasa) (1990, 1996)), *Hyoron nanka kowakunai* (I'm not afraid of criticism) (1992) and editor (under the pen name Yumi Hirosawa) of the pioneering *Onna o aisuru onnatachi no monogatari* (Stories of women who love women) (1987), which was the first book for lesbians to reach mainstream distribution in Japan. She has recently written about the history of lesbian communities in "The Symbolic Tree of Lesbianism in Japan: An overview of lesbian activist history and literary works," in *Sparkling Rain: And Other Fiction from Japan of Women Who Love Women* (2008) and *PA/F Space no ayumi* (The history of PA/F Space) (2008). Her current work-in-progress is *Kimi to itsuma-demo—Koshiji Fubuki to Iwatani Tokiko* (Together with you forever—Fubuki Koshiji and Tokiko Iwatani).

Ikuko Sugiura, who holds an MA in sociology from Chuo University, has been a part-time lecturer at Chuo University, Seikei University, Japan Women's University, Musashi University, and Kanto Gakuin University. She is currently pursuing research on the development of lesbian communities, and in the hope of seeing the establishment of a domestic partnership system in Japan, she is conducting a study into the lives of same-same couples. Her writings include "Lesbian Discourses in Mainstream Magazines of Post-War Japan: Is Onabe Distinct from Rezubian?" in *Journal of Lesbian Studies* (2006), and *Paatonaa-shippu seikatsu to seido: kekkon, jijitsukon, doseikon* (Partnership life and systems: marriage, common-law marriage, same-sex marriage) (2007).

Leny P. Tolentino has spent over twenty years accompanying Filipino migrants in Japan. From 1990 to 2002 she was in charge of the Philippine Desk in the Catholic Yokohama Diocese Solidarity Center for Migrants. In the last ten years she has focused especially on the empowerment of migrant Filipina women and their children, promoting their rights and dignity and facilitating for women to assert their voices. She is a co-founder of Kalakasan Migrant Women Empowerment Center and at present, a member of the steering committee of the Women's Project of the Solidarity Network with Migrants Japan and a committee member of the Campaign Against Racial Discrimination organized by the International Movement Against All Forms of Discrimination and Racism-Japan Committee (IMARD-JC). She received an MA in community building from Yokohama City University.

Masae Torai, a graduate of Hosei University, has been a leading advocate on gender-identity disorder issues as a writer and public speaker. He is the founder and editor of *FTM Nihon* (Female to Male Japan), a magazine for transgendered people launched in 1994, and he is also a member of *Ningen to sei kyoiku kenkyu kyogikai* (Council for education and research on human sexuality and sex education). His publications include *Onna kara otoko ni natta watashi*, (My transformation from woman to man) (1996), *Aru seitenkansha no kiroku* (Chronicles of a transsexual) (1997), *Toransujendaa no jidai* (The age of transgenderism) (2000), *Otoko no koseki o kudasai* (Please change my gender designation to male on the family register) (2003).

Yoko Tsuruta (translator), who holds a PhD in linguistics from the University of Luton, is a professor at the Center for Global Education at Hitotsubashi University. Her research deals with Japanese linguistics communication and Japanese linguistic politeness, and her writings have appeared in *The Language Teacher, International Journal of Pragmatics,* the *SFC Journal of Language and Communication*, and the volume *Hirakareta Nihongo kyoiku no tobira* (Open door to Japanese language education) (2005).

Midori Wakakuwa pursued her undergraduate and graduate studies at the Tokyo National University of Fine Arts and Music (currently the Tokyo University of the Arts) and also studied at the University of Rome. She was a professor at the Tokyo National University of Fine Arts and Music and later at Chiba University and Kawamura Gakuen Woman's University. She wrote extensively about the history of Japanese as well as Western art in both Japanese and Italian, and authored, among other books (in Japanese), *Gui to shocho no joseizo* (The female image of allegory and symbolism), *Manerisumu geijutsuron* (The artistic theory of mannerism). Since the mid-1990s she has written extensively on issues of feminism and gender, and in 2006 founded the Center for Research on Gender Culture. Her many writings in this area include, *Senso ga tsukuru joseizo—dainiji seikaitaisenka no Nihon joseidoin no shikakuteki puropaganda* (Image of women created in wartime—visual propaganda in the mobilization of Japanese women during World War II) (1995), *Shocho to shite no joseizo— jendaashi kara mita kafuchoshakai ni okeru joseihyozo* (Image of women as symbol—representation of women in patriarchal society viewed through the history of gender) (2000), *Ohimesama to jendaa—anime de manabu otoko to onna no jendaa nyumon* (The princess and gender—introduction to study of gender through animation) (2003), and *Senso to jendaa—senso o okosu danseidomei to heiwa o tsukuru jendaa riron* (War and gender—alliance of men who start wars and gender theory that creates peace) (2005). Midori Wakakuwa passed away in 2007.

Yeong-ae Yamashita, who is a second-generation Zainichi Korean, is an adjunct assistant professor at Ritsumeikan University. She received an MA in international studies from Tsuda College, after which she enrolled in the graduate women's studies program at Ewha Woman's University in Seoul, Korea. While studying in Korea, she became active in the movement to resolve the issue of the Japanese military's "comfort women." Her analysis and reflections based on the experience are set forth in *Nashonarizumu no hazama kara—'ianfu' mondai e no mohitotsu no shiza* (From the battlement of nationalism—an alternative perspective regarding the issue of the 'comfort women') (2008). She has translated from Korean to Japanese such books as, *Kankoku josei jinken undoshi* (History of South Korean women's human rights movement), edited by Korean Women's Hotline Alliance (2004), *Kankoku no gunji bunka to jendaa* (South Korea's military culture and gender), by Kwon In-suk (2006), and *Amerika taun no onnatachi* (Women of 'American towns'), by Kim Yeon-ja (2009).

Acknowledgments

Florence Howe, above all, is the person who made the publication of this book possible. Florence's support throughout the long process of bringing this volume to fruition, together with her strong belief in the value of this work, has been an immeasurable source of strength to me. I am also deeply indebted to her for her thoughtful, painstaking, and time-consuming editing of the entire book. In working with Florence I have gained many insights and lessons not only about writing and editing, but also about the possibilities of growth and development that come from having a caring and respectful mentor.

I am indebted to all those who contributed their writings, and for their generous willingness to cooperate with my repeated requests for additions, clarifications, and revisions. Special thanks also go to Minata (Minako) Hara, Kimberly Hughes, and Malaya Ileto, who devoted countless hours to translating the essays that were submitted in Japanese into English. Minata, Kim, and Malaya graciously agreed to take on the project in large part because they shared a strong commitment to the issues taken up in the book, and were eager to take part in disseminating knowledge and understanding of those issues to wider audiences. The translation process entailed numerous discussions, negotiations, revisions, checking, and re-checking to ensure that the texts were not only accurate, but also that they reflected, as much as possible, the voices and styles of the authors. Of course, I, as editor, assume ultimate responsibility for the content.

I am thankful also for the support and advice of Hiroko Hara, Jane Spalding, Miho Watanabe, Kuniko Funabashi, my assistant Akemi Yahagi, and John F. Fanselow. My heartfelt gratitude also extends to the Feminist Press for giving me the opportunity to publish this volume, to the editorial director Amy Scholder, managing editor Jeanann Pannasch for her meticulous copyediting, and Drew Stevens for his thoughtful designing of the book. This book was made possible in part by a generous research grant from Toyo Eiwa University and also the Japan Foundation, to which I extend my deep gratitude.

Kumiko Fujimura-Fanselow
September 2010